APPLYING

EDUCATIONAL

RESEARCH

A Practical Guide
Fourth Edition

JOYCE P. GALL
University of Oregon

M. D. GALL
University of Oregon

WALTER R. BORG
Late of Utah State University

 LONGMAN

An imprint of Addison Wesley Longman, Inc.

New York • Reading, Massachusetts • Menlo Park, California • Harlow, England
Don Mills, Ontario • Sydney • Mexico City • Madrid • Amsterdam

Dedicated to Marie Borg, Adrienne Borg,
Rose Comaduran, and the memory
of Julio Comaduran

Acquisitions Editor: Arthur Pomponio
Associate Editor: Arianne J. Weber
Marketing Manager: Renée Ortbals
Project Coordination and Text Design: Elm Street Publishing Services, Inc.
Cover Designer: Frank Caligiuri
Cover Design Manager: Nancy Danahy
Full Service Production Manager: Valerie Zaborski
Manufacturing Buyer: Denise Sandler
Electronic Page Makeup: Elm Street Publishing Services, Inc.
Printer and Binder: The Maple-Vail Book Manufacturing Group
Cover Printer: Phoenix Color Corp.

Library of Congress Cataloging-in-Publication Data
Gall, Joyce P.
  Applying educational research: a practical guide/Joyce P. Gall,
M. D. Gall, Walter R. Borg.—4th ed.
    p.   cm.
  Borg's name appears first on the earlier edition.
  Includes bibliographical references and indexes.
  ISBN 0-8013-1950-1
    1. Education—Research—Handbooks, manuals, etc.   I. Gall,
  Meredith D.   II. Borg, Walter R.   III. Title.
  LB1028.B59   1999   98-37935
  370'.7'2—dc21   CIP

Please visit our website at http://longman.awl.com

ISBN 0-8013-1950-1

  345678910—MA—010099

CONTENTS

REPRINTED ARTICLES, BY CHAPTER

PREFACE

THE GOALS OF THIS BOOK

Applying Educational Research is designed to help you make your professional practice more effective by explaining how to use the findings and methods of educational research in making decisions. It is written primarily for the student in education who will need to write a research paper that synthesizes and interprets findings from the educational research literature. It is also intended for practicing educators who need to investigate the research relating to an educational issue or problem and to share what they learn with others.

Our aim is not to train you to be an educational researcher but rather to help you learn how to evaluate and interpret educational research and apply its findings to educational practice. This is an important goal because a vast body of information and ideas is contained in the educational research literature. Although educational research rarely results in pat answers, it provides knowledge and insights that are relevant to virtually any practical problem or question in education. If you can locate and interpret research information that relates to the problems that arise in your work, you will be in a position to make sounder decisions than someone who relies solely on personal experience or others' opinions. You will also be able to carry out action research in your work context: reflecting on your practice, generating new strategies to solve practical problems, trying out such strategies with colleagues, and determining the results.

The fourth edition of this book continues the tradition of the earlier editions of making educational research accessible to educational practitioners, especially those who will study this subject in a graduate degree program. We include many actual examples of research studies to illustrate the concepts and procedures of research. Educators today work in increasingly diverse contexts and have a wide variety of responsibilities. For this reason, we have included examples of research from elementary, secondary, and higher education; involving different educator roles, such as staff development, teaching, administration, and education in the private sector; and from varied areas of the curriculum, such as language arts, science, music, and health. Throughout the text, we focus on how educators can apply the methods and findings of educational research in making practical decisions.

This edition maintains the readability and study aids of the book's previous editions. Each approach to educational research that we describe is illustrated by a recent, published research article that is reprinted in full. These 13 research articles are easily identified by their two-column format. They are accompanied by comments written by the individual(s) who conducted the research and by our footnotes that explain technical details and terms that appear in the article. Appendixes 4 and 5 contain questions for evaluating the articles or other quantitative and qualitative research reports.

In this edition, coverage of the methods used in educational research has been broadened. Consistent with recent changes in the field, we have expanded our coverage of qualitative research, so the book now provides balanced treatment of quantitative and qualitative research methods.

WHAT THIS BOOK COVERS

The book has five parts, each preceded by a brief introduction to orient readers to its topics. All the chapters include a vignette, a list of objectives and key terms, and a self-check test to facilitate mastery of their content.

Part I consists of one chapter, in which we explain the important role that research plays in improving educational practice.

Part II describes the process of finding research reports in the published literature that are relevant to specific educational topics. In Chapter 2 we discuss the steps involved in conducting a review of the research literature. In Chapter 3 we explain how to carry out either a hard-copy search or a computer search of the major preliminary sources that index educational research reports. In Chapter 4 we describe procedures for reviewing secondary sources (that is, syntheses of research literature on specific topics), and explain how reading secondary sources can help you identify relevant primary sources (that is, original research reports written by the individuals who conducted the research). Appendixes 1, 2, and 3 at the end of the book provide additional information to help you locate research literature relevant to your needs.

Part III describes the methods and procedures used in conducting quantitative research in education. In Chapter 5 we explain what to look for in each section of a typical report of quantitative research. In Chapter 6 we provide a brief treatment of the statistical analysis of research data, which is central to quantitative research design. Chapters 7, 8, and 9 cover the main methods of quantitative research found in the research literature: descriptive and causal-comparative research in Chapter 7, correlational research in Chapter 8, and experimental research in Chapter 9.

Part IV describes various approaches that are used in conducting qualitative research in education. In Chapter 10 we describe case study research and provide an overview of qualitative research traditions that have influenced education. Chapters 11, 12, and 13 describe three of the traditions that guide many qualitative research studies in education: ethnographic research in Chapter 11, critical-theory research in Chapter 12, and historical research in Chapter 13.

Part V covers applications of educational research that can involve either quantitative or qualitative research methods: evaluation research in Chapter 14, and action research in Chapter 15.

An Instructor's Manual is available to accompany the text. It includes suggestions for designing an introductory or applied research course for graduate students in education and related fields; application problems that can be assigned for each chapter, along with suggested answers; and a test item bank with both open-form (essay-type) and closed-form (objective) items covering the content of each chapter.

In writing this book, we assumed that most readers will have little or no previous instruction in educational measurement or statistics. For this reason, we explain the essentials of statistics and measurement so that you can understand their use in educational research. Everything in the book relates to the goal of helping you become an intelligent consumer of educational research findings and methods. As a result, you need to make a thorough and careful study of the book in order to achieve its specified goals and objectives.

A SUGGESTED STUDY STRATEGY

Most students will find the following strategy effective for studying this book:

Read the vignette, objectives, and key terms. Each chapter begins with a brief vignette, followed by objectives and key terms. These beginning elements are designed to give you a sense of the scope of the chapter and to help you focus on the main concepts that you will be learning.

The objectives are stated in approximately the same order in which they are covered in the chapter, whereas the key terms are listed in alphabetical order. We recommend that you read the objectives and list of key terms to see which ones are new to you and which ones you already know. If you learn well by taking notes, you can use the lists of objectives and key terms to organize your note taking.

Read the body of the chapter. As you read the chapter, try to locate the main ideas related to each objective, and the definitions of key terms. We recommend that you underline or highlight main concepts, but avoid underlining too much.

The body of the chapter gives examples that are designed to help you place the chapter's ideas into a meaningful context. In addition to reading these examples, reflect on what each concept might mean in some specific educational context that is familiar to you. Reread the sections about any ideas that are new to you or that you find difficult to grasp.

Check the meaning of research terms. In reading the text, you probably will encounter some terms with which you are not familiar. If so, we suggest that you first check the glossary at the back of the book. It gives a definition of the research terms in the book, in alphabetical order. You also can check the subject index to find the pages on which each term is discussed in the book. When you are reading a reprinted article, also read the footnotes for the article. These footnotes further explain technical terms that might cause you difficulty in understanding the article. We also suggest that you ask your instructor or your classmates about terms and concepts that you wish to understand more thoroughly.

Check your mastery.   After you finish reading an entire chapter, go back to the objectives and see if you can state the concepts or carry out the activities described in each objective. If you find any objectives that you have not mastered, reread the sections related to the objective that you underlined, and then check yourself again. Review the list of key terms in a similar fashion. Then take the self-check test in the chapter, which includes one or more multiple-choice items related to each of the chapter objectives. If you wish to expand your understanding of particular aspects of educational research, read some of the recommended readings listed for the chapter.

Review previous chapters.   As you progress through the book, review the objectives and the material you underlined in previous chapters before you start to read the next chapter. You will find that each chapter builds on what you learned in previous chapters. To develop your skills in locating and interpreting educational research, we recommend that you read every chapter that is assigned and at least scan any chapters that are not assigned. We also suggest that you review the main concepts in earlier chapters periodically while you are studying the later chapters.

Prepare for tests.   You can prepare for the instructor's tests by rereading the chapter objectives and key terms, the chapter material that you underlined, and any notes that you took. You can prepare even better if you work with a classmate as the last step in your study sequence. Each of you can alternate taking the role of the instructor by making up questions about the chapter content and asking your classmate to answer them.

Complete any assigned application problems.   The Instructor's Manual for this text contains application problems for each chapter, along with suggested answers, which your instructor may choose to assign. We recommend that you work on these problems carefully. They will deepen your understanding of the research process, especially of the many problems and decisions that confront researchers in investigating educational issues and phenomena.

ACKNOWLEDGMENTS

We want to thank our colleagues at Longman for their support in producing this edition, especially Arianne Weber and Art Pomponio. We also thank the authors of the articles reprinted in the book. They not only agreed to allow their research to be shared but also prepared thoughtful comments to help readers appreciate their work and responded promptly to our many requests for information.

We wish to express our deep appreciation to the members of the family of our deceased colleague Walter Borg—his widow, Marie, his daughter, Adrienne, and his granddaughter, Rose. Through them we honor our continued association with Walter as a scholar and a friend.

To the following reviewers of portions of the manuscript, our sincere thanks. We greatly appreciate your willingness to spend your time carefully reading chapter drafts and sending us both critical and constructive comments to refine the manuscript. The book is a better work because of your efforts.

Mariam Jean Dreher, *University of Maryland*
Thomas P. Evans, *Oregon State University*
Gonzalo Garcia, Jr., *Texas A&M University*
Bert A. Goldman, *University of North Carolina at Greensboro*
Bryan W. Griffin, *Georgia Southern University*
Stephen J. Jenkins, *Georgia Southern University*
H. W. Meyers, *University of Vermont*
Alan D. Moore, *University of Wyoming*
Henry B. Reiff, *Western Maryland College*
Donald L. Walters, *Temple University*

Joyce P. Gall
M. D. Gall

PART I
THE CONTRIBUTIONS OF EDUCATIONAL RESEARCH

This part of the book provides an overview of educational research as an organized approach to inquiry about the many facets of teaching, learning, and schooling. You will find that the goals of this inquiry include the discovery of patterns in educational practice, the development of theories to explain such patterns, and the use of research knowledge in the creation and validation of methods to improve educational practice.

You also will learn that educational researchers face important, still unresolved, philosophical issues concerning the nature of social reality and the best means for acquiring knowledge about it. Researchers have taken different positions on these issues, and consequently, they have developed quite different approaches to the investigation of education. We introduce you in Part I of the book to the two main approaches, commonly known as quantitative and qualitative research. Subsequent parts of the book provide detailed explanations of how research studies are conducted according to each approach.

In reading Part I, you will find that research plays an important role in efforts to improve educational practice. At the same time, educational research is a very human process and, therefore, it is prone to error and bias. We describe various procedures that researchers have developed to minimize the influence of such factors on their findings.

CHAPTER 1
USING RESEARCH TO IMPROVE EDUCATIONAL PRACTICE

Mary Gomez has been an elementary school teacher for 20 years. She has taken classes about how to help different types of students learn to read, and has tried to apply this knowledge in her own classroom. She served on a reading curriculum committee for her middle school, but found it frustrating. "Nobody asked about the goals of the different reading programs we looked at, or how we could be sure they would really help our kids learn," she complained to her husband. "They were more concerned about which program looked nicest and would be easiest to use." To another teacher she confided, "We must find some way to improve students' reading skills before they get to middle school and fall further behind. But from now on I want my voice to be heard more. That's why I'm going back to the university for my master's degree. I want to find out what's really known about teaching reading. I want to be able to cite research, not just my experience or opinions."

Mary has designed her master's degree program so that she will learn in depth about research on the reading process and on reading instruction. To understand this body of research knowledge, she will need to develop general research skills. For this reason, she most likely will take a research methods course in which she will study this textbook or one like it. Perhaps there is some similarity between your situation as an educational practitioner and Mary Gomez's.

In this chapter we introduce you to the world of educational research and how it can be used to improve educational practice. Also, you will learn about different types of research and how each type contributes to our understanding of education.

OBJECTIVES

After studying this chapter, you will be able to

1. define research and explain its role in professional work.
2. explain how basic, applied, and action research each contribute to practice.
3. explain how an awareness of research findings and methods can benefit educational practitioners.
4. describe several ways in which practitioners in education can collaborate with researchers.
5. describe the key characteristics of research that differentiate it from other forms of inquiry.

6. describe how quantitative researchers and qualitative researchers differ in their views about the nature of knowledge, and how that difference affects their approach to data collection and analysis.

KEY TERMS

action research	interpretivism	reflexivity
applied research	positivism	refutation
basic research	postmodernism	replication
construct	predictive research	theory
descriptive research	progressive discourse	triangulation
educational research	qualitative research	
epistemology	quantitative research	

THE NATURE OF EDUCATIONAL RESEARCH

Educators are members of a profession. Teachers, school psychologists, principals, and many other types of practitioners who work in the field of education must earn professional licenses or degrees in order to gain employment. Most belong to professional associations in their fields of specialization.

A major characteristic of a profession is that it has a base of research knowledge. For example, the medical profession has a base of research knowledge that derives from research in biology, chemistry, and other physical sciences. In the profession of business management, the knowledge base is informed by research in such disciplines as economics, psychology, and mathematics.

The education profession also has a base of research knowledge. This knowledge base derives primarily from disciplines in the social sciences, including psychology, history, anthropology, and sociology. In addition, many individuals receive training specifically to conduct research investigations of educational issues and practices. Educational research is a substantial enterprise, as evidenced by the large membership of the American Educational Research Association.

If you wish to be a fully informed member of the education profession, you will need to learn about the knowledge generated by researchers. You also will need to develop an understanding of their methods of inquiry and of the problems and practices that they are currently investigating. You would expect no less of a doctor, an engineer, a therapist, an airline pilot, or any other professional on whom you depend.

The Purpose of Educational Research

Educational research can be defined as the systematic collection and analysis of information (sometimes called *data*) in order to develop valid, generalizable descriptions, predictions, interventions, and explanations relating to various aspects of education.

Descriptive research focuses on making careful, highly detailed observations or measurements of educational phenomena. For example, Marilyn Adams's monumental synthesis of research on learning to read includes findings about how an individual's eyes move while reading text (Adams, 1990). Contrary to popular belief, researchers have found that good readers process every word in the text rather than engage in selective scanning. This finding has important implications for teaching children to read. You will study the methods of descriptive research in Chapter 7.

Predictive research involves using data collected at one point in time to predict future behavior or events. For example, important research has been done to study the relationship between parenting practices or family disruptions (e.g., divorce) and children's subsequent academic achievement. This form of predictive research is called correlational research. Another form of predictive research is causal-comparative research: Researchers identify an event of interest that has already occurred (e.g., a group of children has high or low self-esteem), and they try to identify factors that may have caused it. You will study the methods of causal-comparative and correlational research in Chapters 7 and 8, respectively.

Some research seeks to determine whether a phenomenon can be controlled or improved by a particular intervention. Research of this type involves the experimental method. For example, many researchers have conducted experiments to determine whether introducing cooperative learning into a classroom improves students' learning. This important line of experimental research is reviewed in a published literature review that appears in Chapter 4. You will study the methods of experimental research in Chapter 9.

Some individuals believe that the ultimate goal of educational research is to develop theories that explain various aspects of education. A theory is an explanation of particular phenomena in terms of a set of underlying constructs and a set of principles that relates these constructs to each other. Constructs refer to structures or processes that are presumed to underlie observed phenomena.

For example, our local newspaper reported a new research finding with major significance for the teaching of motor skills (Recer, 1997). The researchers, led by a psychiatrist at Johns Hopkins University, used a device to measure blood flow in the brain. They observed consistent changes in the portion of research participants' brains where blood flow was most active during and after motor learning tasks. They used constructs from the information-processing theory of learning to explain these changes in blood flow and motor-skill learning.

The researchers found that it takes approximately six hours for a new motor skill that has been taught to move from short-term memory to long-term memory. If another new motor skill is taught during this six-hour interval, the first motor skill will not move into long-term memory. Short-term memory and long-term memory are constructs in information-processing theory. They are called constructs because they cannot be observed directly, but are inferred to exist on the basis of observed phenomena.

The possible applications of this finding are considerable. For example, say that a teacher is teaching students a new skill (e.g., cutting wood with a power saw). If the students then get a lesson shortly thereafter on another new skill (e.g., serving a volleyball), the memory of the first skill is not likely to be retained. More time must pass before the new skill is introduced, so that the skill studied in the first lesson is permanently learned.

Information-processing theory and other theories are powerful because they not only help to explain educational phenomena but also help educators make predictions and design better forms of instruction or other interventions. For example, information-processing theory has helped educators understand and improve students' ability to read with good comprehension and to prepare for school tests effectively. Some of the research articles that you will read later in this book draw from and in turn contribute to such theories.

Basic and Applied Research

Researchers do not use a single approach to inquiry. Some of their investigations can be characterized as basic research, whereas others can be characterized as applied research. The purpose of basic research is to understand basic processes and structures that underlie observed behavior. For example, medical research currently is making enormous advances by seeking to explain the occurrence of certain diseases (the observed behavior) in terms of underlying differences in gene composition (a basic structure) among individuals. The published article that you will read in Chapter 10 reports basic research on how teachers construct a personal knowledge base to inform their daily work.

In contrast to basic research, the purpose of applied research is to develop and test predictions and interventions that can be used directly to improve practice. In education, the development and testing of a new method to help students engage in mathematical problem solving would be an example of applied research. The published research articles that are included in Chapters 9 (Experimental Research), 14 (Evaluation Research), and 15 (Action Research) are examples of applied research.

Some practitioners believe that applied research is more valuable as a guide to their work than basic research, and that it should therefore have funding priority over basic research. A study of medical research by Julius Comroe and Robert Dripps (1976) raises doubts about this view. Comroe and Dripps studied the advances in research knowledge that were necessary for innovations in the treatment of cardiovascular and pulmonary disease (e.g., cardiac surgery and chemotherapy). Surprisingly, many more basic research studies were instrumental in these innovations than were applied research studies. Basic research leads to theoretical understanding of underlying processes and structures, and this understanding provides a necessary foundation for constructing interventions that are likely to be effective.

THE BENEFITS OF EDUCATIONAL RESEARCH

It is difficult to convince some educators that research benefits practitioners and students. For example, we might point to standardized tests (e.g., intelligence tests and college-entrance tests) as products of research that are in wide use today. However, education and research are value-laden enterprises. While some educators believe that standardized tests are valuable, others believe that these tests are harmful to the teaching-learning process.

In another example, recent research reviewed by Beth Azar (1997) suggests that day care may have adverse effects on children's later social and academic development. These research findings might lead to beneficial changes in day-care practice, but some groups have decried the entire line of research as sexist.

These examples suggest that research can and does contribute to the practice of education, but only to practice based on a particular set of values. In this respect, education is no different than other professions. Research has shown business managers various ways in which to maximize profit. Some individuals might view this research as valuable, but others may view the profit motive as immoral and might therefore reject this type of research. Medical research keeps finding new ways to prolong life in seriously ill patients, but some individuals question the ethics of this goal.

Another reason that it is difficult to claim that research has benefited educational practice is that its influence is rarely direct. The work of education professionals is influenced by many factors, only one of which is research. Also, it often takes a long time for research findings to find their way into practice. The change process in education is very slow.

As you read this textbook, you will study a variety of published literature reviews and research studies, along with comments from the researchers who wrote them. After reading each one, we invite you to consider whether it was worth doing. For example, you can ask yourself the question, "Did I learn anything of value from this study?" In our experience, professional educators who have read studies like these do find value in them. At the same time, they may be hard-pressed to find a *direct* application of these studies' findings to educational practice. Rather, the main benefit of the increased professional knowledge that they gain from reading such studies is that the findings inform their thinking about particular practices. Then they must combine this thinking with other factors (e.g., the budgetary and political realities of schools), and with their own creativity, in order to generate new solutions to problems of practice. In other words, research knowledge usually is a necessary, but not sufficient, condition for the improvement of practice.

Robert Slavin (1989) has demonstrated how the practice of education has swung like a pendulum from one fad to another and back again. The shift from phonics-based reading instruction to whole-language instruction, now reversing back to phonics-based instruction, is one example of the pendulum-swing phenomenon that is so common in educational practice. Although pendulum swings change education, they rarely result in lasting improvement. Slavin argues that practitioners need to learn about research so that they may start to base their decisions more upon evidence and less upon fads promoted by charismatic individuals.

APPLYING EDUCATIONAL RESEARCH TO PRACTICE

Using Research Knowledge to Inform Practice

Educators need a large amount of knowledge in order to carry out their work effectively. For example, they need knowledge about the learning process, knowledge about student characteristics, and knowledge about school management. Where does this knowledge come from? For example, how do teachers, in preparing for the first day of school, decide what to do when their first class of new students arrives?

Some teachers rely on their past experience, perhaps the experience gained during their student teaching. Other teachers base their decisions on the opinion or example of colleagues, or of people whom they consider to be experts. Still others might decide to do whatever occurs to them at the time, believing that they can only learn by trial and error what works and what doesn't work in the classroom.

This book does not discount personal experience, expert opinion, or even the results of trial and error as a knowledge base for professional practice. What it does is show the value of including research as part of your knowledge base.

Let's consider another hypothetical, but typical, example of educational practice. Suppose that you are a high school teacher, and your principal has proposed to offer a study skills class and an after-school study hall with volunteer tutors to incoming freshmen. When asked for his opinion, one of your teacher colleagues (A) tells the principal that study skills classes are a waste of time: "The way I learned study skills was from my mom helping me review for tests. And that's how most of my best students learn study skills, too." Another teacher colleague (B) favors the program because she believes in anything that seems innovative.

You might sense that colleague A is making a decision mainly on the basis of personal experience, while colleague B believes in improvement through trial and error. You, on the other hand, might decide to do some reading about study skills before forming your opinion. With the help of an experienced librarian, you do a literature search. You find articles that reflect expert opinion, but also describe research on the effectiveness of study skills programs and procedures for implementing such programs. At the next faculty meeting, when the topic of the study skills class and study hall is raised, you probably will feel that you have a much better understanding of what the benefits might be for your school's students, and you will know what questions to ask.

Part II of this book will help you develop skills for reviewing the education literature on issues and problems that arise in your work. Some of this literature presents theory, opinions, or the personal experience of practitioners and others, but our focus is on the research literature. You will learn how to conduct a literature review (Chapter 2), and how to use preliminary sources to find literature on particular topics (Chapter 3). You will also learn how to obtain and evaluate published literature reviews on particular topic areas (Chapter 4).

Because there are many types of research studies, you need to understand the specific purposes and methods of each type. The chapters in Parts III, IV, and V will help you develop this understanding. In Chapter 7 and each subsequent chapter, you will read a description of each type of educational research and a published study that illustrates it. In addition, you will read comments written for this book by the authors of these studies. Reading their comments will give you a deeper understanding of how researchers think, why they decide to carry out a particular research study, how they go about designing their research, and what the relevance of their work is to educational practitioners.

Conducting Action Research

Action research is research carried out by practitioners to improve their own practice. There are at least two reasons why practitioners might want to conduct action research rather than relying on findings from others' research. One reason involves the generalizability of research findings, that is, the extent to which the findings are likely to apply to their particular work situation. For example, a program might have been found effective in urban schools, but you may work in a suburban or rural school. In this case you could carry out your own research to determine the program's effectiveness in your situation.

A second reason that practitioners might wish to conduct action research is that they have a question about an idea or method, and the research literature has not provided sufficient information to answer the question to their satisfaction. For example, suppose a counselor has been collecting anecdotes and newspaper articles about the growing problem of drug abuse among younger students. She has ideas for a program to address the problem but cannot find an existing program or set of research findings that relate to her ideas. By carrying out action research, she can develop the program and determine whether it is effective.

Action research does not need to be as formal as the studies that are reported in research journals. The reason is that an action researcher is not concerned with obtaining findings that can be generalized to other settings. Nonetheless, local action research can draw on the methods of data collection and analysis, including the techniques for minimizing bias, that professional researchers have developed.

You will learn procedures for conducting action research in Chapter 15. The placement of the chapter at the end of the book reflects the fact that action researchers can use any of the approaches to research that are presented in the previous chapters. Therefore, reading those chapters first will give you a better understanding of the variety of ways in which you can design your own action research projects.

Collaborating with Researchers

In order for research to inform and improve practice, practitioners need to participate in an ongoing dialogue with research professionals. Maintaining a dialogue can be a challenge, however. One reason is that researchers and practitioners tend to be very different in their views about knowledge and research. According to Lilian Katz and Dianne Rothenberg (1996), researchers' main interest in knowledge is scientific: When confronted with a problem, they seek to explore and discover the nature of the problem, no matter how long that might take. By contrast, practitioners' main interest in knowledge is clinical: When confronted with a problem, they seek information that will allow them to solve it, usually under the pressure of a time limit. Katz and Rothenberg add that effective practice:

> . . . depends to some extent on the certainty with which the practitioner approaches his or her task. And by definition, the researcher's task is to prize doubt and uncertainty and be open to being wrong. . . . (p. 8)

Researchers and practitioners can take steps to understand each other's needs and to communicate clearly with each other. For example, researchers can develop research agendas that are responsive to practitioners' needs and can prepare reports of their findings that are written in nontechnical language and that spell out the implications of the findings for practice.

Practitioners in turn need to make an effort to understand the language and methods used by researchers. The researcher's comments that accompany the articles reprinted in this book were specially prepared by the articles' authors to give you a sense of how researchers think. Some of these researchers are themselves practitioners. For example, the author of the historical research article reprinted in Chapter 13, Terese Volk, is a music teacher in a public school district, and the author of the action research article reprinted in Chapter 15, Beverly Jatko, is a teacher of gifted and talented students at the elementary school level.

In addition to improving lines of communication, practitioners and researchers can strengthen the application of research to practice through collaboration. Several types of collaborative possibilities are described below.

Being a Research Participant.   Researchers often ask practitioners to participate in research studies. The effort required might be minimal (e.g., filling out a questionnaire) or more extensive (e.g., volunteering your class to be part of the experimental or control group in an experiment). By volunteering to participate, you may find that you are eligible to receive special training or consultation, or curriculum materials that can be kept and reused. You also learn about how research is actually done and how it can contribute a fresh perspective about educational phenomena.

Participating in Program Evaluation.   Educational institutions often obtain grants from private or government funding sources to implement experimental programs. These grants typically require the grantee to carry out an evaluation of the program during or at the end of the funding period. If your institution employs evaluation specialists, you can work alongside them to design an evaluation that is appropriate for your experimental program's intended objectives. For this collaboration to happen, however, you need to be knowledgeable about evaluation research. If no evaluation specialists are available to help you in securing a grant and satisfying its requirements for evaluation, you will need to know enough about evaluation research to deal effectively with this aspect of the grant.

Chapter 14 will explain how to conduct an evaluation study, and how to decide whether you can apply the findings of other evaluations to help you make a decision in your own practice. Because evaluation research may involve any of the research approaches described in Parts III and IV of this book, study of the chapters in those parts of the book will be helpful to you, too.

Influencing Policy Agendas.   Various policy-making bodies, ranging from national and state legislatures to local school districts, are constantly proposing changes in educational practice that directly affect practitioners' work. Some changes are sound, but others make little sense to the practitioners who must implement them. For example, many states have implemented or are considering mandatory achievement testing of all students in order to make educators accountable for student learning outcomes. Teachers in particular are concerned about the validity of these tests and whether they respect the large individual differences in students' learning needs and family situations. However, without knowledge about research on achievement testing and student characteristics, teachers and other practitioners are in a poor position to influence statewide testing programs.

Ill-considered policies perhaps could be avoided if practitioners and researchers would collaborate to make their views and knowledge known to policy makers. For this to happen, though, researchers and practitioners must be familiar with each other's knowledge base and perspective.

CHARACTERISTICS OF RESEARCH

In recent years, some scholars have begun to question the relevance of research to understanding human behavior and society. Adherents of this movement, which is called *postmodernism*, acknowledge that science has contributed to an understanding and control of the physical world, but they argue that no one method of inquiry can claim to be true, or better than any other method, in developing knowledge about the human world (Graham, Doherty, & Malek, 1992). Thus postmodernists would argue that the methods of social science inquiry are not superior to personal reflection, or to other forms of inquiry such as artistic or religious study.

The postmodern critique of scientific inquiry has caused social science researchers (including educational researchers) to rethink their claims to authority in the pursuit of knowledge. They have identified several characteristics of research that establish its claim to authority and that differentiate it from other forms of inquiry. We describe these characteristics in the following sections.

Creation of Concepts and Procedures that Are Shared and Publicly Accessible

Social science researchers have developed specialized concepts (e.g., test reliability) and procedures (e.g., purposeful sampling) to help them conduct studies of high quality. They accept responsibility for making their terminology and procedures public and explicit. Everyone is free to learn and use this terminology and these procedures. Indeed, most journals that publish research reports use a "blind" review procedure, meaning that the reviewers do not have access to the names of the authors or other identifying information about them.

Of course, there are power struggles in the arenas of funding and publicity for research findings, but it is highly unlikely that important theories or findings could be suppressed over the long term. This is because researchers generally are committed to progressive discourse (Bereiter, 1994), which means that anyone at any time can offer a criticism about a particular research study or research methodology, and if it proves to have merit, that criticism is listened to and accommodated.

If we compare educational research with practice, we find that many practitioners perform their work at a high level of excellence and have developed many insights from their personal inquiries. However, they lack concepts and procedures for making their ideas for effective practice publicly accessible. Hence, their knowledge cannot be publicly debated, and it generally disappears when they retire. In contrast, new researchers are able to learn from experienced researchers, and the results are available in research journals for all to study.

Replicability of Findings

For researchers to have their findings published, they must make public the procedures by which the findings were obtained. Because the procedures are public, other researchers can conduct similar studies (called replications), to see whether they obtain the same results. Some researchers conduct their own replication studies, and only publish the findings if their original findings are replicated.

Individuals who engage in nonscientific inquiry may obtain potentially important effects and insights. However, their inquiries are of limited value because they do not make their procedures sufficiently explicit for others to replicate them. Thus, we have no way to know whether an individual's claimed effects and insights are unique to that individual or can inform the work of other individuals.

Refutability of Knowledge Claims

Karl Popper (1968) proposes a standard for testing knowledge claims that has won general acceptance among social science researchers. Popper argues that science advances by submitting its knowledge claims (theories, predictions, hunches) to empirical tests that allow them to be refuted, that is, challenged and disproved. If the data are inconsistent with the knowledge claim, we can say that it is refuted. The knowledge claim must then be abandoned or modified to accommodate the negative findings. If the data are consistent with the knowledge claim, we can conclude that it is supported, but not that it is correct. We can say only that the knowledge claim has not been refuted by any of the tests that have been made of it thus far.

The refutation test of knowledge claims is more rigorous than the way we test everyday knowledge claims. For example, suppose a school administrator visits a particular teacher's classroom one day and discovers that (1) the teacher has attended a recent workshop on behavior management, and (2) the teacher's class is unusually quiet and orderly. The administrator might conclude that the workshop is effective, and therefore she advocates that all teachers be required to take it. In effect, this administrator made an observation first and then formulated a broad knowledge claim. In contrast, researchers who follow Popper's logic make a knowledge claim first and then test it by making observations. The tests are cautious in that contrary data can disprove the knowledge claim, but confirmatory data do not prove it. Instead, if the data are confirmatory, we conclude that the knowledge claim thus far has withstood efforts to refute it.

Control for Researcher Errors and Biases

Researchers acknowledge the likelihood that their own errors and biases will affect the data that they collect. Therefore, they design research studies to minimize the influence of such factors. For example, in making observations, researchers often seek to reduce error by using multiple observers and training them beforehand in the system for collecting data on observational variables. In addition, they may use statistical procedures to estimate the observers' level of agreement. While the observations of different observers rarely agree perfectly, a satisfactory level of agreement can be accepted as an indicator of the accuracy of the observations.

Another approach that is sometimes used to validate findings based on the study of particular cases is triangulation of data sources. Triangulation refers to the researchers' attempts to corroborate the data obtained with one data collection method (e.g., observation of individuals) by using other data collection methods (e.g., interviews of individuals or examination of documents).

Researchers are particularly careful to avoid the error of generalizing their knowledge claims beyond the bounds of what their research findings support. Many of these procedures involve sampling logic, which is explained in Chapter 5. For example, researchers who are interested in studying the effects of teachers' enthusiasm on student attendance might first define a population (e.g., fifth-grade teachers in urban school systems) and then study a sample that is representative of the population. The researchers would generalize the findings obtained from the data collected on this sample only to the population that they initially defined. To generalize knowledge claims beyond the defined population is considered speculative until those knowledge claims are supported by evidence from new studies that involve other populations.

Other research procedures that we describe in various chapters of this book are intended to minimize various researcher errors and biases in data collection and analysis. We invite you to compare the rigor of these procedures with the everyday procedures that individuals use in their personal lives or in the workplace to arrive at and justify their knowledge claims.

QUANTITATIVE AND QUALITATIVE RESEARCH

Educational research is not a unified enterprise. For example, the approaches to research described in Part III (called *quantitative*) involve the study of samples and populations, and rely heavily on numerical data and statistical analysis. In contrast, the research traditions described in Part IV (called *qualitative*) make little use of numbers or statistics, but instead rely heavily on verbal data and subjective analysis.

Why does educational research include such diverse approaches? To answer this question, we need to consider the different epistemologies—that is, views about the nature of knowledge—that guide educational researchers. Some researchers assume that features of the human environment have an objective reality, meaning that they exist independently of the individuals who created them or are observing them. The students in a teacher's first-period class are viewed as the same, irrespective of what the teacher is thinking about them or doing with them at the moment. These researchers subscribe to a positivist epistemology. Positivists believe that there is a real world "out there" and that it is available for study through scientific means similar to those that were developed in the physical sciences.

Most quantitative research is carried out by researchers who ascribe to the positivist epistemology. Thus they define their subjects of interest in terms of observable behavior (e.g., "feeling good about one's teacher" might become "students report positive attitudes . . ."). They attempt to define that behavior in terms of the specific operations used to measure it (e.g., "students with positive attitudes gave average ratings of 3 or higher on 5-point scales . . ."). They also are concerned about the probability that what they discover in a research sample would occur in the larger world from which that sample was presumably drawn.

Other researchers take the epistemological position known as *interpretivism* (Erickson, 1986). To them, aspects of the human environment are constructed by the individuals who participate in that environment. Interpretivists believe that aspects of social reality have no existence apart from the meanings that individuals construct for them. For example, the students in a teacher's first-period class might be constructed as "13 boys and 16 girls," or as 29 unique individuals, or as "easier to teach than students I've had other years," depending on when the teacher is thinking about them. If the principal steps into the teacher's classroom, his construction of the students in the class might vary depending on how they are behaving at the moment, how the principal is feeling, or many other factors.

Most qualitative research is carried out by individuals who subscribe to the interpretivist epistemology. These researchers believe that scientific inquiry must focus on the study of the different social realities that individuals in a social situation construct as they participate in it. Qualitative researchers usually study single individuals or situations, each of which is called a *case*, and generalize case findings mainly by comparing the case with other cases that also have been studied in depth.

Qualitative researchers also accept and acknowledge their own role in constructing the social realities that they describe in their research reports. For this reason they often include their own experiences in what they report. This focus on the researcher's self as a constructor of social reality is called *reflexivity*.

While some scholars use the terms *positivism* and *interpretivism* to distinguish these two approaches to research, the terms *quantitative research* and *qualitative research* are more commonly used. For this reason we will refer to quantitative and qualitative research in this book. The terms *quantitative* and *qualitative* highlight the differences in the kinds of data that typically are collected by the researchers, and the ways in which the data are analyzed. Table 1.1 provides a further elaboration of the distinguishing characteristics of quantitative and qualitative research.

Given that both quantitative research and qualitative research are conducted to investigate education, several questions arise. Is one approach better than the other? Do they complement each other in some way? Do they produce conflicting findings?

Some researchers (e.g., Biddle & Anderson, 1986) believe that the methods of qualitative research and quantitative research are complementary, and that

TABLE 1.1 **Differences between Quantitative and Qualitative Research**

Quantitative researchers	Qualitative researchers
Assume an objective social reality.	Assume that social reality is constructed by the participants in it.
Assume that social reality is relatively constant across time and settings.	Assume that social reality is continuously constructed in local situations.
View causal relationships among social phenomena from a mechanistic perspective.	Assign human intentions a major role in explaining causal relationships among social phenomena.
Take an objective, detached stance toward research participants and their setting.	Become personally involved with research participants, to the point of sharing perspectives and assuming a caring attitude.
Study populations or samples that represent populations.	Study cases.
Study behavior and other observable phenomena.	Study the meanings that individuals create and other internal phenomena.
Study human behavior in natural or contrived settings.	Study human actions in natural settings.
Analyze social reality into variables.	Make holistic observations of the total context within which social action occurs.
Use preconceived concepts and theories to determine what data will be collected.	Discover concepts and theories after data have been collected.
Generate numerical data to represent the social environment.	Generate verbal and pictorial data to represent the social environment.
Use statistical methods to analyze data.	Use analytic induction to analyze data.
Use statistical inference procedures to generalize findings from a sample to a defined population.	Generalize case findings by searching for other similar cases.
Prepare impersonal, objective reports of research findings.	Prepare interpretive reports that reflect researchers' constructions of the data and an awareness that readers will form their own constructions from what is reported.

Source. Table 1.3 on p. 30 in: Gall, M. D., Borg, W. R., & Gall, J. P. (1996). *Educational research: An introduction* (6th ed.). White Plains, NY: Longman.

researchers who use a combination of both types of methods can give the fullest picture of the nature of educational phenomena. One study that used this approach was conducted by Stephen Stoynoff (1990), who studied international students. English was the second language for the 77 students in his sample, who had just begun their freshman year at a U.S. university.

First Stoynoff conducted quantitative research to determine how well students' scores on the Test of English as a Foreign Language (TOEFL) and on the Learning and Study Strategies Inventory (LASSI) predicted their first-term grade point average (GPA). The results indicated that TOEFL and LASSI scores yielded only modest predictions of GPA. Stoynoff then conducted qualitative case studies of selected members of his sample to determine whether other factors might be more important to the academic success of international students. Stoynoff made the following discovery from the case studies:

> The LASSI does not measure the compensatory methods that students use to help them negotiate the system. Interviews revealed that students sought social assistance from a wide variety of persons. They used tutors and roommates to explain and review homework. They borrowed lecture notes, previous tests, and papers from classmates and friends. They asked teachers for extra help. Students also learned to carefully select their courses based on the recommendations of others. These compensatory methods are not measured by the LASSI . . . . (p. 112)

Stoynoff's discoveries from his qualitative research could be used to conceptualize what *compensatory method* means. Another researcher might then develop a measure of such compensatory strategies, and administer it to a sample in a quantitative research study to test Stoynoff's insights. Depending on the results, new studies might be done, again combining the approaches of qualitative and quantitative research.

Some researchers would argue that quantitative and qualitative research are incompatible because they are based on different epistemological assumptions. For example, they might argue that it is not possible to believe that social reality exists independently of the observer while also asserting that it is constructed by the observer. In our opinion, both approaches have helped educational researchers make important discoveries. Over time, philosophers of science may gain enough understanding to resolve the seeming contradictions in the epistemological assumptions that underlie qualitative and quantitative research.

CONCLUDING THOUGHT

There are many reform movements and fads in education today. Being knowledgeable about educational research methods and findings can help you evaluate the merits of the many competing claims about what is needed to improve education. Also, knowing about research provides a useful counterpoint to personal experience and expert opinion in the development of your own philosophy about educational practice.

In this chapter we have described the nature of the research knowledge base that is available to educational practitioners and sought to demonstrate the various ways in which research contributes to the practice of education. We have also explained key differences between basic, applied, and action research and between quantitative and qualitative research.

SELF-CHECK TEST

1. An essential characteristic of educational research is its
   a. attempt to prove particular theories of learning.
   b. assumption that the control of human behavior is unethical.
   c. systematic collection and analysis of information.
   d. use of statistical procedures to determine the significance of research findings.

2. The role of theory in educational research is primarily to
   a. develop precise descriptions of educational phenomena.
   b. explain phenomena in terms of constructs and principles.
   c. evaluate the effectiveness of specific instructional interventions.
   d. provide a language that facilitates collaboration between educational researchers and educational practitioners.

3. Unlike applied research, basic research
   a. has a relatively minor role in the education profession.
   b. seeks to develop interventions that can be used directly to improve educational practice.
   c. seeks to prove specific knowledge claims to be true or false.
   d. seeks to develop understanding of the processes and structures underlying observed behavior.

4. Action research is particularly appropriate when educators
   a. want to test a particular theory of education.
   b. are concerned about improving local practice rather than developing generalizable knowledge.
   c. wish to pinpoint the precise causes of an educational phenomenon.
   d. have minimal knowledge about the methods of basic or applied research.

5. For educational practitioners the main benefit of reading research findings is that such findings
   a. provide the best basis for making professional decisions.
   b. can be applied directly to improve practice.
   c. are more effective than political advocacy in bringing about changes in educational policy.
   d. enrich their thinking about particular educational practices.

6. In order to collaborate successfully with researchers, educational practitioners will find it essential to
   a. suspend judgment as to the potential implications of the research for practice.
   b. obtain formal training in how to conduct research.
   c. volunteer as research participants.
   d. make an effort to understand research terminology and procedures.

7. Using multiple observers to collect observational data about a particular phenomenon illustrates researchers' concern for
   a. obtaining generalizable findings.
   b. obtaining different perspectives about the phenomenon.
   c. controlling for researcher errors and biases.
   d. predicting future behavior or events.

8. If the research data that are collected are consistent with the researchers' knowledge claim, we can conclude that the knowledge claim
   a. has practical significance.
   b. is valid.
   c. has not been refuted.
   d. is generalizable beyond the defined population.

9. Qualitative researchers are much more likely than quantitative researchers to
   a. describe in their research reports their personal experiences in conducting the study.
   b. study samples rather than individual cases.
   c. make carefully detailed observations of educational phenomena.
   d. define constructs in terms of observable behavior.

10. Quantitative researchers tend to
    a. subscribe to the belief in an objective reality independent of the observer.
    b. believe that aspects of the human environment are constructed by the participants in that environment.
    c. disregard description as a goal of scientific inquiry.
    d. disregard the possible effects of their own biases on the research findings.

CHAPTER REFERENCES

Adams, M. J. (1990). *Beginning to read: Thinking and learning about print*. Cambridge, MA: MIT Press.

Azar, B. (1997). When research is swept under the rug. *American Psychological Association Monitor, 28* (8), pp. 1, 18.

Bereiter, C. (1994). Implications of postmodernism for science, or, science as progressive discourse. *Educational Psychologist, 29*, 3–12. Quote appears on p. 6.

Biddle, B. J., & Anderson, D. S. (1986). Theory, methods, knowledge, and research on teaching. In M. C. Wittrock (Ed.), *Handbook of research on teaching* (3rd ed., pp. 230–252). New York: Macmillan. Quote appears on p. 239.

Comroe, J. H., Jr., & Dripps, R. D. (1976). Scientific basis for the support of biomedical science. *Science, 192*, 105–111.

Erickson, F. (1986). Qualitative methods in research on teaching. In M. C. Wittrock (Ed.), *Handbook of research on teaching* (3rd ed) (pp. 119–161). New York: Macmillan.

Graham, E., Doherty, J., & Malek, M. (1992). Introduction: The context and language of postmodernism. In J. Doherty, E. Graham, & M. Malek (Eds.), *Postmodernism and the social sciences* (pp. 1–23). Basingstoke, England: Macmillan.

Katz, L. G., & Rothenberg, D. (1996). Issues in dissemination: An ERIC perspective. *The ERIC Review, 5*, 2–9.

Popper, K. (1968). *Conjectures and refutations*. New York: Harper.

Recer, P. (1997, August 8). Learning physical skill requires time. *The Register Guard*, pp. 1A, 10A.

Slavin, R. E. (1989). PET and the pendulum: Faddism in education and how to stop it. *Phi Delta Kappan, 70*, 752–758.

Stoynoff, S. J. (1990). English language proficiency and study strategies as determinants of academic success for international students in U.S. universities. *Dissertation Abstracts International, 52*(01), 97A. University Microfilms No. AAC-9117569.

RECOMMENDED READING

Cooper, H. (1996). Speaking power to truth: Reflections of an educational researcher after 4 years of school board service. *Educational Researcher, 25* (1), 29–34.

The author describes his efforts to include knowledge of educational research as a legitimate component of his service as a member of the school board in a midwestern community. He explains the aspects of research that may have contributed to the skepticism of some board and community members toward research knowledge as a basis for policy making.

Gage, N. L. (1985). Hard gains in the soft sciences: The case of pedagogy. Bloomington, IN: Phi Delta Kappa.

The author demonstrates how research can contribute to practice by describing some of the practical gains that have resulted from a generation of research on teaching. Of the nine experimental research studies reviewed, all designed to improve teaching through inservice teacher education, eight brought about significant improvement in teaching performance as well as in student achievement, attitudes, or behavior. A number of models for the scientific study of teaching are described.

Leutheuser, J. (Ed.). (1994). *Educational programs that work: The catalogue of the National Diffusion Network (NDN)*, 20th ed. (Also available as ERIC Document Reference No. ED 379 219.)

Describes projects approved for national dissemination by the U.S. Department of Education since the last edition was published, including evidence of effectiveness. To be eligible for dissemination approval, the programs had to be subjected to evaluation research that demonstrated their effectiveness.

PART II

THE RESEARCH LITERATURE ON EDUCATION

The knowledge base in educational research continues to expand at an accelerating rate. Similarly, the technology designed to store and access that knowledge in the form of electronic or hard-copy databases is expanding and changing rapidly. Thus, you need to know the current status of these databases, and how to search them to identify research findings that can help guide and improve your educational practice. The chapters in Part II are designed to inform you about sources of research findings and how to search them effectively.

In Chapter 2 we discuss the value of preliminary, primary, and secondary sources of research literature, and how they differ from each other. The chapter also describes a generic strategy for finding educational literature that bears on a problem or question that concerns you.

Chapter 3 describes how to conduct either a hard-copy or computer search of preliminary sources, which are indexes to journal articles, book chapters, conference proceedings, technical reports, and other types of research literature. We place particular emphasis on ERIC, which is the preliminary source most often used by educators.

Chapter 4 explains the value of reading secondary sources, which are reviews of the literature that experts have prepared on particular topics or problems. We describe strategies for locating appropriate secondary sources early in your literature search. Three articles that illustrate different types of secondary sources are reprinted in full at the end of the chapter.

Chapter 2

Conducting a Review of the Research Literature

For seven years, Clara Davis has taught career development and health classes at a community college. Clara wants to expand the career development program to give students more intensive preparation for careers involving technology.

Clara has decided to submit a grant proposal to a foundation that supports innovative educational efforts. The proposal will require her to demonstrate familiarity with research about adult education and technology. Clara recently made a trip to the library of the state university. She tried looking for books on her own, but could not find anything recent that dealt with both technology and adult education. That was when she decided to make an appointment with the reference librarian, David Conners.

David showed Clara how to select descriptor search terms that best reflected her information needs. Then he demonstrated how to use those terms to quickly search the education literature by computer. With David's help, Clara was able to download over 20 citations for recent publications that relate to both technology and adult education. After reading several of these publications, Clara's picture of the theory and previous research related to her topic area was much clearer. In particular, she sensed a great opportunity for, and unique problems in, teaching computer and technology skills to older adults.

In this chapter we present a general process that you can use to locate research findings and other information about any educational topic. We explain each step of the process, from identifying the questions that will guide a search of the educational literature to preparing a report of the literature review. Once you understand this general process, you can adapt it to meet your specific information needs.

OBJECTIVES

After studying this chapter, you will be able to

1. describe the steps involved in carrying out a literature review, and the purpose of each step.

2. explain the value of contacting experts before you begin your literature review.

3. explain the value of reading a few secondary sources on your topic early in your literature search.

4. define a preliminary, secondary, and primary source, and describe how each type of source is used in the conduct of a literature review.

5. outline the information you need to include in writing a report of your literature review.

KEY TERMS

abstract

bibliographic citation

bulletin board

chart essay

descriptor

preliminary source

primary source

publication

secondary source

A SYSTEMATIC PROCESS FOR CONDUCTING A LITERATURE REVIEW

As we explained in Chapter 1, research findings can help educators by informing their thinking about the problems and questions that arise in their work. For research findings to be helpful, though, educators need some way to access them. They also need to be able to interpret and synthesize the findings, and report them to their colleagues in a meaningful, convincing manner.

The purpose of this chapter is to provide you with a general model for accessing, synthesizing, and reporting research findings that you retrieve from the literature. The steps in the model are summarized in Table 2.1. Each step is described in this chapter, and reference is made to other chapters where certain aspects of the steps are discussed in more depth.

In our explanation of how to conduct a literature review, we focus on identifying research findings that can inform and improve educational practice. However, the education literature also includes theories, expert opinions on issues, descriptions of experimental programs, methods that individual practitioners have found useful in their work, and other information of potential value to you. The literature-review process that we present in this chapter will be useful to you in accessing these types of information as well.

TABLE 2.1 **A Systematic Process for Reviewing the Research Literature**

1. Frame your information needs as a set of questions that will guide your literature search.
2. Contact experts who can answer your questions directly or guide you to relevant publications.
3. Read general secondary sources to obtain a broad overview of the research literature pertaining to your questions.
4. Select preliminary sources that index the type of research literature relevant to your questions.
5. Identify descriptors that reflect your information needs, and use these descriptors to search the preliminary sources for relevant publications.
6. Read and evaluate primary sources that are relevant to your questions.
7. Classify all the publications that you have reviewed into meaningful categories.
8. Prepare a report of the findings of your literature review.

STEP 1: FRAMING QUESTIONS TO GUIDE THE LITERATURE SEARCH

The usual problem that you will encounter in seeking information about a particular topic is not a lack of information, but too much of it. For example, *Cabell's Directory of Publishing Opportunities in Education* (1995) lists over 450 journals in education dealing with nearly every conceivable aspect of educational practice. Also, there are many different types of publications. Here we use the term *publication* to include any communication that has been prepared for dissemination, whether in print, on microfiche, in a computer file, or possibly in other forms. The disseminating agency may be a book publisher, professional association, government office, school system, or other type of organization.

To avoid being lost in the information explosion of our era, you will need to focus your literature search. One way to do this is to reflect on your information needs, and then frame them as a set of questions. Here are a few examples of this process:

An inner-city elementary school teacher is concerned about students fighting during and after school. She has heard that anger-management and conflict-resolution programs have been developed for schools, and wants to learn about them. She formulates the following questions to guide her literature search: "What anger-management and conflict-resolution programs, if any, have been developed for use at the elementary-school level? What are the characteristics of these programs? Is there any evidence that they are effective?"

A committee of school superintendents met with officials from the state department of education to learn more about plans for statewide mandatory testing of students' achievement at selected grade levels. The superintendents expressed several concerns about the testing program. State officials worked with the superintendents to frame questions for which the state department agreed to seek answers. The following key questions were framed: "What have other states with mandatory testing programs done to ensure that the tests accurately reflected the school curriculum? What have other states done to ensure that the tests were administered and scored fairly? What is the range of students who failed to earn the states' criterion score on the tests? What remediation programs, if any, have these states developed to help students who failed to achieve the criterion score? How effective are these remediation programs?"

An educator from an Asian country is enrolled in a master's degree program at an American university and wants to learn teaching methods that she can use in a private school that she operates. In particular, she is interested in the latest methods for teaching English as a Second Language (ESL), which is the subject of her final project for the master's degree. She frames the following questions for this project: "What methods are currently used to teach ESL in American schools? What is the theoretical basis, if any, for these methods? How effective are these methods? Are there particular teaching resources that are needed in order to use these methods effectively? Are there any obstacles or disadvantages to using these methods?"

The preceding examples illustrate how framing specific questions can focus a literature search. The more focused your search, the greater the likelihood that you will obtain satisfactory answers to your questions within a reasonable time period. Also, framing your questions clearly will simplify the subsequent steps in the literature search process, especially the last step, which involves preparing a report of your literature review.

The approach of framing questions to guide a literature search can be modified for different circumstances. For example, as you start reading publications identified through an initial literature search, you may think of new questions for which you would like answers. These questions can be added to those that you framed initially, and you can then orient your literature search accordingly. Also, you may wish to find information to prove a point rather than to answer a question. As an example, you might be convinced that students would perform much better in college if they could take their course examinations without the pressure of time limits. In this case, the purpose of your literature search is to find evidence to support a belief—or what technically we would call a *hypothesis*—rather than to answer a question. You could therefore guide your literature search with a purpose statement, for example: "The purpose of this literature search is to determine whether there is research evidence that students perform better on tests under untimed conditions than under timed conditions." Alternatively, you could frame your information need as a question, for example: "Do students perform better on tests under untimed conditions than under timed conditions?"

STEP 2: CONSULTING WITH EXPERTS

Business managers who need information and advice frequently call in consultants who have expert knowledge. Educational administrators, too, make use of experts when they have a pressing need for information and advice. Of course, expert consultants are often hired for a fee. However, many experts are willing to help you as a professional courtesy without charge if your information need is clearly focused and can be addressed quickly. They often are willing—even eager—to tell you their ideas, and can point you to the most important publications relating to your information needs. With their expert knowledge as an initial framework, you can carry out a literature search with greater confidence and efficiency.

Educators in your local community may know an expert in your area of interest, or they may be able to refer you to someone who might know of such an expert. For example, the principal of a high school in Portland, Oregon, recently was planning to switch to block scheduling. (In block scheduling, fewer classes are offered, but they meet for longer time periods than in conventional scheduling of classes.) He wanted information about how best to implement block scheduling so that teachers would buy into it and so that students' learning would benefit. He mentioned his information need to a member of his teaching staff, who in turn called us. We are not experts in the practice of block scheduling, but we knew a colleague who was. We referred the principal to our colleague, and he was able to obtain an orientation to block scheduling from her. Thus, he had a strong initial background of information prior to conducting his own search of the literature on this practice.

A good way to contact experts outside your geographic area is by sending an e-mail message by way of the Internet. Some printed directories now include the e-mail addresses of the individuals or organizations listed in the directory. If not, you can use various search engines available on the Internet (e.g., Yahoo) to help you find the types of people, or specific individuals, with whom you wish to communicate.

Computer users have formed many computer networks through which members carry on electronic discussions or post information of various types, like announcements of upcoming conferences. Called *bulletin boards* or *discussion forums*, these networks on the Internet are managed by a computer software program called *Listserv*. Some Listserv bulletin boards are moderated and others are unmoderated, depending on whether someone monitors the contributed messages to decide which will be posted.

One general bulletin board for educational researchers is the *Educational Research List (ERL-L)*, which is sponsored by the American Educational Research Association (AERA). The topics of its specialized bulletin boards, with the *list-name* stated in caps, are as follows:

AERA-A	Educational Administration
AERA-B	Curriculum Studies
AERA-C	Learning and Instruction
AERA-D	Measurement and Research Methodology
AERA-E	Counseling and Human Development
AERA-F	History and Historiography
AERA-G	Social Context of Education
AERA-H	School Evaluation and Program Development
AERA-I	Education in the Professions
AERA-J	Postsecondary Education
AERA-K	Teaching and Teacher Education
AERA-L	Politics and Policy in Education
AERA-GSL	Graduate Studies List

If you have access to the Internet, you can subscribe to any of these AERA bulletin boards at no cost. As of this writing, it is simply a matter of sending a message to this e-mail address: <listserve@asu.edu>. Your message should state: *<subscribe listname your first name your last name>*. For example, the message might be:

> *<subscribe AERA-C Bill Austin>*

The AERA also maintains a home page on the World Wide Web at the address: <http://aera.net>, which is managed by Ev Shepherd or Gene Glass, editors of the AERA General Listserv. To post messages, you can e-mail them at: <AERA-GEN@asu.edu> or <shepherd@asu.edu>. This bulletin board is for general announcements to the educational research community (e.g., job openings, conferences, announcement of members' publications, relocation of AERA members).

To illustrate the types of information that are posted on ERL-L, here are three messages that we received recently from the AERA-E (Counseling and Human Development) bulletin board:

> The national director of Project Appleseed reminds us that the U.S. president has proposed annual voluntary testing for America's public schools. He suggests that we let our opinions be known by sending a message to Project Appleseed's Web site (the http address is given), and indicates that all received messages will be forwarded to the president and other key government officials.

> A member forwards this message from another Listserv to which she subscribes. It is from a school psychologist and freelance writer in Connecticut describing her new home page on special education, which is accessible from the World Wide Web.

> A professor from Vermont informs us of the date and location of an upcoming conference on authority, leadership, and followership in organizations, and provides telephone numbers and a Web site for obtaining further information.

Identifying the individual who can best answer your questions or give you feedback can be a hit-or-miss affair. There are several ways to make this step more systematic and efficient. Central administrators who have been in their school district for many years often know the various types of expertise that are available nearby. If you live near a college or university, you can examine its catalog, which typically lists all the faculty and their areas of expertise. Reference librarians at a college or university are themselves experts in accessing relevant literature for various information needs. A few minutes speaking with a reference librarian can pay large dividends in helping you identify publications that will provide a good launch to your literature search. In fact, these publications may be sufficient for your needs, in which case you will be able to skip some of the subsequent literature-search steps that are described below.

STEP 3: READING GENERAL SECONDARY SOURCES

Once you have identified the questions that you want to answer through a literature review, it is a good idea to read some secondary sources in order to form a general picture of the research that has been done on your topic. A secondary source is a publication in which the author reviews research that others have conducted. Two publications in education are especially helpful for identifying secondary sources: the *Encyclopedia of Educational Research,* and the *International Encyclopedia of Education.* The articles in these sources cover a wide range of topics that are relevant to educators.

Chapter 4 describes these encyclopedias and other more specialized publications containing secondary sources. It may be that one of these sources will be sufficient for your information needs. If not, at least it may help you refine the questions that you want to answer. It will also help you develop a conceptual framework for making sense of the information that you retrieve when you carry out the subsequent steps of the literature-review process described below.

STEP 4: SELECTING A PRELIMINARY SOURCE

The education literature includes many thousands of publications—books, journal articles, technical reports, papers presented at professional conferences, curriculum guides, and so forth. Even if you limit your literature search to publications that have appeared in the past five or ten years, the number of such publications is overwhelming. For this reason, various preliminary sources have been created to help you navigate the literature. A preliminary source is an index to a particular body of literature. Because the body of literature in different fields grows continually, these indexes are updated periodically.

Chapter 3 explains how to use a preliminary source to identify publications that are relevant to your information needs. First, though, you will need to select an appropriate preliminary source, because each one indexes a different body of literature. For example, *Sport Discus* indexes literature on sport, physical education, physical fitness, and sport medicine; *Child Development Abstracts and Bibliography* indexes literature on child development; and *Educational Administration Abstracts* indexes literature on educational administration. There are also preliminary sources that seek to provide a very broad coverage of topics that are relevant to education. The most widely used of these sources are the indexes maintained by the Educational Resources Information Center

(ERIC): the *Current Index to Journals in Education* (*CIJE*) and *Resources in Education* (*RIE*). Appendix 1 contains a comprehensive list of preliminary sources. You may find it necessary to experiment with some of them before you find the ones that index the types of publications that are most relevant to your information needs.

STEP 5: SEARCHING A PRELIMINARY SOURCE BY USING APPROPRIATE DESCRIPTORS

A typical preliminary source indexes many thousands of publications. The individuals who keep the preliminary source updated have coded each of these publications by using a standard set of descriptors, that is, key terms. For example, consider the report *School and Family Partnerships*, written by Joyce Epstein and Lori Connery and published by the National Association of Secondary School Principals in 1992. This publication was coded by the preliminary source *Resources in Education* using the following descriptors from the *Thesaurus of ERIC Descriptors* (Houston, 1995): *educational cooperation*, *family role*, *family school relationship*, *middle schools*, *parent influence*, *parent role*, *parent school relationship*, *school community relationship*, and *secondary education*. Say that you were interested in how schools and parents might cooperate to improve students' learning. If you had used *Resources in Education* and any of these descriptors, you would have come across Epstein and Connery's report.

It requires skill to identify appropriate descriptors to use in identifying publications that are relevant to your information needs. If you use inappropriate descriptors, you will miss relevant publications. Chapter 3 teaches you how to use descriptors and other features of preliminary sources so that you identify a list of publications that is not unmanageably long, but is sufficiently complete to include all potentially relevant publications. Also, you will learn that some preliminary sources are available in both a computerized and hard-copy (that is, print) format. In Chapter 3 we focus on conducting a computer search of preliminary sources because of the advantages that computer searching provides. We also provide an explanation of how to conduct a manual search of the hard-copy version of a preliminary source, should you need or wish to use that approach.

STEP 6: READING PRIMARY SOURCES

Your search of a preliminary source will yield a list of publications that correspond to your descriptors. The bibliographic citation for each publication typically will include the authors, title, publisher, and publication date. If the publication is a journal article, the page numbers of the article will be included, too. Some bibliographic citations also include an abstract, which is a brief summary (typically, 100 words or less) of the information contained in the publication.

Preliminary sources may also cite other preliminary sources, for example, an annotated bibliography of publications on a specified topic. However, most of the publications indexed by preliminary sources are either secondary or primary sources. As we explained, secondary sources are publications in which the author reviews research that others have conducted. In some secondary sources, the author may review educational programs, curriculum guides and materials, and methods that others have developed.

In contrast to secondary sources, a primary source is a publication written by the individual or individuals who actually conducted the work presented in that publication. The following are examples of primary sources: a journal article that reports a research study conducted by the author of the article, a curriculum guide in the form that its authors prepared it, a diary of reflections and experiences in the form that its author prepared it, and a report describing the author's opinions about a particular educational phenomenon or practice. In short, while a secondary source is a publication that is written by author A about the writings of authors X, Y, and Z, a primary source *is* the writing of author X, Y, or Z.

It sometimes is necessary to read primary sources directly rather than to rely on the summary of the primary source that is contained in a secondary source. For example, if you conduct a research study for a master's thesis or doctoral dissertation in education, you will be required to prepare a literature review as part of the thesis or dissertation. This literature review must include a detailed analysis of primary sources and their relationship to the problem that you investigated.

Other situations also require you to read primary sources. Suppose you read a secondary source that reviews research evidence relating to a program that you want your school or other organization to adopt. Because this research evidence may play a critical role in convincing others to adopt the program, you most likely will want to read the actual primary sources that produced this evidence rather than relying on a secondary-source review of these studies. Similarly, you most likely will want to read program materials and documents written by the program's developers (i.e., primary sources) rather than relying on others' description of them in secondary sources.

Unless you live near a university with a large research library, you will need to order research journals through inter-library loan, or request a reprint of the article from the publisher. Publisher addresses are listed in the front of each issue of *Current Index to Journals in Education* (*CIJE*). You also can order photocopies of journal articles from the following reprint services: the Institute for Scientific Information (call 1-800-523-1850 or send an e-mail message to: <tga@isinet.com>), or UMI InfoStore (call 1-800-248-0360 or send an e-mail message to: <orders@infostore.com>). Curriculum guides, program materials, and other publications of this type also may need to be ordered. After you obtain these types of primary sources, you may find that they require slow reading.

Most primary sources are written in technical language and describe sophisticated research procedures. Therefore, this step of the literature-search process typically is the most time-consuming.

It is frustrating to search for a primary source in a library, or to order it through inter-library loan, only to find once you get hold of it that it is irrelevant to your information needs. Therefore, you need to study carefully the abstracts that are part of the bibliographic citations available from some preliminary sources. These abstracts usually contain sufficient information for you to decide whether particular publications are relevant to your information needs. In some cases, the abstract contains sufficient information that you do not need to obtain and read the actual publication.

Many journal articles start with an abstract of their contents. As with the abstracts in preliminary-source citations, the article's abstract can help you decide whether the article is relevant to your information needs, and may contain sufficient information so that it is not necessary to read the article itself. Even if you do decide to read the article, reading the abstract first gives you a conceptual framework that facilitates your comprehension of the article's contents.

If you plan to read a set of research studies, it usually is a good idea to start with the most recent ones. The reason is that the most recent studies use the earlier research as a foundation, and thus are likely to help you understand what has been learned about the problem under investigation. It will then be much easier to see how older studies relate to this problem.

Most reports of research studies follow a standard format. As you learn this format, you can search more quickly for the information you need. The format typically follows this sequence: (1) an abstract; (2) an introduction that states the problem and discusses important previous research relating to it; (3) a statement of the research questions or hypotheses to be tested; (4) a description of the research method, including subjects, measures, and research design; (5) a presentation of statistical and/or qualitative analyses; and (6) a discussion of the research results that includes interpretations and implications for further research and practice. As you study Parts III, IV, and V of this book, you will learn more about this format and you will see it illustrated in the various reprinted studies.

The introductory and discussion sections of a research report might mention relevant previous studies that did not turn up in your search of preliminary sources. If this is the case, you can add the bibliographic data for these studies to the list that you compiled from your search of preliminary sources.

It is frustrating to take notes on primary and secondary sources while you are at the library, only to find later that your notes omitted important details. The only alternatives are to continue your review without knowing the detail or to make a return trip to the library. Therefore, if you think you will need to take a lot of notes on a particular publication, you should consider photocopying it instead. You can save time by marking relevant information on the photocopy rather than writing notes on a bibliography card or sheet of paper. Also, you can refer back to your photocopies whenever you wish.

STEP 7: CLASSIFYING PUBLICATIONS INTO MEANINGFUL CATEGORIES

While studying the publications identified in your literature search, you should consider developing categories for grouping them. For example, suppose you are reviewing the literature to help your school system plan a staff development program for its administrators. As you read the literature, you may observe that some publications concern school administrators specifically, whereas others concern administrators in business and industry or administrators generally. This observation suggests grouping the publications into three categories: (1) school administrators, (2) administrators in business and industry, and (3) general. You also may find that different publications concern different purposes of staff development, leading you to formulate the following subcategories under each of the three main categories: (a) staff development to help administrators improve staff morale, (b) staff development to help administrators lower their stress and maintain a healthy lifestyle, (c) staff development to help administrators improve organizational effectiveness, and (d) staff development for other purposes.

Developing a set of categories can help you set priorities for reading the publications that you identified in your literature review. It can also suggest the best way to synthesize your findings. A systematic approach to synthesis is important because your literature search can yield a large, and sometimes contradictory, set of findings. Developing a set of categories can help you organize your findings into meaningful clusters that facilitate the process of synthesis. In Chapter 4, you will learn several different approaches to literature synthesis, each of which benefits from having available a set of categories for grouping publications.

It is easier to use categories if you develop a code for each of them. The codes can be written on bibliography cards or photocopies of each publication. Here is a coding system developed by one of us for a review of the literature on ability grouping:

S   Studies dealing with social interaction among children within a particular ability group
A   Studies describing ability-grouping systems and their relationship to student achievement
G   Studies discussing problems involved in ability grouping, such as the range of individual differences within ability groups
B   Studies relating ability grouping to behavior problems in students
P   Studies relating ability grouping to students' social adjustment, personality, and self-concept

The appropriate code was placed in the upper right-hand corner of each bibliography card. Publications that covered several different topics were assigned multiple codes.

STEP 8: PREPARING A REPORT OF THE LITERATURE REVIEW

Depending on your purpose for conducting a literature review, you may or may not need to prepare a report of what you learned from it. First we suggest guidelines for preparing a written report, and then we describe a procedure that is suited to making a more visual and nontechnical presentation.

Preparing a Written Report of a Literature Review

A report of a literature review describes the state of knowledge about the questions that were investigated and makes recommendations based on that knowledge. A formal written report typically contains the following sections:

1. *Introduction*. A description of the situation that created a need for information, the questions that guided your literature search, and the literature search plan that was followed.
2. *Findings*. A presentation of the information that you learned from conducting your literature review. The findings should focus on what is most important and relevant to your information needs. This section of the report should be organized by meaningful categories or by the questions that guided the literature search.
3. *Discussion*. Your conclusions about the state of knowledge relating to the questions you investigated and your recommendations for a course of action.
4. *References*. Complete bibliographical information for all the primary and secondary sources that you cited in the report.

Each of these sections is described below.

The Introduction.   The introduction of the report should state the problem or questions that motivated your literature review (step 1 in Table 2.1) and the reasons why you chose to investigate them. If the information gained from your literature search led you to redefine your problem statement or questions, you can present your new problem statement or questions in the introduction.

The introduction also should include a description of your literature-search procedures. This description should indicate the preliminary sources that you consulted (step 4 in Table 2.1), the years that were covered, the descriptors that were used (step 5 in Table 2.1), and any special situations or problems that you encountered. If you read particular secondary sources that provided a historical background or conceptual framework for your literature review (step 3 in Table 2.1), they can be summarized in the introduction.

The Findings.   You can organize the findings of your literature review by the questions that guided your literature search (step 1 in Table 2.1) or by the categories that you created to organize the publications identified in your search (step 7 in Table 2.1).

You will need to decide on the order in which to present your questions or categories. Then for each question or category, you can decide on the order in which to present relevant research studies, theories, programs, methods, and opinions. By grouping together closely related publications, you can emphasize areas of agreement and disagreement that would be of interest to your audience. A particular publication may be pertinent to several questions or categories, and thus might be cited several times in your report.

Recommendations for writing the findings section of your report are presented in Table 2.2. Chapter 4 includes reprints of three published literature reviews. Studying how each of these reviews is organized will give you additional ideas for organizing the findings of your literature review.

The Discussion.   When you write the findings section of the literature review, it is important to be objective and therefore fairly literal in representing research findings, theories, program characteristics, and other types of information. In the discussion, however, you are free to provide your own interpretation and assessment of this information.

TABLE 2.2   Recommendations for Writing the Findings of a Literature Review

---

1. Use straightforward language that clearly expresses whether you are reporting someone's research findings, theories, or opinions. For example, an author may describe a new program and its advantages, but not report any empirical evidence. In this case you might write, "Jiminez (1991) claims that. . . ." If the author conducted a research study, you might write, "Jiminez (1991) found that. . . ." If the author developed a theory or referred to another's theory, you might write, respectively, "Jiminez (1991) theorized that. . ." or "Jiminez (1991) referred to Piaget's theory of. . . ."

2. Use frequent headings and subheadings to help the reader follow your sequence of topics more easily.

3. Describe the strengths and weaknesses of the methods used in important studies so that readers have enough information to weigh the results and draw their own conclusions.

4. Discuss major studies in detail, but devote little space to minor studies. For example, you might first discuss the most noteworthy study in depth and then briefly cite others on the same topic: "Several other studies have reported similar results (Anderson, 1989; Flinders, 1991; Lamon, 1985; Moursund, 1990; Wolcott, 1990)."

5. Use varied words and phrases, such as: "Chou found that. . .", "Smith studied. . .", "In Wychevsky's experiment the control group performed better on. . .", "The investigation carried out by Gum and Chew showed that. . . ."

6. Use a direct quotation only when it conveys an idea especially well, or when it states a viewpoint that is particularly worth noting.

As an example, suppose that your literature review was aimed at determining the effectiveness of a particular program to help emancipated teens who were previously in foster care to acquire independent living skills. Now you must present a brief report of your literature review to state legislators, who are considering a bill to provide funds for a pilot of this program. In writing the findings section of your report you would need to state objectively what researchers have discovered about this program and what experts think about it. In the discussion section of your report, however, you need to reach your own conclusions based on what you learned in reviewing the literature. For example, you might conclude: "Although the research evidence is consistently positive about this independent living program, in my opinion the gains in student learning are weak relative to the amount of effort required to implement it." Or you might say, "This program has been found to produce positive learning gains, but I am concerned about possible side effects that critics claim the program can produce."

A good procedure for writing the discussion is to start by listing the main findings of your review. You can compile this list by asking yourself, "What did I learn from this review?" and then attempting to answer this question without looking at your report of the findings. By relying on memory, you are more likely to focus on the prominent findings rather than on a variety of specific details. If necessary, you then can read over what you wrote to be sure you did not miss any important findings.

Now list the findings in order of importance, and reflect on each one. You might ask yourself questions such as these: "To what extent do I agree with the overall thrust of the research evidence, theories, descriptions, and expert opinions that I examined? Are alternative interpretations possible? How would I explain the contradictions in the literature, if any? What is the significance of a particular finding for the problem I need to solve or the question I want to answer?"

The discussion also should contain your recommendations regarding the problem or questions that initiated your literature review. The recommendations should be stated clearly and, if possible, without qualification. If you are tentative or indirect, readers of your report will not know where you stand. They want to know your opinions and recommendations because you did a review of the literature, so you are an expert compared to policy makers or colleagues who do not know the literature. Keep in mind, too, that even if you state your opinions and recommendations forcefully, your readers are unlikely to accept them uncritically. They will use your views as one source of input for making up their own minds about a question or problem relating to educational practice.

References.   All the publications that you cite in your report should be included in this section. Conversely, the list should not contain any publications that were not cited in the report. If you should wish to include noncited publications for some reason, you should present them in a separate list, with a heading such as *Supplemental References* and an explanatory note about why they are being cited.

Different preliminary sources use different bibliographic citation styles, and the bibliographies in the secondary and primary sources you read may also be in different styles. For example, in one style all the main words in the title are capitalized, while in another style only the first word is capitalized.

It is important that you convert all your citations to the same style before typing your reference list. Some institutions require that students writing dissertations or theses use a certain style for bibliographic citations, so if your report is being written for this purpose, you will need to check on what style to use. If no particular style is required, we recommend that you use the citation style of the American Psychological Association (APA), because it is the most widely used style in educational and psychological journals. The chapter references and recommended readings sections of this book are written in APA style. To learn APA style, obtain a copy of the fourth edition of the *Publication Manual of the American Psychological Association* (American Psychological Association, 1994).

Because typing errors are easy to make in citations, you should check the reference list once again for accuracy and consistency after it is typed.

Preparing a Visual Presentation of a Literature Review

Perhaps you plan to present the findings of your literature review to educational practitioners or to an audience that includes lay people. In such cases, it is helpful to present your findings in an interesting but nontechnical format that your audience will understand.

In Table 2.3 we give an example of a chart essay, which is a format that uses charts to focus the audience's attention on aspects of the literature review in which they are likely to be interested. The chart essay format was originally designed to summarize the findings of a single research study (see Haensly, Lupkowski, & McNamara, 1987, in the Recommended Reading for this chapter). Here we have adapted it to illustrate the value of a visual format for presenting the findings of a literature review in a nontechnical form. The chart essay in Table 2.3 graphically presents two findings from Robert Slavin's review of cooperative learning, which you will read in Chapter 4.

You can see that the chart poses one research question, immediately followed by the empirical research findings that pertain to it. The second research question is presented in similar fashion. The chart concludes with two trend statements, which are generalizations that can be inferred from the empirical findings. These statements are called *trends* because the evidence pertaining to each question was not always consistent. However, there was sufficient consistency to identify a trend that could serve as a guide to improving educational practice.

The chart essay presented in Table 2.3 is shown as a single chart. However, in showing the chart essay to an audience on overhead transparencies or handouts, the presenter might want to use three charts—one for each of the research questions and a third for the trend statements.

TABLE 2.3   Visual Presentation of Selected Findings from a Literature Review on Cooperative Learning

Research Question 1: How effective is cooperative learning relative to traditional instruction in fostering academic achievement?

In 60 studies, there were 68 comparisons of cooperative learning classes and traditional classes on an achievement measure. Achievement was:

significantly higher in the traditional classes in:	not significantly different in the cooperative learning and traditional classes in:	significantly higher in the cooperative learning classes in:
4%	34%	62%
of the comparisons.	of the comparisons.	of the comparisons.

Research Question 2: How important is it that group goals and individual accountability both be present for cooperative learning to be effective?

Percentage of studies showing significantly positive achievement effects for cooperative learning when group goals and individual accountability are:

Present	Absent
80%	36%

Trends

Cooperative learning is more effective than traditional instruction in promoting student achievement.

Cooperative learning is most effective when it includes both group goals and individual accountability.

Source. Based on data from: Slavin, R. E. (1992). Cooperative learning. In M. C. Alkin (Ed.), *Encyclopedia of educational research*, American Educational Research Association (pp. 235–238). New York: Macmillan.

CONCLUDING THOUGHT

Two of the authors own a Siamese cat named CoCo. Our veterinarian recently diagnosed CoCo as having hyperthyroidism, and recommended radioactive iodine therapy. When we indicated that we would like to know more about this treatment, he gave us a chapter to read from a veterinary textbook (a secondary source).

Because we have some understanding of research procedures and statistics, we were able to read this secondary source. We also sought expert consultation from our vet, who has treated CoCo for many years, and from the specialist who provides this remarkable treatment in our area. On our own we found other information on the Internet and at the library. After we had put all this information together, we felt more assured that we were making the right decision when we gave a "go-ahead" for CoCo's treatment.

As in your personal life, when you face a critical decision in your education practice it is important to be able to access information readily and with assurance that it is sound information. In this chapter we have described a process for reviewing the literature in education that will help you obtain sound, research-based information for decision making and problem solving.

SELF-CHECK TEST

1. One of the most common problems that educational practitioners encounter in conducting a literature search is
   a. a lack of sufficient information relevant to their topic.
   b. an overabundance of information relevant to their topic.
   c. a shortage of preliminary sources pertinent to educational topics.
   d. a shortage of primary sources pertinent to educational topics.

2. Consulting an expert prior to conducting a literature review is particularly helpful for
   a. developing a theory relating to the topic of your review.
   b. identifying critical primary and secondary sources to include in the review.
   c. establishing the credibility of your review.
   d. determining an appropriate bibliographic citation style.

3. A publication that presents a theory that was developed by the author of the publication is a
   a. secondary source.
   b. preliminary source.
   c. literature review.
   d. primary source.

4. The most important criterion for selecting the preliminary source to search in conducting a literature review is that it
   a. is available in hard-copy (print) form.
   b. uses a bibliographic citation style with which you are familiar.
   c. indexes the types of publications that contain information about your topic or problem.
   d. includes citations of annotated bibliographies.

5. In choosing descriptors with which to search a preliminary source, you should try to specify terms that
   a. are used in coding publications that are indexed by that preliminary source.
   b. are unique to your topic area.
   c. are sufficiently nontechnical that policy makers will understand them.
   d. correspond closely to the research methods and procedures that you wish to apply.

6. Reading some of the primary sources identified in your literature search will be of greatest help to you in
   a. developing a conceptual framework for making sense of the publications that you identify through your literature search.
   b. choosing the best descriptors for searching the preliminary source that you have selected.
   c. checking whether the findings of the research studies are accurately reviewed in a secondary source on which you are relying.
   d. deciding whether the preliminary source you used was sufficiently comprehensive.

7. In writing a report of your literature review, the _____ section should describe the preliminary source searched, descriptors used, and range of publication years examined.
   a. introduction
   b. findings
   c. discussion
   d. references

8. The primary advantage of a chart essay over a written report of a literature review is that a chart essay
   a. identifies the particular studies upon which the findings of the literature review are based.
   b. focuses on the statistics that were used to test the significance of the research findings.
   c. highlights the categories that were used to cluster the publications included in the review.
   d. is presented in a form that is more easily comprehended by lay persons.

CHAPTER REFERENCES

American Psychological Association. (1994). *Publication manual of the American Psychological Association*. Washington, DC: American Psychological Association.
Cabell's directory of publishing opportunities in education (4th ed.). (1995). Beaumont, TX: Cabell.
Houston, J. D. (Ed.). (1995). *Thesaurus of ERIC descriptors* (13th ed.). Phoenix, AZ: Oryx.

RECOMMENDED READING

Haensly, P. A., Lupkowski, A. E., & McNamara, J. F. (1987). The chart essay: A strategy for communicating research findings to policy makers and practitioners. *Educational Evaluation and Policy Analysis, 9*, 63–75.
The authors developed the chart essay method to present research findings in a nontechnical format. The method is illustrated in a study that determined the impact of students' participation in extracurricular activities on their high school grades.

Henson, K. T. (1995). *The art of writing for publication*. Boston: Allyn & Bacon.

This book provides useful guidelines for educators who wish to prepare their literature review as a manuscript to submit for publication. It includes a discussion of how to write journal articles, books, and grant proposals in education. An appendix describes the characteristics (e.g., circulation, percentage of accepted manuscripts, manuscript length) of a representative sample of education journals.

Jaszczak, S. (Ed.). (1997). *Encyclopedia of associations: An associations unlimited reference* (32nd ed.). Detroit: Gale.

The latest edition of this annual encyclopedia lists over 1,300 educational organizations. Each entry gives the name, address, telephone number, and fax number of the organization, and its aims or purposes. Available in hard-copy, on-line, and CD-ROM versions. This publication may be useful in identifying educators with expertise on a subject of interest to you.

Macfarlane, T. (Ed.). (1997). *Encyclopedia of associations: International organizations* (31st ed.). Detroit: Gale.

This edition lists over 700 educational organizations worldwide, classified by such categories as administration, cooperative education, educational reform, higher education, students, and teachers.

Mogge, D. (Ed.). (1996). *Directory of electronic journals, newsletters and academic discussion lists* (6th ed). Washington, DC: Association of Research Libraries.

This directory offers readers a brief overview of serials (that is, publications intended to be continued indefinitely) available on the Internet. This edition covers nearly 1,700 journal and newsletter titles and over 3,000 listings of scholarly and professional electronic conferences (e-conferences), bulletin boards, and academic discussions found on Bitnet, Internet, and various other networks. Also, issues and trends in electronic publishing are discussed.

CHAPTER 3

USING PRELIMINARY SOURCES TO SEARCH THE LITERATURE

Jill Novotny is a psychologist who has worked in the field of education throughout her career. She feels that she learned the hard way (mostly by lonely trial and error) what it takes to be a good parent. Now she is writing a book about how parents can support their children's learning both in and out of school.

Jill recently read about research showing that children of authoritative parents—defined as parents who provide both a high level of structure and a high level of nurturance to their children—have more success in school and in their personal lives than other children. She wanted to find out what work was being done to help parents learn this type of parenting.

Jill looked for books on authoritative parenting, but found very little. Then she decided to do an electronic search of a preliminary source

(ERIC) to identify journal articles and other reports on this topic. Her search yielded 26 publications that had been coded as having information about the topic of authoritative parenting. "I thought almost no one else was concerned about this," she confided to a friend. "Now I see that other professionals are working on this style of parenting, and I have much to learn from them."

This chapter takes you through the steps that are involved in using a preliminary source to search the education literature on parenting or any other topic of interest to educators. You will learn how to define your search terms, design and carry out a search, and obtain citations for the publications that appear most likely to contain information relevant to your needs.

OBJECTIVES

After studying this chapter, you will be able to

1. explain how to conduct a literature search using a hard-copy preliminary source.

2. describe the usual types of information about a publication that a preliminary source provides.

3. describe the three most common methods for storing and accessing an electronic preliminary-source database.

4. explain how to conduct a literature search using an electronic preliminary source.

5. explain how truncation and the use of the *and* and *or* connectors affect retrieval of publications when using an electronic preliminary source.

6. describe several options for focusing the search of an electronic version of the ERIC database.

7. compare the advantages of retrieving titles only, brief citations, and full citations for the publications retrieved in a literature search of a preliminary source.

KEY TERMS

and connector	ERIC	on-line database
CD-ROM	free-text search	*or* connector
CIJE	fugitive literature	proximity searching
citation	hard-copy preliminary source	resume
database	identifier	*RIE*
descriptor	indexer	thesaurus
electronic preliminary source	Internet	truncation
entry	literature search	World Wide Web

THE PURPOSE OF PRELIMINARY SOURCES

As we explained in Chapter 2, the education literature contains many thousands of publications. For this reason, preliminary sources have been developed to help you identify the publications that are relevant to your information needs. A preliminary source is an index to a particular body of literature, for example, journals that publish articles about education. The body of literature may contain both publications that have been formally published (e.g., scholarly books and professional journals) and publications that have not been formally published but are intended for distribution to a wide audience (e.g., papers presented at professional conferences and technical reports prepared by a school system). We are using the term *publication* to refer to all the types of items that are indexed in a preliminary source.

A preliminary source provides a citation for each publication that it references. A citation typically includes the publication's authors, title, year of publication, publisher, and possibly an abstract, which is a brief summary of the information in the publication.

In Chapter 2, we described a general process for conducting a literature review. The first three steps of the process involve framing questions to guide the literature review, consulting with experts, and reading general secondary sources. The next two steps involve selecting and searching a preliminary source. This chapter explains how preliminary sources are constructed and how they can be used effectively to identify all the publications in the literature that are relevant to your information needs.

Some preliminary sources are available only in print (also called *hard-copy*) form. Others are available in electronic form (e.g., as a computer file or as a CD-ROM). Still others are available in both hard-copy and electronic forms. We explain how to use both forms in this chapter. Although electronic preliminary sources are rapidly becoming the dominant format, we first explain how to search a hard-copy preliminary source because the process is simpler and easier to learn. Once you understand the logic of a hard-copy search, it will be relatively easy for you to learn how to use electronic preliminary sources.

SEARCHING A HARD-COPY PRELIMINARY SOURCE

You will find it helpful to maintain a record of your search of preliminary sources. You can consult this record to remind yourself of the steps of your search strategy that you still need to complete and to make sure that you do not repeat steps needlessly. Also, you can consult this record if you prepare a report of your literature review and wish to include a description of your search strategy.

Figure 3.1 contains a form for recording the steps followed in conducting a search of a hard-copy preliminary source (also known as a *manual search*). It is

Search question(s): *What are effective ways to help parents of at-risk students increase their support of their children's academic efforts?*
Preliminary source(s) used: *RIE*

Time Period

Descriptors	1992	1993	1994	1995	1996
1. ~~Parents~~					
2. ~~At risk students~~					
3. ~~Academic efforts~~					
4. Parent*	✓	✓	✓	✓	✓
5. High risk students	✓	✓	✓	✓	✓
6. Academic achievement	✓	✓	✓	✓	✓
7.					
8.					
9.					
10.					

FIGURE 3.1 **Manual search record for a literature search on parent involvement**

filled in with information for a sample literature search described in this section of the chapter. You might want to design a form like this, or adapt it as you wish, for conducting your own literature search of a hard-copy preliminary source.

Parent involvement in their children's schooling is currently a major concern of many educators. Therefore, we selected it as a topic for illustrating search procedures in using a hard-copy preliminary source. We framed a specific question to guide our literature search on this topic: "What are effective ways to help parents of at-risk students increase their support of their children's academic efforts?" As we explained in Chapter 2, the framing of questions is a critical step in conducting a literature review.

Once you have framed the question or set of questions that will guide your search, you are ready to begin the process of selecting and using a preliminary source. The steps of this process are described in the next sections.

Step 1: Selecting a Preliminary Source

There are many preliminary sources, each of which indexes a different range and type of publications, related to education. For example, *Children's Books in Print* indexes books for young readers, whereas *Psychological Abstracts* indexes journals and other types of publications covering a wide range of psychological topics, including topics that relate to education. Appendix 1 provides a list and description of preliminary sources that may be useful to you in your work as a professional educator.

The most comprehensive preliminary sources for educators are *Current Index to Journals in Education* (*CIJE*) and *Resources in Education* (*RIE*). Both are published by the Educational Resources Information Center (ERIC), which is funded by the U.S. government. ERIC also provides many publications and services to educators at no cost. The types of publications available from ERIC are described in Chapter 4 and in Appendix 2. To ask a question about ERIC or to access its services, you can contact ACCESS ERIC (Phone: 1-800-LET-ERIC; e-mail address: <ericdb@aspensys.com>).

CIJE indexes more than 1,000 articles in nearly 800 education-related journals each month. It has been in operation since 1969. If you need to identify journal articles and books published prior to 1969, *Education Index* is a useful preliminary source.

Whereas *CIJE* indexes journal articles, *RIE* indexes papers presented at education conferences, progress reports on ongoing research studies, technical reports on studies sponsored by federal research programs, and reports on projects conducted by local agencies such as school districts. These publications sometimes are called *fugitive literature* because they are not widely disseminated or easily obtained. *RIE* has indexed such publications since 1966.

If you choose an inappropriate preliminary source, you will miss many publications that are potentially important to your literature review. Therefore, it is important to select the most appropriate preliminary source. *CIJE* and *RIE* are quite adequate for most literature reviews in education. However, if you wish to do a comprehensive literature review, you most likely will need to search additional preliminary sources for publications not indexed by either *CIJE* or *RIE*.

Because *CIJE* and *RIE* are the preliminary sources most widely used by educators, we will refer to them to explain the next steps of conducting a search of a hard-copy preliminary source. Other preliminary sources generally are organized similarly, so you should be able to apply most of what we say about *CIJE* and *RIE* to them.

Step 2: Selecting Descriptors

The *Thesaurus of ERIC Descriptors* (Houston, 1995) is a reference book that helps you identify appropriate descriptors to use in searching *CIJE* and *RIE* for publications that are relevant to your problem. As we explained in Chapter 2, the term *descriptor* is used to classify all publications that contain information about the topic denoted by the term. Keep in mind, though, that *CIJE* and *RIE* contain not the actual publications, but rather a citation for each publication. ERIC uses the term *entry* in *CIJE* and the term *resume* in *RIE* to refer to these citations.

To identify appropriate descriptors for your literature search, you can start by underlining the most important words or phrases in your problem statement. Using our example about parents, we underlined the following words: "What are effective ways to help *parents* of *at-risk students* increase their support of their children's *academic efforts*?" Next we listed the underlined words in pencil in the section labeled *Descriptors* of the manual search record (Figure 3.1).

The next step is to look up each of our three terms in the Alphabetical Descriptor Display of the ERIC *Thesaurus* to determine whether they are ERIC descriptors. When we look up the term *Parents*, we find the display shown in Figure 3.2. This display has the following features.

1. *Main-entry designation.* The term **PARENTS** is shown in boldface capital letters. This designation indicates that *Parents* is a main-entry descriptor, meaning that it is used to classify *CIJE* entries and *RIE* resumes.

2. *Add date.* The notation *Jul. 1966* indicates when this term was entered into the *Thesaurus*.

3. *Number of* CIJE *entries and* RIE *resumes.* The notations *CIJE: 1286* and *RIE: 1115* indicate that, from July 1966 until this edition of the *Thesaurus*, there were 1,286 *CIJE* entries and 1,115 *RIE* resumes classified by this descriptor.

4. *Descriptor Group Code.* The notation *GC: 510* indicates that the descriptor *Parents* is in Descriptor Group Code 510. This three-digit number indicates the broad category to which this descriptor belongs. The code is useful for identifying other descriptors that are conceptually related to a descriptor, but do not necessarily appear in the descriptor's display. When we look at the categories list on page 678 of the *Thesaurus*, we find that *GC* is the category *Groups Related to HUMAN SOCIETY*, and that *GC 510* concerns *THE INDIVIDUAL IN SOCIAL CONTEXT*. The term *group*, as used here, refers not to groups of people, but to groups of conceptually related descriptors in the *Thesaurus*.

```
PARENTS                              Jul. 1966
        CIJE: 1286      RIE: 1115      GC:510
UF      Catholic Parents (1966 1980)#
NT      Adoptive Parents
        Biological Parents
        Employed Parents
        Fathers
        Grandparents
        Lower Class Parents
        Middle Class Parents
        Mothers
        Parents as Teachers
BT      Groups
RT      Adults
        Child Caregivers
        Daughters
        Early Parenthood
        Family (Sociological Unit)
        Family Environment
        Family Life
        Family Problems
        Heads of Households
        Home Schooling
        Home Visits
        Kinship
        One Parent Family
        Parent Aspiration
        Parent Associations
        Parent Attitudes
        Parent Background
        Parent Child Relationship
        Parent Conferences
        Parent Counseling
        Parent Education
        Parent Financial Contribution
        Parent Grievances
        Parent Influence
        Parent Materials
        Parent Participation
        Parent Responsibility
        Parent Rights
        Parent Role
        Parent School Relationship
        Parent Student Relationship
        Parent Teacher Conferences
        Parent Teacher Cooperation
        Parent Workshops
        Parenthood Education
        Parenting Skills
        Sons
        Spouses
```

FIGURE 3.2   Display for the main entry *Parents* in the alphabetical descriptor display of the *Thesaurus of ERIC Descriptors*

Source. Houston, J. D. (Ed.). (1995). *Thesaurus of ERIC descriptors* (13th ed.), pp. 217–218. Phoenix, AZ: Oryx.

5. *Used for (UF) designation.* The *UF* designation preceding the term *Catholic parents* indicates that the descriptor *Parents* should be used instead of the term *Catholic parents* in doing an ERIC search. The information in parentheses after the term *Catholic parents* indicates that this term was a descriptor only during the period 1966 to 1980. The # designation after the term *Catholic parents* refers to a footnote at the bottom of the page of the Alphabetical Descriptor Display where

the term appears. The footnote states that two or more descriptors are needed to represent this term. By looking in the *Thesaurus* for *Catholic parents* as a descriptor, the reader can learn which descriptors to use instead of this term.

6. *Narrower term (NT) designation*. The *NT* designation identifies narrower descriptors that are included under the main-entry descriptor *Parents*. The nine narrower descriptors shown under *Parents* also can be searched for *CIJE* entries and *RIE* resumes relating to parents.

7. *Broader term (BT) designation*. The *BT* designation identifies broader descriptors that subsume the concept represented by the main-entry descriptor. Thus we see that the broader descriptor *Groups* includes the descriptor *Parents* as a subcategory.

8. *Related term (RT) designation*. The *RT* designation indicates related descriptors that also are main-entry descriptors in the *Thesaurus*. These related descriptors have a close conceptual relationship to the descriptor *Parents*, but do not fit the superordinate/subordinate relationship described by BT and NT. All the related terms listed under *Parents* appear elsewhere in the *Thesaurus* as main-entry descriptors. Thus, any of these descriptors can be used to search for *CIJE* entries and *RIE* resumes relating to parents.

9. *USE designation*. The information shown in Figure 3.2 does not exhaust the descriptors relating to the topic of parents in the *Thesaurus*. Over a page of the Alphabetical Descriptor Display lists main-entry descriptors that include the word *parent* or *parents*, from *PARENT ASPIRATION* to *PARENTS AS TEACHERS*. Another example is *Parent Absence USE ONE PARENT FAMILY*. The *USE* designation tells us that the term *Parent Absence* is not a main-entry descriptor in the *Thesaurus*. If we are interested in searching for entries or resumes relating to parent absence, we will need to use the descriptor *One parent family*.

10. *Scope note*. If we now check the Alphabetical Descriptor Display for our second term, *At-risk students*, we will find the term *AT RISK PERSONS* as a main-entry descriptor, followed by the information shown in Figure 3.3. *SN* is an acronym for *Scope Note*, which is a brief statement of the intended usage of an ERIC descriptor. The scope note clarifies an ambiguous term or restricts the usage of a term, and it may give special indexing information as well. The scope note in this case directs us to a narrower term, *HIGH RISK STUDENTS*. Therefore, we change the term *At-risk students* to *High risk students* on our manual search record (Figure 3.1).

Suppose that our main interest is how teachers can help parents as a group rather than one at a time. If we look at the descriptors under *Parents* in the Alphabetical Descriptor Display, we see four related terms that involve working with parents as a group: *Parent education, Parent workshops, Parenthood education*, and *Parenting skills*. However, there may be only a few or no citations under these subjects in any given monthly issue or cumulated volume of *CIJE* or *RIE*. For this reason, we decide to include in our literature search all the entries or resumes classified by any descriptor that begins with the word *Parent*. Hence

```
AT RISK PERSONS                    Apr. 1990
        CIJE: 600      RIE: 609      GC:120
SN   Individuals or groups identified as possi-
     bly having or potentially developing a
     problem (physical, mental, educational,
     etc.) requiring further evaluation and/or
     intervention (note: if possible, use the
     more specific term "high risk students")
UF   High Risk Persons (1982 1990)
     Risk Populations
NT   High Risk Students
BT   Groups
RT   Developmental Delays
     Disabilities
     Disability Identification
     Early Intervention
     Incidence
     Symptoms (Individual Disorders)
```

FIGURE 3.3   Display for the main entry *At Risk Persons* in the alphabetic descriptor display of the *Thesaurus of ERIC Descriptors*

Source. Houston, J. D. (Ed.). (1995). *Thesaurus of ERIC descriptors* (13th ed.), p. 23. Phoenix, AZ: Oryx.

we cross out the term *Parents* on the manual search record (Figure 3.1) and add the term *Parent**. The asterisk signifies that we want to check all the entries or resumes that have been coded for any descriptors that begin with these six letters (e.g., *Parent Influence, Parenthood Education, Parents, Parenting Skills*).

To determine whether *Academic efforts* is the appropriate descriptor for our search concerning parents of high risk students, we refer to the Rotated Descriptor Display in the *Thesaurus*. A rotated descriptor display takes each descriptor in the *Thesaurus* and shows all other descriptors that share any word in common with it. For example, if we key on the word *Academic* in *Academic efforts*, the Rotated Descriptor Display will show all *Thesaurus* descriptors that also include that word, irrespective of position (e.g., *Summer academic classes* and *Academic achievement*). We could do the same kind of search in the Rotated Descriptor Display for the word *Efforts*.

We scanned all the phrases in the Rotated Descriptor Display beginning with the word *ACADEMIC*. The phrase *ACADEMIC EFFORTS* was not listed, but a related phrase, *ACADEMIC ACHIEVEMENT*, was listed. Therefore we changed the term *Academic efforts* on our manual search record (Figure 3.1) to *Academic achievement*.

Most education topics of any significance are represented in the literature, so if you do not locate any publications in your area of interest, you should reconsider your descriptors and your choice of a preliminary source. Most likely you have framed your search question in terms that are different from the descriptors used by ERIC indexers. Keep in mind, too, that your descriptors might identify some relevant publications but miss others, because the indexer at ERIC who classified the publications used different descriptors than the ones that you used to conduct your search.

Step 3: Using the Subject Index to Identify Entries or Resumes

The hard-copy version of *CIJE* is published as monthly issues and as semiannual cumulated volumes. The hard-copy version of *RIE* is published as monthly issues and as annual cumulated volumes. The semiannual volumes for *CIJE* provide a cumulated set of indexes and all the corresponding main entries. The annual volumes for *RIE* include only cumulated indexes, so you must check the appropriate monthly issue to find the corresponding resumes. Keep in mind that the month of a publication's first printing or presentation is not necessarily the month in which it will appear in *CIJE* or *RIE*. Several months may pass before the publication is processed for inclusion in a preliminary source.

After having selected appropriate descriptors, we are ready to search the subject index in issues of *CIJE* or *RIE* for the time period we wish to review. The headings in the subject index for a particular issue or volume of *CIJE* or *RIE* include all relevant descriptors from the *Thesaurus*, as well as other terms called *identifiers* (e.g., names of tests or organizations), that ERIC indexers used to code the publications that are indexed in that issue or volume. As we stated above, the information provided about each publication is called an *entry* in *CIJE* and a *resume* in *RIE*.

In *CIJE*, the entries constitute most of each issue or volume, and are in the front section labeled *Main Entry Section*. *CIJE* includes three other indexes besides the subject index that you can use to search for relevant articles. You can check the author index to determine whether particular authors have written publications relevant to your problem. The source journal index gives information about each journal from which articles were selected for indexing in that *CIJE* issue. In this index, the journals are grouped by the ERIC clearinghouse that reviews each journal, which helps you determine the journals that are most relevant to a given topic area. The journal contents index lists the titles of the articles in each journal issue that have been indexed in that issue of *CIJE*. For example, the *CIJE* July–December 1996 Semiannual Cumulation lists the titles and ERIC accession numbers for ten articles from the Spring 1996 and Winter 1996 issues of the journal *Review of Educational Research*.

In *RIE* the resumes constitute most of each issue, and are in the front section labeled *Document Resumes*. *RIE* includes four other indexes that you can use to search for relevant publications. If you think that particular authors or sponsoring agencies might be associated with publications relevant to your search, you can check them in the author index or the institution/sponsoring agency index, respectively. If you want to examine certain types of publications (for example, ERIC Digests, which are explained in Chapter 4), you can search for them in the publication type index. You can also examine the publications that have been reviewed by a particular ERIC clearinghouse by using the clearinghouse accession number index.

It is obviously to your advantage to search the cumulated volumes of *CIJE* or *RIE* whenever possible. By looking in the subject index of a *CIJE* semiannual volume, for example, you can find all the publications that were classified by a particular descriptor for that six-month period. All the entries or resumes for those publications are in that same volume. If you used the six monthly issues instead, you would need to repeat the process of searching the subject index and the main-entry section six times in order to cover the same time period.

All main entries in *CIJE* and document resumes in *RIE* are written in the same standard format. Because all *CIJE* main entries are from journals, they tend to have fewer format features than *RIE* document resumes. The publications indexed in *RIE* involve various publication formats (for example, papers presented at conferences and reports by government agencies). Therefore, we will use an *RIE* resume to explain the information that *CIJE* and *RIE* provide about a publication.

To initiate our search concerning parents of high risk students, we turned to the subject index of the 1992 volume of *RIE*. We found two citations under *Parent role* that appeared relevant to our search question.

Family Focus: Reading and Learning Together Packet   ED 347 498
School and Family Partnerships   ED 347 638

We decided to check just the second citation, so we copied down its ED number.

Next we turned to the *Document Resumes* section of the December 1992 *RIE* issue, where the resumes are arranged in numerical order. Reading the resume for ED 347 638, we found that indeed it is relevant to our problem. The document resume is shown in Figure 3.4. Below we refer to it as we explain the typical elements in an *RIE* resume. Understanding these elements will be a great help to you in identifying and reviewing literature that is relevant to your question or topic.

1. *ERIC accession number. ED 347 638* is the identification number for this publication. Accession numbers are sequentially assigned to publications as they are processed for indexing in ERIC. The *ED* indicates that this is a non-journal document rather than a journal article. (Journal articles begin with an *EJ* number instead.) Resumes are placed in the document resumes section of *RIE* in numerical order by their accession number. If a library maintains a microfiche file of ERIC documents, the microfiches also are stored in accession-number order.

2. *Clearinghouse accession number.* The number *EA 024 079* is an accession number assigned to publications by the specific clearinghouse that processed them for entry into the ERIC system. Referring to the list of ERIC clearinghouses in Appendix 2, we find that EA is the designation for the Clearinghouse on Educational Management, housed at the University of Oregon.

3. *Author(s).* The names in italics below the ERIC accession number are the names of the authors of the publication. Thus we learn that this publication was written by Joyce Epstein and Lori Connors.

4. *Title.* The title of the publication is shown next. In this example it is *School and Family Partnerships.*

ED 347 638   **EA 024 079**
Epstein, Joyce L.   Connors, Lori J.
School and Family Partnerships.
National Association of Secondary School Principals, Reston, Va.
Report No.—ISSN–0912–6160
Pub Date—Jun 92
Note—10p.
Available from—National Association of Secondary School Principals, 1904 Research Drive, Reston, VA 22091-1537 ($2; quantity discounts).
Journal Cit—Practitioner; v18 n4 Jun 1992
Pub Type—Collected Works - Serials (022) — Guides — Non-Classroom (055)
EDRS Price — MF101 Plus Postage. PC Not Available from EDRS.
Descriptors—*Educational Cooperation, Family Role, *Family School Relationship, Middle Schools, *Parent Influence, *Parent Role, *Parent School Relationship, School Community Relationship, Secondary Education
 Concerns about and characteristics of family/school partnerships are the theme of this issue of a ''newsletter for the on-line administrator.'' Because of the changing natures of students, families, and schools, school administrators must take a leadership role in facilitating parent involvement in education. The six major types of involvement for comprehensive partnership programs are outlined. These include basic obligations of families; basic obligations of the school; involvement at the school; involvement in home learning; involvement in decision making, governance, and advocacy; and community collaboration. Questions to be considered for organization of partnerships are discussed; some of these include the development of a written policy, a leadership and committee structure, a budget, and an evaluation process. Examples of each type of partnership that has been implemented in middle and high schools are provided. A brief program description and contact information are included. (LMI)

FIGURE 3.4   Document resume from the hard-copy version of *Resources in Education* (RIE)
Source. Resources in Education (1992, December), p. 61. Washington, DC: U.S. Government Printing Office.

5. *Organization where publication originated.* If the publication was available in print form prior to being placed into the ERIC system, the organization where it originated is specified here. We find that our publication originated with the National Association of Secondary School Principals (NASSP) in Reston, Virginia.

6. *Sponsoring agency.* If a different agency from the one in which the publication originated was responsible for initiating, funding, and managing the project described, it is listed after *Spons Agency.* No separate sponsoring agency is shown for this publication.

7. *Report number.* If a report number is given, it is the number assigned to the publication by the originating organization. In this case, the report number ISSN-0912-6160 would be used to request the publication from NASSP.

8. *Date published (Pub Date).* The Pub Date indicates the month and year in which the publication was entered in the ERIC system.

9. *Contract or grant number.* If a contract or grant number is given, it signifies the number assigned by the funding agency to the project or grant described in the publication. No contract or grant number is given for this publication.

10. *Note.* A descriptive note gives additional information about the publication, such as its page length and country of origin. We find that this publication is 10 pages long.

11. *Availability.* If the publication is available from a source other than ERIC, it is listed here. This publication is available from the National Association of Secondary School Principals. It costs $2.00 per copy, with quantity discounts available.

12. *Language of publication.* If the publication is available in a language other than English, this information is indicated. This publication is written in English only, so no language designation is included in the resume.

13. *Journal citation.* If the publication has been cited in a recent journal issue, the journal title and issue number are listed here. We checked the journal issue mentioned in the document resume shown in Figure 3.4, and found a published version of the document that was cited in *RIE*. This example illustrates that occasionally a publication is produced both as a journal article and as an *RIE* document available in microfiche form from the ERIC Document Reproduction Service (EDRS is explained in item 15).

14. *Publication type (Pub Type).* *Pub Type* is a three-digit code that classifies a publication by its form of publication. For example, there are separate codes for research/technical reports, dissertations and theses, and instructional materials for learners. The Pub Type code appears in the printed issues of *RIE*, but not in the printed issues of *CIJE*. Two Pub Types were assigned to our sample publication: *Collected Works—Serials (022)* and *Guides—Non-Classroom (055)*. A list of ERIC's publication types appears later in the chapter.

15. *ERIC Document Reproduction Service (EDRS) availability.* This code indicates whether the publication can be ordered through ERIC's reproduction service facility in Springfield, Virginia (Phone: 1-800-443-ERIC; Web address: <http://edrs.com>). *MF* means the publication can be ordered in microfiche format, and *PC* means the publication is available in regular paper format. In our example, *MF01* means that the publication can be ordered in microfiche format. The *01* part of the code refers to a price code schedule contained in the latest issue of *RIE*. A publication from 1 to 480 pages is in Price Code Number 1, and therefore costs $1.38.

16. *Descriptors.* The descriptors from the ERIC *Thesaurus* that were assigned to this publication by an indexer at an ERIC clearinghouse are listed here. These descriptors classify the substantive content of the publication. Up to six major descriptors, each preceded by an asterisk, are listed to cover the main content of the publication. Minor descriptors also are listed to indicate less important content of the publication, or nonsubject features such as methodology or educational level. A minor descriptor for educational level is mandatory for every publication and journal article indexed in ERIC, unless it is entirely inappropriate. If a publication covers a specific age range, a minor descriptor for age level also may be assigned. A publication is cited in the subject index of *CIJE* or *RIE* under its major descriptors, but not under its minor descriptors.

17. *Identifiers.* Identifiers are key words or "indexable" concepts intended to add depth to subject indexing that is not possible with the ERIC *Thesaurus* descriptors alone. They generally are either proper names or concepts not yet represented by approved descriptors. They appear in *CIJE* entries or *RIE* resumes in a separate field just below the descriptors. Major identifiers are marked with an asterisk and appear in the printed subject indexes of *RIE* and *CIJE*. There are no identifiers for this publication.

18. *Target audience.* If a publication specifies an intended audience, this information is provided in the entry or resume. Eleven different audiences are identified by ERIC: policy makers; researchers; practitioners, which include the five subtypes administrators, teachers, counselors, media staff, and support staff; students; parents; and community members. If more than two practitioner groups are identified, only the generic target audience *practitioners* is catalogued. No target audience is specified for the resume shown in Figure 3.4.

19. *Abstract.* This is a brief summary of the publication's contents, written either by the author or by the indexer at the ERIC clearinghouse.

20. *Indexer's initials.* The initials of the person at the ERIC clearinghouse who indexed each publication are indicated in parentheses at the end of the resume. The indexer for our sample publication is LMI.

In doing a hard-copy search of *CIJE* and *RIE*, we can search for entries or resumes using only one subject heading at a time. In the preceding section, for example, we identified some relevant publications concerning parents, but we do not know if they also are relevant to our other descriptors, *High risk students* and *Academic achievement*. We will need to study each entry or resume to make this determination.

You can take notes on the bibliographic information and abstract of each *CIJE* entry or *RIE* resume that is relevant to your literature search. However, this is time-consuming, and you run the risk of making errors in copying bibliographic citations. A far simpler and more effective method is to make a photocopy of all relevant entries and resumes.

SEARCHING AN ELECTRONIC PRELIMINARY SOURCE

Searching a hard-copy preliminary source is not difficult if you have just a few descriptors and need to cover only a few years of the literature. Suppose, instead, that you are planning to write a master's thesis, a doctoral dissertation, or another type of major report, or that you want comprehensive information for making an important educational decision. In these situations, you need to be able to conduct a thorough review of the literature. The manual search process would be too time-consuming and unreliable to accomplish this task, so it is necessary to know how to use a computer search process.

To understand why a computer might facilitate a search of a preliminary source, consider the case of writing by hand versus using a word processing program. Using just paper and pencil, most people can write a report, but the handwriting process is slow, and some tasks (e.g., revising a draft or checking the accuracy of one's spelling) are laborious and difficult. In contrast, once you have acquired typing skills, you can generate text fairly quickly on a computer screen. Also, the capabilities of a word processor make it easy to edit text, check the spelling of words, print out a professional-looking report, and perform other writing tasks.

Just as a word processor makes writing easier, an electronic preliminary source facilitates most search tasks, as we explain below. It takes some effort to learn how to use an electronic preliminary source, but this effort is rewarded later when you can perform comprehensive, accurate searches of the literature with ease.

To illustrate the steps of an electronic search of a preliminary source, we will use the same question that we used in our example of a hard-copy search: "What are effective ways to help parents of at-risk students increase their support of their children's academic efforts?" This question is written in the space provided in the electronic search record shown in Figure 3.5.

Search question(s): *What are effective ways to help parents of at-risk students increase their support of their children's academic efforts?*
Preliminary source(s) used: *ERIC on-line database*

Search Procedure	# Retrieved	# Downloaded
Search 1: *Parents and High risk students and Academic achievement*	124	
Search 2: *Parents and High risk students and (Academic achievement or Enrichment or Academic persistence or Academic aspiration)*	178	
Search 3: *Search #2 and Elementary education*	65	29
Search 4: *Search #2 and (Pub Date: after 12/31/91 and before 01/01/97)*	92	
Search 5: *Center for the Improvement of Child Caring (free-text search)*	4	
Search 6: *Parents and (Pub Type: Tests, Evaluation Instruments)*	126	
Search 7: *Author: Joyce L. Epstein*	73	
Search 8: *Periodical Title: Practitioner*	26	
Search 9: *Parents and (Target Audience: Teachers)*	68	14
Search 10: *Parents and (Language: Spanish)*	30	

FIGURE 3.5   Electronic search record for a literature search on parent involvement

Step 1: Selecting an Electronic Preliminary Source

An electronic preliminary source has two key components. One of them is the *database*, which consists of the citations for all the publications that the preliminary source indexes. The other component is the software that allows you to search the database. Appendix 1 lists various preliminary sources that index education-related literature, and it indicates which of these sources are available in electronic format.

You will recall that we used *RIE* as the hard-copy preliminary source to be searched for publications related to our search question about parent involvement. In the electronic version of this preliminary source, *RIE* is integrated with *CIJE* into one database, hereon referred to as the *ERIC database*.

Below, we use the ERIC database to illustrate the steps that are involved in an electronic search of a preliminary source. First we will describe the most common methods for storing and accessing the ERIC database. Keep in mind that a particular method may appeal to you, but it may not be available in your vicinity. Also, in different electronic versions of the ERIC database you may find slight variations in the information provided about each publication from that provided in the hard-copy version of *CIJE* or *RIE* (Figure 3.4).

CD-ROM Databases.   Today many college and university libraries contain a variety of dedicated computer terminals, each of which stores the database for a specific preliminary source. Each database is on one or more CD-ROMs. The acronym *CD-ROM* stands for *Compact Disk-Read Only Memory*, which means that the user can only obtain data from the disks, not add new data to them. A dedicated terminal means that the computer can be used only to access the CD-ROMs that are stored in that particular machine.

CD-ROMs may contain part or the whole of the database that is available in their hard-copy counterparts. For example, some sources supply CD-ROMs that contain only the last 10 years of the ERIC database, but CD-ROMs are available from other sources that contain all citations from 1966 to the present. (ERIC itself now offers at relatively low cost a version of the *ERIC* database on CD-ROMs that was developed by the National Information Services Corporation, or NISC.) Because the CD-ROMs integrate *CIJE* and *RIE* into one database, users can search both of these preliminary sources simultaneously.

At many libraries you can search preliminary sources on CD-ROMs for little or no charge. Most of these CD-ROMs contain step-by-step instructions for conducting a literature search. Also, the computer on which the database is stored may have *help* keys that offer assistance when a search question arises. It is advisable to read the instructions carefully and to try various search options and *help* keys before you conduct a formal search.

Internet Databases.   It is possible to access electronic preliminary sources through the *Internet*, an overarching communication network that links computer networks worldwide. At our university library, certain computer terminals are reserved specifically to allow access to the Internet. It also is possible to search the Internet from one's personal computer by using a modem to hook up to an Internet provider.

You can search the ERIC database on the Internet through the World Wide Web (or Web for short), a client/server system that offers access to the resources of the Internet. For example, you can currently access databases for the period from:

(a) 1989 to the present through Syracuse University; Web address <http://ericir.syr.edu/> or e-mail address <eric@ericir.syr.edu>.

(b) 1983 to the present through the University of Saskatchewan library system; Web address <http://library.usask.ca/>.

(c) 1976 to the present through the ERIC Clearinghouse on Assessment and Evaluation (clearinghouse code TM) at Catholic University of America; Web address <http://eric_ae@cua.edu>. You can also access the ERIC Thesaurus through the Search ERIC Wizard that is maintained by this clearinghouse, at Web address: <http://ericae2.educ.cua.edu/scripts/ewiz/amain2.sap>.

On-Line Databases.   Many college and university libraries have downloaded the entire database for the most commonly used preliminary sources into the same computer system that operates the electronic catalog of the library's holdings. A user can conduct an on-line search of any of these databases. An on-line search means that the on-site computer that you are using to initiate your search is connected by a modem to an off-site computer that contains the database for the preliminary source. An on-line search has several advantages: You can access the database at any time, not only during library hours; and you can conduct the search from anywhere, including your residence, if your computer has the appropriate modem hook-up.

If the preliminary source that you want to access is not available on either CD-ROM or your library's on-line system, you probably can access it through a commercial information-retrieval system. Contact ACCESS ERIC for current information about vendors offering such systems. They can be accessed from some libraries, but typically there is a fee for this service.

In carrying out the sample search of the electronic version of the ERIC database described below, we used the University of Oregon Library's on-line system. You will see that we entered this information on the literature search record in Figure 3.5.

If you are in a geographic area with limited access to computer searching, or if your search topic is highly unusual, you may need to pay for an intermediary search, that is, one conducted for you by an information specialist. This person typically will be a librarian in your topic area with special expertise in using on-line databases.

Step 2: Selecting a Search Strategy

In searching a hard-copy version of *CIJE* or *RIE*, you can identify relevant publications by using a particular *Thesaurus* descriptor and the subject index of each issue or volume. You also can search for publications in a particular year or range of years by using issues or volumes of *CIJE* and *RIE* that were published in or around that year or range of years. A computer search of these preliminary sources has the same capabilities, but others as well. You will need to decide which of these capabilities you wish to incorporate as part of your search strategy. The main capabilities are described in the following sections.

Searching by *Thesaurus* Descriptor.   Some electronic versions of the ERIC database include a thesaurus to help you identify the most appropriate descriptors to use in conducting your search. The version that we used for our sample search does not provide a thesaurus. Therefore, we used the hard-copy *Thesaurus of ERIC Descriptors* to identify the descriptors for our electronic search.

The electronic preliminary source that we used to search for publications relating to parents of high risk students refers to both *CIJE* entries and *RIE* resumes as *entries*, so hereon we will use that term. Our first step involved determining the number of entries that had been coded by each of the descriptors listed on our electronic search record (Figure 3.5): *Parent**, *High risk students*, and *Academic achievement*.

Before we describe the results of the search, we need to explain the meaning of the asterisk in the term *Parent**. When we did a manual search, we used the asterisk to mean that we wanted to look at any citation that had been classified by a descriptor beginning with *Parent* (e.g., *Parent Influence, Parenthood Education, Parents, Parenting Skills*). In an electronic search of the ERIC database the asterisk has a similar, but slightly broader, meaning. The asterisk refers to a search procedure called *truncation*, which means that we want to see all instances of any term that includes the "trunk" of a given word, whether it occurs at the beginning of the term or not. For example, the terms *signify, insignificant*, and *resign* all contain the "trunk" *s-i-g-n*.

To demonstrate how truncation affects an electronic search, Figure 3.6 shows a portion of the rotated descriptor display from the *Thesaurus of ERIC Descriptors*. It shows all the descriptors that contain the trunk of the word *parent*, starting with *PARENT ABSENCE* and ending with *MIDDLE CLASS PARENTS*. After *PARENTING SKILLS* we find the descriptor *IN LOCO PARENTIS*. An electronic search of the descriptor *Parent** will retrieve entries coded for all these descriptors. Truncation makes it much easier to do a comprehensive search when one is searching for descriptors or terms that have many variants.

In response to the search for our three descriptors shown in Figure 3.5, the computer screen showed the following information:

Parent*	65156 entries
High risk students	4836 entries
Academic achievement	32803 entries

```
                    PARENT ABSENCE      Use ONE PARENT FAMILY
                    PARENT AS A TEACHER    Use PARENTS AS TEACHERS
                    PARENT ASPIRATION
                    PARENT ASSOCIATIONS
                    PARENT ATTITUDES
                    PARENT BACKGROUND
                    PARENT BEHAVIOR      Use PARENT CHILD RELATIONSHIP
                    PARENT CHILD INTERACTION      Use PARENT CHILD RELATIONSHIP
                    PARENT CHILD RELATIONSHIP
                    PARENT CONFERENCES
         TEACHER    PARENT CONFERENCES      Use PARENT TEACHER CONFERENCES
         TEACHER    PARENT COOPERATION      Use PARENT TEACHER COOPERATION
                    PARENT COUNSELING
                    PARENT EDUCATION
             ONE    PARENT FAMILY
          SINGLE    PARENT FAMILY      Use ONE PARENT FAMILY
             TWO    PARENT FAMILY      Use NUCLEAR FAMILY
                    PARENT FINANCIAL CONTRIBUTION
                    PARENT FORUMS      Use PARENT CONFERENCES
                    PARENT GRIEVANCES
                    PARENT INFLUENCE
                    PARENT INVOLVEMENT      Use PARENT PARTICIPATION
                    PARENT MATERIALS
                    PARENT OPINIONS      Use PARENT ATTITUDES
                    PARENT PARTICIPATION
                    PARENT REACTION (1966 1980)      Use PARENT ATTITUDES
           CHILD    PARENT RELATIONSHIP      Use PARENT CHILD RELATIONSHIP
          SCHOOL    PARENT RELATIONSHIP      Use PARENT SCHOOL RELATIONSHIP
         STUDENT    PARENT RELATIONSHIP      Use PARENT STUDENT RELATIONSHIP
                    PARENT RESPONSIBILITY
                    PARENT RIGHTS
                    PARENT ROLE
                    PARENT SCHOOL RELATIONSHIP
                    PARENT SKILLS      Use PARENTING SKILLS
                    PARENT STUDENT CONFERENCES (1967 1980)      Use PARENT TEACHER CONFERENCES
                    PARENT STUDENT RELATIONSHIP
                    PARENT STUDY GROUPS      Use PARENT CONFERENCES
                    PARENT TALK      Use CAREGIVER SPEECH and PARENT CHILD RELATIONSHIP
                    PARENT TEACHER CONFERENCES
                    PARENT TEACHER COOPERATION
                    PARENT WORKSHOPS
                    PARENTAL ASPIRATION (1966 1980)      Use PARENT ASPIRATION
                    PARENTAL BACKGROUND (1966 1980)      Use PARENT BACKGROUND
                    PARENTAL FINANCIAL CONTRIBUTION (1978 1980)      Use PARENT FINANCIAL CONTRIBUTION
                    PARENTAL GRIEVANCES (1967 1980)      Use PARENT GRIEVANCES
                    PARENTAL OBLIGATIONS      Use PARENT RESPONSIBILITY
           EARLY    PARENTHOOD
                    PARENTHOOD EDUCATION
                    PARENTING      Use CHILD REARING
                    PARENTING MATERIALS      Use PARENT MATERIALS
                    PARENTING SKILLS
        IN LOCO    PARENTIS
           LOCO    PARENTIS      Use IN LOCO PARENTIS
                    PARENTS
      ADOLESCENT    PARENTS      Use EARLY PARENTHOOD
        ADOPTIVE    PARENTS
                    PARENTS AS TEACHERS
      BIOLOGICAL    PARENTS
           BIRTH    PARENTS      Use BIOLOGICAL PARENTS
        CATHOLIC    PARENTS (1966 1980)      Use CATHOLICS and PARENTS
         COTTAGE    PARENTS      Use RESIDENT ADVISERS
     DUAL EARNER    PARENTS      Use EMPLOYED PARENTS
        EMPLOYED    PARENTS
          FOSTER    PARENTS      Use FOSTER FAMILY
     LOWER CLASS    PARENTS
    MIDDLE CLASS    PARENTS
         NATURAL    PARENTS      Use BIOLOGICAL PARENTS
         WORKING    PARENTS (1966 1980)      Use EMPLOYED PARENTS
```

FIGURE 3.6   Display for descriptors containing the "trunk"
Parent **in the rotated descriptor display of the** *Thesaurus of ERIC*
Descriptors

Source. Houston, J. D. (Ed.). (1995). *Thesaurus of ERIC descriptors* (13th ed.), p. 478.
Phoenix, AZ: Oryx.

Clearly we could not look at every one of these entries individually. Even though we anticipate considerable overlap between these entries, we do not know which entries are common to more than one of our descriptors until we combine them. Procedures for combining descriptors and using other search strategies are described in the following sections.

Combining Descriptors.

1. *Using the* and *connector.* In describing the hard-copy search of *CIJE* and *RIE*, we noted the difficulty of searching for entries relevant to all three of our descriptors: *Parent**, *High risk students*, and *Academic achievement*. This task is no problem in searching an electronic database. We simply enter our first descriptor, enter the connector *and*, then enter our second descriptor, again enter the connector *and*, and enter our third descriptor. By using the *and* connector, we are telling the computer that we want to see only entries that have been coded for all three of the descriptors that we have connected by *and*.

Because the term *Parent** combines many descriptors, we decided to use the narrower descriptor *Parents* for this search. When we entered *Parents* as our first descriptor, we learned that 3773 entries have been coded with this descriptor. Then we combined this descriptor with our second and third descriptors as follows (Search 1):

> *Parents* and *High risk students* and *Academic achievement*

The computer screen showed 124 entries with this combination.

2. *Using the* or *connector.* We were pleased to find that a manageable number of entries (i.e., 124) had been coded by all three of our descriptors. We suspected, however, that other entries might also have some relevance to our problem. Therefore we decided to use the *or* connector to combine our third descriptor, *Academic achievement*, with alternate descriptors that are similar to it in meaning. We did the following search (the parentheses show how the third descriptor was grouped together with other descriptors):

> *Parents* and *High risk students* and (*Academic achievement* or *Enrichment* or *Academic persistence* or *Academic aspiration*)

The result of Search 2 was 178 entries. In other words, by including alternate terms for one of our descriptors, we increased the number of entries retrieved from 124 to 178. We know that each of these 178 entries was classified by an ERIC indexer by the descriptors *Parents* and *High risk students* and also by one of these descriptors: *Academic achievement*, *Enrichment*, *Academic persistence*, or *Academic aspiration*.

Searching by Educational Level.   As we mentioned in the section on hard-copy searching, every publication indexed by ERIC is assigned an educational-level descriptor, if appropriate. We can thus focus our search by selecting the specific educational level or levels in which we are most interested. For example, we can take the combination of descriptors used in our previous search and use an *and* connector to limit the citations to those that involve elementary education. This combination of descriptors is shown below (Search 3):

> *Parents* and *High risk students* and (*Academic achievement* or *Enrichment* or *Academic persistence* or *Academic aspiration*) and *Elementary education*

Adding the educational-level descriptor reduced the entries retrieved from 178 entries to 65 entries. Thus we were able to focus our search still further and reduce the number of entries to a more manageable number.

Searching by Publication Date.   When you complete each search of the database, the computer screen will show you the retrieved citations in reverse chronological order, that is, with the most recent citations at the top of the list. You can look only at the items for the time period that interests you. Another option, which yields a faster search, is to initiate the search by entering a specific range of publication dates. To illustrate this procedure, let us take the 178 entries retrieved from the search we did for entries classified by *Parents*, *High risk students*, and the four descriptors relating to academics. Generally it is reasonable to limit a search to entries published during the most recent five years. We limited our search to entries published between 1992 and 1996, as follows (Search 4):

> *Parents* and *High risk students* and (*Academic achievement* or
> *Enrichment* or *Academic persistence* or *Academic aspiration*) and
> (*Pub date* after 12/31/91 and before 01/01/97)

We obtained 92 entries from this search.

Conducting a Free-Text Search.   A free-text search (also called a *natural language* search) involves requesting every entry in which a particular word or set of words appears anywhere in the entry. In the on-line database that we searched, the words can occur anywhere in the title, descriptors, identifiers, or abstract of the entry. Also, the words can be adjacent to each other or separated by other words. For example, if we were conducting a free-text search for entries about constructivist teacher education, we might find an entry in which *constructivist* appeared in the title of the publication, *teacher* in the abstract, and *education* in the list of descriptors.

   Suppose that you want to search for a unique term, like the name of an organization (Parents Anonymous), an acronym (ITIP), or a test name (Learning and Study Skills Inventory). The ERIC database designates many such terms as identifiers, and codes all the publications that include them. Therefore, even if you consider your term unique, first try entering it as an identifier or descriptor to see if entries have been coded with that term. If you find no entries for your term, you can then do a free-text search.

   Some versions of the *CIJE* and *RIE* database allow you to conduct a free-text search in which you specify that the words must appear next to or in close proximity to each other, or in the same field (e.g., both words must be some-where in the title). This method, called *proximity searching*, is useful when you want to search a sharply defined topic or when there are no descriptor terms for the topic. Even though the database we used did not include this option, by examining the entries we could quickly determine which ones included the term for which we were searching.

The value of free-text searching was illustrated for us when we heard about an organization for parents called the *Center for the Improvement of Child Caring*. First we searched for entries that had been coded for this term as a descriptor or identifier, and no entries were retrieved. In Search 5 we did a free-text search and retrieved four entries. The words *center, improvement, child*, and *caring* occurred separately in two of the entries. Neither of these entries had anything to do with the Center for the Improvement of Child Caring. The other two entries, however, listed this center as the institution where the publication orig-inated, and so these two entries were relevant to our search topic.

Other Types of Searching.   If you wish to examine a particular entry and you know its ERIC accession number or title, you can enter either one and view the entire citation on the computer screen. It also is possible to search for entries that have particular features. For example, you can search:

1. *By publication type.* Publications in the *CIJE* and *RIE* database are coded as to the type or types of publication they represent. Table 3.1 shows the publica-tion types in current use. In our literature search about parent involvement, we wanted to know which publications included tests or measures. For Search 6 we entered this publication type exactly as it appears in Table 3.1:

(Parents) and (Pub Type: *Tests, Evaluation Instruments*)

We obtained 126 entries.

2. *By author.* We entered the name of the first author of the *RIE* resume shown in Figure 3.4, that is, Joyce L. Epstein, in Search 7. Four authors were found, with 73 entries as follows:

1.	Epstein, Joyce	6 entries
2.	Epstein, Joyce L.	62 entries
3.	Epstein, Joyce L. and Others	4 entries
4.	Epstein, Joyce Levy Ed	1 entry

In this case it appears that all 73 entries were written by the particular author for whom we were searching. (In the last example, *Ed* indicates that Epstein was the editor of the publication cited in the entry.)

This example shows that, in searching for authors, you may need to try dif-ferent variations of their names, particularly for common names like *Smith* or *Brown*. Then you can examine the entries to see if they concern topics about which the individual for whom you are searching is likely to have written.

TABLE 3.1   Publication Types Used to Code *CIJE* and *RIE* Publications

Code	Publication type	Code	Publication type
010	**BOOKS**	080	**JOURNAL ARTICLES**
	COLLECTED WORKS	090	**LEGAL/LEGISLATIVE/REGULATORY MATERIALS**
020	— General	100	**AUDIOVISUAL/NON-PRINT MATERIALS**
021	— Conference Proceedings		
022	— Serials	101	— Computer Programs
030	**CREATIVE WORKS** (Literature, Drama, Fine Arts)	102	— Machine-Readable Data Files (MRDFs)
	DISSERTATIONS/THESES	110	**STATISTICAL DATA** (Numerical, Quantitative, etc.)
040	— Undetermined		
041	— Doctoral Dissertations	120	**VIEWPOINTS** (Opinion Papers, Position Papers, Essays, etc.)
042	— Masters Theses		
043	— Practicum Papers		**REFERENCE MATERIALS**
	GUIDES	130	— General (use more specific code, if possible)
050	— General (use more specific code, if possible)		
	— Classroom Use	131	— Bibliographies/Annotated Bibliographies
051	— Instructional Materials (for Learner)	132	— Directories/Catalogs
052	— Teaching Guides (for Teacher)	133	— Geographic Materials/Maps
055	— Non-Classroom Use (for Administrative and Support Staff, and for Teachers, Parents, Clergy, Researchers, Counselors, etc.)	134	— Vocabularies/Classifications/Dictionaries
			REPORTS
		140	— General (use more specific code, if possible)
060	**HISTORICAL MATERIALS**		
070	**INFORMATION ANALYSES** (State-of-the-Art Papers, Research Summaries, Literature Reviews, etc.)	141	— Descriptive (i.e., Project Descriptions)
		142	— Evaluative/Feasibility
		143	— Research/Technical
071	— ERIC Information Analysis Products (IAPs)	150	**SPEECHES, CONFERENCE PAPERS**
072	— Book/Product Reviews	160	**TESTS, EVALUATION INSTRUMENTS**
073	— ERIC Digests (selected) in Full Text	170	**TRANSLATIONS**
074	— Non-ERIC Digests (selected) in Full Text	171	— Multilingual/Bilingual Materials

Source. Adapted from: Houston, J. D. (Ed.). (1995). *Thesaurus of ERIC descriptors* (13th ed.), p. xxi. Phoenix, AZ: Oryx.

3. *By periodical title.* If you think a particular journal or magazine is likely to contain publications relevant to your search, you can enter the periodical title. We entered *Practitioner*, the journal cited in the document resume in Figure 3.4. Search 8 located 26 entries, each of which had been published in that journal.

4. *By target audience.* As we noted earlier in describing the information in an *RIE* resume, some of the publications indexed in the ERIC database are coded for one or more target audiences. If you are concerned about a particular target audience, you can retrieve all the entries related to given descriptors or words that have been coded for that target audience. For Search 9 we specified:

Parents and (Target Audience: *Teachers*)

The computer retrieved 68 entries. Upon examination, we found that most of these entries indexed publications that were designed to help schoolteachers work with their students' parents.

5. *By language.* In the electronic version of the ERIC database, each publication is coded for the language or languages in which it is available. You might wish to search for publications written in a language other than English. For example, we searched for Spanish-language publications in Search 10:

Parents and (Language: *Spanish*)

The computer retrieved 30 entries. Some of these publications were available only in Spanish, and others were available in both English and Spanish.

The above examples do not exhaust the search strategies that you can apply to an electronic preliminary source. Once you have become familiar with the basic procedures of a particular source, you can experiment with descriptors, connectors, truncation, and free-text searching to identify a set of citations that satisfy your particular information needs.

Step 3: Specifying the Form of the Entries

After developing your search strategy, you will need to decide the amount of detail that you want about each entry and the form in which you want to receive this information.

ERIC and other databases offer various options for the level of detail that you can retrieve for each entry. The following are three possible levels to consider.

1. *Title only.* If your search results in a substantial list of entries, it will be time-consuming to scan through them on your computer screen or make a hard copy of them on a computer printer. Therefore, you may choose to examine only the titles first. You can read through the titles to decide which entries you want to examine further, and then request more complete entries for only the titles you want.

2. *Brief citation: title, accession number, and bibliographic data.* This option gives you a slightly better basis than just the title for judging the value of a publication. It also gives you sufficient information to obtain the publication from a journal (an accession number beginning with *EJ* indicates a journal article) or from the ERIC microfiche collection (an accession number beginning with *ED* indicates a

document that may be in this collection). We downloaded a brief citation for ERIC entry EJ 397 738 from our search and got the following information:

AUTHOR   Kahn, Ann P.
TITLE   Enlisting Parents' Help with Mathematics
APPEARS IN   Educational Leadership 1989, Oct v47 n2 p37.
PUB DATE   01 JAN 1989.

3. *Full citation, including abstract and descriptors*. The full citation includes all the information available in the database for a particular entry, and is similar to the information shown in Figure 3.4. The complete citation is probably sufficient for you to decide whether the publication is relevant to your literature search.

Step 4: Downloading the Entries

After deciding how much information you want about the entries retrieved in your search, you need to decide how you wish to retrieve and store the information. We decided to download 29 entries from Search 3 and 14 from Search 9, as shown in Figure 3.5.

It may be possible to have the selected entries directly printed on a printer linked to the computer on which you are conducting your literature search. Other options may be to download the entries to a computer disk or forward them to your e-mail address. You then can study the citations on any computer screen and have them printed on any computer printer.

CONCLUDING THOUGHT

Many people's traditional notion of an expert is someone with much greater ability, experience, or leadership capacity than others in a particular profession. In the information age, however, experts are often the individuals who best know how to define and satisfy information needs. You will have a good start to becoming this type of expert if you learn how to carry out a hard-copy or electronic search of preliminary sources as a means to access the education literature.

SELF-CHECK TEST

1. A preliminary source typically does not contain
   a. information about papers presented at professional conferences.
   b. abstracts summarizing the contents of publications.
   c. information about publications more than 15 years old.
   d. the complete text of publications.

2. All the following are customary steps in searching a hard-copy preliminary source, except for
   a. identifying whether the information in monthly issues has been cumulated in semiannual or annual volumes.
   b. identifying relevant descriptors.
   c. taking note of the quality of each publication as rated by the preliminary-source indexer.
   d. using the subject index.

3. The elements of information about a publication that are contained in an *RIE* document resume are designed primarily to
   a. make it unnecessary for users to obtain and read the publication.
   b. suggest other publications about which users might want to get information.
   c. give users sufficient information about the publication to guide them in making a practical decision.
   d. help users determine the relevance of the publication to their information needs.

4. An educator accesses the ERIC database by using a dedicated computer terminal on which the entire database is stored. This is an example of using a(n)
   a. Internet database.
   b. CD-ROM database.
   c. on-line database.
   d. hard-copy database.

5. One option that is available in an electronic version of a preliminary source, but not in a hard-copy version, is
   a. searching for publications over a span of many years.
   b. using standard descriptors established by the preliminary-source indexers.
   c. combining several descriptors so as to obtain only publications relevant to all of them.
   d. searching for publications by specific authors.

6. The use of truncation in searching an electronic preliminary source typically
   a. increases the number of entries retrieved.
   b. decreases the number of entries retrieved.
   c. has no effect on the number of entries retrieved.
   d. limits the search to standard descriptors and identifiers.

7. A good way to broaden the scope of a search of an electronic preliminary source is to
   a. connect several descriptors related to your topic by the *or* connector.
   b. connect several descriptors related to your topic by the *and* connector.
   c. ask for entries that are of a particular publication type.
   d. ask for entries that are directed to a specific target audience.

8. A free-text search of a specific set of words is most desirable when you
   a. are searching for a term that is likely to be an ERIC descriptor or identifier.
   b. want to find every entry that has mentioned the set of words for which you are searching.
   c. want to find entries for publications of a specific publication type.
   d. want to obtain complete citations for the retrieved entries.

9. You plan to obtain the entries retrieved in an electronic search of a preliminary source from the appropriate journal or the ERIC microfiche collection. For this purpose it is sufficient to download the entries'
   a. titles only.
   b. brief citations.
   c. full citations.
   d. abstracts only.

CHAPTER REFERENCES

Houston, J. D. (Ed.). (1995). *Thesaurus of ERIC descriptors* (13th ed.). Phoenix: Oryx.

RECOMMENDED READING

Hahn, H. (1996). *The Internet complete reference* (2nd ed.). Berkeley, CA: Osborne McGraw-Hill.

Covers topics necessary for anyone to understand and use the Internet, including hardware and software requirements, Internet addressing and electronic mail, and use of the World Wide Web and other client-server systems.

Hartley, R. J., Keen, E. M., Large, J. A., & Tedd, L. A. (Eds.). (1990). *On-line searching: Principles and practice*. London: Bowker-Saur.

Contains chapters on basic searching, search strategies, and Boolean logic. Examples are used to illustrate techniques discussed. A bibliography follows each chapter.

Taheri, B. J., Pearce, E., & Boston, C. (1996). *Directory of ERIC resource collections*. Washington, DC: Office of Educational Research and Improvement, National Library of Education, U.S. Department of Education.

Periodically updated, the current edition of this directory lists over 1,000 organizations, organized by state, that provide access to the ERIC database and related resources and services. It includes organizations such as school districts, colleges and universities, state departments of education, ERIC clearinghouses, and regional education agencies.

Another resource for identifying means of local access to the ERIC database is to call ACCESS ERIC at 1-800-LET-ERIC or to send an e-mail message to <ericdb @aspensys.com>.

CHAPTER 4
READING SECONDARY SOURCES

Gene Letterman is a high school principal in a large urban school district that is facing a budget shortfall. Several teachers have been told that their contracts will not be renewed for the next school year, and the school board is considering further reductions in the teaching staff. The board chairman, Jane Rutledge, is worried about parents' reactions to the projected increase in class size, from 29 students to 31 students on average.

"Gene, we want to know how to respond if parents say we will be short-changing their kids," she says. "I know you try and keep up with research in education, so I wonder if you could get some information about whether increasing class size will affect our students' learning."

Gene promises to explore the issue, and agrees to make a presentation to the board at its next meeting. Like most school principals, Gene is pressed for time. Thumbing through the journals that he receives as part of his membership in professional associations, he finds nothing on the topic of class size. He also talks to a few other principals. They provide some ideas and information, but he doesn't feel that he yet has a solid answer for the school board.

At this point, he decides to look for a good secondary source, which basically is a review of the published literature. At a nearby university library he checks the second edition of the *International Encyclopedia of Education*, published in 1994, and reads the entry on "Class Size." It summarizes the important research findings, and concludes that a small change in class size appears to affect student achievement only under very limited conditions. It also notes that a substantial change in class size (an increase or decrease of five or more students) appears to have the greatest effect in the early grades, and for lower-achieving students.

Having read this article, Gene now feels ready to make a presentation to the school board about the effects of class size on learning, and to answer their questions with some confidence.

In this chapter, you will learn about the characteristics of a secondary source, such as the encyclopedia article that Gene Letterman used to meet his need for information about class size. You also will learn about different types of secondary sources, how to go about finding a secondary source for your particular information needs, and how to judge whether the secondary sources that you locate are sound. You also will read three illustrative secondary sources that are available in the professional literature.

OBJECTIVES

After studying this chapter, you will be able to

1. explain how a secondary source differs from a primary source in a literature review.
2. explain how reading appropriate secondary sources can help you develop an understanding of the literature on an educational problem.

3. compare two types of secondary sources that review and synthesize the research literature related to a topic.

4. compare the relative advantages of vote counting, the chi-square test, and meta-analysis for synthesizing quantitative research findings in a primary source analysis.

5. explain how to carry out a review of research that involves primarily qualitative research studies.

6. describe several major secondary sources and their usefulness in doing a literature search.

7. describe several criteria that you can use to evaluate a specific secondary source to determine its soundness and usefulness.

KEY TERMS

artifact
Books in Print
cause-and-effect relationship
chi-square test
construct
control group
criterion measure
Current Index to Journals in Education (CIJE)
Education Index
Educational Resources Information Center (ERIC)
effect size
Encyclopedia of Educational Research

ERIC clearinghouse
ERIC Digest
experimental group
exploratory case study method
fugitive literature
International Encyclopedia of Education
literature search
mean
meta-analysis
narrative summary
NSSE Yearbooks
on-line catalog
preliminary source
primary source

primary source analysis
professional review
Psychological Abstracts
research synthesis
Resources in Education (RIE)
Review of Educational Research
Review of Research in Education
reviewer bias
secondary source
standard deviation
statistical significance
vote counting

THE VALUE OF SECONDARY SOURCES

Secondary sources are publications in which the author is reporting on research that others have carried out, on a theory that others have developed, or on experiences that others have had. Among the most common secondary sources in education are textbooks. For example, a book on educational psychology usually discusses the findings of classical and recent research in areas such as human development, motivation, learning, instructional methods, and assessment. Or an encyclopedia entry that synthesizes research on cooperative learning will summarize the findings of many researchers who have investigated this method. Authors of secondary sources may review their own research as well, but this research usually was originally reported in various primary sources.

Carrying out your own literature review obviously has some advantages over relying on a secondary source. Searching the literature will give you an in-depth familiarity with the research findings that bear on your problem and a better understanding of the educational research process. If you are in a graduate degree or licensure program, you may be expected to conduct a thorough literature search as a program requirement.

There are several disadvantages, however, to conducting your own literature review "from scratch." The biggest problem is the time it takes to do a thorough literature review, especially when you are seeking an immediate answer to a pressing problem. As we described in preceding chapters, you must spend time defining your problem, selecting appropriate preliminary sources (that is, indexes to the professional literature), and using the preliminary sources to identify citations to primary and secondary sources. Next you must judge the relevance of each citation by reading the actual study, once you finish the time-consuming process of locating it. Then you must organize, evaluate, and interpret what each study found. Finally, you must synthesize the various findings, draw conclusions, and prepare a report.

The time and effort involved in this type of literature review are beyond the resources of many practitioners. Nonetheless, most educators, policy makers, and the public believe that educational practitioners should inform their decision making with research findings. Reading the most relevant secondary sources enables practitioners to accomplish this goal with much less effort. Even if you find a relevant secondary source that was written some years ago, you still would save a great deal of time, because you would only need to search for recent sources to update the information contained in the secondary source.

A published secondary source has a special advantage if its authors are well informed and experienced in the area they are investigating. You reap the benefits of their expertise in finding, organizing, and interpreting research, theory, opinion, and experience relevant to your problem. It is difficult for most practitioners to develop the same level of skill as a reviewer who is familiar with the range of methodologies, measures, and statistical tests that have been used to investigate a particular educational topic.

Still another advantage of reading a well-done, published secondary source is that it is authoritative, and so may carry more weight with policy makers than a search you do on your own. If you can cite well-documented research syntheses as the basis for your own opinions, policy makers and your colleagues are likely to give your opinions more weight.

Despite the advantages of good secondary sources, you cannot fully rely on them in forming your opinions. You still need to exercise independent judgment about the literature cited, and use your own reasoning to determine whether the conclusions reached are justified by the body of research evidence reviewed. Reviewers may omit important information from a primary source, or interpret it in a way that reflects their own biases or values. Therefore, it is wise to track down selected studies and read them yourself. Reading primary sources selectively will give you more detailed information than is contained in a secondary source, and will deepen your understanding of the research process.

TYPES OF SECONDARY SOURCES

There are two main types of secondary sources: primary source analyses and professional reviews. We discuss them in the following sections.

Primary Source Analyses

Primary source analyses have a limited scope, involve a comprehensive search process, and focus on primary sources. As we explained in Chapter 3, primary sources are reports written by the individual or individuals who actually did the research study, developed the theory, or witnessed or participated in the experiences described in the report. The purpose of a primary source analysis is to draw diverse findings together into a coherent picture of the state of research knowledge, theoretical understanding, and professional practice relating to a particular aspect of education.

Reviewers who do primary source analyses use various techniques to synthesize findings from quantitative research studies that have investigated the same problem, but with different types of participants, measures, and statistical techniques. A simple technique is vote counting, which was recommended by Gregg Jackson (1980). First, studies are identified in which the effect of one variable on another variable, or the relationship between two variables, has been measured. Then all the studies are classified into four categories depending upon the statistical significance and direction of the results obtained. (As we explain in Chapter 6, if a result is statistically significant, it means that the result is probably true of the population, not just of the sample studied in the research.) Studies with statistically significant positive results (that is, in the direction hypothesized) are coded ++; studies with nonsignificant positive results are coded +; studies with statistically significant results opposite to the hypothesized direction are coded −−; and studies with nonsignificant results opposite to the hypothesized direction are coded −.

Barak Rosenshine (1971) used a form of vote counting in his review of the relationship between specific teaching behaviors and student achievement. Before vote counting, he made careful judgments about which studies were relevant to a particular teaching behavior. Once this determination was made, Rosenshine designed tables to show the significant and nonsignificant results from each relevant study. He then discussed the overall trend of the results, and drew conclusions. For example, having examined nine studies that concerned teachers' use of student ideas, Rosenshine concluded that

. . . not one yielded a significant linear correlation between the use of this variable and student achievement. However, there was a positive trend . . . in eight of the nine studies. . . . Although a great deal has been written about the importance of teacher use of student ideas . . . the significance of this variable alone is not as strong as has been claimed. (p. 71)

Other approaches to quantitative research synthesis are more mathematically precise than vote counting. N. L. Gage (1978) recommended a procedure called the chi-square test. It involves use of a particular statistical measure (chi-square) to test the statistical significance of two or more results across studies of a particular program or method. This procedure takes into account both the size of the sample and the magnitude of the relationship or difference reported in each study. Gage reviewed individual studies of how teaching techniques such as teachers' praise, criticism, and acceptance of student ideas affect student learning. Gage demonstrated that while individual studies tended to show weak, nonsignificant effects for these techniques, combining the results across studies using the chi-square test led to strong, generalizable conclusions about their effectiveness.

In recent years, meta-analysis has become the most widely used method for combining results from different quantitative research studies. Meta-analysis involves translating the findings of a set of research studies on the same phenomenon into a statistic called an *effect size*. Most meta-analyses in education follow the procedures developed by Gene Glass (1976).

Suppose that the individual studies are experiments that test the effectiveness of a particular program. In this case the effect size indicates the degree to which participants in the experimental program show superior performance compared to a comparison group (called the control group) that receives either no treatment or an alternative program. The effect size is computed by this formula: The numerator is the difference between the mean score of the experimental group and the mean score of the control group on a criterion measure (for example, an achievement test), and the denominator is the average of the two groups' standard deviations (a measure of score variability) on the criterion measure.

For example, imagine a study of the effect of small cash rewards on the achievement of students in an inner-city high school. For one school year, experimental students receive cash rewards for passing weekly quizzes, and control students receive no rewards. At the end of the year both the experimental and control group students take the XYZ Mathematics Test, which is the criterion measure. For the experimental group the mean score is 46.2 and the standard deviation is 4.0. For the control group the mean score is 41.2 and the standard deviation is 3.6. The effect size would be 46.2 minus 41.2 divided by 3.8, or 1.32. An effect size of 1.32 means that a student who scores at the 50th percentile in the experimental group has a score equivalent to a student who scores at the 91st percentile in the control group. Thus, based on the findings described here, we would conclude that giving students cash rewards for passing quizzes is substantially more effective than not giving them cash rewards.

There is some consensus among practitioners and researchers that an effect size of .33 or larger has practical significance. An effect size of .33 indicates that a student in the group with a higher mean score whose score is at the 50th percentile would be at the 63rd percentile of the other group's score distribution.

Calculating an effect size for every relevant study included in a primary source analysis transforms the results from various studies into a comparable unit of measure. It does not matter that one study used the XYZ Mathematics Test, on which scores can vary from 0 to 70, and another study used the ABC History Test, on which scores can vary from 0 to 100. An effect size can be calculated for the results of both studies, and these effect sizes can be directly compared. An effect size of 1.00 is twice as large as an effect size of .50, irrespective of the measures and scoring systems that were used. The mean of the effect sizes from different studies can be calculated to yield an estimate of the average effect that the experimental program or method produces relative to a comparison intervention.

Not all studies in the research literature report the means and standard deviations for calculating effect size in the manner described above. However, there are procedures for estimating effect size from virtually any statistical data reported in the primary sources included in the meta-analysis.

Meta-analysis has gained much popularity in different disciplines, among them medicine, psychology, and education. However, you should be aware of the potential limitations of this technique. One of them is the reviewer's basis for selecting studies. For example, in a meta-analysis of the effects of metacognitive instruction on reading comprehension, Eileen Haller and her colleagues state that they examined 150 references but limited their analysis to 20 studies (Haller et al., 1988). These 20 studies met certain criteria: the use of metacognitive intervention, employment of a control group for comparison, and provision of statistical information necessary to compute effect sizes. Gene Glass, one of the primary developers of meta-analysis, probably would have advised Haller and her colleagues to include as many of the 150 original studies as possible in their analysis, even though some are methodologically more sound than others. Glass argues that either weaker studies will show the same results as stronger studies and thus should be included, or that a truer picture will emerge if weak studies are also analyzed.

By contrast, Robert Slavin (1986) argues against including every possible study in a meta-analysis. Slavin examined eight meta-analyses conducted by six independent teams of reviewers and compared their procedures and conclusions against the studies they analyzed. Slavin reported that he found errors in all eight meta-analyses that were serious enough to invalidate or call into question one or more of the major conclusions of each study. Slavin therefore recommends including in a meta-analysis only studies providing "best evidence," that is, those that meet criteria such as methodological adequacy and relevance to the issue at hand. He also makes a strong case for calculating not only an overall mean effect size, but also separate effect sizes for subsets of studies—for example, those that used the same measure of the dependent variable or those that studied a specific ethnic group.

Consistent with Slavin's recommendations, we advise you not to accept an effect size in a meta-analysis at face value, but to examine at least a few of the primary sources that contributed findings to the calculation of the effect size. By taking this extra step, you can check exactly how the primary source investigated the particular educational practice or issue of interest to you.

The first of three secondary sources reprinted at the end of this chapter is a published meta-analysis by Molly Weinburgh (1995). Her meta-analysis reviewed 18 research studies on differences between boys and girls in their attitudes toward science and their level of achievement in science. In the "Data Sources" section of her article, Weinburgh gives a brief explanation of the procedure that she used to identify these 18 studies. Although the mean effect sizes reported by Weinburgh are relatively low, the fact that the findings of gender differences in students' science attitudes and achievement are derived from 18 studies allows us to be fairly confident that they represent real gender differences, and are not merely the artifact of an atypical sample or measure of attitudes and achievement. To help readers make sense of the findings, Weinburgh also reports the results of subanalyses of the studies based on the type of science studied, students' ability level, and the studies' publication dates.

Thus far we have considered procedures for reviewing primary sources that involve quantitative research. As we explain in Chapter 1, qualitative research represents another approach to scientific inquiry. It involves the study of individual cases in an effort to understand the unique character and context of each case. Rodney Ogawa and Betty Malen (1991) suggested a method for synthesizing qualitative research studies that enables the reviewer to acknowledge the unique characteristics of each case, but also to identify concepts and principles that are present across cases. Although the primary focus is qualitative studies, Ogawa and Malen's method (called the *exploratory case study method*) allows reviewers to include quantitative studies and nonresearch accounts of a phenomenon in their synthesis of the literature on a particular educational topic.

The article by Nathan Bos, Joseph Krajcik, and Helen Patrick, also reprinted later in this chapter, illustrates several of the procedures that Ogawa and Malen recommend for reviewing qualitative research. Their review article appeared in a special issue of the *Journal of Computers in Mathematics and Science Teaching*, devoted to the topic of telecommunications. It was intended to clarify the potential role of computer-mediated communications (CMC) in improving teaching practice in mathematics and science. The report describes research on a selective number of projects (13) about which sufficient research was available. The research consisted primarily of case studies of the projects, but some quantitative survey data were collected and analyzed, too.

One procedure recommended by Ogawa and Malen is to clarify the focus of the review and define key constructs used in the review. Consistent with this recommendation, Bos et al. (1995) state a specific focus for their literature review:

"This review will focus on computer networking projects that have been designed to support teacher practice" (p. 188 in the original article). They define computer-mediated communications (CMC) as "e-mail networks, bulletin boards, listservers, and ftp libraries for teachers" (p. 188 in the original article).

Ogawa and Malen recommend that reviewers classify the types of documents that they have identified in their search of the literature, for example: qualitative case studies, quantitative research experiments, and position statements. Bos and his colleagues do not present a document classification scheme in their article, probably because all the documents were similar in nature, being descriptions of specific CMC projects.

Qualitative case studies typically are reported in narrative form. Ogawa and Malen recommend that reviewers analyze the case studies by developing narrative summaries and coding schemes that take into account all the pertinent information in the documents. In reading the literature review on CMC, you will come across a table that provides a narrative summary of the 13 CMC projects that were reviewed. The table contains three columns: (1) the name of each CMC network, (2) the network's uses and purposes, and (3) research findings relating to the network.

Ogawa and Malen view the goals of a review of qualitative research as to increase understanding of the phenomena being studied and to guide further research. These goals are achieved by searching the documents included in the review for relevant constructs and cause-and-effect relationships. A quantitative research review also has the goal of guiding further research, but its other goal is quite different, namely, to make generalizations based on statistical findings.

When you read the literature review by Bos and his colleagues, you will find that they identified several key constructs that helped them understand the potential benefits of CMC networks for teachers. Among these constructs are *reflective practice, support for innovation, professional isolation,* and *communities of learning.* In addition, the authors developed several cause-and-effect propositions from their analysis of findings reported in the documents that they reviewed. For example, they proposed that CMC (the presumed causal agent) helps to create "a uniquely egalitarian online 'classroom' for mutual reflection and idea-sharing" (p. 190 in the original article), which is the presumed effect.

Ogawa and Malen caution reviewers of qualitative research to be aware of possible bias in their literature review procedures. For example, various statements in the literature review on CMC networks make evident that the authors strongly believe that these networks have great potential as a support for teachers. The reviewers therefore needed to be careful not to overlook or minimize any limitations of the positive effects, or possible negative effects, reported by the researchers. To provide an unbiased account, Bos and his colleagues include highlighted sections called "issues" that draw the reader's attention to several such limitations. They also suggest future directions for CMC development and research.

Professional Reviews

Some primary source analyses draw implications for educational practice, but this is not their main purpose, as they generally are written for researchers, not practitioners. By contrast, professional reviews do draw this type of implication, because they are intended for practitioners and policy makers. Many of them are intended for a particular audience of practitioners, such as elementary school teachers.

Professional reviews typically use nontechnical language to describe research findings. They also tend to be brief and selective in their citations of primary sources. For example, the *Encyclopedia of Educational Research* primarily consists of professional reviews. Each review is about four pages and lists 10 to 15 references.

The article by Robert Slavin that is reprinted later in this chapter originally appeared in the 1992 edition of the *Encyclopedia of Educational Research* as the entry on the topic of cooperative learning. Slavin presents a brief review of the research that has been carried out to test the effects of cooperative learning on various student outcomes.

The reviewers who are invited to write articles for an encyclopedia like the *Encyclopedia of Educational Research* typically are recognized as experts on particular topics. For example, Slavin's research and development in the area of cooperative learning is well known among educational practitioners. In the article Slavin summarizes not only his own work, but that of several other researchers and practitioners who have extensively promoted and studied cooperative learning strategies.

Authors of professional reviews generally examine published research studies, primary source analyses, and theoretical writings to determine their implications for improving professional practice. Slavin, for example, cites a number of research studies that found positive effects of cooperative learning methods on various student outcomes, and notes the conditions that are necessary to produce these effects in actual classrooms.

A good professional review is beneficial to you because it contains both research evidence and explicit implications and recommendations for practice. Unless a professional review is recent, however, it may not provide a good basis for making a decision about practice. The reason is that, over time, new advances in research and the changing conditions of educational practice might invalidate the reviewer's conclusions. Even so, a professional review can be useful as a reflection of the state of knowledge and practice that prevailed at the time it was prepared. You can supplement it by conducting your own literature search for publications that appeared subsequent to the review.

As with primary source analyses, some professional reviews focus on quantitative research, others focus on qualitative research, and still others review both types of research. Whatever their research focus, most professional reviews rely primarily on a narrative approach to synthesize the varied findings in the literature. The value of the implications for practice presented in professional reviews thus depends almost entirely on the authors' judgment and experience and their understanding of conditions in real-world educational settings.

Slavin's article includes an example of vote counting, and he also refers to an effect size in an earlier literature review that he conducted. For the most part, however, Slavin states findings about cooperative learning in general terms, without giving specific information about the statistical results that formed the basis for those findings.

Professional reviews generally lack the rigor of a good primary source analysis, so you need to consider whether the reviewer's conclusions and recommendations are warranted. Also, some professional reviews are written by individuals with limited experience in the conduct or interpretation of research. Therefore, you are advised to read for yourself some of the primary and secondary sources cited in a professional review before basing important educational decisions on the review's conclusions.

HOW TO LOCATE SECONDARY SOURCES

To identify relevant secondary sources, you may need first to consult preliminary sources, which are indexes to the literature on education and other disciplines. Four preliminary sources that are particularly useful to educators are ERIC, *Education Index*, *Psychological Abstracts*, and *Books in Print*. Each of these sources is described briefly in the next section.

Using Preliminary Sources to Locate Secondary Sources

ERIC.   The Educational Resources Information Center (ERIC) publishes two of the main preliminary sources in education: *Resources in Education* (*RIE*) and *Current Index to Journals in Education* (*CIJE*). If you do a computer search of these sources, you can combine *meta analysis* and *literature reviews* as descriptor terms with your primary descriptor terms to identify relevant secondary sources. (These computer search procedures are described in Chapter 3.)

ERIC also operates 16 clearinghouses focused on different educational topics. The name and address of each clearinghouse are presented in Appendix 2. Each clearinghouse is responsible for cataloging, abstracting, and indexing relevant documents in its subject area. The clearinghouses also publish newsletters, bulletins, annotated bibliographies, and literature reviews on high-interest topics. You can obtain copies of these publications by contacting the appropriate clearinghouse.

For example, we recently read an ERIC Digest from the ERIC Clearinghouse on Educational Management on the school practice of block scheduling (Trmsher, 1996). In two pages it defines block scheduling, covers the advantages and challenges of this instructional practice, and summarizes research and expert advice on how schools can implement it. The Digest includes eight references dated from 1990 to 1995.

You can search a database of over 1500 ERIC Digests, which are short reports on current educational topics produced by each of the 16 ERIC clearinghouses. This database, which is maintained by the U.S. Department of Education, can be accessed from this Web address: <http://www.ed.gov/databases/ ERIC_Digests/index/>. If you want to order a copy of the complete ERIC Digest, you can use the e-mail address or toll-free telephone number provided.

We carried out a search using the keyword *computer,* which resulted in 20 "hits," all marked either 100 percent or 98 percent for relevance. Three of the hits are listed below:

> 100%   ED392463 Mar 96 Computer Skills for Information Problem-
> Solving: Learning and Teaching Technology in Context. ERIC
> Digest. (summary)
> 98%   ED382409 May 95 The Internet and Early Childhood Educators:
> Some Frequently Asked Questions. ERIC Digest. (summary)
> 98%   ED376734 Dec 94 Internet for Language Teachers. ERIC Digest.
> (summary)

By clicking on the term "summary" next to any Digest, you can call up a brief summary of the information in that Digest. When we clicked on the ERIC Digest *Internet Basics 1996* (Tennant, 1996), we received the following summary:

> ELECTRONIC MAIL
> Electronic mail, or e-mail, is a fast, easy, and inexpensive way to communicate with other Internet users around the world. In addition, it is possible for Internet users to exchange e-mail with users of other independent networks such as CompuServe, Applelink, the WELL, and others. Another type of electronic communication that is growing in popularity is the electronic journal, or "e-journal." FILE TRANSFER Another application of the Internet is the ability to transfer files from one Internet-connected computer to another. To locate files, Internet users can use the Archie service, which indexes files from over 900 separate anonymous FTP sites (Tennant, 1993).

Education Index and Psychological Abstracts.   The main use of these preliminary sources is to locate primary sources. However, they also can be used to identify secondary sources on particular practices and issues in education. See Appendix 1 for more information on these preliminary sources.

Books in Print.   Some of the major secondary sources described in the next section, such as encyclopedias, are not published sufficiently often to present the current status of a particular educational practice or issue. If this is true of the topic you wish to review, your best chance of finding an up-to-date secondary source may lie in checking recent scholarly books, monographs, and textbooks.

The best source for locating such publications is the most recent edition of *Books in Print*. Most major libraries and bookstores have either a hard-copy set or on-line version of *Books in Print*, which includes a yearly index by title, author, and subject to books published in the United States or elsewhere. Start by looking up specific key terms related to your topic in the Subject Guide to *Books in Print*. For example, suppose you want to learn more about the academic achievement of minority students. In the 1995–96 edition, six recent books that appear to deal with this topic are listed under the heading "Academic Achievement." Under "Prediction of Scholastic Success" another relevant book is listed, and under "Minorities Education" four titles are listed. Thus, by using *Books in Print* you would promptly identify several potentially useful books, all currently in print.

If you find no scholarly books that relate closely to your topic, you may be able to find reports of research, theory, and practice in a recent textbook on educational administration, child development, educational psychology, or other field of education. For example, a check of three randomly selected textbooks in educational psychology revealed that all of them contained brief discussions of such topics as motivation, reinforcement, sex roles, and reading instruction. Because most textbooks cover a broad subject, discussion of specific questions is usually brief, often less than a page. Scholarly books cited in *Books in Print* usually deal with a more limited topic, but cover it in much greater depth.

Say that you have identified a book through *Books in Print* or some other means, but the book is not available in your library. It might be possible to obtain it through inter-library loan from a nearby library. At the University of Oregon Library, for example, the on-line catalog allows us to enter the title of a book and see whether it is available at any of a number of universities in the Pacific coastal states. If so, we can request that it be sent to us on loan. Check with the reference librarian at your library to see what procedures to use.

Publications Containing Secondary Sources on Specific Educational Topics

An extensive list of publications containing secondary sources is provided in Appendix 3. The following is a description of some of the most important of these publications.

Encyclopedia of Educational Research.   The sixth edition of this monumental work, published in 1992, includes 237 articles representing the work of over 300 contributors. The contents are organized in alphabetical order by such broad topic headings as educational measurement and assessment, levels of education, and teachers. If your topic is not in the alphabetical listing, you can check the 56-page index. This is an excellent source for getting a brief review of topics related to your area of interest.

International Encyclopedia of Education.   Published in 1994, the second edition of this encyclopedia presents an overview of research and scholarship on educational problems, practices, and institutions worldwide. The encyclopedia entries are grouped into 21 major clusters, such as administration of education, organization of schools, and teaching.

NSSE Yearbooks.   Each year the National Society for the Study of Education (NSSE) publishes two yearbooks. Each covers recent research and theory related to a major educational topic and contains 10 to 12 chapters that deal with different aspects of that topic. The chapters are written by experts in their field. The titles of recent yearbooks of the NSSE are:

1997	Part 1	Service Learning
	Part 2	The Construction of Children's Character
1996	Part 1	Performance-based Student Assessment: Challenges and Possibilities
	Part 2	Technology and the Future of Schooling
1995	Part 1	Creating New Educational Communities
	Part 2	Changing Populations, Changing Schools
1994	Part 1	Teacher Research and Educational Reform
	Part 2	Bloom's Taxonomy: A Forty-year Retrospective
1993	Part 1	Gender and Education
	Part 2	Bilingual Education: Politics, Practice, and Research

Review of Educational Research.   This journal consists entirely of reviews of research literature on educational topics. It is published quarterly, and each issue typically contains four to seven reviews. Each review includes an extensive bibliography, which may list primary source articles relevant to your problem. For example, the Spring 1997 issue includes a review of research by Kathleen V. Hoover-Dempsey and Howard M. Sandler titled "Why Do Parents Become Involved in Their Children's Education?" The text of this article covers 40 pages and cites more than 100 publications.

Review of Research in Education.   This is an annual series of books that was started in 1973. Each volume contains chapters written by leading educational researchers who provide critical surveys of research on important problems and trends in education. For example, Volume 22, published in 1997, includes 7 chapters grouped into three topic areas. The chapters include "The Political Economy of Urban Education," "Critical Race Theory and Education: History, Theory, and Implications," and "Professional, Personal, and Political Dimensions of Action Research."

Handbooks.   An increasing number of handbooks (listed in Appendix 3) have been published to address specific areas of education. For example, the *Handbook of Research on Teacher Education* (2nd ed.) was published in 1996.

Sample articles from this publication are "Selecting and Preparing Culturally Competent Teachers for Urban Schools" by M. Huberman, "The Moral Responsibilities of Teachers" by K. Strike, and "Needed Research in Teacher Education" by E. R. Ducharme and M. K. Ducharme.

A good way to find professional reviews in the educational literature is to examine the types of journals that are intended for education professionals. For example, *The Reading Teacher* periodically publishes reviews that synthesize research findings relevant to school teachers. *Phi Delta Kappan* contains articles citing research and drawing practical implications on many important educational issues, such as standards-based schooling, educational technology, school choice, and recent trends in national assessments of student achievement.

CRITERIA FOR EVALUATING SECONDARY SOURCES

The following criteria are intended to help you identify the most useful and valid secondary sources as you search for information related to your area of interest.

1. *The reviewer's credentials.* The reviewer's reputation and experience with the topic are factors to consider when reading a secondary source. One way to make this determination is to examine the reference list at the end of the source to see whether the author has done research on the topic, and if so, where and when it was published. You can also check for information in the article itself about the author's affiliation, title, and experience related to the topic.

2. *The search procedures.* In older published reviews, it was not customary for reviewers to specify their search procedures. Thus, it was difficult for readers to determine whether the research cited in the review resulted from a comprehensive search or whether it was haphazardly selected. Now reviewers often identify the preliminary sources examined, the descriptors used, and the years covered. This is more likely to be the case in a primary source analysis than in a professional review.

3. *The breadth of the search.* Research reviews vary widely in their breadth, from an exhaustive search for all primary sources on a topic to a highly selective search. The advantage of a comprehensive search is that you have some assurance that no significant research evidence or theoretical framework has been overlooked. A narrower search may be just as useful for your purposes, but in this case it is even more important to know how the reviewer selected the documents included in the review. The following dimensions reflect the breadth of the reviewer's search of the literature.

   a. The period of time covered by the search. The publication dates of the most recent and oldest sources provide an indication of this time period. Keep in mind, though, that the time period may span beyond these dates, but the search may not have yielded older or more recent publications that were relevant to the topic.

b. The types of documents reviewed. For example, the report might include only published journal articles, or it also may include dissertations and so-called "fugitive" literature, such as technical reports produced by a research team for its funding agency.

c. The geographical scope of the search. Some reviewers examine only studies carried out in the United States, whereas others also include studies conducted in other countries.

d. The range of grade levels and types of students, teachers, educational institutions, or other entities that were studied in the reviewed research.

e. The range of theoretical or ideological perspectives on the topic. For example, did the reviewer consider both studies based on behavioral theory and studies based on cognitive theory? Were different ideological perspectives, such as critical theory (see Chapter 12) and the accountability movement, considered?

f. The use of criteria to exclude any of the reports that were initially examined. For example, the reviewer might exclude research studies that involved atypical students or experiments that did not employ random assignment procedures. (Random assignment is explained in Chapter 9.)

4. *The amount of information provided about the studies reviewed.* Authors of research reviews have a challenging task: to summarize findings of a large number of studies briefly so as to be readable, yet in sufficient detail that the basis for their conclusions and interpretations is reasonably clear. Simply citing a reference or two in parentheses after making a sweeping generalization does not accomplish this goal. A better approach is for the reviewer to describe briefly the relevant information from a research study that demonstrates how it supports the generalization.

5. *The exercise of critical judgment.* Research reviews range from those that reflect uncritical acceptance of research findings to those in which the reviewer finds flaws in every research study and asserts that no conclusions can be drawn from them. Neither extreme is justified for topics that have been extensively researched.

Another aspect of critical judgment is whether the reviewer tended to lump studies together or discriminated among studies that appeared to deal with the same question, but that were actually quite different in design or purpose. The latter approach generally reflects better critical judgment.

6. *The resolution of inconsistent findings.* Nearly every research review will reveal that the results obtained in some studies do not agree with those found in other studies. You should examine carefully how the reviewer dealt with these inconsistencies. Earlier we described several approaches that can be used to synthesize varied findings from quantitative and qualitative research studies. These approaches are used most commonly in primary source analyses. Another approach is to make more holistic judgments based on one's expertise. This approach is used more commonly in professional reviews.

CONCLUDING THOUGHT

People judge professionals, such as doctors, accountants, and engineers, by how well they know the current literature in their field, and their ability to access that literature to satisfy specific information needs. Also, because their time is valuable and limited, professionals must know how to access publications that synthesize research, theory, and current practice rather than try to do such a synthesis on their own.

In this chapter, we have sought to contribute to your professional skills as an educator by describing the types of secondary sources that are available in the field of education, procedures for locating these sources, and criteria for judging their usefulness and validity.

SELF-CHECK TEST

1. In contrast to primary sources, secondary sources
   a. do not describe the findings of research studies.
   b. are often technical and difficult to read.
   c. are not indexed in preliminary sources.
   d. are written by someone other than the person who carried out the research being described.

2. Reading a secondary source is particularly helpful when
   a. no original studies have been carried out on your research topic.
   b. you want to learn the researcher's own perspective about the meaning of the research findings.
   c. you want to see how an authoritative reviewer has summarized the literature related to your topic.
   d. all of the above.

3. Unlike a primary source analysis, a professional review
   a. tends to rely on secondary sources.
   b. is written mainly for other researchers.
   c. does not draw implications for practice.
   d. is written by someone who writes reviews for a living.

4. Unlike vote counting, meta-analysis
   a. involves a quantitative technique to synthesize findings across research studies.
   b. examines the statistical significance of the findings of different research studies.
   c. provides a standard unit of measure for comparing the results of different studies.
   d. enables researchers to determine the cause of an observed effect.

5. In a review of research involving primarily qualitative research studies, the reviewer typically seeks to
   a. discover the unique characteristics of each case.
   b. identify concepts and principles that are present across cases.
   c. avoid limiting the focus of the literature review.
   d. do all of the above.

6. To synthesize the varied findings from the research studies that were reviewed, the author of a professional review usually
   a. employs a narrative approach.
   b. conducts a meta-analysis.
   c. employs vote counting.
   d. does a comprehensive literature search.

7. To locate recent scholarly books and textbooks related to your topic, probably the most useful preliminary source is
   a. ERIC.
   b. *Education Index.*
   c. *Psychological Abstracts.*
   d. *Books in Print.*

8. The publication most likely to contain professional reviews about school instruction is
   a. *The Review of Educational Research.*
   b. *The Journal of Experimental Education.*
   c. *The Reading Teacher.*
   d. *Books in Print.*

9. All of the following except _____ are relevant criteria for judging the usefulness and validity of a secondary source.
   a. specification of the reviewer's credentials
   b. identification of the search procedures
   c. limitation of the breadth of the search
   d. exclusion of fugitive documents from the literature review

CHAPTER REFERENCES

Curry, L. (1990). A critique of the research on learning styles. *Educational Leadership,* *48*(2), 50–55.

Gage, N. L. (1978). *The scientific basis of the art of teaching.* New York: Teachers College Press.

Glass, G. V (1976). Primary, secondary, and meta-analysis of research. *Educational Researcher, 5*(10), 3–8.

Haller, E. P., Child, D. A., and Walberg, H. J. (1988). Can comprehension be taught? A quantitative synthesis of "metacognitive" studies. *Educational Researcher, 17*(9), 5–8.

Jackson, G. B. (1980). Methods for integrative reviews. *Review of Educational Research, 50,* 438–460.

Ogawa, R. T., & Malen, B. (1991). Towards rigor in reviews of multivocal literatures: Applying the exploratory case study method. *Review of Educational Research, 61*, 265–286.

Rosenshine, B. (1971). *Teaching behaviors and student achievement*. London: National Foundation for Educational Research in England and Wales.

Slavin, R. E. (1986). Best-evidence synthesis: An alternative to meta-analytic and traditional reviews. *Educational Researcher, 15*(9), 5–11.

Tennant, R. (1992). Internet basics. ERIC Digest. Syracuse, NY: ERIC Clearinghouse on Information Resources. (ERIC Document Reference No. ED 348 054).

Tennant, R. (1996). Internet basics: Update 1996. ERIC Digest. Syracuse, NY: ERIC Clearinghouse on Information and Technology. (ERIC Document Reference No. ED 392 466).

Trmsher, K. (1996). Block scheduling. ERIC Digest, No. 104. Eugene, OR: ERIC Clearinghouse on Educational Management. (ERIC Document Reference No. ED 393 156).

RECOMMENDED READING

Buttlar, L. J. (1989). *Education: A guide to reference and information sources*. Englewood, CO: Libraries Unlimited.

An index to over 900 preliminary and secondary sources relevant to education in general and to 14 specific areas of education, for example, elementary and secondary education, special education, and career and vocational education.

Cooper, H. M. (1989). *Integrating research*. Newbury Park, CA: Sage.

This book emphasizes the importance of using rigorous methodology in reviewing and integrating previous research findings. Each stage of the research review process is discussed in depth.

Cooper, H., & Hedges, L. V. (Eds.). (1994). *The handbook of research synthesis*. New York: Russell Sage Foundation.

Includes 32 chapters in which various authors cover quantitative approaches to research synthesis and describe the procedures, benefits, and limitations of these approaches. Organized by the stages of research synthesis, from formulating a problem to reporting the results.

Hunter, J. E., & Schmidt, F. L. (1990). *Methods of meta-analysis*. Newbury Park, CA: Sage.

The authors provide an overview of various methods that can be used to obtain average results across studies. Much of the book focuses on psychometric meta-analysis, an approach developed by the authors to integrate research findings. This approach is unique in that it provides a means of estimating how much variance across studies is due to various artifacts. Their approach appears to overcome most of the problems that have been raised about meta-analytic procedures by providing methods to adjust for the effects of these artifacts.

SAMPLE REVIEW OF QUANTITATIVE RESEARCH:
GENDER DIFFERENCES IN STUDENT ATTITUDES TOWARD
SCIENCE: A META-ANALYSIS OF THE LITERATURE FROM
1970 TO 1991

Weinburgh, M. (1995). Gender differences in student attitudes toward science: A meta-analysis of the literature from 1970 to 1991. *Journal of Research
in Science Teaching, 32,* 387–398.

> In this section of the chapter you will read a published secondary source that
> illustrates a review of quantitative research. It is preceded by comments written
> especially for this book by the author of the article. Then the article itself is
> reprinted in full, just as it appeared when originally published. Where appro-
> priate, we have added footnotes to help you understand the information con-
> tained in the article.

Researcher's Comments, Prepared by Molly Weinburgh

When I began work on this meta-analysis, I had just completed a study that examined
students' attitudes toward biology laboratory (Weinburgh & Engelhard, 1991). Thus I
was very much aware of the conflicting data as to whether there was a gender difference in attitude toward science.

Much of the research cited in the literature review section of the report had served
as a background and theoretical base for the research reported in the 1991 paper.
ERIC searches and searches of *Dissertation Abstracts* produced the references. The
ones chosen to be cited were either well known and often cited, or showed the inconsistent findings that were not being reported. Narrative reviews of the literature were
useful, but they did not seem to capture the true study of what was happening in science education. I had never done a meta-analysis, but it seemed to be the answer to
provide an accurate picture of the existing research findings about whether boys or
girls with more positive attitudes toward science have higher levels of achievement in
science classes.

I began by using the suggestions of Glass, McGaw, & Smith (1981), who recommend
using several sources for finding articles. I selected ERIC, *PsycLit,* and *Comprehensive
Dissertation Abstracts* because they seemed to be the most comprehensive databases
dealing with science education. In addition, I did a manual search of the most prestigious
science education journals. I found the manual search to be the most rewarding. I
would just sit in the library stacks and flip through each journal volume from 1970 to
1991. I often got sidetracked with interesting articles that did not relate to the topic,
but eventually this strategy produced the greatest number of usable sources.

The bibliographies of reviewed articles also guided me to obscure research studies
that had not surfaced in either my manual or database searches. I firmly believe that
one should use a search strategy that identifies as many articles related to the topic as
possible.

After the coding criteria were set, it was fairly easy to read each article and code it. I met with the graduate students who helped establish the inter-rater reliability coefficients before they began coding. We discussed the rating criteria, rated one article together, and discussed differences in our ratings. Then each of us rated several of the selected articles. When we compared our ratings, we found that the criteria worked well.

I had hoped that after 21 years of research (the period for which I sought research articles) showing a problem with gender differences in classrooms, the effect size would decrease over time. A decrease would suggest that females and males are approaching equity in their attitudes toward science. Based on the results of my meta-analysis, however, that has not occurred. The effect size in the early 70s and late 80s was about the same. I believe that my finding of no change over time indicates that much still needs to be done to turn research into practice. Educators know about the gender inequities in science, yet they do not appear to have changed their instruction to reduce or eliminate these inequities.

I would like to see more research studies that report the effect size when presenting statistical analyses of research data. I also believe that researchers need to analyze and report research data separately by gender and ethnicity. Too often research is analyzed to describe the sample as a whole, instead of examining the possible effects of these important variables.

At the end of my report I mentioned three individuals who gave me helpful comments. George Engelhard, Robert Jensen, and Donald Reichard were the members of my doctoral dissertation committee. It is they who encouraged me to use meta-analysis as my research design. They also recommended that I review the past 20 years of the research literature instead of the more typical review of only the past 10 years of research. My receipt of the Distinguished Paper Award for this research from the Georgia Educational Research Association in 1992 validates the importance of meta-analysis as an approach to synthesizing research findings. More meta-analyses about other important problems and issues in education are needed.

References

Glass, G. V, McGaw, B., & Smith, M. L. (1981). *Meta-analysis in social research*. Beverly Hills, CA: Sage.

Hedges, L. V., Shymansky, J. A., & Woodworth, G. (1989). Gender differences in mathematics performance: A meta-analysis. *Psychological Bulletin, 107*, 139–155.

Weinburgh, M. H., & Engelhard, G., Jr. (1991, March). *Gender, prior academic performance and beliefs as predictors of attitudes toward biology laboratory experiences*. Paper presented at the meeting of the Georgia Educational Research Association conference, Decatur, GA.

GENDER DIFFERENCES IN STUDENT ATTITUDES TOWARD SCIENCE: A META-ANALYSIS OF THE LITERATURE FROM 1970 TO 1991

Molly Weinburgh
Georgia State University, College of Education, MSIT, Atlanta, Georgia 30303

Abstract

A meta-analysis covering the literature between 1970 and 1991 was conducted using an approach similar to that suggested by Glass, McGaw, and Smith (1981) and Hedges, Shymansky, and Woodworth (1989). This analysis examined gender differences in student attitudes toward science, and correlations between attitudes toward science and achievement in science. Thirty-one effect sizes and seven correlations representing the testing of 6,753 subjects were found in 18 studies. The mean of the unweighted effect sizes was .20 ($SD = .50$) and the mean of the weighted effect size was .16 ($SD = .50$), indicating that boys have more positive attitudes toward science than girls. The mean correlation between attitude and achievement was .50 for boys and .55 for girls, suggesting that the correlations are comparable. Results of the analysis of gender differences in attitude as a function of science type indicate that boys show a more positive attitude toward science than girls in all types of science. The correlation between attitude and achievement for boys and girls as a function of science type indicates that for biology and physics the correlation is positive for both, but stronger for girls than for boys. Gender differences and correlations between attitude and achievement by gender as a function of publication date show no pattern. The results for the analysis of gender differences as a function of the selectivity of the sample indicate that general level students reflect a greater positive attitude for boys, whereas the high-performance students indicate a greater positive attitude for girls. The correlation between attitude and achievement as a function of selectivity indicates that in all cases a positive attitude results in higher achievement. This is particularly true for low-performance girls. The implications of these finding are discussed and further research suggested.

Weinburgh, M. (1995). Gender differences in student attitudes toward science: A meta-analysis of the literature from 1970 to 1991. *Journal of Research in Science Teaching, 32,* 387–398. Copyright © 1995 by the National Association for Research in Science Teaching. Reprinted by permission of John Wiley & Sons, Inc.

Historically, research on science education has focused on specific educational outcomes. Until about 20 years ago, the major focus of this research was on educational objectives in the cognitive domain. Recently, the affective domain, as defined by Krathwohl, Bloom, and Masia (1964), has not only been accepted as a relevant part of education, but has also become the focus of considerable research. One of the key variables within the affective domain that has drawn attention is attitudes.

Of early interest was the relationship of attitudes to behavior. Fishbein and Ajzen (1975) proposed a theory of reasoned action that describes the relationship of attitude to behavior. They suggested that a person's attitude toward any object is a function of his or her beliefs about the object and the implicit evaluative responses associated with those beliefs. Ajzen (1989) extended the theory of reasoned action to the prediction of behavioral goals in his theory of planned behavior. Based on this model, many researchers have examined attitudes by studying the variables that influence it or by examining its relationship to a specific behavioral goal such as achievement (Albert, Aschenbrenner, & Schmalhofer, 1989).

In addition to the growing interest in student attitudes and their relationship to student behavior, there has developed a real concern about gender differences as expressed in the academic area. Since Sells (1973) reported that mathematics acts as the "critical filter" for many women, there has been an increased focus on gender differences in mathematics and science. Eccles (1987) reported that gender roles are related to women's achievement-related decisions. Stage, Freinberg, Eccles, and Becker (1985) examined the importance of increasing the participation and achievement in mathematics, science, and engineering for women. The American Association of University Women (AAUW, 1991) reported that as girls grow up they loose [sic] confidence in their academic abilities and lower their career aspirations.

Research in science education indicates that gender may also influence attitudes toward science. Schibeci (1984) reported in a review of the literature that of all the variables that may influence attitudes toward science, gender has generally been shown to have a consistent influence. If individual studies are examined, a range of conflicting conclusions are reported. Studies that examine science in general, rather than a specific discipline, suggest that boys have more positive attitudes than girls. Simpson and Oliver (1985), in an ongoing multidimensional study among approximately 4,000 students in Grades 6 through 10, found that boys exhibited significantly more positive attitudes towards science than girls. This was true within each grade level. Baker (1983) found girls to have more negative attitudes toward science than boys, but still to have higher science grades. Handley and Morse (1984) reported that both attitudes and achievements in science are related to the variables of self-concept and gender role perceptions. These relationships are more evident in association with attitudes than achievement. They reported that, over time, the female attitude toward science became more related to their concept of male dominance in science. Pogge (1986) found, in a study of 1,200 students enrolled in Grades 4, 5, and 6, that a majority of the students have a positive attitude toward science. This was true for all grade levels. Okebukola (1986) explored the effects of cooperative learning on the attitude of students toward laboratory work and found a significant difference in gender for both the cooperative and noncooperative group with boys having more positive attitudes than girls. Lowery, Bowyer, and Padillia (1980), although suggesting that a curriculum can have a measurable effect on students' attitudes, did report the maintenance of attitudinal differences between the sexes within both the control and the experimental groups. In both groups, the boys showed more positive attitudes toward science than the girls.

It appears that, in general, boys have a more positive attitude toward science than girls. However, if specific disciplines of science are studied, this is not always the case. Schibeci (1984) reported that girls show a more positive attitude toward biology and boys toward physics and chemistry. Weinburgh and Engelhard (1991) examined biology laboratory experiences in high school students and reported a small, negative relationship between attitude toward biology laboratory experiences and gender, indicating that girls have a more positive attitude than boys. In a similar study, Al-Hajji (1983) examined the attitudes of middle school students in Kuwait to science laboratory work. He found that girls have more positive attitudes toward science laboratory work than boys. In contrast to what has been previously reported, Barrington and Hendricks (1988) found no gender differences with respect to attitudes toward science with gifted and average students.

Few studies were found that examined the correlation between attitude toward science and achievement in science by gender.[a] Cannon (1983)

---

a. A correlation is a statistic that indicates the degree to which variations in one set of scores (e.g., students' scores on a measure of attitude toward science) are related to variations in another set of scores (e.g., the same students' scores on a measure of science achievement).

examined seventh-grade students in basic, general, and advanced life science classes. Using a criterion-referenced life science achievement test to obtain achievement scores, he reported a higher correlation between positive attitudes in science and higher achievement scores for basic and advanced-performance girls and general performance boys.[b] Stoner (1981) examined the relationship of psychological and skill factors to science attitude and achievement in 5th- and 10th-grade students using teacher-given grades for achievement. She found the correlation between attitude toward science and achievement in 10th-grade students to be stronger for girls than boys. Schibeci and Riley (1986), using a National Assessment of Educational Performance (NAEP) data set, investigated the influence of student background and perceptions on science attitude and achievement. They found that gender had an influence on attitudes and achievement, with girls having less positive attitudes than boys, as well as having lower scores in achievement. Cannon and Simpson (1983), using a teacher-made test for achievement, reported that general ability boys show a slightly higher correlation between attitude toward science and achievement in science than girls. They also reported that the correlation appears to become stronger for boys from basic ability to general ability to advanced ability. For girls, the strongest correlation is for the low ability followed by advanced ability and then general ability.

The conflicting results from different studies make it difficult to determine whether, in general, there are gender differences in student attitudes toward science, or whether there are gender differences in correlations between attitude toward science and achievement in science. This is particularly true because attitude and achievement are not measured using the same instrument for all studies. Diamond and Tittle (1985) offered a word of caution when examining studies of sex differences in test performances. They attributed many of the differences between men and women in test performance

to the socialization process. A recent AAUW report (1992) pointed out that there appears to be a difference in performance levels of boys and girls depending on whether an instrument used to measure achievement is teacher-made or standardized.

Although the narrative reviews of the literature, such as Schibeci (1984) and Gallager (1987) are useful, meta-analytic techniques offer the potential for rigorous and parsimonious summaries of evidence from many studies. Applied to the topic of gender differences in attitudes toward science, meta-analysis may lead to a clearer view of the magnitude of observed gender differences, and may also be a useful way to examine whether or not the gender differences generalize across subject area, publication date, and selectivity of the sample.

Purpose

The purpose of this study was to examine gender differences in student attitudes toward science. The meta-analysis focused on gender differences in attitudes, and on gender differences in the relationship between attitude toward science and achievement in science. The goal was to answer the following questions:

1. Are there gender differences in student attitudes toward science?
2. Do gender differences vary as a function of subject area, publication date, and selectivity of the sample?
3. Are the correlations between attitudes toward science and achievement in science comparable for boys and girls?
4. Do the correlations between attitudes toward science and achievement in science for boys and girls vary as a function of subject area, publication date, and selectivity of the sample?

---

b. The higher the correlation between two measures, the better you can predict an individual's score on one measure by knowing his or her score on the other measure.

Data Sources

The following sources were used to get the sample of studies: (a) a computerized database search of ERIC, PsychLit[sic][c], and Comprehensive Dissertation Abstracts[sic][d]; (b) manual search of *Science Education, School Science and Mathematics, Journal of Research in Science Teaching,* and *School Science Review;* and (c) examination of bibliographies in the review articles retrieved by the computer and manual searches. By inspecting the abstracts, citations that did not promise to yield data necessary to compute effect sizes or the Pearson correlation coefficients between attitude toward science and achievement in science were eliminated.[e]

If it was possible to obtain several independent effect sizes or correlations from a single article, for example, data from several age groups or disciplines, these were reported as separate samples (Hyde, Fennema, & Lamon, 1990). This happened in 10 of the 18 cases for effect size and 2 of the 3 cases for correlations.

The result was 18 usable sources, yielding 31 independent effect sizes. This represents the testing of 6,753 students (3,337 boys and 3,416 girls). Seven attitude–achievement correlations were reported separately by gender. Each of these seven correlations used a teacher-made test for the achievement score, allowing comparison between studies to be made with more confidence. This represents the testing of 561 boys and 623 girls.

Coding

Each study was coded using five categories, as suggested by Glass, McGaw, and Smith (1981). These are (a) identification items, (b) study demographics, (c) study conditions, (d) outcome variables and (e) other comments. A chart was developed to record the necessary information.

Outcome Measures

The outcomes measured were student attitude toward science and the correlation between attitudes and achievement. As recommended by Glass et al. (1981) and Hedges, Shymansky, and Woodworth (1989), each attitude outcome was coded as an effect size (d), defined as the mean of the boys minus the mean[f] of the girls divided by the standard deviation[g] of the girls. Thus, a positive value represented more positive attitudes for boys and a negative value represented more positive attitudes for girls. The values of d were then corrected for bias in estimation of the population effect size,[h] using the formula provided by Hedges et al. The outcome measure for the relationship between student attitudes toward science and achievement in science was the Pearson product moment correlation coefficient. Table 1 gives a complete listing of the unbiased effect sizes of all studies in this meta-analysis.

Because there is the possibility of variation in excess of sampling fluctuation among studies, a test

---

c. PsychLit (correct spelling: *PsycLIT*) is the CD-ROM version of *Psychological Abstracts*, which is a preliminary source that indexes reports of psychological studies (see Appendix 1).

d. Comprehensive Dissertation Abstracts (correct title: *Comprehensive Dissertation Index*) is a preliminary source that indexes doctoral dissertations completed between 1861 and 1972.

e. Pearson correlation coefficients represent one approach to measuring the strength of the relationship between two sets of scores.

f. The mean (*M*) is the average of a set of scores.

g. The standard deviation (*SD*) is a measure of how much a set of scores deviates from the mean score. The larger the *SD*, the wider is the range of scores around the mean score.

h. An effect size (*d*) is calculated by using the data collected on the sample of research participants investigated by the researcher. This *d* value is a biased estimate of the effect size that would be obtained if the researcher had investigated the entire population of participants that the sample is intended to represent. The Hedges et al. formula corrects for the bias in the estimate. The corrected effect size is labeled *D*, as in Table 1.

TABLE I   **Study of Gender Differences in Science Attitude and Achievement**

Study	Date	Boys n	Girls n	D	Male r	Female r	Science[a]	Selectivity[b]
Burke	1983	87	77	0.00	NA	NA	7	2
Burke	1983	120	102	0.03	NA	NA	7	2
Burke	1983	125	91	0.03	NA	NA	7	2
Cannon	1983	87	78	0.11	.48	.65	2	1
Cannon	1983	91	95	0.13	.50	.46	2	2
Cannon	1983	35	50	0.48	.61	.64	2	3
Cannon & Simpson	1983	87	78	0.11	.48	.65	2	1
Cannon & Simpson	1983	91	95	0.13	.50	.46	2	2
Cannon & Simpson	1983	35	50	0.47	.61	.65	2	3
Cornett	1981	951	950	0.48	NA	NA	7	2
Daume	1981	26	24	0.12	NA	NA	7	2
Daume	1981	24	26	0.66	NA	NA	7	2
Hamilton	1982	248	328	0.11	NA	NA	7	2
Harty & Beall	1984	13	12	0.48	NA	NA	6	3
Harty & Beall	1984	13	12	0.11	NA	NA	6	2
Harty, Samuel, & Beall	1986	110	118	0.19	NA	NA	6	2
Hasan	1985	153	160	−0.35	NA	NA	6	2
Hofman	1977	21	17	−0.46	NA	NA	1	2
Hofman	1977	19	22	−0.09	NA	NA	1	2
Lowery, Bowyer, & Padillia	1980	27	28	1.39	NA	NA	7	2
Lowery, et al.	1980	27	28	0.61	NA	NA	7	2
Novak	1980	147	129	0.07	NA	NA	7	2
Okebukola	1986	58	55	1.59	NA	NA	2	2
Okebukola	1986	52	56	0.93	NA	NA	2	1
Scott	1982	77	77	0.29	NA	NA	4	2
Shrigley	1972	62	53	0.84	NA	NA	1	2
Squiers	1983	59	68	0.26	NA	NA	5	2
Squiers	1983	60	69	−0.61	NA	NA	5	2
Stoner	1981	135	177	0.04	.34	.37	4	2
Stoner	1981	139	155	0.07	NA	NA	7	2
Weinburgh & Engelhard	1991	158	136	−0.30	NA	NA	2	3

Note. D = unbiased effect size with positive numbers indicating that boys are more positive than girls and negative numbers indicating that girls are more positive than boys.

[a] 1 = earth science; 2 = biology; 3 = chemistry; 4 = physical science; 5 = not currently enrolled; 6 = not reported; 7 = general science.

[b] 1 = low performance; 2 = general performance; 3 = high performance.

for heterogeneity was performed. This was done by comparing Q, a measure of heterogeneity, to the percentile of the chi-squared distribution with $k - 1$ degrees of freedom (Hedges et al., 1989).[i] The determination of heterogeneity meant that the effect sizes could be divided into subgroups for further examination.

Interrater Reliability

Interrater reliability was determined by selecting two samples that were coded independently by two graduate students.[j] Each of the new codings was compared to the original in order to see if the coding matched. Agreement rates of 97% and 98% were found, indicating that the coding was highly reliable.

RESULTS

Gender Differences in Attitude Toward Science

Thirty-one independent effect sizes and seven achievement–attitude correlations for each gender were found between 1970 and 1991. The mean of the unweighted effect sizes was .20 ($SD = .50$) based on 6,753 students. This indicates that boys have a more positive attitude toward science than girls. Of the 31 effect sizes, 25 (81%) were positive, reflecting more positive attitudes by boys and 8 (19%) were negative, reflecting more positive attitudes by girls. When the weighted mean effect size was computed with weights proportional to the number of subjects in each study (Hedges et al., 1989), the mean was .16

($SD = .50$). In both cases, this small positive value indicates that boys have a more positive attitude toward science than girls. Although the magnitude of effect is small, Linn and Petersen (1985) pointed out that small differences may be of "interest at the extremes of score distribution and may interact with other factors to have greater impact" (p. 55).

Homogeneity analyses using procedures described by Hedges et al. (1989) indicated that the set of 31 effect sizes was significantly nonhomogeneous ($H = 284.0$), compared with a critical value of χ^2 (30, $N = 6753$) = 59.7, $p < .001$.[k] Therefore, it can be concluded that the set of effect sizes is heterogeneous and can be partitioned into more homogeneous subgroups. Because two or more populations are reasonable, a search using the variables of the studies that have been hypothesized to predict effect size is reasonable. The variables examined in the study are subject area, date of publication, and selectivity of the sample.

The mean correlation was .50 for boys ($n = 561$) and .55 for girls ($n = 623$).[l] This indicates that for both boys and girls there is a strong, positive relationship between attitude toward science and achievement in science. The relationship is stronger for girls than for boys.

Science Type

The results for the analysis of gender differences in attitude as a function of science type reported are shown in Table 2. No studies were found in the field of chemistry. For all types of science with the exception of the two cases in which the students were not currently enrolled in a science, boys showed a more

---

i. Even if a set of samples is randomly drawn from the same population, the samples will yield different effect sizes because of random variations in the composition of each sample. However, if the effect sizes differ substantially, as they do in Table 1, one can conclude that the variations in the effect sizes do not reflect random variations in samples drawn from the same population, but instead that the samples were drawn from different populations. The test of heterogeneity conducted by Weinburgh indicated that this was the case for the samples included in the meta-analysis. Q and other statistical values (chi-square and k) are calculated as part of this test.

j. Inter-rater reliability is the extent to which the two raters exercise the same types of judgment in classifying characteristics of each study (e.g., selectivity of the sample). If the reliability is high, it means that the raters consistently used the same criteria.

k. This homogeneity analysis is similar in meaning to the analysis explained in footnote i.

l. Mean correlations of .50 and .55 indicate that, for both boys and girls, there is a moderate tendency for higher attitude scores to be associated with higher achievement scores and for lower attitude scores to be associated with lower achievement scores.

TABLE 2   **Magnitude of the Gender Differences as a Function of Science Type**

Science type	k	d	SE_M
Biology	9	.03	.05
Physics	2	.12	.09
Earth science	3	.34	.15
General science	10	.34	.04
Not now enrolled	2	.22	.12
Not reported	5	.00	.06

Note. k = number of effect sizes; d = weighted mean effect sizes; SE_M = standard error of weighted mean.[m]

positive attitude toward science than girls. The order from smallest effect sizes to largest is (a) not currently enrolled, (b) biology, (c) physics, (d) not now enrolled, (e) general science, and (f) earth science. This indicates that there is a wider gap between male and female attitudes in general science and earth science.

The results of the analysis of the correlation between attitude and achievement for boys and girls as a function of science type are shown in Table 3.

TABLE 3   **Correlation between Attitude and Achievement as a Function of Science Type, Date of Publication, and Selectivity of Sample**

Function	k	Male	Female
Type			
Biology	6	.53	.59
Physics	1	.34	.37
Date			
1981	1	.34	.37
1983	6	.53	.59
Selectivity			
Low performance	2	.48	.65
General	3	.45	.43
High performance	2	.61	.65

Note. k = number of effect sizes.

m. The standard error of the weighted mean provides an estimate of the true d value for each science type. For example, as shown in the first row of Table 2 in the column labeled k, Weinburgh's review of the literature provided nine estimates of the effect size of gender differences in biology. The weighted mean of these estimates (shown in the d column of Table 2) is .03. (The mean is weighted to take into account the fact that the nine estimates are based on varying numbers of students.) The standard error of the weighted mean (shown in the SE_M column of Table 2) is .05. These statistics indicate that if the entire population of boys and girls had been measured, the "true" weighted mean might be as high as .08 (.03 + .05) or as low as −.02 (.03 − .05).

TABLE 4   **Magnitude of the Gender Differences as a Function of Date**

Sample	k	d	SE_M
1972	1	.84	.20
1977	2	−.26	.22
1980	3	.28	.11
1981	5	.38	.04
1982	2	.15	.07
1983	11	.07	.05
1984	2	.29	.29
1985	1	−.35	.11
1986	3	.06	.10
1991	1	−.30	.12

Note. k = number of effect sizes; d = weighted mean effect size; SE_M = standard error of weighted means.

Correlations were only reported in studies examining students in biology and physics. For each of these disciplines, the correlation is positive and slightly stronger for girls than for boys. As pointed out earlier, the relationship between attitudes and achievement in biology is higher than in physics. However, in each case, those students with a more positive attitude toward the science type investigated showed greater achievement.

Date of Publication

The analysis for the magnitude of gender differences as a function of date of publication is shown in Table 4. Only 10 of the 21 years designated for this study produced research that could be included. The largest number of studies were reported in 1981 and 1983. Seven of the 10 dates reported a positive effect size, reflecting a more positive attitude by boys. In looking at the variation in scores, no pattern of change can be seen across the 21 years.

Table 3 shows the correlation between attitude and achievement by gender as a function of the date of publication. Studies in 1981 and 1983 reported the correlation between attitude and achievement by gender. For both years, the correlation was positive with a stronger correlation being seen for the girls.

Sample Selectivity

The results for the analysis of gender differences as a function of the selectivity of the sample are shown in Table 5. The high-performance students reported a small, negative effect size (−.02), indicating that girls have a slightly more positive attitude toward science than boys. For the low-performance and general performance students, boys showed more positive attitudes than girls. The difference between the two effect sizes is small, but general performance students do reflect a greater positive attitude by the boys.

The correlation between attitude and achievement as a function of the selectivity of the sample is shown in Table 3. The correlation in all cases is positive, indicating that as attitude become [sic] more positive, achievement tended to increase. It was lowest for both boys and girls in the general performance group. Of interest is the fact that this is the only group where the correlation between attitude and achievement is lower for the girls than the boys.

TABLE 5 **Magnitude of the Gender Differences as a Function of Selectivity**

Sample	k	d	SE_M
Low performance	2	.11	.11
General	25	.21	.03
High performance	4	−.02	.10

Note. k = number of effect sizes; d = weighted mean effect size; SE_M = standard error of the weighted means.

The correlation is strongest among the high-performance and low-performance girls. Also interesting is the span between low-performing boys and girls.

DISCUSSION

It appears that, in general, boys do have a more positive attitude toward science than girls, as has been suggested by narrative reviews of the literature (Gallager, 1987; Schibeci, 1984). However, if specific disciplines are examined, the magnitude of the effect varies. The small positive effect size (.03) for biology was expected. Schibeci reported that girls may have a more positive attitude toward biology, whereas boys may have a more positive attitude toward physics and chemistry. Johnson (1987) supported this in her study of gender differences in 11-, 13-, and 15-year-olds. Increasingly, she noted that girls have a greater interest in parts of plants, growing seeds, how animals have young, and medical applications of knowledge, whereas boys have a greater interest in speed, electric circuits, floating and sinking, and technological application in the physical sciences. It was somewhat surprising to find a small effect size (.12) for physics. Physics has earned the reputation of requiring a high level of mathematical skill and of being a "hard" science. From prior studies (Schibeci, 1984), it would have been hypothesized that the effect size would be much larger. Johnson's study, which reported that girls show less interest in physical science concepts, did not examine students beyond the 10th grade, at which time girls selectively decide to continue with science electives, one of which is physics. This may help explain the small effect size found in this study. General science (d = .34) and earth science (d = .34) appear to be viewed much more positively by boys than girls. It has been suggested by Johnson (1987) and Kahle and Lakes (1983) that from an early age, girls, in general, read fewer books about science and technology than do boys, and that boys in greater numbers claim to engage in "tinkering" activities outside school. The topics covered in general science, earth science, and physical science may be perceived to be "male" topics.

No pattern was suggested by the effect sizes as a function of date of publication of the study. This may suggest that although gender differences in attitudes have been recognized, nothing substantial has been done in 21 years to change attitudes in students, especially for girls. The one area where girls showed more positive attitudes toward science than boys was in studies selected for gifted or high-performance students. This may be explained by the fact that gifted students for the past decade have been removed from the regular class and given special instruction. The smaller effect seen for low-performance students over general performance students may be explained in somewhat the same manner, because students designated as low-performance are often removed from the regular class and given additional instruction.

The data suggest that, in general, the correlation between attitude toward science and achievement in science is moderate. This would be expected from the theory of planned behavior (Ajzen, 1989), which suggests a link between attitude and behavior. The correlation is somewhat stronger for girls than for boys, indicating that a positive attitude is more necessary for girls in achieving high scores. In looking at the type of science, only two disciplines were found that reported correlations, biology and physics. In both cases, the correlation for the girls was higher than for boys, with the correlation being stronger in biology than in physics. The correlation of attitudes toward science and achievement in science as a function of date of publication of the study reveals the same trend as noted previously. Girls again exhibit a stronger correlation than boys. However, it must be remembered that only two dates were reported.

The only exception to girls having a stronger correlation than boys was seen when the correlation was viewed as a function of selectivity. General level students reported a higher correlation for boys than for girls. For high- and low-performance students, girls reported a higher correlation. This suggests that for girls in these two groups, doing well or "achieving" in science is closely linked with "liking" science.

Limitations

There are several limitations in this study. The major limitation is the small number of studies that reported the correlation between attitude toward science and achievement in science by gender (only seven cases). A second limitation is the lack of information reported on how achievement measures were determined. A third is the relatively small number of total cases ($n = 31$) reported in this study for gender differences.

CONCLUSION

In conclusion, the findings from this study suggest that over the last 21 years, boys have consistently shown a more positive attitude toward science than girls. This has not appeared to change over time if the date of publication of the studies is used as an indictor. The selectivity of the sample does affect the results, with high selectivity reporting more positive attitudes for girls than for boys. However, more research is need [sic] in the field of attitudes toward science, particularly in reference to gender differences. Also, more research is needed to determine why different types of science produce less positive attitudes in students.

The correlation between attitudes toward science and achievement in science are comparable for boys and girls. The correlation is somewhat stronger for girls than for boys, indicating that a positive attitude is more necessary for girls in achieving high scores. The correlations did vary as a function of selectivity and type, but not date of publication.

Three implications for further research are noted. The first is the practical need to continue research that examines strategies in the classroom for improving all students' attitudes toward science, especially those of female students. The second is the need to continue research that examines attitudes, gender, and grade level. Research needs to address the question of when attitudes begin to decline and then try to determine why. The third, gender differences, needs to be examined by race in order to determine differences in girls of different ethnic backgrounds.

Earlier versions of this article were presented at the annual meeting of the Georgia Educational Research Association and the American Educational Research Association. This article received the Distinguished Paper Award from the Georgia Educational Research Association (Fall 1992). I acknowledge the helpful comments of George Engelhard, Robert Jensen, and Donald Reichard.

References

Ajzen, I. (1989). Attitude structure and behavior. In A.R. Pratkanis, S.J. Breckler, & A.G. Greenwald (Eds.), *Attitude structure and function* (pp. 241–274). Hillsdale, NJ: Erlbaum.

Albert, D., Aschenbrenner, K.M., & Schmalhofer, F. (1989). Cognitive choice processes and the attitude–behavior relation. In A. Upmeyer (Ed.), *Attitudes and behavioral decisions* (pp. 61–99). New York: Springer-Verlag.

Al-Hajji, Y.Y. (1983). Attitudes of students and science teachers toward science laboratory work in the middle schools of Kuwait (Doctoral dissertation, Boston University, School of Education, 1983). *Dissertation Abstracts International, 43,* 12A.

American Association of University Women. (1991). *Summary: Shortchanging girls, shortchanging America.* Washington, DC: Author.

American Association of University Women. (1992). *How schools shortchange girls.* Washington, DC: Author.

Baker, D.R. (1983, April) The relationship of attitude, cognitive abilities, and personality to science achievement in the junior high school. Paper presented at the annual meeting of the National Association of Research in Science Teaching, Dallas, TX.

Barrington, B.L., & Hendricks, B. (1988). Attitudes toward science and science knowledge of intellectually gifted and average students in third, seventh, and eleventh grades. *Journal of Research in Science Teaching, 25,* 679–687.

Burke, P.A.Y. (1983). A study to determine the trends in attitude toward science among fourth-, fifth-, and sixth-grade male and female students (Doctoral dissertation, State University of New York at Buffalo, 1983). *Dissertation Abstracts International, 44,* 09A.

Cannon, R.K., Jr. (1983). Relationships among attitude, motivation, and achievement of ability-grouped, seventh-grade, life science students (Doctoral dissertation, University of Georgia, 1983). *Dissertation Abstracts International, 44,* 05A.

Cannon, R.K., Jr., & Simpson, R.D. (1983). Relationships among attitude, motivation, and achievement of ability-grouped, seventh-grade life science students. *Science Education, 69,* 121–138.

Cornett, L.M. (1981). A study of the relationship between the elementary science study (ESS) and attitudes towards science of urban sixth-grade students (Doctoral dissertation, University of Rochester, 1981). *Dissertation Abstracts International, 12,* 08A.

Daume, R.J. (1981). The use of selected variables to compare science content achievement and science process skill achievement in two junior high school science programs: ISCS and traditional (Doctoral dissertation,

University of Southern Mississippi, 1981). *Dissertation Abstracts International, 42,* 06A.

Diamond. E.E., & Tittle C.K. (1985). Sex equity in testing. In S.S. Klein (Ed.), *Handbook for achieving sex equity through education* (pp. 167–188). Baltimore, MD: Johns Hopkins University Press.

Eccles, J.S. (1987). Gender roles and women's achievement-related decisions. *Psychology of Women Quarterly, 11,* 135–172.

Fishbein, M., & Ajzen, I. (1975). *Belief, attitude, intention, behavior: An introduction to theory and research.* Reading, MA: Addison-Wesley.

Gallager, J.J. (1987). A summary of research in science education-1985. *Science Education, 71,* 271–273.

Glass, G.V., McGaw, B., & Smith, M.L. (1981). *Meta-analysis in social research.* Beverly Hills, CA: Sage.

Johnson, S. (1987). Gender differences in science: Parallels in interest, experience and performance. *International Journal of Science Education, 9,* 467–481.

Kahle, J. B., & Lakes, M.K. (1983). The myth of equality in science classrooms. *Journal of Research in Science Teaching, 20,* 131–140.

Hamilton, M. (1982). Jamaican students' attitude to science as it relates to achievement in external examinations. *Science Education, 66,* 155–169.

Handley, H.M., & Morse, L.W. (1984). Two-year study relating adolescents' self-concept and gender role perceptions to achievement and attitudes toward science. *Journal of Research in Science Teaching, 21,* 599–607.

Harty, H., & Beall, D. (1984). Attitudes toward science of gifted and nongifted fifth graders. *Journal of Research in Science Teaching, 21,* 483–488.

Harty, H., Samuel, K.V., & Beall, D. (1986). Exploring relationships among four science teaching-learning affective attributes of sixth-grade students. *Journal of Research in Science Teaching, 23,* 51–50.

Hasan, O.E. (1985). An investigation into factors affecting attitudes toward science of secondary school students in Jordan. *Science Education, 69*(1), 3–18.

Hedges, L.V., Shymansky, J.A., & Woodworth, G. (1989). *Modern methods of metaanalysis.* Washington, DC: National Science Teachers Association.

Hofman, H.H. (1977). An assessment of eight-year-old children's attitude toward science. *School Science and Mathematics, 77,* 662–670.

Hyde, J.S., Fennema, E., & Lamon, S.J. (1990). Gender differences in mathematics performance: A meta-analysis. *Psychological Bulletin, 107,* 139–155.

Krathwohl, D.R., Bloom, B.S., & Masia, B.S. (1964). *Taxonomy of educational objectives. Handbook 2: Affective domain.* New York: David McKay.

Linn, M.C., & Petersen, A.C. (1985). Facts and assumptions about the nature of sex differences. In S.S. Klein (Ed.), *Handbook for achieving sex equity through education* (pp. 53–77). Baltimore, MD: Johns Hopkins University Press.

Lowery, L.R., Bowyer, J., & Padillia, M.J. (1980). The science curriculum improvement study and student attitude. *Journal of Research in Science Teaching, 17,* 327–355.

Novak, J.A. (1980). *Investigation of the relationships between personality types of eighth-grade science students and cognitive preference.* (ERIC Document Reproduction Service No. ED 194 366)

Okebukola, P.A. (1986). Cooperative learning and students' attitudes to laboratory work. *School Science and Mathematics, 86,* 582–590.

Pogge, A.F. (1986). The attitudes toward science and science teaching of the teachers and students at Baldwin Intermediate School, Quincy, Illinois (Doctoral dissertation, University of Iowa, 1986). *Dissertation Abstracts International, 17,* 07A.

Schibeci, R.A. (1984). Attitudes to science: An update. *Studies in Science Education, 11,* 26–59.

Schibeci, R.A., & Riley, J.P., II. (1986). Influence of students' background and perceptions on science attitudes and achievement. *Journal of Research in Science Teaching, 23,* 177–187.

Scott, L.E.U. (1982). The effects of mixed-sex and single-sex cooperative grouping and individualization on science achievement and attitudes of early adolescent females (Doctoral dissertation, University of Minnesota, 1982). *Dissertation Abstracts International, 43,* 08A.

Sells, L.W. (1972). High school mathematics as the critical filter in the job market. In R.T. Thomas (Ed.), *Developing opportunities for minorities in graduate education* (pp. 37–39). Berkeley: University of California Press.

Shrigley, R.L. (1972). Sex differences and its implications on attitude and achievement in elementary school science. *School Science and Mathematics, 72,* 789–79.

Simpson, R.D., & Oliver, J.S. (1985). Attitude toward science and achievement motivation profiles of male and female science students in grades six through ten. *Science Education, 69,* 511–526.

Squiers, S.M.M. (1983). An analysis of attitudes of high school seniors towards science and scientists in a southern metropolitan high school (Doctoral dissertation, Auburn University, 1983). *Dissertation Abstracts International, 11,* 03A.

Stage, E.K., Freinberg, N.M., Eccles, J.R., & Becker, J.R. (1985). Increasing the participation and achievement of girls and women in mathematics, science, and engineering. In S.S. Klein (Ed.), *Handbook for achieving sex equity through education* (pp. 237–269). Baltimore, MD: Johns Hopkins University Press.

Stoner, D.K. (1981). The relationship of psychological and skill factors to science attitude and achievement of fifth- and tenth-grade students (Doctoral dissertation, Claremanot Graduate School, 1981). *Dissertation Abstracts International, 42,* 03A.

Weinburgh, M.H., & Engelhard, G., Jr. (1991, October). Gender, prior academic performance and beliefs as predictors of attitudes toward biology laboratory experiences. Paper presented at Georgia Educational Research Association conference, Decatur, GA.

Sample Review of Qualitative Research: Telecommunications for Teachers: Supporting Reflection and Collaboration among Teaching Professionals

Bos, N. D., Krajcik, J. S., & Patrick, H. (1995). Telecommunications for teachers: Supporting reflection and collaboration among teaching professionals. *Journal of Computers in Mathematics and Science Teaching, 14,* 187–202.

In this section of the chapter you will read a published secondary source that illustrates a review of qualitative research. It is preceded by comments written especially for this book by the first author of the article. Then the article itself is reprinted in full, just as it appeared when originally published. Where appropriate, we have added footnotes to help you understand the information contained in the article.

Researcher's Comments, Prepared by Nathan Bos

The hardest thing about writing a review article is getting the categories right. By categories I mean the overall structure of an article: how the topic is divided, what is emphasized, what is de-emphasized, and so forth. There's something intimidating about taking a large collection of research articles written by other people and imposing your own order on them. But it's also the hump that you have to get over, and it's downhill on the other side.

The "uphill" side of writing this article started near the end of my first year of graduate school, when my advisor Joe Krajcik asked me to coauthor a review article for his "Research Notes" column in the *Journal of Computers in Mathematics and Science Teaching*. I was nervous, though honored with the opportunity. Although before starting graduate school I wrote for a living (as a newspaper journalist and freelance writer), academic writing is a different sort of thing, and I was inexperienced in it. However, it was a great opportunity not only to have a published article, but also to do a thorough review of current telecommunications research.

Joe and I were preparing for a year when we would be putting teacher support via telecommunications to the test. Approximately 100 teachers from across the state of Michigan had attended workshops put on by our research group, and we hoped to keep in contact with them through telecommunications.

These teachers had attended workshops on Project-Based Science, which is a particular approach to inquiry-oriented science teaching. (See our research group's WWW page if you'd like to know more: <http://www.umich.edu/~pbsgroup>.) Teaching science in this way can be a revolutionary improvement for both teachers and students, but it's also difficult and requires a great deal of support beyond one-time workshops. Aware of this, our group was sponsoring a series of follow-up work sessions throughout the following year. But we also hoped that our teachers could provide each other some of the day-to-day advice, practical information, and moral support that teachers need, either through an e-mail group or some other form of telecommunications.

With this goal in mind, we set out to take a serious look at all the ways that telecommunications had been used for teacher support in the published research literature. Writing a review article was a great way to get a broader sense of what we were trying to do, to spur our creativity, and to help us avoid some of the mistakes that others had made.

Gathering Information

By the time classes started in the fall of 1994, my cubicle was quite literally covered with articles and books. I was either going to have to write this review article, or move. During my spare time all summer I had been collecting materials, starting with what Joe thought were a few key articles and expanding from there.

Reviewing the field of telecommunications in 1994 at first sounded like a simple enough thing—after all, the technology had barely existed five years before, and decent educational applications of it were just beginning to be developed. However, as with any topic, the more I learned about telecommunications the more I could see how it connects to everything else, and it was hard to know where to stop. Although telecommunications is a fairly new technology, ideas about teacher support were not new, and we would be foolish to ignore that literature. Also, researchers in the business community were in some ways ahead of researchers in education in thinking about how new technology might revolutionize communications. Throughout this process I was concerned that we might miss good research articles that had been published in different areas (like business, rural education, or engineering), but did not happen to use the same keywords that I was using to search the research literature.

One of the first things that I did was to meet with a colleague, John, who was in the midst of reviewing the literature on teacher support. John explained to me some of the basic concepts of interest in that field, such as encouraging reflective practice and structuring school-university collaboration. I left John's office with a much better sense of how telecommunications fits into the larger picture of teacher support, and with another medium-sized stack of articles in my hands.

By chance we found out that Helen Patrick (the third author of this review) was already engaged in reviewing the literature on telecommunications and teachers as a project for another professor. Helen generously let me look through her work in progress. I found that she had taken the topic in some new directions that Joe and I hadn't thought of, including preservice teaching and teacher education. Helen also had constructed comprehensive tables (the basis for the table that appears in the review article) to analyze the research she had found into categories. Her efforts gave us a good direction for moving into the next phase of writing the article.

Choosing Categories

When I was a newspaper reporter, the first sentence of an article was always the key. Once I had that right, the rest of the article would tend to spill out onto the page. In academic writing, however, first sentences are much less important than overall structure. The categories are the key.

I spent a considerable amount of time trying to decide how to reorganize the clutter of articles on my desk into meaningful piles. I seriously considered grouping the articles by the type of technology used. If we had gone that route, we would have put all the articles dealing with e-mail in one section, bulletin boards in another, file-transfer in a third, and so forth. However, I think this would have sent the wrong message that the article was about technology, when it was really about education.

Instead, we organized the articles according to recognized problems in education. We wanted to emphasize that telecommunications is not a novelty or a distraction from the rest of educational research, but a new set of tools that can solve both old and new problems. By bringing problem solving to the forefront, I hoped that we could help people make the leap from asking, "What is this neat new technology?" to "What is this really good for?"

When choosing categories, every gain also has a corresponding loss. By de-emphasizing the technology, we did not cover some topics as well as we might have liked to. What is most glaringly missing is any mention of a nascent technology that Joe and I had seen in "demo" form a few months earlier: the World Wide Web. (We removed a brief mention of the WWW from the final version of the article.) At the time I didn't think that the WWW was going to provide any new solutions to educational problems, because I believed (incorrectly) that it couldn't be made interactive and would be basically identical to the established "gopher" technology with pictures. Given the hindsight of the past few years, we should probably have investigated the potential of WWW technology a little bit further!

Writing

As we were writing, describing how different researchers had used telecommunications to solve the large conceptual problems of education, I realized that some of the more important things that I had learned while doing this research weren't coming through. Recall that Joe and I were still trying to figure out how best to support the 100 Project-Based Science teachers, and certain issues were paramount in our minds. Was technical support going to be a problem? Would teachers who had initially attended different work sessions, and thus had never met each other, be inclined to collaborate on-line? Did we have to worry about people "flaming" each other on our network? These smaller details did not qualify as large problems, but we wanted to include them because we suspected that others would face the same issues that we did. We decided to include smaller "issues" sections within each category, where we discussed some of the things that were of most concern to us. After we submitted the article to *JCMST*, the journal editor commented that he especially liked our "issues" sections.

Afterwards

The special issue of *JCMST* that includes our review came out about six months after we sent in our final draft. During that time, much had happened with the 100 Project-Based Science teachers. We had set up our own e-mail list, helped many of them get signed up with Labnet on America Online, and run a telecommunications weather project where students tracked bleak February weather in Michigan and across the country. We also put together a set of project-based science WWW pages and learned how to distribute software and register users over the WWW.

According to the Project-Based Science teachers, the most valuable on-line support we provided that year was getting them involved with the LabNet group, which was an existing network of about 1500 teachers. Our teachers who used LabNet regularly reported that they were getting timely support, materials, and a chance to reflect on practice within that active and larger group. LabNet, which is sponsored by TERC and supported by the National Science Foundation, has since moved to the WWW and is accessible at <http://labnet.terc.edu/labnet/labnet.html>.

Since then, Joe and I have continued researching educational uses of telecommunications, focusing more on K-12 students. We are both currently involved in the University of Michigan's Digital Libraries initiative (<http://mydl.soe.umich.edu>), designing new tools and pedagogical techniques to make the World Wide Web usable and useful in K-12 classrooms.

TELECOMMUNICATIONS FOR TEACHERS: SUPPORTING REFLECTION AND COLLABORATION AMONG TEACHING PROFESSIONALS

Nathan D. Bos, Joseph S. Krajcik, and Helen Patrick
University of Michigan
Ann Arbor, MI 48109-1259

This review article describes a number of Computer-Mediated Communications (CMC) networks that have been designed to support K-12 teachers. In order to demonstrate that CMC is a valuable means of teacher support, rather than a game-like add-on to the teacher support process, we have structured the article around a number of existing strands of education research. We argue that CMC networks are uniquely well suited to support "reflective practice" in both preservice and inservice teachers, preservice teachers in the student teaching phase of their education, inservice teachers undertaking some educational innovation, school-university collaborations, teachers in rural areas online, and "communities of learning" in which teachers collaborate with students and outside learners, according to constructivist models of learning.

This article also discusses the unique attributes of CMC communication, factors that contribute to or inhibit network success, and future directions for both technology and research.

A table gives a brief overview of the purposes and research results of 13 networks mentioned in the review.

Telecommunications is transforming education. The "information superhighway" is radically changing the way many people work and play, and will not pass by the neighborhood school—networking has been given too high a priority by many educators and policy makers for that to happen.

Bos, N. D., Krajcik, J. S., & Patrick, H. (1995). Telecommunications for teachers: Supporting reflection and collaboration among teaching professionals. *Journal of Computers in Mathematics and Science Teaching, 14,* 187–202. Reprinted with permission of the Association for the Advancement of Computing in Education.

However, in 1994, the current standard for a well-networked classroom is still one computer in the front of class, attached (if the class is lucky) to one phone line. The box that promises marvelous interactivity, access, and motivation for students becomes less effective if 20, 30, or 40 students have to interact through it. (Of course, there are many clever uses of telecommunications in the one-computer classroom, such as the Inter-Cultural Learning Network projects—see Riel, 1993—and TERC's KidsNet curriculums—see Lenk, 1992, and Julyan & Wiske, 1994.)

The one-computer classroom does offer great interactive potential for one class member, however—the teacher. This review will focus on computer networking projects that have been designed to support teacher practice.

Far from being an expensive "extra" with artificial, game-like uses, a networked computer can help solve many recognized difficulties in teaching practice:

- A number of recent theorists and teacher educators have written about the value of teachers' reflecting on their practice, and sharing these reflections with other teachers.
- Teachers in preservice or early inservice especially can benefit from moral support, curriculum guidance and the opportunity for joint reflection.
- Teachers undertaking new innovations, working closely with teachers in a [sic] another location, or collaborating with University researchers have a need for ongoing contact and support.

TABLE 1   Summary of Major Computer-Mediated Communications Projects Reviewed (displayed in the order in which they are discussed in this article)

Reference/name of network	Users and purpose of network	Findings
DCE (Dialogic Community Exercise) (Harrington, 1992)	Encourage preservice teachers' reflection and conversation	Network participation was time-consuming, but did provide a safe, convenient opportunity for reflection and conversation
BTCN (Beginning Teacher Computer Network) (Merseth, 1991)	Provide an electronic medium for reflection and exchange between newly-graduated Master's students for one year with a computer network	Participants rated network most effective in: 1) providing moral support 2) developing broader perspective on teaching 3) keeping in touch with friends
Science Teacher's Network Harvard (Katz, McSwiney, & Stroud, 1987)	Reduce teacher isolation, provide a vehicle for staff development, and promote collegial exchange among 45 inservice science teachers	1) Networking appealed more to professionally isolated teachers 2) Teachers who knew others wrote largely social messages. Those who didn't wrote on discrete topics.
School Renewal Network (NEA sponsored 'Mastery in Learning project') (Watts & Castle, 1992)	Support inservice teachers and promote educational transformation (change) via 'dialogic exchange' between practitioners, administrators, and researchers	Networking judged to be an effective support tool for professional development, educational change, and the breaking down of institutional barriers and hierarchies
Star Schools TERC (Weir, 1992)	Provide curriculum, technical, and personal support for teachers involved in networked science projects. Measure educational change	Of 932 participating teachers, 78% reported trying new techniques such as using cooperative learning.
LabNet TERC (Ruopp, Gal, Drayton, & Pfister, 1993)	Provide ongoing support for high school physics teachers (and now, others) using new technology and new methods. Support educational change	Labnet was successful in promoting use of MBL software, and to a lesser degree successful in supporting a change to project-enhanced science.
B.E.S.T. (Better Elementary Science Teaching) (Jinks & Lord, 1990)	Overcome rural isolation problem for Montana science teachers	Network recorded much use, both social and professional, 10 months after the 50 participants attended an intensive, month-long workshop.
Virginia's PEN (Public Education Network) (Robin, 1994)	Electronically link every school (elementary, high school, university) in the state of Virginia, and promote online collaboration	'Pavilion curators' (network facilitators) could significantly increase network participation.
ICLN Learning Circles AT&T Inter-Cultural Learning Network (Riel & Levin, 1992)	To create 6–10 classroom 'learning circles.' Teachers, students, and outside learners participate in collaborative learning.	By organizing network projects with clear purposes and expectations, this model overcomes problems that have plagued less structured networks.
National Geographic KidsNet (TERC) (Julyan & Wiske, 1994)	Demonstrate a curriculum model for widely scattered classrooms to share data and engage in collaborative science learning	KidsNet useful as a model and tool for teachers transitioning to more constructivist (project-based) teaching practices
PSNet (Univ. Michigan Project-Based Science) (Soloway et al., 1994)	Provide file-transfer capability, along with specialized project planning software, to create both a language and medium for high-level professional exchange	not yet implemented
CoVis (Collaborative Visualization) (Pea, 1993)	Enable live video collaboration between science learners, teachers, and professional scientists	early in implementation phase
Noah Webster school Wall Street Journal, 9/16/94	Provide curriculum and professional support for home schooling parents	not yet implemented

103

- Rural isolation magnifies the need for teachers to have contact with other teachers and with content experts.

All of these needs can be and are being addressed by the use of computer-mediated communications (CMC)—email networks, bulletin boards, listservers, and ftp libraries for teachers, widely ranging in design, purpose, and accessibility.

This review focuses on literature relevant to these areas. Table 1 presents a summary of the major CMC projects we describe.

SUPPORTING THE "REFLECTIVE PRACTITIONER"

Computer-mediated communications provide radically new means and opportunities for teachers to reflect collaboratively on their practice.

The recent surge in the use of telecommunications comes on the heels of a movement in teacher education that calls for teachers to become "reflective practitioners" (Munby, 1989; Richardson, 1990; Schon, 1992). It is argued that, for teachers, reflecting on their practice is a crucial step for enacting meaningful innovations. By taking the time to verbalize what they do and why they do it, teachers can more effectively integrate their theoretical knowledge into their day-to-day and minute-to-minute classroom decisions. Reflecting collaboratively with other teachers can be especially effective (Munby, 1989; Richardson, 1990), providing a supportive audience for reflection and a source of new perspectives.

CMC can provide the right medium to fulfill this recognized need in teaching. Electronic messaging tends to be less formal (and therefore less time-consuming) than other forms of writing. But because it happens asynchronously (Harasim, 1990), CMC provides the writers more time for reflection and response than does face-to-face communication. Participants in a network can take part in discussions any time it is convenient, 24 hours a day, and can take as much time as they want or need to mull over postings and formulate responses.

CMC FOR PRESERVICE TEACHING

Computer-mediated communications can contribute to inservice teaching by providing a flexible means of communicating between preservice teachers and professors, and by creating a uniquely egalitarian online "classroom" for mutual reflection and idea-sharing.

A number of preservice university teacher-education programs have begun to make use of CMC to provide a cooperative learning environment for student teachers (Harrington, 1992; Merseth, 1991; Sunal & Sunal, 1992). Networks can provide emotional support (Lowe, 1993), curriculum support (Weir, 1992), and a place to reflect on issues of teaching with peers in the same situation (Yan, Poage, Munson, & Anderson, 1994). Also, the ability to access the network at any time, from multiple locations (Harasim, 1990), may be particularly well-suited to student teachers, whose activities are no longer centralized on the University campus.

The Dialogic Community Exercise (DCE) at the University of Michigan is an example of CMC being well-integrated with the specific goals of a teacher education program (Harrington, 1992; Harrington & Quinn-Leering, 1994). Situated within a program heavily focused on reflective practice, the DCE attempts to make use of another characteristic of CMC—its potential for breaking down barriers in the classroom. The uniquely democratic exchange made possible by CMC (see below) has been a good setting for DCE's stated goals: helping students examine "taken-for-granted assumptions," promoting openness to new perspectives, and examining moral issues of teaching practice. To promote openness, student participants sign onto DCE with pseudonyms. The DCE organizers also made the unorthodox decision not to include any kind of moderator in early discussions, and they banned professors from the forum altogether. (In later exercises, students have been appointed as facilitators.) In anonymous post-class surveys, 85% of participants judged the DCE to have been a worthwhile activity, and several commented on the freedom of discussion. Previous research has also noted the capability of CMC to transform classroom discussion:

Issue: Democratization of the online classroom. In an online discussion group, there is no competition for "air time"—everyone can contribute to whatever extent they feel comfortable (Harasim, 1990). It is much less likely for any member or group of members to dominate discussion. Because CMC also strips away the social clues of gender, ethnicity, age, and so forth, CMC tends to encourage participation from class members who would be reticent to participate in a face-to-face seminar (Harris, 1993; Sproull & Kiesler, 1993). Also, Levin, Kim, and Riel's (1990) analysis of patterns of conversation-responses on a bulletin board showed that CMC conversations tend to break the teacher-centered IRE (Interaction-Response-Evaluation) pattern of exchange.

Issue: Negative characteristics of CMC. It is only fair to point out that CMC has some negative characteristics as well. The lack of nonverbal clues and face-to-face contact can lead to misunderstandings. This is often blamed for the propensity toward hostile interactions ("flaming") in CMC (Sproull & Kiesler, 1993). Flaming seems to be less of a problem in educational settings (none of the educational literature reviewed report this as a problem), but some users have reported that the lack of personal contact and the delayed feedback of CMC can be unsettling to participants (Harasim, 1990).

Another reported weakness of CMC is the difficulty of achieving consensus. The same asynchronous quality that promotes reflection also makes timely group decisions difficult (even for such simple tasks as setting a meeting time) (Harasim, 1990; Sproull & Kiesler, 1993). One technological way around this problem is the use of live online conferencing, whereby a number of participants can exchange short text messages in real time.

CMC FOR INSERVICE TEACHERS

Inservice teachers can use computer-mediated communications to reflect on issues of practice with peers, to solicit and provide materials, ideas, or advice, and to receive the kind of day-to-day support necessary for innovative teaching.

Teachers' need for support and reflection does not end with certification, of course. Harvard's Beginning Teacher Computer Network (BTCN) provided equipment and a network server to 39 newly graduated Masters students for one year (Merseth, 1991). The network included private email and subject-oriented bulletin boards for posting messages to the group. In evaluation surveys and structured interviews, participants reported that the most important function of the network was providing moral support. Keeping in touch with friends and developing a broader perspective on teaching also ranked high. Lesson and curricular planning needs were significantly lower; Merseth believes this kind of support might require a network with file-transfer capability.

Issue: Access and technical support. Lack of access to technology and lack of adequate technical support are still two of the most crucial determiners of teachers' network participation (Katz, McSwiney, & Stroud, 1987). Common networking problems include lack of phone lines into classrooms, lack of computer access at work or at home, balky or difficult software, or incompatibilities between network software and the school's computers.

SUPPORTING EDUCATIONAL INNOVATION

Teachers who are undertaking difficult changes in their practice require time, sustained contact with mentors and outside resources, and support from peers. Likewise, successful school-university collaborations also require time and sustained contact. Computer-mediated communication is a means to provide this scaffolding.

Just as CMC can help beginning teachers continue relationships and revisit issues of practice, so it can also be a means of supporting experienced teachers undertaking new innovations. There has been much interest in what factors help teachers take new ideas, perhaps developed at a summer seminar or inservice, and put them into practice (Dwyer, Ringstaff, & Sandholtz, 1991). There has also been much study of what successful school-university collaborations look like (Denton & Metcalf, 1993). Both of these literatures pinpoint ongoing support as essential factors.

Watts and Castle (1992) describe how the School Renewal Network grew out of an earlier, non–computer-based Mastery-in-Learning project. Teachers who used the earlier resource—to receive research, model programs, bibliographies and lists of other schools by U.S. mail—often found the material difficult to interpret or use. When the project went online, teachers could network with each other to trade practical advice, encouragement, and innovations. When educational researchers were added to the network, both teachers and researchers benefited: "The linking of research to practice has become much more natural, flowing from the needs of the users" (Watts & Castle, 1992, p. 686).

Being part of an online "community of practice" can also support teacher innovation in more human ways. Lieberman and McLaughlin (1992) believe that "dialogic communities" can be especially empowering for urban teachers: "Members of networks report an intellectual and emotional stimulation that gives the courage to engage students differently in the classroom" (Lieberman & McLaughlin, 1992, p. 674).

Studying how telecommunications can support teachers' changing practice was a major assessment goal of TERC's two-year Star Schools project. Star Schools provided teacher support and training in technology and telecommunications software, along with curriculums and organized online projects and contests. Classrooms across the country participated in contests and data collection over the network.

The Star Schools project had 932 teacher participants. In a survey evaluation of the project, 78% of teachers also reported that the Star Schools activity had changed their teaching style, in such areas as use of cooperative learning techniques. Fifty-six percent of the teachers reported having collaborated with one or more other teachers over the network, and teachers also reported increases in student motivation and involvement (Weir, 1992). Use of

CMC alone did not bring about these changes, but it did provide an unprecedented means of interaction between teachers, students, and support personnel.

Another TERC-sponsored project, LabNet, is ongoing (Ruopp, Gal, Drayton, & Pfister, 1993). Begun in 1989 as part of a training and support mechanism for high school physics teachers using Microcomputer-Based Laboratory software, Labnet's scope and ambitions have expanded to the broader purpose of introducing and sustaining constructivist, project-based science teaching. LabNet's philosophy emphasizes that teacher change is a never-ending process, rather than a discrete event, and the use of CMC as a support mechanism fits neatly with that orientation. Labnet's research results are presented mostly in the form of case studies (fitting with their philosophy, they eschew one-time measures such as surveys) and these case studies emphasize the constant adaptation and flexibility teachers need to keep up with changes in their schools, and concurrently bring about changes in practice. Labnet currently sponsors an area on the private service America Online (keyword "LabNet" for membership information), where the 1,500 LabNet member teachers can go online at any time to ask for and give advice, and become involved in projects, as well as discuss issues (Ruopp, Gal, Drayton, & Pfister, 1993).

OVERCOMING RURAL ISOLATION

Teachers who are isolated by geography have been some of the first beneficiaries of CMC.

Rural isolation not only tends to separate teachers from other teachers, but also makes contact with content experts more difficult, and additionally, sparse staffing tends to force teachers to teach out of their area of specialization (Jinks & Lord, 1990). The increasing availability of telecommunications can help bridge these gaps. In their study of networked science teachers in Massachusetts, Katz, McSwiney, and Stroud (1987) noted that the geographic isolation of a teacher was a predictor of network involvement. It should not be surprising, then, that early successes in teacher networking were recorded in such geographically dispersed states as Alaska (Bruce & Rubin, 1992), Texas (Stout, 1992), Montana (Jinks & Lord, 1990), and Indiana (Lehman, Campbell, Halla, & Lehman, 1992). Programs such as the Indiana STEPS network (Students and Teachers Electronic Productivity System) can bring teachers in contact with peers and outside experts and encourage both general-participation conferencing on topics of interest and one-to-one mentoring relationships across distances (Lehman et al., 1992).

Issue: Must teachers know each other In order to network? The Jinks and Lord research raised an interesting issue about networking. These researchers intended to set up a network to connect rural educators in Montana (the Better Elementary School Science Teaching Project, or B.E.S.T). They judged that participants must get to know each other face-to-face before networking can be effective, so they conducted a summer seminar following a military model of team building. Their 50 participants were sequestered in one dormitory, isolated even from family, for an intensive month-long workshop on science content and computer use. And this strategy did produce results: Ten months after the workshop, the group's attrition rate was minimal, and participants had used the network to exchange over 15,000 messages on both social and professional topics.

Jinks and Lord are not the only researchers to assume that networkers must know each other personally before they can collaborate professionally. The successful BTCN and DCE networks both report high levels of social interaction that sustained the networks. This contrasts with many other networks that tend to dwindle and disappear, for lack of participation (Riel & Levin, 1992).

Anecdotal evidence suggests that networks of strangers can succeed, however. Private services such as CompuServe, American [sic] Online, and the WELL support many discussion areas for the non-acquainted. Most glaring, perhaps, is the existence of over 2,000 usenet and bitnet newsgroups, where participants from all over the world gather to discuss topics ranging from beer making to operating systems. In fact, it has been observed that on newsgroups, the more obscure the topic (and therefore the fewer and more dispersed the participants), the more collegial the exchange seems to be. Providing a narrow topic of common interest seems to provide a gateway into acquaintanceship and more sustained conversation.

And perhaps here lies a key point: Weir (1992, citing Katz, McSwiney, & Stroud, 1987) also reports that, in Harvard's Science Teacher's Network project, participants who did not already have acquaintances on-line tended to contribute on more narrow topics, inquiring or responding to the specifics of requests for information on specific topics. Perhaps this is a useful model: Participants engage in discussions of a more reflective, philosophical, or social nature only after establishing relationships with other participants. So, a successful network might be one that includes opportunities for new participants to link into narrow, practical topics, but also allows regular users to discuss broader or more personal ones.

Another factor that can promote dialogue among non-acquaintances is the presence of an active moderator. Robin (1994) found a statistically significant increase in participation at the math-science pavilion of Virginia's Public Education Network (PEN) when a moderator (or "curator") began to manage the area according to a particular strategy. The curator in this model was responsible for tending the discussion threads, sometimes by transplanting inappropriate posts to other locations, sometimes by summarizing and prompting. The curator also helped users with technical problems, arranged for training, and perhaps most importantly, personally contacted and encouraged participants and actively cultivated a core group of frequent users.

Other groups have their own takes on the proper role of a moderator. A handbook published for teacher moderators of LabNet (Spitzer, Wedding, & DiMaurio, 1994) maintains that there are many effective moderating styles: "What makes for a good moderator is having the confidence to put forth your own style in order to 'grow' network conversations" (p. 4).

The presence of a strong moderator is also one of the factors that Riel and Levin (1990) point to in their study of successful and unsuccessful teacher networks—but there is another variable that these authors emphasized more. Riel and Levin's best advice to would-be network administrators is to involve teachers in collaborative projects. Projects should be well structured, with set beginnings, endings, and deadlines, and clearly defined roles and expectations for participants (see also Lenk, 1992).

Riel has helped implement this advice within AT&T's Inter-Cultural Learning Network (ICLN) using Riel's model of "learning circles" (Riel, 1993). Six to ten ICLN classrooms come together via electronic mail to introduce themselves, plan a project, and produce an end product (typically a newsletter.) In this model, the teacher-student roles become blurred: Teachers collaborate along with the students and are exposed to new ideas at the same time the students are.

TEACHERS AND ONLINE "COMMUNITIES OF LEARNING"

Education visionaries foresee a classroom without walls, made possible partly by CMC, in which students and teachers will become co-learners and collaborators with outside scientists and learners, unhindered by geographical separation.

The blurring of the student/teacher roles into a "community of learning" is one of the more exciting prospects of educational CMC. This change in the role of the teacher is a desired outcome of recent educational literature on constructivist teaching practice (Blumenfeld, Soloway, Marx, Krajcik, Guzdial, & Palincsar, 1991; Pea & Gomez, 1992; Ruopp, Gal, Drayton, & Pfister, 1993). Programs such as the National Geographic Kids Network show how CMC can lead the way toward this goal.

The KidNet project (developed by TERC and published by National Geographic) was principally a network for students, and as such would be outside the scope of this review, but as we saw in TERC's research on the similar Star Schools project, classroom networking activities can also affect teaching. The Kids Network provided for large-scale data-sharing projects between geographically dispersed students. For example, one of the most popular Kids Network units was *Acid Rain* (National Geographic, 1989); in the telecommunications component of *Acid Rain*, students tested their local rainwater and compared their data with that of their cross-country or international peers (Julyan & Wiske, 1994). In this model of classroom learning, students and teachers take on the roles of authentic scientists. KidsNet also expanded the horizon of classroom-to-classroom collaboration by including professional scientists into the mix. The inclusion of outside scientists into network collaboration may provide more opportunity for teacher change, allowing teachers to further distance themselves from the role of all-knowing information source and to move toward the roles of co-collaborator, facilitator, and learner.

FUTURE DIRECTIONS FOR TEACHER SUPPORT AND COLLABORATION

One of the near-term changes in teachers' networking capability will be the increasing availability of file-transferring tools (ftp) to augment the purely textual message capability of email and electronic bulletin boards. In her 1987 study, Merseth complained that lack of such capability limited their network's usefulness as a means of curriculum support. Networks such as Virginia's PEN are now making use of these tools, providing sites where teachers can upload and download lesson plans, information, or educational software. Private services such as America Online, CompuServe, and Prodigy also have online libraries of software and non-text files, as do an increasing number of sites on the internet. As network connections become faster and teacher access improves, sharing documents over the network may soon be as easy a source of material as swapping documents over the photocopy machine.

Here at the University of Michigan, the Project-Based Science group is making plans for a telecommunications network that would make heavy use of ftp capability in combination with our in-house curriculum-planning software, PIViT (Project Integration Visualization Tool) (Brade, Krajcik, Soloway, & Blumenfeld, 1994). The 300-plus educators using the software would be able to swap PIViT's concept maps, calendars, and graphical project plans easily and quickly, sharing with other teachers not only ideas and concerns, but specific curriculum components (Soloway, Krajcik, Blumenfeld, & Marx, 1994).

An even more radical addition to the capabilities of CMC is live video communications. The CoVis (Collaborative Visualization) project at Northwestern University has been experimenting with science-related collaborations ("collaboratories") between schools using live video (Pea, 1993). The team is working on capabilities that would allow learners in different locations to simultaneously work on projects that require advanced data visualization tools—tools that are valuable in such fields as meteorology, oceanography, or molecular biology.

Live video communications between individuals overcomes some of the limitations of CMC, such as lack of visual clues and asynchronicity. However, live video would also not have some of the strengths of asynchronous text CMC that makes it a good medium for reflective and egalitarian conversations, so video should not be seen as a replacement for other CMCs. Addition of this exciting medium will simply open another window out of the classroom, with its own set of unique possibilities to be explored.

An experimental charter school in the state of Michigan is also pushing the frontiers of online possibilities for teacher support. The Noah Webster Academy has no classrooms and plans to hire only a few certified teachers, yet it has 2,000 students across Michigan. Noah Webster is set up to provide curriculum and other support to home-schooling parents. When and if it is approved to receive state education funds, the academy's first purchases will be a network server and home computers for all of its participating families to provide ongoing support, consultation, collaboration, and curriculum resources to the home-schooling parent/teachers (*Wall Street Journal*, 9/16/94, front page, midwest edition).

FUTURE RESEARCH DIRECTIONS

Clearly, the field of telecommunications will provide fertile ground for researchers to till for a long time to come. None of the uses of CMC described in this paper have been studied to the point where further research would be redundant; in most areas, there is a paucity of research data. In particular, we see the following questions as particularly fertile for exploration:

- What are the effects of current uses of CMC on teaching practice? Most evaluations of educational computer networks, when they report any data at all, rely on either (a) access frequency data from the network server or (b) survey data collected from teachers. But research must keep developing methods that go beyond this, to study how networks are used (not just whether they are accessed) and how teachers' practice is changed as a result.
- What are the limits of CMC in providing a forum for preservice and inservice teachers to reflect on their practice? Will increasing availability and ease of use lead to ubiquitous "communities of practice," or are there psychological limits to the usefulness of this new technology? Will CMC be equally valuable to all practitioners or to only a few whose communications styles and response to technology make them likely users? What yet-unseen barriers may prevent the formation of new online "communities of practice"?
- How will technological advances affect teaching practice? Will increased network bandwidth, together with file-transferring capability, dramatically improve the usefulness of networks for teachers? How can synchronous, two-way video reshape the nature of networked collaboration?

Divergence and convergence of future research. We expect that, in the future, the study of CMC will both converge and diverge. Hopefully, the field will converge on accepted methods for evaluation of networks (Riel & Levin's 1992 analysis of participant structures seems a promising start), and a body of research will be available from which to further categorize and situate networking efforts. But we would also expect the field to diverge, as computers become ubiquitous on the teacher's desk (and maybe even the students'!). Research will need to focus less on the technology, which will be taken for granted, and more on the radically creative and divergent means by which the technology will be used to improve education at all levels.

References

Blumenfeld, P.C., Soloway, E., Marx, R.W., Krajcik, J.S., Guzdial, M., & Palincsar, A. (1991). Motivating project-based learning: Sustaining the doing, supporting the learning. *Educational Psychologist, 26*(3 & 4), 369–398.

Brade, K., Krajcik, J., Soloway, E., & Blumenfeld, P. *Project integration visualization tool* [Computer software]. Ann Arbor, MI: Regents of the University of Michigan.

Bruce, C., & Rubin, A. (1992). *Electronic Quills: A situated evaluation of using computers for writing in classrooms.* Hillsdale, NJ: Lawrence Erlbaum Associates.

Denton, J.J., & Metcalf, T. (1993). *Two school-university collaborations: Characteristics and finding from classroom observations.* Paper presented at the Annual Meeting of the American Educational Research Association, Atlanta, GA. (ERIC Document Reproduction Service No. ED 361 850)

Dwyer, D.C., Ringstaff, C., & Sandholtz, J. H. (1991). Change in teachers' beliefs and practices in technology-rich classrooms. *Educational Leadership 48*(8), 45–52.

Harasim, L.M. (1990). Online education: An environment for collaboration and intellectual amplification. In L. M. Harasim (Ed.), *Online education: Perspectives on a new environment* (pp. 39–64). New York: Praeger.

Harasim, L.M. (Ed.). (1993). *Global networks: Computers and international communications.* Cambridge, MA: MIT press.

Harrington, H. (1992). Fostering critical reflection through technology: Preparing prospective teachers for a changing society. *Journal of Information Technology for Teacher education, 1*(1), 67–82.

Harrington, H., & Quinn-Leering, K. (1994). Computer conferencing, moral discussion, and teacher develop-ment. In J. Willis, B. Robin, & D.A. Willis (Eds.), *Technology and teacher education annual 1994* (pp. 661–665). Charlottesville, VA: Association for the Advancement of Computing in Education.

Harris, J.B. (1993). An internet-based graduate telecomputing course: Practicing what we preach. In D. Carey, R. Carey, D.A. Willis, & J. Willis (Eds.), *Technology and teacher education annual 1993* (pp. 641–645). Charlottesville, VA: Association for the Advancement of Computing in Education.

Jinks, J., & Lord, R. (1990). The better elementary science teaching project: Overcoming the rural teacher's professional and academic isolation. *School Science and Mathematics, 90*(2), 125–133.

Julyan, C., & Wiske, S. (1994). *Learning along electronic paths: Journeys with the NGS Kids Network.* Cambridge, MA: Technical Education Research Center (TERC).

Katz, M.M., McSwiney, E., & Stroud, K. (1987). *Facilitating collegial exchange among science teachers: an experiment in computer-based conferencing.* Cambridge, MA: Education Technology Center. (ERIC Document Reproduction Service No. ED 291 597)

Lehman, J.D., Campbell, J.P., Halla, M., & Lehman, C.B. (1992). Doing science in the electronic school district. *Journal of Computers in Mathematics and Science Teaching, 11*(2), 193–198.

Lenk, C. (1992). The network science experience: Learning from three major projects. In R. F. Tinker & P. M. Kapisovsky (Eds.), *Prospects for educational telecomputing: Selected readings* (pp. 51–60). Cambridge, MA: Technical Education Research Center (TERC).

Levin, J.A., Kim, H., & Riel, M.M. (1990). Analyzing instructional interactions on electronic message networks. In L.M. Harasim (Ed.), *Online education: Perspectives on a new environment* (pp. 185–214). New York: Praeger.

Lieberman, A., & McLaughlin, M. (1992, May). Networks for educational change: Powerful and problematic. *Phi Delta Kappan,* pp. 673–677.

Lowe, M.E. (1993). 911 for student teachers. In D. Carey, R. Carey, D.A. Willis, & J. Willis (Eds.), *Technology and teacher education annual 1993* (pp. 672–674). Charlottesville, VA: Association for the Advancement of Computing in Education.

Merseth, K.K. (1991). Supporting beginning teachers with computer networks. *Journal of teacher education, 42*(2), 140–147.

Merseth, K.K. (1992, May). First aid for first-year teachers. *Phi Delta Kappan,* pp. 678–683.

Munby, H. (1989). Reflection-in-action and reflection-on-action. *Current Issues in Education, 9,* 31–42.

National Geographic Kids Network. (1989). *Acid Rain.* Washington, DC: National Geographic Society.

Pea, R.D., & Gomez, L.M. (1992). Distributed multimedia learning environments: Why and how? *Interactive Learning Environments, 2*(2) 73–109.

Pea, R.D. (1993). The collaborative visualization project. *Communications of the ACM, 36*(5), 60–63.

Richardson, V. (1990). Significant and worthwhile change and teaching practice. *Educational Researcher, 19*(7), 10–18.

Riel, M. (1993). Global education through learning circles. In L. M. Harasim (Ed.), *Global networks.* Cambridge, MA: MIT press.

Riel, M.M., & Levin, J.A. (1992). Building electronic communities: Success and failure in computer networking. In R.F. Tinker & P.M. Kapisovsky (Eds.), *Prospects for educational telecomputing: Selected readings* (pp. 61–86). Cambridge, MA: Technical Education Research Center (TERC).

Robin, B. (1994). The influence of conference moderator strategies on the participation of teachers in collaborative telecomputing projects. In J. Willis, B. Robin, & D.A. Willis (Eds.), *Technology and teacher education annual 1994* (pp. 693–698). Charlottesville, VA: Association for the Advancement of Computing in Education

Ruopp, R., Gal, S., Drayton, B., & Pfister, M. (Eds.). (1993). *Labnet: Toward a community of practice.* Hillsdale, NJ: Lawrence Erlbaum Associates.

Schon, D.A. (1992). The theory of inquiry: Dewey's legacy to education. *Curriculum Inquiry, 22*(2), 119–139.

Soloway, E., Krajcik, J., Blumenfeld, P., & Marx, R. (1994). *Technological support for teachers transitioning to project-based science practices.* Unpublished manuscript, University of Michigan School of Education.

Spitzer, W., Wedding, K., & DiMaurio, V. (1994). *Fostering reflective dialogues for teacher professional development* (Handbook for LABNET teacher moderators). Technical Education Research Center (TERC).

Sproull, L., & Kiesler, S. (1993). Computers, networks, and work. In L.M. Harasim (Ed.), *Global networks.* Cambridge, MA: MIT Press.

Stout, C. (1992). TENET: Texas education network. In R.F Tinker & P.M. Kapisovsky (Eds.), *Prospects for educational telecomputing: Selected readings* (pp. 135–140). Cambridge, MA: Technical Education Research Center (TERC).

Sunal, D.W., & Sunal, C.S. (1992). The impact of network communication technology on science teacher education. *Journal of Computers in Mathematics and Science Teaching, 11*(2), 143–153.

Tinker, R.F., & Kapisovsky, P.M. (Eds.). (1992). *Prospects for educational telecomputing: Selected readings.* Cambridge, MA: Technical Education Research Center (TERC).

Watts, G.D., & Castle, S. (1992, May). Electronic networking and the construction of professional knowledge. *Phi Delta Kappan,* pp. 684–689.

Weir, S. (1992). Electronic communities of learners: Fact or fiction. In R.F. Tinker & P.M. Kapisovsky (Eds.), *Prospects for educational telecomputing: Selected readings* (pp. 87–110). Cambridge, MA: Technical Education Research Center (TERC).

Yan, W., Poage, J.A., Munson, D., & Anderson, M. (1994). The integration of telecommunications into special education student teaching. In J. Willis, B. Robin, & D.A. Willis (Eds.), *Technology and teacher education annual 1994* (pp. 675–679). Charlottesville, VA: Association for the Advancement of Computing in Education.

SAMPLE PROFESSIONAL REVIEW: COOPERATIVE LEARNING

Slavin, R. (1992). Cooperative learning. In M. C. Alkin (Ed.), *Encyclopedia of Educational Research*, American Educational Research Association (pp. 235–238). New York: Macmillan.

In this section of the chapter you will read a published secondary source that illustrates a professional review. It is preceded by comments written especially for this book by the author of the article. Then the article itself is reprinted in full just as it appeared when originally published. Where appropriate, we have added footnotes to help you understand the information contained in the article.

Researcher's Comments, Prepared by Robert Slavin

Research on cooperative learning represents one of the greatest success stories in the history of educational research—and also one of its greatest failures. As recently as the 1970s, cooperative learning methods were rarely used, little known, and considered "fringe" methods by most educators. By 1993, a national survey (Puma et al., 1993) found that 79 percent of third-grade teachers and 62 percent of seventh-grade teachers reported making sustained use of cooperative learning methods in teaching mathematics. The proportions in reading/language arts were 74 percent at both grade levels. Even though these figures are certainly overestimates, it is true that hundreds of thousands of teachers are making daily use of cooperative learning methods. Research rarely has anything like this impact on practice.

The research itself is an extraordinary success story. Field experiments comparing experimental and control groups using different teaching methods are relatively rare in educational research. Yet for a recent review (Slavin, 1995) I was able to locate 99 experimental studies of cooperative learning in elementary and secondary schools that met high methodological standards, including a duration requirement of at least four weeks. Further, the research has been remarkably consistent in showing the benefits of cooperative learning on a broad range of student outcomes, including achievement.

The problem with this success story, however, is that the cooperative learning methods most often used in classrooms are not those that the research has found to be effective. Teachers generally use quite informal forms of cooperative learning, in which students may be assigned common tasks or projects with a single product, or may simply be allowed to sit together and help each other as needed. The problem with these structures is fairly obvious. Often, one group member can do all the work for the group. In some project groups, for example, some members do most of the thinking, while other members cut and paste, color, or type—and may even be *assigned* such nonthinking tasks by the teacher. Sometimes low-status members whom other members feel have little to contribute to the group are ignored or shut out of group activities or discussions. These forms of so-called "cooperative learning" fail to meet the criteria that have been established and validated, through considerable research, as necessary for the effectiveness of cooperative learning.

Since the 1970s, researchers have generally agreed that for cooperative learning to be effective, especially in promoting student achievement, two elements must be in place so that cooperative learning does not degenerate into one or a few students doing the work for other students.

One element is *group goals*. Group goals mean that recognition is provided for, small rewards are given for, or a small proportion of students' grades are based on, the performance of the entire group.

The second element is *individual accountability*. Individual accountability means that the success of the group requires individual learning by all the members of the group. For example, effective methods may recognize groups based on the sum or average of individuals' scores on quizzes that are taken with group mates' help. Alternatively, effective methods can recognize a group's success based on the quality of a group report or book to which each group member contributes a (signed) chapter or distinct portion. The goal here is to motivate students to be concerned about the learning of all the members of the group, and to make it impossible for the group to succeed unless all group members learn satisfactorily. For cooperative learning to be effective, the interaction within each group should focus on teaching and learning, discussing and debating, assessing and filling in gaps in understanding, and so forth. It should *not* consist of students sharing unexplained answers, students doing work for each other, or students simply carrying out make-work tasks that do not foster their learning. See Webb & Palincsar (1996), which reviews research on behaviors associated with achievement gain in cooperative learning.

My own research on cooperative learning has moved toward the development and evaluation of comprehensive school-based programs that build curriculum, instruction, school organization, and support elements around a cooperative learning base. I have had many disappointments observing the way cooperative learning is usually structured in classrooms. My experiences have led me to try to create cooperative learning approaches that are so well worked out and complete, from student materials to teachers manuals to professional development procedures, that teachers can use them with confidence and integrity on a consistent basis. I have come to believe that instructional reform must be tied to curriculum reform so that teachers will fully understand how instructional ideas like cooperative learning can play out in practice.

To give readers a picture of what the result might be, imagine an elementary school built around the notion that cooperative learning is a regular feature of the curriculum in all classrooms throughout the school year. As part of this notion, students, teachers, administrators, and community groups are all committed to working *cooperatively* to make the school a better place for working and learning. Here is a brief list of the major components of the school's operation that follow from this commitment, with some examples of what each might involve (see Slavin, 1987).

1. *Cooperative learning in the classroom.* On any school day, cooperative learning methods can be observed in most classrooms and in all or most of the basic subjects. Learning is based more on cooperation among students than on competition between them.

2. *Integration of special education and remedial services with the regular program.* Special education and regular teachers team-teach on a regular basis. Students with handicaps are integrated with nonhandicapped students in cooperative learning teams.

3. *Peer coaching.* Teachers learn new cooperative learning methods together. Experienced teachers get release time to visit one another's classes and give assistance and exchange ideas when teachers implement new methods.

4. *Cooperative planning.* Teachers plan goals and strategies together and prepare common libraries of instructional materials. Teachers make joint decisions about cooperative learning activities that involve more than one class.

5. *Building-level steering committees.* Teachers and administrators work together through a steering committee to determine the direction that the school takes. Parents and other staff are represented on the committee.

6. *Cooperation with parents and community members.* The school supports the notion that children's school success is everyone's responsibility. Parental and community participation in school is SOP (standard operating procedure).

This set of practices was the basis for what we called the Cooperative Elementary School, which we successfully evaluated in the mid-1980s (Stevens & Slavin, 1995). They were then incorporated into our Success for All program, which as of the fall of 1997 will be in use in more than 700 elementary schools serving 350,000 children (see Slavin, Madden, Dolan, & Wasik, 1996, for more details). Research on Success for All finds substantial positive effects on student achievement.

In closing, let me return to cooperative learning as it exists in most schools today. Despite the lack of correspondence between the forms of cooperative learning found to be effective in research and the forms used in most classrooms, this has still been an exciting and fruitful area of research that has had an enormous impact on practice, and that will undoubtedly continue to do so for many years. If nothing else, kids love to work together, and it's great to be involved in research on something that makes so many kids (and teachers) so happy!

References

Puma, M. J., Jones, C. C., Rock, D., & Fernandez, R. (1993). *Prospects: The congressionally mandated study of educational growth and opportunity.* Interim Report. Bethesda, MD: Abt Associates.

Slavin, R. E. (1987). Cooperative learning and the cooperative school. *Educational Leadership, 45* (3), 7–13.

Slavin, R. E. (1995). *Cooperative learning: Theory, research, and practice* (2nd ed.). Boston: Allyn & Bacon.

Slavin, R. E., Madden, N. A., Dolan, L. J., & Wasik, B. A. (1996). Every child, every school: Success for All. Thousand Oaks, CA: Corwin.

Stevens, R. J., & Slavin, R. E. (1995). The Cooperative Elementary School: Effects on students' achievement, attitudes, and social relations. *American Educational Research Journal, 32,* 321–351.

Webb, N. M., & Palincsar, A. S. (1996). Group processes in the classroom. In D. C. Berliner & R. C. Calfee (Eds.), *Handbook of educational psychology* (pp. 841–873). New York: Simon & Schuster Macmillan.

COOPERATIVE LEARNING

Cooperative learning refers to instructional methods in which students of all levels of performance work together in small groups, usually toward a group goal. The many cooperative learning methods differ considerably from one another. The most extensively researched are described.

Slavin, R. (1992). Cooperative learning. In M. C. Alkin (Ed.), *Encyclopedia of educational research,* American Educational Research Association (pp. 235–238). New York: Macmillan. Reprinted with permission of Macmillan Library Reference USA, a Simon & Schuster Macmillan Company, from *Encyclopedia of Educational Research,* Sixth Edn., Marvin C. Alkin, Editor in Chief, Vol. 1, pp. 235–238. Copyright © 1992 by the American Educational Research Association.

COOPERATIVE LEARNING METHODS

Student Teams-Achievement Divisions (STAD). In STAD (Slavin, 1986), students are assigned to four-member learning teams that are mixed in performance level, gender, and ethnicity. The teacher presents a lesson, and then students work within their teams to make sure that all team members have mastered the lesson. Finally, all students take individual quizzes on the material, at which time they may not help one another.

Students' quiz scores are compared to their own past averages, and points based on the degree to which students can meet or exceed their own earlier performance are awarded. These points are then summed to form team scores, and teams that meet certain criteria earn certificates or other rewards. The whole cycle of activities—from teacher presentation to team practice to quiz—usually takes 3–5 class periods.

The STAD method has been used in most subjects, from mathematics to language arts to social studies, and has been used from Grade 2 through college. It is most appropriate for teaching well-defined objectives with single right answers, such as mathematical computations and applications, language usage and mechanics, geography and map skills, and science facts and concepts.

Teams-Games-Tournament (TGT). The TGT method (DeVries & Slavin, 1978; Slavin, 1986) uses the same teacher presentations and team work as in STAD but replaces the quizzes with weekly tournaments, in which students compete with members of other teams to contribute points to their team scores. Students compete at three-person-*tournament tables* against others with similar past records in mathematics. A *bumping* procedure keeps the competition fair by changing assignments to tournament tables each week based on student performance. As in STAD, high-performing teams earn certificates or other forms of team rewards.

Team Assisted Individualization (TAI). The TAI method (Slavin, 1985a; Slavin, Leavey, & Madden, 1986) shares with STAD and TGT the use of four-member, mixed ability learning teams and certificates for high-performing teams. But whereas STAD and TGT use a single pace of instruction for the class, TAI combines cooperative learning with individualized instruction. The TAI method is designed specifically to teach mathematics to students in Grades 3–6 (or older students not ready for a full algebra course).

In TAI, students enter an individualized sequence according to a placement test and then proceed at their own rates. In general, team members work on different units. Teammates check each others' work against answer sheets and help each other with any problems. Final unit tests are taken without teammate help and are scored by student monitors. Each week, teachers total the number of units completed by all team members and give certificates or other team rewards to teams that exceed a criterion score based on the number of final tests passed, with extra points for perfect papers and completed homework.

Cooperative Integrated Reading and Composition (CIRC). In CIRC (Stevens, Madden, Slavin, & Farnish, 1987), teachers use basal readers and reading groups, much as in traditional reading programs. However, students are assigned to teams composed of pairs of students from two different reading groups. While the teacher is working with one reading group, students in the other groups are working in their pairs on a series of cognitively engaging activities, including reading to one another, making predictions about how narrative stories come out, summarizing stories to one another, writing responses to stories, and practicing spelling, decoding, and vocabulary. Students work in teams to master main idea and other comprehension skills. During language arts periods, students write drafts, revise and edit one another's work, and prepare for "publication" of team books.

Jigsaw. In the original jigsaw method (Aronson, Blaney, Stephan, Sikes, & Snapp, 1978), students are assigned to six-member teams to work on academic material that has been broken into sections. For example, a biography might be later divided into early life, first accomplishments, major setbacks, later life, and impact on history. Each team member reads a section. Next, members of different teams who have studied the same sections meet in "expert groups" to discuss their sections. Then the students return to their teams and take turns teaching their teammates about their sections. Because the only way that students can learn sections other than their own is to listen carefully to their teammates, they are motivated to support and show interest in one another's work. Several modifications of Jigsaw have also been designed (Slavin, 1986; Kagan, 1989).

Learning Together. The learning together model of cooperative learning (Johnson & Johnson, 1987) was developed at the University of Minnesota. The methods that they researched involve students working in four- or five-member heterogeneous groups on assignment sheets. The groups hand in a single sheet, and receive praise and rewards based on the group product.

Group Investigation. Developed at the University of Tel-Aviv (Sharan & Shachar, 1988), group investigation is a general classroom organization plan in which students work in small groups using cooperative inquiry, group discussion, and cooperative planning and projects. Students form their own two- to six-member groups. After choosing subtopics from a unit being studied by the entire class, the groups further break their subtopics into individual tasks and carry out the activities necessary to prepare group reports. Each group then makes a presentation or display to communicate its findings to the entire class.

RESEARCH ON COOPERATIVE LEARNING

More than 70 high-quality studies have evaluated various cooperative learning methods over periods of at least 4 weeks in regular elementary and secondary schools; 60 of these have measured effects on student achievement (Slavin, 1990). These studies compared effects of cooperative learning to those of traditionally taught control groups on measures of the same objectives pursued in all classes. Teachers and classes were randomly assigned to cooperative or control conditions, or they were matched on pretest achievement level and other factors.

Academic Achievement. Overall—of 68 experimental–control comparison studies of the achievement effects of cooperative learning in 60 different studies—42 (62%) found significantly greater achievement in cooperative than in control classes.[a] Twenty-three (34%) found no differences, and in only three studies did a control group outperform the experimental group. However, the effects of cooperative learning vary considerably according to the particular methods used. Two elements must be present if cooperative learning is to be effective: group goals and individual accountability (Davidson, 1985; Newmann & Thompson, 1987; Slavin, 1990). That is, groups must be working to achieve some goal or earn rewards or recognition, and the success of the group must depend on the individual learning of every group member. In studies of methods of this kind (e.g., STAD, TGT, TAI, and CIRC), effects on achievement have been consistently positive; 32 of 40 such studies (80%) found significantly positive achievement effects with a median effect size of +.30 (Slavin, 1990).[b] In contrast, only 10 of 28 studies (36%) lacking group goals and individual accountability found positive effects on student achievement, and only 3 studies (11%) found effects favoring control groups, with a median effect size of only +.06.

Research on behaviors within groups that contribute to learning gains has found that students who provide and receive elaborated explanations are those who gain the most from the activities (Webb, 1985). Successful forms of cooperative learning have

---

a. The word "significantly" refers to statistical significance (see Chapter 6). A research study typically investigates a small sample that is intended to represent a much larger population. If a statistically significant difference is found between the experimental and control groups, one can conclude with some confidence that a similar difference will be found in the population represented by the sample.

b. A median effect size of +.30 means that half the 40 studies found an effect size of +.30 or lower. In other words, an effect size of +.30 corresponds to the 50th percentile in the distribution of effect sizes.

generally been equally effective with high-, average-, and low-achieving students (Slavin, 1990).

Intergroup Relations. Social scientists have long advocated interethnic cooperation as a means of ensuring positive intergroup relations in desegregated settings. The famous social science statement submitted as part of the *Brown v. Board of Education* school desegregation decision strongly emphasized that positive intergroup relations would rise from school desegregation if and only if students were involved in cooperative equal-status interaction sanctioned by the school (Slavin, 1985b, 1990). Research has borne out this expectation. Positive effects on intergroup relations have been found for the STAD, TGT, TAI, jigsaw, learning together, and group investigation models (Slavin, 1985b). Two of these studies, one on STAD and one on jigsaw II included follow-ups of intergroup friendships several months after the end of the studies. Both found that students who had been in cooperative learning classes still named significantly more friends outside their own ethnic groups than did students who had been in control classes. Two studies of the group investigation method found that students' improved attitudes and behaviors toward classmates of different ethnic backgrounds extended to classmates who had never been in the same groups.

Mainstreaming. The research on cooperative learning and mainstreaming has focused on the academically handicapped child. In one study, STAD was used to attempt to integrate students performing two years or more below the level of their peers into the social structure of the classroom. The use of STAD significantly reduced the degree to which the normal-progress students rejected their mainstreamed classmates and increased the academic achievement and self-esteem of all students—mainstreamed and normal progress. Similar effects have been found for TAI, and other research using cooperative teams has also shown significant improvements in relationships between mainstreamed academically handicapped students and their normal-progress peers (see Madden & Slavin, 1983).

Self-Esteem. Several researchers working on cooperative learning techniques found that use of teams increases students' self-esteem. Students in cooperative learning classes have more positive feelings about themselves than do students in traditional classes. These improvements in self-esteem have been found for TGT, STAD, and jigsaw, for the three methods combined, and for TAI (Slavin, 1990).

Other Outcomes. In addition to effects on achievement, positive intergroup relations, greater acceptance of mainstreamed students, and self-esteem effects of cooperative learning have been found on a variety of other important educational outcomes. These effects include liking of school, development of peer norms in favor of doing well academically, feelings of individual control over the student's own fate in school, time on task, and cooperativeness and altruism (Slavin, 1990).

Current Research. Research on cooperative learning is proceeding in several directions. One involves research on schoolwide applications of cooperative learning principles, including peer coaching, mainstreaming, and teacher collaboration, as well as widespread use of cooperative learning methods (Madden, Slavin, Karweit, & Livermon, 1989; Slavin, 1987). Another involves continuing research on the cognitive and motivational bases for the achievement effects of cooperative learning (Dansereau, 1988). Applications of cooperative learning to the education of Hispanic and Native American children are being studied. Some of the many topics in need of further study include methods for training, maintenance, and institutionalization of cooperative learning in schools and why cooperative learning increases student achievement and critical elements contributing to this effect. Further applications of cooperative learning to complex problem solving and to senior high schools are needed.

CONCLUSION

The positive effects of cooperative learning methods on a variety of student outcomes are not found in every study or for every method. The overall conclusion to be drawn from this research, however, is that when the classroom is structured to allow students to work cooperatively on learning tasks, students benefit academically as well as socially.

Robert E. Slavin

See also Deinstitutionalization and Mainstreaming; Exceptional Children; Grouping Students for Instruction; Minorities, Education of; Peer and Cross-Age Tutoring; School Desegregation.

References

Aronson, E., Blaney, N., Stephan, C., Sikes, J., & Snapp, M. (1978). *The jigsaw classroom.* Beverly Hills, CA: Sage.

Dansereau, D. (1988). Cooperative learning strategies. In C. E. Weinstein, E. T. Goetz, & P. A. Alexander (Eds.), *Learning and study strategies: Issues in assessment, instruction, and evaluation* (pp. 103–120). New York: Academic Press.

Davidson, N. (1985). Small-group learning and teaching in mathematics: A selective review of the research. In R. E. Slavin, S. Sharan, R. Hertz-Lazarowitz, C. Webb, & R. Schmuck (Eds.), *Learning to cooperate, cooperating to learn* (pp. 211–230). New York: Plenum.

DeVries, D. L., & Slavin, R. E. (1978). Teams-Games-Tournament (TGT): Review of ten classroom experiments. *Journal of Research and Development in Education, 12,* 28–38.

Johnson, D. W., & Johnson, R. T. (1987). *Learning together and alone* (2nd ed.). Englewood Cliffs, NJ: Prentice-Hall.

Kagan, S. (1989). *Cooperative learning resources for teachers.* San Juan Capistrano, CA: Resources for Teachers.

Madden, N. A., & Slavin, R. E. (1983). Mainstreaming students with mild academic handicaps: Academic and social outcomes. *Review of Educational Research, 53,* 519–569.

Madden, N. A., Slavin, R. E., Karweit, N. L., & Livermon. B. J. (1989). Restructuring the urban elementary school. *Educational Leadership, 46*(5), 14–18.

Newmann, F. M., & Thompson, J. (1987). *Effects of cooperative learning on achievement in secondary schools: A summary of research.* Madison: University of Wisconsin, National Center on Effective Secondary Schools.

Sharan, S., & Shachar, C. (1988). *Language and learning in the cooperative classroom.* New York: Springer-Verlag.

Slavin, R. E. (1985a). Team Assisted Individualization. In R. E. Slavin, S. Sharan, S. Kagan, R. Hertz-Lazarowitz, C. Webb, & R. Schmuck (Eds.), *Learning to cooperate, cooperating to learn* (pp. 77–209). New York: Plenum.

Slavin, R. E. (1985b). Cooperative learning: Applying contact theory in desegregated schools. *Journal of Social Issues, 41,* 45–62.

Slavin, R. E. (1986). *Using student team learning* (3rd ed.). Baltimore: The Johns Hopkins University, Center for Research on Elementary and Middle Schools.

Slavin, R. E. (1987). Cooperative learning and the cooperative school. *Educational Leadership, 45*(3), 7–13.

Slavin, R. E. (1990). *Cooperative learning: Theory, research, and practice.* Englewood Cliffs, NJ: Prentice-Hall.

Slavin, R. E., Leavey, M. B., & Madden, N. A. (1986). *Team Accelerated Instruction—Mathematics.* Watertown, MA: Charlesbridge.

Stevens, R. J., Madden, N. A., Slavin, R. E., & Farnish, A. M. (1987). Cooperative Integrated Reading and Composition: Two field experiments. *Reading Research Quarterly, 22,* 433–454.

Webb, N. (1985). Student interaction and learning in small groups: A research summary. In R. E. Slavin, S. Sharan, S. Kagan, R. Hertz-Lazarowitz, C. Webb, & R. Schmuck (Eds.), *Learning to cooperate, cooperating to learn* (pp. 148–172). New York: Plenum.

PART III
QUANTITATIVE RESEARCH IN EDUCATION

To apply relevant research findings to your practice, you need a basic understanding of quantitative research methods. Therefore, Part III shows you how quantitative researchers design, analyze, and report an educational research study. It also introduces you to the major quantitative research designs used in educational research.

Chapter 6 provides an introduction to the statistical techniques that researchers use to describe educational phenomena, to determine the validity and reliability of their research measures, and to test whether their findings generalize to a population of interest.

Chapter 7 and all the remaining chapters of the book include a reprinted research article to illustrate the research design described in that chapter. Chapter 7 shows how researchers conduct investigations that yield precise quantitative descriptions of educational phenomena. It also explains causal-comparative research, which involves comparing two or more groups that naturally differ in order to explore possible cause-and-effect relationships among phenomena.

Correlational research, the subject of Chapter 8, also has the purpose of exploring possible cause-and-effect relationships, but it involves different statistical techniques than those used in causal-comparative research.

In Chapter 9 we discuss various types of experimental research. Unlike causal-comparative and correlational research, experimental research involves the manipulation of variables to determine their effects on other variables. This chapter contains two reprinted research articles.

CHAPTER 5

READING REPORTS OF QUANTITATIVE RESEARCH STUDIES

Bill Calvecchia is a student counselor who has worked in schools and colleges. He has been asked to do an extensive review of the literature on attention-deficit disorders in order to receive credit toward renewal of his counseling license. Most of his previous reading in the counseling field has been in textbooks and practitioner journals. Understandably, he is anxious about his ability to read and evaluate studies about attention-deficit disorders published in research journals. These journal articles have a format that he has not seen previously, and they include unfamiliar terminology and statistics.

Bill's apprehension about reading research articles will be reduced greatly once he learns how these articles are organized and the meaning of the technical terms commonly used in them. In this chapter, we explain the organization of quantitative research reports and their technical features. We also provide criteria and questions for evaluating the soundness of the studies they report.

OBJECTIVES

After studying this chapter, you will be able to

1. describe how a typical report of a quantitative research study is organized.
2. explain the purpose served by constructs, variables, and hypotheses in a quantitative research study.
3. explain how a researcher's biases might adversely affect the literature review and findings in a quantitative research study.
4. describe the characteristics of simple random sampling and stratified random sampling, and their advantage over nonrandom sampling.
5. explain how an analysis of the target population, accessible population, and research sample is used in judging the population validity of findings obtained from a nonrandom sample.
6. describe the distinguishing features of paper-and-pencil tests and scales, questionnaires, interviews, and direct observation in quantitative research.
7. explain the meaning of test validity, and distinguish between the four types of test validity.
8. explain the meaning of test reliability, and distinguish between the three types of test reliability.
9. describe the types of information and interpretation that are included in the research-design section, results section, and discussion section of a quantitative research study.

KEY TERMS

accessible population
concurrent validity
constant
construct
construct validity
content validity
correlation coefficient
direct observation
face validity
high-inference variable
hypothesis
inter-observer reliability

inter-rater reliability
interview
item consistency
low-inference variable
parameter
performance measure
population validity
predictive validity
proportional random
  sampling
questionnaire
reliability

sampling error
scale
simple random sampling
stratified random sampling
target population
test-retest reliability
test stability
validity
variable
volunteer sample

ORGANIZATION OF A QUANTITATIVE RESEARCH REPORT

In Chapter 1, we explained that quantitative research and qualitative research are two different approaches to scientific inquiry in education. Among the primary characteristics of quantitative research are an epistemological belief in an objective reality, the analysis of reality into measurable variables, the study of samples that represent a defined population, and a reliance on statistical methods to analyze data.

These characteristics of quantitative research affect the way in which researchers write their research reports. Quantitative research reports generally are much more impersonal and objective than reports of qualitative research. You will read several quantitative research reports—reprinted articles from research journals—in this part of the book. This initial chapter shows you how to read these reports and, in the process, develops your understanding of the main procedures of quantitative research.

Most reports of quantitative research studies are organized similarly. This is because researchers typically follow the style guidelines in the *Publication Manual of the American Psychological Association* (1994). These guidelines specify the sections of a quantitative research report and the order in which they are to be presented, as follows:

> Abstract
> Introduction
> Methods
>   Sampling Procedures
>   Measures (or Materials)
>   Research Design and Procedures
> Results
> Discussion

Each of these sections is explained in this chapter.

Of course, it is not sufficient to be able to read a research report with good comprehension. You also need to be able to evaluate the soundness of the study that it reports. Therefore, as we explain the parts of a research study that are reported in each section of the report, we also will explain how to judge whether each part is sound or flawed. To make these judgments, it is helpful to ask yourself questions as you read each section of the report. A set of questions for this purpose is presented in list form in Appendix 4. You can use this list to guide your evaluation of any quantitative research study.

ABSTRACT AND INTRODUCTORY SECTION

A research report begins with an abstract, which is a brief summary (typically about 100 words) of the contents of the report. Reading the abstract first will give you an idea of the purpose of the study, the method of inquiry that was used, and the major findings. With this information in mind, reading the full report will be substantially easier.

The introductory section of a quantitative research report explains the purpose of the study, the relevant variables, and the specific hypotheses, questions, and objectives that guided the study. In addition, the introductory section includes a review of previous research findings and other information that is relevant to the study. You also may be able to learn something about the researchers' qualifications. These different types of information are explained in the following sections.

Constructs and Variables

The introductory section of a research report should identify and describe each of the concepts that was studied. Examples of the concepts studied in educational research are learning style, aptitude, academic achievement, intrinsic motivation, top-down management, and implicit curriculum. Researchers usually refer to these concepts as constructs or variables.

A construct is a structure or process that is inferred from observed phenomena. For example, social scientists have observed that some individuals tend to speak about themselves in consistent ways, such as, "I'm very good at sports," "I am attractive," "I don't like to draw attention to myself." The consistency of these self-perceptions over time and situations led the social scientists to infer that individuals have a psychological structure that they called *self-concept*. Self-concept, then, is a construct inferred from observed behavior; it cannot be observed directly. Other related constructs have been inferred as well, such as positive self-concept, negative self-concept, and self-esteem. Some constructs are tied to a particular theory. For example, logical operations and sensorimotor intelligence are integral constructs in Piaget's theory of human development.

Quantitative researchers generally use the term *variable* rather than *construct*. A variable is a quantitative expression of a construct. For example, we can think of self-concept as ranging from highly negative to neutral to highly positive. In thinking this way, we are viewing self-concept as a variable. Variables usually are measured in terms of scores on a measure, such as an achievement test or attitude scale. Variables also can take the form of categories, for example, tall versus short, public versus private schools, or authoritarian versus democratic versus laissez-faire styles of leadership.

If a construct is part of the design of a research study but does not vary, it is called a *constant*. For example, suppose an experiment compares the effectiveness of teaching method A and teaching method B for community college students. The educational level of the students (that is, community college) is a constant because no other educational level is included in the research design. Suppose, however, that the experiment compares the effectiveness of the two teaching methods to see which is most effective for community college students and which is most effective for high school students. In this experiment, educational level is a variable because it takes on two values: community college and high school.

In reviewing a research report, you should examine carefully how each of the variables is defined and measured. If the definitions are unclear or nonexistent, the significance of the research results is cast into doubt. Similar doubts are created if the definitions of the variables are inconsistent with the methods used to measure them.

Research Hypotheses, Questions, and Objectives

A hypothesis in a research study is a speculation—an educated guess—about how two or more variables are related to each other. For example, researchers might hypothesize that birth order of children is related to their level of leadership in school activities, or that method A is more effective than method B for promoting the academic achievement of students involved in distance education. After formulating a hypothesis, researchers collect data to test it and then examine the data to decide whether or not to reject it.

Hypotheses usually are formulated on the basis of theory and previous research findings. If theory or previous research do not provide an adequate basis for formulating specific hypotheses, however, researchers will instead formulate questions or objectives to guide their investigation. For example, suppose a research team wondered about the effect of higher-cognitive questions on students' learning in social studies classes, but were not prepared to make an educated guess (i.e., a hypothesis) about what that effect might be. In this case they could pose a question such as "What is the effect of higher-cognitive questions on students' learning in social studies classes?" Or they could state an objective: "The objective of this study is to determine whether higher-cognitive questions improve students' learning in social studies classes."

The choice of research questions or objectives is generally a matter of personal preference. Both formats guide the study design, but neither expresses a prediction about what the research findings will show. By contrast, a research hypothesis makes a specific prediction before data are collected. If the researchers are willing to make predictions about some of the phenomena they are studying but are unwilling to make predictions about other phenomena, they will often specify both hypotheses and questions (or objectives).

Formulating hypotheses, questions, or objectives is one of the first steps researchers take in planning a quantitative research study. These formulations guide the rest of the planning process, data collection, and data analysis. Therefore, you should look for hypotheses, questions, or objectives in the introductory section of the report. If none are present, you have reason to be concerned about the quality of the study and the validity of its findings. You also should be concerned if you find that hypotheses, questions, or objectives are stated, but the research design and statistical analyses do not deal with them directly.

The variables and their relationship to each other should be made explicit in the hypotheses, questions, or objectives. For example, consider this hypothesis: "There is a positive relationship between peer-group acceptance and attitude toward school among sixth-grade boys." This is a good hypothesis because the two variables (peer-group acceptance and attitude toward school) are made explicit. Furthermore, the hypothesized relationship between the two variables is made explicit: The researcher expects a positive relationship, meaning that boys who have greater peer-group acceptance will have better attitudes toward school, and boys who have less peer-group acceptance will have more negative attitudes.

This example can be contrasted with the following hypothesis: "The lecture method will have a different effect than the discussion method on students' performance on essay tests." Only one of the variables in this example is explicit: teaching method (lecture versus discussion). The other apparent variable, essay test performance, is actually a measure, but the variable being measured is not identified. Furthermore, the predicted effects of the teaching methods on essay test performance are not made explicit.

If the researchers have done a good review of the literature, they should be able to provide a good rationale for each of their hypotheses, questions, or objectives. This rationale should be made explicit. For example, Randall Eberts and Joe Stone (1988) did a research study, the objective of which is included in the following statement: "Using nationally representative data . . . we tested the major conclusions drawn from case studies regarding principal effectiveness" (p. 291). This objective developed from their observation that published case studies showed that school principals who displayed certain behaviors (e.g., setting clear priorities and organizing and participating in staff development programs) had a positive effect on the learning of students in their school. However, Eberts and Stone noted a weakness in the case studies:

> Case studies have many advantages in generating hypotheses, in evaluating the implementation of new techniques, and in providing detailed explanations and backgrounds for observed phenomena, but they are not necessarily representative and often suffer from weak controls for individual student and teacher attributes. (p. 291)

These researchers' rationale for their objective, then, was that nationally representative data would provide a stronger test of the principals' influence on student achievement than that provided by case studies.

Hypotheses, questions, and objectives that lack a rationale pose a problem for interpretation. For example, suppose a study is done to identify teachers' testing practices. If no rationale for this objective is provided, the readers have no basis for understanding why particular testing practices were studied or whether testing practices identified as important in previous research were ignored in this study. Also, the readers, as well as the researchers who conducted the study, will find it difficult to judge whether the observed testing practices are desirable or undesirable.

Literature Review

If you are doing a comprehensive review of the research literature on a particular problem, you will soon notice that a few key studies are cited in most research reports. If these key studies are not reviewed in a particular research report, it might indicate that the researchers were careless in reviewing the literature. If important studies that disagree with the researchers' findings are omitted, bias may be involved.

Most research journals allow researchers limited space for reviewing previous research, so you should not expect detailed reviews. However, the five to ten most relevant previous studies should be cited, if only briefly. Research reports not appearing in journals, such as doctoral dissertations, usually provide much more detailed reviews because they are not subject to space limitations.

The Researchers' Qualifications

Because quantitative researchers strive to be objective, they generally reveal little or nothing about themselves in their reports. Their institutional affiliation typically is listed beneath their name at the start of the report, and there may be a note indicating their title. The literature review may refer to reports of other studies or scholarly work that they have written.

Knowledge about the researchers may provide some indication of whether researcher bias affected their study. For example, some research studies involve experimental tests of the effectiveness of an educational program or method. If we know that the researchers have a stake in the program or method (which is often the case), we need to be concerned that the design of the experiment was not slanted in favor of it.

Whenever researchers have reason for wanting their research to support a particular viewpoint, the likelihood of bias is greatly increased. Occasionally, the bias becomes so great that the researchers slant their findings or even structure their research design to produce a predetermined result. A famous case of emotional involvement is the research into intelligence based on studies of twins that was conducted by Sir Cyril Burt. It appears that Burt was so intent on proving that intelligence is inherited that he slanted, or even fabricated, the research data to support his hypothesis (Evans, 1976).

METHODS SECTION: SAMPLING PROCEDURES

In conducting a study, researchers ideally would investigate all the individuals to whom they wish to generalize their findings. These individuals constitute a population, meaning that they make up the entire group of individuals having the characteristics that interest the researchers. Because of the great expense involved in studying most populations of interest, researchers are limited to studying a sample of individuals who represent that population.

For example, suppose the researchers wish to study the effect of a new reading program on the reading comprehension of visually impaired children in U.S. elementary schools. Because the researchers cannot try out the new reading program with the entire population, they must select a sample from this population. The researchers now have solved the problem of making the study feasible to conduct, but they have created a different problem in the process, namely, whether they can generalize their findings from this limited sample to the entire population. As we explain below, researchers can use various sampling procedures to make their findings more generalizable.

Samples very rarely will have the exact same characteristics as the populations from which they are drawn. For example, suppose that you randomly select three male students from each class in a large high school and measure their height. Your sampling procedure is random, because each member of the population has an equal and independent chance of being included in the sample. Nonetheless, it is unlikely that the mean height of this sample would be identical to the mean height of all male students in the school (defined to be the population in this example). The difference between the sample's mean height and the population's mean height is a random sampling error. In technical terms, a sampling error is the difference between a statistic (e.g., a mean score) for a sample and the same statistic for the population. (The technical term to describe a statistic for the population is *parameter*.)

Sampling errors are likely to occur even when the sample is randomly drawn from the population. The size of the errors tends to become smaller as we select a larger random sample. For this reason, we can be more confident in generalizing results from studies with a large random sample than studies with a small random sample. The likelihood of sampling errors for a sample of a given size can be estimated by using a mathematical procedure.

Despite the advantages of a random sample, researchers often must study nonrandom samples. Sampling errors in nonrandom samples cannot be estimated by mathematical procedures. Therefore, generalizations about populations based on nonrandom samples need to be viewed as tentative.

Types of Sampling

Researchers have developed various techniques for drawing random samples from a defined population. Two of the most common techniques are simple random sampling and stratified random sampling.

In simple random sampling, all the individuals in the defined population have an equal and independent chance of being selected as a member of the sample. By *independent*, we mean that the selection of one individual does not affect in any way the chances of selection of any other individual. A simple random sample can be selected by assigning a number to each individual in the population and using a computer-based random number generator, or a hard-copy table of random numbers, to select the needed number of individuals.

Simple random sampling is most feasible in survey research. For example, if researchers wish to know the opinion of psychologists on some educational issue, they can obtain a directory of a national organization for psychologists, such as the American Psychological Association. They then can draw a simple random sample of psychologists from the directory list, and request the sample to complete a mailed questionnaire or phone interview. Not everyone in the sample may agree to participate, however. In this case, the resulting sample of participants is no longer a random sample. If the response rate to the question-naire or phone interview is below 70 percent, you should be concerned about the randomness of the sample.

Stratified random sampling is a procedure for ensuring that individuals in the population who have certain characteristics are represented in the sample. By constructing the sample in this manner, the researchers ensure that they will study these characteristics and their relationship to other variables. For example, suppose researchers are interested in whether boys and girls from three different home environments (single parent, mother; single parent, father; both parents together) have different attitudes toward mathematics. If the researchers draw a simple random sample from a school district's list of students, there is a chance that they will get few or no students in one of these six classifications: (1) boys with single parent, mother; (2) girls with single parent, mother; (3) boys with single parent, father; (4) girls with single parent, father; (5) boys with both parents together; and (6) girls with both parents together.

To ensure that all six groups are represented in the sample, the researchers can use stratified random sampling. They would consider each group (called *strata* in sampling terminology) as a separate population. They then would draw a random sample of a given size from each group, thereby ensuring that each population is represented adequately in the sample. Another option is to draw random samples of different sizes (but each size being an adequate number) so that the proportion of students in each group in the sample is the same as their proportion in the population. This procedure is called *proportional random sampling*.

Volunteer Samples

Educational research usually requires face-to-face interaction with individuals, as when the researcher needs to administer tests under standardized conditions or to try out a new instructional method. However, it is expensive to define a population that covers an extensive geographical area, to randomly select a sample from that population, and then travel to the individuals in the sample in order to collect the necessary data. Therefore, researchers typically work with nonrandom samples.

Sampling is further complicated by the fact that researchers have the legal and ethical requirement to obtain informed consent from individuals or their legal guardians before involving them in a research project. An individual can refuse to participate for any reason. As a result, nearly all educational research is conducted with nonrandom samples comprised of volunteers.

The main difficulty with volunteer samples is that systematic sampling errors can occur such that members of a sample have different characteristics from the population that the sample is intended to represent. If the sampling error is large, the sample is said to have low population validity. The term *population validity* refers to the degree to which the sample of individuals in the study is representative of the population from which it was selected.

Population validity is established by showing that the selected sample is similar to the accessible population, which is the immediate population from which the researchers drew their sample. The researchers also must demonstrate that the accessible population is similar to the target population, which is the population to which the researchers want to generalize or apply their research findings. For example, if researchers were interested in investigating career planning among high school seniors, the target population could be defined as all seniors in U.S. public and private high schools. This target population most likely would be too large from which to draw a sample. The researchers might then limit themselves to their local community—let's say, Denver, Colorado. In this case, Denver high school seniors would be the accessible population from which the sample would be drawn.

To establish population validity, the researchers must show how (1) the sample, (2) the accessible population (Denver high school seniors), and (3) the target population (all U.S. high school seniors) are similar on variables that are relevant to their research problem. For example, it seems reasonable to expect that career planning would vary by gender, socioeconomic status, and ethnicity. Therefore, the researchers should determine the extent to which their sample, the accessible population, and the target population are similar on these variables. Evidence of similarity helps to establish the population validity of their study.

In making a critical evaluation of a research report, you should pay close attention to the accessible population and to the sample. It also is important to determine the degree to which students, teachers, or other groups in the research sample are similar to the groups in the local setting to whom you wish to apply the research findings. As the similarity between the research sample and the local group decreases, the research results are less likely to apply.

Comparison of the research sample with your local group is a difficult task for several reasons. First, researchers often include very little information in their reports about the sample and the accessible population from which it was drawn. Second, local educational organizations often can provide only limited information about the characteristics of the local group that is of interest to you. Third, it is difficult to decide which differences between the research sample and the local population would actually affect the applicability of the research findings.

Given these problems, the best test of population validity may be to try out the course of action suggested by the research findings and see how well they generalize to your local groups. This approach involves using action research, which we discuss in Chapter 15.

METHODS SECTION: MEASURES

Research results can only be as sound as the measures used to obtain them. For this reason, you should pay special attention to the description of the measures in a research report. This description hopefully will give you basic information about the measures: the constructs that they are intended to measure, scoring procedures, and their validity and reliability. If the measures are ones that have been commonly used in educational practice or research, you can obtain more information about them by examining the recommended readings listed at the end of this chapter or by searching a preliminary source (see Chapter 3 and Appendix 1).

Another way to learn about a measure used in a research study is to examine a copy of it. Some school systems and universities maintain collections of commonly used tests and the manuals that accompany them. Otherwise you may be able to order a copy from the publisher. In the case of a measure developed specifically for a research study, you can write the researchers to request a copy of the measure. They should be willing to send you a copy if you state a reasonable purpose for your request and if you provide assurances that you will maintain the confidentiality of the measure.

Types of Measures

Four types of measures are commonly used in quantitative research studies: (1) paper-and-pencil tests and scales; (2) questionnaires; (3) interviews; and (4) direct-observation. Each type is described in the following sections.

Paper-and-Pencil Tests and Scales. Tests measure an individual's knowledge, depth of understanding, or skill within a curriculum domain. They typically yield a total score, which is the number of items answered correctly. Scales measure an individual's attitudes, personality characteristics, emotional states, interests, values, and related factors. They typically yield a total score, which is the sum of the individual's responses to item scales. For example, a Likert-type scale item typically has five response options (e.g., 5 points for "strongly agree" and 1 point for "strongly disagree").

Paper-and-pencil measures can be contrasted with performance measures. An example of a performance measure is the driving test in which you drive a car while being evaluated by a state examiner. Performance measures typically must be individually administered. Paper-and-pencil measures are used much more frequently in educational research than performance measures because they generally are cheaper to administer and require less time. Also, because of the huge number and variety of paper-and-pencil measures, researchers usually can find at least one such measure for virtually any variable.

Paper-and-pencil tests and scales also have limitations. First, most of them require that the person being tested be able to read and write. Thus, individuals who are lacking in these abilities will be unable to show what they know or think about the variables measured by tests and scales. Another limitation of these measures is that they rely on self-report. This is not a serious problem when measuring academic achievement, but in attitude measurement, for example, individuals may wish to hide their true attitude in order to get a more socially acceptable score. The third limitation is that many tests and scales are group-administered. Thus, it is difficult for the researcher to determine the physical and mental state of the persons being assessed. If they happen to be ill, tired, or emotionally upset, they are likely to perform atypically on the measure.

Questionnaires.   Paper-and-pencil tests and scales usually measure one or two variables, such as knowledge of vocabulary or attitude toward school. In contrast, questionnaires typically measure many variables. For example, a questionnaire might ask respondents about the type of computer they use, the software programs that they use, the frequency of use of each program, their previous training in computers, and their intentions to expand their use of computers in the future. The response to each question may constitute a separate variable in the research study.

In evaluating the use of a questionnaire in a research study, you should consider the following questions.

1. *Was the questionnaire pretested?* It is impossible to predict how the items will be interpreted by respondents unless the researcher tries out the questionnaire and analyzes the responses of a small sample of individuals before starting the main study. Results of this pilot study should be used to refine the questionnaire and locate potential problems in the interpretation or analysis of the data. If a pilot study was done, you can have more confidence that the findings reported in the main study are valid.

2. *Did the questionnaire include any leading questions?* A copy of the questionnaire sometimes is included in the research report. You should check it carefully

for leading questions, which are questions framed in such a way that individuals are given hints about the kind of response that is expected. Results obtained from leading questions are likely to be biased, so they should be interpreted with caution.

3. *Were any psychologically threatening questions included in the questionnaire?* In constructing items, the researcher should avoid questions that may be psychologically threatening to the respondents. For example, a questionnaire sent to school principals concerning the morale of teachers at their schools would be threatening to some principals, because low morale suggests that they are failing in part of their job. Many individuals who receive a questionnaire containing threatening items will not return it. If they do return it, little confidence can be placed in the accuracy of their responses because of their ego involvement in the situation.

4. *Were the individuals who received the questionnaire likely to have the information requested?* Researchers inadvertently may send a questionnaire to a group of persons who do not have the desired information. For example, a researcher seeking data on school financial policies sent questionnaires to a large number of elementary school principals. Many of the questionnaires returned were incomplete and contained few specific facts of the sort that the researcher wanted. This problem occurred because the trend in recent years has been for superintendents and their staffs to handle most matters concerning school finance.

Interviews.   Unlike paper-and-pencil tests, scales, and questionnaires, interviews involve the collection of data through direct interaction between the researcher and the individuals being studied.

The main advantage of interviews is their adaptability. The well-trained interviewer can alter the interview situation at any time in order to obtain the fullest possible response from the individual. For example, if the individual makes an interesting remark, the interviewer can ask a follow-up question on the spot. Another advantage of interviews is that they elicit data of much greater depth than is possible with other measurement techniques. For example, most questionnaires tend to be shallow; that is, they fail to probe deeply enough to produce a true picture of the respondents' opinions and feelings.

The major disadvantage of interviews is that the direct interaction between researcher and interviewee makes it easy for subjectivity and bias to occur. The eagerness of the interviewee to please the interviewer, a vague antagonism that sometimes arises between interviewer and interviewee, and the tendency of interviewers to seek out answers that support their preconceived notions are a few of the factors that may contribute to biasing of interview data. As a result, the validity of findings based on the interview method is highly contingent on the interpersonal skills of the interviewers.

The following questions will help you evaluate research studies that use interviews to collect data.

1. *How well were the interviewers trained?* The level of training required for interviewers is directly related to the type of information being collected. Less

training is required in structured interviews, because the interviewer asks specific questions from an interview guide and does not deviate from these questions. More training is required in semistructured and unstructured interviews, because the interviewer does not employ a detailed interview guide but instead has a general plan and decides on the spot what questions and comments to use in order to lead the interviewee toward the interviewer's objectives. Information on the training of interviewers should be included in the research report.

2. *How was information recorded*? Audiotaping is the most accurate method of recording interview information. If interviewers take notes instead of audiotaping the interview, they may overlook important information or take biased notes.

3. *Were the interview procedures tried out before the study began*? Because interviewing tends to be highly subjective, the researcher must use many controls and safeguards to obtain reasonably objective and unbiased data. A careful pilot study is necessary to develop these controls and safeguards before data for the main study are collected. The pilot study should be described in the research report.

4. *Were leading questions asked*? As with questionnaires, leading questions can invalidate interview data.

If an interview was a primary measure in a research study, the report should include at least the main questions that were asked. You should study these questions for signs of bias.

Direct Observation.   Direct observation, as its name implies, involves collecting data while an individual is engaged in some form of behavior or while an event is unfolding. Standard observation forms generally are used for this purpose. If the forms are well developed, the variables listed on the forms will be carefully defined. Also, there will be evidence that the researchers' inferences from the observational data are valid and reliable.

Direct observation tends to yield more accurate data about particular variables than can be obtained from questionnaires or interviews. However, a disadvantage of direct observation is that it tends to be very time-consuming. Also, the observer tends to change the situation being observed, albeit unintentionally.

In evaluating the use of observational procedures in a research study, you should consider the following questions.

1. *Were high-inference or low-inference variables observed*? Observational variables differ in the amount of inference required by the observer. For example, an observer will need to use a greater degree of inference to decide how much enthusiasm a teacher is exhibiting during a lesson than to decide how many verbal praise statements the teacher made. Thus, the validity of the observer's data will be more of an issue if the observational variables are high-inference than if they are low-inference.

2. *Were observers trained to identify the variables to be observed*? The researcher should describe the kind and extent of training given to the observers, and whether they used a standard observation form or procedure.

3. *How long was the observation period*? The observation period should be sufficiently long to obtain a representative sample of the behaviors being studied. Otherwise the observation data will yield atypical results. The necessary period of observation will depend on such factors as the nature of the behaviors being observed, the circumstances under which the behavior occurs, and its frequency of occurrence.

4. *How conspicuous were the observers*? Observers ideally would be stationed behind a one-way screen, and their presence would not be known to the research participants. A few researchers are able to achieve these conditions, but, for ethical reasons, most need to be visible to the individuals being studied. Consequently, they are likely to have some impact on the persons being observed. This problem can be overcome to a certain extent if the observers do not record any observational data initially. In many situations, individuals—for example, students in a classroom—become accustomed to the observers after a while and engage in their customary behavior. It also helps if the observers remain as unobtrusive as possible. You should examine the research report to determine whether the researchers were sensitive to this problem in direct observation and took steps to minimize it.

Validity of Measures

The validity of tests and other measures refers to the "appropriateness, meaningfulness, and usefulness of the specific inferences made from test scores" (American Education Research Association et al., 1985). For example, if we administer a science achievement test to a group of students, each student earns a score on the test. We then might *infer* that this score represents how much each student has learned about science relative to other students. It is helpful to think about this inference as a "claim" that we make about the test scores.

Four types of evidence can be used to demonstrate the validity of test score inferences: (1) content-related evidence, (2) construct-related evidence, (3) predictive evidence, and (4) concurrent evidence of validity. Validity evidence should be studied carefully because the soundness of research results hinges on the validity of the measures used to generate them. Each of these four types of evidence is explained below.

Content Validity.   A test has content validity to the extent that its items represent the content that the test is designed to measure. For example, the XYZ Test of Algebra Achievement would have content validity if the researchers can demonstrate that it measures what students were taught in the algebra classes that the researchers are studying. Content validity is important primarily in achievement testing and various tests of skill and proficiency, such as occupational skill tests.

Content validity should not be confused with face validity, which is concerned with the degree to which the test *appears* to measure what it claims to measure. For example, we may examine the items of the XYZ Test of Algebra Achievement and conclude that the test has face validity because the items correspond to our view of what students typically are taught in an algebra course. By contrast, content validity is determined by systematically comparing the test content with the course content. This comparison may reveal, for example, that the XYZ Test of Algebra Achievement has high content validity for algebra courses taught in school district A and low content validity for courses taught in school district B.

Content validity is particularly important in research in which the effect of different teaching methods on students' learning is investigated. The test of learning should measure precisely the curriculum content that was taught by the method under investigation.

Construct Validity.   A test has construct validity to the extent that it can be shown to measure a particular hypothetical construct. As we explained earlier in the chapter, psychological concepts such as intelligence, anxiety, and creativity are considered hypothetical constructs because they are not directly observable, but rather are inferred on the basis of their observable effects on behavior.

To obtain evidence of construct validity, the test developer often starts by formulating hypotheses about the characteristics of persons who would obtain high scores on the measure as opposed to those who would obtain low scores. Suppose, for example, that the test developers publish a test that they claim is a measure of anxiety. What kind of evidence can they collect to support this claim? One approach might be to draw on the theory that anxiety causes an individual's performance to deteriorate. Assuming the theory is true, we would expect that high-anxious students' performance would deteriorate faster under conditions of stress than would low-anxious students' performance. Our reasoning would proceed to the next step, which is to predict that students who score high on the test that purportedly measures anxiety should demonstrate more deterioration of performance than students who score low on the test. If the results conform to this prediction, this constitutes evidence that the test indeed measures the hypothetical construct called anxiety. You should keep in mind, though, that if the results do not conform to prediction, it does not mean necessarily that the test is an invalid measure of anxiety. It may mean instead that the theory used to assess the test's construct validity is unsound.

A good measure of a hypothetical construct will have multiple sources of evidence to support its construct validity. Therefore, in the case of the anxiety measure, the test developers would seek additional ways to check its construct validity besides the method described above. For example, they might hypothesize that if the new test measures anxiety, it should correlate with already validated measures of anxiety. They could test this hypothesis by administering the new test and several validated measures of anxiety to a sample of individuals. If scores on the new test correlate well with scores on these measures, this finding provides additional evidence in support of its construct validity.

Predictive Validity.   A test has predictive validity if scores on the test predict individuals' subsequent performance on a criterion measure. For example, it may be that students' scores on the XYZ Test of Algebra Achievement predict well the grades they will earn in courses on geometry and calculus. If so, we can say that the XYZ Test of Algebra Achievement has good predictive validity for students' performance in these two courses.

Some research studies are designed for the specific purpose of investigating a test's predictive validity. (The research article reprinted in Chapter 8 reports a study of this type.) A sample of individuals takes the test at one point in time, and their performance on some criterion (e.g., level of success in an occupation) is measured at a subsequent point in time. The two sets of scores—test scores and criterion scores—are related to each other by a statistic called a *correlation coefficient* (see Chapter 8). The higher the value of the correlation coefficient, the better is the test's predictive validity.

Concurrent Validity.   A test has concurrent validity if it can be shown that individuals' scores on the test correlate with their scores on another test administered at the same time or within a short interval of time. Concurrent validity studies are often carried out in an effort to locate simple, easy-to-use tests that can be administered in place of complex, expensive tests. For example, suppose that research demonstrated that young children's scores on a brief, group-administered test correlate well with their scores on a lengthy, individually administered test of school readiness. We can conclude on the basis of this evidence that the brief test has good concurrent validity with the long test. This information would be of great help to early childhood educators because it means that the brief test can be administered as a substitute for the long test. The savings in time and money involved in testing would be substantial.

Concurrent validity and predictive validity are determined by similar procedures. The main difference is that, to determine concurrent validity, researchers calculate the correlation between individuals' scores on test A and their scores on test B, and both tests are administered within a short time of each other (typically a few days to a week). By contrast, predictive validity involves correlating individuals' scores on test A with their scores on test B (in this case, the criterion) when test B is administered substantially later (typically months or years later).

Reliability of Measures

A test or other measurement tool is reliable to the degree that it is free of measurement error. For example, if two testers score an individual's test and obtain different total scores, measurement error has occurred. Less obviously, suppose a student takes the same achievement test on two different days and obtains two different scores. These different results also constitute measurement error. They are not errors in the usual sense of the word, that is, mistakes resulting from students' lack of skill. Instead, they reflect shortcomings in the test's ability to accurately measure the students' performance.

It is difficult to develop a measure that is perfectly reliable, meaning that it is completely free of error, because a variety of factors can create error. Possible factors are differences in the skill of persons who administer the test or other measure, changes in testing conditions from one day to the next, temporary fluctuations in how individuals respond to the testing situation, and features of the test items that affect different individuals differently. It is virtually impossible to eliminate all these sources of error.

Tests and other measurement tools with very low reliability will produce large errors of measurement. These errors will obscure the effects of methods and programs, or the extent of a relationship between variables. This problem can be understood by considering the case of a completely unreliable test. After the test is administered, the resulting scores will consist entirely of measurement error, meaning that they are essentially random numbers. Random numbers obviously cannot reveal the true effects of educational programs or the true relationships between variables. For this reason you need to check how reliable a measure is before you reach conclusions about findings based on its use.

The degree of reliability of an educational measure is usually expressed by a correlation coefficient. For present purposes it is sufficient for you to know that reliability coefficients range from 0, which indicates no reliability, to 1.00, which indicates perfect reliability. In other words, a reliability coefficient of .00 means that the test scores are meaningless because they consist entirely of measurement error; in contrast, a reliability of 1.00 means that the measure has absolutely no measurement error. As a rough rule of thumb, a measure is considered reliable for most research and practical purposes if its reliability coefficient is .80 or higher. (In the case of one type of reliability coefficient, Cronbach's alpha, a value of .70 or higher usually is sufficient.)

Procedures have been developed to estimate the extent of the different types of measurement errors in a test. In describing each procedure, we use the term *test* to refer generally to various forms of measurement, such as achievement tests, attitude scales, and direct observation.

Item Consistency.   One type of measurement error is caused by inconsistencies in the items that make up the test. For example, if a test of visual creativity contains some items that measure this construct and other items that measure a somewhat different construct, the total score will be an inaccurate indicator of visual creativity. Therefore, test developers want all the items on the test to measure the same construct. In other words, they want the items to be consistent. If the items are perfectly consistent, individuals who score one way on an item should score the same way on all the remaining items. The test's reliability reflects the extent to which the test items are consistent with one another, and it can be determined by several statistical methods.

Stability of Measurement. As we observed above, measurement error will occur if the individuals being tested vary in their performance from one testing occasion to the next. These variations can occur for many reasons. For example, an individual may be fatigued on one testing occasion and rested on the next. Or an individual may have reviewed a relevant item of information just before one testing occasion, but not just before the next.

If a test is free of this type of measurement error, individuals should earn the same score on each testing occasion. To determine the extent to which this is the case, researchers administer the test to a sample of individuals, and then after a delay they administer the same test again to the same sample. Scores obtained from the two administrations are then correlated to determine their reliability. This type of reliability is called *test-retest reliability* or *test stability*.

Consistency of Administration and Scoring. Individuals who administer or score tests can cause measurement errors because of carelessness or for some other reason, such as not knowing the correct procedures. Highly objective measures, such as multiple-choice tests, tend to be free of this type of measurement error. However, even test-scoring machines have been known to make scoring mistakes because of mechanical defects. Less objective measures, such as individually administered intelligence and personality tests or direct observation, are more subject to administration and scoring errors.

The presence of test-administration errors can be determined by having several individuals administer the same test, or alternate forms of the same test, to the same sample. Their scores are then correlated with one another to yield a reliability coefficient. The presence of scoring errors can be determined quite simply by having several individuals or machines score the same set of tests. A reliability coefficient is calculated on the sets of scores to determine how well they agree. The degree of reliability among the individuals who administer or score measures is sometimes called *inter-rater reliability* or *inter-observer reliability*.

Evaluating Researchers' Determination of Reliability. We discussed above three types of test reliability: item consistency, test stability, and consistency of test administration and scoring. It is unlikely that researchers will determine all three types of reliability for each measure used in a study. One type of reliability is typically of most concern, depending on the measure involved and the research situation. You will need to determine whether the researcher made the appropriate reliability check for each measure.

Researchers sometimes determine the reliability or validity of their measures by using evidence from other studies. If these studies involve a different population from the one used in the researcher's study, the reliability and validity evidence may not be applicable. In other words, a measure may be reliable and valid for one population, but not for another. Therefore, you need to check the source of the reliability and validity evidence that is presented in a research report.

METHODS SECTION: RESEARCH DESIGN AND PROCEDURES

Research reports should describe the research design that was used to obtain the data needed to test the research hypotheses, answer the research questions, or achieve the research objectives. Depending on the research design, the description of the procedures might be brief or it might need to be quite detailed. Descriptive research designs (see Chapter 7) generally are simple. The researchers might consider it sufficient to mention who administered the measures and how and when they were administered. If descriptive data were collected periodically, as in longitudinal research, the time intervals should be specified.

Other research designs, especially experimental designs (see Chapter 9), require more detailed explanations. For example, the report should indicate the time line of the experiment so that readers know when the various measures and treatments were administered. Also, each of the experimental treatments (for example, a new teaching method) should be described so that other researchers could implement them as intended, if they wish to replicate the study. It is especially important that the researcher describe how long the treatments (e.g., different teaching methods) were implemented. In some experiments, the treatments are of such brief duration that it is not reasonable to expect an effect on the research participants' learning or other outcomes. Any flaws in the research design and procedures will weaken the conclusions that can be drawn from the statistical findings.

You will need a basic understanding of various research designs in order to evaluate the adequacy of the research design used in a particular quantitative research study. The remaining chapters in Part III are intended to help you develop this understanding. In addition to explaining each design, we present a report of an actual research study that used it.

RESULTS SECTION

The results section of a quantitative research report presents the results of the statistical analyses of the data generated from the researchers' administration of measures to their sample.

We explain commonly used statistical techniques and conditions for their appropriate use in Chapter 6. Then in Chapters 7, 8, and 9, we explain the statistical techniques that are commonly used in conjunction with particular quantitative research designs.

DISCUSSION SECTION

The final section of a quantitative research report is the discussion section (sometimes called *Conclusions*). The purpose of the discussion section is to clarify the meaning and implications of the results. Thus, the researchers are expected to express their interpretations of the results, draw conclusions about the practical and theoretical significance of the results, and make recommendations for further research. While the results section should present an objective account of the statistical analyses, a more personal perspective is necessary in the discussion section.

In evaluating the discussion section, you must decide whether you agree with the researchers' judgments about how the results should be interpreted and their implications for theory and practice. The most critical factor in this evaluation is whether you think the researchers' judgments are supported by their research results and the results of the previous research that they cite. Your ability to make this evaluation will improve as you develop an understanding of research methodology and knowledge of the research literature to which a particular study contributes.

CONCLUDING THOUGHT

Many people experience research only by reading about research findings in newspapers, magazines, and books. They have little understanding of the dynamic process of scientific inquiry that led to these findings. Some people also believe that no research can be trusted, or that statistics distort the truth. In this chapter, we have given you the tools for reading primary sources that are reports of quantitative research studies written by the researchers who conducted them. The ability to read these reports brings you much closer to the heart of the research process than merely reading second-hand accounts of isolated research findings.

In this chapter, we also have tried to convey the fact that, while quantitative research is not perfect, neither is it fatally flawed. Random sampling and the determination of the validity and reliability of measures are among the technical procedures that researchers have developed to avoid bias and inaccuracy in their own studies. Furthermore, these technical procedures provide criteria for judging the soundness of their colleagues' studies.

SELF-CHECK TEST

1. Reports of quantitative research studies typically
   a. are written in a more personal style than are reports of qualitative research studies.
   b. follow the style guidelines of the American Psychological Association.
   c. do not include an abstract.
   d. begin with a description of the research design that was employed.

2. Some research studies have found that direct instruction is more effective than other instructional styles. In this research, direct instruction is a
   a. constant.
   b. hypothesis.
   c. construct.
   d. stratified variable.

3. In reporting a quantitative research study, researchers typically
   a. include a statement of their qualifications to conduct the study.
   b. include a brief list of their work history and publications.
   c. do not mention their institutional affiliation.
   d. provide few details about their professional lives.

4. In simple random sampling, researchers
   a. select individuals at random from different populations.
   b. identify a sample of populations, and select one of them at random to be studied.
   c. ensure that each individual in the population has an equal chance of being in the sample.
   d. do all of the above.

5. To evaluate population validity, researchers must analyze
   a. the selected sample, the accessible population, and the target population.
   b. the selected sample and the target population.
   c. the accessible population and the target population.
   d. the membership list used to define the target population.

6. A research questionnaire typically
   a. contains several leading questions.
   b. measures many variables.
   c. does not require pretesting.
   d. is ideal for obtaining psychologically threatening information.

7. Evidence that a test measures the curriculum taught by a research sample of teachers can be used to demonstrate the test's
   a. predictive validity.
   b. content validity.
   c. concurrent validity.
   d. construct validity.

8. If a measure has high reliability, it means that the measure
   a. has been endorsed by the editors of the *Mental Measurements Yearbook.*
   b. has face validity among those who use it in research.
   c. has yielded valid results over a period of many years of use.
   d. is relatively free of measurement error.

9. All of the following typically appear in the discussion section of a quantitative research report, except for
   a. the statistical results.
   b. an interpretation of the results.
   c. the practical significance of the results.
   d. recommendations for further research.

CHAPTER REFERENCES

American Educational Research Association, American Psychological Association, and National Council on Measurement in Education. (1985). *Standards for educational and psychological testing.* Washington, DC: American Psychological Association.

Eberts, R. W., & Stone, J. A. (1988). Student achievement in public schools: Do principals make a difference? *Economics of Education Review, 7,* 291–299.

Evans, P. (1976). The Burt affair: Sleuthing in science. *APA Monitor, 12,* pp. 1, 4.

American Psychological Association. (1994). *Publication manual of the American Psychological Association* (4th ed.). Washington, DC: Author.

RECOMMENDED READING

Borich, G. D., & Madden, S. K. (1977). *Evaluating classroom instruction: A sourcebook of instruments.* Reading, MA: Addison-Wesley.

This book reviews a large number of instruments, including many observation forms, that can be used to evaluate teacher and student behavior.

Conoley, J. C., & Kramer, J. J. (Eds.). (1994). *Tenth mental measurements yearbook.* Lincoln, NE: The Buros Institute of Mental Measurements.

This standard reference work includes information about many of the measures used in education. A CD-ROM version is also available. For some of the measures, there is a critical review of its strengths and weaknesses. Because new editions appear periodically, you will find it helpful to consult: Buros Institute of Mental Measurements. (1994). *Tests in print* (5th ed.). Lincoln, NE: Author. This reference work serves as a comprehensive bibliography to measures that are included in one or more editions of the *Mental Measurements Yearbook.*

Doolittle, P., Halpern, M., & Rudner, L. M. (1994). The ERIC/AE Test Locator Service. *Educational Researcher, 23*(7), 34–35.

The authors describe an ERIC service that makes it possible to conduct a computer search for information about tests.

Fowler, F. J., Jr. (1993). *Survey research methods* (2nd ed.). Beverly Hills, CA: Sage.

  The author provides an overview of the use of questionnaires and interviews in research.

Gall, M. D., Borg, W. R., & Gall, J. P. (1996). *Educational research: An introduction* (6th ed.). White Plains, NY: Longman.

  This book explains many of the topics covered in this chapter, but in more depth.

Kalton, G. (1983). *Introduction to survey sampling*. Beverly Hills, CA: Sage.

  The author explains the major sampling techniques and addresses issues such as sample size and nonrandom sampling.

CHAPTER 6

STATISTICAL ANALYSIS OF RESEARCH DATA

After many years of teaching, Henry Wu has returned to the university to obtain an administrator's license. His scheduled course work includes classes on educational statistics, assessment, and research methods.

New state assessment tests are scheduled to be given throughout Wu's state to students at three grade levels. Henry has some concerns about the upcoming state assessment. For example, he wonders whether repeated administrations of state tests can be used to measure learning gains, and whether administering the tests to samples of students—even large samples—will yield results that can be generalized to all students in the state at those grade levels.

His deepest concern is whether statistics such as mean scores and percentile scores can present an honest picture of what students know, and whether they will reflect the large individual differences among students. Henry hopes that these concerns will be addressed in his licensure courses.

In this chapter, you will learn how educational researchers use statistics to summarize and describe the data obtained from administering tests and other measures to groups of individuals. You also will learn how researchers use statistics to help them make valid generalizations of statistical results obtained from a small sample to a much larger population.

OBJECTIVES

After studying this chapter, you will be able to

1. explain the role of statistics in educational research.

2. describe the types of continuous scores yielded by tests and measures.

3. describe the characteristics of rank scores, categories, and gain scores, and explain their limitations.

4. explain how the mean, median, mode, frequency counts, and percentages can be used to summarize a set of numerical data.

5. explain the meaning of a standard deviation and its relationship to the normal curve.

6. compare the use of bivariate correlational statistics and multivariate correlational statistics in analyzing research data.

7. explain the purpose of inferential statistics and the sampling logic on which they are based.

8. explain the meaning of a *p* value.

9. describe the types of statistical inference that are made possible by the *t* test, analysis of variance, analysis of covariance, and the chi-square test.

10. explain the difference between parametric and nonparametric tests of statistical significance.

11. explain the difference between the statistical significance and practical significance of a research result.

KEY TERMS

age equivalent
analysis of covariance
analysis of variance
average variation
bivariate correlational
 statistics
categorical score
ceiling effect
chi-square (χ^2)test
continuous score
correlational statistic
derived score
descriptive statistics
dichotomy
effect size
F value
factor
frequency count
gain score
grade equivalent

inferential statistics
interaction effect
interval scale
Kruskal-Wallis test
Mann-Whitney *U* test
mean
median
mode
multiple linear regression
multivariate correlational
 statistics
nonparametric test of
 significance
normal curve
normal probability
 distribution
norming sample
null hypothesis
p value
parametric test of significance

percentage
percentile score
practical significance
r value
range
rank score
raw score
replication study
Scheffé's test
standard deviation
standard deviation unit
standard score
statistic
statistical significance
t test
t value
test of statistical significance
Tukey's test
variance
Wilcoxon signed-rank test

THE PURPOSE OF STATISTICAL ANALYSIS

Most research studies, whether quantitative or qualitative, generate data that can be expressed in numerical form. For example, if the researchers administer an aptitude test to their sample, the analysis of the sample's performance on the test will generate numerical scores. There might be a total test score for each individual in the sample, as well as scores for subsections of the test (e.g., verbal aptitude and mathematical aptitude). In addition, the researchers might have collected numerical data about each individual's personal background (e.g., age and number of years of professional work experience).

Qualitative research studies usually yield verbal data (e.g., transcripts of interviews) or visual data (e.g., videorecordings of events). These data are analyzed in their original state by the researchers. However, this method of analysis sometimes is supplemented by transforming the data into numerical form. For example, suppose that the researchers made transcripts of a set of interviews. The transcripts can be analyzed by counting the frequency with which certain words or themes are mentioned. The frequency counts constitute numerical data.

Even though statistical procedures sometimes are used in qualitative research, they are used much more intensively in quantitative research. For this reason, we introduce the use of statistical analysis in educational research in this part of the book.

The numerical data in a quantitative research study are subjected to various statistical analyses. One purpose of these analyses is to summarize the scores on a particular measure that are obtained by all the individuals who constitute the sample. In some research studies, the sample includes hundreds or even thousands of individuals. Without statistical tools for summarizing these data, it would be virtually impossible to make sense of them. Other statistical tools, as you will learn in this chapter, help researchers determine whether conclusions based on the numerical data for a sample can be generalized to the population that the sample is intended to represent.

Statistical analysis is a branch of mathematics, and therefore you need to have some understanding of mathematics in order to understand the assumptions and computational procedures for the statistical tools used in educational research. Development of this understanding typically requires taking one or more courses in statistics and its applications in educational research. Coursework in statistics will also help you make better judgments about the appropriateness of the statistics that are used in published research studies, and to use appropriate statistical techniques in your own research.

Because you might not yet have taken statistics courses, we have minimized presentation of the mathematical basis for statistical analysis in this chapter. Each statistical procedure is described in nontechnical rather than in mathematical terms. We focus on the purpose of each statistical procedure, its appropriate use in research studies, and the information that it yields. You might be able to follow the discussion better if you have scratch paper handy as you read, so that you can see for yourself how we did certain calculations with the data that are presented in tables.

TYPES OF SCORES IN STATISTICAL ANALYSIS

In reviewing statistical analyses in a research report, you should start by determining what type of score was used in each analysis. These scores will be of different types depending on the type of variable that was measured. For example, a student's score on a typical achievement test is of a different type from the student's "score" on the variable of gender.

Three types of scores are computed in educational research studies: (1) continuous scores, (2) gain scores, and (3) categorical scores. You need to understand each of these types of scores, because different statistical analyses are appropriate for each type.

Continuous Scores

Continuous scores are values of a measure that has an indefinite number of ordered points. Most achievement and aptitude tests, attitude scales, and personality measures yield scores of this type. For example, suppose a test has 50 items, with a score of 1 point for each item answered correctly. Thus, scores on this test have 51 continuous points, ranging from 0 to 50. The points are ordered so that each value is greater than the value preceding it. The points are not truly indefinite in number but only approximately so, because on most standardized tests the continuous scores are limited to whole numbers. To be truly indefinite, the test could yield fractional values, such as 41.25.

One type of continuous score is the raw score, which is simply the total score obtained by following the test developers' scoring procedures. Raw scores by themselves are difficult to interpret. For example, a score of 30 on a 50-item test might be interpreted as high or low, depending on how difficult the test is and on how well other individuals in the research sample performed on it. Therefore, researchers often report derived scores in addition to raw scores. Derived scores provide a quantitative comparison of each individual's performance relative to a comparison group. Five types of derived scores are commonly reported: age equivalents, grade equivalents, percentiles, standard scores, and rank scores.

Age Equivalents.   A student's age equivalent score is the age level of other students who typically earn the same raw score that the student did. This type of derived score is commonly used with academic achievement tests. The other students to whom the student's score is compared usually are a large sample, called a *norming sample*, which typically represents a national, regional, or state population. The raw score of each student in the research sample can be found in the table of norms, which will report the age of students in the norming sample who earned that score, on average. For example, if the age equivalent for a student who earned a raw score of 30 is 12.0, it means that this student earned the average raw score of students in the norming sample who were 12 years old. (Later in this chapter, you will find that *average* in this context refers to a statistic called the *mean*.)

Grade Equivalents.   These derived scores are similar in meaning to age equivalents. The only difference is that the table of norms reports the average raw score earned by students at each grade level in the norming sample. For example, if the grade equivalent for a student who earned a raw score of 20 is 3.5, it means that this student performed at the average level of students in the norming sample who were in the middle of the third grade.

Percentile Scores.   These derived scores represent the percentage of individuals whose raw score falls at or below the raw scores of other individuals in the research sample. For example, suppose that 40 percent of the students in the research sample earn a raw score of 27 or below. In this case, a raw score of 27 would represent a percentile score of 40. More commonly, we would state that the student scored at the 40th percentile of the research sample.

Test developers often construct a table of norms in percentile form. If such a table is available, researchers can use percentile scores in addition to, or instead of, age and grade equivalents to express how well individuals in their sample performed relative to the norming sample. In the above example, a raw score of 27 might be at the 40th percentile in relation to other students in the research sample but at, say, the 35th percentile with respect to the norming sample.

Standard Scores.   These derived scores are similar in meaning to percentiles. However, they have mathematical advantages over percentile scores, and therefore are commonly used in statistical computations. An individual's standard score is derived by subtracting his or her raw score from the mean score earned by the research sample and then dividing that result by the standard deviation of the scores of the research sample. (Mean scores and standard deviations are explained later in the chapter.) Some test manuals include a table of norms in which the sample's raw scores can be converted to standard scores derived from a norming sample.

Intelligence test scores are a common example of standard scores. For example, the mean score on the Stanford-Binet Intelligence Scale is set at 100, meaning that half of the norming sample obtained a score that is at or below this standard score. The standard deviation is set at 16. By referring to the normal probability curve (discussed later in this chapter), you can determine the percentage of individuals in the sample who earned at or below a particular IQ score.

Rank Scores.   A rank score expresses the position of an individual on a measure relative to the positions held by other individuals. Rank scores are used by educators for various purposes. For example, a school might rank the students at a particular grade level with respect to academic achievement, or athletes might be ranked with respect to performance in a sports contest (e.g., first place, second place, and third place). These examples illustrate the educational or social significance of some measures that yield rank scores. Because of their significance, rank scores sometimes are collected and analyzed by educational researchers.

Rank scores typically have unequal intervals. For example, in one classroom there might be very little difference in academic achievement between the first-ranked and second-ranked student. In another classroom, however, these two ranks might reflect substantial differences in academic achievement. This limitation of rank scores should be kept in mind when interpreting statistical results based on this type of score.

Gain Scores

Individuals' learning and development are the focus of much educational research. Both processes involve change in an individual from one time to another. These changes can be detected by administering the same measure to individuals at two or more points in time. A gain score is simply the difference in an individual's score on the measure from one time to the next. Gain scores often are positive, but they also can be negative, as when an individual forgets information learned earlier.

Gain scores are sometimes reported by researchers, but you should view them with caution. For example, they are subject to a ceiling effect. To understand this effect, suppose that a student scores 95 out of 100 possible points on initial testing. The student can improve by a maximum of only 5 points on this test when it is readministered. These 5 points might be inadequate (the ceiling is too low) to measure all the new information or skills that the student has learned during the intervening time interval.

Another limitation of gain scores is that most tests tend to have unequal intervals. For example, suppose a test has 50 items, and each item answered correctly earns a score of 1. Suppose, though, that the items vary in difficulty. Now consider the case of two students who earn the same gain score of 5, but one goes from a raw score of 10 to a raw score of 15, whereas the other goes from a raw score of 40 to a raw score of 45. It probably is more difficult for the second student to make a gain score of 5 than it is for the first student, because he or she will need to answer correctly more difficult items on the test. Thus the gain score does not have the same meaning for both students.

Still another problem is that most tests contain different types of items. For example, suppose that two students earn the same gain score on a subtraction test, but they do it by making gains on different types of subtraction items. Once again, the gain score is the same, but it does not mean the same thing for the two students.

Despite these problems and others not described here, gain scores continue to be used in educational research and practice. To determine whether they provide meaningful information, you need to check for possible ceiling effects and determine whether similar gain scores for different individuals reflect similar learning or development.

Categorical Scores

Categories are variables that yield values that are discrete and nonordered when measured. An example would be students' parental status. We could assign categorical scores for different types of parental status, such as: (a) two parents together, (b) mother only, (c) father only, and (d) other. These categories are discrete, meaning that each student can be assigned to only one category; the categories do not overlap. Note, too, that the categories do not form an ordered continuum. For example, it would not make sense to say that a father-only family is "more" or "less" than a mother-only family or that either is "more" or "less" than a family categorized as "other." Because categories cannot be ordered, categorical scores must be analyzed by different statistical techniques than continuous or rank scores.

A dichotomy is a special type of categorical variable. It yields only two values. Gender, for example, is a dichotomous variable because only two values are possible: male and female. Gender is a natural dichotomy, but other dichotomies are artificial, meaning that the values are defined by the researchers or by other individuals. For example, researchers might classify school districts as having a centralized or a decentralized administration, or students might classify themselves as college bound or not college bound.

DESCRIPTIVE STATISTICS

Research studies often yield a large amount of numerical data. Descriptive statistics serve a useful purpose by summarizing all the data in the form of a few simple numerical expressions, called *statistics*. A statistic is a number that describes the characteristic of a sample's scores on a measure. To illustrate, we created data for a hypothetical research study, which is shown in Table 6.1. The

TABLE 6.1   **Interest in History and History Course Grade for Employed and Nonemployed Students**

	Employed students			Nonemployed students	
ID	**Interest in history**	**Course grade**	**ID**	**Interest in history**	**Course grade**
01	31	2	11	25	2
02	30	3	12	37	3
03	27	0	13	41	3
04	38	2	14	42	3
05	18	1	15	32	3
06	34	3	16	47	4
07	29	3	17	33	3
08	25	2	18	38	4
09	33	1	19	44	1
10	42	4	20	37	2
	$M = 30.70$	$M = 2.10$		$M = 37.60$	$M = 2.80$
	$SD = 6.73$	$SD = 1.20$		$SD = 6.43$	$SD = .92$

Total Sample ($N = 20$)

Interest in history	Course grade
$M = 34.15$	$M = 2.45$
$SD = 7.32$	$SD = 1.10$

main purpose of this study was to determine whether there is a relationship between employed and nonemployed students' interest in history and their final grade in a history course.

The data in Table 6.1 constitute the raw data of the study. The students were classified as having part-time jobs or as not having any jobs, and the scores of these groups are shown separately. Data for employed students are shown on the left side of the table, and data for nonemployed students are shown on the right side. The ID column in this table is an identification code to distinguish each individual in the sample from the others. The ID numbers are in consecutive order, from 01 to 20.

The first data column of the table shows students' scores on the interest measure, with higher scores indicating greater interest. The second data column shows students' course grades (A = 4; B = 3; C = 2; D = 1; F = 0).

Raw data like these seldom are included in a research report. Journals, which are the primary medium in which research reports are published, lack space to include raw data. Even if they had space, however, they would not do so, because conclusions drawn from raw data tend to be imprecise. For example, one would be limited to statements such as, "It appears that students who are more interested in history tend to do better in a course on this subject," or, "Employed students tend to be less interested in history than nonemployed students." These statements do not tell us precisely how strong the tendency to do better is or precisely how much less interested employed students are than nonemployed students. Therefore, descriptive statistics are reported instead. They lead to mathematically precise statements such as, "There is a strong positive correlation of .57 between students' interest in history and their grades in a course on this subject," or, "Employed students scored an average of 6 points less than nonemployed students on a 20-item measure of interest in history."

The following is an explanation of the descriptive statistics that are commonly used in educational research.

Mean, Median, and Mode

Researchers are interested in the individuals who make up their sample, but they also are interested in the sample as a whole. In our hypothetical study, they would want to know the typical interest level of the sample and whether the typical interest level of employed students differs from that of nonemployed students. A statistic known as the *mean* usually is computed to represent the typical score in a distribution of scores. The mean is calculated by summing the individual scores of the sample and then dividing the total sum by the number of individuals in the sample. Table 6.1 reports the means (represented by the symbol *M*) for the total sample and separately for employed students and nonemployed students for the two variables: interest in history and course grade. The mean is misleading as a typical score if the distribution of scores is markedly asymmetrical. (A symmetrical distribution is shown in Figure 6.1.)

The median is another statistic that can be used to describe a sample's typical score on a measure. The median is the middle score in the distribution of scores, meaning that half the individuals in the sample score at or below the median score. (If there is an even number of individuals in a sample, the median is the score halfway between the scores of the two middle individuals.)

The median for the total sample on the interest measure is 33.5, and the median course grade is 3.0. The median grade for the employed students is 2.0, and for the nonemployed students it is 3.0. You will note that the medians are similar to, but not identical with, the corresponding means. If the distribution of scores is markedly asymmetrical, the median provides a better representation of the typical score than does the mean.

The mode is simply the most frequently occurring score among the scores for the sample. It is seldom reported, because it usually has little meaning. For example, the mode for course grades in our hypothetical study is 3, which corresponds to a grade of B. Without further information, we do not know whether this grade was assigned to slightly more students, or to many other students, than any of the other grades.

The mean is most often included in research reports because it is more stable than the median or mode. In other words, if one selected many samples at random from a population with scores on a certain measure, the means for the samples would be more similar to one another than would the medians or the modes.

The mean, median, and mode are appropriate descriptive statistics for continuous scores and rank scores.

Frequency Counts and Percentages

Suppose that the data for our hypothetical sample include the variable of type of employment. The three categories are (1) food service worker, (2) gas station attendant, and (3) store clerk. The mean, median, and mode are inappropriate statistics for data of this type. Instead, the frequency or percentage of individuals in each category is determined. Table 6.2 reports these statistics for the employed students in our hypothetical sample. The frequency is simply the total number of individuals in the sample who fit a particular category. The percentage is the frequency of individuals in a particular category divided by the

TABLE 6.2 **Type of Employment for Employed Students**

Type of employment	Frequency	Percentage
Food service worker	5	50
Store clerk	4	40
Gas station attendant	1	10

total number of individuals in the sample. (For example, for food service work-ers, 5 divided by 10 = .5, or 50 percent.) Some research reports include only fre-quencies or only percentages rather than reporting both, because the other statistic can easily be calculated by readers if they wish to know it.

Range and Standard Deviation

The mean provides a mathematically precise and succinct description of the sample's average performance on a measure. This information, however, is not sufficient. We also want to know how much variation is present in the individ-ual scores. Did most of the individuals in the sample obtain scores at or near the mean, or did they vary widely from the mean?

One way to answer this question is to determine the range of scores. The range is calculated as the difference between the lowest and highest score plus 1 in the distribution of scores for a measure. Referring to Table 6.1, we see that the range for the interest measure is 30 (47 – 18 + 1), and the range of course grades is 5 (4 – 0 + 1).

Some research reports include the range of scores for each measure, but if so, they also should report the standard deviation of scores, which is a more stable and mathematically meaningful measure of variability. The standard deviation is a statistical expression of how much individual scores vary around the mean score. Table 6.1 reports the standard deviation (abbreviated as *SD*) for each mean that was calculated.

A simple way to understand the standard deviation is to imagine taking each individual score and subtracting it from the mean score of the sample. Following this procedure for the first student (ID = 01), we calculate a variation of 4.15 points from the total sample mean (34.15 – 31.00). Suppose we followed this procedure for the entire sample, ignoring whether the subtraction process yielded a negative or positive score. We then could sum these difference scores and divide the total sum by the number of individuals in the sample. The result is called the *average variation*, that is, the average amount by which individual scores deviate from the mean score. This result approximates the standard devi-ation. (The actual formula for calculating the standard deviation involves squar-ing the individual difference scores, and a few other procedures.)

The standard deviation is a particularly useful statistic if the individual scores on the measure form a normal probability distribution. A normal probability distribution of scores, known more commonly as a normal curve, is shown in Figure 6.1. To understand this figure, suppose that a large number of individu-als were measured on a particular variable. The height of the curve at any point along the horizontal line would indicate the number of individuals who obtained the score represented by that point. You will note that the mean of the sample's scores is indicated on the horizontal line. If the sample's scores are nor-mally distributed, more individuals will obtain the mean score than any other score in the distribution of scores.

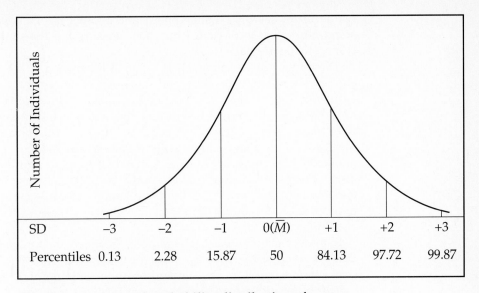

FIGURE 6.1   Normal probability distribution of scores
Source. Adapted from Figure 5.1 on p. 179 in: Gall, M. D., Borg, W. R., & Gall, J. P. (1996).
Educational research: An introduction (6th ed.). White Plains, NY: Longman.

You will note, too, that actual scores for a measure are not shown in Figure 6.1. Instead, the scores are represented immediately below the curve as standard deviation units (–3, –2, –1, etc.). To understand what these units mean, consider the hypothetical data set shown in Table 6.1. The standard deviation for the total sample on the interest measure is 7.32, and the mean is 34.15. If an individual scored 1 standard deviation unit above the mean, it indicates that he or she obtained a score of 41 (34.15 + 7.32 = 41.47, rounded to the whole number of 41). This score corresponds to the +1 in Figure 6.1. Individuals who score 1 standard deviation unit below the mean score would obtain a score of 27 (34.15 – 7.32 = 26.83). This score corresponds to the –1 in Figure 6.1.

Now consider the case of an individual who scores 2 standard deviations (7.32 × 2 = 14.64) above the mean. That individual's score would be 49 (34.15 + 14.64 = 48.79). This score corresponds to the +2 in Figure 6.1. No individual in the sample actually obtained that score, because the distribution of scores did not follow the normal curve perfectly.

The standard deviation units immediately beneath the normal curve shown in Figure 6.1 include a zero (0). The zero is the mean score of the sample or population. In our hypothetical study, the mean score of the sample on the measure of interest in history is 34.15. There is no deviation of a mean score from itself. Therefore, it has a value of zero when expressed in standard deviation units.

The advantage of standard deviation units in constructing the normal curve shown in Figure 6.1 is that scores for any measure can be represented on it, assuming that the scores are normally distributed. It does not matter whether one measure has 100 possible points and another has 20 possible points. The standard deviation of scores for each measure has the same meaning with respect to the normal curve.

The normal curve has practical value in interpreting the results of research studies. If you know the mean and standard deviation for the scores on a measure, you can use these two bits of information to determine the amount of variability in the scores (assuming the scores are normally distributed). Referring to Figure 6.1, you will see that scores 1 standard deviation below the mean are at approximately the sixteenth percentile, and scores 1 standard deviation above the mean are at approximately the eighty-fourth percentile. Thus, approximately 68 percent of the sample (84 − 16) will earn scores between +1 and −1 standard deviations. By a similar procedure, we can determine that approximately 96 percent of the sample (98 − 2) will earn scores between +2 and −2 standard deviations.

Suppose that, for a particular sample, the mean of their scores on a measure that has 50 possible points is 25 and the standard deviation is 2. Assuming the scores form a normal curve, we can conclude that most of the sample (approximately 96 percent) earned scores between 21 (−2 *SD* units) and 29 (+2 *SD* units). In other words, the scores are clustered tightly around the mean score, and so the mean is a good representation of the performance of the entire sample.

Suppose that, for another sample, the mean is again 25 but the standard deviation is 10. The variation in scores is quite large. If we consider only those individuals who scored within the range of +1 and −1 standard deviation units (approximately 68 percent of the sample), their scores are expected to vary from 15 (25 − 10) to 35 (25 + 10) if the distribution of scores follows the normal curve. In this case the mean does not represent closely the performance of the sample. In interpreting the research results, we need to keep in mind that in this research sample the individuals are more different than alike with respect to the variable that was measured.

The mean and standard deviation are mathematically elegant, because these two statistics together provide a succinct summary of the raw data. Even if the sample includes 1,000 individuals, we can tell much about how they performed on a measure just by knowing the mean and standard deviation.

Keep in mind, however, that the standard deviation is interpretable only if the scores are normally distributed (as shown in Figure 6.1) or approximately so. If the distribution of scores deviates substantially from normality, the standard deviation cannot be interpreted in terms of the normal curve. For this reason, researchers should state in their reports whether scores for any measure deviate substantially from the normal curve. Fortunately, it seems to be a law of nature that most variables of educational significance are normally distributed.

The range and standard deviation are meaningful descriptive statistics for continuous scores and gain scores. They are not appropriate for categorical scores. The variability in distribution of these scores can be determined simply by looking at the frequency counts or percentages in each category. For example, if the variable being measured has five categories, you need only inspect the frequency counts or percentages to determine whether individuals are evenly distributed across the categories or whether a disproportionate number are in a few of the categories.

Bivariate Correlational Statistics

A major purpose of research is to explore the relationship between variables. In the case of our hypothetical research study, the purpose is to determine the relationship between high school students' interest in history and their final grade in a history course. Correlational statistics can be used to describe the extent of this relationship in mathematically precise terms. If only two variables are involved, a bivariate correlational statistic is calculated. This type of statistic is discussed at length in Chapter 8, which is concerned with the correlational research method. Therefore, we provide only a brief description of this topic here.

Correlational statistics involve the calculation of a correlation coefficient, which is represented by the symbol r, for the r value. Larger r values indicate greater magnitudes of relationship between the variables that have been measured. Different types of correlation coefficients can be calculated, depending on whether continuous scores, rank scores, dichotomous scores, or categorical scores are involved.

The two variables in Table 6.1 both involve continuous scores, so the product-moment correlation coefficient is appropriate for describing the magnitude of their relationship. Positive values of this coefficient can vary between 0 and 1.00. The obtained coefficient ($r = .49$) for this sample indicates a moderately positive relationship, meaning that students with more interest in history tend to earn somewhat higher grades in a history course than students with less interest. For example, the student with ID 05 has an interest score of 18 and a course grade of D (numerical value = 1), whereas the student with ID 10 has a higher interest score of 42 and a higher course grade of A (numerical value = 4). The relationship between the two variables is less than perfect, however, as illustrated by the student with ID 19, who has a high interest score (44) but a course grade of D.

Multivariate Correlational Statistics

Advances in research methodology have enabled researchers to explore the relationship between more than two variables at the same time. In our hypothetical study, students' scores on a measure of interest in history were used to predict their grades in a history course. Suppose that we included several more measures to make this prediction, for example, measures of students' verbal aptitude and their study habits. It might be that a combination of the three measures (interest in history, verbal aptitude, and study habits) yields a better prediction of course grades than any one measure alone. A correlational procedure known as *multiple linear regression* can be used for this purpose. It determines which measure, or combination of measures, to use and how to weight students' scores on each measure to produce the best prediction of the criterion variable (in this case, students' course grades).

Multiple linear regression and other multivariate correlational techniques are discussed in Chapter 8.

INFERENTIAL STATISTICS

In Chapter 5 we explained procedures for selecting samples for quantitative research studies. The ideal procedure is to select a sample at random from a defined population. If random selection is not possible, researchers still should attempt to select a sample that represents a population of interest. In either case, the goal is to generalize from the sample to the population, that is, to make inferences about the population from the results obtained with the sample.

As the name implies, inferential statistics help in the process of making inferences. More specifically, inferential statistics enable researchers to make inferences about a population based on the descriptive statistics that are calculated on data from a sample that represents this population.

The mathematical basis for inferential statistics is complex. Therefore, we will provide a nontechnical explanation here by considering one of the results of the hypothetical study shown in Table 6.1.

If you examine this table, you will see that the mean of employed students on the measure of interest in history ($M = 30.70$) is lower than the mean of nonemployed students ($M = 37.60$). The question we must ask is whether a similar difference would be found if we studied the entire population of students taking this type of history course. In other words, can we generalize the results from our small sample to the population of students that it represents? (Let's assume that the population is all U.S. high school students, and that this sample is representative of that population.)

To conclude that the results are generalizable, we first must reject the possible explanation that the results are a chance finding. One way to reject this explanation would be to conduct replications, that is, to carry out the same study repeatedly with different samples representing the same population. If these replications consistently yielded approximately the same direction and degree of difference between employed and nonemployed students, this would constitute strong evidence of generalizability.

Replication studies, in fact, are commonly carried out for important findings. In medicine, for example, positive findings about a new drug obtained by one group of researchers rarely are accepted. Other laboratories around the world must test the drug to confirm the original results. The consequences of using a drug claimed to be effective, but actually not so, are far too serious to rely on the results of a single research study. In education, too, important findings are replicated across many studies. For example, hundreds of research studies on the effects of class size have been done, because class size is an important consideration in educational policy and budgetary decisions.

Inferential statistics are not as strong a test of generalizability as replication studies. However, they require only a tiny fraction of the effort required for a single replication study. As with replications, inferential statistics test the possible explanation that an observed result for a sample is a chance finding. What do we mean by a chance finding? To answer this question, imagine that we have two populations whose members have identical sets of scores on the measure of interest in history. These sets of scores are shown in Table 6.3. We labeled one population "employed students" and the other, "nonemployed students." Because the populations are identical with respect to interest in history, the mean of the scores for each population must be identical.

Now let's draw a random sample of 10 individuals from one population and then do the same with the other population. Then we can compute the mean score of each sample on the measure of interest in history and determine the difference. The results of these computations are shown in the first row of Table 6.4. Note that even though the population means are identical, the two sample means differ from each other. In this case the mean score of the employed students, by chance, is greater than the mean score of the nonemployed students.

Table 6.4 shows the results of repeatedly drawing new samples of size 10 from each population and computing their mean scores. In some samples the employed students score higher; in other samples the nonemployed students score higher; and in one sample there is no difference. The important thing to note is that, whenever a difference between employed and nonemployed students is obtained, it is a chance difference. Even though the population means are identical, differences between samples drawn from the two populations occur simply by chance.

We see, then, the possibility that the difference between the mean scores of employed and nonemployed students shown in Table 6.1 could have occurred by chance. Now the question arises, just how likely is it that the result occurred by chance? The answer to this question is obtained by using inferential statistics. In nonmathematical terms, inferential statistics are the equivalent of creating identical populations and then drawing many pairs of samples of a given size—just as we did in Table 6.4—and computing the difference between the mean scores. These difference scores will form a normal probability distribution, also known as a *normal curve* (an example is shown in Figure 6.1).

Researchers can determine how often the difference they obtained in their sample occurs in the normal distribution. Suppose we calculated this number for our hypothetical study and found that our obtained difference of 6.90 points (employed students' M minus nonemployed students' M) occurs only once in 100 times when we draw samples of the same size as our samples from two identical populations. In this case, we can conclude that our obtained difference in mean scores might be a chance finding, but that this is not very likely. Therefore, we reject the explanation that our obtained result occurred by chance. Instead, we accept the alternative explanation that our obtained result came about because the two samples (employed students and nonemployed students) represent different populations, and the population mean of nonemployed students is greater than the population mean of employed students.

TABLE 6.3   Hypothetical Populations of Employed Students and Nonemployed Students with Identical Mean Scores on a Measure of Interest in History

Population of employed students ($N = 100$; $M = 32.28$)

27	31	29	28	40	42
26	32	37	36	39	21
31	29	38	33	26	39
28	36	31	26	27	32
28	30	43	32	40	36
35	37	37	24	24	33
30	29	26	27	27	35
45	36	37	29	28	30
29	32	40	31	23	19
38	34	32	34	28	25
22	29	40	39	25	28
35	39	35	23	34	42
37	31	41	29	38	41
38	37	21	38	36	33
34	36	35	33	28	25
35	34	32	26	27	44
20	41	30	30		

Population of nonemployed students ($N = 100$; $M = 32.28$)

27	37	36	30	23	36
26	38	34	28	29	28
31	34	41	36	38	27
28	35	29	33	33	42
28	20	37	26	26	21
35	31	38	32	30	39
30	32	31	24	28	32
45	34	43	27	23	36
29	29	37	29	28	33
38	39	26	31	25	35
22	31	37	34	34	30
35	37	40	39	38	19
32	29	41	39	27	41
29	36	21	26	25	33
36	32	35	27	28	25
30	40	32	40	42	44
37	35	40	24		

TABLE 6.4 **Results of Taking Random Samples of Size 10 from Populations of Employed and Nonemployed Students Having Identical Scores on a Measure of Interest in History**

Employed M	Nonemployed M	Difference
33.2	31.4	+1.8
32.0	35.4	−3.4
34.0	29.8	+4.2
32.3	32.3	.0
34.4	30.3	+4.1
30.4	35.0	−4.6
31.8	32.9	−1.1
29.2	31.1	−1.9
32.0	31.1	+.9
31.3	29.6	+1.7

In reflecting on this deductive process, you might come to the realization that it is not perfect by any means. Even though our obtained difference between employed and nonemployed students would occur by chance only once in 100 times if the populations were identical, our samples might constitute that once-in-100-times occurrence. Also, even if we are correct in concluding that the obtained difference reflects real population differences, our sample means might not be the actual population means. For example, the mean score of the employed students in our sample on the measure of interest in history might not be the actual population mean score. The actual mean score might be somewhat higher or lower than the obtained mean score. (A particular inferential statistic, not discussed here, can be used to determine the range of mean scores within which the population mean score is likely to fall.)

The foregoing explanation of inferential statistics should be sufficient to help you understand several technical terms that you are likely to encounter in research reports. One term is *null hypothesis*, which simply is the explanation that an observed result for a sample is a chance finding. The basic purpose of any inferential statistic is to test the null hypothesis. The findings of this test are used to accept the null hypothesis (that is, attribute the obtained result to chance) or to reject the null hypothesis (that is, conclude that the obtained result can be generalized to the population).

Other technical terms you are likely to see in research reports are *p* and statistical significance. In the example that we have been considering, a *p* value refers to the percentage of occasions that a chance difference between mean scores of a certain magnitude will occur when the population means are identical (see the previous discussion). The lower the *p* value, the less often a chance difference of a given magnitude will occur; therefore, the more likely it is that the null hypothesis is false. For example, a *p* value of .001 indicates that it is much more likely that the null hypothesis is false than would a *p* value of .01. A *p* value of .001 indicates that a mean score difference as large as the obtained mean score difference would occur only once in 1,000 drawings of two samples from identical populations. A *p* value of .01 indicates that a mean score difference as large as the obtained mean score difference would occur only once in 100 drawings.

In educational research, a *p* value of .05 generally is considered sufficient to reject the null hypothesis. This high a *p* value makes it fairly easy to reject the null hypothesis because the researcher's obtained difference between mean scores would need to exceed the difference that would occur only once in 20 times in samples drawn from identical populations. Therefore, some obtained results with *p* = .05 might be chance findings. For this reason, you should be cautious about generalizing results from a sample to a population if the *p* value is .05 or higher. You have less need for caution, though, if other research studies in the literature reported similar findings, that is, replicated the study results.

Some researchers will report *p* as < .05 rather than = .05. Usually the *p* value is not exactly .05 but rather some value less than that. The symbol "<" means "less than," and is a shorthand way of expressing this information.

When the obtained result is statistically significant, the null hypothesis is rejected. For this reason the various inferential statistics sometimes are called *tests of statistical significance*. In reading research reports, you should be careful not to confuse statistical significance with practical significance. A statistically significant result only means that it is likely to be generalizable beyond the sample, or in other words, that it is not a chance finding. Although generalizable, the obtained result might reflect such a small difference between groups that it has little practical significance.

We describe below the main types of inferential statistics used in educational research. Different types are necessary to test the generalizability of the different types of results obtained in research studies. In the above example, we considered only one of many possible results, that is, the difference between two mean scores.

The *t* Test

The *t* test is used to determine whether an observed difference between the mean scores of two groups on a measure is likely to have occurred by chance or whether it reflects a true difference in the mean scores of the populations represented by the two groups. In our hypothetical study of high school history instruction, the *t* test could be used to determine whether the mean score of employed students on the interest measure is truly different from the mean score of nonemployed students. Similarly, the *t* test could be used to determine whether the mean course grade of these two groups is truly different.

The computations involved in a *t* test yield a *t* value. Researchers look for this value in a table of the *t* distribution. A *t* value of 2.10 is statistically significant at the .05 level for a sample of 20 individuals, meaning that only 5 times in 100 ($5 \div 100 = .05$) will a difference in mean scores as large as or larger than the observed difference occur when drawing samples of a given size from identical populations. Researchers generally agree that *t* values yielding a *p* of .05 or lower are sufficient to conclude that a difference in mean scores of two groups can be generalized to the populations represented by the samples used in the study.

In our hypothetical study, the *t* value for the difference in mean scores on the interest measure for employed students ($M = 30.70$) and nonemployed students ($M = 37.60$) is 2.35. Because our obtained *t* of 2.35 exceeds the *t* value of 2.10 required for statistical significance at the .05 level, we would reject the null hypothesis that this is a chance finding. Instead, we would conclude that nonemployed students in other settings with characteristics similar to those of the research sample would display more interest in history than employed students.

The distribution of scores for one or the other group being compared sometimes deviates substantially from the normal curve (see Figure 6.1). The *t* test cannot be used under this set of conditions. Alternative tests of statistical significance can be used instead: the Mann-Whitney *U* test or the Wilcoxon signed-rank test. They do not require the same assumptions about score distribution as the *t* test.

The *t* test also can be used to determine whether observed correlation coefficients occurred by chance. For example, we could determine whether the correlation coefficient value of .49, representing the level of relationship between interest in history and history course grade in Table 6.1, occurred by chance. The null hypothesis to be tested is that the true relationship between interest and course grade in the population represented by the sample is .00 and that the observed coefficient of .49 is a chance deviation from that value. The test of this null hypothesis yields a *t* value of 2.39 ($p < .05$), and therefore we conclude that the relationship between interest and course grade would be found in other groups similar to the research sample.

Analysis of Variance

In our hypothetical study the students were classified as employed or as nonemployed. Suppose, instead, that we had three classifications: (1) nonemployed, (2) working 10 hours a week or less, and (3) working 11 hours a week or more. This research design would yield three mean scores on the measure of interest in history, one for each of the three groups. The *t* test can compare only two means at a time. Therefore, another test of statistical significance, known as *analysis of variance*, must be used. This test determines the likelihood that the differences between the three mean scores occurred by chance, in other words, that they are chance values generated by drawing repeated samples from three populations having identical scores. (Analysis of variance also can be used to compare four or more mean scores.)

Analysis of variance yields an inferential statistic called an *F value*. If the *F* value exceeds a certain value determined by examining a particular statistical table (a table of the *F* distribution), we would reject the null hypothesis and conclude that the difference between the three mean scores is generalizable. However, analysis of variance does not tell us which of the differences between the three mean scores is generalizable. If we represent the three mean scores by the symbols A, B, and C, we see that three comparisons are possible: A versus B, A versus C, and B versus C. One or more of these comparisons might be generalizable. To make these comparisons, a special form of the *t* test is applied to each comparison. The most common of these special tests is Tukey's test and Scheffé's test.

Another application of analysis of variance is to determine the likelihood that differences in the standard deviations of two or more groups occurred by chance. For example, we could use analysis of variance to test whether the standard deviations of the interest scores for the two groups of employed students ($SD = 6.73$) and nonemployed students ($SD = 6.43$) differ by chance. More accurately, we would be testing whether the variances in the two sets of scores differ by chance. (Variance is a measure of the variability in a set of scores; it is calculated by squaring the standard deviation.)

Analysis of variance plays an important role in drawing conclusions from data yielded by experiments. To understand its role in this context, we constructed data for a hypothetical experiment comparing two types of text. Two groups of students were formed prior to the experiment: (1) students with high reading ability and (2) students with low reading ability. Students in each group were randomly assigned to the experimental and control treatments. Students in the experimental treatment read a text passage with inserted questions inviting them to relate the information being presented to something they already knew. Students in the control treatment read the same text passage but with no inserted questions. A multiple-choice test covering the content of the text passage was administered a day before students read the passage (the pretest) and a day after (the posttest).

Table 6.5 shows descriptive statistics for each subgroup (e.g., high-reading-ability students in the experimental group) on the posttest. Also shown are descriptive statistics for combinations of subgroups, for example, the mean score and standard deviation for all experimental-group students, ignoring whether they have high or low reading ability.

Many comparisons are possible for the mean scores shown in Table 6.5, for example, all experimental-group students versus all control-group students; high-ability students versus low-ability students in the experimental group; high-ability students in the experimental group versus high-ability students in the control group. One could do *t* tests for all these comparisons. However, not only is this procedure tedious, but as the number of comparisons increases so does the likelihood of false conclusions. (It can be shown mathematically that, as the frequency of inferential statistics calculated for a set of data increases, so does the likelihood of falsely rejecting the null hypothesis.) Analysis of variance is a more elegant and accurate method of making all the comparisons at once to determine which ones are likely to be chance differences.

TABLE 6.5 Posttest Scores for Students Classified by Reading Ability and Experimental or Control-Group Assignment

Experimental group		Control group	
High reading ability	Low reading ability	High reading ability	Low reading ability
23	18	19	3
14	17	12	7
16	9	16	1
18	10	14	6
16	17	7	4
17	19	8	7
19	8	13	6
20	20	10	5
17	15	19	3
17	16	9	2
$M = 17.70$	$M = 14.90$	$M = 12.70$	$M = 4.40$
$SD = 2.50$	$SD = 4.33$	$SD = 4.32$	$SD = 2.12$

	Subgroup statistics		
Subgroup	**N**	**M**	**SD**
Experimental group	20	16.30	3.73
Control group	20	8.55	5.39
High-reading-ability group	20	15.20	4.29
Low-reading-ability group	20	9.65	6.33

Table 6.6 shows a summary of the *F* values generated by the analysis of variance of the data presented in Table 6.5, and whether each *F* value is statistically significant ($p = .05$ or less). The first line of results shows the *F* value (49.88) for the comparison of all experimental-group students ($M = 16.30$) and all control-group students ($M = 8.55$) on the posttest, ignoring whether the students have high or low reading ability. This *F* value is statistically significant ($p < .001$), meaning that the difference is generalizable. The second line shows the *F* value (25.58) for the comparison of all high-reading-ability students ($M = 15.20$) and all low-reading-ability students ($M = 9.65$) on the posttest. The *F* value, too, is statistically significant ($p < .001$).

The next line shows an *F* value of 6.28 ($p. < .05$) for the interaction effect. In educational practice, an interaction effect is implied when we claim that different instructional methods are effective for different types of students. In

TABLE 6.6   **Summary of Analysis of Variance for Posttest Scores in Hypothetical Experiment on Inserted Questions in Text**

Source	F	p
Treatment (T)	49.88	< .001
Reading ability (R)	25.58	< .001
T × R reaction	6.28	< .05

statistics, an interaction effect is said to have occurred when the difference between two groups on variable *B* varies according to the value of variable *A*. To understand what this means, consider the research results shown in Table 6.5. For students with low reading ability (one level of variable *B*), the difference in the posttest mean scores of the experimental and control groups (variable *A*) is substantial (14.90 − 4.40 = 10.50 points). For students with high reading ability (the other level of treatment variable *B*), the difference in the posttest mean scores of the experimental and control students (variable *A*) is much smaller (17.70 − 12.70 = 5.00 points). Thus, it appears that the experimental text passage helped poor readers much more than it helped good readers. The inclusion of both variables in the experimental design yielded a better understanding of the experimental treatment's effectiveness than if the design had only compared an experimental group and a control group.

The experiment described above is fairly simple. There are two levels of each variable (sometimes called a *factor*). The first factor is the type of reading passage, and it has two levels: inserted questions versus no inserted questions. The other factor is reading ability, and it also has two levels: high versus low. Some experiments reported in the research literature have more complex designs, for example, three factors with three or more levels of one or more of the factors. Analysis of variance is capable of testing the statistical significance of group differences on each factor and also the statistical significance of the various interaction effects.

Analysis of variance is widely used in educational research because of its versatility. However, it can produce inaccurate results if the distribution of scores for any of the measures deviates substantially from the normal curve. Another condition that can produce inaccurate results is large differences in the size of the groups being compared.

Analysis of Covariance

We have ignored up to this point the pretest results for our hypothetical experiment. (The pretest was administered in order to determine how much students

TABLE 6.7 Pretest Means for Students in Hypothetical Experiment on Inserted Questions in Text

	Experimental group M	Control group M
High-ability readers	10.10	7.70
Low-ability readers	4.30	2.90

knew about the text passage content prior to the experiment.) The pretest mean scores for each group are shown in Table 6.7. These results complicate our interpretation of the posttest results, because they show that the experimental group had higher scores on the pretest than did the control group. The experimental group's superior knowledge of the text passage content beforehand, rather than the inserted questions in the text passage, might be responsible for its higher score on the posttest.

We could eliminate superior preknowledge as an explanation for the results by doing another experiment in which the students selected for the experimental and control groups were equivalent on the pretest. This solution, however, is time-consuming and expensive. Another solution is to use gain scores, which are computed by subtracting the pretest score from the posttest score for each student in the experiment. However, as we discussed earlier in the chapter, gain scores have several limitations, and so they are rarely used to analyze experimental data.

The best solution to the problem is to make the groups equivalent on the pretest by applying a statistical technique known as analysis of covariance. In this method, each student's posttest score is adjusted up or down to take into account his or her pretest performance. Statistical tables in research reports sometimes show both the actual posttest means and the adjusted posttest means after analysis of covariance has been applied. There is no need to do an analysis of variance if an analysis of covariance has been conducted. Analysis of covariance yields F values similar in meaning to those described above.

The procedure used in analysis of covariance is somewhat similar to the handicapping procedure used in sports such as golf. Poor golf players can compete with good golf players by being assigned a handicap based on their past performance. Each golf player's score in a tournament is determined by how much better or worse she does than her handicap (that is, her previous performance).

Analysis of covariance requires certain conditions and mathematical assumptions to yield valid results. If the research data do not satisfy these assumptions, the results of the analysis of covariance are likely to be invalid. In reading a research report, you should look for a statement by the researchers that they checked at least the key assumptions before using this statistical method. If there is no such statement, you should view the F values and p values associated with them with caution.

We explained analysis of covariance and analysis of variance by referring to hypothetical experiments. The same techniques can be used to test the statistical significance of results yielded by research designs that do not involve experimentation. These designs are explained in Chapter 7.

The Chi-Square Test

The *t* test, analysis of variance, and analysis of covariance are appropriate inferential statistics for data that are in continuous or rank score form. They are not appropriate for categorical data. The chi-square test is the appropriate test of statistical significance in this case.

To illustrate the use of this test, suppose that we want to determine whether urban school districts are more likely to employ female school superintendents than are rural school districts. A random sample of 100 urban school districts and 100 rural school districts is drawn from a population of school districts. The gender of each district's superintendent is determined.

The two variables involved in this study are gender (male vs. female) and type of school district (urban vs. rural). Both variables are categorical because they cannot be ordered on a continuum. For example, a rural district is neither "more" nor "less" than an urban district.

Table 6.8 shows hypothetical data relating to our research question. The descriptive statistics are in the form of frequencies, each frequency being the number of superintendents in each gender category for a particular type of district. Table 6.7 shows that the distributions of male and female superintendents vary across districts. We need to determine whether these differences occurred by chance or are characteristic of other districts similar to those used in the study.

The chi-square test is used to make this determination. It yields an inferential statistic known as *chi*, which is squared and represented by the symbol χ^2. The χ^2 value for the distributions shown in Table 6.8 is 7.42. This value is associated with a *p* value that is less than .01. Therefore, we reject the null hypothesis that these results occurred by chance. Instead, we conclude that they can be generalized to the population of districts having similar characteristics to those in the study.

TABLE 6.8   **Distribution of Male and Female Superintendents in Urban and Rural School Districts**

	Urban	Rural
Males	65	82
Females	35	18

Parametric versus Nonparametric Tests

All the tests of statistical significance described above, with the exception of the chi-square test, are parametric tests. These tests make several assumptions about the measures being used and the populations that are represented by the research samples. These assumptions are that there are equal intervals between the scores on the measures, that the scores are normally distributed about the mean score, and that the scores of the different comparison groups have equal variances.

Suppose the assumptions underlying parametric tests, especially the assumption of equal intervals, cannot be satisfied. In this case, researchers might use a parametric test anyway if the assumptions are not violated seriously. They could instead use a nonparametric test of statistical significance. The chi-square test is the most commonly used nonparametric test, because many variables are in the form of categories, which do not form an interval scale.

Other nonparametric tests sometimes found in the research literature are the Mann-Whitney *U* test and the Wilcoxon signed-rank test. These are nonparametric counterparts of the *t* test. Another nonparametric test is the Kruskal-Wallis test, which is the nonparametric counterpart of analysis of variance.

PRACTICAL SIGNIFICANCE AND EFFECT SIZE

As previously noted, statistical significance should not be confused with practical significance. If a result is statistically significant, it means only that the result probably did not occur by chance, and so one can generalize from the sample to the population that it represents. Even a trivial result can be statistically significant if the sample is sufficiently large, because the calculation of inferential statistics is affected by sample size. The larger the sample, the smaller the observed result required for statistical significance.

The practical significance of statistical results is a matter of judgment. For example, an experimental treatment might have only a small effect on learning relative to conventional instruction, but the type of learning might be so important that even small increments of learning are worthwhile.

Researchers have developed a statistical approach to determining practical significance. This approach involves the calculation of a statistic known as *effect size*. It is discussed in Chapter 4, which concerns procedures for synthesizing research findings. For present purposes, we will note only that the effect size statistic is most commonly used as an aid in determining the practical significance of the results yielded by experiments. It provides a numerical expression of how well the experimental group learned or otherwise performed relative to the control group. Effect sizes of .33 or larger generally are considered to have practical significance.

Although the effect size statistic provides useful information, it should not be the sole basis for making judgments about the practical significance of statistical results. You should examine the total context of the research study, especially the measures that were used and the scores they generated, in judging whether an observed result is sufficiently large to have implications for practice.

CONCLUDING THOUGHT

Numbers are important in the education profession. They are used to represent demographic characteristics of communities, students' performance on tests, school expenditures, and other important variables. Numbers are equally important to researchers as representations of the educational phenomena that they seek to understand. In this chapter, we have shown how statistics can be used to summarize numerical data in ways that are meaningful to educators and other groups, to explore relationships among variables, and to check the validity of inferences based on data from a sample to a large population.

SELF-CHECK TEST

1. Statistics
   a. are never used in qualitative research.
   b. are frequently used in quantitative research.
   c. are only used to analyze achievement test data.
   d. cannot be used to analyze interview and video data.

2. Percentile scores
   a. are a type of derived score.
   b. are a type of raw score.
   c. yield the same information as grade equivalents.
   d. are used in educational practice, but not in educational research.

3. Ceiling effects are most likely to be found when
   a. the median is used as an indicator of average performance on a test.
   b. a large percentage of the sample scores low on a test.
   c. the distribution of scores deviates from the normal curve.
   d. raw scores are converted to gain scores.

4. If a distribution of test scores deviates substantially from the normal curve, the average score is best represented by the
   a. mean.
   b. median.
   c. mode.
   d. average variation.

5. A student who scores two standard deviation units above the mean on a test would be approximately
   a. between the 50th and 60th percentiles of the score distribution.
   b. between the 61st and 75th percentiles of the score distribution.
   c. between the 76th and 90th percentiles of the score distribution.
   d. above the 90th percentile of the score distribution.

6. If researchers wish to know how well the combination of students' high school GPA and college aptitude test scores predicts their college GPA, they most likely would use
   a. analysis of variance.
   b. analysis of covariance.
   c. multivariate correlational statistics.
   d. bivariate correlational statistics.

7. The purpose of inferential statistics is to determine whether
   a. a set of scores forms a normal distribution.
   b. the sample size is sufficiently large to detect real differences between the experimental and control group.
   c. an observed result is a chance finding.
   d. the results of one study constitute a non-chance replication of the results of another study.

8. The likelihood that the null hypothesis is false is greatest when the p value is
   a. .001.
   b. .01.
   c. .10.
   d. 1.00.

9. If the pretest scores of two groups in an experiment differ, researchers usually can compensate for this problem by
   a. using analysis of covariance.
   b. using analysis of variance.
   c. converting the pretest and posttest scores to gain scores.
   d. using a nonparametric test of statistical significance.

10. Nonparametric tests of statistical significance
    a. assume that the scores to be analyzed form an interval scale.
    b. do not assume that the scores to be analyzed form an interval scale.
    c. must be used even if the scores constitute a minor violation of the assumptions underlying analysis of variance.
    d. can be used only with continuous scores.

11. Decisions about the practical significance of research findings are aided by the calculation of a(n)
    a. *p* value.
    b. *F* value.
    c. standard deviation.
    d. effect size statistic.

RECOMMENDED READING

Bruning, J. L., & Kintz, B. L. (1990). *Computational handbook of statistics* (3rd ed.). Reading, MA: Addison-Wesley Educational.

This book provides easy-to-follow computational procedures for most of the statistical techniques presented in this chapter.

Linn, R. L. (1986). Quantitative methods in research on teaching. In M. C. Wittrock (Ed.), *Handbook of research on teaching* (3rd ed.) (pp. 92–118). New York: Macmillan.

The author provides a mathematical discussion of the statistical techniques covered in this chapter and also of more sophisticated aspects of statistical analysis. The relationship among research design, causal inference, and statistical analysis is discussed.

Shaver, J. P. (1985). Chance and nonsense: Part 1. *Phi Delta Kappan, 67*(1), 57–60; Chance and nonsense: Part 2. *Phi Delta Kappan, 67*(2), 138–141.

This is an interesting and easily understood series of two articles written as a conversation between two teachers. Such concepts as statistical significance, practical significance, statistical power, and effect size are discussed in the context of one teacher's thesis study.

Vogt, W. P. (1993). *Dictionary of statistics and methodology: A nontechnical guide for the social sciences.* Thousand Oaks, CA: Sage.

This is a helpful guide to statistical and methodological terms that you are likely to encounter as you read reports of educational research studies.

CHAPTER 7

DESCRIPTIVE AND CAUSAL-COMPARATIVE RESEARCH

Sue Griffin is a middle school teacher whose daughter Bethany started high school two months ago. Bethany has always loved school, and done well. But now she's staying up late, and Sue has to coax, threaten, and shake her to get her out of bed each morning. Bethany's first-period teacher noted on her midterm report card, "Sleeping in class."

Then Sue read a newspaper article titled, "Your teenager might not be lazy, just sleepy." It described the research of several professors showing that most adolescents need more sleep than adults, but do not become sleepy until later at night. It quoted a principal who noted positive effects on students' energy and learning after his school district shifted its start time two hours later for its middle schools and high schools.

Sue suggested that Bethany adjust her class schedule to keep first period free so that she can sleep longer in the morning. Next she plans to do a literature search on the professors who were mentioned in the article. Sue thinks, "I'll look for other ideas to help my own kids. And if what I learn convinces me that a later start time really works, I may ask my principal to consider it for our middle school."

In this chapter you will learn how educational researchers conduct descriptive studies to help educators like Sue understand more about the behavior and needs of the groups involved in education, including students, teachers, administrators, and policy makers. You also will learn about causal-comparative research, in which researchers explore possible cause-and-effect relationships among variables (like the relationship between the amount of sleep that teenagers get and their school achievement) that are difficult to manipulate experimentally.

OBJECTIVES

After studying this chapter, you will be able to

1. distinguish between descriptive, relationship, and experimental research.
2. describe the purpose and data collection methods of survey research.
3. state an advantage of direct observation as a method of gathering descriptive information.
4. describe procedures that can be used to increase the validity and reliability of research findings based on direct observation.
5. explain the purpose and methods of longitudinal and cross-sectional research.
6. name and give an example of each of the two types of descriptive statistics that are used to analyze research data.

7. explain why causal-comparative research sometimes is used instead of experimental research to examine possible cause-and-effect relationships between two variables.

8. explain why the selection of comparable groups is important in causal-comparative research.

9. name and give an example of each of the two types of inferential statistics that are used to analyze causal-comparative or experimental research data.

10. describe three possible interpretations that can be made when causal-comparative research finds a significant relationship between two variables.

11. describe two conditions under which inferences about cause-and-effect relationships from causal-comparative research are nearly as sound as those from experimental research.

12. describe the similarities and differences between causal-comparative and correlational research.

KEY TERMS

ability test	direct observation	paper-and-pencil test
causal-comparative research	experimental research	parametric statistics
cause-and-effect relationship	independent variable	questionnaire
central tendency	inferential statistics	relationship research
comparison group	inter-observer agreement	sampling bias
correlational research	interview	self-report
cross-sectional research	longitudinal research	survey research
dependent variable	nonparametric statistics	variability
descriptive research	observer bias	

THE NATURE OF DESCRIPTIVE, RELATIONSHIP, AND EXPERIMENTAL RESEARCH

Most quantitative research studies can be placed in one of three broad categories: descriptive, relationship, and experimental research. Descriptive research aims to provide a clear, accurate description of individuals, events, or processes. For example, descriptive research might identify how reading teachers plan their lessons and how much time they spend in planning.

Relationship research includes both causal-comparative research, which is described in this chapter, and correlational research, the subject of Chapter 8. Relationship research is more complex than descriptive research because it explores observed relationships among variables. An example would be a study to determine whether the students of reading teachers who spend more time planning their lessons (variable 1) develop better reading comprehension skills (variable 2).

Experimentation is the most complex type of research, because the researchers manipulate one or more variables and measure the effect on another variable or set of variables. For example, an experiment might involve training one group of teachers (the experimental group), but not training another group of teachers (the control group), in effective lesson planning techniques (the independent variable). Then the effects of lesson planning on students' reading comprehension skills (the dependent variable) might be measured.

DESCRIPTIVE RESEARCH

Descriptive research involves the collection and analysis of quantitative data in order to develop a precise description of a sample's behavior or personal characteristics. (Qualitative descriptive research is discussed in Chapter 10.) Researchers can describe a sample at one point in time only, or they can use longitudinal or cross-sectional research designs to describe a sample over time. Below we explain the various methods used in descriptive research.

Survey Research

Survey research is a form of descriptive research that involves collecting information about research participants' beliefs, attitudes, interests, or behavior through questionnaires, interviews, or paper-and-pencil tests. Opinion polls are a well-known example of survey research. Surveys can be used to explore many topics of interest to educators, for example: the extent to which cooperative learning occurs in elementary school classrooms, school district policies for serving students for whom English is a second language, and parents' preferences for various alternatives for schooling their children.

Descriptive studies that deal with highly sensitive topics, such as students' attitudes about sexuality, or that attempt to elicit deeper responses than can be elicited by questionnaires, frequently employ interviews. Some surveys use both questionnaires and interviews, the former to collect basic descriptive information from a large sample and the latter to follow up the questionnaire responses in depth with a smaller sample.

Because survey research is based on self-report, respondents can conceal information that they do not want others to know. Also, even if respondents want to give accurate information, they may not have the self-awareness to do so. For these reasons, the data obtained through survey research are likely to be distorted or incomplete to an unknown degree.

If researchers establish good rapport with the research participants and demonstrate that they are using some system to ensure the confidentiality of responses, self-report data will produce more accurate results. In addition, researchers can use the strategies described in Chapter 5 to design questionnaires, interviews, or tests so as to minimize leading questions or questions that give respondents clues as to what answers are socially desirable.

The procedure that is used to select the research sample is very important in survey research. For example, if survey researchers drew their sample from the telephone directory to predict the outcomes of a bond election, the resulting sample would be biased, because many individuals have unlisted telephone numbers or do not have telephones. Sampling bias also occurs when the response rate is low, because nonrespondents tend to differ from respondents, as explained in Chapter 5.

In some descriptive studies, tests of ability or achievement are administered to the research participants. The test scores provide a picture of individuals' ability to perform particular intellectual tasks. However, intellectual performance is dependent to some extent on motivation. For example, if students do not have a good reason to perform at their best level, they may not take the test seriously.

Some descriptive studies involve the administration of measures of personality and other personal characteristics. Most of these measures involve self-report and thus, like questionnaires or interviews, they may provide biased responses. Therefore, in reading descriptive research studies, you must consider the question of whether any conclusions about individuals based on self-report data are likely to be accurate.

Direct Observation

You were introduced to direct observation as a measurement procedure in Chapter 5. Direct observation involves gathering "live" data about individuals' behavior as the behavior occurs. Observations are more objective than surveys because they do not depend on research participants' self-report. For example, we probably could learn much more about students' racial attitudes by observing students of different ethnic groups during actual interactions with one another than by analyzing their answers to questions on a paper-and-pencil test about how they would behave in various situations involving interracial interactions.

Direct observation is especially effective when researchers want to study specific aspects of human behavior in detail. For example, the following questions are well suited for study by observation: How do school psychologists interact with parents when reporting their children's test results? How do preschool children behave after watching a television program that contains a large number of violent acts? How do parents interact with their children when discussing homework assignments?

In reviewing studies that employ direct observation, you should pay particular attention to the procedures used by the researchers to avoid the potential for observer bias. For example, suppose that observers record the social behavior of kindergarten children during free play. They might perceive more social behavior in those children who the observers know have higher verbal aptitude. The best approach to reduce observer bias is to design the observational procedures so that observers do not have prior knowledge of the research participants' backgrounds or characteristics.

To increase the validity of observational research data, researchers should use narrow, specific definitions of the behavior to be observed rather than broad, general definitions; measure low-inference variables (e.g., counting the number of times that specific actions occur during a game instead of rating each individual's sports performance from poor to excellent); and require observers to record only as many aspects of behavior as they can effectively attend to.

To collect reliable observational data, it is desirable to train observers carefully. Most good reports of observational research describe the procedures that were used to train the observers. They also include information on inter-observer agreement, that is, the extent to which the observations of two or more observers agree when the observers have independently observed the same events.

Description of a Sample Over Time

Most descriptive research involves reporting the characteristics of a sample at one point in time. In some descriptive studies, however, researchers want to examine patterns of stability or change in individuals from one point in time to another. This research helps us understand changes within individuals due to maturation or significant life experiences, or changes common to many individuals from one time period to another.

In longitudinal research, researchers collect data from either the same or a different sample from a given population at two or more separate points in time. For example, C. C. Carson, R. M. Huelskamp, and T. D. Woodall (1993) studied a cohort of high school students who were projected to complete their senior year in 1982. The researchers contacted the individuals in the sample in 1982 and again in 1984 and 1986, in order to determine how many had completed high school by then. At the first data-collection point (1982), only 82.7 percent of the students had completed high school, which represents a dropout rate of 17.3 percent. However, by 1984, 5.2 percent more of the students had completed high school, either by returning to high school or by earning a General Equivalency Degree (GED). By 1986, another 2.8 percent of the students had completed high school. On this expanded time frame, a total of 90.7 percent of the students had completed high school. The 9.3-percent dropout rate found in this cohort study is substantially lower than the rate reported in nonlongitudinal studies (typically, 25 to 30 percent).

Researchers also can study a sample at different points in time by using a cross-sectional research design. In cross-sectional research, researchers collect data at the same time from groups of individuals who are of different ages or at different stages of development. Let's say that researchers want to examine changes in female students' attitudes toward mathematics as they mature. It would take a long time to follow a group of first-grade girls through 12 years of education and measure their attitudes every few years. Instead they could select samples of girls in, for example, the first, fourth, eighth, and twelfth grades, and, on a given date, measure each sample's attitudes toward mathematics. Differences between mean attitude scores at different grade levels could be interpreted as reflecting developmental changes in female students' attitudes toward mathematics. However, in order to reach this conclusion it is important to ensure that the samples do not differ on some other key characteristic besides grade level. For example, if instructional practices changed over time, the samples also would differ in the nature of their mathematics instruction. Perhaps the twelfth graders received no instruction in estimation during elementary school, for example, whereas the current sample of fourth graders may have been taught estimation as part of their instruction in mathematics.

Data Analysis in Descriptive Research

The procedures used to analyze descriptive research data are fairly simple to understand. Table 7.1 summarizes common statistics that are often presented in descriptive research reports. You will note that all of the statistics are measures of central tendency or measures of variability.

Several of these descriptive statistics were used in the study reprinted at the end of this chapter. The two researchers, David Conley and Paul Goldman, sent a 99-item questionnaire to over 2,000 educators in 20 Oregon school districts, to assess their reactions to state legislation mandating new high school graduation requirements and other reforms.

Table 7.2 shows several of the descriptive statistics that are reported in the article. The main columns of the table show the sample's responses to four scales: (1) Change orientation (the belief that the schools need to change and that the legislation will foster that change), (2) Resistance to change (skepticism about and opposition to the mandated changes), (3) Learning outcomes (belief

TABLE 7.1   Statistical Techniques Used to Analyze Descriptive Research Data

Procedure	Purpose
Measures of central tendency	**Provide a quantitative measure of the most representative or typical score in a score distribution**
Mean (*M*)	Equals the sum of the scores divided by the number of scores (*N*). Reported in almost all descriptive research studies.
Median (Med)	The middle score in the score distribution. Used when extreme scores would distort the mean.
Mode	The most frequently obtained score in the score distribution. A crude measure of central tendency that is seldom used in research.
Measures of variability	**Provide a quantitative measure of the distribution of individual scores around the mean**
Range	The difference between the lowest and highest scores in the distribution, plus 1.
Standard deviation (*SD*)	Based on the deviations of individual scores from the mean. Most widely used measure of group variability.
Variance	The square of the standard deviation.

TABLE 7.2   Scale Means for Educators' Reactions to State Restructuring Legislation

	Change orientation	Resistance to change	Learning outcomes	Changes in practices	N
Sample					2,257
Mean	41.0	34.7	63.9	60.7	
SD	30.3	22.7	23.2	32.2	

Source. Taken from Table 3 on p. 525 in: Conley, D. T., & Goldman, P. (1995). Reactions from the field to state restructuring legislation. *Educational Administration Quarterly, 31,* 512–538. Reprinted by permission of Sage Publications, Inc.

that specific features of the legislation will lead to increased student learning), and (4) Changes in practices (belief that the legislation will lead to specific changes in educators' practices in the schools).

Each scale is composed of 5 to 16 items in the questionnaire. For example, the Change Orientation scale consists of five items. The researchers summed the number of items to which each respondent expressed agreement, and divided the sum by the total number of items (in this case, five) to yield a percentage score for each respondent. Thus if a respondent agreed with three of the five items concerning change orientation, that respondent's percentage score would be 60 percent. The percentage scores for all 2,257 educators in the sample then were summed and divided by 2,257 to yield the mean percentage score.

Looking at Table 7.2, we find that, on average, the educators' mean percentage of agreement with the items in the Change Orientation scale was 41.0 percent, and the mean percentage of agreement with the items in the Resistance to Change scale was 34.7 percent. We find, too, that, on average, the educators showed greater agreement with the items in the Learning Outcomes scale (63.9 percent) and the Changes in Practices scale (60.7 percent).

The researchers reported another descriptive statistic, the standard deviation, for most of the mean scores presented in their article. The standard deviation is a measure of how much the individuals in a sample vary in their scores. Looking at Table 7.2, we find that the standard deviation for the educators' percentage-of-agreement scores on the Change Orientation scale is 30.3. This is a rather large standard deviation. It indicates that many of the educators in the sample had a much higher percentage of agreement, or a much lower percentage of agreement, with the items on the Change Orientation scale than the mean percentage of 41 percent.

The descriptive statistics shown in Table 7.2 at first might seem to you to be somewhat abstract, or even "cold." However, keep in mind that these statistics summarize an enormous amount of data, namely, over two thousand educators' responses on four different scales. It would be very difficult to make sense of these data by considering them for one educator at a time. By examining the means and standard deviations that the researchers used to condense the data, we quickly can see the main patterns in these educators' attitudes toward state legislative methods for school reform.

CAUSAL-COMPARATIVE RESEARCH

In many research projects, investigators want to examine the possible effects of variables that are difficult or impossible to manipulate experimentally. A study by Gary Green and Sue Jaquess (1987) illustrates this point. These researchers were interested in the effect of high school students' part-time employment on their academic achievement. The sample included 477 high school juniors, some of whom were unemployed and some of whom were employed at least 10 hours a week. It would not be feasible to manipulate student employment experimentally, requiring some students to work part time and others not to work at all. Instead, through careful sampling, the researchers were able to select two comparable groups of students and then assess the effects of natural variations in their employment.

In causal-comparative research, a variable that is hypothesized to cause an observed difference is called an *independent variable*. The variable in which the difference is observed is called the *dependent variable*. In the study described above, employment is the independent variable because it is hypothesized to affect students' academic achievement, which is the dependent variable.

In reviewing causal-comparative studies, you should examine whether there is any evidence that the two groups are similar except for the independent variable on which they are being compared. If two groups are formed because they differ on independent variable X, but they also happen to differ on variable Y, the researchers will not know whether group differences on the dependent variable are caused by variables X or Y. In the study by Green and Jaquess, the employed students were found to have lower scores on a measure of scholastic aptitude. Thus we do not know whether their lower academic achievement (the dependent variable) is the result of their employment (independent variable X) or their lower academic aptitude (independent variable Y). To rule out independent variable Y, the researchers would have to select groups of employed and nonemployed students with similar aptitude. Another possibility is to use a statistical technique that can determine the relative effects of independent variable X and independent variable Y on the dependent variable. (Analysis of covariance or multiple regression typically is used for this purpose.)

Examples of other situations amenable to causal-comparative research include comparisons of the academic motivation of adolescent boys and girls, the test performance of students with adequate nutrition and students with inadequate nutrition, and the duties and work satisfaction of special educators who work in large school districts and those who work in small school districts.

In all these examples the causal-comparative research design permits study of the effects of variables that are difficult to manipulate experimentally with human research participants. Even if it were possible to manipulate such variables, it might be unethical to do so. For example, researchers could not ethically withhold adequate nutrition from one group of research participants in order to study the effect of nutrition on academic performance.

Forming Comparison Groups

Sometimes the independent variable used to form comparison groups is in the form of discrete categories. Gender is an example of such a variable; an individual is either male or female. In the world of work, job classifications are typically discrete. For example, an individual might be classified as a custodian, teacher, secretary, or counselor.

In other situations, the independent variable forms a continuum, and researchers select comparison groups depending on which parts of the continuum they wish to study. For example, suppose that some researchers are interested in whether there is a relationship between students' nutrition (the hypothesized independent variable) and school performance (the hypothesized dependent variable). The researchers might obtain a measure of the nutritional adequacy of the diets of all the students in a school. The scores probably would range along a continuum of high to low. The researchers might choose to compare students at the extremes of the continuum, that is, students with very good nutrition and students with very poor nutrition. Alternatively, they could form multiple comparison groups that sample the entire continuum, for example, students with excellent nutrition, students with adequate nutrition, and students with poor nutrition.

Data Analysis in Causal-Comparative Research

In causal-comparative research, the typical first step in data analysis is to compute the mean score of each group on the dependent variable. Next, inferential statistics are used to determine whether any differences between the means are statistically significant. (Inferential statistics are explained in Chapter 6.)

Table 7.3 summarizes the inferential statistics that are most widely used in causal-comparative research. The same statistics also can be used to analyze data from experimental research, which is discussed in Chapter 9. Table 7.3 shows both parametric and nonparametric statistics for analyzing the data from causal-comparative or experimental research. As we stated in Chapter 6, nonparametric statistics are appropriate when the sets of data to be compared do not meet three assumptions: equal intervals between scores, normal distribution of scores about the mean score, and equal variances in the scores of the different comparison groups.

The study of school reform by Conley and Goldman that is reprinted in this chapter made extensive use of inferential statistics. For example, Conley and Goldman used analysis of variance to examine differences between elementary, middle, and high school educators in the responses to the four scales measuring beliefs and attitudes about school reform. Table 7.4 shows the mean score of each of these groups on each of the four scales. (You will note that the middle school group also included some junior high school educators, who serve a similar age range of students.) In general, high school educators express more

TABLE 7.3   Statistical Techniques Used to Analyze Causal-Comparative and Experimental Research Data

Test of statistical significance	Purpose
Parametric	
t test	Used primarily to determine whether two means differ significantly from each other; also used to determine whether a single mean differs significantly from a specified population value.
Analysis of variance	Used to determine whether mean scores on one or more variables differ significantly from each other and whether the variables interact significantly with each other.
Analysis of covariance	Similar to analysis of variance but permits adjustments to the post-treatment mean scores of different groups on the dependent variable to compensate for initial group differences on variables related to the dependent variable.
Nonparametric	
Mann-Whitney *U* test	Used to determine whether two uncorrelated means differ significantly from each other.
Wilcoxon signed-rank test	Used to determine whether two correlated means differ significantly from each other.
Kruskal-Wallis test	Used to determine whether the mean scores of three or more groups on a variable differ significantly from one another.
Chi-square test	Used to determine whether two frequency distributions or sets of categorical data differ significantly from each other.

positive attitudes and beliefs about state-legislated school reforms in Oregon than do elementary or middle school educators.

The *F* value below each column of mean scores in Table 7.4 indicates the results of an analysis of variance. The purpose of this statistical analysis is to determine whether the mean scores of the groups on a particular variable are

TABLE 7.4   Scale Means by School Level for Educators' Reactions to State Restructuring Legislation

	Change orientation	Resistance to change	Learning outcomes	Changes in practices	*N*
High school	45.0	32.1	64.3	64.8	802
Junior high and middle	38.7	35.1	63.3	54.0	596
Elementary	39.1	38.5	63.1	61.0	768
F	9.2**	10.3**	0.3	16.1**	

$^*p < .05$; $^{**}p < .01$.

Source. Taken from Table 3 on p. 525 in: Conley, D. T., & Goldman, P. (1995). Reactions from the field to state restructuring legislation. *Educational Administration Quarterly, 31,* 512–538. Reprinted by permission of Sage Publications, Inc.

significantly different from each other. Two asterisks after an *F* value signify statistical significance at the .01 level. If an observed difference is statistically significant, that means that it probably did not occur by chance. (Statistical significance is explained in more detail in Chapter 6.)

When three or more mean scores are being compared, the finding of a significant *F* value can be followed by a statistical test to determine which pairs of means differ significantly from each other. Conley and Goldman used one of these tests (Tukey's HSD test) for this purpose. For example, on the Change Orientation scale, they found that the difference between the mean scores of high school educators (45.0) and middle school educators (38.7) was statistically significant. The difference between the mean scores of high school educators and elementary school educators (39.1) also was statistically significant. However, the difference between the mean scores of the middle school educators and the elementary school educators was not statistically significant.

Interpreting Causal-Comparative Research Findings

Causal-comparative research is valuable in identifying possible causes or effects, but it usually cannot provide definitive support for the hypothesis that one of the variables being studied caused the observed differences in the other variable. When we find that different scores on variable *A* are associated with different scores on variable *B*, three possible interpretations can be made: that differences in variable *A* caused the observed differences in variable *B*; that differences in variable *B* caused the observed differences in variable *A*; or that the differences in both variables *A* and *B* were caused by differences in a third variable, *C*.

Under certain conditions, the findings from causal-comparative research can be accepted as supporting a hypothesized cause-and-effect relationship with nearly the same level of confidence as experimental findings. These conditions are:

1. When the variables are time-ordered, meaning that variable *A* always occurs before variable *B*. In this sequence of events, variable *A* could cause variable *B*, but it is impossible for variable *B* to have caused variable *A*. For example, consider studies of the relationship between cigarette smoking and lung cancer. In such studies the smoking (variable *A*) always occurs before the incidence of lung cancer (variable *B*), so it is impossible to say that lung cancer caused the smoking. Thus, we can conclude that if a causal relationship exists, it can occur in only one direction.

2. When many causal-comparative studies have been conducted by different researchers working with different samples in different settings, and consistent results emerge from these studies. Again, this is the case with causal-comparative research on smoking and lung cancer. When the combined evidence from

these studies is considered, the probability that these results could occur if smoking does not cause lung cancer is so slight that most scientists who have worked in the area have accepted the combined results as definite evidence of a causal relationship.

The interpretation of causal-comparative findings can be illustrated by examining one finding of the study reprinted in this chapter. As shown in Table 7.4, Conley and Goldman found that educators who work in high schools had a more positive orientation toward school change and expected more positive results from the mandated changes than educators who work in junior high, middle, or elementary schools. These findings contradicted the researchers' predictions, based on earlier research, "that high school educators would be more wary than those in elementary schools" (Conley & Goldman, 1995, p. 523 in the original article). Their data led them to conclude that there is apparent support for large-scale change in high schools.

What are the possible causal implications of high school educators' greater apparent willingness to undertake the changes required by these legislated reforms? One might reason that it is in high school that the current system of education breaks down most severely for many students. If so, the high school teachers in this research sample might have had more direct experience with the problems of the current system, and hence could be expected to have greater openness to proposed changes. The presumed cause-and-effect relationship, then, is that level of schooling (variable A) directly affects attitudes toward proposed school reform (variable B). However, if this hypothesis is true for this sample, the results might not generalize to school districts in which only a small proportion of high school students were dropping out or experiencing other learning problems or personal difficulties.

A second possibility is that variable B (attitudes toward proposed school reform) causes variable A (level of schooling). Because of the time-ordered nature of variables A and B (that is, specific proposals for school reform came after the educators who were surveyed had been hired into their current positions), this presumed cause-and-effect relationship is not realistic.

Another possibility is that educators who generally are more flexible and open to change are attracted to work at the high-school level. In this case, variable C (flexibility and openness to change) can be hypothesized to cause both variable A (level of schooling) and variable B (attitudes toward proposed school reform). If this were true, even educators in high schools in which students were experiencing very few learning problems or personal difficulties would presumably be supportive of the proposed school reforms.

How researchers interpret their findings with respect to the presumed cause-and-effect relationship between variables such as school level and the respondents' survey responses will influence the direction of their future research. Indeed, Conley's comments preceding the reprinted article suggest that he and his colleagues have shifted to qualitative research methods (e.g., focus groups) in order to examine more closely the causal connections between educators' characteristics and their receptivity to school reform.

Similarities between Causal-Comparative Research and Correlational Research

Like correlational research, which you will study in Chapter 8, causal-comparative research involves the determination of a relationship between two or more variables. However, causal-comparative research is more often used to examine variables that involve dichotomies (such as male and female) or categories (such as administrators of elementary, middle, and high schools). Correlational research is better for examining relationships between continuous variables, which can be scored on a dimension from high to low (such as most measures of personality traits or aptitude).

In addition, causal-comparative research typically involves examining the relationship between only two variables at a time. By contrast, correlational techniques enable researchers to study and precisely quantify the nature of the relationship between three or more variables at the same time.

CONCLUDING THOUGHT

In this chapter we have asked you to frame your thinking about important issues in education in the way that educational researchers do. We began with descriptive research, which relies on straightforward forms of measurement (tests, questionnaires, interviews, and direct observation) and simple descriptive statistics. Applied properly, these research tools can identify meaningful patterns of beliefs, attitudes, and behavior in groups ranging from a small sample to an entire population. We also showed how researchers use causal-comparative research to explore possible cause-and-effect relationships involving educational variables. With increased knowledge of the variables that affect important educational outcomes (e.g., improved student learning and school reform), practitioners can design programs and other interventions that are more likely to achieve their intended outcomes.

SELF-CHECK TEST

1. Researchers plan to study whether students whose teachers ask more higher-cognitive questions are more attentive in class than other students. This study is an example of
   a. relationship research.
   b. survey research.
   c. experimental research.
   d. descriptive research.

2. Survey data are likely to be distorted or incomplete primarily because the data
    a. are obtained at only one point in time.
    b. are based on self-report.
    c. involve direct observation.
    d. cannot be analyzed by inferential statistics.

3. Direct observation is especially effective for studying
    a. research participants with highly developed verbal skills.
    b. research participants' beliefs and interests.
    c. specific details of human behavior.
    d. variables that form natural categories.

4. The best way to minimize the effects of observer bias in collecting observational data is to
    a. provide broad, general definitions of the behaviors to be observed.
    b. prevent the observers from having contact with one another.
    c. use observers who are well known to the research participants.
    d. ensure that observers have no prior knowledge about the research participants.

5. Researchers send a questionnaire to the parents of all the first graders in one school to measure their interest in participation in school site management activities. Two years later they send the same questionnaire to the same parents. This study is most clearly an example of
    a. observational research.
    b. experimental research.
    c. cross-sectional research.
    d. longitudinal research.

6. Researchers examine the distribution of scores on a test that was administered to a sample, and they determine the score that was most commonly obtained. This score is an example of a
    a. measure of central tendency.
    b. standard score.
    c. measure of variability.
    d. percentage.

7. Experimental research is preferable to causal-comparative research primarily when
    a. the researchers have not stated a hypothesis about which of two behaviors is the cause and which is the effect.
    b. the groups to be compared are known to be widely different on a number of variables.
    c. the variables being investigated are easily manipulated.
    d. it would be viewed as unethical to withhold an intervention from one of the comparison groups.

8. In forming comparison groups for causal-comparative research, researchers usually
   a. take steps to ensure that the groups are similar except with respect to the dependent variable.
   b. take steps to ensure that the groups are similar except with respect to the independent variable.
   c. select individuals whose scores on the independent variable are within one standard deviation above or below the mean score.
   d. select individuals whose scores on the independent variable fall at the high extreme of possible scores.

9. A nonparametric test of statistical significance should be used to analyze data from a causal-comparative study whenever
   a. the independent and dependent variables are time-ordered.
   b. the researchers hypothesized in advance that differences in one variable are the probable cause of differences in another variable.
   c. the variances in the scores of the different comparison groups on the dependent variable are grossly unequal.
   d. there are equal intervals between possible scores on the independent variable.

10. A researcher finds that parents who earned good grades in high school more often attend social activities at their sons' and daughters' high school than parents who earned poor grades in high school. What is the least plausible interpretation of this finding?
    a. High scholastic achievement causes parents to value their children's school activities.
    b. Participating in their children's school activities causes parents to do better in high school.
    c. Both parents' scholastic achievement and their participation in their children's school activities are caused by a third variable—for example, parents' socioeconomic status.
    d. There is a positive relationship between parents' own scholastic achievement and their participation in their children's high school activities.

11. Accepting causal-comparative research findings as supportive of a hypothesized cause-and-effect relationship is not possible when
    a. the comparison groups differ on a variable other than the independent variable that could affect the dependent variable.
    b. the researchers did not state their research hypothesis before collecting data.
    c. the independent variable necessarily occurs before the dependent variable in given individuals.
    d. other researchers have investigated the same phenomena and have obtained similar results.

12. Unlike correlational research, causal-comparative research
    a. studies possible cause-and-effect relationships between variables.
    b. is ideal for examining relationships between continuous variables.
    c. enables researchers to study the relationship between three or more variables at the same time.
    d. focuses on independent variables that involve categories.

CHAPTER REFERENCES

Carson, C. C., Huelskamp, R. M., & Woodall, T. D. (1993). Perspectives on education in America. *The Journal of Educational Research, 86,* 259–311.

Green, G., & Jaquess, S. N. (1987). The effect of part-time employment on academic achievement. *Journal of Educational Research, 80,* 325–329.

RECOMMENDED READING

Bruning, J. L., & Kintz, B. L. (1990). *Computational handbook of statistics* (3rd ed.). Reading, MA: Addison-Wesley Educational.
Provides a step-by-step computational guide for the statistical analyses commonly conducted in descriptive and causal-comparative studies.

Campbell, D. T., & Stanley, J. C. (1981). *Experimental and quasi-experimental designs for research.* Boston: Houghton Mifflin.
This classic work focuses on experimental research, but also discusses the causal-comparative method and the problems involved in drawing causal inferences from research results.

Croll, P. (1986). *Systematic classroom observation.* Philadelphia: Falmer Press.
Explains the design and conduct of observational research and the analysis of observational data, with many useful examples.

De Vaus, D. A. (1992). *Surveys in social research* (3rd ed.). Concord, MA: Paul & Company.
Covers all the major steps in survey research, from formulating a research question to analyzing data.

Fowler, F. J., Jr. (1993). *Survey research methods* (2nd ed.). Newbury Park, CA: Sage.
Covers a wide range of survey research topics, including sampling, nonresponse bias, data collection, questionnaire design, interviewing, and data analysis.

Stewart, C. J., & Cash, W. B., Jr. (1996). *Interviewing: Principles and practices* (8th ed.). Madison, WI: Brown & Benchmark.
Describes the process and structure of research interviewing and how to phrase questions. Various kinds of interviews are explained, including the survey interview.

SAMPLE DESCRIPTIVE AND CAUSAL-COMPARATIVE RESEARCH STUDY: REACTIONS FROM THE FIELD TO STATE RESTRUCTURING LEGISLATION

Conley, D. T., & Goldman, P. (1995). Reactions from the field to state restructuring legislation. *Educational Administration Quarterly*, 31, 512–538.

> In the rest of this chapter you will read a research article that illustrates the use of both the descriptive and causal-comparative research methods. It is preceded by comments written especially for this book by David Conley, the first author of the article. Then the article itself is reprinted in full, just as it appeared when originally published. Where appropriate, we have added footnotes to help you understand the information contained in the article.

Researcher's Comments, Prepared by David Conley

> The following study reports data on the perceptions of Oregon educators in late 1992 concerning school reform legislation passed by the Oregon legislature in 1991. I became interested in this research because of my concurrent work with schools in Oregon that were engaged in educational redesign, and my personal involvement in the formulation and passage of the legislation. I was most interested in how schools would react to the state's call for what amounted to fundamental restructuring.
>
> The legislation, termed the Oregon Educational Act for the 21st Century, or House Bill 3565, has several components that would dramatically affect schools. It mandates Certificates of Mastery, one to be obtained by all students at age 16 and the other at age 18, that are to be based on demonstrated student performance in comparison to state standards. The Certificate of Initial Mastery (CIM) focuses on skills that are cumulative throughout a student's educational career, to be assessed via "benchmarks" at grades 3, 5, and 8. The Certificate of Advanced Mastery (CAM) focuses the last two years of high school around work readiness in the form of six broad "endorsement" areas, or career pathways. Students are expected to have experiences in the world of work before leaving high school.
>
> The law specifies numerous changes to be made in school operations, including an extended school year, a statewide "report card" in which school performance would be reported annually, and site councils at every school. In terms of instruction, it mandates more emphasis on preschool programs to increase readiness, alternative learning centers for students who do not achieve certificates through traditional programs, and the use of different instructional strategies for students not making adequate progress toward benchmark performance levels. This was to be educational reform on a grand scale.
>
> Passed quickly, with little dissent or amendment, the law sprung upon Oregon educators with suddenness and surprise when they returned to their schools in the fall of 1991. I was interested in how they would react to such a comprehensive blueprint for change and

challenge to existing practice. I hoped that my research might inform the policy development process and be influential as future modifications to the law were considered.

In response to the proposed legislation, other, more partisan groups were conducting their own surveys. By contrast, my purpose was not to advocate through my research, but to establish some clear reference point for determining how educators perceived the law. With my coauthor, Paul Goldman, I took pains to report simplified versions of our results in formats much more accessible to practitioners and policy makers than research journals. We sent summaries to each school that we surveyed and published articles with graphs and summary tables in an in-state publication, the *Oregon School Study Council Bulletin*.

I consider my research to be in the area of policy analysis. While descriptive research studies fall within this category, policy analysis has, by definition, an interpretive strain that may go beyond what the data at hand support. In this article we tie all conclusions directly to the data that we report, consistent with the descriptive/causal-comparative research method. However, that method leaves out a good deal. As I worked with the legislature, key interest groups, and a range of schools, I developed my own hypotheses that sometimes exceeded our data but were consistent with already available data. We supplemented our survey data with comments and focus groups to provide more texture. But at a certain point, the researcher's ability to synthesize and hypothesize becomes an additional dimension of the study.

Policy analysis requires more than formulating a question, developing a data collection strategy, and reporting the data. There is a crucial "value-added" dimension that derives from the researcher's deep understanding of the phenomenon that she or he is studying. Of course, this understanding must be tempered with an awareness of one's individual biases and assumptions. For this reason I often conduct my research with a colleague, and I depend heavily on outside readers to detect possible biases.

The editors of the journal in which this article appeared pushed us toward a tight quantitative focus. Most of the questions and critiques we received during the revision process had to do with our statistical methods for interpreting the data, not with our conclusions. As a result, the study makes several significant generalizations about the dangers of stereotyping educator reactions to reform based on age, gender, or grade level taught. We also uncovered some important information on differences between school buildings and reaffirmed the importance of individual school sites as the locus of educational reform and restructuring. But we are aware that some important observations may have been lost in the process, and we ourselves question whether our study had any effect on policy making.

Although this article reports one year's data, the study is longitudinal. We have equivalent data for each year through 1995. We found that the same general trends we identified in 1992 continued through 1994, but that educators' support for the proposed reform dropped precipitously in 1995. We have reported the results from each year's surveys in state publications and at national conferences. In addition, I have provided personal briefings to key educators and members of the state education agency.

I have come to several conclusions about the overall effects of this research and our reports about it to the field. In general, I find that few individuals outside the research community seem to be interested in using empirical data to do anything other than justify the point of view they already hold. Little in the way of policy modification was undertaken based on the opinions from the several thousand Oregon educators whose views we recorded and analyzed over four years.

However, interest can arise suddenly and without warning. Recently, some key work groups who are attempting to implement reform have requested reports of the results from our studies. At the same time, concern has been expressed that our reports of a decrease in support for reform while the state legislature is in session could be "dangerous," because such information might jeopardize legislative support for reform.

I should hasten to add that we are continuing this line of research, but have directed it toward a new series of questions that arose from the conclusions presented in this study. I have now focused my investigations on how and why a school site responds to state restructuring legislation. I ask the more fundamental question: Can state legislatures effect fundamental change in schools via legislative programs? I also seek to understand in greater depth how teachers process state mandates. I want to know why it is that educators, who would be expected to respect authority and comply readily with government dictates, feel free to resist or ignore state legislation that directs them to change their practices toward new state goals for education.

In almost every research study that I have conducted, I have sought to incorporate a wide range of data sources. This study is no exception. More and more, I realize the need to capture subtleties and highlights in reporting my research—facets that would be obscured if only broad outlines and contrasts are allowed to be viewed. The nature of the phenomenon under investigation here necessitates a wider palette of data from which to paint the picture that emerges. In subsequent reports, Paul Goldman and I have included comments, focus group data, and document analysis in order to help readers better appreciate the complexity of educational reform efforts.

REACTIONS FROM THE FIELD TO STATE RESTRUCTURING LEGISLATION

David T. Conley
Paul Goldman

Can state legislatures mandate fundamental school reform when local control is prevalent and other legislative actions and policies may not be consistent with the goals of reform? This article examines teacher reactions to an Oregon law (H.B. 3565) designed to restructure public education around Certificates of Initial

and Advanced Mastery and other changes. Over 2,000 educators in 92 schools completed surveys to determine their attitudes toward mandated reforms. Their reactions can be categorized as cautious support for the ideas contained in the reforms tempered with skepticism that the reforms can be implemented successfully. Individual schools varied greatly in their responses, but demographic groupings did not. States that mandate change may have to provide systematic supports—funding, demonstration projects, networks, consultation services—that enable educators to interpret, adapt, and act upon state mandates at the site level, and that are compatible with and supportive of the structures and strategies that emerge in schools.

Authors' Note: Partial funding for this study was provided through a grant from the University of Oregon's Scholarly and Creative Development Award program.

Conley, D. T., & Goldman, P. (1995). Reactions from the field to state restructuring legislation. *Educational Administration Quarterly, 31,* 512–538. Copyright © 1995 by The University Council for Educational Administration. Reprinted by Permission of Sage Publications, Inc.

In this article we explore educator reactions to the Oregon Educational Act for the 21st Century, known also as the "Katz bill" or as House bill 3565. We attempt here to understand the reactions of teachers and administrators to this comprehensive educational restructuring legislation, which portends fundamental changes in Oregon's K–12 educational system, especially for secondary schools. We pose one basic question in two parts: (a) Can a state legislature mandate educational restructuring when evidence suggests large-scale educational change is a school-by-school phenomenon? and (b) What are the factors that may be related to site-specific responses to such legislation?

TWO VIEWS ON THE STATE'S ROLE IN REFORM AND RESTRUCTURING

There are two basic views on the state's role in school reform and restructuring. One focuses on the state's ability to set standards and mandate the context and procedures of schooling. The other emphasizes the individual school site as the nexus for restructuring and argues that the state has difficulty effecting the conditions necessary for this site-based transformation to take place. We consider each of these perspectives as they help to frame the interactive relationship between state and school site actions, intentions, and goals.

In reaction to the issues raised by *A Nation at Risk* (U.S. Department of Education, 1983) and rising public concern, a significant amount of state-level education reform legislation was enacted during the 1980s. Key questions have been raised regarding the degree to which such legislation actually improved student learning (Wilson & Rossman, 1993). Studies of these reforms conclude that they have tended to mandate more of the same at the school site level, meaning more required courses in academic core areas, heightened teacher certification requirements, a lengthened school day or year, or more defined teacher evaluation practices (Center for Policy Research, 1989; Conley, 1986; Fuhrman, 1988; Grossman, Kirst, & Schmidt-Posner, 1986). This type

of reform requires little change in fundamental practices or organizational structures. Teachers can merely continue their current practices or adapt them incrementally. Underlying assumptions and beliefs about teaching and learning are not challenged or modified. School structures need change little.

Many state legislatures have also noted the relatively weak effect of these mandated reform programs. State lawmakers have heard the steady call for large-scale redesign of schools from the business community, educational reformers, and, most recently, even the federal government. Simultaneously, many legislatures have gained much greater control over school finance as a result of lawsuits challenging or overturning local funding of school districts. As legislators revisit school reform in the 1990s, they often have much greater control over education and more responsibility for financing it than they did during the round of reforms in the 1980s. Increasingly centralized funding generally leads to greater scrutiny of schooling and a more activist stance by state lawmakers who feel more entitled (and obligated) to set statewide educational policy when they are providing the funds.

Although educational policy scholars have posited the relative merits and limitations of state intervention as the engine for fundamental school reform (Elmore, 1983; Elmore & McLaughlin, 1988; Firestone, Fuhrman, & Kirst, 1990, 1991; Fuhrman, Clune, & Elmore, 1991; Fuhrman & Elmore, 1990; Kirst, 1992; Smith & O'Day, 1991), there are relatively few studies that systematically examine the process by which educators interpret reform and mediate state-level initiatives. Although many reformers believe that real restructuring must be initiated at the state level, there is little evidence that current programs will actually lead to significant change in individual schools. To the contrary, 20 years of research on educational innovations beginning with Berman and McLaughlin's 1974 study suggests the opposite; educational change is idiosyncratic and uneven, regardless of the initiating source. Schools respond opportunistically, not systemically, to externally designed and mandated reform or improvement programs.

Fuhrman and her colleagues (Fuhrman, 1993; Fuhrman et al., 1991) have presented evidence that state-level initiatives can lead to change at the level of the school district, but the issue of whether and how these initiatives get translated to individual school sites remains largely unanswered. Although it is possible to achieve adherence to clearly stated rules or regulations, particularly at the district level (special education being a prime example), compliance to regulations does not necessarily translate into significant change within schools, or, more important, achievement of the goals that the regulations were designed to achieve. School sites and individual teachers may adapt to the new requirements without changing their educational practices in any significant fashion.

Fuhrman and others examined the adaptive incremental reforms of the 1980s. Larger scale, more fundamental programs of educational restructuring remain largely unexamined, primarily because states have just begun to initiate such programs. Mazzoni (1991) stated that "scholars have had little opportunity until recently to analyze the legislative initiation of structural reforms, because relatively few laws of this sort were enacted" (p. 115). There is evidence that a number of states are implementing or considering more fundamental structural reform, making it possible to consider the effects of large-scale changes initiated at the state level.

A second body of research examines how individual school sites are self-starting engines of school restructuring (Conley, 1991; David, 1990; Eberts, Schwartz, & Stone, 1990; Elmore, 1988; Glen & Crandall, 1988; Goldman, Dunlap, & Conley, 1991; Hallinger, Murphy, & Hausman, 1991). These researchers tend to report that educators who are restructuring view state intervention as a problem, nuisance, or barrier to change rather than as an initiator or facilitator of it. These studies focus on how educators at individual school sites develop unique, nonstandardized solutions to educational problems (Goldman, Dunlap, & Conley, 1993), and how educators at individual school sites are interpreting and responding to the restructuring movement (Conley, Dunlap, & Goldman, 1992; Goldman & Conley, 1994).

The data we have gathered provide us with an opportunity to examine and assess how state legislation designed to foster site-level restructuring is being perceived by those charged with the transformation. These perceptions can suggest the effect state legislation is having on the site-level school restructuring process which the legislation mandates. These data do not tell us whether or how much schools are changing, but do provide valuable insight into the first stage of what most Oregon educational leaders anticipate will be a multistep process of educational redesign. To provide a better sense of the magnitude of the changes being attempted, we begin with a brief overview of the legislation's major provisions.

MAJOR PROVISIONS OF THE OREGON EDUCATIONAL ACT FOR THE 21ST CENTURY

In 1991, the Oregon legislature passed House bill 3565, laying out a new vision of schooling for the state's 1,200 public elementary and secondary schools. Oregon's educators were neither prepared for nor participated in the development of this legislation. Instead, their attention had been focused on the state's recently enacted tax limitation measure and its implications for education funding. Oregon's reform legislation is far reaching, encompassing policies from early childhood to postsecondary education, from accountability to school governance. The act presents a complex framework for systemic redesign of education, preschool through postsecondary. Its stated intention is to create a "restructured educational system . . . to achieve the state's goals of the best educated citizens in the nation by the year 2000 and a work force equal to any in the world by the year 2010" (Oregon Educational Act, 1991).

Oregon's reforms are not incremental changes to be implemented gradually and sequentially year by year from early childhood to secondary education. In this regard, they differ fundamentally from legislation in other states. The Oregon legislation's emphasis on secondary education departs dramatically from major reform efforts elsewhere that have mandated changes first and foremost in primary education. The best examples of those approaches are Kentucky's Education Reform Act and British Columbia's Year 2000 Program (which began to lose provincial government commitment about 5 years after its 1988 enactment). House bill 3565's author and primary sponsor, Vera Katz, had been deeply influenced by the National Center for Education and the Economy's (1990) report "America's Choice: High Skills or Low Wages," which dealt explicitly with high schools and the school-to-work transition. Although the act contains provisions for full funding of early childhood education programs, it offers little more that relates to presecondary education.

The act emphasizes two performance- and skill-based milestones, the Certificate of Initial Mastery (CIM) and the Certificate of Advanced Mastery (CAM). The new educational system is designed to work downward as elementary and middle schools look specifically to ways in which they can adapt their programs to the requirements of the CIM and the CAM. Every student will have the opportunity to obtain the CIM by age 16 or the end of 10th grade. Students are then expected to pursue the CAM, which might take anywhere from 2 to 4 years to achieve.

To obtain a CIM, a student must demonstrate mastery in 11 performance areas at approximately 16 years of age. Benchmarks at Grades 3, 5, and 8 track student progress. Assessments must include "work samples, tests and portfolios . . . culminating in a project or exhibition that demonstrates attainment of required knowledge and skills" (Oregon Educational Act, 1991, p. 54). Performances are to be geared to world-class levels.

The CAM follows the CIM and is organized around six broad occupational categories. The CAM is designed to facilitate school-to-work transition by causing students to give more thought to their career choices as well as to investigate the world of work firsthand while still in school. There is an emphasis on professional-technical programs in addition to college preparation. Students are provided "opportunities for structured work experiences, cooperative work and study programs, on-the-job

training and apprenticeship programs in addition to other subjects" in combination with "a comprehensive educational component" (Oregon Educational Act, 1991). The CAM can be earned in a high school or community college up to the age of 21.

There are several other provisions of interest and concern to Oregon educators. Site-based school councils were to be established in every school no later than September 1995. Teachers will form a majority, but parent and classified employees must be represented as well. These councils are to set school goals, approve school staff development programs, and support implementation of the act. Enhanced public accountability for education is achieved through the Oregon Report Card, a comprehensive report on performance on a school-by-school basis, accompanied by an increase in the frequency of external accreditation team visits, coupled with local school and district self-evaluations every 2 years, and increased parental involvement. The act contains provisions for lengthening the school year from the current 175 days to 185 in 1996, 200 in the year 2000, and 220 days by 2010.

The act defines how help and assistance will be provided to students who are not succeeding in public education. Included are requirements that schools identify in the primary years students who are not succeeding and employ alternative instructional approaches with them. Additional support for at-risk students is mandated through alternative learning centers. Social service agencies are required to coordinate their services with those of the public schools and to offer them at the site closest to the client. Learning centers will offer "teaching strategies, technology, and curricula that emphasize the latest research and best practice" to help students develop mastery in defined areas.

In essence, the act lays out a framework of expectations for student performance and calls on schools to redesign their programs to enable students to meet performance standards. The law does not prescribe the means or structures educators should employ to achieve the act's goals. Its sponsors envisioned it as a "trigger mechanism" to engage educators in serious redesign of schools. The law's principal sponsor stated she was attempting to use top-down legislation to catalyze bottom-up school restructuring. Hence Oregon would seem to provide a strong test of this top-down/bottom-up model of reform as well as of a state's capacity to mandate fundamental educational reform. Our data shed light on how educators interpret this type of reform legislation, and whether they are likely to initiate new programs and practices in school districts, buildings, and classrooms as a result of such legislation.

DATA COLLECTION AND METHODOLOGY

The methodology and design of this study applies a policy analysis perspective to this investigation. Although no formal hypothesis is posed per se, we are attempting to shed light on a specific issue, that is, the relationship between state policy and teacher reactions as aggregated into various demographic groupings and school-by-school findings. We did enter this study with certain untested assumptions that did not have the structure of hypotheses. These assumptions were based on our previous research in the state over several years (Conley, 1991; Conley et al., 1992; Conley, Goldman, & Dunlap, 1993; Goldman et al., 1991, 1993) and conversations, formal and informal, that we had regularly with a wide range of Oregon educators and policymakers through our professional relationships and other ongoing research projects we were conducting. Furthermore, we sought to examine some of what passed for common knowledge in the state and, to some degree, nationally, regarding teacher attitudes toward school reform.

Data come from a self-administered questionnaire distributed and returned during fall 1992, approximately 15 months after the passage of the act. The eight-page questionnaire consisted of 99 forced-choice items, one open-ended question, a comments section, three items on personal characteristics, and five items describing the respondent's school building and school district. The forced-choice items were grouped into the following areas: (a) knowledge of the legislation's major provisions; (b) beliefs about the law's *intent;* (c) assessment of the law's potential *effects;* (d) predictions about the success of implementation; (e) personal reactions, including how much each respondent might have to *change;* (f) what resources would be required for the law to be implemented; and (g) whether specific provisions will improve student learning. We pretested the survey on Oregon educators during summer 1992.

We employed a stratified sampling technique in which the sampling units were school districts and school buildings.[a] This strategy provided a correction factor to overcome the extreme skewness in the size distribution of Oregon's 297 school districts, many of which are extremely small. Based on the number of students served, the state was divided into four groups each having roughly the same number of students, plus Portland, the one large urban district. Within each of the four categories, districts were randomly selected so that each category would proportionally represent its share of the state's student population. Hence two districts each were selected in the two largest categories, four from the medium-sized group of school districts, and nine from the smallest ones. Within each school district, individual school buildings were randomly selected as follows: one high school, two middle schools or junior highs, and three elementary schools. In districts with fewer schools, all buildings were included in the study. We also designated two midsized districts as "case study districts," in which we surveyed all schools in the district.[b] A total of 92 schools were included in the sample, 64 from the

a. Stratified sampling is a sampling strategy to ensure that certain subgroups are adequately represented in the sample. As the researchers explain, they used stratified sampling to ensure that larger school districts were adequately represented, and also to give proportional representation to elementary, middle (or junior high), and high schools.

b. The researchers use the term "case study" in a different sense than the way in which this term is used in qualitative research (see Chapter 10). Here it means that these two school districts were surveyed comprehensively, with questionnaires being sent to every school in the district. As Table 1 indicates, the response rate was higher for the case study districts than for other districts, which might indicate that the researchers had greater involvement with the educators in those districts before or during the research study.

TABLE I **Sample Description and Response Rates**

District size (ADM)	Total Oregon districts	Number sample districts	ADM in Oregon	Percentage Oregon ADM	Total surveys	Total surveys returned	Percentage returned surveys	Return rate (percentage)
30,000+	I	I	53,700	11.6	225	140	9.2	62.2
10,400–29,999	4	2	83,100	17.9	562	374	24.7	66.5
5,000–10,399	15	2	113,300	24.4	504	271	18.0	53.8
2,000–4,999	35	4	113,700	24.5	757	478	31.7	63.1
Under 2,000	242	9	100,200	21.6	390	247	16.4	63.3
State of Oregon sample	297	18	464,000	100	2,438	1,510	100	61.9
Case study districts (5,000–10,000 ADM)					1,007	747		74.2
Total		20			3,445	2,257		65.6

Note: ADM is the average daily membership.

state sample and an additional 28 from those two districts. Except where otherwise noted, statistical tabulations present data from both the 18 randomly sampled districts and the 2 case study districts. Table I illustrates the parameters of the sample.

In each school, questionnaires were distributed to all certified staff. The principal was first approached with a request that the school participate in the study. In some cases, the request was referred to the district office. After permission was granted, appointments were scheduled so that a member of the research staff could make a brief presentation at a faculty meeting. In some cases, the principal personally requested faculty participation in a meeting or through a letter to the staff. Staff returned the anonymous completed questionnaires to a drop box in the school office, and members of the research team either picked them up or they were mailed directly to the researchers' university office.

The questionnaires were distributed, completed, and collected between October 1, 1992 and December 15, 1992. No district refused to partici-

pate, but one school did decline to participate and was replaced by another from the same district. Of the 3,445 questionnaires distributed, a total of 2,260 were returned, a rate of just under 66%. Return rates were above 60% for all but one of the subsamples. The subsample proportions closely approximate the distribution of the state's teachers and schoolchildren. It is worth noting that response rates exceed by a substantial margin those from a similar type of survey conducted in British Columbia during the first year of that province's mandated school reform. Researchers surveying teachers there reported an individual response rate of 30% (2,547 distributed, 770 returned) and a school participation rate of 67% (Silns, 1992).

Four separate additive scales were distilled from the 99 individual questions.[c] The scales were developed through careful analysis of the language of individual items and through statistical analysis, specifically item correlations and factor analysis.[d] The scales and the individual questionnaire items they contain are displayed in Table 2. Scale scores were

c. The scales shown in Table 2 are additive in that each individual's responses to all the items on the scale were summed to yield a total scale score for that individual.

d. Item correlations and factor analysis are statistical techniques for determining which subsets of items in a total set of items elicit a consistent response from a sample of individuals. A consistent response suggests that the subset of items measure the same construct. Four subsets of items in the 99-item questionnaire to which the educators responded consistently were identified in this manner, and these items defined the four scales shown in Table 2.

TABLE 2   Scales and Scale Items

Item number	Item description	Mean (percentage agree)	SD
Change orientation			
39	It is time for fundamental change in education	56.1	49.6
42	Many schools are already doing much of what law mandates	30.4	46.0
43	Ideas make sense	32.7	46.9
44	Current system isn't working for many kids	58.8	49.2
67	Opportunity to do things I've always wanted to do	27.0	44.4
	Scale alpha		.68
Resistance to change			
50	Unrealistic	34.3	47.5
51	Not good ideas for education	10.0	30.0
52	Unfair to some types of student	34.4	47.5
54	Too much change too fast for schools	43.4	49.6
63	Am skeptical	51.5	50.0
70	Will take it seriously when it is adequately funded	65.3	47.6
72	Have too much else to do to give it much thought	24.9	43.2
84	Rewrite it to make timelines more reasonable	41.8	49.3
	Scale alpha		.73
Learning outcomes			
15	Will benefit all students	40.5	49.1
16	Will benefit college bound	62.9	48.3
17	Will cause more children to enter kindergarten prepared	45.1	49.8
25	CIM will lead to decrease in dropouts	45.0	49.8
27	Alternative learning centers will help decrease dropouts	69.4	46.1
89	Site councils will lead to learning	69.1	46.2
90	Increased accountability will lead to learning	66.8	47.1
91	Funding for preschool will enable all students to enter school ready to learn	84.1	36.6
92	Extended school year will lead to learning	35.1	47.7
93	CIM will lead to learning	65.9	47.4
94	CAM will lead to learning	65.4	47.6
95	Alternative learning centers will lead to learning	86.0	34.7
96	Parental choice for students who are not succeeding in a school will lead to learning	61.8	48.6
97	Coordination of social services at the school site for those who need such services will lead to learning	80.5	39.6
98	Mixed age classrooms in Grades 1–3 will lead to learning	58.9	49.2
99	Educational philosophy of developmentally appropriate practices in Grades 1–3 will lead to learning	79.9	40.1
	Scale alpha		.82

(continued)

TABLE 2   *continued*

Item number	Item description	Mean (percentage agree)	SD
Changes in practices			
11	Will promote more developmentally appropriate practice in elementary schools	66.4	47.3
14	Will increase teacher control over instructional program at school	38.6	48.7
18	Will cause teachers to increase number of instructional strategies they employ	61.8	48.6
19	Will lead to greater integration of social services in schools	60.7	48.9
20	Will lead to greater curriculum integration	74.3	43.7
21	Will lead to new and diverse ways to organize or group students for learning	77.0	42.1
22	Will lead to increased teacher involvement in decision making	55.5	49.7
23	Will lead to increased teacher collegiality and cooperation	51.3	50.0
	Scale alpha		.72

Note: CIM = Certificate of Initial Mastery. CAM = Certificate of Advanced Mastery.

derived first by calculating the mean number of affirmative responses to the total number of items in each scale, then converting this score into a percentage figure. Each of the scales displays internal consistency, and this is reflected by the alpha statistic shown in Table 2.[e]

Scale 1 is change orientation, consisting of items that suggest a general sense that schools should be changing and that the Oregon act provides an opportunity for change to occur. Scale 2, resistance to change, reflects both skepticism and disengagement. Although negatively correlated with change orientation ($r = -.31$), this scale seems to measure slightly different attitudinal dimensions, reflecting doubts that changes should or can be made.[f] Scale 3,

learning outcomes, is taken directly from specific consecutive questions in one section of the questionnaire. These items asked educators whether, in their opinion, specific features of the act would lead to increased student learning. Scale 4 measures anticipated changes in practices, specifically in such areas as developmentally appropriate practices, integrating curriculum, and increased teacher collegiality and cooperation. Scales 3 and 4 are strongly intercorrelated ($r = .60$), but appear to measure somewhat different dimensions of response to House bill 3565.[g] Moreover, the two correlate with somewhat different demographic variables.

Statistically significant and conceptually interesting findings consisted primarily of comparisons of scale

e. The alpha statistic is a means of testing whether the items comprising a measure (in this case, the items in the four scales shown in Table 2) consistently measure the same attitude, ability, or other construct. If a scale has a high alpha coefficient (typically, .60 or higher, with the highest possible coefficient being 1.00), it means that individuals who respond in a certain way to one item on the scale are likely to respond in the same way to the other items on that scale.

f. When two measures are negatively correlated, individuals with higher scores on one measure tend to have lower scores on the other measure. The magnitude of the relationship is indicated by a correlation coefficient such as r. The r value of $-.31$ indicates that educators with higher scores on the Change Orientation scale tend to have lower scores on the Resistance to Change scale. Conversely, educators with lower scores on the Change Orientation scale tend to have higher scores on the Resistance to Change scale.

g. An r value of .60 indicates that there is a positive correlation between these two measures. Educators with higher scores on Scale 3 also tend to have higher scores on Scale 4. Conversely, educators with lower scores on Scale 3 tend to have lower scores on Scale 4.

means between different values of categorical variables.[h] Statistical significance was assessed using *F* tests, and these are reported, as appropriate, in individual tables as recommended by Blalock (1972).[i] The *F* values reported in Table 3 have been verified by a post hoc pairs analysis using Tukey's Honest Statistical Difference test.[j] Readers should note, however, that with large sample size, statistical significance may be reported when actual differences are small and, conversely, the lack of statistical significance where sample means show little difference between them may indicate "nonfindings" that are nonetheless suggestive or important (Cohen, 1990).

RESULTS AND INTERPRETATIONS OF THE DATA

We thought that teachers would be opposed to, or at the least suspicious of, state-level restructuring legislation, because the objection that teachers had not participated in the design of House bill 3565 in any significant fashion had been voiced by many teacher representatives. Furthermore, we assumed that some demographic groups might be more resistant to the requirements and intent of the legislation than others. For example, recent surveys elsewhere suggest that high school educators would be more wary than those in elementary schools, and that more veteran staff would be less receptive than younger or less experienced teachers (Auriemma, Cooper, & Smith, 1992; Harris & Wagner, 1993; King & Peart, 1992). In particular, we thought male high school teachers in the 45- to 50-year range might be expected to be less enthusiastic or supportive of such large-scale change.

Teachers in rural districts might be more critical because elements of the reform such as the CAM seemed much more difficult for small schools to implement. Correspondingly, staff in larger districts might be more responsive because Oregon's larger school districts see themselves as lighthouses. They tend to keep abreast of important state (and federal) legislation and could be expected to be more likely to make sure teachers and administrators understood the act and its implications.

Because we had previously conducted research at schools that had received competitive school improvement grants from the state through its "2020" program, we believed these schools would be more receptive to the act (Goldman et al., 1993). And, finally, we felt that the attention educators were paying to budget cuts brought on by the phased implementation of a property tax reduction measure passed in 1990 might seriously affect educators' willingness to take on anything new. Cuts were being made in nearly all districts, and we wondered if a district's relative wealth would be a factor in its professional staff's reactions to the act.

The results of the data analysis parallel these issues. The data suggest the ways in which educators are interpreting the legislation, as well as the types of action that a state might take to enhance the ability of sites to implement this and similar reforms. Policy analysis of this sort is designed to serve an "enlightenment function" (Majchrzak, 1984; Weiss, 1977), the purpose of which is to highlight the effects, both intended and unintended, of policy as it is put into practice. Therefore, we present an analysis of the data and provide an interpretation of its meaning and implications first in a more limited statistical sense, and then in a broader policy context.

In presenting the study's findings, we first lay out the highlights of the frequency distributions, summarizing previously reported findings (Conley et al., 1993) and setting the context for more detailed analysis. Second, we discuss and analyze the four

---

h. If a difference between groups is statistically significant, it means that we can generalize beyond this sample and conclude that a similar difference would be found in other samples from the same population as this sample.

i. *F test* is another term for the statistical technique of analysis of variance.

j. The Tukey Honest Statistical Difference (HSD) test is used when an analysis of variance reveals that the differences among three or more groups on a measure can be generalized to a larger population. The Tukey procedure enables researchers to determine which pairwise comparisons are generalizable in this sense. (If there are three groups, A, B, and C, there are three possible pairwise comparisons: A versus B, A versus C, and B versus C.)

scales in the context of individual, school, and district demographic characteristics. Third, we move from an individual to an organizational level of analysis, presenting and discussing how school buildings and school districts seem to differ from one another.

Questionnaire responses indicate that educators believed the act was well intended and had student interests at heart, but 15 months after enactment, they did not yet feel fully informed about the bill's details and its implications. A substantial majority believed that the most innovative programs, the CIM and CAM, would be implemented (88% and 86%, respectively), and almost as many (82%) expected site-based decision making would become the norm. They were very skeptical that preschool programs and the extended school year, the most expensive components of the act, would actually come to pass. Moreover, with virtual unanimity (92%), they believed that funding and time for staff development were essential prerequisites for successful implementation of the act.

Three quarters of the respondents thought the act would result in new ways to group students as well as greater curriculum integration, and that the new alternative learning centers for failing or at-risk adolescents would decrease dropout rates. A majority of educators believed both that the current system is not working for many kids (59%) and that it is time for fundamental change in education (56%). About half the respondents considered themselves skeptical but, at the same time, 66% expected to make at least a "little" change and another 29% expected to change "a lot."

In general, Oregon's educators seem more positive about the concepts embodied in the reform legislation than their counterparts who have been experiencing systemic educational reform elsewhere in North America (Harris & Wagner, 1993). Both

the general intent of the law and its specific elements are apparently not in conflict with the ways educators perceive both current problems and the potential solutions to them. This conclusion is consistent with the findings of Fuhrman et al. (1991) that "suggest strongly that policy maker and educator support for reform, which is key to successful implementation, does not depend on participation in reform initiation and design" (p. 215). Our analysis tends to validate the proposition that most teachers and administrators in Oregon are ready philosophically to address the broad restructuring implied by Oregon's legislation. They are, however, quite skeptical that the state will follow through with either the funding or the sustained commitment over time necessary to put these changes into practice.

Individual Differences

Table 3 displays one-way ANOVAs for each of the scales as they are distributed among individual and organizational characteristics.[k] The table is organized in three sections: characteristics of individuals, characteristics of school buildings, and characteristics of school districts.

There are substantial differences in attitudes between classroom teachers and administrators. Each scale showed a differential of at least 10 points between the two. Teachers appear to be less oriented to change generally and less likely to believe reformers' pleas that the educational system is in crisis; correspondingly, teachers are more resistant to change, at least the changes embodied in the act. A much lower proportion of teachers believe that the restructuring program will either change educational practices or make significant improvements in outcomes. Certified staff who are not classroom teachers present intermediate attitudes, but these

---

k. Analysis of variance is a statistical procedure to determine the likelihood that a difference in the mean scores of two or more groups on a measure would also be found if the researchers studied the entire population. A one-way analysis of variance (ANOVA) involves one independent variable. For example, one of the first comparisons shown in Table 3 involves the independent variable of position, which includes three categories: teachers, other certified staff, and administrators. The *F* values show the effect of this independent variable on each of the four scales. For example, on the Change Orientation scale the analysis of variance yields an *F* value of 20.1, which is statistically significant. This means that if the three populations represented by these three sample groups had been studied, they likely would differ in a similar way on this scale.

TABLE 3 **Scale Means by Individual, Building, and District Demographics**

	Percentage agree responses				
	Change orientation	**Resistance to change**	**Learning outcomes**	**Changes in practices**	**N**
Sample					2,257
Mean	41.0	34.7	63.9	60.7	
SD	30.3	22.7	23.2	32.2	
Individual characteristics					
Position					
Teachers	39.6	36.4	62.5	58.7	1,750
Other certified staff	44.0	34.2	66.7	63.7	317
Administrators	55.4	32.6	73.2	76.9	153
F	20.1**	29.0**	23.5**	17.9**	
Gender					
Men	40.6	33.3	60.8	58.5	872
Women	42.0	35.8	65.9	62.4	1,310
F	0.2	6.7*	22.8**	7.4*	
Age					
20–29	37.4	38.4	63.1	59.2	162
30–39	40.0	35.2	63.3	62.2	526
40–49	42.9	33.7	64.9	61.8	1,009
50–59	41.5	35.2	63.6	58.9	478
60+	43.0	40.9	54.4	49.4	27
F	1.6	2.2	1.7	1.5	
Building characteristics					
School level					
High school	45.0	32.1	64.3	64.8	802
Junior high and middle	38.7	35.1	63.3	54.0	596
Elementary	39.1	38.5	63.1	61.0	768
F	9.2**	10.3**	0.3	16.1**	
Student SES					
Highest quartile	41.9	34.8	62.8	62.4	476
2nd quartile	42.8	32.7	66.1	62.6	454
3rd quartile	39.9	35.5	62.4	58.9	475
4th quartile	40.8	35.3	64.9	60.9	498
F	0.9	0.7	1.3	2.7	

(continued)

TABLE 3   *continued*

	Percentage agree responses				
	Change orientation	Resistance to change	Learning outcomes	Changes in practices	N
2020 Grant					
Yes	44.2	36.1	63.5	59.1	673
No	39.7	31.8	64.7	64.2	1,549
F	10.2**	16.7**	1.2	10.8**	
District characteristics					
Size					
15,000+	38.9	37.5	63.5	55.6	458
5,000–14,999	41.9	33.5	64.3	62.1	928
2,000–4,999	41.6	32.3	63.7	65.7	440
100–1,999	40.9	38.7	63.9	55.9	234
F	1.3	8.1**	0.2	9.9**	
Region					
Portland Metro	38.3	37.4	62.1	55.9	933
Willamette Valley	46.6	32.0	67.8	67.6	728
Southern Oregon	41.4	30.2	65.2	63.0	246
Central/Eastern Oregon	31.8	41.2	56.5	55.3	137
Oregon Coast	39.4	33.0	61.2	59.4	210
F	9.0**	11.8**	10.3**	13.9**	
Per student expenditure					
Highest quartile	30.4	38.8	63.2	60.3	484
2nd quartile	37.1	38.3	67.0	66.0	518
3rd quartile	34.1	35.6	64.9	65.0	504
4th quartile	28.7	42.0	60.3	51.5	518
F	13.6**	13.9**	22.6**	7.66**	

$*p < .05; **p < .01.$

TABLE 3A   **Statistically Significant Pairs**

	Change orientation	Resistance to change	Learning outcomes	Changes in practices
Position	All	All	All	All
School level	HS:MS HS:ELEM	All	HS:MS	HS:ELEM
District size		15K:5–14.9K 15K:2–4.9K 2–4.9K:.1–1.9K	15K:5–14.9K 15K:2–4.9K 2–4.9K:.1–1.9K	

(continued)

TABLE 3A   *(continued)*

	Change orientation	Resistance to change	Learning outcomes	Changes in practices
Region	Metro:Valley	Metro:Valley	Metro:Valley	Metro:Valley
	Metro:South	Valley:East	Valley:East	Metro:South
	Valley:East	Valley:Coast	Valley:Coast	Valley:East
	Valley:Coast	South:East	South:East	Valley:Coast
	South:East			South:East
	East:Coast			
Per student expenditure	1st:2nd	1st:2nd	1st:2nd	1st:2nd
	1st:3rd	1st:3rd	1st:3rd	1st:3rd
	2nd:4th	2nd:4th	2nd:4th	2nd:4th
	3rd:4th	3rd:4th	3rd:4th	3rd:4th

Note: Post hoc paired comparisons were computed employing Tukey's HSD test with a significance level of .05.

specialists, counselors, and special educators have outlooks similar to teachers. A note of caution may be in order. These differences are relative: The typical teacher still thought 60% of the reform proposals would change practices and improve outcomes.

Comparisons between Oregon's female and male educators reveal only very small differences. Women express marginally more agreement with statements that describe resistance to change. However, this finding runs in the opposite direction from the differences on the outcomes and practices scales. Women are more optimistic both about the possible beneficial effects of the act on student learning and about the likelihood that teachers will change their instructional practices. These differences may be partially explained by differences between elementary and secondary teachers, but this is probably only part of the story. Note that there are virtually no differences in the response pattern between schools with male and female principals.

Contrary to both conventional wisdom and to recent findings by Auriemma and colleagues (1992) and the Canadian Teachers Federation (King & Peart, 1992), there appears to be virtually no relationship between reactions to Oregon's restructuring legislation and educator age or experience. Oregon's teaching force is predominantly middle aged (median age is 45) and experienced. This sample seems to be a reliable approximation of the state; almost one half are in their 40s. Except for teachers in their 60s who present views less favorable to Oregon's educational reforms, no age group is noticeably more or less change oriented or change resistant.

If individual responses are not correlated with personal demographic characteristics, does the fact that the school serves elementary or secondary level children make a difference? As Table 2 indicates, high school and elementary school teachers do differ somewhat from one another, especially in the degree to which they embrace change.[1] Middle

1. This information is shown in Table 3A, not in Table 2. Table 3A is a supplement to Table 3. It notes only the specific pair comparisons that were found to be statistically significant. The authors of the article informed us of two corrections that should be made to Table 3A: (1) for School level, under Learning Outcomes, *HS:MS* should be deleted; (2) for School level, under Changes in Practices, *HS:ELEM* should be deleted, and *HS:MS* and *MS:ELEM* should be inserted.

school and junior high teachers are in the middle. For example, two thirds of high school teachers but only one half of elementary teachers agree that "the system isn't working for many kids." Differences narrow when we ask whether teachers will change their instructional practices and whether this set of school reforms will improve learning outcomes. In addition, the gradation running from elementary to middle to high school breaks down when we consider how much teachers say they know about the act and how much they expect their own practices to change. Middle-level teachers believe they are less informed than both other groups and less likely to anticipate changed practices. The act does not specify or mandate program changes for the middle level, but many are clearly implied by other sections of the act, such as the CIM and the alternative learning centers.

We investigated whether school averages on student socioeconomic status might be related to how teachers view school reform. In general, schools with middle- and upper middle-class students have had somewhat more resources of all kinds, whereas schools with students from working and lower class families contain a higher proportion of children with learning problems who may have to be educated with relatively fewer resources. Whatever the differences between these types of schools in practices, workloads, or morale, we found no differences in their faculty's beliefs about school reform. These similarities were echoed by comparisons of district-level differences in funding. In our sample, educators in the poorest districts are a bit less optimistic about the act and its possible effects, but their responses are more similar to those of educators in the richest districts than to those in the middle.

Geography and district size appear to explain some differences. Over 80% of Oregon's population is within an hour's drive of I-5, the interstate highway that bisects the state from Portland to the California border. Educators in districts on the I-5 corridor are more knowledgeable about, and more receptive to, reform than those in less populated and more remote areas of the state. The findings for eastern Oregon indicate that these districts are less supportive of reform and see it as less relevant to them. The possible sources of these differences, and whether the apparent skepticism actually results from geographic isolation, or from a real and perceived distance from state policy makers, are discussed in the Conclusions section.

The data on district size reveal some differences as well. The largest and smallest districts are very similar to one another on two of the four scales: resistance to change, and the expectation that the legislation's consequences will include changed classroom practices. Teachers in the largest districts are on the lower extreme of the change orientation scale. If these results reflect a larger reality, they suggest that large districts may be having more difficulty translating broad policy initiatives, especially those originating externally, to staff in the schools, than medium-sized districts, that is, those below 15,000 students.

One final factor appears to have had an impact on attitudes: Educators in schools that had previous and current state-funded school improvement grants were more receptive to the restructuring legislation. These staffs were also more likely to expect that the school reform legislation might have an effect on instructional practice. Between 1987 and 1993, Oregon's State Department of Education funded competitive school improvement and professional development grants. The funding, called 2020 grants after the legislative bill number, allowed schools considerable latitude but required that the monies be managed by a committee where teachers comprised the majority. Among the wide range of funded projects were those focused on creating readiness for restructuring, developing new assessment techniques, creating programs for at-risk students, implementing cooperative learning, developing new decision-making or governance structures, designing interdisciplinary curriculum, enhancing multiculturalism, improving school climate, addressing needs of special education students, and integrating technology (Conley, 1991). Schools that had already experimented with restructuring, whether or not they were successful, were more favorable to reform.

School Districts and School Buildings as Units of Analysis

What the data above suggest is that, aside from differences that seem to stem from job titles and job responsibilities, demographic factors are not strong predictors of individual responses. Even where the literature suggests possible individual explanatory factors—for instance, those associated with age, experience, or gender—personal characteristics appeared to have little effect. Similarly, at a broader more contextual level, district size and even the economic status of the district's students and the money the district spent on those children made little difference. When districts, and especially school buildings, are taken as units of analysis, however, the findings are different. Table 4 presents a nested analysis of variance comparing school and districts effects in the 12 districts for which we collected data in five or more schools.[m]

Between district differences on all four scales are large and statistically significant, indicating that district variations may nurture attitudes that are receptive to or skeptical about Oregon's school restructuring legislation. The range in expectations about whether schools will change their practices was especially large: In one large district, the mean was 48; in another (less large) the mean was 73, a substantial difference when we consider that these were measures aggregated over 210 and 125

TABLE 4 Multischool Districts: Nested Building and District Effects

District/school	Change orientation	Resistance to change	Changed practices	Learning outcomes
Model				
df	53	53	53	53
Mean square	1,551.05	1,203.05	3,265.07	1,180.75
F value	2.88**	2.47**	3.57**	2.41**
Error				
df	1,230.0	1,203.0	1,129.0	1,120.0
Mean square	538.8	486.62	913.8	489.3
R^2	.11	.10	.14	.10
District				
df	9	9	9	9
Mean square	2,527.67	2,950.74	8,311.95	2,327.92
F value	4.69**	6.06**	9.10**	4.76**
School (district)				
df	44	44	44	44
Mean square	1,351.3	845.6	2,232.8	946.1
F value	2.51**	1.74*	2.44**	1.93**

$*p < .01; **p < .001.$

m. Analysis of variance can determine the effect of several independent variables on a dependent variable. In Table 4, the two independent variables are school district and school building. These two independent variables are not independent of each other, however, because the schools are located in (that is, nested in) specific school districts. The analysis of variance is designed to reflect the nested relationship between these two independent variables.

respondents, respectively. Comparable differences on the three other scales were less dramatic: from 30 to 41 on resistance to change, 31 to 47 on change orientation, and 58 to 71 on expectations for learning outcomes. There were, however, no patterns suggesting that particular types of districts—larger or smaller, richer or poorer, close to or distant from the state capital and the major metropolitan center—produce environments that encourage staff to be more or less positive or optimistic about the restructuring legislation.

School-level data demonstrate similar patterns. In some districts, differences between schools are also large. Although overall school effects are smaller than district effects, there are several districts in which variation between individual schools is large enough to generate questions about how districts interpret state policy for schools. One example illustrates this phenomenon. One district near the Portland metropolitan area had school means ranging from 32 to 84 on change orientation, from 62 to 85 on expectation of changed practices, and from 48 to 85 on outcome expectations.

OBSERVATIONS, CONSIDERATIONS, AND IMPLICATIONS

We discuss these findings in three subsections: general observations from the survey; demographic, district, and site-level considerations; and implications.

General Observations From the Survey

The first year of the Oregon experience suggests that legislation mandating fundamental school reform can, at the very least, cause considerable reflection and self-examination by teachers. One indication was the fact that about 55% of responding teachers completed an optional comments section where they identified those activities they personally would have to change in their teaching practice as a result of passage of the act. Furthermore, the Oregon experience suggests that, even without teacher input, states can develop school restructuring legislation that teachers will accept if, and perhaps only if, it captures key themes that respond to concerns already felt by teachers. Fuhrman and colleagues (1991) reached similar conclusions.

The conventional wisdom, expressed frequently by administrators, policymakers, and policy pundits, and seemingly felt by the general public, that teachers are unresponsive to the need to change schooling may be somewhat overstated. A sizable number of teachers in Oregon seem to be very ready to enter into discussions about school restructuring and to consider changing what they do and how they do it. In the same breath, it is worth noting that our data do not capture the intensity of feeling very well. Subsequent research we conducted using focus groups (Goldman & Conley, 1994) suggests there is a group of teachers who oppose reform strongly. Although smaller in number, their impact may ultimately be disproportionally large.

Oregon's educators believe strongly that fiscal issues will influence their ability to remake schooling on a large scale. However, the state policy-making and policy-implementation structures, experienced by educators as legislative mandates translated and enforced by state officials, have not sent coherent or consistent messages to the field about the relationship between funding and reform. In practice, there is no relationship, or even an inverse relationship: Funding decreases whereas expectations for enhanced performance, professional development, and systems redesign increase.

Teachers express skepticism that the act can be implemented without additional targeted funding to buy the time and expertise they perceive as necessary for their own training, learning, and changing. Teachers view the state's lack of financial commitment as a reason to wait before jumping onto the reform bandwagon. This suggests the interconnection between school finance reform and school restructuring programs. Radical school finance reform continues at a rapid pace in a number of states. Any new funding strategy and formula is likely to have significant interaction effects with any program of restructuring. Rarely are these finance reforms being designed and implemented in concert with educational restructuring programs. Our data suggest that a potentially strong magnifying or multiplier effect could be achieved if the two were linked, and if teachers in particular perceived the connection, a possibility suggested by Verstegen (1994).

Educators in this study express a willingness to entertain change, but do not believe they will necessarily be given the authority or resources they need to adapt successfully. Their ambivalence fosters a wait-and-see attitude. As they wait, the deadline for implementing key provisions of the act draws nearer. This creates a situation where more change will be required in less time. Few teachers plan for the changes; instead, they wait to see what each new legislature does to provide time, money, and guidance. Will teachers be able to adapt to the requirements of a standards-based system with extensive performance assessment requirements within the time remaining and with the resources that are currently available?

Demographic, District, and Site-Level Considerations

Our data suggest that both researchers and policymakers must be cautious when generalizing about the relationships between resistance to change and demographic factors such as age, gender, and locality, or distinctions between elementary and secondary schools. Resistors and enthusiasts exist in most schools and districts, but do not seem to come disproportionately from specific demographic categories. However convenient generalizations might be, it appears educator attitudes toward large-scale reform defy simple categorization.

Equally significant is the apparent potential support for large-scale change in high schools. We found this particularly striking, given the widely held view that the high school level is most resistant to change. This finding suggests that it may be more possible than supposed to redesign high schools. Current thinking on reform often emphasizes a focus on preschool and early childhood as the starting point for system redesign. Such an approach implies grade-by-grade restructuring as a student cohort moves through the system.

Our findings hint that it may not be necessary to take 12 or more years to reshape education by redesigning curriculum and instruction one grade level at a time, as was planned in the British Columbia Year 2000 design (Sullivan, 1988). The finding that a majority of teachers at all levels indicate support for fundamental change suggests that elementary, middle, and high schools might engage in reform and redesign more or less simultaneously. Interestingly, one of the several factors that contributed to a reappraisal of the Year 2000 program in British Columbia was resistance from secondary teachers, who expressed more concerns as the time approached for them to receive students educated under the Year 2000 program (Kuehn, 1993).

Differences in reaction that appear to be based on geography suggest that smaller schools, especially those in rural areas, may view reform with a cautious eye. Aside from possible staff selection factors, educators in the smallest districts may have problems scanning externally generated initiatives because administrative staffs are already stretched in so many directions. The problem would be exacerbated for those located at a distance from policy centers. People in these districts may also be more suspicious of state-level initiatives that they perceive as threatening to local autonomy. These educators apparently do not see the reforms the way the Department of Education presents them—as an opportunity to exercise more discretion in the operation of their schools. They do not interpret the act as an invitation to greater local control of their educational programs in exchange for improved student performance as defined by state standards.

Lower levels of support in larger districts may be attributable to the law's lack of procedural specificity. Schools in these districts could not simply wait to be told how to implement the law by central administration. Many of the large districts in this sample have an administrative structure and organizational culture that emphasizes strong central authority and standardization across schools within the district. Individual schools in these districts have less of a capacity to interpret and respond locally to broad policy frameworks. For these schools, a generalized call to restructure with few specific required activities will be viewed with much greater caution, particularly if large-scale change is implied. It would not be surprising if educators at the school level had difficulty taking initiative instead of waiting to be directed how to respond, which has been their previous practice.

Small districts may have had concerns regarding the lack of specificity, but for a different reason. The smaller districts have indicated they will be unable to meet some of the law's requirements, such as offering CAM programs in six "broad occupational categories" for all students or identifying work-based experiences for all students.

The lack of distinctive differences among almost all demographic groupings contrasted with clear differences among school sites. These findings reinforce the conclusions of many others over the past decade and a half that schools are the appropriate unit of analysis when considering policy implementation or reform in public education (Berends, 1992; David, 1990; Mortimore & Sammons, 1987; Muncey & McQuillan, 1993; Purkey & Smith, 1983). As difficult and inconvenient as it is to conceive of a public school system as thousands of individual school buildings rather than as one integrated system, it seems necessary to consider policy development from this perspective. In fact, well-constructed policy would require that sites be both able and expected to engage in a process of interpreting policy. State bureaucracies tend to prefer standardized reforms, whereas contextual effects and efforts at the building level tend to create nonstandardized responses. Resistance to and acceptance of change is more complex and subtle than demography or status suggest and is probably as connected to contextual as to personal characteristics.

Differences among schools may flow from the interaction among individual characteristics rather than organizational effects. Although demographic characteristics may not seem important when viewed in the aggregate, these same characteristics and others not sampled in this study may create

dynamics—essentially an interaction effect—that does not occur when people express themselves individually. Characteristics such as a comparatively old or young staff, one that is predominantly male or female, or one where the principal has a strong vision can have a powerful effect individually or in combination within the context of a school building. Understanding how attitudes about school restructuring are formed at the school site is important because there are strong indicators that educational restructuring is a building-by-building process, not primarily a state phenomenon (Goldman et al., 1993; Louis & Miles, 1990; Murphy & Hallinger, 1993).

These findings taken in their entirety suggest that some combination of district-level actions and factors specific to each school affects attitudes toward the act. Possibly factors at the school such as history and culture, staff composition, leadership, and experience with school improvement combine to provide filters through which both state mandates and district policy pass as they are being understood, interpreted, and adapted. In other districts where school differences are much smaller, it is most likely that the school-level contextual factors described above are being influenced, at least modestly, by actions at the district level. Although restructuring is and likely will continue to be primarily a school-by-school phenomenon, districts do apparently influence attitudes toward reform at the site level as well. State actions merely initiate a series of complex interactions leading to a wide range of interpretations and responses.

Implications

Schools may serve as the locus for change, but the more crucial issue is whether they can create or sustain staff willingness and energy for change without external pressure for reform and improvement. Based on our findings, states that mandate change may have to provide systematic supports—funding, demonstration projects, networks, consultation services—that enable educators to interpret, adapt, and act on state mandates at the site level, and that are compatible with and supportive of the structures and strategies that emerge in schools. This observation is consistent with the findings of Teddlie and Stringfield's (1993) longitudinal study of school effects.

The movement toward national and state standards only sharpens the need to focus on the capacity of individual schools to meet externally imposed performance expectations. The national standards model is based on the assumption that once standards are developed, individual schools will have both the capacity and will to reshape their educational programs so that more students meet the standards. Oregon educators do not appear to accept this premise. They seem concerned that *any* action by the state will result in reduced local control. There is little evidence that teachers currently feel capable of making changes of the magnitude required for all students to reach high standards, nor that they even feel the most important factors could ever be under their control. For example, a common teacher response to poor student performance is to cite unsupportive or dysfunctional family environments. Serious resistance can be expected if teachers feel they are being given an impossible task.

Teachers may be more likely to accept the notion of externally designated learning standards if they believe that the conditions under which they teach and their students learn will somehow be modified substantially. The extent to which teachers participate in the decisions that operationalize restructuring may be key in determining their acceptance of externally designed frameworks for school organization (Conley & Goldman, 1994; Merwin, 1993). States may find themselves in the unfamiliar position of nurturing rather than mandating policy implementation.

If a state were to develop educational restructuring policy that responded to these findings, the policy would contain provisions to require or at least encourage individual school sites to respond to the state's policy in at least four ways: (a) by creating provisions that ensured each school determined the policy's likely effects on that school; (b) by enabling the site to tailor its responses or implementation in some important ways; (c) by making

sure there were exemplars or models that showed educators how the new policy might play out in practice; and (d) by demonstrating to teachers that they will likely be able to adapt successfully to the demands of the policy.

Can states restructure their public education systems through comprehensive legislative programs, particularly when traditions of local control and school-based change are strong? Can legislative action spur and support change at school sites? Our data suggest that educators are much more receptive than might be expected, particularly considering their lack of involvement and the state's fiscal crisis. But they are realists. They are unlikely to proceed too far down this path if they believe there is little probability of success. Reform legislation has initiated a profound reexamination of current practice and has opened the door to a new vision of education. In that sense it has served the catalyst function desired by its initiators. It remains unclear whether policymakers and educators are now poised to walk through the door, or to close it after glimpsing what lies ahead.

References

Auriemma, F., Cooper, B., & Smith, S. (1992). *Graying teachers: A report on state pension systems and school district early retirement incentives.* Eugene, OR: ERIC Clearinghouse on Educational Management.

Berends, M. (1992). *A description of restructuring in nationally nominated schools.* Madison, WI: University of Wisconsin, Center on Organization and Restructuring of Schools.

Berman, P., & McLaughlin, M. (1974). *Federal programs supporting educational change: Vol. 8. Implementing and sustaining innovations.* Santa Monica, CA: RAND.

Blalock, H. (1972). *Social statistics.* New York: McGraw-Hill.

Center for Policy Research. (1989). *The progress of reform: An appraisal of state education initiatives.* Rutgers, NJ: Author.

Cohen, J. (1990). Things I have learned (so far). *American Psychologist, 45*(12), 1304–1312.

Conley, D. (1986). *Certificated personnel evaluation in Colorado: A policy study of practices and perceptions at the time of the implementation of the Certificated Personnel Performance Evaluation Act (H.B. 1338).* Unpublished doctoral dissertation, University of Colorado, Boulder.

Conley, D. (1991). Lessons from laboratories in school restructuring and site-based decision-making: Oregon's 2020 schools take control of their own reform. *OSSC Bulletin, 34*(7), 1–61.

Conley, D., Dunlap, D., & Goldman, P. (1992). The "vision thing" and school restructuring. *OSSC Report, 32*(2), 1–8.

Conley, D, & Goldman, P. (1994). Ten propositions for facilitative leadership. In J. Murphy & K. S. Louis (Eds.), *Reshaping the principalship: Insights from transformational reform efforts* (pp. 237–262). Newbury Park, CA: Corwin.

Conley, D. T., Goldman, P., & Dunlap, D. M. (1993, April 14). *Radical state legislation as a tool for fundamental educational reform and restructuring: Reactions from the field to Oregon's H.B. 3565.* Paper presented at the annual conference of the American Educational Research Association, Atlanta, GA.

David, J. (1990). Restructuring in progress: Lessons from pioneering districts. In R. Elmore (Ed.), *Restructuring schools: The next generation of educational reform.* San Francisco: Jossey-Bass.

Eberts, R., Schwartz, E., & Stone, J. (1990). School reform, school size, and student achievement. *Economic Review (Federal Reserve Bank of Cleveland), 26*(2), 2–15.

Elmore, R. F. (1983). Complexity and control: What legislators and administrators can do about implementing public policy. In L. S. Shulman & G. Sykes (Eds.), *Handbook of teaching and policy.* New York: Longman.

Elmore, R. F. (1988). *Early experience in restructuring schools: Voices from the field.* Washington, DC: Center for Policy Research, National Governors' Association.

Elmore, R. F., & McLaughlin, M. W. (1988). *Steady work: Policy, practice, and the reform of American education.* Santa Monica, CA: RAND.

Firestone, W., Fuhrman, S., & Kirst, M. (1990, February). Implementation, effects of state education reform in the '80's. *NASSP Bulletin,* pp. 75–84.

Firestone, W., Fuhrman, S., & Kirst, M. (1991). State educational reform since 1983: Appraisal and the future. *Educational Policy, 5*(3), 233–250.

Fuhrman, S. (1993). The politics of coherence. In S. Fuhrman (Ed.), *Designing coherent policy: Improving the system.* San Francisco: Jossey-Bass.

Fuhrman, S., Clune, W., & Elmore, R. (1991). Research on education reform: Lessons on the implementation of policy. In A. Odden (Ed.), *Educational policy implementation* (pp. 197–218). Albany: SUNY Press.

Fuhrman, S., & Elmore, R. (1990). Understanding local control in the wake of state education reform. *Educational Evaluation and Policy Analysis, 12*(1), 82–96.

Fuhrman, S. O. (1988). Research on education reform: Lessons on the implementation of policy. *Teachers College Record, 90*(2), 237–57.

Glen, H., & Crandall, D. P. (1988). *A beginning look at the what and how of restructuring.* ERIC Document Reproduction Service No. ED 294 326.

Goldman, P., & Conley, D. (1994, April 4). *School responses to state-level restructuring legislation.* Paper presented at the annual conference of the American Educational Research Association, New Orleans.

Goldman, P., Dunlap, D., & Conley, D. (1991, April). *Administrative facilitation and site-based school reform projects.* Paper presented at the annual conference of the American Educational Research Association, Chicago.

Goldman, P., Dunlap, D., & Conley, D. (1993). Facilitative power and non-standardized solutions to school site restructuring. *Educational Administration Quarterly, 29*(1), 69–92.

Grossman, P., Kirst, M., & Schmidt-Posner, J. (1986). On the trail of the omnibeast: Evaluating omnibus education reforms in the 1980s. *Educational Evaluation and Policy Analysis, 8*(3), 253–266.

H.B. 3565: Oregon Educational Act for the 21st Century (1993). In *Oregon Laws Relating to Public Schools and Community Colleges,* pp. 43–80. Salem, OR: Oregon Department of Education.

Hallinger, P., Murphy, J., & Hausman, C. (1991, April). *Restructuring schools: Principals' perceptions of fundamental educational reform.* Paper presented at the annual conference of the American Educational Research Association, Chicago.

Harris, L., & Wagner, R. F. (1993, September). *Testing assumptions: A survey of teachers attitudes toward the nation's school reform agenda.* Ford Foundation.

King, A.J.C., & Peart, M. (1992). *Teachers in Canada: Their work and quality of life.* Ottawa, Ontario: Canadian Teachers Federation.

Kirst, M. (1992). The state role in school restructuring. In C. Finn & T. Rebarber (Eds.), *Education reform in the 90's.* New York: Macmillan.

Kuehn, L. (1993). *Teaching in the '90s: Rep. No. 1. Changing teaching practice: Teachers' aspirations meet school realities.* Vancouver: British Columbia Teacher's Federation.

Louis, K. S., & Miles, M. (1990). *Improving the urban high school: What works and why.* New York: Teachers College Press.

Majchrzak, A. (1984). *Methods for policy research*. Beverly Hills, CA: Sage.

Mazzoni, T. (1991). Analyzing state school policymaking: An arena model. *Educational Evaluation and Policy Analysis, 13*(2), 115–138.

Merwin, G. (1993). *Facilitative power: Strategy for restructuring educational leadership*. Unpublished doctoral dissertation, University of Oregon.

Mortimore, P., & Sammons, P. (1987). New evidence on effective elementary schools. *Educational Leadership, 45*(1), 4–8.

Muncey, D., & McQuillan, P. (1993). Preliminary findings from a five-year study of the coalition of essential schools. *Phi Delta Kappan, 74*(6), 486–489.

Murphy, J., & Hallinger, P. (Ed.). (1993). *Restructuring Schooling: Learning from ongoing efforts*. Newbury Park, CA: Corwin.

National Center for Education and the Economy, Commission on the Skills of the American Work Force. (1990). *America's choice: High skills or low wages!* Rochester, NY: Author.

Purkey, S., & Smith, M. (1983). Effective schools: A review. *Elementary School Journal, 83*, 427–452.

Silns, H. C. (1992). Effective leadership for school reform. *Alberta Journal of Educational Research, 38*(4), 317–334.

Smith, M. S., & O'Day, J. (1991). Systemic school reform. In S. H. Fuhrman & B. Malen (Eds.), *The politics of curriculum and testing: The 1990 yearbook of the politics of education association* (pp. 233–267). Philadelphia: Falmer.

Steffy, B. (1993). *The Kentucky Education Reform Act: Lessons for America*. Lancaster, PA: Technomics.

Teddlie, C., & Stringfield, S. (1993). *Schools make a difference*. New York: Teachers College.

U.S. Department of Education. (1983). *A nation at risk: The imperative for educational reform*. Washington, DC: Author.

Verstegen, D. A. (1994). Reforming American education policy. *Educational Administration Quarterly, 30*(3), 365–390.

Weiss, C. H. (1977). Research for policy's sake: The enlightenment function of social research. *Policy Analysis, 3*, 531–545.

Wilson, B., & Rossman, G. (1993). *Mandating academic excellence*. New York: Teachers College Press.

CHAPTER 8

CORRELATIONAL RESEARCH

Joseph Wright heads the history department of a large urban high school. He believes that many of his students do poorly in history because they lack good study skills. In talking with a professor of education at a nearby university, Joseph learned about a measure of study skills that is appropriate for high school students. The professor encouraged Joseph to test his theory by giving this measure to all the students enrolled in his history classes at the beginning of the term. According to the professor, if Joseph's theory is correct, the students' scores on the study skills measure should be related to their history course grades. This sounds reasonable to Joseph, but he does not fully understand the logic of the research

design and how to analyze the data in order to test his theory.

By reading this chapter, you will develop an understanding of the data-collection procedures that were recommended for Joseph's study of the possible relationship between his students' study skills and their history course grades. These procedures constitute a type of investigation called *correlational research*. You will learn how correlational research makes it possible to investigate the precise extent of the relationship between two or more variables, or to predict an important criterion from variables that are related to the criterion. A reprint of a published correlational study is included at the end of the chapter.

OBJECTIVES

After studying this chapter, you will be able to

1. describe the advantages of correlational research compared to causal-comparative or experimental research.

2. describe the possible interpretations of a significant correlation between variables *A* and *B*.

3. explain the difference between bivariate and multivariate correlational statistics.

4. explain how characteristics of the research data affect researchers' choice of a correlational statistic for analyzing the data.

5. describe two potential problems in research studies in which correlations are calculated among a large number of variables.

6. draw appropriate inferences from given correlation coefficients about the degree, direction, and possible causal nature of the relationship between two variables.

7. describe how relationship and prediction studies differ in design and in their interpretation of the significance of correlational research findings.

KEY TERMS

bivariate correlational
   statistics
canonical correlation
correlation coefficient
correlational research
criterion variable
descriptive research
differential analysis
discriminant analysis
explained variance

factor analysis
line of best fit
moderator variable
multiple regression
multivariate correlational
   statistics
negative correlation
path analysis
positive correlation
practical significance

prediction study
predictor variable
relationship study
scattergram
statistical significance
structural equation modeling
variance

THE NATURE OF CORRELATIONAL RESEARCH

Both correlational research and causal-comparative research investigate relationships between variables. As you learned in Chapter 7, causal-comparative studies determine relationships by examining whether groups that differ on a specific characteristic (typically an independent variable) also differ on another characteristic (typically a dependent variable). For example, students scoring high on a variable such as popularity with peers might be compared with students scoring low on the variable. Having selected groups that differ on this independent variable, the researcher then determines whether these groups also differ on other variables, such as academic achievement and attitude toward school.

By contrast, correlational research examines all the levels of the variables that are measured. For example, when students take a test of verbal aptitude, their scores typically range on a continuum from high to low, with many students falling between the extremes. In correlational research, the relationship of all these scores (not just high versus low) to students' scores on other variables is calculated. The statistical procedure used for this purpose is correlation.

Correlational research has an advantage over causal-comparative research because it allows researchers to determine not only whether a relationship between variables exists, but also the degree of the relationship between them. An additional advantage is that correlational research allows researchers to analyze how several variables, either singly or in combination, might affect a particular pattern of behavior. In contrast, the causal-comparative method and the experimental method are best suited to studying the effects of only one or two variables at a time.

To determine the degree of the relationship between two variables with the correlational method, researchers calculate a statistic called a *correlation coefficient*. To understand the correlation coefficient, it is helpful to think about individual differences. For example, students differ in their level of artistic ability. If everyone had the same level of artistic ability, there would be little interest in studying its determinants or in predicting it. Yet people do differ in this ability, and these variations can have important personal and social consequences. If researchers could discover the causes of individual differences in artistic ability, this knowledge might prove useful in helping individuals maximize their artistic potential.

Let us consider the role of the correlation coefficient in this kind of investigation. Imagine that a group of students earned scores varying from 40 to 100 on a measure of artistic ability. We want to determine whether students' scores on another variable, such as intelligence as measured by an IQ test, are related to their scores on the measure of artistic ability. Suppose that all students who received a score of 40 on artistic ability had an IQ score of 85, whereas those with an artistic ability score of 41 had an IQ score of 86. Imagine that this pattern continued through the entire range of scores, so that students with an artistic ability score of 100 had IQ scores of 145. In this case there is a perfect positive relationship between the two variables of artistic ability and intelligence. On the basis of this finding, we would have reason to believe that artistic ability and intelligence are causally related in some way.

Suppose, by contrast, that students obtaining a particular artistic ability score had widely varying IQ scores. For example, students with scores of 40 on the artistic ability measure had IQ scores ranging from 85 to 145, and students with scores of 100 on the artistic ability measure also had IQ scores across the same range. Thus there is no relationship between the two variables. Still another possibility is that students with progressively higher artistic ability scores could earn progressively lower IQ scores. In this case, there is a negative relationship between artistic ability and intelligence.

A correlation coefficient is a precise mathematical expression of the types of relationships between variables described above. In other words, the coefficient indicates the extent to which scores on one variable covary with scores on another variable. The correlation between two variables also can be pictorially represented by a scattergram. A scattergram plots each individual's score on one variable on the horizontal, or x, axis of a chart and plots each individual's score on another variable on the vertical, or y, axis. The two scores of each individual in the sample are thus represented by a single point on the scattergram, the point where that individual's scores on the two variables intersect.

Figure 8.1 presents several scattergrams. The first shows a perfect positive correlation. Each point marks one individual's scores on the two variables. All the points fall on a straight diagonal line, which is called the *line of best fit*. The line starts at the low end of both the x-axis and the y-axis, and it moves up at a 45-degree angle to the high end of both the x-axis and the y-axis. This graph indicates that each unit of increment, or increase, in the x-axis variable is accompanied by a unit of increment in the y-axis variable. The correlation coefficient is 1.00, meaning that if we know the individual's score on one variable, we can predict perfectly that individual's score on the other variable.

The second scattergram indicates a perfect negative correlation. Here again, as in scattergram 1, all the points fall on a straight diagonal line. In this case, however, the line starts at the high end on the y-axis and the low end on the

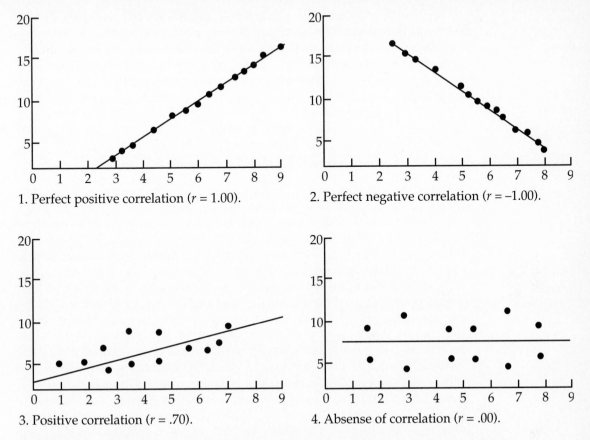

FIGURE 8.1   Scattergrams showing different degrees and directions of relationship between two variables

Source. Adapted from Figure 11.1 on p. 410 in: Gall, M. D., Borg, W. R., & Gall, J. P. (1996). *Educational research: An introduction* (6th ed.). White Plains, NY: Longman.

x-axis and moves down at a 45-degree angle to the low end of the y-axis and the high end of the x-axis. This scattergram corresponds to a correlation coefficient of −1.00, indicating that each unit of increment on the y-axis is accompanied by a decrement, or decrease, of one unit on the x-axis. As with a perfect positive correlation, we can predict perfectly an individual's score on one variable if we know that individual's score on the other variable.

The third scattergram indicates a fairly high positive correlation between the two variables. If we know an individual's score on the x-axis variable, we cannot predict that individual's score on the y-axis variable perfectly, but we can make a fairly accurate prediction. A mathematical formula can be used to calculate the line of best fit, which is shown on the scattergram. If we know the individual's score on one variable, we can use the line of best fit to estimate the individual's score on the other variable.

The fourth scattergram is a graphic representation of a complete lack of relationship between two variables. Knowing a person's score on the x-axis variable is of no value in predicting that person's score on the y-axis variable. This relationship is graphically depicted by a line of best fit that is parallel to the x-axis. The correlation coefficient for this relationship would be .00, or close to it.

BIVARIATE AND MULTIVARIATE CORRELATIONAL STATISTICS

If the relationship between only two variables is being investigated, bivariate correlational statistics are used to determine the correlation between them. The specific statistic that is used depends mainly on the types of scores to be correlated. (Score types are discussed in Chapter 6.) The data for many educational variables are in the form of continuous scores, such as individuals' total score on an achievement test containing many items. Sometimes the data are in the form of ranks, such as placing students in the order of their overall grade point average. Some data are available in the form of a dichotomy, meaning that individuals are classified into two categories based on the presence or absence of a particular characteristic. For example, students can be classified as passing or failing a course, which is an artificial dichotomy because selection of the cutoff point for passing is arbitrary. Individuals also can be classified as female or male, which is a true dichotomy because it is based on a naturally occurring difference. Finally, some data are available in the form of categories. For example, students could be classified by the sport they most like to play: volleyball, football, soccer, tennis, and so on. These sports cannot be placed on a scale from high to low or less to more; rather, each sport is a separate, discrete category.

Table 8.1 briefly describes the most widely used types of bivariate correlational statistics. Probably the best-known bivariate correlational statistic is r, also called the *Pearson product-moment correlation coefficient*. Because r has a small standard error, researchers often compute r for any two sets of scores, even if they are not continuous scores. The other bivariate correlational statistics in Table 8.1 are used less frequently, but are more appropriate under the conditions listed in the "Remarks" column. Although a correlation coefficient theoretically can vary only from −1.00 to +1.00, for some of these statistics its value may be greater than 1.

If the relationship between more than two variables is being investigated, multivariate correlational statistics are used. Table 8.2 provides a brief summary of the major multivariate correlational statistics and their uses.

Multiple regression probably is the most commonly used multivariate correlational statistic. It is appropriate in situations where researchers have scores on two or more measures for a group of individuals and want to determine how well a combination of these scores predicts their performance on an outcome or criterion measure. For example, suppose that researchers have the scores of a

TABLE 8.1   **Bivariate Correlational Techniques for Different Forms of Variables**

Technique	Symbol	Variable 1	Variable 2	Remarks
Product-moment correlation	r	Continuous	Continuous	The most stable technique, i.e., smallest standard error
Rank-difference correlation (*rho*)	ρ	Ranks	Ranks	A special form of product-moment correlation, used when the number of cases is under 30
Kendall's *tau*	τ	Ranks	Ranks	Preferable to *rho* for numbers under 10
Biserial correlation	r_{bis}	Artificial dichotomy	Continuous	Values can exceed 1, and have a larger standard error than r; commonly used in item analysis
Widespread biserial correlation	r_{wbis}	Widespread artificial dichotomy	Continuous	Used when researchers are interested in individuals at the extremes on the dichotomized variable
Point-biserial correlation	r_{pbis}	True dichotomy	Continuous	Yields a lower correlation than r_{bis}
Tetrachoric correlation	r_t	Artificial dichotomy	Artificial dichotomy	Used when both variables can be split at critical points
Phi coefficient	ϕ	True dichotomy	True dichotomy	Used in calculating inter-item correlations
Contingency coefficient	C	Two or more categories	Two or more categories	Comparable to r_t under certain conditions; closely related to chi-square
Correlation ratio, *eta*	η	Continuous	Continuous	Used to detect nonlinear relationships

Source. Adapted from Table 11.3 on p. 428 in: Gall, M. D., Borg, W. R., & Gall, J. P. (1996). *Educational research: An introduction* (6th ed.). White Plains, NY: Longman.

group of teachers working overseas on three measures: number of years of teaching experience, extent of travel while growing up, and tolerance for ambiguity. The researchers wish to know whether these measures can accurately predict the teachers' scores on a measure of adaptation to the overseas culture in which they are working. One approach to this question is to compute a separate correlation coefficient between each of the three predictor variables and the outcome measure. A more precise approach is a multiple regression analysis, which will determine whether some combination of the three predictor measures correlates better with the outcome measure than any one predictor variable alone.

Discriminant analysis and canonical correlation are specialized forms of multiple regression. Suppose that the outcome measure in the above example were a dichotomous variable (i.e., adapted well to the overseas culture versus adapted poorly) rather than a continuous variable (i.e., degree of adaptation to the overseas culture). In this case the researchers would use discriminant analysis to determine the correlation between teachers' scores on the three predictor variables and their adaptation to the overseas culture.

Canonical correlation would be used if there were multiple measures of the outcome variable. For example, suppose that the researchers administer

TABLE 8.2   Multivariate Correlational Statistics and Their Uses

Multiple regression	Used to determine the correlation (R) between a criterion variable and a combination of two or more predictor variables
Discriminant analysis	Used to determine the correlation between two or more predictor variables and a dichotomous criterion variable
Canonical correlation	Used to predict a combination of several criterion variables from a combination of several predictor variables
Path analysis	Used to test theories about hypothesized causal links between variables that are correlated
Structural equation modeling	Used to test theories about hypothesized causal links between variables that are correlated; yields more valid and reliable measures of the variables to be analyzed than does path analysis
Factor analysis	Used to reduce a large number of variables to a few factors by combining variables that are moderately or highly correlated with one another
Differential analysis	Used to examine correlations between variables among homogeneous subgroups within a sample; can be used to identify moderator variables that improve a measure's predictive validity

several measures of adaptation, each assessing adaptation to a different aspect of the culture (e.g., the food, the climate, or the local customs). Canonical correlation enables researchers to determine which combination of predictor measures best correlates with a composite factor that represents the various outcome measures.

Path analysis and structural equation modeling are sophisticated multivariate techniques for testing causal links among the different variables that have been measured. For example, suppose that the researchers hypothesize that, among teachers, (1) childhood travel experiences lead to (2) tolerance for ambiguity and (3) desire for travel as an adult, and that (2) and (3) make it more likely that a teacher will (4) seek an overseas teaching experience and (5) adapt well to the experience. Path analysis and structural equation modeling are methods for testing the validity of the hypothesized causal links involving these five factors.

Researchers sometimes wish to determine whether the variables they have measured reflect a smaller number of underlying factors. Factor analysis is a multivariate correlational statistic that allows them to do so. For example, suppose that researchers have developed measures of eight study skills: (1) organizing one's study materials, (2) time management, (3) classroom listening, (4) classroom note-taking, (5) planning for assigned papers, (6) writing assigned papers, (7) preparing for tests, and (8) taking tests. The researchers wonder whether these are related skills, meaning that students who are high on one skill are likely to be high on all or some subset of the other skills.

Factor analysis is a correlational technique that can examine all eight measures and determine whether they cluster into a smaller number of factors. Perhaps the eight study skills reflect three underlying factors: (1) skills that involve writing, (2) skills that involve planning, and (3) skills that involve recall of learned information. Factor analysis can reveal this underlying structure of factors.

The final multivariate technique shown in Table 8.2 is differential analysis, which sometimes is used in prediction research. Differential analysis is the technique of using moderator variables to form subgroups when examining the relationship between two other variables. For example, suppose that we have reason to believe that self-esteem has more effect on school performance for students of lower socioeconomic status (SES) than for students of higher SES. Socioeconomic status, then, is a third variable—called a *moderator variable*—that is thought to mediate the relationship between the first two variables. Let's say that the correlation coefficient for the relationship between self-esteem and school performance is .40 for low-SES students and .25 for high-SES students. These results demonstrate that SES moderates (or mediates) the relationship between self-esteem and school performance.

INTERPRETING CORRELATION COEFFICIENTS

The same limitations in making inferences from causal-comparative findings apply to making inferences from correlational findings. Suppose that we obtain an *r* of .63, indicating a significant positive correlation between students' popularity with peers (variable *A*) and their grade point average (GPA, which is variable *B*). This correlation coefficient indicates that the more popular students are with their peers, the higher their GPA. Note that the correlation is not perfect, however. That is, sometimes a student has a higher or lower GPA than we would expect based on that student's popularity.

Now let's speculate about the causal relationship between these two variables. Because the finding is based on a correlation coefficient, we cannot conclusively determine whether peer popularity causes higher achievement (*A* causes *B*), whether higher achievement causes students to be more popular (*B* causes *A*), or whether both peer popularity and academic achievement are caused by a third variable (*C* causes both *A* and *B*). An experiment is necessary to determine which of these explanations is valid. For example, we could test the first explanation (popularity causes higher achievement) by teaching a group of students social skills that are likely to increase their popularity with peers. We would then follow them over time to see whether their grades improved.

A major advantage of correlational research is that researchers can explore a wide variety of relationships in the same study. Suppose that we wish to study the relationship between specific teaching behaviors and elementary school students' mathematics achievement. We could conduct a correlational research study in which observers record the degree to which a sample of elementary teachers uses 10 different teaching techniques while teaching mathematics over a period of several weeks. At the end of the observation period, each teacher would have been scored on each of the 10 specific techniques that were observed. Achievement tests would be administered to the students in these teachers' classrooms before and after the observation period. To estimate the degree to which each technique predicted students' achievement in mathematics, a correlation coefficient would be computed between each predictor variable (that is, a particular teaching technique) and students' postobservation achievement, which is the criterion variable. (The researchers might use partial correlation, a special form of correlation, to correct for initial differences in students' preobservation mathematics achievement.) Thus, the researchers can study the potential effects of 10 teaching techniques in a single correlational study, whereas only a few of these techniques feasibly could be manipulated in an experimental study.

Correlation coefficients are easy to compute, and as a result, researchers may correlate a large number of variables with one another or with a single criterion variable. The resulting large number of correlation coefficients can cause two problems in interpreting the study findings.

The first problem is that it is difficult to interpret the results, unless the selection of variables to be correlated is guided by a theoretical rationale. For example, suppose that researchers correlate a large number of variables with students' GPA. Further suppose that one of these variables, students' body weight, is correlated with GPA. What does this finding mean? Does higher weight cause students to get better grades? Does getting better grades cause students to weigh more because it leads them to get less exercise or to eat more, and thus gain weight? Or are weight and grade level both caused by some other variable, such as family SES? After the fact, researchers usually can give several plausible explanations for any correlational result, be it a low or a high, a positive or a negative, or a near-zero correlation, between two or more variables. Unless their rationale for examining the relationship between specific variables was sound to begin with, you have reason to suspect such explanations. For example, if researchers concluded from the hypothetical correlation between weight and GPA that students should eat more in order to get better grades, many educators would question the value of educational research!

The second problem with correlating many variables with each other is statistical in nature. When a large number of measures are administered, some will correlate with one another by chance alone. If the study were repeated, these chance findings would not be found again; that is, they would not be replicated. In the hypothetical example of a correlation between weight and GPA, the correlation likely is a chance finding that would not recur if another sample were studied.

RELATIONSHIP STUDIES AND PREDICTION STUDIES

Correlational statistics are used for two primary purposes in educational research: (1) to explore the nature of the relationship between variables of interest to educators, and (2) to determine variables that can be used to predict important educational or personal characteristics of individuals that will not occur until later. Correlational research studies usually have one or the other of these purposes, and differ in design accordingly. Hereafter we distinguish such studies as either relationship studies or prediction studies.

In some relationship studies, researchers use the correlational method to examine possible cause-and-effect relationships between variables, such as whether parents' educational level affects their children's success in school. In other relationship studies, the researchers want to gain a better understanding of factors that contribute to a complex characteristic, such as artistic ability. For example, if researchers were to find that observational skills, visual acuity, small-muscle dexterity, and creative imagination are all related to artistic ability, they would have gained some insight into the nature of this complex characteristic. Relationship studies usually explore the relationships between measures of different variables obtained from the same individuals at the same point in time.

In contrast to relationship studies, in prediction studies some variables (the predictor variables) are measured at one point in time, and other variables (the criterion variables) are measured at a later point in time. This procedure is followed because the goal of prediction studies is to forecast important future behavior. The correlational research study that is reprinted in this chapter is a prediction study. The study involved development of a shortened version of a test of prekindergarten children's printing errors, which could be used to predict their later school performance.

Good predictor variables are important whether or not we understand why they predict well. For example, the U.S. Air Force has developed a battery of tests that can be given to applicants for pilot training. Prediction studies have shown that each of these tests is correlated with later success in pilot training. By administering this battery of tests and studying the correlations obtained in previous research, the researcher can predict the likelihood that any given individual will successfully complete the pilot-training program.

STATISTICAL AND PRACTICAL SIGNIFICANCE
OF CORRELATION COEFFICIENTS

A correlation coefficient basically is a descriptive statistic, because it expresses quantitatively the precise extent of the relationship between two or more variables. Let us say that the correlation between students' liking for school (variable *A*) and students' GPA (variable *B*) equals .50. If we square the correlation coefficient, we have a measure of the explained variance, which is the amount of variance that these two variables have in common. In this case, variables *A* and *B* have 25 percent of their variance in common, because .50 squared equals .25. As a statement of prediction, we can say that the variance in variable *A* predicts 25 percent of the variance in variable *B*, or vice versa. The higher the correlation, whether in a positive or a negative direction, the more accurately we can predict an individual's score on variable *A* from the individual's score on variable *B*, or vice versa.

A correlation coefficient can be tested to determine whether it is statistically significant. If it is statistically significant, we can conclude that a correlation coefficient this great is unlikely to have occurred by chance if there is in fact no relationship between variables *A* and *B* in the population from which the sample was drawn. Whether or not a correlation coefficient of a particular size is statistically significant depends on several factors, including the significance level selected, the number of participants in the research sample, whether the researchers predicted the (positive or negative) direction of the relationship, and the variability of the scores.

Because its focus is on exploration and understanding, a relationship study is meaningful whether the correlation coefficient obtained is low or high, positive or negative. Any correlation coefficient contributes to an understanding of the educational phenomena involved. Therefore, in a relationship study the statistical significance of the correlation coefficient is far more important than its practical significance.

In prediction studies, researchers are concerned with both the statistical significance of the correlation coefficient and its practical significance. If the coefficient is sufficiently large to achieve statistical significance, we can be fairly confident that the observed relationship is not a chance finding. If the predictor variable explains a substantial proportion of the variance in an important criterion variable, it will be useful for improving educational practice, and thus the correlation coefficient also has practical significance. For example, an aptitude measure that has been shown to relate to later school performance has many practical applications. School counselors could use students' scores on the aptitude measure to counsel students about what subjects to take or what careers they might want to explore. Scores also could be used to identify children who might need special education, or to assign students to remedial or advanced classes.

CONCLUDING THOUGHT

Educators hold many beliefs about how the different characteristics of the groups or individuals with whom they work relate to one another. They also are constantly searching for attributes that help them predict the future success of their students, or of individuals for whom they have administrative responsibility.

The techniques of correlational research provide a precise means for testing these beliefs and for improving predictions. For these reasons, correlational research plays an important role in the quest to improve the knowledge base upon which educational practice rests.

SELF-CHECK TEST

1. Correlational research is superior to causal-comparative research in
   a. determining the causal relationship between two variables.
   b. determining the precise extent of the relationship between two variables.
   c. studying the effects of only one variable at a time.
   d. studying variables that involve discrete categories.

2. A scattergram is helpful in indicating all of the following except
   a. the direction of the relationship between two variables.
   b. the extent of the relationship between two variables.
   c. whether there is a curvilinear relationship between two variables.
   d. whether there is a causal relationship between two variables.

3. A perfect negative correlation between variables A and B means that
   a. there is no relationship between individuals' scores on variable A and their scores on variable B.
   b. the higher an individual's score on variable B, the higher that individual's score on variable B.
   c. the higher an individual's score on variable A, the lower that individual's score on variable B.
   d. variations in individuals' scores on variable A caused the observed variations in individuals' scores on variable B.

4. If researchers wish to determine whether 10 measured variables cluster into a smaller set of underlying characteristics, they are likely to use
   a. multiple regression.
   b. structural equation modeling.
   c. path analysis.
   d. factor analysis.

5. The most important consideration in choosing a bivariate correlational statistic is
   a. the form of the scores for each variable.
   b. the number of variables to be correlated.
   c. whether one is trying to study a cause-and-effect relationship or predict a criterion variable.
   d. the size of the research sample.

6. Researchers calculated correlations between each pair of 20 variables and found several statistically significant correlations. When they repeated the study, none of these pairs of variables were significantly correlated. This occurrence is most likely due to the
   a. selection of variables to be correlated based on a theoretical rationale.
   b. likelihood that when many variables are intercorrelated, some statistically significant correlations will occur by chance.
   c. failure to hypothesize in advance which variables had a causal effect on which other variables.
   d. selection of inappropriate predictor variables.

7. If variable *A* is significantly correlated with variable *B* in the research sample, we can conclude that
   a. there is likely to be a relationship between variables *A* and *B* in the population.
   b. variable *A* is a suitable predictor of variable *B*.
   c. no other variables are likely to correlate positively with variable *A*.
   d. variable *A* causes variable *B*.

RECOMMENDED READING

Gall, M. D., Borg, W. R., & Gall, J. P. (1996). *Educational research: An introduction* (6th ed.). White Plains, NY: Longman.
   See Chapter 11 of the book for a more extensive discussion of the correlational topics and issues covered in this chapter.

Bruning, J. L., & Kintz, B. L. (1990). *Computational handbook of statistics* (3rd ed.). Reading, MA: Addison-Wesley Educational.
   Provides easy-to-follow computational procedures for the most commonly-used correlational techniques.

Cohen, J., & Cohen, P. (1983). *Applied multiple regression/correlation analysis for the behavioral sciences* (2nd ed.). Hillsdale, NJ: Erlbaum.
   Presents computational procedures and research applications for many of the statistical techniques presented in this chapter. The authors also discuss procedures for handling missing data, computer analysis of data, and the relationship between analysis of variance and multiple regression.

Jackson, D. H., & Messick, S. (Eds.). (1978). *Problems in human assessment*. Melbourne, FL: Krieger.
   The articles reprinted in this book can help students planning a prediction study, including: Thorndike, R. L., The analysis and selection of test items; Guilford, J. P., Some lessons from aviation psychology; Saunders, D. R., Moderator variables in prediction; and Cureton, E. E., Validity, reliability, and baloney.

SAMPLE CORRELATIONAL RESEARCH STUDY: PREDICTIVE VALIDITY OF AN ABBREVIATED VERSION OF THE PRINTING PERFORMANCE SCHOOL READINESS TEST

Simner, M. L. (1989). Predictive validity of an abbreviated version of the Printing Performance School Readiness Test. *Journal of School Psychology,* 27, 189–195.

In the rest of this chapter you will read a research article that illustrates a correlational research study involving prediction. It is preceded by comments written especially for this book by the author of the article. Then the article itself is reprinted in full, just as it appeared when originally published. Where appropriate, we have added footnotes to help you understand the information contained in the article.

Researcher's Comments, Prepared by Marvin Simner

Every beginning kindergarten class contains a few children whose spontaneous name printing looks like the examples in Figure 8.2. For many children, "form errors" such as these are merely bothersome mistakes that occur from time to time and interfere with

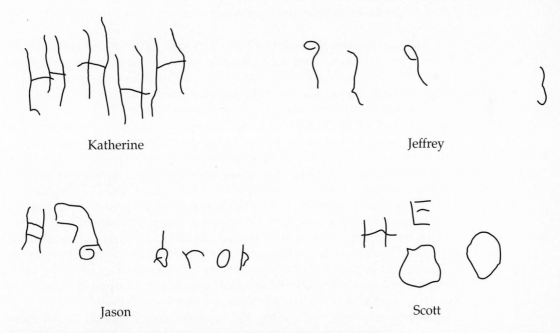

Katherine   Jeffrey

Jason   Scott

FIGURE 8.2   **Examples of kindergarten children's name printing**

Source. Taken from p. 156 in: Simner, M. L. (1982). Printing errors in kindergarten and the prediction of academic performance. *Journal of Learning Disabilities, 15,* 155–159. Reprinted by permission of Pro-Ed, Inc.

the legibility of the children's printing. The research described in my article indicates, however, that children who produce an excessive number of form errors are at high risk of experiencing serious learning problems when they enter school.

I discovered the relationship between form errors and school achievement when, in a study of the development of printing skills, I asked beginning kindergarten children to reproduce a series of letters from slides shown one at a time on a screen. Standing behind the children as they copied this material, I was struck by the odd mistakes that some of them made. I wondered why, for example, a child who seemed to be looking directly at the letter *E* would a moment later use four, five, or even six horizontal lines when attempting to reproduce it. I also was curious as to why a few children continued to make errors of this type for almost every one of the letters shown on the screen. I wondered whether this persistence of form errors revealed anything of importance about these children, so I asked permission to obtain the teachers' evaluations of the children's command of the kindergarten curriculum.

By comparing the teachers' evaluations with the children's protocols (that is, the papers on which they printed their letters), I found that the children who had produced the largest number of form errors were those who seemed to be having the greatest difficulty learning. After replicating this finding with additional kindergarten children followed through the end of first grade, I launched an extensive study that eventually involved more than 850 kindergarten children, many of whom were followed for periods of up to three years. This longitudinal work culminated in the development of the Printing Performance School Readiness Test (PPSRT; Simner, 1990). The PPSRT appears to have considerable value in predicting those children who are at risk for later school failure.

It eventually became apparent to me that a shorter version of this test would be desirable, for two reasons. First, a shorter version would be easier for younger children to complete. Second, it could be administered at the start of prekindergarten, giving an earlier indicator of possible problems in later school performance.

As the research report indicates, the Abbreviated Printing Performance School Readiness Test (APPSRT) proved to be as effective as the longer version of the test in predicting those students whom teachers would later judge to be poor performers in first or second grade. Three questions, however, remain unanswered: Why do these errors occur? Why do they predict future school performance? How can we help children who produce an excessive number of form errors avoid academic difficulty?

Previous accounts of similar drawing errors (e.g., Berry & Buktenica, 1967; Koppitz, 1963) suggest that these printing errors may be due to perceptual/motor difficulties. If this is true, perhaps children who habitually exhibit form errors should be placed in perceptual/motor training intervention programs such as those described by McCarthy and McCarthy (1976). However, my other studies (Simner, 1979; 1986) showed that when children print while looking directly at the letters rather than from memory, or when they are asked to trace the letters rather than copy them, they reduce their error rate considerably. Thus it seems that form errors do not occur because children are suffering from a perceptual deficit (being unable to see the letters as they actually appear), nor from a motor deficit (being unable to execute the fine muscle movements required to reproduce the letters), nor from a visual/motor integration problem (being unable to combine the visual information they receive from the letters with the motor output required to make a correct reproduction of the letters).

I thus was led to consider two alternative explanations for why form errors occur and why they are related to poor school performance (see Simner, 1986; Simner, 1991). The first explanation is that form errors reflect a problem with short-term memory and attention. Possible evidence for this explanation is that the letters and numbers having curved features in Figure 1 of the article tend to generate form errors that are largely curved, while those with linear features tend to produce mostly linear form errors. This error pattern suggests that children might start printing a letter with the proper visual memory image in mind, but that the memory image fades as printing continues, leaving them without an appropriate model to follow. I also found that children who produce many form errors tend to have short attention spans (Simner, 1982).

A second explanation for excessive form errors is that they reflect difficulty in planning and organizing the sequence of pencil movements that are needed to generate proper renditions of the letters. This difficulty may be indicative of a more general deficit in problem solving or strategy planning, which affects subsequent school performance.

Both of these explanations are supported by research findings that many young children who are unable to master the school curriculum have memory as well as planning problems (Hughes, 1988; Smith, 1981). These children often benefit by placement in structured, academically oriented preschool programs such as those based on the Direct Instruction Model (Gersten, Darch, & Gleason, 1988) or the Cognitively Based Curriculum (Schweinhart & Weikart, 1988).

My prediction, then, is that children who produce high scores on the PPSRT or APPSRT are more likely to avoid school failure if they are placed in academically oriented preschool programs rather than in perceptual/motor training programs. Although this prediction is supported by the research discussed above, the evidence is indirect. Further research is needed to test the prediction directly.

References

Berry, K. E., & Buktenica, N. (1967). *Developmental test of visual-motor integration.* Chicago: Follett.

Gersten, R., Darch, C., & Gleason, M. (1988). Effectiveness of a direct instruction academic kindergarten for low-income students. *The Elementary School Journal, 89,* 227–240.

Hughes, J. N. (1988). *Cognitive behavior therapy with children in schools.* New York: Pergamon.

Koppitz, E. M. (1963). *The Bender Gestalt Test for young children.* New York: Grune & Stratton.

McCarthy, J. J., & McCarthy, J. F. (1976). *Learning disabilities.* Boston: Allyn & Bacon.

Schweinhart, L. J., & Weikart, D. P. (1988). Early childhood education for at-risk four-year-olds? Yes. *American Psychologist, 43,* 665–667.

Simner, M. L. (1979). Mirror-image reversals in children's printing: Preliminary findings. (ERIC Document Reference No. ED 174 354).

Simner, M. L. (1982). Printing errors in kindergarten and the prediction of academic performance. *Journal of Learning Disabilities, 15,* 155–159.

Simner, M. L. (1986). Further evidence on the relationship between form errors in preschool printing and early school achievement. In H. S. R. Kao, G. P. van Galen, & R. Hoosain (Eds.), *Graphonomics: Contemporary research in handwriting* (pp. 107–120). Amsterdam: NorthHolland.

Simner, M. L. (1990). *Printing performance school readiness test*. London, Ont., Canada: Phylmar.

Simner, M. L. (1991). Estimating a child's learning potential from form errors in a child's printing. In J. Wann, A. M. Wing, & N. Sovik (Eds.), *Development of graphic skills: Research perspectives and educational implications* (pp. 205–222). London: Academic Press.

Smith, D. D. (1981). *Teaching the learning disabled*. Englewood Cliffs, NJ: Prentice-Hall.

PREDICTIVE VALIDITY OF AN ABBREVIATED VERSION OF THE PRINTING PERFORMANCE SCHOOL READINESS TEST

Marvin L. Simner
University of Western Ontario

When preschool children print, it is not unusual to find a letter such as the capital *E* containing four or more horizontal lines, an *S* drawn in the shape of a backward three, or *Q* appearing without a diagonal. These errors are known as form errors because they involve the addition, deletion, or misalignment of parts, thereby producing a distortion in the overall shape or form of the intended letter or number (see Figure 1 for other examples).

In the past, errors of this nature generated very little interest among educators and psychologists except for those concerned with developing instructional procedures to improve legibility. Recently, though, we discovered that an excessive number of form errors in a kindergarten child's printing can be an important early warning sign of later school failure (Simner, 1982). Incorporating procedures derived from this work, we then developed the Printing Performance School Readiness Test (PPSRT) to provide a standardized means for

Simner, M. L. (1989). Predictive validity of an abbreviated version of the Printing Performance School Readiness Test. *Journal of School Psychology, 27,* 189–195. Reprinted with permission from Elsevier Science Ltd., Oxford, England.

identifying kindergarten children who exhibit this warning sign (Simner, 1985). Although the PPSRT is quite appropriate for use at the kindergarten level, the task is unfortunately too long and too demanding to employ with younger children. Hence, the present longitudinal investigation was undertaken to determine if form errors, measured with a shorter, less taxing version of the PPSRT, can be employed as effectively at the start of prekindergarten as they can during the kindergarten year to help identify children at risk for school failure.

METHODS

Subjects

Two samples of children were employed. Sample 1 contained 104 prekindergarten children (60 male, 44 female) tested in October/November, 1983. Sample 2 consisted of 67 prekindergarten children (38 male, 29 female) tested in October/November, 1984. Detailed information describing the procedure used to obtain the children and the population from which both samples were drawn can be found in

Letter	FORM ERRORS	Letter / Number	FORM ERRORS
B	ß ß ß ᵦ ß ᵬ	s	ᵌ 8 ᵋ 9 3
C	6 Ȿ ᒐ α	u	Ʊ Ʊ 4 ſ ५ ५
D	O C P □	y	Y X ⊣ h ५
E	Ḗ ᵴ Ϝ	z	Ʒ ₽ Ɔ ₹ ₴
F	E Ϝ	2	ᒐ ₹ c ᵬ ₴ Ƹ
G	C ℭ ℭ G ᵬ ᵬ	3	₹ ₴ ₴ ᵴ Ǝ
J	Ʊ ⅃	4	H ✗
K	Ⅸ ᴎ Ϝ Ϝ ᵏ	5	Ƈ Ϛ Ƨ ᵭ
L	∠ ⊥	6	ᵠ Ͻ ₽ Ϛ
N	M ⌐ ℳ	7	ᵭ ₽ ᵴ Ƴ)

FIGURE I   **Examples of form errors in children's printing**

Source. From p. 156 in: Simner, M. L. (1982). Printing errors in kindergarten and the prediction of academic performance. *Journal of Learning Disabilities, 15,* 155–159. © 1982 by Pro-Ed, Inc. Reprinted by permission.

Simner (1987). The mean age of the children at the time testing took place was 52 months (*SD* = 2.9).[*, a]

Test Instrument

To select as few letters and numbers as possible with which to construct an effective yet shorter, or abbreviated, PPSRT (APPSRT), we followed recommendations by Anastasi (1982, pp. 203–210) and performed an item analysis on results from our earlier investigations at the kindergarten level, in which all 41 letters and numbers in the PPSRT were employed.[b] The aim of this analysis was to determine which letters and numbers were most predictive of later school failure. On the basis of the outcome of this work, 18 letters and numbers were

* Original notes to the article appear as numbered endnotes. The footnotes written by the authors of this text are ordered alphabetically from a to h.

a. *SD* is an abbreviation for standard deviation, which is a statistical measure of how much the obtained test scores vary around the mean score. An *SD* of 2.9 means that approximately two-thirds of the children in the sample are between 49 months (mean score of 52 minus 1 *SD* of 2.9) and 55 months (mean score of 52 plus 1 *SD* of 2.9) of age.

b. An item analysis, as its name implies, involves the analysis of individual test items for various purposes. In this case, the purpose was to determine which items best predicted school failure. These items were selected for the abbreviated version of the test.

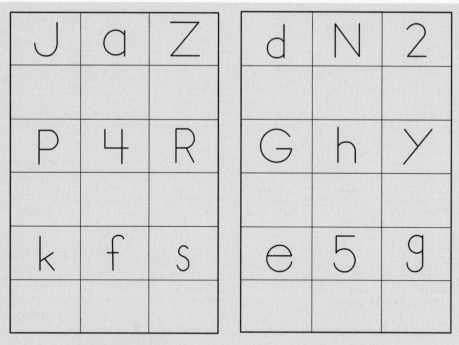

Response Sheet 1   Response Sheet 2

FIGURE 2   **Response sheets making up the APPSRT.**

chosen and presented to the prekindergarten children on two 22-cm × 28-cm response sheets using the fixed but random order illustrated in Figure 2.

Procedure

The children, tested one at a time, were asked to copy each letter and number in the spaces provided below the letters and numbers on the response sheets. No time limit was employed; however, all of the children completed the task without difficulty in less than 3 min. The resulting protocols were scored for the presence of form errors according to the instructions in the PPSRT manual. Because each of the children's attempts at reproducing a letter or number received a score of 0 (form error absent) or 1 (form error present), total scores ranged from 0 through 18.

As in our earlier work, all of the children in both samples were followed for 3 years. To assess the children's academic achievements at the end

of this period and to permit a direct comparison between the present findings and our previous results, we employed the same sets of criteria as those used in our earlier investigations. The first set made use of the children's report card marks in reading and arithmetic issued in June of first grade. These marks ranged on a 12-point scale from D to A+ and reflected the teacher's judgments of the children's command of the core curriculum established by the board of education.[1] The second set of criteria consisted of the children's raw scores at the end of first grade on two standardized achievement tests. Here we employed, as before, the word identification subtest from the Woodcock Reading Mastery Test (WRMT) by Woodcock (1974) along with the addition, subtraction, numerical reasoning, word

1. This information was not available for seven children who either failed or were placed in special education classes prior to entering first grade.

problem, and time subtests from the Keymath Diagnostic Arithmetic Test (KDAT) by Connolly, Nachtman, and Pritchett (1971). Both tests were administered to 93% of the children who completed first grade by a tester who was unaware of the children's classroom performance evaluations.

RESULTS

Interrater and Test-Retest Reliability

To evaluate interrater reliability, all of the protocols from Sample 1 were scored independently by two people.[c] The results yielded a product-moment correlation of .95 ($p < .001$).[d] Furthermore, the total scores generated by both raters differed by three points or less in 90% of the cases.

Test-retest reliability was evaluated by a different tester, who was unaware of the scores the children obtained the first time they were given the APPSRT.[e] Because of budget restrictions, however, it was not possible to retest all of the children. Therefore, 44 of the 67 children in Sample 2 were selected at random and tested on a second occasion 1 month later. Here the product-moment correlation was .87 ($p < .001$) and the total scores on each occasion differed by three points or less in 78% of the cases. Together, these findings agree with the evidence we obtained with the PPSRT.

Follow-Up Results

Table 1 contains, for Sample 1 and Sample 2, the product-moment correlations between the children's total scores on the APPSRT and the children's performances, 3 years later, on the two criteria. As the evidence in Table 1 shows, when in-class performance was the criterion the correlations ranged from −.42 through −.58, and when the criterion was achievement test performance the correlations extended from −.40 through −.60.[2,f] Hence, the predictive validity correlations obtained from both samples are also in line with the predictive validity correlations that we obtained earlier with the PPSRT. In that work, the samples of kindergarten children followed through the end of first grade produced scores on the PPSRT that correlated from −.40 to −.70 with the two achievement tests and from −.43 to −.56 with the two measures of classroom performance (see Table 1 in Simner, 1986).

Next we asked if scores on the APPSRT could be used with the same accuracy as scores on the PPSRT to identify children who later had serious learning problems. In our previous work the cutoff on the PPSRT correctly identified, on average, 81% of those kindergarten children who subsequently experienced considerable difficulty mastering the curriculum (true

2. Separate correlations were calculated for males and females in each sample, but no reliable sex differences were found.

c. The scoring of children's errors in printing requires some judgment. Inter-rater reliability is the extent to which two raters exercise the same kind of judgment in scoring. If the reliability is low, it means that the raters are using different or inconsistent criteria, and so the children's scores have little meaning.

d. A product-moment correlation is a statistical measure of how well two sets of scores agree. Perfect agreement would yield a correlation of 1.00, so a correlation of .95 in this situation means that the two raters were in near-perfect agreement in their scoring of children's printing errors. The expression "$p < .001$" is a way of showing the results of a test of statistical significance. In this case, the obtained p value of < (less than) .001 means that we can generalize with confidence beyond these two raters and conclude that other, similar raters would agree highly in their scoring of children's printing errors.

e. Test-retest reliability is an analysis of how consistently students perform on a test from one administration of it to another. If test-retest reliability is low, interpretation of a student's score is difficult because the student's score on the same test at a different point might be quite different. In fact, students' performance on the abbreviated test is quite stable (the correlation is .87).

f. A negative correlation means that as students' scores on one measure increase, their scores on another measure decrease. Negative correlations in this instance make sense because it means that students who have few printing errors (yielding lower scores on the APPSRT) are likely to have high grades and achievement test scores. Conversely, students who have many printing errors (yielding higher APPSRT scores) are likely to have low grades and achievement test scores. Correlations in the range between .40 and .60 mean that we can make moderately good predictions about a student's grades and achievement test scores from knowing the student's score on the APPSRT.

TABLE 1   Product-Moment Correlations (*p* < .001) Between Children's Scores on the APPSRT Administered in the Fall of Prekindergarten and Children's Subsequent Academic Performances at the End of First Grade

	June report card marks		Achievement test performance	
	Reading	Arithmetic	WRMT[a]	KDAT[b]
Sample 1	−.42	−.44	−.40	−.49
Sample 2	−.58	−.51	−.57	−.60

[a]Woodcock Reading Mastery Test.

[b]Keymath Diagnostic Arithmetic Test.

positives) while, at the same time, achieving an average false-positive rate of 23%.[g]

To compare these previous findings with the present data, we adhered to our earlier procedure and chose as a cutoff on the APPSRT a score that corresponded to somewhat less than 1 *SD* above the mean for Sample 1 (*M* = 11.80, *SD* = 5.33) and Sample 2 (*M* = 11.80, *SD* = 5.27). This procedure resulted in a score of 16 form errors as the cutoff. Also as before, the children were divided into two categories reflecting the teachers' end-of-year overall evaluations of the children's command of the curriculum. Children whom we placed in the *Poor performance* category were the ones who either failed, were promoted to a slower or junior section of the next grade, or were recommended for some type of special education class. The second category, labeled *Good performance,* contained children who received an overall rating of *B−* to *A+* on their report cards at the end of first grade. According to the children's teachers, these ratings were awarded only to children who were not experiencing any major problem with the core curriculum. The remaining children who received *C* ratings were not included in the present analysis, because these ratings were assigned when there was some uncertain-

ty with regard to the child's mastery of the curriculum. In other words, this uncertainty prevented us from applying the true-positive/false-positive, true-negative/false-negative designations to this group of children in an unambiguous fashion.[h]

Table 2 contains the number and percentage of prekindergarten children in Sample 1 and Sample 2 who were placed either in the Poor performance or in the Good performance category and whose scores on the APPSRT were either above or below the cutoff of 16 form errors. For the sake of completeness, Table 2 also contains the number of children who were given *C* ratings. Once again the findings were similar in the two samples and were nearly identical to the results we obtained previously. Specifically, with this cutoff we correctly identified 70–78% of the children in the Poor performance category (true-positives) while achieving, on average, a false-positive rate of 19%.

CONCLUSIONS

In short, the outcome of this 3-year longitudinal investigation demonstrates that form errors in children's printing, even as early as the start of prekindergarten, can be scored reliably, and that

g. A true positive is a student who the APPSRT predicts will experience difficulty in school and who in fact experiences difficulty. A false positive is a student who the APPSRT predicts will experience difficulty in school but who in fact experiences success.

h. A true negative is a student who the APPSRT predicts will not experience difficulty in school and who in fact does not experience difficulty. A false negative is a student who the APPSRT predicts will not experience difficulty in school but who in fact experiences difficulty.

TABLE 2   Prediction of Children's Classroom Performance Evaluations from the Cutoff Score on the APPSRT Administered in the Fall of Prekindergarten

	Poor performance	C ratings	Good performance
Sample 1			
Poor prognosis (16 errors or more)	(True-positive) 14 (70%)	13	(False-positive) 8 (18%)
Good prognosis (15 errors or less)	(False-negative) 6 (30%)	26	(True-negative) 37 (82%)
Sample 2			
Poor prognosis (16 errors or more)	(True-positive) 7 (78%)	9	(False-positive) 9 (20%)
Good prognosis (15 errors or less)	(False-negative) 2 (22%)	5	(True-negative) 35 (80%)

they remain stable over time and are tied to children's performances in first grade. Hence, the present findings not only agree with the results we obtained in our previous work at the kindergarten level, they also extend this work by suggesting that form errors can provide a useful source of additional information to consider when deciding which prekindergarten children may require special academic assistance before school entry.[3]

References

Anastasi, A. (1982). *Psychological testing* (5th ed.). New York: Macmillan.

Connolly, A. J., Nachtman, W., & Pritchett, E. M. (1971). *Keymath Diagnostic Arithmetic Test.* Circle Pines, MN: American Guidance Service.

3. Some possible reasons for the relationship between form errors and school achievement are given in Simner, 1982, 1985, and 1986. Recommendations for assisting children who produce an excessive number of form errors also can be found in these sources.

Simner, M. L. (1982). Printing errors in kindergarten and the prediction of academic performance. *Journal of Learning Disabilities, 15,* 155–159.

Simner, M. L. (1985). *Printing Performance School Readiness Test.* Toronto, Ontario: University of Toronto, Guidance Centre, Faculty of Education. A revised version of the Printing Performance School Readiness Test is available from Phylmar Associates, 191 Iroquois Avenue, London, Ontario, Canada N6C 2K9.

Simner, M. L. (1986). Further evidence on the relationship between form errors in preschool printing and early school achievement. In H. S. R. Kao, G. Van Galen, & R. Hoosian (Eds.), *Graphonomics: Contemporary research in handwriting* (pp. 107–119). Amsterdam: North-Holland.

Simner, M. L. (1987). Predictive validity of the Teacher's School Readiness Inventory. *Canadian Journal of School Psychology, 3,* 21–32.

Woodcock, R. W. (1974). *Woodcock Reading Mastery Tests.* Circle Pines, MN: American Guidance Service.

CHAPTER 9

EXPERIMENTAL RESEARCH

Greg Evans is in a school psychology doctoral program at a university, and he spends one day a week in an elementary school for his psychology internship. Greg and a teacher at the school want to help one of the teacher's special education students, Manny, who is trying hard to improve his reading skills. However, Manny gets angry whenever he comes to a word that he doesn't know, and then begins acting aggressively toward the teacher or other students.

The teacher told Greg that when Manny is allowed to play a computer game for a few minutes, he seems to calm down and enjoy the game, and then will readily return to his reading. So Greg and the teacher set up an experiment. After establishing a baseline for Manny's aggressive behavior during class, they will introduce the opportunity for Manny to play a computer game for a few minutes following a specified period of reading instruction. If they can reduce Manny's aggressiveness, they think he will learn more, and also be less of a threat to the teacher or other students.

In this chapter you will learn how researchers carry out experiments with groups of research participants, or single-case experiments with individuals like Manny. You will learn about various procedures that researchers can use to demonstrate that the experimental treatment, rather than some uncontrolled variable, caused the desired change in the target behavior that is being studied. You will also learn how to determine whether the findings of an experimental research study can be applied to your local setting.

OBJECTIVES

After studying this chapter, you will be able to

1. explain three essential steps involved in conducting an experiment.
2. explain the difference between a true experiment, a quasi-experiment, and a single-case experiment.
3. explain how extraneous variables can threaten the internal validity of experiments.
4. describe three aspects of external validity that affect the extent to which the findings of experimental research can be applied to local settings.
5. describe two common experimental research designs.
6. describe two common quasi-experimental research designs.
7. describe three common designs used in single-case experiments.

KEY TERMS

A-B design
A-B-A-B design
attrition
baseline
cause-and-effect relationship
control group
dependent variable
differential selection
experiment
experimental group
experimental mortality

external validity
extraneous variable
history effect
independent variable
instrumentation effect
internal validity
inter-observer agreement
inter-rater reliability
maturation effect
posttest
pretest

quasi-experiment
random assignment
reversal
selection-maturation
  interaction
single-case experiment
statistical regression
target behavior
testing effect
treatment

THE NATURE OF EXPERIMENTAL RESEARCH

In doing experiments, researchers manipulate one variable (e.g., a teaching technique) to determine its effect on another variable (e.g., students' on-task behavior in class). If the experiment is well done, the researchers can conclude that the first variable caused or did not cause a change in the second variable. No other type of quantitative research (descriptive, correlational, or causal-comparative) is as powerful in demonstrating the existence of cause-and-effect relationships among variables as experimental research.

After research participants have been selected, an experiment typically involves three steps:

1. Research participants are randomly assigned to either the experimental or the control group. Random assignment means that each participant has an equal chance of being in either group. Thus, researchers can rule out previously existing group differences as the cause of observed differences in the outcome variable.

2. The experimental group is exposed to an intervention (also called the *treatment* or the *independent variable*), while the control group either is exposed to an alternate treatment or receives no treatment.

3. A comparison is made of the experimental and control groups' performance on the variable that the experiment is designed to affect. This variable is called the *dependent variable*, because it is presumed to be dependent on the treatment introduced by the researchers.

This chapter covers three related types of research that all are based on the experimental research model. The first type, a true experiment, involves all three of the essential characteristics of an experiment: random assignment, administration of a treatment to an experimental group and an alternative or no treatment to a control group, and comparison of the groups' performance on a post-treatment measure.

The second type of research, a quasi-experiment, approximates the treatment and post-treatment procedures of a true experiment, but it does not involve random assignment. As in other applied disciplines, in education it often is difficult to assign research participants randomly to different experimental conditions. As a result, quasi-experiments are probably more common than true experiments in educational research, but they present more problems in the interpretation of the research results.

The third type of research, single-case research, involves administration of a treatment to one individual, or to a small number of individuals who are treated one at a time, with each individual's behavior under nontreatment conditions serving as the control for comparison purposes.

Let us consider an example of a simple educational experiment. Suppose that a new program has been developed to reduce ethnic stereotyping among students in ethnically diverse first-grade classrooms. This program is the experimental treatment, so the independent variable is exposure or nonexposure to the treatment.

The first step in carrying out the experiment would be to select a sample of, let's say, 20 ethnically diverse first-grade classrooms and randomly assign 10 of them to receive the program on reducing ethnic stereotypes. Students in the other 10 classrooms would receive the control treatment, which could be either an alternative program dealing with ethnic stereotypes, or no program.

At the end of first grade, a measure of ethnic stereotyping would be administered to children in all 20 classrooms. This measure is the dependent variable, that is, the variable that the researchers expect will be affected by the experimental treatment. Statistical analyses would be done to determine whether students in the experimental classes showed a lower level of ethnic stereotyping on the measure than students in the control classes. Assume that, at the conclusion of the experiment, the ethnic stereotyping scores of the experimental students and those of the control students were different at a previously selected level of statistical significance. Then the researchers could generalize their findings. That is, they could conclude, with some certainty, that administering the same program to other students who are similar to those who participated in the experiment would have a positive effect on their stereotyping behavior.

Researchers have created many variations on this basic experimental design. For example, in some studies a pretest is administered before a program starts, and a posttest (the measure of the dependent variable) is administered at the end of the experimental program. The pretest data can be analyzed to check whether the experimental and control groups were similar at the outset of the experiment and to measure pretest-to-posttest gains. In some experiments, several treatments might be compared. For example, an experiment might be designed to compare the effectiveness of three different computer-generated test formats.

In some experiments, more than one independent variable is studied. For example, in the experiment described above, the researchers might include both the new program and gender as independent variables. By doing so, the researchers could determine the effect of gender on ethnic stereotyping and whether the new program is more effective for one gender than the other.

Analysis of experimental research data typically involves computing the mean scores of each group on the dependent variable and then comparing the mean scores to determine whether the differences obtained are statistically significant. See Table 7.3 for a summary of the inferential statistics commonly used in causal-comparative, experimental, and quasi-experimental research.

THE VALIDITY OF EXPERIMENTS

Some factors affect an experiment's internal validity, that is, the level of certainty that the experimental treatment has a causal influence on the dependent variable. Other factors affect an experiment's external validity, that is, the extent to which the experimental findings can be generalized beyond the research sample to other groups. Below we describe both types of validity and the factors that need to be controlled in order to maximize it. These factors have been studied primarily in relation to their effects on true experiments and quasi-experiments, both of which involve groups of research participants. We will refer back to validity when we examine the nature of single-case experiments, because they too are subject to certain threats to their validity.

Internal Validity

The observed effects in an experiment can be caused partly by the treatment variable and partly by extraneous variables. Extraneous variables are nontreatment factors that are present while the experiment is in progress. If extraneous variables are present, the researchers will be unable to determine the extent to which any observed difference between the experimental and control groups on the dependent variable are caused by the treatment or by one or more extraneous variables. The practical implication is that educators might implement the treatment in their local situation expecting to achieve the same positive effects that occurred in the experiment, but they might not achieve these effects because the effects resulted from extraneous variables, not from the treatment.

To demonstrate the importance of controlling for extraneous variables, we will consider a research problem that can be studied through a simple experimental design. Suppose that researchers are evaluating the effectiveness of a newly developed reading program for slow learners. At the beginning of the school year, they select 100 students for participation in the program. All the students meet the selection criterion of scoring at least two grades below the age norm on a standard test of reading achievement. After participation in the program for a school year, the students are once again given a reading achievement test.

Suppose that the researchers find a large, statistically significant gain in reading achievement, as determined by a *t* test. Can the researchers conclude that this achievement gain was caused by the experimental treatment, that is, the new reading program? The answer depends on how well various extraneous variables were controlled.

Donald Campbell and Julian Stanley (1963) identified eight types of extraneous variables that can affect the internal validity of experiments. We will explain how each of these threats to internal validity could affect the results of the experiment described above. Other extraneous variables have been identified, but these eight reflect common challenges to researchers in designing and conducting experiments.

1. *History*. The fact that experimental treatments extend over a period of time provides an opportunity for other events besides the experimental treatment to cause changes in the experimental group. The students in our example participated in the reading program for an entire school year. Therefore, other factors, such as the students' other instruction from teachers, could have accounted for all or part of their achievement gain in reading.

2. *Maturation*. While an experimental treatment is in progress, certain biological or psychological processes occur within the research participants. For example, participants become older, and they might experience increased fatigue, comfort, or some other emotional or physical change, all of which are forms of maturation as defined by Campbell and Stanley. During the year of the experimental reading program, students were developing physically, socially, and intellectually. Perhaps maturation in one of these areas, rather than the reading program itself, enabled students to overcome their reading deficiency.

3. *Testing*. In many educational experiments a pretest is administered, followed by the treatment, and concluding with a posttest. If the pretest and posttest are similar or are administered close together in time, research participants might show an improvement on the posttest simply as a result of their experience with the pretest. In other words, they have become "test-wise." It is unlikely that this extraneous variable was operating in the hypothetical experiment on a new reading program. Because of the long period of time between the pretest and posttest, students are not likely to have remembered enough about the pretest for it to have affected their posttest performance.

4. *Instrumentation*. An apparent learning gain might be observed from the pretest to the posttest due to changes in the nature of the measuring instrument. Suppose that the students in our example were administered a posttest of reading achievement that was easier than the pretest that they took. The gain in reading achievement then would be caused by differences in the testing instruments rather than by the experimental treatment.

5. *Statistical regression*. Whenever a pretest-posttest procedure is used to assess learning in an experiment, the individuals scoring high or low on the pretest will tend to have scores somewhat closer to the mean on the posttest. This phenomenon is known as statistical regression. For example, suppose that the students in the experimental group on average scored at the 15th percentile on a pretest of reading achievement. When this group of students is tested again on the same or a similar test, they are likely to earn a higher mean score, with or without any intervening experimental treatment. The reason is that their lower initial score likely results from not only lower ability but also chance factors (e.g., they were feeling ill on the day of the test, or they made unlucky guesses on some test items). Upon retesting, these chance factors are unlikely to be present again. Consequently, their test scores will improve independently of the effect of the experimental treatment. Similarly, due to chance factors, when students with very high scores on the pretest are retested, their scores also are likely to regress, that is, move towards the mean.

6. *Differential selection*. In some experiments, participants are selected for the experimental and control groups by a procedure other than random selection. (Such experiments, called *quasi-experiments*, are discussed later in the chapter.) Because the participants in the two groups are differentially selected, the effects of the treatment can be distorted. For example, suppose that the students receiving the experimental treatment (the new reading program) came from schools whose principals were instructional leaders and wanted to try the new program. The control group subsequently was formed by recruiting schools opportunistically until the desired sample size was achieved. Their principals might, or might not, be instructional leaders. If the experimental group of students subsequently showed greater achievement gains than the control group, the effect could be attributed to the principals' instructional leadership rather than to the experimental treatment itself. The best way to avoid the difficulties of interpretation caused by differential selection is to assign participants randomly to the two groups, a condition that is essential to a true experiment.

7. *Selection-maturation interaction*. This extraneous variable is similar to differential selection, except that maturation is the specific confounding variable. Suppose that, in our example, first-grade students from a single school district are selected to receive instruction in the new reading program, while the control group is drawn from the population of first-grade students in another school district. Because of different admissions policies in the two school districts, the mean age of students in the control group is six months higher than the mean age of students in the experimental group. Now, suppose that the experiment shows that the experimental group made significantly greater achievement gains than the control group. Do these results reflect the effectiveness of the experimental treatment, or the effects of maturation? Due to differential assignment of students to the experimental and control groups, the researchers would not be able to provide a clear answer to this question.

8. *Experimental mortality* (sometimes called *attrition*). Experimental mortality is the loss of research participants over the course of the experimental treatment. This extraneous variable can bias the results, because the participants who discontinue their participation usually differ in important ways from those who remain. For example, suppose that there was a systematic bias in the type of students who dropped out of the reading program during the school year: The students who left the school district happened to be the lowest-achieving students. If the researchers measured the achievement gains of only the students who completed the program, the effectiveness of the experimental treatment would be exaggerated.

External Validity

Experiments are externally valid to the degree to which their results can be generalized to other individuals, settings, and times. Glenn Bracht and Gene Glass (1968) described three aspects of external validity to consider when you wish to apply the findings of an experimental study to your particular conditions.

1. *Population validity.* You will recall from our discussion of sampling in Chapter 5 that population validity is the degree to which the results of a research study can be generalized from the specific sample that was studied to the population from which the sample was drawn. To determine population validity, one must assess the degree of similarity among the research sample that was used in the study, the accessible population from which the research sample was drawn, and the larger target population to which the research results are to be generalized. The more evidence the researcher provides to establish links among the sample, the accessible population, and the target population, the more confident you can be in generalizing the research findings to the target population.

In practice, however, educators who want to apply research findings to their own setting are interested not so much in the similarity between the research sample and the target population, but rather between the research sample and the individuals in their local setting. To determine this type of similarity, you should note all relevant information in the research report about the research sample, such as age, gender, academic aptitude, ethnicity, socioeconomic status, and the characteristics of the communities in which they live. You then should compare the resulting profile with information about individuals in the local setting to which you want to apply the research findings.

2. *Personological variables.* Another factor affecting external validity is the possibility that various personal characteristics of the research sample will interact with the experimental treatment. An interaction is present if the experimental results apply to research participants with certain characteristics (e.g., those who have high test anxiety) but not to those with other characteristics (e.g., those who have low test anxiety). For example, the Beginning Teacher

Evaluation Study sought to relate specific teaching strategies to the achievement of second- and fifth-grade pupils in mathematics and reading (Fisher et al., 1978). The researchers found that some teaching strategies were significantly related to academic achievement at both grade levels and in both subject areas, but the majority were not. For example, academic feedback was positively related to achievement at both grade levels and for both subject areas. However, academic monitoring was negatively correlated with second-graders' reading achievement, but was positively correlated with second-graders' mathematics achievement. At grade 5, correlations between academic monitoring and achievement in both subject areas were virtually zero.

These results demonstrate that even though a teaching strategy might have merit, it might vary greatly in its effectiveness at different grade levels, in different subject areas, or for students with different personal characteristics. In generalizing from the results of a specific experiment, you need to look carefully at any differences in the findings for different subcategories of research participants.

3. *Ecological validity*. Ecological validity depends on the extent to which the situational conditions that were present during the experiment are similar to the conditions that exist in the setting to which you wish to apply the results. As a rule, you can assume that the larger the difference between the experimental environment and the local environment, the less confidence you can have that the results will apply. Keep in mind, however, that not all experimental results are situation-specific. Thus, the results of an experiment on the effects of a classroom management program conducted with fifth-grade children in a small town in the South might generalize quite well to small towns, rural communities, and medium-sized cities in other regions. By contrast, suppose that all the classrooms in the study of classroom management included 20 or fewer students, and each teacher had a part-time aide to help with instruction. If your classroom has 28 students and there are no teacher aides, the generalizability of the experimental results is questionable.

Research Tradeoffs

Often the procedures that researchers use to improve an experiment's internal validity tend to reduce its external validity. The reason is that the procedures make the research environment considerably different from a typical educational setting. For example, the best method of ensuring internal validity is random assignment of research participants to different treatments. In practice, however, students seldom can be randomly assigned to classrooms, so if the experimental treatment is administered in classrooms, the internal validity of the experiment is immediately compromised. Yet the solution of randomly assigning students to experimental and control treatments and taking them to a laboratory-like setting for short periods of time is likely to decrease the experiment's external validity.

Researchers must continually weigh the advantages of more rigorous control of extraneous variables against the advantages of doing research in educational environments that are as natural as possible. They often must compromise in their attempts to provide acceptable levels of both internal and external validity.

EXPERIMENTAL DESIGNS

The following symbols commonly are used to describe both experimental designs (discussed below) and quasi-experimental designs (discussed in the next section):

R   (Represents random assignment of the research participants.)
X   (Represents the experimental treatment.)
O   (Represents observation of the dependent variable, by administering either a pretest or a posttest.)

Below, we describe two true experimental designs that often are used in educational research. We also discuss the threats to internal validity that each design presents.

Pretest-Posttest Control Group Design

The pretest-posttest control group design is written

$$R \quad O_1 \quad X \quad O_2$$
$$R \quad O_1 \qquad O_2$$

The top line represents the experimental group, and the second line represents the control group. The symbols have this meaning:

R   (Research participants are randomly assigned to the experimental or control group.)
O   (Both the experimental and the control group are given the pretest, O_1.)
X   (The experimental group is given the treatment, while the control group is given no treatment or receives an alternative treatment.)
O   (Both the experimental and the control group are given the posttest, O_2.)

This design is excellent for controlling the threats to internal validity that were described earlier in the chapter. For example, the effects of differential selection are minimized, because there is no systematic bias in the assignment of individuals to the experimental and control groups. Testing effects are controlled, because the experimental and control groups take the same tests. If the experimental group performs better on the posttest, this result cannot be attributed to pretesting, because both groups had the same pretesting experience.

The only extraneous variable that cannot be ruled out by this design is experimental mortality. Differences in the demands made on the research participants in the experimental and control groups can lead to differences in the number of participants who are lost from each group during the course of the experiment. Thus, posttreatment differences between the groups on the dependent variable could be due to differences in such characteristics as the motivation and ability of the remaining experimental group members compared to the control group members.

Posttest-Only Control Group Design

The posttest-only control group design is written

        R   X   O
        R   O

which means:

     R   (Research participants are randomly assigned to the experimental or control group.)
     X   (The experimental group is given the experimental treatment.)
     O   (Both the experimental group and the control group are given a posttest that measures the dependent variable.)

This design is useful in studies in which the administration of a pretest could influence the research participants' behavior either during the experiment or on the posttest. For example, suppose that the pretest is a measure of students' attitudes toward students who are developmentally disabled. After completing the pretest, the research participants view a film about developmental disabilities. It is possible that the pretest would dispose the participants to respond to the film differently from the way that they would respond if they had not taken the pretest. If so, any differential change between the experimental and control groups can be attributed to both the film and the pretest. By using the posttest-only control group design, the researchers can determine the effect of the film by itself.

QUASI-EXPERIMENTAL DESIGNS

Quasi-experiments are similar to true experiments, except that research participants are not randomly assigned to the treatment and control conditions. Researchers do not intentionally avoid random assignment, but often they are unable to assign research participants randomly because of circumstances beyond their control.

The experimental study by William Lan that is described in the first reprinted article in this chapter is a quasi-experiment. Lan wished to determine whether teaching students to carry out a self-monitoring procedure during a statistics class would improve their course grades and other learning outcomes. Specifically, he compared the post-course performance of students taught self-monitoring (the experimental treatment) with students who carried out instructor-monitoring during the course (an unrelated alternate treatment) and students who received no treatment (the control group). As Lan explains in the article, he felt it necessary to design his experiment without random assignment in order to avoid a perception of unfairness toward students in the treatment conditions compared to those in the control condition. Therefore he randomly assigned students to the experimental treatment or alternate treatment in some classes, but used a different class of students as the control group.

Many experiments carried out in the public schools do not permit random assignment of research participants. School administrators generally will not allow students to be randomly assigned to classrooms, even though that is the best way to ensure that students receiving the treatment are not systematically different from those not receiving the treatment. When this happens, researchers usually must consider each class as an intact group. For example, two classes could be randomly assigned, so that students in one class comprise the treatment group, while the students in the other class comprise the control group. This procedure still does not qualify as random assignment, because each student does not have an equal chance of being in either group.

Researchers sometimes select students in one school as the treatment group and students in another school as the control group. School administrators often prefer this arrangement, because the control group is unlikely to know what the treatment group is doing. As a result, teachers and parents are unlikely to question why the students in the control group are not getting the presumed benefits of the experimental treatment. Again, the drawback of this arrangement is that students are not randomly assigned to the treatment or control group. Thus, there is a risk that the two groups may differ on some important variable at the outset of the experiment.

Below we discuss two common designs used in quasi-experimental research.

Pretest-Posttest Design with Nonequivalent Groups

The pretest-posttest design with nonequivalent groups is probably the most widely used quasi-experimental design in educational research. It is represented by the following diagram:

$$O_1 \quad X \quad O_2$$

$$O_1 \qquad O_2$$

The symbols mean:

O_1 (Both the experimental group and the control group are given a pretest.)

X   (The experimental group is given the experimental treatment.)

---   (The broken line indicates that the experimental and control groups were not formed randomly.)

O_2 (Both the experimental group and the control group are given a posttest that measures the dependent variable.)

The pretest scores in this experimental design can be used to determine whether the two groups were initially equivalent on the pretest variable, even though the groups were not formed by random assignment. However, we have no evidence that the groups are initially comparable on other unmeasured variables that could influence the results of the study. For example, some systematic bias of which we are unaware might cause more research participants who score high on variable X to be placed in one group, whereas more participants with low scores on variable X would be placed in the other group.

If researchers must use a quasi-experimental design, they should attempt to draw their experimental and control groups from very similar classrooms, schools, or other situations. Also, they should report as much descriptive data as possible about the experimental and control groups, such as the location and socioeconomic level of the participating schools, teachers' experience level, and mean achievement scores of students in the different classrooms or schools. This kind of information helps clarify the degree of similarity between the experimental and control groups. If the treatment and control groups are demonstrated to be similar, results of a pretest-posttest design with nonequivalent groups can be given nearly as much weight as the results of a true experimental design.

Posttest-Only Design with Nonequivalent Groups

The posttest-only design with nonequivalent groups is similar to the posttest-only control group design that we described earlier, except for the assignment procedure. Assignment of participants to experimental and control groups is random in the former design, but not in this design. The posttest-only design with nonequivalent groups is written:

X O

O

where:

    X   (The experimental group is given the experimental treatment.)

    −− (The broken line indicates that the experimental and control groups were not formed randomly.)

    O   (Both groups are given a posttest that measures the dependent variable.)

The main threat to internal validity in this design is differential selection. That is, posttest differences between the experimental and control groups can be attributed to characteristics of the groups as well as to the experimental treatment. For example, suppose that the teachers in one school receive an experimental treatment and then are given a posttest, while the teachers in another school simply are given the posttest. If differences on the posttest are found, it can be argued that they are due to initial differences between the teachers in the two schools rather than to the effect of the experimental treatment. Because no pretest was given, it is not possible to determine whether the two groups were similar or different prior to the experimental treatment. For this and other reasons, it is difficult to make strong cause-and-effect inferences from the results of a posttest-only experiment with nonequivalent groups.

SINGLE-CASE DESIGNS

Single-case designs are favored over true experimental designs or quasi-experimental designs when researchers want to make a quantitative study of the effects of interventions on specific behaviors of individuals. Using a single-case design, for example, researchers can diagnose a dyslexic student's reading problem, devise an individualized strategy to solve it, and rigorously test the effectiveness of the strategy through repeated phases of data collection.

While both single-case experiments and qualitative case studies (see Chapter 10) focus on one case, they differ greatly in design and purpose. Single-case designs use procedures to achieve tight control over, and precise description of, the experimental situation: frequent observations of the behaviors targeted for change, description of the treatment in sufficient detail to permit replication, tests of the reliability of observations of the individual's behavior, and replication of treatment effects within the experiment. In contrast, case studies explore much broader phenomena, focus on perceived reality as well as on behavior, usually are carried out in a field setting, and rely heavily on qualitative data.

Because single-case designs involve the treatment and study of individuals one at a time, it is not necessary to form groups of individuals who have the same characteristic before researchers can conduct an experiment. In fact, no matter how unique the individual's concern, a single-case design will permit investigation of the research problem. Also, single-case designs allow teachers, counselors, or others to function simultaneously as both treatment providers and researchers. By contrast, these functions often are handled by different people when a group experiment is conducted.

Some researchers perceive the single-case experiment as a watered-down version of one of the group designs presented earlier in this chapter. However, single-case designs are rigorous and time-consuming, and often they involve as much data collection as a design involving experimental and control groups. Furthermore, researchers who conduct single-case experiments are just as concerned with the issues of internal and external validity as researchers who conduct group experiments.

Single-case designs often lack external validity, that is, the ability to generalize the findings to other individuals in the population of interest. This is because the research participants are not randomly selected, and the experiment involves only one or a few individuals. Replication thus is the best way to increase the external validity of single-case experiments. Replication involves repeating the experiment with other individuals, perhaps with variations in the investigators, the settings, and the measures.

The following symbols are used in describing single-case designs:

> A = baseline, meaning that an individual's behavior is observed under normal conditions.
> B = treatment, meaning that an individual's behavior is observed under treatment conditions.

We describe three common single-case research designs in the following sections.

A-B-A-B Design

The A-B-A-B single-case experiment includes two or more baseline periods (condition A) and two or more treatment periods (condition B). During the baseline period, the individual's behavior is observed under normal conditions. The A-B-A-B design was used by Glen Dunlap and his colleagues in the single-case study that is reported in their article at the end of this chapter.

Figure 9.1 is a reproduction of Figure 2 in the article by Dunlap and his colleagues. Its five columns, divided by dashed vertical lines, show clearly how the level of on-task and problem behavior changed for the research participant Jill during each phase of the experiment.

The first condition A, or baseline, is shown in the first column in Figure 9.1 (labeled *Standard Outcome*). During these five data points, Jill shows a slight decline in on-task behavior and a slight increase in problem behavior. The first condition B, or treatment, is shown in the second column in Figure 9.1 (labeled *Functional Outcome*). During these eight data points, Jill's on-task behavior shows some variation but tends to be even more consistent, while her problem behavior declines to almost zero.

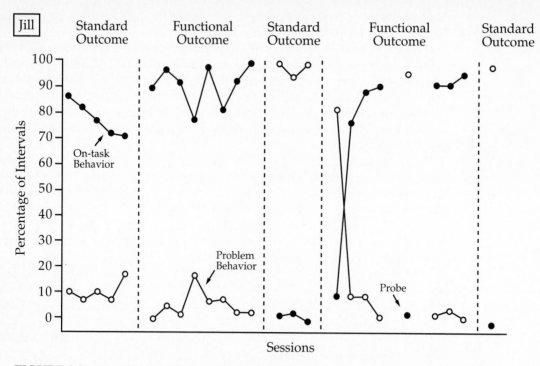

FIGURE 9.1   Results for Jill showing the effects of the standard versus functional-outcome assignments on on-task and problem behavior: an example of the A-B-A-B single-case design

Source. Figure 2 on p. 254 in: Dunlap, G., Foster-Johnson, L., Clarke, S., Kern, L., & Childs, K. E. (1995). Modifying activities to produce functional outcomes: Effects on the problem behaviors of students with disabilities. *Journal of the Association for Persons with Severe Handicaps, 20*, 248–258. Reprinted with permission of the Association for Persons with Severe Handicaps.

The second condition A, which involves treatment reversal, is shown in the third column of Figure 9.1 (labeled *Standard Outcome*). During this time period the treatment was withdrawn, meaning that Jill was asked to return to performing the original, minimally relevant task. The change in Jill's behavior is dramatic, with all three data points showing a very high level of problem behavior and a near-zero level of on-task behavior.

The second condition B, or treatment, is shown in the fourth column of Figure 9.1 (labeled *Functional Outcome*). During this time period the treatment was reinstated, meaning that Jill again was asked to perform the modified, functional-outcome task. After the first data point, Jill's on-task behavior increases to a high level while her problem behavior drops to a low level. During this second condition B, however, one data point (labeled *Probe*) represents a return to condition A, the standard-outcome task. For this data point Jill's problem behavior soars to nearly 100 percent, while her on-task behavior drops to near zero. When condition B is resumed, shown in the last three data points of the fourth column,

Jill's on-task behavior returns to near 100 percent and her problem behavior returns to near zero.

As a final check, condition A is again reinstated for one data point, shown in the fifth column of Figure 9.1 (labeled *Standard Outcome*). Once again Jill's problem behavior reaches near 100 percent and her on-task behavior drops to zero.

Figure 9.1 shows a clear pattern of high levels of problem behavior and low levels of on-task behavior during the baseline conditions, and high levels of on-task behavior and low levels of problem behavior during the treatment conditions. This pattern occurs irrespective of whether each condition is one, three, four, five, or eight data points in length. This graph is typical of the type used by researchers to report the results of single-case experiments using the A-B-A-B design.

By returning to conditions A and B in turn, this design enables researchers to demonstrate that the individual's behavior is not changing by chance, but varies consistently with the presence or absence of the treatment. The graphic display of the descriptive data obtained in such studies usually is sufficiently clear that no test of statistical significance is needed. Looking at the graph, the researchers would be justified in concluding that instituting the experimental intervention is effective in promoting on-task behavior and reducing problem behavior.

Because research results based on a single individual cannot be generalized to other individuals with confidence, single-case research is weak in external validity. The solution to this weakness is replication, that is, repeating the study with other individuals. This approach was used in the study by Dunlap and his colleagues. The researchers applied a variation of the same treatment (modification of a standard outcome to a functional outcome), to three individuals who differed in age and in the nature of their learning-associated disabilities. All three students showed increased on-task behavior and decreased problem behavior during the treatment phases.

Caution is needed in using the A-B-A-B design, because not all behaviors can be readily reversed (that is, returned to condition A after condition B) during a research study. For example, a teacher's goals for an individual student might include learning various social skills such as cafeteria manners, or academic skills such as taking multiple-choice tests. Learning such skills is similar to learning to ride a bicycle: although individuals may get rusty without practice, once they learn how, they never completely forget. Because these skills are not completely reversible, it is necessary to use a design other than the A-B-A-B design. Two such designs are described in the next sections.

Single-Case Design Involving Multiple Baselines across Behaviors

In this single-case design, baseline measurements are taken on two or more behaviors exhibited by the same individual. After baselines are stable, a treatment condition is applied to one of the behaviors. The treatment is continued until a noticeable change occurs in that behavior. Then the treatment condition is applied to the second behavior until a change is observed.

An important requirement for using the across-behaviors design is the discreteness of the behaviors to be observed. If the occurrence of one behavior is relatively dependent on the occurrence of the other, treatment of one behavior may cause a change in both. If so, explanations other than the treatment could account for the change.

To understand this design further, suppose that you want to train a teacher in using three behaviors designed to provide reinforcement for correct student responses during a question-and-answer lesson. The three behaviors to be learned are as follows:

1. The teacher smiles at the student who gives a correct response.
2. The teacher gives the responding student a token that can be exchanged for free time.
3. The teacher praises the responding student.

Here are the steps a researcher would take in conducting this study:

1. The researcher would first collect baseline data on the number of times that the teacher exhibited each behavior during five half-hour lessons (i.e., one a day for one week) and record the results, as in Figure 9.2.

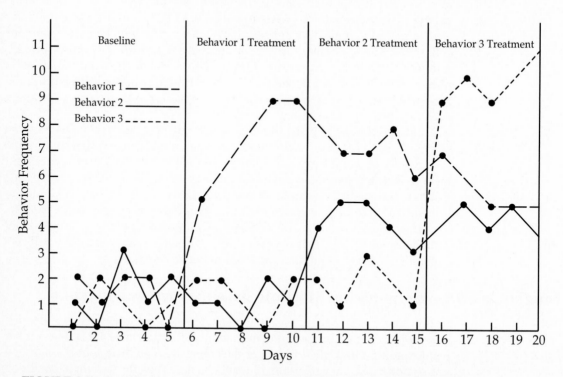

FIGURE 9.2 **Results of a single-case experiment involving multiple baselines across behaviors**

2. The researcher then would train the teacher to use behavior 1.
3. Over the subsequent five days the researcher would record the number of times the teacher used each of the three reinforcement behaviors during half-hour lessons. If the training has been effective, the teacher will increase use of behavior 1 but will not change noticeably on behaviors 2 or 3 (see Figure 9.2).
4. The researcher then would train the teacher to use behavior 2.
5. Again the researcher would record the teacher's use of all three behaviors during five half-hour lessons and record the results, as in Figure 9.2. At this point, behaviors 1 and 2 should be higher than baseline, but behavior 3 should stay about the same.
6. The researcher then would train the teacher to use behavior 3.
7. The researcher again would record the teacher's use of all three behaviors during five half-hour lessons. If the training has been effective, all three behaviors should occur more frequently than was the case during the baseline condition.

Inspection of Figure 9.2 indicates that the training in all three behaviors was effective. However, notice that behavior 1 gradually decreases near the end of the study. This decrease might indicate that the researcher's training program for this behavior is weak and needs to be strengthened, or follow-up instruction may be needed to achieve more permanent results. Notice also that the frequency of behavior 2 never reaches the levels of behaviors 1 and 3. This result could lead to one of several possible interpretations: (a) the teacher needs more training in behavior 2; (b) teachers give tokens less frequently as a reinforcement strategy than smiles or praise, perhaps because giving tokens takes more class time; (c) teachers sense that students respond better to smiles and praise than to tokens.

Of course, other explanations of the observed results are possible. In many cases, the researcher will conduct additional research to test alternate hypotheses. As alternate hypotheses are supported or rejected in subsequent studies, the researcher learns more about the phenomenon being studied.

Single-Case Design Involving Multiple Baselines across Individuals

In this single-case design, two (or more) individuals are selected for whom the behavioral goal of treatment is the same. After the baseline rates of behavior have become stable for both individuals, a treatment condition is applied with one individual. If a change is noted in the behavior of the individual to whom treatment was applied but the behavior of the other individual remains constant, the researchers can conclude that their treatment had an effect. The treatment then is applied to the second individual to see if that individual's behavior now changes. If change does occur, this result represents a replication of the treatment's effect on that behavior.

The across-individuals design is invalidated if the intervention for one individual influences the behavior of the other individual who still is in the baseline condition. This problem can occur, for example, when an intervention is provided to several children in the same classroom, to members of the same family, or to employees in the same work location.

Selecting the Appropriate Single-Case Design

Just as you learned in our discussion of group experiments and quasi-experiments, the choice of a single-case design depends largely on the researchers' efforts to balance the internal and external validity of the experimental findings.

The A-B-A-B design presents fewer threats to the internal validity of a single-case experiment than the two multiple-baseline designs we discussed. It is a more powerful design, because the reversal phase (the second A condition) demonstrates active control of the individual's target behavior by removing the treatment that is hypothesized to have caused the initial change (the initial B condition). Reinstatement of the treatment (the second B condition) provides additional evidence of the effect of the treatment.

Despite the power of the A-B-A-B design, it cannot be used in all situations. For example, in many counseling situations it is not appropriate to attempt to bring a client back to baseline. For example, if a client's anxiety level has been reduced during the course of treatment, a counselor could not ethically withdraw the successful treatment in order to observe whether the client's anxiety level returned to its pre-treatment level. Multiple-baseline designs give educators the advantage of studying the effects of a treatment without having to withhold it from a distressed client, and of allowing the study of treatment-induced behaviors that are not reversible or that have a high resistance to extinction. By using experimental procedures that better reflect real-life treatment conditions designed to modify individuals' behavior, these designs seek to improve the external validity of their research findings.

CONCLUDING THOUGHT

This chapter has described experimental research designs, which represent the type of quantitative research that is best suited to establishing a cause-and-effect relationship between a treatment variable and an outcome variable. You have learned that various experimental designs are used in educational research, each with its own strengths and weaknesses. Although the findings of a single experiment rarely are conclusive, a well-done experiment can provide strong evidence that a particular educational program or method does, or does not, improve learning or other valued educational outcomes. Additional experiments can then be conducted to rule out any threats to the internal validity of the original experiment, and to determine whether the findings are generalizable to other settings.

SELF-CHECK TEST

1. Experiments typically involve all the following steps except for
   a. random assignment of research participants to an experimental or control group.
   b. administration of an intervention to an experimental group.
   c. administration of an intervention to a control group.
   d. comparison of the experimental and control group's performance on the dependent variable.

2. Unlike a quasi-experiment, only a true experiment
   a. involves comparison of a control group with an experimental group.
   b. involves random assignment of research participants to the experimental and control groups.
   c. involves administration of a treatment to some of the research participants.
   d. can produce findings with a high degree of external validity.

3. Unlike single-case experiments, true experiments and quasi-experiments
   a. can establish cause-and-effect relationships.
   b. involve the study of groups rather than individuals.
   c. need to control for possible threats to internal validity.
   d. involve the administration of a treatment designed to affect research participants' behavior.

4. Students with the highest pretest scores in the class tended to have more moderate posttest scores. This phenomenon demonstrates the effect of
   a. experimental mortality.
   b. testing.
   c. maturation.
   d. statistical regression.

5. To determine the generalizability of experimental findings to his local setting, an educator should look mainly for evidence of similarity between
   a. the research sample and the target population.
   b. the accessible population and the target population.
   c. the target population and the individuals in the local setting.
   d. the research sample and the individuals in the local setting.

6.
$$R \; O_1 \; X \; O_2 \qquad R \; X \; O$$
$$R \; O_1 \qquad O_2 \qquad R \qquad O$$

   The symbols above represent two different research designs that are commonly used in true experiments. The main difference between the design on the left and the design on the right is in whether
   a. a control group is included in the experiment.
   b. research participants are randomly assigned to the experimental and control groups.
   c. a pretest is given to the experimental and control groups.
   d. a treatment is administered to the experimental group and withheld from the control group.

7. Probably the most widely used quasi-experimental design in educational research is the
   a. posttest-only design with nonequivalent groups.
   b. pretest-posttest design with nonequivalent groups.
   c. pretest-only design.
   d. pretest-posttest control group design.

8. Probably the best way to increase the generalizability of the findings of a single-case experiment is to
   a. replicate the experiment with other individuals.
   b. add more baseline and treatment conditions.
   c. end the experiment with reinstatement of the pretreatment conditions.
   d. have the research conducted by someone other than the treatment provider.

CHAPTER REFERENCES

Bracht, G. H., & Glass, G. V (1968). The external validity of experiments. *American Educational Research Journal, 5,* 437–474.

Campbell, D. T., & Stanley, J. C. (1963). Experimental and quasi-experimental designs for research on teaching. In N. L. Gage (Ed.), *Handbook of research on teaching* (pp. 171–246). Chicago: Rand McNally.

Fisher, C. W., et al. (1978). Teaching and learning in the elementary school: A summary of the beginning teacher evaluation study. San Francisco: Far West Laboratory for Educational Research and Development. (ERIC Document Reference No. ED 165 322.)

RECOMMENDED READING

Campbell, D. T., & Stanley, J. C. (1966). *Experimental and quasi-experimental designs for research.* Boston: Houghton Mifflin.

This monograph, now more than thirty years old, still provides useful guidelines for understanding experimental research methods. Many research designs are described and analyzed in terms of their internal and external validity.

Gall, M. D., Borg, W. R., & Gall, J. P. (1996). *Educational research: An introduction* (6th ed.). White Plains, NY: Longman.

Chapters 12 and 13 provide comprehensive coverage of experimental, quasi-experimental, and single-case designs used in educational research.

Kratochwill, T. R., & Levin, J. R. (Eds.). (1992). *Single-case research design and analysis.* Hillsdale, NJ: Lawrence Erlbaum Associates.

Provides an overview of the most promising designs and methods of data analysis that have emerged in single-case research. Among the topics covered are typical errors of application and the use of meta-analysis in interpreting single-case research findings.

Linn, R. L. (1986). Quantitative methods in research on teaching. In M. C. Wittrock (Ed.), *Handbook of research on teaching* (3rd ed., pp. 92–118). New York: Macmillan.

The chapter cited discusses important topics concerning random and nonrandom assignment of research participants in experimental research. Includes a discussion of the strengths and weaknesses of different procedures for measuring change in research participants' behavior following an experimental treatment.

Shaver, J. P. (1983). The verification of independent variables in experimental procedure. *Educational Researcher, 12*(8), 3–9.

This article identifies weaknesses in the conventional research procedures that are used to assess treatment fidelity, that is, whether an experimental treatment was implemented in accordance with the researchers' specifications.

SAMPLE QUASI-EXPERIMENTAL RESEARCH STUDY: THE EFFECTS OF SELF-MONITORING ON STUDENTS' COURSE PERFORMANCE, USE OF LEARNING STRATEGIES, ATTITUDE, SELF-JUDGMENT ABILITY, AND KNOWLEDGE REPRESENTATION

Lan, W. Y. (1996). The Effects of Self-Monitoring on Students' Course Performance, Use of Learning Strategies, Attitude, Self-Judgment Ability, and Knowledge Representation. *The Journal of Experimental Education, 64*, 101–115.

In this section of the chapter you will read a research article that illustrates a quasi-experimental research study. It is preceded by comments written especially for this book by the author of the article. Then the article itself is reprinted in full, just as it appeared when originally published. Where appropriate, we have added footnotes to help you understand the information contained in the article.

Researcher's Comments, Prepared by William Lan

I am glad to have this opportunity to share my experience in conducting this research study, because authors are not usually able to do that in research articles.

As most researchers will tell you, a research project starts with the researcher's interests. My interest in self-monitoring began with my experiences as an instructor of an introductory statistics course for graduate students in education. As I mentioned in the article, many graduate students consider statistics to be the most difficult part of their program, and some of them wait until the last minute to take the statistics course.

After teaching the course for several semesters, I noticed a pattern in students' learning. Most students did pretty well on the material in the first several chapters of the textbook, which cover topics like frequency distribution, central tendency, dispersion, and normal distribution. However, strange things happened starting with the chapters on regression and correlation.

As the class moved into these chapters, which cover gradually more difficult course content, it seemed as if many students began to lose track of what they were doing in class. For example, in the chapter on regression, students need to conduct cumbersome calculations to find the intercept and slope for a regression equation. As they carried out these calculations, some of the students lost the purpose of the calculation. The textbook author, and I as the instructor, both emphasized that the final product of a regression analysis is a regression equation that can be used to predict one variable from another variable. Nonetheless, many of the students would stop after finding only one of the two parameters of the equation, assuming that they had finished the regression problem.

Some students found values for both the intercept and the slope, as required, but then failed to put them into an equation or could not grasp how to solve a sequential problem involving prediction. In the chapter on correlation, some students who clearly had learned the fact that the range of possible correlation coefficients could vary between −1 and +1 still handed in assignments with unreasonable correlation coefficients, such as 32.06.

Some of the students said that they felt more confident in learning inferential statistics than descriptive statistics, because the former are based on logical thinking whereas the latter require tedious calculations. However, their performance on tests covering inferential statistics was worse than that on tests covering descriptive statistics.

During the period of time that I was teaching this course, I was also reading the literature on self-regulated learning. I wondered if I could use self-monitoring, an important self-regulated learning strategy, to help my students overcome the problems I had observed in my statistics classes. After reviewing various operational definitions of self-monitoring that other researchers had utilized to manipulate this variable, I developed the self-monitoring protocols used in my original study (Lan et al., 1993) and in the replication, which is the study reprinted in this book.

One lesson I learned from conducting the research is the importance of conducting a pilot study prior to the real one. A pilot study will help a researcher discover problems in the research design, research materials, research procedure, and data collection procedure. During the first semester that I introduced the self-monitoring protocols into my statistics class, I found that most students did not use the protocols as soon or as regularly as I had expected. Some of them did not use the protocols that they received at the beginning of the semester until right before the end of the semester, when I collected them. Then they filled out the protocols with any number they could think of, just before handing them in. The pilot study made me realize that I could not engage my students in self-monitoring merely by providing a protocol. I needed to do more than that in order to strengthen my manipulation of the independent variable.

Results from the pilot study indicated that I should prepare two copies of the protocol for each student, have students exchange copies, and then check students' protocol responses almost daily to ensure that the different treatments were successfully being delivered to the different conditions. Without the pilot study, my manipulation of self-monitoring would have been in vain. I doubt that I would have found any effect of self-monitoring on students' learning in class.

I wish that I could have done a true experimental study in which students were randomly assigned to the three experimental conditions (treatment, alternative treatment, and control conditions) during the same semester. For reasons discussed in the article, I instead taught the treatment and alternative conditions first, and then assigned all the students who took the course during the last semester of the school year to the control condition. This procedural limitation was the focus of a critique I received from one of the journal reviewers. However, considering the problems I faced in conducting the study in a real-life instructional situation, I believe that I had to make the compromises that I did.

Say that I had tried to conduct a true experiment. I still do not see how I could have had some students in the control condition, earning bonus points for doing nothing, without making the students in the two other two conditions feel that they were being treated unfairly. I tried to think of ways to circumvent this potential problem— for example, randomly assigning students into the three conditions simultaneously and having students in the control condition do tasks that were remotely related to statistics. But then I would have had to show that the tasks were remote enough that they had no effect on students' learning of statistics. Otherwise I would have just created another alternative treatment condition. I was also afraid that, if I added extra tasks to the control condition, it would no longer be a true control condition, because it would be different from my regular statistics class. If any of you future educational researchers can help me figure out a solution to this problem, please let me know. I would greatly appreciate your input, because I could use your suggestions in another study that I am currently planning.

When both my original study and the replication showed that self-monitoring enhances students' learning in a statistics course, the next question for me was how to apply these research findings in my subsequent teaching of the statistics class. A possible application strategy would be to give the self-monitoring protocol to every student who takes the class. I chose not to do so, because I felt that the protocol was not yet sufficiently "user-friendly." During both research studies, I heard many positive comments from students on how helpful the self-monitoring protocol was to their learning, and I reported those comments in both research articles. However, that was not the whole story. There were also some negative comments about the protocol, which I did not report. For example, some students complained that the protocol contained too many details and that it distracted them from learning. From a cognitive perspective, I think that the students' complaints deserve consideration. A detailed protocol for self-monitoring makes a heavy demand on students' information-processing capacity, and thus leaves less capacity available for learning statistical concepts and procedures.

One solution that I tried was to modify the self-monitoring protocol by including a sheet in the course syllabus for every student, titled, "*Have you spent enough time studying for the statistics class?*" The sheet listed 75 basic statistics concepts that were used in the two self-monitoring protocols. Beside each concept, instead of a row of boxes in which students could record the duration or frequency with which they engaged in each learning activity, I listed the estimated amount of time that an average student would need to spend to learn the concept. The time estimates were based on data that I collected from students who had used the self-monitoring protocols in the two research studies that I had conducted. I told the students that this sheet was designed to give them an idea of how much time they should spend studying for the course. I also included a column for rating self-efficacy with regard to each concept in the protocol, in order to enhance students' self-evaluation of their understanding of the course content. This sheet appears to be more user-friendly than the protocol, because I have heard only positive feedback on it from my students.

I hope that my article and the experiences that I have shared here will help readers to become better educational researchers themselves. More importantly, I appreciate being able to share my enthusiasm for educational research with you. Let me end by paraphrasing a slogan I have seen on television: "Research is a journey; enjoy the ride."

Reference

Lan, W. Y., Bradley, L., & Parr, G. (1993). The effects of a self-monitoring process on college students' learning in an introductory statistics course. *The Journal of Experimental Education*, 62, 26–40.

THE EFFECTS OF SELF-MONITORING ON STUDENTS' COURSE PERFORMANCE, USE OF LEARNING STRATEGIES, ATTITUDE, SELF-JUDGMENT ABILITY, AND KNOWLEDGE REPRESENTATION

William Y. Lan
Texas Tech University

Abstract

Self-monitoring, defined as deliberate attention to some aspect of one's behavior, is considered to be an important self-regulatory process in learning. In the present experiment, 72 graduate students in a statistics class were assigned to a self-monitoring group, an instructor-monitoring group, or a control group to investigate the effects of self-monitoring on students' learning strategies, motivation, knowledge representation, self-judgment ability, and course performance. During the course, the self-monitoring group recorded the frequency and intensity of their various learning activities, the instructor-monitoring group evaluated the instructor's teaching, and the control group took the course without any treatment. The self-monitoring group performed better than the other two groups on course tests, used more self-regulated learning strategies, and developed better knowledge representation of the course content. Psychological processes are suggested through which self-monitoring increases students' learning and provides a prototype of a self-monitoring protocol that has potential for improving students' course performance.

Lan, W. Y. (1996). The effects of self-monitoring on students' course performance, use of learning strategies, attitude, self-judgment ability, and knowledge representation. *The Journal of Experimental Education, 64,* 101–115. Reprinted with permission of the Helen Dwight Reid Educational Foundation. Published by Heldref Publications, 1319 Eighteenth Street, NW, Washington, DC 20036-1802. Copyright © 1996.

Recent research has drawn attention to the importance of self-regulation in the learning process. As defined by Schunk and Zimmerman, self-regulation is "students' self-generated thoughts, feelings, and actions, which are systematically oriented toward attainment of their goals" (1994, p. ix). Researchers have demonstrated that self-regulation influences whether students succeed or fail in school. For example, self-regulation has been found to play a major role in the school success of minority students (Wibrowski, 1992) and poor immigrant children from Southeast Asia (Caplan, Choy, & Whitmore, 1992). Conversely, lack of self-regulation has been found to be associated with student underachievement (Borkowski & Thorpe, 1994; Krouse & Krouse, 1981). Some researchers (e.g., Zimmerman, 1994) believe that improving students' self-regulated learning processes holds considerable promise as a remedy for the increasing national concern about the low achievement of many American students.

Two distinctive approaches can be followed in examining the relationship between self-regulation and learning. One approach is correlational: Researchers identify students who naturally engage or do not engage in self-regulation and compare them on various factors related to learning processes and academic achievement. The other approach is experimental: Researchers manipulate the variable of self-regulation and then examine the effects of the manipulation on student learning processes and academic achievement.

The positive effects of self-regulation are well documented in correlational research. For example, researchers have found that self-regulation is positively related to students' academic achievement and challenge-seeking behaviors in learning activities (Zimmerman & Martinez-Pons, 1986), intrinsic motivation (Pintrich & De Groot, 1990; Zimmerman & Martinez-Pons, 1988), self-efficacy (Schunk, 1986; Zimmerman & Martinez-Pons, 1990), and self-awareness (Zimmerman & Martinez-Pons, 1988).

Whereas the correlational approach is helpful in identifying variables related to self-regulation, the experimental approach is necessary to identify causal relationships between self-regulation and learning variables. By manipulating students' self-regulation processes as independent variables and examining learning processes and outcome as dependent variables, we can determine how these processes affect student learning.[a]

Self-monitoring, defined as "deliberate attention to some aspect of one's behavior" (Schunk, 1991, p. 267), has been found to be a key process in self-regulated learning (Corno, 1986; Corno & Mandinach, 1983; Mace & Kratochwill, 1988; Nelson, 1977; Shapiro, 1984). Researchers have hypothesized that self-regulated learning is possible only when

individuals self-monitor their learning activities. In a review of research on self-monitoring, Pressley and Ghatala (1990) depicted the self-monitoring process as one in which the learner evaluates the effectiveness of a particular cognitive strategy by using such criteria as (a) how the strategy helps them make progress toward a goal and (b) how much expenditure of time and effort the strategy requires. Applying these two criteria enables the learner to determine whether the strategy should be continued or abandoned in favor of another strategy. Self-monitoring, therefore, is "an executive process, activating and deactivating other processes, as a function of on-line evaluation of thought processes and products as they occur" (Pressley & Ghatala, 1990, p. 19). Because self-monitoring is the initial and sometimes the sole process of self-regulation in a learning situation, I selected it as the independent variable in the present study.

Researchers have manipulated self-monitoring in different ways. In studies involving students with learning disabilities, self-monitoring was manipulated by having students monitor the number of errors in their performance (McCurdy & Shapiro, 1992) and dysfunctional behavior (e.g., DiGangi, Maag, & Rutherford, 1991; Lloyd, Bateman, Landrum, & Hallahan, 1989; Maag, Rutherford, & DiGangi, 1992). The authors found improvements in students' academic performance and classroom behavior. In a study involving fifth- and sixth-grade students, Delclos and Harrington (1991) manipulated self-monitoring by asking students to monitor their problem-solving strategies in a computer-based logic task. Students in the self-monitoring condition were able to solve more complex problems in less time than were those who did not monitor their problem-solving strategies.

Self-monitoring in these studies typically was operationalized as a one-shot intervention, and only

a. Independent variables and dependent variables represent the presumed cause and effect, respectively, in an experiment. Here students' self-regulation processes are the independent variables, because each is hypothesized to improve students' learning. Students' learning processes and outcomes are the dependent variables, because they are hypothesized to be affected by the experimental manipulation of the independent variables.

one aspect of learning was investigated.[b] In contrast, self-monitoring in the present study was manipulated for an entire semester and various learning variables were measured for that period of time. The learning variables generally corresponded to those used in previous research on self-monitoring: students' performance on class examinations, use of learning strategies, mastery-seeking behavior, intrinsic motivation, perceived control over the learning environment, knowledge representation, and self-judgment ability.

Following the recommendations of Mace and Kratochwill (1988), I manipulated self-monitoring by asking students to record the frequency and intensity of their learning activities. Specifically, students in a statistics course monitored their own learning activities with a self-monitoring protocol. In an alternative treatment condition, students monitored teaching activities of a statistics course instructor with an instructor-monitoring protocol. The experiment also included a control condition in which students took the statistics course with no experimental manipulation. I hypothesized that, compared with the instructor-monitoring and control groups, the self-monitoring group would perform better on course examinations, use self-regulated learning strategies more frequently, take more initiative in seeking mastery in learning, express more interest in the course, perceive stronger control over their learning environment, demonstrate more accurate self-judgment ability, and develop better knowledge representation of the course content.

METHOD

Sample

Data were collected from students enrolled in a graduate-level introductory statistics course in a university in the southwestern United States during four successive semesters to cumulate a sufficient number of participants. Eighty-one students were recruited as participants at the beginning of the study. Of this initial sample, 1 student terminated her participation in the study and 8 dropped the course, resulting in a final sample of 72 graduate students (40 females and 32 males). Forty-two of the students were enrolled in the College of Education, 16 in the College of Human Sciences, 6 in the School of Nursing, 5 in the College of Arts and Sciences, and 3 in an interdisciplinary program. Twenty-five students were in the self-monitoring group, 28 in the instructor-monitoring group, and 19 in the control group.

The statistics class met twice a week for 1.5 hr per session. I taught the course for the four semesters, with the same textbook and supplementary materials, same homework assignments, and identical examinations.

Students enrolled in the course were informed that by participating in the study, they could earn 10 out of a total of 200 points on which their course grade would be based. Every student in the course agreed to participate. I realized that if students were assigned to the treatment condition, the alternative treatment condition, and the nontreatment control condition the same semester, students in the control condition would earn the bonus points without doing anything. This situation might cause resentment among the students in the two treatment conditions, who would be asked to engage in extensive monitoring work. To avoid this potential problem, I decided that students enrolled in the first three semesters would be participants in the treatment and alternative treatment condition, and students in the fourth semester would be participants in the control condition.

Students enrolled in the course during the first three semesters were assigned randomly to the self-monitoring and instructor-monitoring conditions and were given a self-monitoring or instructor-monitoring protocol during the first class meeting. Students were informed that because more than one research project was being conducted in this class, their pro-

---

b. To operationalize a behavior or characteristic of research participants is to define it in terms of the specific operations by which it is measured. In earlier studies, self-monitoring was operationally defined as a one-occasion intervention designed to stimulate students' attention to a single aspect of learning.

tocol might differ from that of their classmates. Students in the control group took the course without any experimental treatment.

Procedure

The self-monitoring protocol was designed for students in the self-monitoring group to use in monitoring their learning activities during the statistics course. A sample section of this protocol is shown in Figure 1. A total of 75 statistical concepts derived from the statistics textbook used in the course (Pagano, 1990) were listed in the left column of the protocol. Accompanying each concept was a row of boxes in which students recorded the amount of time spent and frequency in reading the textbook, completing required assignments, voluntarily participating in group discussion after class, receiving tutoring, and engaging in other activities needed to master the concept. The last box in the row asked students to rate on a 10-point scale their self-efficacy in solving problems related to the concept. The purpose of this self-efficacy scale was to strengthen the effects of self-monitoring. I expected that students in the

self-monitoring group would use this scale as one more opportunity to monitor their learning and evaluate their understanding of the concept.

I questioned whether exposing students to the list of 75 statistical concepts might influence their learning by helping them to organize and review course content so that the amount of exposure to the course content, rather than the self-monitoring procedure, would be responsible for any observed effects. To control for this possibility, I designed an instructor-monitoring protocol. This protocol exposed students to the same list of 75 statistical concepts, but it directed them to monitor the instructor's teaching activities rather than their own learning activities. Each concept was accompanied by a row of boxes in which students evaluated the instructor's pace of instruction, sufficiency of examples and assignments, and time allowed for students' questions. Students rated the instructor on a 10-point scale, with a value of 1 representing an *inadequate amount of instruction* (faster instructional pace, fewer examples and assignments, and less time for students to ask questions than they needed) and a value of 10 representing an *excessive*

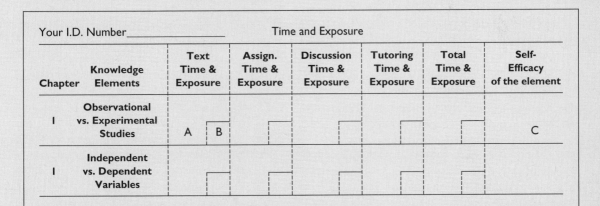

Note. In the box with the letter A, students recorded the amount of time in minutes that they spent using various techniques to understand the concept. In the box with the letter B, students recorded the number of times they exposed themselves to the concept. In the box with the letter C, students filled in a number from 1 to 10 to indicate their self-efficacy to solve problems regarding the concept, with 1 signifying *low confidence* and 10 signifying *high confidence*.

FIGURE 1 **Sample section of the self-monitoring protocol.**

amount of instruction (slower instructional pace, more examples and assignments, and more time for students to ask questions than they needed). The design of the instructor-monitoring protocol paralleled the self-monitoring protocol, the only difference being that the columns referred to the instructor's teaching activities rather than to the students' learning activities.

Regularity and proximity are considered to be important characteristics of effective self-monitoring (Bandura, 1986; Shapiro, 1984). Regularity means that students continuously, rather than intermittently, monitor their own behavior. Proximity means that behavior is monitored close in time to its occurrence, rather than a long time afterward. These characteristics were incorporated in the self-monitoring treatment to maximize its effectiveness. To increase regularity and proximity, I encouraged students to record their protocol responses every time they studied for the statistics course. In addition, two copies of the protocol (Copy A and Copy B) were prepared for each student. During the first day of class, students were given Copy A; at the next class, they exchanged Copy A for Copy B. I checked the protocols to make sure that students followed directions and completed the protocols correctly. The procedure of recording responses and exchanging protocols continued throughout the semester.

Measures

Various measures were administered to all students before and after the experimental treatment.

Mathematics Ability Test. This test included 22 multiple-choice items, with difficulty varying from elementary mathematics to college algebra. The students were asked to respond to all problems on the test.

This test was administered before the experiment; I used it to check the equivalence of mathematics ability among the three groups. The reliability coefficient for the mathematics ability test was .86.[c]

Course Examinations. Each of the four course examinations contained 40 multiple-choice questions, covering three or four chapters from the statistics textbook adopted for the course. The examinations were designed to measure students' understanding of statistical concepts and ability to perform statistical calculations. Computation formulas were provided, and calculators were allowed during the examinations. I used the four test scores, each with a possible range between 0 and 40, and an average test score (the mean of the four test scores) as measures of the students' academic performance in the statistics course. The KR-20 reliability coefficients for the four examinations during the period of the experiment ranged from .73 to .86.[d]

Self-regulated Learning Strategies. This scale assessed students' use of 13 self-regulated learning strategies identified by Zimmerman and Martinez-Pons (1986): self-evaluation; organizing instructional materials; goal-setting; seeking information; keeping records and monitoring; environmental structuring; self-consequences; rehearsal and memorization; seeking assistance from peers; seeking assistance from teachers; and reviewing the textbook, notes, and previous tests and assignments in preparation for a test. Students indicated the frequency of use of each strategy when studying statistics on a 5-point scale: *never* (1), *rare* (2), *sometimes* (3), *often* (4), and *always* (5).

Mastery Seeking. After receiving feedback from the instructor, students were allowed to resubmit their

---

c. A reliability coefficient is a statistical expression of the amount of measurement error present in the scores yielded by a test. A reliability coefficient of .86 means that a test is substantially free of measurement error.

d. The KR-20 formula is a method of calculating the reliability of a measure containing items that are scored dichotomously (e.g., correct-incorrect). A high reliability coefficient (i.e., approaching 1.00) indicates item consistency, meaning that individuals who choose one answer to some items tend to choose the same answer to other items. Correlation coefficients between .73 and .86 indicate that the course examinations have good but not perfect reliability in terms of the consistency with which they measure students' course-related understanding and ability.

homework assignments on 10 chapters for 40 points (20% of the course grade). Also, they were provided with 5 sets of mastery problems for the first 5 chapters of the course if they felt the problems in the textbook were not challenging enough. The students' performance on these mastery problems did not affect their final course grade. The number of students in each of the three conditions who resubmitted homework or did mastery problems was recorded and used as a measure of mastery-seeking behavior.

Perceived Control over Learning. The measure of this variable included six statements such as "I know what I am doing when studying for this course." Students completed a 6-point Likert scale to indicate the extent to which they agreed or disagreed with the statements.[e] A value of 1 indicated *weak perceived control,* and a value of 6 indicated *strong perceived control.* Cronbach's alpha for the scale was .52.[f]

Intrinsic Motivation toward Statistics. The measure of this variable included six statements such as "I would like to take more statistics classes, even if I am not required to do so." Students completed the same type of 6-point Likert scale used in the measure of perceived control over learning. Cronbach's alpha for the scale was .60.

Self-judgment Accuracy. When taking the examinations, students were instructed to assign a value from 1 to 10 to each problem to indicate their level of confidence that their answer was correct. A value of 1 signaled no confidence, and a value of 10 signaled complete confidence. I calculated and compared students' confidence in correct answers and in incorrect answers. My reasoning was that students with good self-judgment ability would express greater confidence when the answers were correct and less confidence when the answers were wrong than would students with poor self-judgment ability.

Knowledge Representation. At the end of each examination, three extra questions were asked to investigate students' knowledge representation. In each question, several related and unrelated statistics concepts were listed, and students were asked to find relevant concepts, organize them in an outline format, and indicate the headings of the outline. My reasoning was that students with a well-organized knowledge representation of statistics would he able to delete irrelevant concepts and organize the related concepts in a meaningful way. If the heading of the outline was properly indicated, students scored 1 point for that question. Because there were three such questions for each of the four examinations, the total score on this measure could range from 0 to 12.

The four course examinations, each accompanied by the measures of self-judgment accuracy and knowledge representation, were administered during the semester at intervals of 3 to 4 weeks. The scales measuring use of self-regulated learning strategies, perceived control, and intrinsic motivation were administered at the end of the semester. The instructor recorded data for the two measures of mastery-seeking behavior (resubmitting homework and doing mastery problems) throughout the semester.

RESULTS

Mean scores on the mathematics test were 13.09 (SD = 4.47), 12.07 (SD = 4.55), and 14.11 (SD = 5.62) for the instructor-monitoring, self-monitoring, and control groups, respectively.[g] Analysis of variance

---

e. A Likert scale is a measure that asks individuals to check the extent of their agreement or disagreement with various statements about a topic (e.g., strongly agree, agree, neither agree nor disagree, disagree, strongly disagree).

f. Named after its developer, Cronbach's alpha, also called the *alpha coefficient,* is a statistical measure of the degree to which the items in a measure consistently measure the same construct or ability. The use of alpha typically yields a lower correlation coefficient than the KR-20 formula. An alpha of .52 is low, but sufficient for an instrument used in exploratory research.

g. *SD* is an abbreviation of *standard deviation,* which is a measure of the degree to which the scores of a sample vary around the mean score. Here, an *SD* of 4.47 means that about 17 (68 percent) of the 25 students in the instructor-monitoring group scored between 8.62 (mean score of 13.09 minus 1 *SD* of 4.47) and 17.56 (mean score of 13.09 plus 1 *SD* of 4.47).

(ANOVA) revealed that the differences were not statistically significant.[h]

Table I contains the means and standard deviations of the four examination scores and the average examination score for the three experimental groups. To compare academic performance on the four course examinations across the three groups, I conducted a 4×3 mixed design ANOVA, with a within-subject [sic] variable of examination and a between-subjects variable of treatment.[i] The procedure yielded a significant within-subject [sic] effect, $F(3, 207) = 25.01$, $p < .001$, for the variable of examination and a significant between-subjects effect, $F(2, 69) = 3.88$, $p < .025$, for the treatment variable.[j]

The significant examination effect revealed that students' test scores decreased during the course, suggesting that the tests gradually became more dif-

TABLE I   Means and Standard Deviations of Course Examination Scores by Condition

Experimental condition	Score				
	Exam I	Exam 2	Exam 3	Exam 4	Average
Self-monitoring (n = 25)					
M	36.32	35.80	35.00	32.68	34.95
SD	2.56	3.75	3.80	3.81	2.50
Instructor-monitoring (n = 28)					
M	34.32	33.61	33.14	29.75	32.71
SD	4.56	3.75	4.50	5.30	3.80
Control (n = 19)					
M	34.42	33.26	32.79	29.63	32.53
SD	4.07	5.79	3.41	4.52	3.66
Combined (n = 72)					
M	35.04	34.28	33.69	30.74	33.44
SD	3.90	4.89	4.06	4.77	3.50

h. Analysis of variance is a statistical procedure to determine the likelihood that a difference between two or more groups in a research sample also would be found if the entire population were studied. Here the researcher found that differences between the mathematics test scores of the instructor-monitoring, self-monitoring, and control groups were not statistically significant, meaning that we cannot generalize beyond this sample and conclude that there would be a difference between the mathematics test scores of individuals in the three experimental conditions if the entire population were studied.

i. The 4×3 mixed-design ANOVA is an analysis of variance that was used in this instance to examine the effect of two independent variables on examination scores (the dependent variable). One independent variable, the treatment, is a between-subjects variable because each subject (i.e., research participant) participated in only one of the three experimental conditions. The other independent variable, the specific examination (Exam 1, 2, 3, or 4) that the students took, is a within-subjects variable, because each student took all four examinations. The phrase *4 X 3* indicates that there were four levels of one independent variable (the specific examination) and three levels of the other independent variable (two treatment conditions and one control condition). The experimental design is mixed because it incorporated both a between-subjects independent variable and a within-subjects independent variable.

j. The significant within-subjects effect for the variable of examination means that individuals' mean scores on the four examinations differed significantly, which indicates that differences in the mean scores on the four examinations would be found if the entire population represented by the research sample were studied. The significant between-subjects effect for the treatment variable indicates that differences in the mean scores for the individuals in the three experimental conditions also would be found if the entire population represented by the research sample were studied.

ficult.[k] I examined the significant treatment effect by post hoc comparisons with the Tukey-Kramer procedure.[l] The difference between the self-monitoring and instructor-monitoring groups was significant, $q(3, 69) = 3.43$, $p < .05$, and the difference between the self-monitoring group and the control group barely failed to achieve the specified alpha level of .05, $q(3, 69) = 3.37$, $p > .05$.[m] The effect size of this treatment effect, measured by the coefficient of partial eta squared was .10.[n] According to Cohen (1977), a treatment effect of this magnitude is considered between medium and large.

Table 2 contains descriptive and inferential statistics for the frequency scores for the 13 self-regulated learning strategies for each treatment group. The correlation matrix for the 13 self-regulated learning strategies revealed that most of them were intercorrelated.[o] Therefore, I analyzed the 13 sets of scores by multivariate analysis of variance (MANOVA) with treatment as the independent variable.[p] With Wilks's lambda equal to .53, the treatment effect approached the specified alpha level of .05, $F(26, 108) = 1.55$, $p = .056$.[q] Individual ANOVAs for the 13 frequency scores revealed significant group differences on 5 self-regulated learning strategies (see Table 2). Post hoc comparisons revealed that the self-monitoring group used the strategies of self-evaluation and environmental structuring more frequently than did the instructor-monitoring and control groups. They also used the strategies of rehearsal, memorization, and reviewing previous tests and assignments in preparation for a test more frequently than did the control group. The instructor-monitoring group sought assistance from peers more frequently than did the self-monitoring and control groups.

I analyzed the frequency of mastery-seeking behaviors by chi-square tests.[r] The frequency of resubmitting homework did not reveal significant group differences because almost everyone resubmitted

k. The significant examination effect is equivalent to the within-subjects effect mentioned in footnote i.

l. Post hoc comparisons involve comparing the mean score of individuals in each experimental condition with the mean score of individuals in each of the other experimental conditions to determine which groups differ significantly from each other in their examination scores. They are post hoc because they were carried out only after the ANOVA revealed a significant treatment effect. Named after its developers, the Tukey-Kramer procedure involves a special form of the t test for multiple comparisons; it adjusts for the probability of finding a significant difference between mean scores simply because many comparisons are made on the same data.

m. In the formula $q(3, 69) = 3.37$, q is the value obtained from the Tukey-Kramer comparison between the mean examination scores of the self-monitoring and the instructor-monitoring groups. The numbers 3 and 69 represent certain features of the data set that are used to determine the alpha level of the obtained q value. An alpha level of .05 means that the researcher chose the probability level $p = .05$ as the level of statistical significance that he would accept in order to conclude that any difference observed between the mean scores of the individuals in the three experimental conditions also would be found if the entire population represented by the research sample had been studied.

n. An effect size is a statistic based on a formula involving both the mean scores and standard deviations of the scores of two groups. It allows a precise calculation of how different the score distributions of the two groups are, and is adjusted so that it can be directly compared to effect sizes involving other samples or based on other measures. The coefficient of partial eta squared (η^2) is a special correlation coefficient that enables researchers to estimate the strength of the observed treatment effect, that is, the treatment's effect size.

o. A correlation matrix is an arrangement of correlation coefficients in rows and columns that shows the correlation between each pair of a set of measured variables.

p. Multivariate analysis of variance is a form of analysis of variance that is used when the dependent variable is a composite index of two or more measured variables (here, the 13 self-regulated learning strategies) that are correlated with one another.

q. Wilks's lambda is a statistic yielded by multivariate analysis of variance. Its magnitude indicates whether the treatment effect is statistically significant.

r. The chi-square (χ^2) test is a nonparametric test of statistical significance that is used when the research data are in the form of category frequencies.

TABLE 2   **Descriptive Statistics and ANOVA for Treatment Group Scores on Use of Self-Regulated Learning Strategies**

Variable	Self-monitoring group (*n* = 25)	Instructor-monitoring group (*n* = 28)	Control group (*n* = 19)	*F* (*df* = 2, 69)	Contrast (Tukey-Kramer)
Self-evaluation					
M	4.56	3.70	3.88	3.76*	S > I
SD	0.65	1.41	1.36		
Organizing materials					
M	3.24	3.41	3.53	.25	—
SD	1.48	0.97	1.13		
Goal setting					
M	3.36	3.26	3.06	1.42	—
SD	1.15	0.98	0.83		
Seeking information					
M	3.52	3.07	3.18	.92	—
SD	1.39	1.27	0.95		
Keeping records					
M	3.20	2.93	2.88	.32	—
SD	1.58	1.34	1.11		
Environmental structuring					
M	4.64	3.85	3.71	5.76**	S > I, C
SD	0.91	1.23	1.31		
Self-consequences					
M	2.64	2.48	2.65	.16	—
SD	1.38	1.16	1.00		
Rehearsing/memorization					
M	3.96	3.63	3.24	3.60*	S > C
SD	0.94	1.04	1.20		
Seeking peers' help					
M	2.60	3.52	2.82	3.70*	I > S, C
SD	1.50	1.28	1.19		
Seeking teachers' help					
M	2.56	2.70	3.18	1.06	—
SD	1.33	0.82	1.24		
Reviewing textbook					
M	4.72	4.00	4.24	2.72	—
SD	0.61	1.39	1.30		
Reviewing notes					
M	4.40	4.48	4.00	1.71	—
SD	1.04	1.01	1.12		
Reviewing tests/assignments					
M	4.36	3.89	3.35	5.41**	S > C
SD	0.76	1.01	1.46		

Note. S = self-monitoring group, I = instructor-monitoring group, and C = control group.

*p < .05. **p < .01.

assignments for the full credit, $\chi^2(2, N = 72) = .24$, $p = .90$. However, 4 of 25 students in the self-monitoring group worked some mastery problems, whereas only 1 of 28 students in the instructor-monitoring group and 1 of 19 students in the control group did so. The chi-square test indicated that this effect was not significant, $\chi^2(2, N = 72) = 3.26$, $p = .20$.

The self-monitoring group reported more perceived control ($M = 4.55$, $SD = .57$) than the instructor-monitoring group did ($M = 4.33$, $SD = .63$) but less control than the control group did ($M = 4.67$, $SD = .71$). ANOVA revealed that this effect was not significant, $F(2, 69) = 1.75$, $p = .18$. Similarly, the self-monitoring group reported higher intrinsic motivation toward statistics ($M = 3.88$, $SD = .60$) than did the instructor-monitoring group ($M = 3.71$, $SD = .67$) and the control group ($M = 3.84$, $SD = .80$), but the ANOVA for this effect was not significant, $F(2, 69) = .45$, $p = .64$.

As predicted, the self-monitoring group developed better knowledge representation than did the instructor-monitoring group and the control group, $F(2, 69) = 3.92$, $p = .02$. Of the 12 knowledge representation questions, the self-monitoring group answered an average of 7.68 ($SD = 1.82$) problems correctly, compared with averages of 5.89 correct answers ($SD = 2.27$) for the instructor-monitoring group and 6.63 correct answers ($SD = 2.93$) for the control group. Post hoc comparisons showed that only the difference between the self-monitoring and instructor-monitoring groups was significant, $q(3, 69) = 3.43$, $p < .05$.

I differentiated and averaged students' self-judgment responses on their correct and incorrect answers on four exams to create two variables: their confidence in correct answers and confidence in incorrect answers, with a value of 1 signaling *low confidence* and a value of 10 signaling *high confidence*. The self-monitoring group demonstrated slightly greater confidence in their correct answers ($M = 8.13$, $SD = 1.38$) than did the instructor-monitoring group ($M = 8.03$, $SD = 1.76$) and the control group ($M = 8.01$, $SD = 1.50$). The mean scores for

confidence in incorrect answers for the self-monitoring, instructor-monitoring, and control groups were 6.59 ($SD = 1.94$), 6.64 ($SD = 1.95$), and 6.13 ($SD = 2.49$), respectively. I analyzed the average confidence scores across the four examinations through a 3×2 ANOVA with a within-subject variable of item correctness and a between-subjects variable of treatment condition. Results of this analysis revealed that the students had higher confidence in their correct answers ($M = 8.06$, $SD = 1.53$) than in their incorrect answers ($M = 6.49$, $SD = 2.07$), $F(1, 69) = 197.67$, $p = .001$. However, neither the treatment effect, $F(2, 69) = .18$, $p = .84$, nor the interaction effect, $F(2, 69) = 1.36$, $p = .26$, was significant.

DISCUSSION

The hypothesis that self-monitoring students are more actively involved in their learning activities and have better academic performance than non–self-monitoring students was partially supported. Students in the self-monitoring condition performed better than students in non–self-monitoring groups on each course examination. This finding demonstrates the importance of self-regulated learning strategies in course work. The specific strategies that the students were asked to monitor were frequent self-evaluation, structuring of the learning environment, memorizing of important information, and review of previous assignments and tests in preparation for examinations.

Contrary to prediction, there was no difference in the mastery-seeking behavior of self-monitoring and non–self-monitoring groups. An explanation for this finding is that students' interest in their course grade was so intense that it overpowered the effects of self-monitoring. When homework assignments were rewarded with grade points, everyone across experimental conditions resubmitted homeworks for full credit. Inasmuch as the mastery problems were not related to grading, not many students were interested in doing them.

The prediction that self-monitoring students would be more motivated in the statistics course than non–self-monitoring students was not supported, although the group differences were in the predicted direction. The lack of a treatment effect can be explained by the particular characteristics of this course. Many students consider statistics to be one of the most difficult courses in their graduate studies and enter it with a high level of anxiety. The course instructor tried several ways to reduce students' anxiety levels and change their attitudes toward statistics, including a slow pace of instruction at the beginning of the semester, ample opportunity for individualized interaction between students and the instructor, and a policy that homework could be resubmitted for full credit. These instructional practices appeared to affect students' attitude toward statistics. When evaluating the course at the end of semester, many students expressed their appreciation of statistics as a tool of scientific inquiry and indicated that their understanding of statistical reasoning had improved. Many of them said that the policy of allowing them to resubmit homework was their favorite class policy because it gave them at least some control over the course grade. Their positive attitudes also were reflected in the fact that all the treatment group means on the intrinsic motivation and perceived control scales fell above the midpoint. These positive feelings among students might have prevented the self-monitoring intervention from further boosting students' intrinsic motivation and perceived control. Another possibility is that the relatively low reliability of the two motivational scales (reliability coefficients were .60 and .52 for the scales of intrinsic motivation and perceived control, respectively) obscured motivational effects.

The prediction that self-monitoring students would develop better knowledge representations than would non–self-monitoring students was supported. Students in the self-monitoring group demonstrated a greater ability to organize the course content than did students in the non–self-monitoring groups. However, the treatment groups did not differ in self-judgment accuracy. A possible explanation is that graduate students, after many years of academic experience, are able to accurately judge their performance in academic activities to such an extent that a self-monitoring intervention would have no additional effect. In fact, students in all three conditions demonstrated significantly higher confidence in their correct answers than in their incorrect answers.

The finding of a positive effect of self-monitoring on academic performance replicates the findings of previous research, most of it involving young students or students with learning disabilities as participants. In the present study, I extended this line of research to the population of graduate students.

The behavior demonstrated by self-monitoring learners in this study can be regarded as evidence of the importance of self-monitoring as a key process of self-regulated learning. When students in the self-monitoring group were involved in the self-monitoring process, the frequency with which they used other self-regulated learning strategies, such as self-evaluation, environmental structuring, rehearsal and memorization, and reviewing previous tests and assignments for testing, also increased. It appears that when students are involved in a self-monitoring process, they are alert to the effectiveness of the currently used learning strategies and appropriateness of their learning environment. This alertness helps them select the most effective strategies and arrange the environment to maximize learning.

Self-regulated learning strategies, like other cognitive skills and strategies, occupy a learner's limited information-processing capacity. In other words, they are *controlling processes* (Schneider & Shiffrin, 1977; Shiffrin & Schneider, 1977) that compete with other cognitive learning processes for the learner's attention. When a learner is engaged in an easy task, self-regulation is likely to be carried out because the information-processing capacity is available. When a learner is involved in a difficult task where self-regulation is most needed and can be most helpful, self-regulation is least likely to happen because the learner must devote most or all information-processing capacity to the learning activities. For this reason, it is important for self-monitoring and other self-regulatory processes to become increasingly automatic through repetition and practice (Anderson, 1987; Cheng, 1985). Therefore, to help students to use self-regulation processes in their learning, educators need to create opportunities for students to practice them.

Researchers have found that college students are deficient in their self-monitoring processes (Lan, Bradley, & Parr, 1993; Pressley & Ghatala, 1988, 1990; Pressley, Ghatala, Woloshyn, & Pirie, 1990). The present results indirectly support this finding in that a self-monitoring intervention increased students' academic performance. It appears that even graduate students, the experienced veterans of higher education, need assistance in engaging self-monitoring processes to improve their learning. We cannot expect self-monitoring or other self-regulated learning strategies to be automatic products of course work. Students at all levels, from learning-disabled students to graduate students, need systematic help to learn and use self-regulated learning strategies. This need is being recognized by an increasing number of educational researchers and practitioners who are developing courses that teach learning strategies explicitly (Ellis, Sabornie, & Marshall, 1989; McKeachie, Pintrich, & Lin, 1985; Pintrich, McKeachie, & Lin, 1987; Stahl, Brozo, Smith, & Henk; 1991; Wood, Fler, & Willoughby, 1992).

Teaching students' to use a self-monitoring protocol of the type used in this study should be considered as a possible element of these learning strategies courses. The protocol functions to elicit and maintain students' self-monitoring on a continuous basis. This intensive self-monitoring may be especially important for difficult classes, such as a graduate statistics course, that include students without a strong prior background in mathematics. When students are taking this course, their limited information-processing capacity is focused on learning processes (e.g., computing, grasping new concepts, or integrating new information into existing knowledge), and they experience frequent state-oriented worry, anxiety, and frustration (Kuhl, 1981, 1985). Consequently, it probably is difficult for them to devote adequate attention to applying self-regulating strategies in their learning process. The self-

monitoring protocol that was examined in the present study reminds students to engage in self-monitoring and helps them to do it regularly and proximately.

Note

Correspondence can be sent to the author at College of Education, Texas Tech University, P.O. Box 41071, Lubbock, Texas 79409-1071.

References

Anderson, J. R. (1987). Skill acquisition: Compilation of weak-method problem solutions. *Psychological Review, 94,* 192–210.

Bandura, A. (1986). Self-regulatory mechanisms. *Social foundations of thought and action: A social cognitive theory.* (pp. 335–389). Englewood Cliffs, NJ: Prentice Hall.

Borkowski, J. G., & Thorpe, P. K. (1994). Self-regulation and motivation: A life-span perspective on underachievement. In D. H. Schunk & B. J. Zimmerman (Eds.), *Self-regulation of learning and performance: Issues and educational applications* (pp. 45–73). Hillsdale, NJ: Erlbaum.

Caplan, N., Choy, M. H., & Whitmore, J. K. (1992, February). Indochinese refugee families and academic achievement. *Scientific American, 266,* 37–42.

Cheng, P. W. (1985). Restructuring versus automaticity: Alternative accounts of skill acquisition. *Psychological Review, 92,* 414–423.

Cohen, J. (1977). *Statistical power analysis for the behavioral sciences.* New York: Academic Press.

Corno, L. (1986). The metacognitive control components of self-regulated learning. *Contemporary Educational Psychology, 11,* 333–346.

Corno, L., & Mandinach, E. B. (1983). The role of cognitive engagement in classroom learning and motivation. *Educational Psychology, 18,* 88–108.

Delclos, V. R., & Harrington, C. (1991). Effects of strategy monitoring and proactive instruction on children's problem-solving performance. *Journal of Educational Psychology, 83,* 35–42.

DiGangi, S. A., Maag, J. W., & Rutherford, R. B. (1991). Self-graphing of on-task behavior: Enhancing the reactive effects of self-monitoring on on-task behavior and academic performance. *Learning Disability Quarterly, 14,* 221–230.

Ellis, E. S., Sabornie, E. J., & Marshall, K. J. (1989). Teaching learning strategies to learning disabled students in post-secondary settings. *Academic Therapy, 24,* 491–501.

Krouse, J. H., & Krouse, H. J. (1981). Toward a multi-modal theory of academic achievement. *Educational Psychologist, 16,* 151–164.

Kuhl, J. (1981). Motivational and functional helplessness: The moderating effect of state versus action orientation. *Journal of Personality and Social Psychology, 40,* 155–170.

Kuhl, J. (1985). Volitional mediators of cognition-behavior consistency: Self-regulatory processes and action versus state orientation. In J. Kuhl & J. Beckmann (Eds.), *Action control: From cognition to behavior* (pp. 101–128). Heidelberg, NY: Springer-Verlag.

Lan, W. Y., Bradley, L., & Parr, G. (1993). The effects of a self-monitoring process on college students' learning in an introductory statistics course. *The Journal of Experimental Education, 62,* 26–40.

Lloyd, J. W., Bateman, D. F., Landrum, T. J., & Hallahan, D. P. (1989). Self-recording of attention versus productivity. *Journal of Applied Behavior Analysis, 22,* 315–323.

Maag., J. W., Rutherford, R., & DiGangi, S. A. (1992). Effects of self-monitoring and contingent reinforcement on on-task behavior and academic productivity of learning disabled students: A social validation study. *Psychology in the School, 29,* 157–172.

Mace, F. C., & Kratochwill, T. R. (1988). Self-monitoring: Application and issues. In J. Witt, S. Elliott, & F. Gresham (Eds.), *Handbook of behavior therapy in education* (pp. 489–502). New York: Pergamon.

McCurdy, B. L., & Shapiro, E. S. (1992). A comparison of teacher-, peer-, and self-monitoring with curriculum-based measurement in reading among students with learning disabilities. *Journal of Special Education, 26,* 162–180.

McKeachie, W. J., Pintrich, P. R., & Lin, Y. G. (1985). Teaching learning strategies. *Educational Psychologist, 20,* 153–160.

Nelson, R. O. (1977). Methodological issues in assessment via self-monitoring. In M. Hersen, R. M. Eisler, & P. M. Miller (Eds.), *Progress in behavior modification* (pp. 263–308). New York: Academic Press.

Pagano, R. R. (1990). *Understanding statistics in the behavioral sciences.* St. Paul, MN: West.

Pintrich, P. R., & De Groot, E. V. (1990). Motivational and self-regulated learning components of classroom academic performance. *Journal of Educational Psychology, 82,* 33–40.

Pintrich, P. R., McKeachie, W. J., & Lin, Y. G. (1987). Teaching a course in learning to learn. *Teaching of Psychology, 14,* 81–86.

Pressley, M., & Ghatala, E. S. (1988). Delusions about performance on multiple-choice comprehension test items. *Reading Research Quarterly, 23,* 454–464.

Pressley, M., & Ghatala, E. S. (1990). Self-regulated learning: Monitoring learning from text. *Educational Psychologist, 25,* 19–33.

Pressley, M., Ghatala, E. S., Woloshyn, V., & Pirie. J. (1990). Sometimes adults miss the main ideas and do not realize it: Confidence in responses to short-answer and multiple-choice comprehension questions. *Reading Research Quarterly, 25,* 232–249.

Schneider, W. & Shiffrin, R. (1977). Controlled and automatic human information processing: I. Detection, search, and attention. *Psychological Review, 84,* 1–66.

Schunk, D. H. (1986). Verbalization and children's self-regulated learning. *Contemporary Educational Psychology, 11,* 347–369.

Schunk, D. H. (1991). *Learning theories: An educational perspective.* New York: Merrill/Macmillan.

Schunk, D. H., & Zimmerman, B. J. (1994). Preface. In D. H. Schunk & B. J. Zimmerman (Eds.), *Self-regulation of learning and performance: Issues and educational applications* (pp. ix–xi). Hillsdale, NJ: Erlbaum.

Shapiro, E. S. (1984). Self-monitoring procedure. In T. H. Ollendick, & M. Hersen (Eds.), *Child behavioral assessment: Principles and procedures* (pp. 148–165). New York: Pergamon Press.

Shiffrin, R., & Schneider, W. (1977). Controlled and automatic human information processing: II. Perceptual learning, automatic attending, and a general theory. *Psychological Review, 84,* 127–190.

Stahl, N. A., Brozo, W. G., Smith, B. D., & Henk, W. A. (1991). Effects of teaching generative vocabulary strategies in the college developmental reading program. *Journal of Research and Development in Education, 24,* 24–32.

Wibrowski, C. R. (1992). *Self-regulated learning processes among inner city students.* Unpublished doctoral dissertation, Graduate School City University of New York.

Wood, E., Fler, C., & Willoughby, T. (1992). Elaborative interrogation applied to small and large group contexts. *Applied Cognitive Psychology, 6,* 361–366.

Zimmerman, B. J. (1994). Dimensions of academic self-regulation: A conceptual framework for education. In D. H. Schunk & B. J. Zimmerman (Eds.), *Self-regulation of learning and performance: Issues and educational applications* (pp. 3–21). Hillsdale. NJ: Erlbaum.

Zimmerman, B. J., & Martinez-Pons, M. (1986). Development of a structured interview for assessing student use of self-regulated learning strategies. *American Educational Research Journal, 23,* 614–628.

Zimmerman, B. J., & Martinez-Pons, M. (1988). Construct validation of a strategy model of student self-regulated learning. *Journal of Educational Psychology, 80,* 284–290.

Zimmerman, B. J., & Martinez-Pons, M. (1990). Student differences in self-regulated learning: Relating grade, sex, and giftedness to self-efficacy and strategy use. *Journal of Educational Psychology, 82,* 51–59.

SAMPLE SINGLE-CASE EXPERIMENTAL RESEARCH STUDY: MODIFYING ACTIVITIES TO PRODUCE FUNCTIONAL OUTCOMES: EFFECTS ON THE PROBLEM BEHAVIORS OF STUDENTS WITH DISABILITIES

Dunlap, G., Foster-Johnson, L. Clarke, S., Kern, L., & Childs, K. E. (1995). Modifying activities to produce functional outcomes: Effects on the problem behaviors of students with disabilities. *Journal of the Association for Persons with Severe Handicaps*, 20, 248–258.

In the rest of this chapter you will read a research article that illustrates the use of the single-case experimental research method. It is preceded by comments written especially for this book by Glen Dunlap, the first author of the article. Then the article itself is reprinted in full, just as it appeared when originally published. Where appropriate, we have added footnotes to help you understand the information contained in the article.

Researcher's Comments, Prepared by Glen Dunlap

The analyses presented in this article represent a line of inquiry that our research group has pursued for over six years. The focus of this research is the effects of antecedent and curricular variables on the problem behaviors of students with disabilities. We have attempted to illustrate the impact that curricular and instructional procedures exert on problem behaviors. We also have sought to demonstrate that teachers can reduce students' undesirable behavior patterns by individualizing curricula on the basis of functional assessment information (Dunlap & Kern, 1993; 1996).

Our initial commitment to this line of research occurred in 1990 when we were asked to consult on the extreme behavior problems of a 12-year-old girl with multiple disabilities. Jill (a pseudonym) was in danger of being institutionalized, because her disruptive behaviors were very frequent and intense and had proved resistant to years of multidisciplinary interventions.

We first conducted a thorough assessment of the interactions between Jill's behavior and events in the school environment (Foster-Johnson & Dunlap, 1993; O'Neill et al., 1997). Eventually we were able to identify associations between her most serious behavior problems and certain curricular variables. When we modified Jill's curriculum based on the assessment findings, her problem behaviors were eliminated, her adaptive behavior improved, and she was able to remain in school (Dunlap, Kern-Dunlap, Clarke, & Robbins, 1991). This positive experience convinced us of the untapped power of assessment-based curricular interventions. It led to a series of studies in special education programs for children with developmental, emotional, and behavioral disabilities.

Our research team is based at the Florida Mental Health Institute (FMHI) of the University of South Florida, and we have conducted all these studies in association with local school systems. This research has been supported by FMHI and by several grants from the U. S. Department of Education. For the most part, the data have been collected by members of our team who have worked on a daily basis in partnership with classroom teachers. Together they have sought to solve problem behaviors with approaches that are effective, feasible, and sensitive to the individual student's needs and characteristics.

Some of the studies have involved detailed analyses of a single student, with data being collected over many months. Jill's story was an example of this approach, as was a study with Eddie (a pseudonym), a boy identified as severely emotionally disturbed (Kern, Childs, Dunlap, Clarke, & Falk, 1994). Eddie had above-average intelligence, but during academic instruction he displayed emotional outbursts and occasional self-injury.

The functional assessment process revealed several instructional and curricular variables that affected Eddie's behavior. These included long academic sessions, assignments that required handwriting, the lack of reminders to self-monitor his engagement, and the visible presence of possible distractors. Each of these factors was shown in brief single-subject research designs to produce low levels of task engagement and high rates of problem behaviors. Eddie's three teachers then used this information (with our assistance) to create small changes in the way they delivered instruction to him. Eddie's problem behaviors decreased dramatically, his engagement increased, and he subsequently moved to a regular class, where he continued to succeed.

Another type of study that we have conducted involves collecting data from large numbers of students in order to evaluate the potential relationship between the general quality of a curriculum and the presence of problem behaviors. In one investigation, we obtained data from students in 64 classrooms and measured the quality of the curricular activity as well as the occurrence of desirable and problem behaviors. The analyses showed that each of the quality dimensions that we measured was related to the behavior patterns, indicating that curriculum and student behavior are related to one another (Ferro, Foster-Johnson, & Dunlap, 1996).

We have observed that many students with acting-out behaviors seem to engage in disruption to obtain desired activities, or to exert some control over their environment. Our studies and those of other researchers show that providing students the option of selecting among scheduled assignments, materials, or sequences can reduce problem behaviors significantly, at least for some students in some circumstances. Similarly, we have seen that the provision of preferred activities or materials can reduce behavior problems. In two recent studies (Clarke et al., 1995; Foster-Johnson, Ferro, & Dunlap, 1994) we demonstrated that the identification and infusion of curriculum elements matched to students' preference helped decrease behavior problems and produce desirable, successful student performance.

The study that is reprinted here is closely aligned with the investigations on student preference. This set of data has a little twist that we felt was important to convey, and therefore we assembled these analyses to emphasize the similarity of the interventions. That is, in the curricular modifications for each of the three students, the activity was modified such that its natural outcome would be one that the individual student would perceive as meaningful and pleasing. Importantly, the integrity of the instructional objective in each case was not abridged; instead, the manner in which it was addressed was changed. The interventions show how instructional activities can be tailored to individual students in order to produce improved responding and deportment, without compromising the curriculum.

Some features of this study are important. For one, the three students were identified as having different disabilities, including autism, mental retardation, emotional and behavioral disorder, and multiple disabilities. This diversity indicates explicitly that the approach has external validity, meaning that its applicability is not limited to a particular kind of disability or circumstance. Similarly, the interests that were identified for the three students were quite different. What motivated one student would not necessarily have motivated another. Repeatedly, we have confirmed through our observations and systematic analyses that an individualized understanding of a student's interests and characteristics is essential for effective interventions.

Another feature that deserves mention is that none of the interventions required a specific alteration of programmed rewards or other consequences. There is no question that contingency management is an important element of motivational and disciplinary systems. However, it is also important to recognize that significant improvements can be achieved with antecedent manipulations, including carefully designed curricula. In fact, that is a core message of the above-mentioned line of research.

As I write these comments, our group is continuing to pursue applied research issues that involve richer and more effective interventions and supports for children with disabilities. Some members of our team have taken other positions. Lynn Foster-Johnson has moved to Dartmouth College, and Lee Kern is now at the University of Pennsylvania. Others of us remain at the University of South Florida, where we are beginning to work increasingly with students with disabilities in the context of their family lives and community participation. We believe that the same ideas and practices that are expressed in this article will have relevance in these expanded domains.

References

Clarke, S., Dunlap, G., Foster-Johnson, L., Childs, K. E., Wilson, D., White, R., & Vera, A. (1995). Improving the conduct of students with behavioral disorders by incorporating student interests into curricular activities. *Behavioral Disorders, 20,* 221–237.

Dunlap, G., dePerczel, M., Clarke, S., Wilson, D., Wright, S., White, R., & Gomez, A. (1994). Choice making to promote adaptive behavior for students with emotional and behavioral challenges. *Journal of Applied Behavior Analysis, 27,* 505–518.

Dunlap, G., & Kern, L. (1993). Assessment and intervention for children within the instructional curriculum. In J. Reichle & D. Wacker (Eds.), *Communicative approaches to the management of challenging behavior* (pp. 177–203). Baltimore: Paul H. Brookes.

Dunlap, G., & Kern, L. (1996). Modifying instructional activities to promote desirable behavior: A conceptual and practical framework. *School Psychology Quarterly, 11*, 297–312.

Dunlap, G., Kern-Dunlap, L., Clarke, S., & Robbins, F. R. (1991). Functional assessment, curriculum revision, and severe behavior problems. *Journal of Applied Behavior Analysis, 24,* 387–397.

Dunlap, G., White, R., Vera, A. G., Wilson, D., & Panacek, L. (1996). The effects of multi-component, assessment-based curricular modifications on the classroom behavior of children with emotional and behavioral disorders. *Journal of Behavioral Education, 6,* 481–500.

Ferro, J., Foster-Johnson, L., & Dunlap, G. (1996). Relation between curricular activities and problem behaviors of students with mental retardation. *American Journal on Mental Retardation, 101,* 184–194.

Foster-Johnson, L., & Dunlap, G. (1993). Using functional assessment to develop effective, individualized interventions. *Teaching Exceptional Children, 25,* 44–50.

Foster-Johnson, L., Ferro, J., & Dunlap, G. (1994). Preferred curricular activities and reduced problem behaviors in students with intellectual disabilities. *Journal of Applied Behavior Analysis, 27,* 493–504.

Kern, L., Childs, K. E., Dunlap, G., Clarke, S., & Falk, G. D. (1994). Using assessment-based curricular intervention to improve the classroom behavior of a student with emotional and behavioral challenges. *Journal of Applied Behavior Analysis, 27,* 7–19.

O'Neill, R. E., Horner, R. H., Albin, R. W., Sprague, J. R., Storey, K., & Newton, J. S. (1997). *Functional assessment and program development for problem behavior: A practical handbook.* Pacific Grove, CA: Brooks/Cole.

MODIFYING ACTIVITIES TO PRODUCE FUNCTIONAL OUTCOMES: EFFECTS ON THE PROBLEM BEHAVIORS OF STUDENTS WITH DISABILITIES

Glen Dunlap, Lynn Foster-Johnson, Shelley Clarke, Lee Kern, and Karen E. Childs
University of South Florida and University of Pennsylvania

This research was supported by Cooperative Agreement No. H133B2004 from the U.S. Department of Education (National Institute on Disability and Rehabilitation Research); however, opinions expressed are those of the authors and no official endorsement should be inferred. Reprint requests should be sent to Glen Dunlap, Department of Child and Family Studies, Florida Mental Health Institute, University of South Florida, 13301 Bruce B. Downs Blvd., Tampa, FL 33612.

This article presents three empirical demonstrations of desirable effects that accrued from modifying curricular activities in accordance with individual students' interests. Participants were three elementary students with disabilities and diverse labels including autism, mental retardation, and emotional and behavioral disorder. In each case, the instructional objective was held constant; whereas, the context of the activity was modified so that it produced an outcome that was judged to be meaningful and reinforcing to the student. Reversal designs showed that each student exhibited less problem behavior and more on-task responding when the modified activity was presented. These results are discussed in relation to the applied and conceptual literatures on curricular design, student preference, and the expanding enterprise of positive behavioral support.

DESCRIPTORS: challenging behavior, curricula, developmental disabilities, functional assessment, positive behavioral support, research, school-age subjects, special education

For some time, curriculum has been acknowledged as a crucial ingredient in the education of students with disabilities (Brown et al., 1979). There has been widespread encouragement to develop curricula that are age appropriate and that develop skills that will be used in students' daily lives in the community (e.g., Falvey, 1986). Some authors have also indicated that curricula should be constructed so that activities are interesting and lead to outcomes that have meaning, or relevance, in the lives of individual students (Neel & Billingsley, 1989). In this regard, there has been some indication that curricula that are designed to meet these criteria will produce improvements in student behavior.

Horner, Sprague, and Flannery (1993) described features of a functional curriculum that they argued should be associated with programs of positive behavioral support. These authors indicated that curriculum should be referenced to activities of peers and to the demands of the local community. They also indicated that curricula should focus on immediate effects and that the content should be functional from a social and from a behavioral (i.e., reinforcement) perspective. In a recent study that investigated several of these features, Ferro, Foster-Johnson, and Dunlap (1994), collected observational data in 64 classrooms to determine possible relationships between curricular characteristics (age appropriateness, social functionality, and student preference) and student behavior. The authors found significant correlations between each of these curricular features and measures of desirable responding and problem behavior.

The past few years have produced a number of within-subject [sic] investigations that have shown empirical associations between instructional and curricular characteristics and the behavior of students who are engaging in the activities (Dunlap & Kern, 1993; Munk & Repp, 1994).[a] For example, one variable that has been studied is the relative preference that a student demonstrates for stimuli that are included in activities (e.g., Green et al., 1988; Pace, Ivancic, Edwards, Iwata, & Page, 1985; Parsons, Reid, Reynolds, & Bumgarner, 1990; Wacker, Berg, Wiggins, Muldoon, & Cavanaugh, 1985).[b] Beneficial effects of student preference have been reported when the stimuli are used as reinforcers or activities (Koegel, Dyer, & Bell, 1987).

Foster-Johnson, Ferro, and Dunlap (1994) used a systematic assessment to determine preferences that individual students with intellectual disabilities showed for activities in their curriculum. In this study, the student responses and the instructional objectives were held constant, while the context and the materials that were used in the activities were adjusted. The results demonstrated that the sessions with the preferred activities contained elevated levels of task engagement and reduced levels of problem behavior for each of the three participants. Clarke and colleagues (1995) also reported data showing that curricular activities that incorporated student interests were associated with reductions in disruptive responding. This latter study was conducted with four participants who were described as having serious emotional and behavioral disorders. In a related line of research, several authors have described positive effects of allowing students to make choices among curricular activities (Bambara, Ager, & Koger, 1994; Dyer, Dunlap, & Winterling, 1990; Guess, Benson, & Siegel-Causey, 1985). This phenomenon has been shown to apply to students who exhibit a diversity of challenging characteristics, including developmental, emotional, and behavioral disabilities (e.g., Dunlap et al., 1994; Dunlap et al.,

---

a. Within-subjects investigations involve comparisons of an individual's behavior under one experimental condition with the same individual's behavior under another experimental condition.

b. A variable is a behavior or characteristic that varies across individuals and that is measured for the purpose of investigation.

1993: Seybert, Dunlap, & Ferro, in press; Sigafoos & Dempsey, 1992).

Dunlap, Kern-Dunlap, Clarke, and Robbins (1991), working with an adolescent female with multiple disabilities, eliminated the student's severe problem behavior by thoroughly revising her curriculum. After 5 weeks of a detailed and comprehensive functional assessment, four curricular variables were implicated and then modified for intervention.[c] One of the variables involved the functionality of the curriculum from the point of view of the student. The authors hypothesized and demonstrated that the student would be better behaved if the curriculum was based on the student's interests and if it led to concrete outcomes that were valued by the student. For example, instead of completing typical subtraction problems from a workbook, the student was asked to use methods of subtraction and a bus schedule to calculate times of the day that a bus would pass by a nearby location. This student was fascinated by busses and other forms of transportation and, thus, this manipulation made the activity relevant to her interests and her daily routine. This modification was shown in a process of functional analysis to be associated with improved behavior.

This issue of relevance in an educational curriculum is, of course, a major concern that is being addressed throughout the panorama of instructional efforts, from early childhood through continuing education programs. Although there are surprisingly few data, there have been frequent reports that an instructional content and educational process that students can relate to their daily lives leads to improved motivation, greater attention, reduced drop outs, and improved performance. Therefore, the concern about this issue appears to transcend special education and the instruction of students with challenging behaviors and severe disabilities.

Aside from the Dunlap et al. (1991) example, there are very few data that relate directly the notion of relevant outcomes to student behavior or motivation. Therefore, in this report, we bring together data from three students whose curricular activities were modified so that the outcomes of the activities would be of relevance to each student's interests and daily lives. As in Foster-Johnson et al. (1994) and Clarke et al. (1995), we held the instructional objectives constant and modified only the context and outcome that the activity produced. To extend the external validity of the approach, we included students who were described as exhibiting a diversity of challenges that included developmental, emotional, and behavioral disabilities.[d]

METHOD

Participants

Data obtained from three students are presented in this article. All of the students were described as having severe disabilities; however, they displayed very different characteristics, and their disability labels indicated a range of developmental to emotional and behavioral challenges. All of the participants had been referred for assessment and behavioral consultation because of persistent and extensive problem behaviors in their school settings.

Jary was a 13-year-old boy with autism and mental retardation. Various tests of performance and intelligence estimated his functioning to be more than 3 standard deviations below the mean.[e] Despite his label of autism, Jary enjoyed social interactions

c. Intervention here refers to modifying the standard or baseline condition to determine whether the modification results in changes in the individual's behavior. In this study the variable of functionality of the curriculum was modified for all three students.

d. External validity is the extent to which the experimental findings can be generalized to other similar individuals. By selecting students with a diversity of challenges for their single-case experiment, the researchers hoped to make their findings more widely generalizable.

e. A standard deviation is a measure of the degree to which the scores of a sample vary around the mean score. A student who is performing more than 3 standard deviations below the mean score on a test is at the first percentile of students who have taken such tests.

with his peers. Jary was enrolled in a self-contained classroom for children with autism and related disabilities. His teachers were concerned with his low level of task engagement and high frequency of inappropriate and disruptive verbalizations and noises.

Jill was a 13-year-old girl who was described with multiple disability labels including severe emotional disturbance, mild mental retardation, schizophrenia, and attention deficit disorder. Test scores showed her intellectual functioning as a 63 full-scale score on the Wechsler Intelligence Scale for Children–Revised (WISC-R), and her performances in reading and mathematics were about 3 years behind grade level.[f] On the Vineland Adaptive Behavior Scales, Jill's adaptive behavior composite was estimated at an age equivalency of 5 years, 4 months. Her teachers were concerned about Jill's extensive history of very severe disruptive behavior, negative and inappropriate affect, and immature social relations. She was enrolled in a classroom for students with severe emotional disturbance; however, her activities were highly individualized, and a personal aide was assigned to her on a full-time basis. Prior to the current analysis, Jill had participated in a functional assessment that had identified the influence of several antecedent variables on her problem behaviors (Dunlap et al., 1991).[g]

Natalie was a 9-year-old girl who was described as having behavioral and emotional challenges and had received a diagnosis of Oppositional Defiant Disorder by the public school system. She was a third grader enrolled in a school program for students with severe emotional disturbance. Natalie was given a full-scale score of 71 on the WISC-R.[h] She participated on a daily basis in four elementary

school classrooms, each of which was designed to support approximately eight students in special education. Her teachers were concerned with Natalie's noncompliance and acting out behaviors during instructional sessions.

Settings

Data for this study were collected in the context of the students' routines in their school settings. Jary's sessions were conducted in his classroom, by his classroom teacher, during regularly scheduled vocational and pre-vocational training activities. Jill's sessions were conducted in a separate room by a familiar aide, and Natalie's sessions were held in the ongoing context of a classroom in which she and her classmates were instructed in handwriting and English composition. The majority of the sessions for Jary and Jill were videotaped.

General Procedures

A first step in this investigation was to determine particular tasks that were associated with high levels of problem behaviors. The second step was to identify the instructional objectives that were the purpose of the tasks. Then, assessments were conducted to ascertain interests of the students and, in particular, interests that could be matched with the existing instructional objectives. The tasks were then modified such that they produced outcomes that were functional for the students, in the sense that the results of the activity were relevant to the students' interests. Although the tasks were modified, the instructional purpose of each task was

---

f. A WISC-R full-scale score of 63 is more than 2 standard deviations below the mean score, because the derived mean score of this test is set at 100 and the standard deviation is set at 15. A score this low signifies that a student is at the first percentile of students who have taken this test.

g. Antecedent variables are characteristics of an individual that have been previously measured. In this experiment they are variables that are presumed to cause the problem behaviors observed in this student.

h. A full scale score of 71 on the WISC-R is close to 2 standard deviations below the mean score, because the derived mean score of this test is set at 100 and the standard deviation is set at 15. A score this low signifies that a student is at the second percentile of students who have taken this test.

maintained. Reversal analyses were conducted to determine experimentally if the tasks with functional outcomes were associated with more desirable student behavior.[i]

Assessments of Tasks and Interests

Tasks associated with high levels of problem behavior and relatively low levels of on-task responding were identified by interviewing the teachers and confirming the reports by direct observation. When a problematic task was identified, the purpose of the task (i.e., the instructional objective) was determined. These were described by the teachers and included on the students' individual educational plans.

Student interests were assessed in a number of ways. First, teachers were asked in an interview to identify preferred activities, materials, and reinforcers for each student. Second, direct observations of the students were conducted in each setting. These observations were intended to identify those activities and stimuli that were associated with the most positive affect, the highest level of engagement, and the most student initiations (Dyer, 1987; Foster-Johnson et al., 1994). For example, these observations showed that Jary appeared to be highly motivated during snack and lunch time when he was interacting with his peers. A third method of assessing interests for Jill and Natalie was simply to ask the students to identify activities that they favored (e.g., Kern, Dunlap, Clarke, & Childs, 1994). A final method of assessment for Jill and Natalie was to conduct brief probes in which hypotheses regarding preferred, functional outcomes were tested empirically (Dunlap & Kern, 1993).[j] The combination of these assessments yielded a number of identified preferences for each participant. These were then related to the instructional objectives to find an expeditious means of incorporating outcomes that would be functional for the students.

Modified Tasks and Functional Outcomes

This process of assessment determined that Jary experienced difficulties when he was asked to assemble component parts of ballpoint pens, in which the instructional objective was to complete a multistep assembly task until a set number of assembled items was completed. The assessment of interests revealed that Jary enjoyed sharing snacks with his peers and, thus, it was determined that an assembly task could be developed from this interest. A functional outcome associated with assembly was established by having Jary prepare cracker sandwiches with peanut butter and jelly. This modified task required a multistep assembling process, and it produced the snacks that Jary and his classmates would consume later in the day.

The assessment for Jill indicated that she experienced tremendous problems when she was asked to complete handwriting assignments, where the objective was to demonstrate correct letter formation and spacing in writing sentences. Among her interests was an activity in which she took photographs of her classmates and teachers in her school environment. She enjoyed looking at and commenting on the photographs. Therefore, the modified task, incorporating a functional outcome, required Jill to use handwriting to prepare captions for her photo album.

Natalie's assessment also implicated handwriting, and her instructional objective was identical to Jill's. The interest assessment for Natalie determined that she enjoyed engaging in activities that were helpful and useful to others. Therefore, the modified task simply required Natalie to use her handwriting period to copy dittos that would later be laminated and used by students as they completed their lessons in another class.

The instructional objectives, standard tasks, and tasks with functional outcomes for each student was [sic] summarized in Table 1 and described in greater detail below.

---

i. Reversal analyses involve the shift from the treatment condition (condition B) in an A-B-A experiment back to the baseline condition (condition A). Here the functional-outcome task for each student represents condition B, and the standard-outcome task represents condition A.

j. As used here, a probe is a brief intervention to test hypotheses (i.e., hunches or educated guesses) about the students' interests.

TABLE I   Descriptions of Instructional Objectives, Standard, and Functional Assignments and Outcomes

Name	Instructional objective	Standard assignment	Standard outcome	Functional assignment	Functional outcome
Jary	To perform a multistep assembly task.	Six parts of a pen were presented in individual pieces. The student assembled each pen by placing parts of the pen together and then placing completed object in a bin.	Completion of task. Student placed completed task in designated area, indicated completion by checking off activity on board, and continued with another activity.	A five-step task to make peanut butter and jelly cracker sandwiches. Pieces of the task were laid out sequentially, and the student was required to complete the steps and put the finished sandwich on a plate.	The student placed the plate of sandwiches aside to be given to the class for snack later in the day. He then checked off the activity on the board, and continued with another activity.
Jill	To demonstrate the correct use of letter formation and spacing in manuscript handwriting	For 15 min, the student was expected to copy words from a handwriting book onto a blank sheet of lined paper.	After completing the assignment, Jill raised her hand to inform instructor, turned in completed assignment, and went on to next scheduled activity.	For 15 min, Jill developed and wrote captions related to photographs that she had taken earlier in the week, onto a blank sheet of lined paper.	After completing the assignment, Jill added her completed captions to a photo album she was creating.
Natalie	To demonstrate the correct use of letter formation and spacing in cursive handwriting	Copy four to five cursive sentences from a ditto onto a blank sheet of lined paper.	Teacher acknowledged completion of task. Student then placed sheet in a bin. It was later graded and returned by the teacher.	Copy four to five cursive sentences from a ditto onto a blank sheet of lined paper.	Teacher acknowledged completion of task. Then Natalie took the finished product to another teacher's room, where it would later be laminated and used by other students.

Procedures

Once the assessment phase was completed, experimental comparisons were conducted to evaluate the effects that the assignments with the standard versus functional outcomes would have on students' behavior. As indicated above, the standard outcome assignments were those activities that had been associated with problem behavior and in which the result of the activity did not relate to the student's interests. The functional outcome assignments addressed the same objectives as the standard outcome assignments, and they were presented to the students in the same fashion. However, the modifications involved the incorporation of functional outcomes as products of the activity.

For Jary, the standard outcome activity consisted of a task composed of the assembly of 18 pens. During the functional outcome conditions, Jary completed an assembly activity, during which he assembled 18 peanut-butter cracker sandwiches for snack time later in the day. Sessions were conducted in the classroom by the classroom teacher and ranged in length from 8 to 15 min. Each session began with the teacher presenting the activity and providing instructions for Jary. During the sessions, the teacher circulated around the classroom providing reinforcement, directions, and feedback for all students in the room on an intermittent schedule. Following every session in both conditions, Jary was given a cracker sandwich as a reward for participation.

For Jill, the standard outcome sessions involved 15 min of handwriting. The sessions began when Jill was given a Merrill handwriting book along with a blank sheet of paper and instructed to copy manuscript from an assigned page (averaging 35 words) to the blank sheet of paper. For sessions in the functional outcome condition, Jill was presented with photographs that she had taken at an earlier time and instructed to develop a caption for each picture, and then to write the caption on blank paper. The task was structured so that Jill was expected to write captions of approximately 35 words during the session. The sessions were 15 min and ended with Jill being given an opportunity to glue the captions and the photos into a photo album. In all sessions, the instructor was available to provide assistance upon request and encouragement on an intermittent schedule.

For Natalie, the standard outcome assignment consisted of copying cursive sentences from a ditto to a blank sheet of paper. The functional outcome assignment was identical to the standard outcome assignment in terms of the work that was performed. The only difference was the outcome associated with the assignment. After each of the functional outcome sessions, Natalie took her completed assignment to another teacher, who would use the finished product with his students during the handwriting activities for that class later in the day. During the first five sessions of the functional outcome condition, Natalie was also able to choose which ditto she would copy out of a pool of five dittos. However, this choice option was then removed, so that the conditions then differed only with respect to their outcomes. In all sessions, Natalie was given 15 min to complete the assignment.

In conducting experimental sessions, no changes other than those indicated above distinguished one condition from the other. A behavior management system was in place in all three classrooms with the same schedules of reinforcement and error correction in effect in all phases of the study.

Each participant experienced a reversal design, beginning with sessions in the standard outcome condition and including at least two additional phases (i.e., a minimum of an ABA).[k] In addition, a brief probe was inserted during the second functional outcome condition for Jill. Because of unavoidable scheduling conflicts, the final phase for each participant was limited to a single session.

Dependent Variables—Desirable and Problem Behavior

The principal dependent variables for each participant included categories of desirable and problem behaviors.[l] Definitions for these categories were

---

k. A reversal design here involves the standard-outcome task during condition A followed by the functional-outcome task during condition B, and then a reversal back to the standard-outcome task, that is, a repeat of condition A. Thus each student experienced a minimum of an A-B-A single-case design, although the experiment included additional manipulation of the functional-outcome (B) condition and in one case also the standard-outcome (A) condition.

l. Dependent variables are the behaviors or characteristics of individuals that are presumed to be affected by the experimental treatment. The experimental treatment constitutes the independent variable.

developed by the participants' teachers and research staff. The behavioral definitions for desirable behavior were the same for all three students. Desirable behavior was scored whenever the student was engaged in the assigned activity according to the teacher's instructions for the majority of an interval. This included eyes on materials during assignments requiring physical manipulation or on the teacher during verbal instruction.

Problem behaviors were defined for each child individually. For Jary, problem behavior consisted of any occurrence of inappropriate vocalizations (e.g., inappropriate giggling, talking about things unrelated to task), inappropriate use of materials (e.g., mouthing, rubbing, or hitting material on the desk), or leaving the instructional area. Problem behaviors for Jill were recorded when she exhibited any of the following behaviors: aggression (e.g., kicking, hitting, spitting, throwing objects), inappropriate vocalizations (e.g., perseverative or delusional speech, cursing), noncompliance (failure to follow instructions within 5 sec), or elopement (running around or out of the room). Natalie's problem behaviors included inappropriate initiations directed at her teacher (e.g., threatening, grabbing, snapping fingers), talking out to peers, noncompliance, and noise making.

Measurement

For all three participants, data for desirable and problem behaviors were collected using a 15-sec partial interval recording system in which the first 10 sec were devoted to observation and the remaining 5 sec were used to record data. Observers were cued using a tape recording that signaled the beginning and ending of each interval. At the end of the interval, observers recorded whether desirable or problem behavior occurred or did not occur. The data on these dependent variables were recorded in vivo for all participants.[m]

Observers and Reliability

All data were collected by observers who had been trained previously to record desirable and problem behaviors of students within special education programs. Observer training involved attaining at least 80% agreement during in vivo classroom practice observations.

Interobserver agreement was calculated for occurrences and nonoccurrences of each dependent variable. Agreements between observers were defined as intervals scored in an identical manner by two observers. Percentage agreement was calculated by dividing the number of agreements by the number of agreements plus disagreements and multiplying by 100.

Interrater reliability was collected for Jary during 87% of the sessions across all conditions.[n] Reliability estimates for occurrence of desirable behavior averaged 95% (77–100).[o] The reliability for nonoccurrence of desirable behavior was 85% (72–100). Interobserver agreement for problem behavior averaged 89% (84–100) for occurrences and 97% (91–100) for nonoccurrences. For Jill, interobserver agreement was obtained during 71% of the sessions across all conditions of the study. Reliability calculations for Jill produced the following results: occurrences of desirable behavior, 98% (98–100), nonoccurrences, 96% (50–100); occurrences of problem behavior, 92% (0–100), and nonoccurrences, 99% (98–100). For Natalie, interobserver agreement was assessed during 45% of the sessions

m. Recording in vivo means that observers rated the students' behavior live, as it occurred.

n. Inter-rater reliability, also called *interobserver agreement* in this study, is a measure of the degree to which two or more observers are consistent in their ratings of the same individual. Here the degree of reliability is expressed as the percentage of the total number of ratings that were the same for all observers.

o. The numbers in parentheses (77–100) represent the range of agreements across sessions. In this case, the lowest reliability for a session was 77 percent inter-observer agreement, and the highest reliability for a session was 100 percent inter-observer agreement.

across all conditions. Agreement on occurrences for desirable behavior averaged 93% (82–100). Reliability for nonoccurrences of desirable behavior averaged 89% (67–100). Interrater agreement for occurrences of problem behavior averaged 93% (67–100), with nonoccurrences averaging 97% (90–100).

Measurement of Student Productivity and Affect

In addition to data on the participants' desirable and problem behavior, other dependent measures were assessed for all three students. Productivity was evaluated in Jary's analysis to determine if the functional outcome condition influenced his rate of responding as compared to the standard outcome task. Prior to recording these data, an empirical comparison of the average time required to assemble a single object (ballpoint pen or cracker sandwich) showed that the assembly generally required similar amounts of time. During the sessions, rate was computed by dividing the number of correctly completed objects (pens or sandwiches) by the time it took to complete each session.

Productivity for Natalie was evaluated in two ways. First, observers noted the percentage of sessions in which she completed her assignment within the expected period of time (15 min). Also, for those sessions in which her assignment was completed within 15 min, a comparison was made of the number of minutes that were required from the time she was presented with the assignment until the assignment was completed.

Productivity was not considered to be a particular problem for Jill; however, her affect was a concern. Therefore, data were obtained on Jill's happiness and interest in the task using six-point Likert-type rating scales (Dunlap, 1984).[p] These data were collected from videotapes. The videotaped sessions were divided into 1-min intervals for scoring purposes. The raters were graduate students who did not know Jill and who were not informed of the purpose of the study. The raters were asked to score each interval according to their judgments of Jill's "interest" and "happiness." Scores ranged from 0 (very unhappy or very uninterested) to 5 (very happy or very interested). Interobserver agreement occurred during 91% of the sessions with agreements defined as either exact number matches or ratings differing by only one number. Mean agreements were 96% (86–100) for interest, and 98% (87–100) for happiness.

RESULTS

Figures 1 through 3 depict the results of the reversal analyses for the three students in this study. The percentage of intervals with on-task (desirable) responding and problem behavior are shown on the ordinate; whereas, sessions are on the abscissa.[q]

During the first standard outcome condition, Jary (Figure 1) demonstrated variable levels of on-task and problem behavior, averaging 59% and 31%, respectively. The functional outcome condition resulted in an immediate increase in on-task responding that was maintained throughout the condition, averaging 98%. Problem behavior showed a corresponding decrease to an average of 8%. The third phase, returning to the standard outcome condition, produced a reduction in on-task responding ($M = 71\%$) and an increase in problem behavior ($M = 17\%$). The final phase contained only one data point, but that session yielded data that were consistent with the previous data functions.

The data for Jill (Figure 2) show relatively slight improvements from the first standard outcome condition to the first functional outcome condition for on-task and problem behaviors. However, the

---

p. A Likert scale is a measure that asks individuals to check the extent of their agreement or disagreement with various statements about a topic (e.g., strongly agree, agree, neither agree nor disagree, disagree, strongly disagree). The scales in this study were a variation of Likert scales (i.e., they were "Likert-type"), because the individuals rated other individuals rather than themselves. Also, rather than rating degree of agreement, they rated degrees of interest and happiness.

q. The ordinate is the vertical dimension of Figures 1 through 3, and the abscissa is the horizontal dimension of the figures.

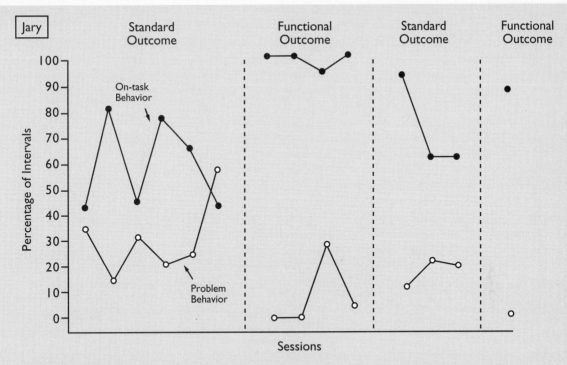

FIGURE I **Results for Jary showing the effects of the standard versus functional outcome assignments on on-task and problem behavior.**

return to the standard outcome condition resulted in a dramatic reversal of data functions, with extremely low levels of on-task responding and with problem behavior being exhibited during virtually every interval. After an initial session of continued problems, the next phase of the functional outcome assignment restored desirable patterns of behavior. A probe session with the standard outcome assignment, as well as the final phase of the analysis, replicated the effects of the second standard outcome condition.[r]

The data for Natalie (Figure 3) resemble those that were obtained with Jill. That is, the first condition change, from the standard to the functional outcomes, produced changes in amplitude and slope, but these initial effects were not as prominent as they were for Jary.[s] However, the subsequent condition changes were associated with very distinct differences, all of which were consistent with the other participants' data.

The data on productivity for Jary and Natalie showed that the functional outcome assignments were accompanied by increased rates of task completion. For Jary, the ballpoint pens were assembled at an average rate of 1.5 pens per minute; whereas, the cracker sandwiches were prepared at an average rate of 2.8 per minute. For Natalie, whose work in the two conditions was essentially identical, completion of

r. The probe was a one-trial reversal from the functional-outcome task back to the standard-outcome task. This reversal is labeled *Probe* in Figure 2.

s. The term *amplitude* refers to the height of the data points on the ordinate. Inspection of Figure 3 shows that the data points for the first functional-outcome condition are generally higher than the data points for the first standard-outcome condition. Also, the slopes of the data points in these two conditions go in the opposite direction.

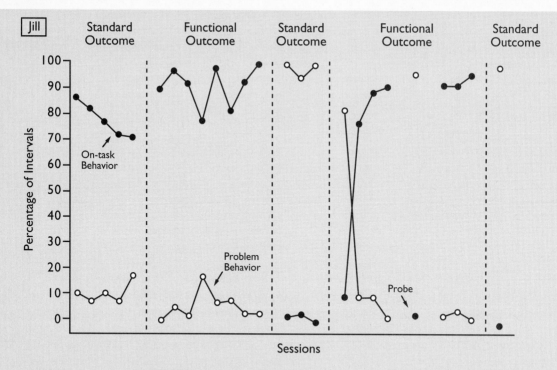

FIGURE 2 **Results for Jill showing the effects of the standard versus functional outcome assignments on on-task and problem behavior.**

her assignment within the expected 15-min period occurred during only 25% of the standard outcome sessions, but it happened during 100% of the functional outcome sessions. Of those sessions in which the task was completed, she required an average of 14.85 min in the standard outcome condition, and only 8.15 min in the functional outcome condition. As noted above, the increased rate of task completion in the functional outcome sessions for Jary and Natalie meant that these sessions were of shorter duration. An analysis of within-session trends for problem and on-task behavior showed no consistent association between these variables and session duration, indicating that the shorter sessions were not responsible for the improved responding depicted in Figures 1–3.

The data on Jill's affect also indicated positive results with the functional outcome assignments. During the standard outcome assignments, the scores for Jill's happiness averaged 2.1, but this

increased to an average of 3.5 during the functional outcome sessions. The ratings for Jill's interest averaged 1.94 during the standard outcome condition, and 3.5 during the functional outcome condition.

DISCUSSION

The data reported in this article demonstrate that the behavior of each student improved when a curricular activity was modified such that it produced an outcome that was judged to be in accordance with the student's interests. The procedures were the same across the three students. That is, observations and interviews were conducted to identify classroom contexts and outcomes that were considered to be more relevant and that might evoke enhanced motivation from the students. These contexts and outcomes were then used to modify existing curricular activities that had been associated with

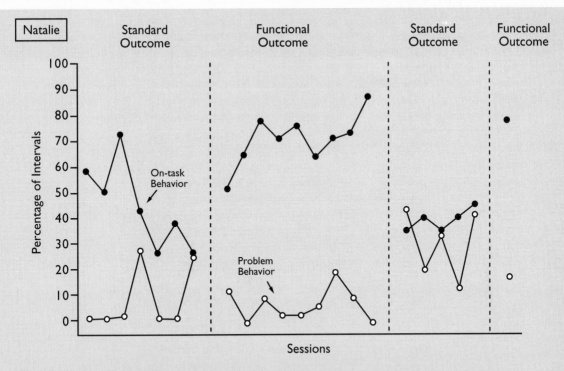

FIGURE 3   **Results for Natalie showing the effects of the standard versus functional outcome assignments on on-task and problem behavior.**

low levels of engagement and relatively high levels of problem behavior. When the activities were modified, the students' behavior improved. This was apparent across different tasks, with students who exhibited a diversity of characteristics and disability labels and with a variety of dependent measures (including task engagement, problem behavior, productivity, and affect).

The applied implications of these data are clear. That is, instructional activities can be modified, or individualized while maintaining the integrity of the instructional objective, and these modifications can produce notable improvements in student behavior. Although the ultimate value of the particular objectives that were targeted in this study (e.g., handwriting) may be questioned and although it is quite possible that the student's behavior may have been improved by simply eliminating these objectives, the important point is a more general one. Curricula for

all students must include instructional objectives, and there is a probability that some agreed upon objectives will be addressed through activities that are considered irrelevant or tedious. Indeed, many people's opinions of typical school activities might very well be characterized in that manner. This study offers an empirical demonstration that modifying curricula to align with students' interests can produce more desirable patterns of responding.

Although the procedural approach that was used in this study is straightforward, the conceptual basis for the effects are less clear. On one hand, it is possible to explain the phenomenon by describing it in terms of reinforcement. Some tasks are more reinforcing than others, and when the task is reinforcing, the student spends time engaged in the task and tends not to engage in problem behavior that is competitive and, quite likely, escape-motivated (Carr, Robinson, & Palumbo, 1990; Horner &

Billingsley, 1988). From this perspective, the operations of this investigation are conceptually similar to those described in the literature on preference (e.g., Dyer, 1987; Foster-Johnson et al., 1994) and, perhaps, choice making (e.g., Bambara et al., 1994; Dyer et al., 1990; Dunlap et al., 1994).

The notion that tasks differ in their properties of reinforcement does not explain the specific means that determine such distinctions. Tasks can differ along many dimensions including materials, response requirements, outcomes, familiarity, and the social context in which they are performed. Any combination of these variables, as well as their interaction with individual student characteristics, could affect the extent to which a task is reinforcing. Although the procedural operations in this investigation focused on the functionality of task outcomes, other ingredients could have contributed to results. For example, one possibility is that social reinforcers were more distinct in the experimental conditions for two of the participants. The outcome of Natalie's modified task was that she delivered her product to a second teacher who presumably expressed gratitude and appreciation that was not experienced in the standard activity. Jary's products, the cracker sandwiches, were consumed by his classmates later in the day. At that time, it is likely that some acknowledgement of Jary's role in preparing the sandwiches was announced. It would have been interesting to see if comparable results had occurred if the pens that were assembled in the standard activity condition had been similarly dispensed to the class. Although social reinforcers were not an obvious component in Jill's intervention, this, nevertheless, is an interpretation that must be regarded as partly responsible for the desirable effects. The effects that an activity or response has on the social environment, of course, must be considered as an important component in the relevance of most tasks and, therefore, the possible contribution of social reinforcement is compatible with an explanation that emphasizes curricular congruence with valued, real-life experiences.

The procedural variables in this study may suggest other explanatory perspectives. For example,

some investigations involving children with autism have demonstrated that responses leading directly to reinforcers were associated with enhanced performances, compared with more arbitrary response-reinforcer connections (Koegel & Williams, 1980; Williams, Koegel, & Egel, 1981). Although the procedures in this study did not manipulate response-reinforcer relationships explicitly or intentionally, it is reasonable to interpret the activities' outcomes as reinforcing events and, in this way, the tasks with the more functional outcomes could be viewed as being more direct.

It is important to recognize that this investigation was not designed to sort out the conceptual basis for the observed phenomenon. Indeed, when one examines the differences in the tasks and the ways in which they were manipulated, it is clear that a number of different variables might have been responsible for the beneficial effects. Future research on this topic would be well directed if it controlled for all variables (e.g., social reinforcement, preference for materials, etc.) aside from the perceived relevance of the tasks.

The contributions of the present data need to be qualified in certain respects. For example, even though the current participants displayed diverse characteristics including cognitive, emotional, and behavioral challenges, none experienced intellectual disabilities in the severe to profound range. It is not clear how such disabilities might limit the direct applicability of the present strategies. Another limitation may be that the functional assessment in this study did not include a functional analysis of the operant motivations for problem behavior. Although it is probable that the problem behaviors were governed by escape, this is an inference that was not specifically demonstrated. Future research could add a preliminary functional analysis (Iwata, Vollmer, & Zarcone, 1990) to help delineate the functions of individual topographies and, perhaps, help explain some of the response variability. In this respect, additional data would also be useful to substantiate the presence of functional relations, especially with respect to the governance of problem behaviors. Some of the present analyses for this category of dependent variable should be considered suggestive rather than definitive. Another stipulation pertains to the range of dependent variables that were included. In this study, data were collected on those variables (e.g., productivity, affect) that were identified as concerns for the individual students, without a priori consideration for their contribution to a unified research endeavor. Greater consistency across participants could facilitate comparison and synthesis of data across individuals.

The methods from this study produced another phenomenon that might warrant further investigation. In the second phases of the standard activity sessions for Jill and Natalie, the data show levels of problem behavior that were greater amplitude than the first phases. This is similar to a phenomenon described by Parsonson and Baer (1986) as "postreversal intensification," and appears to be a contrast effect (cf., Reynolds, 1961). After Jill and Natalie experienced the modified task condition, they apparently found the standard condition to be even more undesirable, probably because of the contrast with the more desirable condition. Although this particular manifestation of contrast differs from previous reports, in which reinforcement schedules vary across settings (Koegel, Egel, & Williams, 1980), this kind of pattern undoubtedly has many practical analogies and might merit further study.

The central argument that these data have to offer, however, pertains to curriculum design. The findings show that increased relevance contributed directly to improved behavior by three children with severe emotional, behavioral, and/or developmental needs. It should be noted that this verdict most likely applies to all children and, indeed, to all people who find themselves in instructional circumstances that are nebulous, tedious, or seemingly immaterial. It is hoped that further research will document the generality of these data and that educational practice will continue to infuse additional meaning into all instructional endeavors.

References

Bambara, L. M., Ager, C., & Koger, F. (1994). The effects of choice and task preference on the work performance of adults with severe disabilities. *Journal of Applied Behavior Analysis, 27,* 555–556.

Brown, L., Branston, M. B., Baumgart, D., Vincent, L., Falvey, M., & Schoeder, J. (1979). Using the characteristics of current and subsequent least restrictive environments as factors in the development of curricular content for severely handicapped adolescents and young adults. *Journal of Special Education, 13,* 81–90.

Carr, E. G., Robinson, S., & Palumbo, L. W. (1990). The wrong issue: Aversive versus nonaversive treatment. The right issue: Functional versus nonfunctional treatment. In A. C. Repp & N. Singh (Eds.), *Perspectives on the use of nonaversive interventions for persons with development disabilities* (pp. 361–379). DeKalb, IL: Sycamore.

Clarke, S., Dunlap, G., Foster-Johnson, L., Childs, K. E., Wilson, D., White, R., & Vera, A. (1995). Improving the conduct of students with behavioral disorders by incorporating student interests into curricular activities. *Behavioral Disorders, 20,* 221–237.

Dunlap, G. (1984). The influence of task variation and maintenance tasks on the learning and affect of autistic children. *Journal of Experimental Child Psychology, 37,* 41–64.

Dunlap, G., dePerczel, M., Clarke, S., Wilson, D., Wright, S., & Gomez, A. (1994). Choice making to promote adaptive behavior for students with emotional and behavioral challenges. *Journal of Applied Behavior Analysis, 27,* 505–518.

Dunlap, G., & Kern, L. (1993). Assessment and intervention for children within the instructional curriculum. In J. Reichle & D. Wacker, (Eds.), *Communicative approaches to the management of challenging behavior problems* (pp. 177–203). Baltimore: Paul H. Brookes.

Dunlap, G., Kern-Dunlap, L., Clarke, S., & Robbins, F. R. (1991). Functional assessment, curricular revision, and severe behavior problems. *Journal of Applied Behavior Analysis, 24,* 387–397.

Dunlap. G., Kern, L., dePerczel, M., Clarke, S., Wilson, D., Childs, K., White, R., & Falk, G. D. (1993). Functional analysis of classroom variables for students with emotional and behavioral disorders. *Behavioral Disorders, 18,* 275–291.

Dyer, K. (1987). The competition between autistic stereotyped behavior with usual and specially assessed reinforcers. *Research in Developmental Disabilities, 8,* 607–626.

Dyer, K., Dunlap, G., & Winterling, V. (1990). Effects of choice making on the serious problem behaviors of students with severe handicaps. *Journal of Applied Behavior Analysis, 23,* 515–524.

Falvey, M. A. (1986). *Community based curriculum.* Baltimore: Paul H. Brookes.

Ferro, J., Foster-Johnson, L., & Dunlap, G. (1994). *The relationship between curricular activities and problem behavior in students with intellectual disabilities.* Manuscript submitted for publication.

Foster-Johnson, L., Ferro, J., & Dunlap, G. (1994). Preferred curricular activities and reduced problem behaviors in students with intellectual disabilities. *Journal of Applied Behavior Analysis, 27,* 493–504.

Green, C. W., Reid, D. H., White, L. K., Halford, R. C., Brittain, D. P., & Gardner, S. M. (1988). Identifying reinforcers for persons with profound handicaps: Staff opinion versus systematic assessment of preferences. *Journal of Applied Behavior Analysis, 21,* 31–43.

Guess, D., Benson, H. S., & Siegel-Causey, E. (1985). Concepts and issues related to choice-making and autonomy among persons with severe disabilities. *Journal of the Association for Persons with Severe Handicaps, 10,* 79–86.

Horner, R. H., & Billingsley, F. F. (1988). The effect of competing behavior on the generalization and maintenance of adaptive behavior in applied settings. In R. H. Horner, G. Dunlap, & R. L. Koegel (Eds.), *Generalization and maintenance: Lifestyle changes in applied settings* (pp. 197–220). Baltimore, MD: Paul H. Brookes.

Horner, R. H., Sprague, J. R., Flannery, K. B. (1993). Building functional curricular for students with severe intellectual disabilities and severe problem behaviors. In R. Van Houten & S. Axelrod (Eds.), *Behavior analysis and treatment* (pp. 47–71). New York: Plenum Press.

Iwata, B. A., Vollmer, T. R., & Zarcone, J. R. (1990). The experimental (functional) analysis of behavior disorders: Methodology, applications, and limitations. In A. C. Repp & N. N. Singh (eds.) *Perspectives on the use of nonaversive and aversive interventions for persons with developmental disabilities* (pp. 301–330). Sycamore, IL: Sycamore Press.

Kern, L., Dunlap, G., Clarke, S., & Childs, K. E. (1994). Student-assisted functional assessment interview. *Diagnostique, 19,* 29–39.

Koegel, R., Dyer, K., & Bell, L. (1987). The influence of child-preferred activities on autistic children's social behavior. *Journal of Applied Behavior Analysis, 20,* 243–252.

Koegel, R. L., Egel, A. L., & Williams, J. A. (1980). Behavioral contrast and transfer across settings in teaching autistic children. *Journal of Experimental Child Psychology, 30,* 422–437.

Koegel, R. L., & Williams, J. A. (1980). Direct vs. indirect response-reinforcer relationships in teaching autistic children. *Journal of Abnormal Child Psychology, 8,* 537–547.

Munk, D. D., & Repp, A. C. (1994). The relationship between instructional variables and problem behavior: A review. *Exceptional Children, 60,* 390–401.

Neel, R. S., & Billingsley, F. F. (1989). *Impact: A functional curriculum handbook for students with moderate to severe disabilities.* Baltimore: Paul H. Brookes.

Pace, G. M., Ivancic, M. R., Edwards. G. L., Iwata, B. A., & Page, T. J. (1985). Assessment of stimulus preference and reinforcer value with profoundly retarded individuals. *Journal of Applied Behavior Analysis, 18,* 249–255.

Parsons, M. B., Reid, D. H., Reynolds, J., & Bumgarner, M. (1990). Effects of chosen versus assigned jobs on the work performance of persons with severe handicaps. *Journal of Applied Behavior Analysis, 23,* 253–258.

Parsonson, B. S., & Baer, D. M. (1986). The graphic analysis of data. In A. Poling & R. W. Fuqua (Eds.), *Research methods in applied behavior analysis: Issues and advances* (157–186). New York: Plenum Press.

Reynolds, G. S. (1961). Behavior contrast. *Journal of the Experimental Analysis of Behavior, 4,* 57–71.

Seybert, S., Dunlap, G., & Ferro, J. (in press). The effects of choice making on the problem behaviors of high school students with intellectual disabilities. *Journal of Behavioral Education.*

Sigafoos, J., & Dempsey, R. (1992). Assessing choice making among children with multiple disabilities. *Journal of Applied Behavior Analysis, 25,* 747–755.

Wacker, D. P., Berg, W. K., Wiggins, B., Muldoon, M., & Cavanaugh, J. (1985). Evaluation of reinforcer preferences for profoundly handicapped students. *Journal of Applied Behavior Analysis, 18,* 173–178.

Williams, J. A., Koegel, R. L., & Egel, A. L. (1981). Response-reinforcer relationships and improved learning in autistic children. *Journal of Applied Behavior Analysis, 14,* 53–60.

PART IV

QUALITATIVE RESEARCH IN EDUCATION

For a complete understanding of the findings and methods of educational research, you need to know how qualitative researchers carry out studies of educational phenomena. Therefore, Part IV of the book describes the typical characteristics of qualitative research studies and several specialized qualitative research traditions.

Chapter 10 explains how qualitative researchers design and carry out case studies to explore educational phenomena. The chapter also introduces specialized qualitative research traditions.

Chapter 11 describes the qualitative research tradition of ethnographic research. It explains how ethnographers make in-depth studies of individuals in their natural settings in order to explore the cultural context of educational phenomena.

In Chapter 12 we describe the qualitative research tradition of critical-theory research. We show how criticalists' commitment to the emancipation of oppressed groups from dominant power structures operating within a culture contributes to educational research and practice.

Chapter 13 covers historical research, a primarily qualitative research endeavor that involves the study of past phenomena and their relationship to present conditions.

CHAPTER 10
CASE STUDIES IN QUALITATIVE RESEARCH

Nitza Goldberg is returning to the university to earn an administrator's license and master's degree so that she can become a school principal. During Nitza's program of studies, she developed an interest in the problems faced by principals of language-immersion schools, which provide some content instruction in English and other content instruction in a second language.

While taking a research course, Nitza decided that for her master's research project she might do a quantitative study of language-immersion school principals, involving administration of a questionnaire to a nationwide sample of such principals. However, she saw two drawbacks to that approach: (a) there are still only a few language-immersion schools in the country, so her sample would be very small; (b) a questionnaire is poorly suited for some of the questions that interest her, including: What unique problems arise in administering language-immersion schools? What solutions do principals typically try, and with what success? How do principals cope with problems that linger on, with no easy solution?

As Nitza's research class proceeded, its focus shifted from quantitative research to qualitative research and the case study method. It was then that she realized that a case study would be an ideal master's project for addressing her questions and promoting her professional development.

In this chapter, you will learn why qualitative research and the case study method is particularly appropriate for Nitza's interests. Also, the chapter will broaden your view of what constitutes educational research and will enable you to comprehend and evaluate case study reports.

OBJECTIVES

After studying this chapter, you will be able to

1. describe the primary characteristics and purposes of case studies.
2. describe how qualitative researchers select cases for study.
3. describe the data-collection methods that typically are used in case study research.
4. compare the purposes and procedures of interpretational, structural, and reflective data analysis.
5. describe criteria that can be used to judge the soundness of case study findings.
6. explain two approaches to determining the applicability of case study findings to other settings.
7. describe the characteristics of a qualitative research tradition.
8. describe three broad areas of investigation with which qualitative research traditions are concerned.

KEY TERMS

applicability
audit trail
case
case study
causal pattern
chain of evidence
coding check
construct
contact summary form
disconfirming case analysis
document analysis
emic perspective
etic perspective

fieldwork
in-depth study
interpretational analysis
interpretivist epistemology
key informant
member checking
multiple-case design
multivocality
outlier
phenomenon
positivism
purposeful sampling
qualitative research tradition

reflective analysis
reflexivity
relational pattern
representativeness check
structural analysis
tacit knowledge
theme
thick description
triangulation
unit of analysis
verisimilitude

THE NATURE OF QUALITATIVE RESEARCH

As we explained in Chapter 1, much of qualitative research is based on an inter-pretivist epistemology. In this view of knowledge, social reality is seen as a set of meanings that are constructed by the individuals who participate in that reality. Any social phenomenon, such as a high school football game, does not have an independent existence apart from its participants; rather, it will have different meanings for the individuals who participate in the phenomenon or who sub-sequently learn about it. A major purpose of qualitative research is to discover the nature of those meanings. The primary method of investigation is in-depth, field-based studies of particular instances of the phenomenon, known as *cases*.

Qualitative research involves a very different world view than positivist epistemology, which characterized most prior investigation in philosophy and science until late in the twentieth century. Positivist epistemology assumes that there is a real world "out there" that can be known by using similar investigative strategies as those that guide the physical sciences. The growth of qualitative research reflects in part a reaction against the intellectual and scientific constraints of positivism, and an embrace of more naturalistic ways of knowing that typify non-Western cultural perspectives.

We suggest that you review Table 1.1 in Chapter 1, which summarizes the ways in which qualitative researchers characterize and investigate the social environment. Qualitative research sometimes is called *case study research* because of its focus on cases, but not all case studies reflect the interpretivist epistemology. In this book we use the term *qualitative research* to refer to the entire body of research that is guided by interpretivist epistemology.

The Purposes of Case Studies

Researchers conduct case studies in order to describe, explain, or evaluate particular social phenomena. Let us consider each of these purposes as they apply to educational research.

1. *Description*. In many case studies the researchers' main purpose is to depict and conceptualize a phenomenon clearly. These case studies usually provide a thick description of the phenomenon, that is, a set of statements that re-create the situation and its context, and give readers a sense of the meanings and intentions inherent in that situation. The term *thick description* originated in anthropology to refer to a complete, literal description of a cultural phenomenon, but it now is widely used in qualitative research.

2. *Explanation*. The purpose of some case studies is to explain particular phenomena. The researchers look for patterns among phenomena within a case or across cases. For example, researchers might observe that American teachers in international schools vary in (a) their perceptions of teaching in such schools and (b) their perceptions of the local culture. If the researchers find that the teachers' perceptions of teaching are related to their perceptions of the culture, they can say that a pattern has been discovered. If one variation appears to have a causal effect on the others, it is referred to as a *causal pattern*. If the cause is not specified, it is referred to as a *relational pattern*.

3. *Evaluation*. Case study researchers have developed several qualitative approaches to evaluation (see Chapter 14). In each approach, researchers conduct a case study about certain phenomena and make judgments about those phenomena. For example, a historical case study carried out by Larry Cuban (1997) bears a title reflecting the case study's evaluative flavor: "Change Without Reform: The Case of Stanford University School of Medicine, 1908–1990."

As we just explained, case studies vary in purpose. They also vary in the degree to which they rely on particular qualitative research traditions. Many case studies are not guided by a specific theoretical framework, nor do they use a particular substantive discipline, such as linguistics or philosophy, in their attempts to clarify the meaning of the case. Other case studies are embedded within one or more qualitative research traditions. Evelyn Jacob (1987) describes a qualitative research tradition as "a group of scholars who agree among themselves on the nature of the universe they are examining, on legitimate questions and problems to study, and on legitimate techniques to seek solutions" (pp. 1–2). In this book we use the term *tradition* also to refer to the body of research and theory generated by those scholars. Later in the chapter we introduce the primary traditions that have been used in qualitative educational research.

How Case Studies Can Be Applied

As an educational practitioner, you might ask what you can learn from qualitative research case studies. We would respond by noting that case studies resemble stories in works of literature or "human interest" accounts that enliven news reporting, because they reflect the nature of reality as experienced by those who have been there. Reading about cases that are either similar to or different from your own experience in education can deepen your understanding of the educational phenomena that you experience in your work. Although case studies tend not to make definite claims about preferred courses of action, their insights and speculations can help you develop the capacity to explore and refine your educational practice.

Discovery of Constructs, Themes, and Patterns

Case study researchers often look for constructs to bring order to descriptive data and to help them relate their data to other research findings reported in the literature. A construct is a concept that is inferred from observed phenomena and that is assumed to underlie those phenomena. For example, Jean Piaget made sense of the case study data that he collected about children's thinking by developing such constructs as assimilation, conservation, and operational thinking.

The discovery of constructs in qualitative data can be a significant outcome of a case study. In the case study that is reprinted in this chapter, Paul Schempp (1995) used constructs from an existing theory to classify his data about the professional knowledge used by the teacher he studied (Bob), but he also developed other constructs. One construct, labeled *knowledge acquired to manage classroom organization and operation*, helped Schempp understand certain aspects of Bob's knowledge-seeking behavior.

Case study researchers add further depth to their descriptions by searching for themes present in the phenomena they investigate. A theme is a salient, recurrent feature of a case. One such theme reported by Schempp is Bob's habitual search for practical pedagogical knowledge: "Content that could be incorporated into [Bob's] existing classroom routines and rituals was highly valued" (p. 243 in the original article). Schempp found, too, that concern for the practical was a recurrent theme in other research on teachers' knowledge construction: ". . . Bob is not alone in his regard for knowledge that is easily imported into existing classroom practices. . ." (p. 243 in the original article).

Patterns represent possible relationships among phenomena, some of which may be causal in nature. Schempp's description of Bob's activities in and outside of class serve to clarify aspects of Bob's definition of his professional role. As you will discover in reading the case study, the demands on Bob as a sports coach appear to have an effect on his teaching activities. Thus a presumed causal pattern has been identified.

Key Characteristics of a Case Study

To explain the characteristics of a case study, we will refer to a study by Dona Kagan, Mary Beth Dennis, Mary Igou, Polly Moore, and Karen Sparks (1993). The study involved the effects of a staff development program on the professional lives of the teachers who participated in it. Kagan conducted an audio-taped interview with four teachers who were in or had recently completed the program, and these teachers subsequently became coauthors of her research report.

In the following sections we show how this study reflects four key character-istics of case study research: (1) study of a phenomenon by focusing on specific instances, or cases; (2) in-depth study of each case; (3) study of a phenomenon in its natural context; and (4) representation of both the researchers' (etic) per-spective and the participants' (emic) perspective.

The Study of Particular Instances.   A case study is conducted to shed light on a particular *phenomenon*, that is, a set of processes, events, individuals, or other things of interest to the researchers. Examples of educational phenomena are instructional programs, curricula, staff roles, and school events. The researchers must first clarify the phenomenon of interest before they can select for intensive study a particular instance of the phenomenon, that is, a case.

In the Kagan study, the phenomenon of interest was school-university part-nerships, and more specifically partnerships that strengthen the staff-develop-ment capacity of local school districts. The case selected for study was the Teacher in Residence (TIR) Program at the University of Alabama. Experienced elementary teachers become teachers in residence at the university for two years, teaching and supervising in the university's preservice teacher education program. They then return to their districts with knowledge to help them design in-service staff development programs.

A phenomenon has many aspects, so researchers must select a focus for investigation. The focus is the aspect, or aspects, of the phenomenon on which data collection and analysis will concentrate. Previous research on school-uni-versity partnerships tended to focus on their policies and structures. The focus of the Kagan study was different: It focused on the effects of the partnership program on the professional lives of the teachers.

In some case studies, multiple instances of the phenomenon are studied. Each instance might be analyzed as a separate unit. If Kagan had studied several school-university partnerships around the United States, school-uni-versity partnerships would be the unit of analysis. In fact, four teachers from the TIR program at Kagan's university were selected for study. Therefore, the unit of analysis was the participating teacher, and four such units were studied.

In-Depth Study of the Case.   A case study involves collection of a substantial amount of data about the specific case, or cases, selected to represent the phenomenon. These data are mainly verbal statements, images, or physical objects, but some quantitative data also might be collected. Data typically are collected over an extended time period, with several methods of data collection.

In Kagan's study, the researcher conducted 90-minute interviews with each teacher. Kagan audiotaped, transcribed, and analyzed each interview in order to provide a coherent narrative of the teacher's experience. She returned two pre-liminary drafts of the narrative to the interviewees for correction, amendment, and editing. Thus, both the researcher and the teachers were involved in "an iterative process of constructing meaning. . ." (p. 428). As coauthors, the four teachers also were invited to modify and edit the entire article.

We can infer from this description that the narratives were developed by the researcher after the interviews, but they then involved continuing dialogue between the teachers and the researcher and among the teachers. The data thus reflect in-depth study of the teachers' experience of the TIR program, although involving a relatively brief period of data collection.

Study of a Phenomenon in Its Natural Context.   Jerome Kirk and Marc Miller (1986) define qualitative research as an approach to social science research that involves "watching people in their own territory and interacting with them in their own language, on their own terms" (p. 9). Consistent with this definition, case studies typically involve fieldwork in which the researchers interact with research participants in their natural settings.

The final report of Kagan's case study includes a narrative for each teacher ("Mary Beth's Experience," "Karen's Story," "Mary's Reflections," and "Polly's Story"). These narratives position each teacher's interview statements about her program experience in the context of her past and current life as an elementary school teacher. For example, the segment on Mary reveals that her motivation to serve as a teacher in residence was to give more realism to the university's teacher education preservice program. The narrative describes Mary's positive and negative experiences as a teacher in residence, and how they affected her perceptions of classroom teaching and her plans upon returning to the elementary school classroom. This narrative, and the others, reflect the teachers' language rather than a reconstruction of that language in particular pedagogical or theoretical terminology.

Representation of Both the Emic and Etic Perspectives.   Case studies seek to develop an understanding of a complex phenomenon as experienced by its participants. In other words, the researcher must come to view the phenomenon as the participants view it. The participants' viewpoint is called the *emic perspective*. Typically, researchers obtain the emic perspective through informal conversations with the case study participants, and by observing them as they behave naturally in the field.

At the same time, the researchers maintain their own perspective as investigators of the phenomenon. Their viewpoint as outsiders, which is called the *etic perspective*, helps them make conceptual and theoretical sense of the case, and to report the findings so that their contribution to the research literature is clear.

The last section of the university-school partnership study ("Dona's Commentary and Analysis") reflects Kagan's use of her own past experience as a professor of education in the analysis and interpretation of the data obtained from the teachers. This commentary provides the etic perspective. The four teachers' involvement in data collection and in the report of the findings ensured that the emic perspective was represented as well.

SELECTION OF CASES FOR STUDY

Michael Patton (1990) describes the procedures that case study researchers use to select their cases as purposeful sampling. The goal of purposeful sampling is to select individuals for case study who are likely to be "information-rich" with respect to the researchers' purposes. Thus, instead of trying to spend time with every individual in the field setting, case study researchers usually search for key informants. These are individuals who have special knowledge or perspectives that make them especially important in obtaining the emic perspective. In Schempp's case study, the case was a male high school physical education teacher. The researcher spent considerable time talking to him and also to a key informant—a female physical education teacher at the same high school.

Researchers generally follow a systematic sampling strategy to select the case or cases to be studied. As you read a case study, you should look for information that will help you determine the sampling strategy that was used. Having this information will help you decide whether and how to apply the case findings to your specific situation.

Table 10.1 summarizes 15 purposeful sampling strategies described by Patton. All these strategies can be used to select multiple cases for study. If the researchers choose to study just one case, only some of them are appropriate (i.e., the 11 strategies for which the "Cases selected" listed in column 2 begin with the word *Cases* rather than with the words *Multiple cases*). In examining Table 10.1, you will see that the strategies are grouped into four categories based on their underlying rationale.

The first category of sampling strategies in Table 10.1 involves selecting cases that represent a key characteristic of the phenomenon that the researchers wish to study. For example, suppose that the researchers are interested in studying teachers' power.

In extreme or deviant case sampling, a case, or cases, would be selected that possess the characteristic to a very high or low extent. In one case study of teacher power, George Noblit (1993) selected an elementary school teacher who was an opinion maker in her building, was highly regarded by students' parents, and was the teacher who assumed charge of the school whenever the principal was out of the building. Thus she could be viewed as a model teacher who exhibits an extremely high degree of power. The findings for an extreme case can provide understanding of both "model" cases and of more typical cases. By contrast, another researcher might choose to study teachers who exhibit high, but not extreme, power (intensity sampling), teachers who are perceived as "average" in their display of power (typical case sampling), or teachers who fit other sampling strategies in the first category.

The second category in Table 10.1 includes five sampling strategies reflecting a conceptual rationale. Researchers choose among these strategies based on the particular rationale that they have chosen to guide their research. The first three strategies involve rationales related to the researchers' theoretical conceptions of the meaning of the case. To return to our example of power among teachers, researchers might select teachers who make it possible to test whether a program

TABLE 10.1   **Purposeful Sampling Strategies Used in Qualitative Research**

Sampling strategy	Cases selected
Strategies to select cases representing a key characteristic	
1. Extreme/deviant case	Cases that exhibit the characteristic to an extreme high or low extent
2. Intensity	Cases that exhibit the characteristic to a high or low, but not extreme, extent
3. Typical case	Cases that exhibit the characteristic to an average or typical extent
4. Maximum variation	Multiple cases that exhibit the entire range of variation in the characteristic
5. Stratified	Multiple cases that exhibit the characteristic at predefined points of variation
6. Homogeneous	Multiple cases that represent the characteristic to a similar extent
7. Purposeful random	Multiple cases selected at random from an accessible population
Strategies reflecting a conceptual rationale	
8. Critical case	Cases that provide a crucial test of a theory, program, or other phenomenon
9. Theory-based/operational construct	Cases that manifest a particular theoretical construct
10. Confirming/disconfirming case	Cases that are likely to confirm/disconfirm findings from previous case studies
11. Criterion	Cases that satisfy an important criterion
12. Politically important case	Cases that are well known/politically important
Emergent strategies	
13. Opportunistic	Cases that are selected based on the data already collected in the case study
14. Snowball/chain	Cases identified by cases who have already been studied
Strategy lacking a rationale	
15. Convenience	Cases that are selected simply because they are available

designed to empower teachers was effective (critical case sampling), teachers who illustrate a particular conceptualization of power in organizations (theory-based/operational construct sampling), teachers who enable the researchers to test the replicability of previous research findings (confirming/disconfirming case sampling), teachers who satisfy a specific criterion, or politically important teachers.

We describe the next group of two strategies as emergent, because both involve a decision to select cases based on data that already have been collected. For example, the researchers might make initial observations of teachers rated as high, medium, and low in power. They then might decide to focus only on the teachers rated unusually high and low in power. Thus they have made an opportunistic switch from a maximum variation sampling strategy to an extreme case strategy.

Another emergent strategy shown in the table is snowball sampling, in which researchers ask individuals from whom they already have collected data to recommend others who can provide useful information about the phenomena of interest. Thus, the sample increases in size (i.e., it "snowballs") as individuals mention other individuals as potential key informants.

The final strategy listed in Table 10.1 acknowledges that some researchers might select cases for study based primarily on convenience. For example, they might select teachers at a school where they formerly worked, because they believe that it will be easy to obtain the teachers' agreement to participate in the study. Patton observes that convenience is the least desirable basis for selecting cases to study.

DATA COLLECTION IN CASE STUDY RESEARCH

In collecting data, qualitative researchers use whatever methods are appropriate to their purpose. They might begin a case study with one method of data collection and gradually shift to, or add, other methods. They might use multiple methods to collect data about the same phenomenon in order to enhance the soundness of their findings—a process called *triangulation* (explained later in the chapter). Below we describe the methods of data collection most often used in case studies.

1. *Observation*. In observing field participants, some researchers might tape-record or videotape the sessions, or take extensive field notes. Many researchers strive to become participant observers, meaning that they personally interact with the field participants in field activities in order to build empathy and trust and to further their understanding of the phenomenon. These researchers generally take notes on their observations only after they have left the field.

Case study researchers might also make observations of material culture. For example, Peter Manning and Betsy Cullum-Swan (1994) did a case study of McDonald's restaurants using the qualitative research tradition of semiotics, which investigates how both verbal and configural sign systems convey meaning. They studied the meaning of McDonald's sign systems as conveyed by such elements as the design of the menu board, lighting, outdoor playgrounds, food containers, and utensils, and the use of the prefix "Mc-" to label food items.

2. *Interviews*. Researchers often conduct interviews of field participants in case studies. Usually the questions are open-ended, meaning that respondents can answer freely in their own terms rather than selecting from a fixed set of responses. An open-ended interview can be informal, occurring in the natural course of conversation. If many respondents are being interviewed, or if more than one interviewer is involved, the researchers might choose to use a general interview guide that outlines a set of topics to be explored with each respondent, or a standardized interview format.

Focus groups are a form of group interview in which a number of people participate in a discussion that is guided by a skilled interviewer. Because the respondents can talk to and hear each other, they are likely to express feelings or opinions that might not emerge if they were interviewed individually. Focus groups sometimes are used by researchers to explore such phenomena as individuals' reactions to educational programs and practices.

3. *Document and media analysis.* Case study researchers often study written communications that are found in field settings. Consistent with interpretivist epistemology, many of these researchers believe that the meaning of a text can vary depending on the reader, the time period, the context in which the text appears, and so forth. For example, G. Genevieve Patthey-Chavez (1993) used documents in her case study of the cultural conflict between Latino students and their mainstream teachers in a Los Angeles high school. In one of her analyses, she interpreted a local newspaper article as revealing the schools' mission to assimilate immigrant students into the mainstream, whether the students wanted to be assimilated or not.

Official records and personal documents are widely used in historical research. For example, in the case study of medical education that we mentioned earlier in the chapter, Cuban (1997) described his main sources as the annual announcements and bulletins of courses published at Stanford University every year since 1910.

4. *Questionnaires.* Case study researchers typically choose to use questionnaires when individual contact with every research participant is not feasible, and the research data to be collected are not deeply personal. A well-designed questionnaire also can elicit in-depth information, as illustrated in a study by Ismail Yahya and Gary Moore (1985). These researchers designed a questionnaire to collect qualitative data that included open-form questions calling for lengthy replies. They sent the respondents an audiotape with the questionnaire, asking respondents to record their responses on the tape.

5. *Tests and other self-report measures.* While more typical of quantitative research, tests can serve a useful purpose in qualitative research. For example, in a case study of the mismatch between a teacher's expectations and the actual reading achievement of two of her first-grade students, Claude Goldenberg (1992) combined qualitative and quantitative methods of data collection. The researcher made qualitative observations of each child's classroom behaviors, and administered two standardized tests of reading achievement to each child. Data from both types of measures yielded key findings. The teacher's greater involvement with the child about whom she initially had low expectations based on the child's achievement test score actually appeared to help this girl to improve her reading achievement. The other girl, about whom the teacher initially had positive expectations, remained in a low reading group.

Reflexivity in Data Collection

The role of case study researchers in data collection is complex. The researchers themselves are the primary "measuring instruments," relying heavily on personal observation, empathy, intuition, judgment, and other psychological processes to grasp the meaning of the phenomenon as it is experienced by the individuals and groups in the field.

In some case study reports the researchers make explicit their role in the data-collection process by describing their personal experiences and reactions in the field. They might also describe how their beliefs and personal background influence the phenomena that they are studying. The researchers' analysis of their own role as constructors and interpreters of the social reality being studied is called *reflexivity*.

Alan Peshkin (1988) illustrates the process of reflexivity in his case study of a multi-ethnic high school. In his published report, he describes a number of "I's" that he had listed during data collection to characterize different aspects of himself, and explains how they affected his findings. The *Ethnic Maintenance I*, based on his identity as a Jew, approved of individuals maintaining their ethnic identity. The *Justice-seeking I* was aroused when Peshkin repeatedly heard the community in which the high school was located being criticized by both residents and nonresidents. This aspect of Peshkin's self strengthened his desire to convey the community in a more generous light.

DATA ANALYSIS IN CASE STUDY RESEARCH

Even a modest case study is likely to generate many pages of field notes, interview transcripts, and documents obtained from the field setting. Suppose there are 200 such pages, each containing 250 words. That totals 50,000 words. How do the researchers analyze all those words in order to produce significant, meaningful findings? Several approaches can be used, which Renata Tesch (1990) classified into three types: interpretational, structural, and reflective analysis. Each is explained below.

Interpretational Analysis

Interpretational analysis involves a systematic set of procedures to code and classify qualitative data to ensure that the important constructs, themes, and patterns emerge. These procedures can be carried out manually, but use of a computer with appropriate software programs makes the task much more manageable.

The steps of interpretational analysis are: (1) preparing a database containing all the data (field notes, documents, transcripts, records, etc.) collected during the case study; (2) numbering each line of text sequentially and then dividing the text into meaningful segments (e.g., in the analysis of interview data, each question plus the participant's response might be a separate segment); (3) developing meaningful categories to code the data; (4) coding each segment by any and all categories that apply to it; (5) cumulating all the segments that have been coded by a given category; and (6) generating constructs that emerge from the categories.

We will refer to the case study reprinted in this chapter to illustrate the process of interpretational analysis. Schempp defined his research problem as an effort to discover the criteria used by an experienced teacher to acquire the knowledge necessary to teach. In exploring this research problem, Schempp used several data-collection methods to create a thick description of the case: nonparticipant observation of the teacher, Bob, during the school day; analysis of artifacts and documents, including a curriculum guide to which Bob occasionally referred; videotaping some of Bob's classes and asking Bob to comment on what he was thinking about during the videotaped events; and interviews of Bob and of one of his teaching colleagues.

In analyzing the data obtained from his case study, Schempp began with a model of seven types of knowledge that teachers need. Schempp used four of these types of knowledge as categories, along with a category that he defined, to code his data. He revised the category scheme until all the data could be classified within the scheme with no redundancy of categories.

Schempp states that the use of constant comparison helped him clarify the meaning of each category, create sharp distinctions between categories, and decide which categories were most important to the case study. In the method of constant comparison, the researchers identify a set of empirical indicators (behavioral actions/events) that are contained in the data; make comparisons to identify similarities and differences between the indicators; and tentatively define categories and related concepts that emerge from the process. This process continues until all the indicators have been categorized.

We can infer that Schempp, in carrying out his case study, recorded many instances (i.e., indicators) of Bob's teaching practice. In using the method of constant comparison, he would have compared each instance with other instances to determine what tentative category of Bob's knowledge-seeking behavior it fit best. As he explains in his report, he continued to refine the set of categories until he was able to code all the data into the five categories he describes.

Schempp describes the category of classroom organization and operation as "a dominant form of Bob's knowledge" (p. 238 in the original article). This category reflects an important construct that emerged from Schempp's analysis of Bob's knowledge acquisition. Another important construct involved Bob's coaching responsibilities, which created competing demands on Bob's school time:

> Bob did not actively pursue knowledge that directly affected his instructional practices. . . . Bob's teaching behavior was a nonissue with almost everybody in the school. . . . His work environment conspired to inform Bob that the operation of the school as a system took precedence over student learning in a physical education class (pp. 240–241 in the original article).

This inference represents a causal pattern, namely that Bob's coaching responsibilities influenced his apparent choice to assign a lower priority to the acquisition of knowledge to inform his teaching behavior.

Schempp's data analysis also identified themes, which in this case refer to the criteria that Bob used to determine what knowledge he needed to carry out various aspects of his professional role as a high school teacher and coach. With regard to Bob's in-class teaching behavior, for example, Schempp inferred that "Much of Bob's teaching behavior was characterized by well rehearsed, time-worn rituals" (p. 240 in the original article).

Figure 10.1 illustrates the blending of data collection and interpretational analysis that is typical of case study research. It shows a contact summary form used in a case study described by Matthew Miles and A. Michael Huberman (1994). The form summarizes eight salient points from the contact. Some points probably were taken from the researchers' field notes, and others might have come to mind when they reviewed the notes. The researchers treated each point on the contact summary form as a data chunk and coded it, using a theme coding system.

The right column in Figure 10.1 shows how each point was coded by the specific "theme/aspect" to which it relates. Some points were coded with more

Contact Summary

Type of contact: Mtg. **Principals**   **Ken's office**   **4/2/76**   Site **Westgate**
                     Who, what group   place   date

               Phone _____   _____   _____   Coder   **MM**
                     With whom, by whom   place   date

               Inf. Int. _____   _____   _____   Date coded **4/18/76**
                     With whom, by whom   place   date

1. Pick out the most salient points in the contact. Number in order on this sheet and note page number on which point appears. Number point in text of write-up. Attach theme or aspect to each point. Invent themes where no existing ones apply and asterisk those. Comment may also be included in double parentheses.

Page	Salient Points	Themes/Aspects
1	1. Staff decisions have to be made by April 30.	Staff
1	2. Teachers will have to go out of their present grade-level assignment when they transfer.	Staff/Resource Mgmt.
2	3. Teachers vary in their willingness to integrate special education students into their classrooms—some teachers are "a pain in the elbow."	*Resistance
2	4. Ken points out that tentative teacher assignment lists got leaked from the previous meeting (implicitly deplores this).	Internal Communic.
2	5. Ken says, "Teachers act as if they had the right to decide who should be transferred." (would make outcry)	Power Distrib.
2	6. Tacit/explicit decision: "It's our decision to make." (voiced by Ken, agreed by Ed)	Power Distrib/ Conflict Mgmt.
2	7. Principals and Ken, John, and Walter agree that Ms. Epstein is a "bitch."	*Stereotyping
2	8. Ken decides not to tell teachers ahead of time (now) about transfers ("because then we'd have a fait accompli").	Plan for Planning/ Time Mgmt.

FIGURE 10.1   **Contact summary form: salient points in a field contact, with theme codes assigned**

Source. Adapted from Figure 4.2 on p. 54 in: Miles, M. B., & Huberman, A. M. (1994). *Qualitative data analysis: An expanded sourcebook* (2nd ed.). Thousand Oaks, CA: Sage. Reprinted by permission of Sage Publications, Inc.

than one theme; e.g., point #6 was judged to relate both to power distribution and to conflict management. Thus the researchers must already have made a list of themes/aspects to describe the phenomenon that they were investigating, from which they obtained these two codes. To code point #7 the researchers invented a new theme (signified by the asterisk), labeled *stereotyping*. Thus the researchers were continuing to identify themes as they collected and analyzed new data.

Structural Analysis

Like interpretational analysis, structural analysis involves a precise set of procedures for analyzing qualitative data. In structural analysis, however, the patterns that are identified do not need to be inferred from the data. Instead, they are inherent features of the discourse, text, or events that the researchers are studying.

To understand the distinction between inherent and inferred patterns, consider this segment of conversation between a Spanish teacher and a student:

Teacher: What does *la casa* mean?
Student: House.
Teacher: That's right. *La casa* means house.

A qualitative researcher conducting a structural analysis of this interaction might note certain features of it, such as:

1. The sequence of speakers within this instructional event was teacher, student, teacher.
2. Each of the teacher's utterances contained more words than the student's utterance.
3. Four Spanish words were uttered.
4. Three words (*la, casa, house*) were uttered twice, and the other six words were uttered once.

You will note that these features are inherent in the data. The researchers need to engage in very little, if any, inference to arrive at these findings.

In contrast, researchers using interpretational analysis overlay a structure of meaning on the data. For example, suppose that researchers were conducting an interpretational analysis of how students receive feedback in the classroom. To analyze their data, they might develop several feedback categories, such as informational feedback, praise, criticism, and ambiguous feedback. Using this category scheme, the researchers might code the segment of conversation as an instance of informational feedback, because of the utterance, "That's right. *La casa* means house." This classification is not inherent in the teacher's utterance, but rather it is an inference from the data made by the researchers.

Structural analysis is used in narrative analysis, ethnoscience, and other qualitative research traditions. It can be used to investigate a variety of educational phenomena, for example, changes in students' speech patterns over the course of schooling, the sequence of events in children's stories, the organization of the parts of textbooks, and movement patterns within a school building.

The reporting of findings from structural or interpretational analyses of case study findings typically follows a conventional format (introduction, review of literature, methodology, results, and discussion), and the researcher's voice is silent or subdued. This reporting style thus is similar to that used in reporting quantitative research studies (see Chapter 5).

Reflective Analysis

Reflective analysis refers to a process in which qualitative researchers rely mainly on their own intuition and personal judgment to analyze the data that have been collected. It does not involve the use of either an explicit category system or a prescribed set of procedures.

One way to understand reflective analysis is to compare it with artistic endeavors. The artist reflects on phenomena and then portrays them so as to reveal both their surface features and essences. Many case study researchers engage in similar reflections and portrayals. Reflective analysis also can involve criticism. Art critics might study a piece of art in order to develop an appreciation of its aesthetic elements and "message," but also to make critical judgments about its artistic merit. Some case studies that are carried out as educational evaluations (see Chapter 14) follow a similar process of critical appreciation. These evaluative studies help educators and policy makers understand the features and purposes of educational programs, products, and methods, and also to appreciate their strengths and weaknesses. Just as an art or literary critic develops reflective ability with experience, an educational evaluator must build up a store of experience in order to use reflective analysis wisely.

In reflective reporting, researchers often weave case study data into a story. For example, Harry Wolcott (1990) conducted an extensive case study of a school dropout, whom he called Brad. The story of Brad starts in present time, and then recounts earlier events in his life to clarify the broader and narrower themes around which the story is organized. One theme is "in the chute," a phrase to describe living in a situation that appears to be leading the individual toward prison. Wolcott's voice is heard clearly in the last two sections of the report, where he presents his interpretation of the case. Wolcott (1994) notes that he used this sequence so that, "By the time readers arrive at the point where I offer *my* thoughts as to what might be done [about school dropouts], I want to be sure they have a sufficient background to form their own assessment of Brad and his circumstances" (p. 64).

Much of Wolcott's report consists of direct quotes of Brad's statements, made in informal conversations with the researcher. For example:

I guess being sneaky means I always try to get away with something. There doesn't have to be any big reason. I used to tell the kid I was hanging around with, "I don't steal stuff because I need it. I just like to do it for some excitement" (p. 77).

Some case study researchers use more dramatic methods to convey findings, including poetry, oral readings, comedy, satire, and visual presentations. Laura Richardson (1992) includes a poem that she wrote to convey her understanding of an unmarried mother whom she had studied. The poem uses only the mother's language, as arranged by Richardson. It begins:

> The most important thing
> to say   is that
> I grew up in the South.
> Being Southern shapes
> aspirations   shapes
> what you think you are
> and what you think you're going to be.
>
> (*When I hear myself, my Ladybird*
> *kind of accent on tape, I think, OH Lord.*
> *You're from Tennessee* (p. 126).*

Richardson observed that case study researchers who use unconventional reporting genres typically have a postmodern sensibility. As we explained in Chapter 1, postmodernism questions all claims to authoritative methods of inquiry and reporting, including mainstream scientific reports. A postmodernist thus would view poetry as just as legitimate for reporting case study findings as the standard journal-article format used by case study researchers writing in an analytic reporting style.

CRITERIA FOR EVALUATING CASE STUDIES

Researchers who conduct case studies differ in their views about whether case study methods and findings should meet the criteria of validity, reliability, and generalizability that are used to judge the soundness of quantitative research. This chapter focuses on case studies carried out according to interpretivist epistemology, which rejects the notion of an external reality that can be discovered through objective means. Interpretivists believe that all the researchers, research participants, and readers of a case study report will have their own unique interpretation of the meaning and value of a case study. Researchers who embrace interpretivism do not judge their case studies using traditional notions of validity and reliability, but instead use criteria that are meant to demonstrate the credibility and trustworthiness of their findings and methods. Below we describe 11 such criteria that will help you evaluate case studies. We have grouped them into three categories: criteria reflecting sensitivity to readers' needs, criteria based on the use of sound research methods, and criteria reflecting thoroughness of data collection and analysis. Appendix 5 contains a list of questions that also can be used in evaluating qualitative research.

Criteria Reflecting Sensitivity to Readers' Needs

1. Strong Chain of Evidence. The readers of case study reports need to be able to make their own assessment of the soundness of the findings that are reported. Researchers can help readers do so by providing clear, meaningful links between the research questions, the raw data, the analysis of these data, and the conclusions drawn from the data. Robert Yin (1989) refers to these links as a *chain of evidence*. The principle underlying a chain of evidence is that readers of the case study should be able to easily follow the derivation of any evidence from the initial research questions to the ultimate case study conclusions.

Researchers can make the chain of evidence explicit by providing an audit trail in the case study report. An audit trail is a complete documentation of the research process used in the case study. The items to document might include: (1) the sources and methods of recording raw data, (2) process notes, (3) the development of the instruments and procedures used to collect data, (4) data reduction and analysis products, and (5) data reconstruction and synthesis products. A case study report would be very long if it included all these materials, but small, representative samples of the most important materials can be provided in a methodology section or appendix.

2. Truthfulness. Readers of a case study report want some assurance that the researchers' descriptions are faithful representations of the phenomena that were studied. The goal is to achieve verisimilitude, which Patricia Adler and Peter Adler (1994) describe as "a style of writing that draws the reader so closely into subjects' worlds that these can be palpably felt" (p. 381). As we explained earlier in the chapter, some case study researchers consider literary structures—for example, the telling of tales, one-act plays, or poetry—especially good formats for portraying the emic perspective.

3. Usefulness. An important criterion to consider in evaluating a case study is its usefulness to the reader. A case study can be useful if it enlightens the individuals who read the report of its findings. Another way it can be useful is that it liberates or empowers the individuals being studied. Critical theory, a qualitative research tradition described in Chapter 12, emphasizes this aspect of usefulness. Still another aspect of usefulness is that the findings can be applied to the readers' settings and used to make meaningful changes in how they deal with the phenomena that the case study involved.

Criteria Reflecting Use of Sound Research Methods

4. Triangulation.   Imagine that you are studying youth gangs, and a gang member tells you that he engages in acts of vandalism because he is bored. Is this a truthful statement of the individual's state of mind? If this person also indicates a habitual state of boredom on a structured questionnaire or personality measure, this evidence would strengthen the truthfulness of his statement. If the researchers report that other gang members make similar statements, this finding would be further evidence of truthfulness. Still another type of evidence would be finding that this causal attribution is consistent with a well-supported theory of aggression.

What has been done in each of these instances is to test the soundness of a case study finding by drawing on corroborative evidence. Case study researchers call this process *triangulation*: It is the process of using multiple data-collection methods, data sources, analysts, or theories to check case study findings.

Triangulation in social science research sometimes does not produce convergence, but instead illustrates inconsistencies or contradictions among findings about the same phenomenon. For example, in studies of controversial, stressful, or illicit phenomena, self-report data might be inconsistent with, or even directly contradict, data resulting from more direct methods of data collection such as observation or document analysis. When this happens, it still may be possible to validate the conflicting data by reconciling them within an explanatory framework.

5. Coding Checks.   In describing interpretational analysis, we explained how researchers develop a category system to code the segments into which interview transcripts, field notes, documents, and other materials have been divided. The reliability of the coding process can be checked with methods similar to those used for determining inter-rater reliability for quantitative measures (see Chapter 5). Because ethnographers rarely rate or code data for enumeration, the form of inter-observer agreement they generally seek is agreement among observers on the nature of the description of, or the composition of, the events that have been observed, not on the frequency of occurrence of events (LeCompte & Preissle, 1993). Besides using multiple observers, they can increase the reliability of their coding schemes by such strategies as using low-inference descriptors and mechanical recording of data.

6. Disconfirming Case Analysis.   Rather than ignoring or explaining exceptions away, Miles and Huberman (1994) recommend using extreme cases as a way to test and thereby strengthen the basic findings: "You need to find the outliers, and then verify whether what is present in them is absent or different in other, more mainstream examples . . ." (p. 269). As we explained in Chapter 5, an outlier is a score at either the high or low extreme of the score distribution. In case study research, an outlier is an individual or situation that differs greatly from most other individuals or situations that are studied. Several of the sampling strategies listed in Table 10.1 could lead the researchers to such cases, including extreme/deviant case, maximum variation, critical case, and disconfirming case sampling.

An example of disconfirming case analysis occurred in a case study of school innovation (Miles and Huberman, 1994). In one site a new practice was evaluated by many teachers as a miraculous cure for local ills. The researchers also discovered two outliers among the field participants at this site, that is, individuals who had not adopted the practice or had expressed strong criticism of it. The researchers learned that these individuals had not mastered the innovation as intended, and that their reasons for not adopting the innovation were opposite to those given by adopters. The outliers' comments thus strengthened the researchers' interpretation that technical mastery of an innovative practice by users leads to positive results.

Miles and Huberman also recommend seeking out individuals who have the most to gain or lose by affirming or denying something. If such individuals give an unexpected answer (e.g., a person who has much to gain by denying a statement affirms it), the researchers can be more confident that they are answering truthfully. A related tactic is to look for negative evidence, that is, to actively seek disconfirmation of what the researchers think is true. For example, asking skeptical colleagues to look at the raw data and independently come up with their own conclusions is a good way to test the soundness of the researchers' analyses and interpretations.

7. Member Checking.   A major purpose of case study research is to represent the emic perspective, that is, reality as constructed by the individuals who were studied. Researchers can check their reconstruction of individuals' emic perspective by member checking, which is the process of having individuals review statements in the researchers' report for accuracy and completeness. Member checking was the primary strategy that Kagan and her colleagues used in their study of teachers in residence to ensure the accuracy of the findings.

Member checking might reveal factual errors that are easily corrected. In other instances, the researchers might need to collect more data in order to reconcile discrepancies. It is possible, too, that the opportunity to read the report will cause participants to recall new facts or to have new perceptions of their situation. The report would be rewritten accordingly.

Criteria Reflecting Thoroughness of Data Collection and Analysis

8. Contextual Completeness.   In order for case study phenomena to be fully understood, they must be set within a context. The more comprehensive the researchers' contextualization of the case, the more credible are their interpretations of the phenomena. David Altheide and John Johnson (1994) recommend that case study researchers consider the following contextual features in interpreting the meaning of the phenomena they investigate: history, physical setting, and environment; the number of participants; specific activities; the schedules and temporal order of events; divisions of labor; routines and variations from routines; significant events and their origins and consequences; members' perceptions and meanings; and social rules and basic patterns of order.

Altheide and Johnson stress that thorough contextualization requires collecting data about the multivocality and the tacit knowledge of field participants. Multivocality refers to the fact that, in many field settings, participants do not speak with a unified voice; they have diverse interests and viewpoints. Tacit knowledge refers to the implicit meanings that the individuals being studied either cannot find the words to express, or that they take so much for granted that they do not refer to them in everyday conversation or in research interviews. Case study findings that reflect multivocality and tacit knowledge are more likely to be complete, and thus more credible.

9. Long-Term Observation.   Gathering data over a long period of time and making repeated observations of the phenomenon can increase the trustworthiness of case study findings. For example, students' perceptions of school are known to vary depending upon the time of year due to such factors as tests, the weather conditions, and whether a school vacation is coming or has just passed. Changing conditions in their own lives also affect participants' perspective, such as problems on the job or in personal relationships. If data are collected over an extended time period, the researchers might be able to distinguish situational perceptions from more consistent trends. The researchers' own perceptions of the phenomenon also develop over time, allowing them greater opportunities to reconfirm or refine their interpretations.

10. Representativeness Check.   Researchers should determine whether a finding is typical of the field site from which it was obtained. They can do so by reflecting on whether they relied too much on accessible or elite informants in collecting data. Researchers might also describe how they ensured that unusual occurrences, or the fact that the researchers were present on some occasions but not on others, did not skew the findings.

11. Researchers' Self-Reflection.   Researchers' interpretations are more credible if they demonstrate reflexivity, which, as explained earlier in the chapter, is self-reflection with respect to their qualifications to conduct the study and their relationship to the situation being studied. For example, David Thomas (1993) demonstrated the use of self-reflection in his case study of cross-race relationships between managers and their protégés in a corporation. Thomas described two major concerns he had about conducting the study: the potential impact of his being an African-American male of junior rank, and his ability to develop effective interview rapport with Caucasian senior managers. Thomas explained the steps he took to manage these concerns, including asking two Caucasian senior managers with expertise in clinical supervision and race relations research to serve as his research supervisors. This sensitivity to his possible effect on the data-collection and analysis process contributed to the soundness of the research findings.

CHECKING THE APPLICABILITY OF CASE STUDY FINDINGS

In reading a case study, one of the main concerns that an educational practitioner might have is the extent to which the study's findings can be applied to the individuals or situations in the practitioner's setting. Applicability thus is similar to generalizability, which is an important goal of quantitative research.

Sampling techniques used in quantitative research (see Chapter 5) allow for precise determination of the generalizability of a study's findings. Determining the applicability of case study findings is less direct. Some researchers would argue that the findings of a case study depend on the ongoing interaction between the data and the creative processes of the researcher, and thus are unique to the case that was studied. However, most qualitative researchers believe that case study findings can be applied to other settings besides those that were studied.

One approach to determining the applicability of case study findings is to consider the sampling strategy that the researchers used to select the case. If the researchers studied a typical or extreme case, the results should be applicable to other similar cases. If the researchers used a multiple-case design, they usually conduct a cross-case analysis to help readers determine whether there was generalizability of findings among the cases that they studied. The presence of cross-case generalizability is strong evidence that the findings are applicable to other situations and individuals than those studied by the researchers.

Another position on the issue of applicability is to place the responsibility for making this judgment on readers of the case study findings. In other words, it is the responsibility of the readers, not the researchers, to determine the similarity of the cases that were studied to the situation of interest to them. Researchers can help readers make this determination by providing a thick description of the participants and contexts that comprise the case.

QUALITATIVE RESEARCH TRADITIONS

Some case study research in education draws from qualitative research traditions in the social sciences (e.g., anthropology, sociology, psychology), the humanities (e.g., art, literature, and philosophy), and interdisciplinary studies. As we explained earlier in the chapter, a qualitative research tradition represents the work produced by a group of investigators who hold a similar view of the nature of the universe and are in agreement as to legitimate questions to ask and techniques to use in its exploration. The literature of a particular tradition can be searched by using terms and descriptors specific to that tradition (see Chapter 2).

Qualitative research traditions generally involve the study of cases. It is possible, therefore, to examine any qualitative research study from this perspective. For this reason, we began this part of the book, which concerns qualitative research, with a discussion of case studies. Although some case studies in education are not grounded in a particular qualitative research tradition, others are.

Table 10.2 presents 17 qualitative research traditions organized into three categories. The traditions in each category study similar phenomena. Those in the first category seek to understand language and communication phenomena, those in the second category focus on understanding the nature of inner

TABLE 10.2   Phenomena Investigated by Qualitative Research Traditions

Research tradition	Phenomena investigated
	Communication
1. Ethnographic content analysis	The content of documents from a cultural perspective
2. Ethnography of communication	How members of a culture use speech in their social life
3. Ethnoscience	A culture's semantic systems
4. Semiotics	Signs and the meanings they convey
5. Narrative analysis	Organized representations and explanations of human experience
6. Structuralism	The systemic properties of language, text, and other phenomena
7. Hermeneutics	The process by which individuals arrive at the meaning of a text
	Inner experience
8. Cognitive psychology	The mental structures and processes used by individuals in different situations
9. Phenomenology	Reality as it is subjectively experienced by individuals
10. Phenomenography	Individuals' mental conceptions of reality
11. Life history	Individuals' life experiences from their own perspective
	Society and culture
12. Ethnomethodology	The rules that underlie everyday social interactions
13. Event structure analysis	The logical structures of social events
14. Symbolic interactionism	The influence of social interactions on social structures and individuals' self-identity
15. Ethnography	Characteristic features and patterns of a culture
16. Critical-theory research	Oppressive power relationships in a culture
17. Action research	Practitioners' self-reflective efforts to improve their effectiveness

Source. Adapted from Table 15.1 on p. 593 in: Gall, M. D., Borg, W. R., & Gall, J. P. (1996). *Educational research: An introduction* (6th ed.). White Plains, NY: Longman.

experience, and those in the third category investigate social and cultural phenomena. Some have played a major role in educational research, while others have been applied to education rarely but clearly have potential for educational application. The list is not exhaustive, because the field of qualitative research is undergoing rapid growth and continual reconceptualization. Also, the list of traditions shown in Table 10.2 does not include historical research, because the subjects of historical research cut across the three categories shown in the table. Historical research is a strong qualitative research tradition, and is the focus of Chapter 13.

Below we briefly explain how investigation of each of the three types of phenomena that these research traditions involve can contribute to the study of education.

Traditions Involving the Investigation of Communication

Instruction in schools and other educational institutions always involves verbal, and nonverbal, communication between or among teachers and students. Even when lone individuals engage in self-instruction, some of the time they are likely to be reading a book or a computer screen, viewing a film or a videotape, or reflecting mentally on some significant experience. Each of these activities involves either reacting to, or generating, language or some other form of communication.

Qualitative research traditions involving the investigation of communication have contributed to educational research in many ways. Researchers have investigated such topics as the philosophy of education conveyed by curriculum guides; the presence of gender bias in textbooks as reflected in the frequency of the use of the terms *he* versus *she* and other pronouns; the symbolic meanings conveyed by physical phenomena in a school building such as school uniforms, sports paraphernalia, and the arrangement of desks in a classroom; and the ways in which teachers exert guidance or control of students through their verbal and nonverbal acts in the classroom. Some researchers study the meaning of texts and artifacts from the perspective of various cultures or subcultures.

Four qualitative research traditions that have focused on communication as it reflects cultural phenomena are ethnographic content analysis, the ethnography of communication, ethnoscience, and semiotics. Three other qualitative research traditions that focus on the investigation of language or other texts are narrative analysis, structuralism, and hermeneutics.

Traditions Involving the Investigation of Inner Experience

All acts of teaching and learning in human beings involve changes in the teachers' or students' inner experience. Thus qualitative researchers who investigate inner experience can shed light on the meaning of education as experienced by various participants.

Quantitative researchers typically ignore the study of inner experience. For example, B. F. Skinner's views of learning had a great impact on educational research, yet Skinner viewed the human mind as a "black box" between a defined stimulus and an observable response, not accessible to scientific study. Qualitative researchers, by contrast, view human thoughts and feelings as phenomena worthy of investigation. They have developed research traditions that focus on the thought processes of individuals and on ways that different individuals apprehend and describe their experiences. These traditions have been used to study the lives of individuals from various subcultures, to explore the life history of exemplary teachers and scholars, and to compare the thinking processes of different types of people (e.g., experts versus novices in a field of inquiry such as art or science).

Four qualitative research traditions that involve the study of inner experience are cognitive psychology, phenomenology, phenomenography, and life history.

Traditions Involving the Investigation of Society and Culture

Here we use the term *society* to refer to the various groups and social categories to which individuals perceive themselves or other human beings as belonging. The term *culture* refers to all the ways of living (e.g., values, customs, rituals, and beliefs) that groups of human beings develop, and that are transmitted from one generation to the next, or from current members to newly admitted members, over time. Education is one of the most powerful factors in cultural transmission, and it has profound effects upon the maintenance of, and changes in, the groups and social categories with which individuals identify. Therefore, the qualitative research traditions that directly investigate societal and cultural phenomena have a great deal to offer educational research.

Three qualitative research traditions involving the study of society and culture are ethnomethodology, event structure analysis, and symbolic interactionism. Three other qualitative research traditions that investigate society and culture have influenced many educational researchers, and therefore each of them is the subject of a separate chapter in this book. Specifically, ethnographic research is discussed in Chapter 11, critical-theory research is discussed in Chapter 12, and action research is discussed in Chapter 15.

CONCLUDING THOUGHT

In this chapter you have learned the key characteristics of a qualitative case study and glimpsed at various qualitative research traditions that build upon the case study's model of in-depth exploration of particular instances of a phenomenon in their natural context. Although educators disagree about the relative value of quantitative research and qualitative research, there is a general consensus that good case study research brings individuals, institutions, programs, and events to life in a way that is not possible using the statistical methods of quantitative research. By reading case studies, you can gain valuable insights for understanding your own professional practice, designing educational interventions, developing theories, or taking other action.

SELF-CHECK TEST

1. In a qualitative research case study, the researchers strive to do all of the following except
   a. conduct an in-depth study of the phenomenon.
   b. study the phenomenon in its natural context.
   c. maintain an objective perspective on the phenomenon.
   d. reflect the research participants' perspective on the phenomenon being studied.

2. Looking for relational patterns in a case study reflects the goal of _____ a phenomenon.
   a. describing
   b. explaining
   c. evaluating
   d. generalizing

3. Qualitative researchers use purposeful sampling in order to
   a. reduce the chances of selecting atypical cases of the phenomenon to be studied.
   b. eliminate the need to study more than one case.
   c. select cases that are the most convenient for in-depth study.
   d. select cases that are "information-rich" with respect to the purposes of the study.

4. In qualitative research, the main measuring instrument is
   a. the questionnaire or other self-report measure used to collect data.
   b. audiotape or videotape recordings of field events.
   c. the researchers themselves.
   d. the researchers' key informants.

5. In interpretational data analysis, the researchers
   a. search for patterns inherent in the data.
   b. impose meaning on the data.
   c. search for naturally occurring segments in the data.
   d. use categories developed by other researchers.

6. Researchers who wish to rely on their own intuition and judgment in analyzing case study data will most likely use
   a. interpretational analysis.
   b. structural analysis.
   c. reflective analysis.
   d. narrative analysis.

7. Reflective reporting of a case study tends to involve
   a. an objective writing style.
   b. computer analysis of the data.
   c. a conventional organization of topics.
   d. the strong presence of the researchers' voice.

8. Researcher bias in case studies is best handled by
   a. honest exploration of one's identity and beliefs as possible biasing factors.
   b. exclusive use of objective data-collection methods.
   c. using data collectors who are similar to the field participants.
   d. studying phenomena in which one has minimal interest.

9. If researchers want to increase the applicability of their case study findings to other settings, it is not wise to
   a. study an atypical case.
   b. use a multiple-case design.
   c. compare their case to similar cases studied by other researchers.
   d. provide a thick description of their case.

10. Qualitative research traditions
    a. do not typically use case study methods to investigate phenomena.
    b. are grounded in positivism.
    c. use the techniques of various academic disciplines in the study of phenomena.
    d. are based primarily on models from the physical sciences.

11. Ethnography primarily involves the investigation of
    a. inner experience.
    b. society and culture.
    c. language and communication.
    d. historical phenomena.

CHAPTER REFERENCES

Adler, P. A., & Adler, P. (1994). Observational techniques. In N. K. Denzin & Y. S. Lincoln (Eds.), *Handbook of qualitative research* (pp. 377–392). Thousand Oaks, CA: Sage.

Altheide, D. L., & Johnson, J. M. (1994). Criteria for assessing interpretive validity in qualitative research. In N. K. Denzin & Y. S. Lincoln (Eds.), *Handbook of qualitative research* (pp. 485–499). Thousand Oaks, CA: Sage.

Cuban, L. (1997). Change without reform: The case of Stanford University school of medicine, 1908–1990. *American Educational Research Journal, 34,* 83–122.

Goldenberg, C. (1992). The limits of expectations: A case for case knowledge about teacher expectancy effects. *American Educational Research Journal, 29,* 517–544.

Jacob, E. (1987). Qualitative research traditions: A review. *Review of Educational Research, 57,* 1–50.

Kagan, D. M., Dennis, M. B., Igou, M., Moore, P., & Sparks, K. (1993). The experience of being a teacher in residence. *American Educational Research Journal, 30*, 426–443.

Kirk, J., & Miller, M. L. (1986). *Reliability and validity in qualitative research.* Beverly Hills, CA: Sage.

LeCompte, M. D., & Preissle, J. (1993). *Ethnography and qualitative design in educational research* (2nd ed.). San Diego: Academic.

Manning, P. K., & Cullum-Swan, B. (1994). Narrative, content, and semiotic analysis. In N. K. Denzin & Y. S. Lincoln (Eds.), *Handbook of qualitative research* (pp. 463–477). Thousand Oaks, CA: Sage.

Miles, M. B., & Huberman, A. M. (1994). *Qualitative data analysis: An expanded sourcebook* (2nd ed.). Thousand Oaks, CA: Sage.

Noblit, G. W. (1993). Power and caring. *American Educational Research Journal, 30*, 23–38.

Patthey-Chavez, G. G. (1993). High school as an arena for cultural conflict and acculturation for Latino Angelinos. *Anthropology and Education Quarterly, 24*, 33–60.

Patton, M. Q. (1990). *Qualitative evaluation and research methods* (2nd ed.). Newbury Park, CA: Sage.

Peshkin, A. (1988). In search of subjectivity—one's own. *Educational Researcher, 17*(7), 17–21.

Richardson, L. (1992). The consequences of poetic representation: Writing the other, rewriting the self. In C. Ellis & M. G. Flaherty (Eds.), *Investigating subjectivity: Research on lived experience* (pp. 125–140).

Schempp, P. G. (1995). Learning on the job: An analysis of the acquisition of a teacher's knowledge. *Journal of Research and Development in Education, 28*, 237–244.

Tesch, R. (1990). *Qualitative research: Analysis types and software tools.* New York: Falmer.

Thomas, D. A. (1993). Racial dynamics in cross-race developmental relationships. *Administrative Science Quarterly, 38*, 169–194.

Wolcott, H. F. (1990). *Writing up qualitative research.* Newbury Park, CA: Sage.

Wolcott, H. F. (1994). *Transforming qualitative data: Description, analysis, and interpretation.* Thousand Oaks, CA: Sage.

Yahya, I. B., & Moore, G. E. (1985, March). On research methodology: The cassette tape as a data collection medium. Paper presented at the Southern Research Conference in Agricultural Education, Mobile, AL. (ERIC Document Reference No. ED 262 098.)

Yin, R. K. (1989). *Case study research design and methods* (Rev. ed.). Thousand Oaks, CA: Sage.

RECOMMENDED READING

Denzin, N. K., & Lincoln, Y. S. (Eds.). (1994). *Handbook of qualitative research.* Thousand Oaks, CA: Sage.

A major overview of various topics in qualitative research, including case study research. The contributors' chapters are organized into six parts that cover the nature of qualitative research, qualitative research paradigms, strategies of inquiry, data collection and analysis, interpretation and reporting, and the future of qualitative research.

Glesne, C., & Peshkin, A. (1992). *Becoming qualitative researchers: An introduction.* New York: Longman.

Covers each stage of the qualitative research process: planning the study, data collection, data analysis, and reporting. The authors emphasize the researcher's personal involvement in the study and the ethics of qualitative research.

Stake, R. E. (1995). *The art of case study research*. Thousand Oaks, CA: Sage.

A primer on how to do case studies in education. The author explains such matters as how to select a case, how to generalize from one case to another, and how to triangulate case study findings.

Wolcott, H. F. (1994). *Transforming qualitative data*. Thousand Oaks, CA: Sage.

Using selections from his own previously published ethnographic case studies, the author explains various approaches to the organization and reporting of case study data. The author also provides guidelines for teaching and learning qualitative inquiry that should be particularly helpful to novice researchers.

Yin, R. K., and Campbell, D. T. (1994). *Case study research design and methods* (2nd. ed.). Newbury Park, CA: Sage.

Discusses the design and conduct of single-case and multiple-case studies. The new edition gives expanded coverage to the role of theory, the rationale for using multiple methods of data collection, and the use of both qualitative and quantitative methods in case study research. (See also Yin, R. K. (1993). *Applications of case study research*. Thousand Oaks, CA: Sage.)

Sample Case Study: Learning on the Job: An Analysis of the Acquisition of a Teacher's Knowledge

Schempp, P. G. (1995). Learning on the job: An analysis of the acquisition of a teacher's knowledge. *Journal of Research and Development in Education*, 28, 237–244.

In the rest of this chapter you will read a research article that illustrates a case study based on qualitative research. It is preceded by comments written especially for this book by the author of the article. Then the article itself is reprinted in full, just as it appeared when originally published. Where appropriate, we have added footnotes to help you understand the information contained in the article.

Researcher's Comments, Prepared by Paul Schempp

Background

Three key events, all of which occurred about the same time, led me to undertake this study. First, I had listened to Lee Shulman's eloquent Presidential Address at the 1985 American Educational Research Association meeting in Chicago (Shulman, 1985). His remarks, later expanded in the *Harvard Educational Review* (Shulman, 1987), vividly described the fundamental importance of teachers' knowledge to their teaching practice. I later read the work of Shulman's students who followed his call for more research in this area (Grossman, 1990; Marks, 1990). These works convinced me that the study of teachers' knowledge held useful insights for understanding the practice of teaching.

The second event involved my experience in reading and reflecting on two books about knowledge. One book was Donald Schon's *The Reflective Practitioner* (Schon,

1983). In the book, Schon identifies the critical distinguishing characteristic of a profession to be its construction and application of a specialized body of knowledge. At the same time, a colleague and I were involved in a protracted discussion of Michel Foucault's book *Power/Knowledge* (Foucault, 1980). These books convinced me that knowledge was a significant force in every profession and social institution.

The third event that led me to undertake this study occurred on a windy May morning at the top of a high hill overlooking the Mediterranean Sea. Sitting in Freema Elbaz's office at the University of Haifa in Israel, I asked her why she undertook her study *Teacher Thinking: A Study of Practical Knowledge* (Elbaz, 1983). Freema told me the story of her difficult first year of teaching and her feelings of inadequacy as a teacher—a story common to many first-year teachers. Freema wanted to discover, "What is it that good teachers know that I don't know?" When she entered the doctoral program at the University of Toronto, that question became her dissertation topic. Freema's story convinced me of the practical value of studying teachers' knowledge.

While the works of Shulman, Schon, Foucault, and Elbaz represent considerable diversity, each underscores the remarkable power of knowledge in directing and giving meaning to human endeavor. I was curious to learn more, and I wanted to learn it for myself. So I headed off to the schools in search of a teacher who was willing to answer my many questions. I found that person in Robert Halstop at Hillcrest High School (pseudonyms).

Experiences

When we negotiated the conditions under which the study would take place, Bob and I discussed the purpose of the study, time lines, the methodology (including access and the use of interviews, observations, and videotaping), and plans for reporting the study. I wanted Bob to know everything I was planning to do, and why. I hoped that he would learn as much as I did from the study, and that it would be empowering for him in his subsequent work as a high school teacher. I also hoped that Bob and I would write the report of the study together. Accordingly, I granted him equal editorial control as to what would and would not be reported.

As the study progressed, Bob and I enjoyed a friendly relationship. I found him to be helpful, honest, and open. Although he never said so, I think he enjoyed my company. In the often isolated world of school teaching, I was someone he could talk to who was interested in what he had to say.

I enjoyed my time with Bob as well. My experiences added a valuable dimension and perspective to my work as a teacher educator. While I was formerly a schoolteacher myself, several years had passed since I spent significant portions of each day in a school. I began to better appreciate and understand schools from the different perspectives of the students, the teachers, the administrators, and even the parents. My increased understanding of these diverse viewpoints was an unanticipated benefit of the study to me.

Problems began, however, when Bob read the first draft of the research report that I wrote. I had asked him to check the accuracy of the events described and to give his opinion on whether the report reflected the way in which he had acquired his professional knowledge. The report was not what Bob expected, and he became angry. Bob told me that he thought I was studying "how good teachers do their work." I was surprised by his comment. I showed him the informed consent form he had signed, which clearly stated that this was a study of "the acquisition of a teacher's knowledge." He didn't see the difference.

Bob then informed me that he didn't like the report. He felt that it was written in a negative tone, and that it didn't reflect well on him or his school. I had not perceived it as negative, so I asked for examples. He was particularly upset over a section in which I described how some of Bob's personal biases influenced his knowledge construction. Because I had granted Bob editorial control, this section and some others had to come out.

It was at this point that I discovered the critical importance of a peer debriefer. Harry Wolcott is well known in the field of educational research for his work in ethnography, and is also a friend of mine. Harry knew about my study with Bob, and I sought his counsel on the problems I was encountering. The events unfolding in my research covered a range of topics that researchers often face, and about which Harry has written eloquently (Wolcott, 1990; 1994): ethics, methodology, report writing, and so forth. Harry listened. He also provided insight, perspective, humor, and when absolutely pressed, advice.

Subsequently I submitted a second draft of the research report to Bob. He thought it was better, but still negative. He did, however, agree that it was accurate. I offered him the opportunity to write a section to be called "Bob's Response." He declined. I then asked him if he felt that he had learned anything about teaching from the study, or whether he felt he was now a better teacher. He told me no.

Two years later, in a nearby city, I ran into Kathy, the person described in my report as Bob's teaching colleague and my key informant. We talked briefly, and as she prepared to leave she said, "You know, Bob is a better teacher because of your study." Surprised by her comment, I asked her how. She told me that since the study ended Bob had begun attending more in-service activities, appeared to be planning his lessons more thoroughly, and was teaching more content in his classes. She assured me that these changes had all started with my study.

I like to think that both Bob and I learned from this study, but in retrospect I regret allowing him editorial control. That decision did not result in the empowerment of Bob that I had desired, and it required me to eliminate an important section from the final manuscript. As a result of this experience, I continue to share research data (for example, transcripts and vignettes) with my participants, and I ask them to comment on the accuracy of the data. But I do not share manuscript drafts, and I no longer give away my rights and responsibilities as a researcher and the main author.

This study also taught me the importance of having a competent and compassionate debriefer such as Harry Wolcott. The study might not have been completed had I not found an individual so well qualified on both these counts. Finally, I learned much more about the work of teachers and students in schools than I could possibly report in a single manuscript—lessons that have helped me to become a better teacher myself. It is in the learning of such lessons that I find the true purpose of educational research.

References

Elbaz, F. (1983). *Teacher thinking: A study of practical knowledge.* London: Croom Helm.

Foucault, M. (1980). *Power/knowledge: Selected interviews and other writings 1972–1977.* New York: Pantheon.

Glaser, B., & Strauss, A. (1967). *The discovery of grounded theory: Strategies for qualitative research.* Chicago: Aldine.

Grossman, P. L. (1990). *The making of a teacher: Teacher knowledge and teacher education.* New York: Teachers College Press.

Marks, R. (1990). Pedagogical content knowledge: From a mathematical case to a modified conception. *Journal of Teacher Education, 41*(3), 3–11.

Schon, D. A. (1983). *The reflective practitioner.* New York: Basic Books.

Shulman, L. S. (1985, April). Knowledge growth in teaching. Presidential address for the annual meeting of the American Educational Research Association, Chicago, IL.

Shulman, L. S. (1986). Those who understand: Knowledge growth in teaching. *Educational Researcher, 15*(2), 4–14.

Shulman, L. S. (1987). Knowledge and teaching: Foundations of the new reform. *Harvard Educational Review, 57,* 1–22.

Wolcott, H. F. (1990). *Writing up qualitative research.* Newbury Park, CA: Sage.

Wolcott, H. F. (1994). *Transforming qualitative data.* Thousand Oaks, CA: Sage.

LEARNING ON THE JOB: AN ANALYSIS OF THE ACQUISITION OF A TEACHER'S KNOWLEDGE

Paul G. Schempp
The University of Georgia

This study analyzed the criteria used by an experienced teacher to acquire the knowledge necessary to teach. An interpretive analytic framework and case study methodology were used in this year-long project with a midcareer high school teacher.[a] Data were collected using a variety of ethnographic techniques including: nonparticipant observations, artifact and document analysis, stimulated recall from videotapes, and formal and informal interviews.[b] Data analysis followed the conventions described by Glaser and Strauss (1967). Five distinct knowledge categories were identified, each with unique selection criteria. These knowledge forms included: class organization and operation, teaching behavior, subject matter, pedagogical content knowledge (Shulman, 1986), and external conditions. In matters of class organization and operation, Bob (the teacher) looked to his experience for those things that worked (i.e., insured classroom order). The acquisition of

Schempp, P. G. (1995). Learning on the job: An analysis of the acquisition of a teacher's knowledge. *Journal of Research and Development in Education, 28,* 237–244. Reprinted with permission of the College of Education, the University of Georgia. Copyright © 1995 by the College of Education, the University of Georgia.

---

a. An interpretive analytic framework corresponds to interpretational analysis as described in this chapter.

b. Ethnographic techniques are data-collection methods that originated in the study of non-Western cultures by anthropologists, and that have been adopted for use in case study research generally; Chapter 11 provides a comprehensive discussion of ethnographic research in education. Nonparticipant observations involve a method of collecting data in which the researchers act primarily as observers, entering the setting only to gather data and minimizing other forms of interaction with the field participants.

instructional behavior came largely from observations of other teachers (e.g., cooperating teacher, peers) or from experience. Bob selected subject matter knowledge based upon previous knowledge, current personal interests, resource availability, and student interest. Pedagogical-content knowledge was comprised in three phases: demonstrations, drills and activities. External conditions were influences outside the classroom (e.g., laws, school policy). Years of occupational service have left Bob with a well developed set of criteria upon which he acquires the knowledge to teach.

A distinguishing characteristic of any profession is the body of knowledge for practicing that profession. Professionals are called into service because they bring a unique understanding and critical insight to a situation that is inaccessible to the uninitiated. It is the body of professional knowledge that explains what those in a particular occupation do and why (Schon, 1983). The body of knowledge currently used in a profession is, therefore, of major concern to those practicing the profession and preparing future practitioners.

Contemporary literature on teaching lacks substantive information on the knowledge base teachers use in their professional practice. As Shulman (1986) noted, important questions such as "Where do teacher explanations come from? How do teachers decide what to teach, how to represent it and how to deal with problems of misunderstanding?" (p. 8) have gone unanswered. There has been a growing recognition in teacher education that the understanding of the knowledge used by teachers will lead to a better understanding of pedagogical practice.

Within the last decade, educational researchers have studied rules and principles used in teacher thinking (Elbaz, 1983), teachers' classroom images (Clandinin, 1985), the experience of classroom cycles and rhythms (Clandinin & Connelly, 1986), subject matter expertise (Leinhardt, & Smith, 1985), and pedagogical-content knowledge (Grossman, 1989; Gudmundsdottir & Kristjansdottir, 1989). These studies, and other similar work, represent the start of a growing trend in research into what teachers know and how they use that knowledge in their classrooms. This study continues that line of inquiry by offering a glimpse into the world of an experienced high school teacher. Specifically, this case study examines the criteria one teacher employed in acquiring the knowledge he found necessary for his professional practice.

METHOD

Teacher

Robert Halstop has taught high school physical education for the past 14 years at Hillcrest High School (HHS). Over those years, Bob has coached many sports and been involved in numerous school clubs, groups, and projects. At the time of this study, he was coaching the girls' varsity basketball team. Besides teaching and coaching, he performed normal student counseling activities and other school duties assigned by the administrators. Bob worked at a local lumber mill during the summers, but did not work outside the school during the academic year. Bob's school day officially began at 7:30 a.m. and ended at 3:30 p.m., but he was usually in school much earlier and it was common for him to stay later. There were seven instructional periods in the day. Bob was assigned six classes, one planning period, and had a 30 minute lunch break. Bob was presented with an initial draft of this report for his review and comment. His comments were incorporated into subsequent drafts and used to validate the accuracy of the events and quotes reported.

Setting

Hillcrest is a small, rural community in the Pacific Northwest. Education was held in high esteem as evidenced by the town having one of the highest tax bases in the state. Hillcrest High School enrolled approximately 470 students. Two years before this study, HHS received an educational excellence award from the United States Department of Education. All first-year students were required to take physical education for one year and could elect physical education after that. The freshman physical education classes were separated by gender and were taught as a survey course to cover many subject areas. The other physical education classes were coeducational and defined by student interest (e.g., recreational sports, weight training). HHS had two physical education teachers; one for boys (Bob) and one for girls (Kathy).

Data Collection

Data were collected and analyzed using a variety of qualitative techniques. Among these techniques were participant observation, artifact and document analyses, stimulated recall using videotaped classes and both formal and informal interviews.[c] Besides Bob, Kathy and other school personnel (e.g., students, teachers, administrators) were also interviewed. Field notes were recorded during and after observations and a summary statement was made off site after each day of data collection. Data collection began 2 days before the start of school and officially ended just before the Christmas break. I was present in the school on a daily basis for the first month of the study and made field trips twice a week on average after that.

Data Analyses

Data analysis began on the first day of the study and ended approximately 1 year later. Concurrently collecting and analyzing data allowed me to develop data summary themes and check the emerging themes against recurring field activities. Analyzing data during the study also allowed data collection techniques to be tailored to gather data that were amenable to testing and understanding the emerging themes. Specific strategies employed to insure data trustworthiness included triangulation of methods, member checks (particularly the use of key informants and the constant use of follow-up interviews

to check consistency of responses), disconfirming case analyses (the investigation of responses and/or occurrences that were incompatible with emerging themes), and cultivating reactions from the case-study teacher to the themes, categories and events to be included in the final report.

My key informant was Bob's teaching colleague, Kathy. At the time of this study, Kathy and Bob had been teaching physical education together at Hillcrest for 3 years. Kathy was particularly helpful in cross checking stories and events described by Bob. In cases where discrepant information occurred (e.g., differences between what Bob told me and what I observed) Kathy often provided valuable insights.

Data analysis involved summarizing data into themes and categories using procedures recommended by Miles and Huberman (1984) Goetz and LeCompte (1984) and Patton (1980). The construction of these categories was influenced by Shulman's (1987) theory of a knowledge base for teaching. He identified seven categories of teachers' knowledge: subject matter, general pedagogical, curriculum, pedagogical content, learners, contexts, and purposes. As themes emerged and clustered into categories, these categories were checked against Shulman's propositions. Four of Shulman's seven categories were ultimately used to describe the forms of knowledge Bob acquired in pursuit of his professional practice: subject matter, general pedagogical (renamed teaching behavior), pedagogical content, and context (renamed external conditions). Classroom organization and operation was a category constructed independent of Shulman's theory as it appeared to better describe a dominant form of Bob's knowledge.

The themes and categories identified forms of knowledge as well as the criteria Bob used in acquiring pedagogical knowledge. The categories allowed the data to be summarized and reported in a suc-

---

c. In participant observation, researchers interact with field participants during their observations in order to establish a meaningful identity within their group, although usually not engaging in activities that are at the core of the group's identity. Stimulated recall is a method of data collection in which a teaching episode is recorded on videotape; while viewing the tape, the teacher is asked to describe the thoughts and decisions that were occurring during the episode.

cinct, yet accurate, manner. The first step was to review the collected data to determine tentative categories. Next, the data were coded using the tentative scheme. The category scheme underwent revisions until the data were able to be classified within the scheme with no redundancy of categories. The constant comparison method of analysis (Glaser & Strauss, 1967) was used to identify these patterns and relationships.

The final step of the analytic procedure was to present a copy of the report to Bob for his comments and reactions. The findings were brought back to the case study teacher so that he could: (a) check the accuracy of the data (reliability), and (b) validate the findings of the report.[d] This procedure was considered a critical component for establishing the validity and trustworthiness of the study's findings (Lather, 1986). Additional revisions were then made based on the responses and reactions from the teacher. Events contained in the report seen by Bob as either inaccurate or threatening to confidentiality were rechecked and eliminated where appropriate. Bob's comments and additional supporting evidence were incorporated into the final draft of the report to lend strength to the propositions put forth.

FINDINGS

From years of contact with many sources of occupationally useful information, Bob had constructed a comfortable set of criteria for evaluating and selecting knowledge necessary for his day-to-day classroom operation. He seemed to have a clear sense of both the expectations others held for him, and his own purpose for being in the school. These criteria formed a screen through which all potential pedagogical knowledge passed. Bob's knowledge acquisition represented an intersection between the demands of his day-to-day practice and the knowledge available to meet those demands. Thus, Bob appropriated knowledge based upon his perception of the power and quality of its source, and his perception of its potential to solve a recurring problem or improve a current practice.

In analyzing the data, five knowledge categories emerged: (a) classroom organization and operation, (b) teaching behavior, (c) subject matter, (d) pedagogical-content knowledge, and (e) external conditions. Each category was unique in terms of the problems it addressed, the sources from which it came, and the criteria that determined knowledge selection and rejection.

Class Organization and Operation

Like many teachers (West, 1975; Yinger, 1980), classroom order and control were predominant concerns for Bob. The concern for classroom organization and controlled operation rose from Bob's belief that, if order was not established and the classroom not operated in the manner he needed, little could be accomplished. In his own words,

> I'm going to get across more to kids in a structured setting. Otherwise kids are pretty much allowed to go where they want to and pick and choose what they want to take and what they don't want to take . . . I have more kids working at a higher level than I would otherwise.

Although he had spent much time formulating, writing and explaining his operational policies and procedures, the complex and fluid nature of his classes required constant interpretation and reevaluation of the codes of operation and organization. The variety of students with varying levels of interest, responsibilities, motivations, and attitudes demanded adaptations in the organization and management of the class. Similarly, different subject matter, teaching stations, or equipment would also signal a change in class organization and operation. Bob, like many

---

d. The author here equates reliability with accuracy of the data, meaning in this case that the data reflected what Bob actually said and did. To validate the findings of the report in this instance means to seek feedback from the case study teacher that the findings are correct, that is, truthful from the case study teacher's perspective.

teachers (Clandinin, 1985; Clandinin & Connelly, 1986), relied on practical rules and principles, routines, and habits to guide classroom operation rather than inflexible standards or absolute rules.

Bob perceived the ability to organize and operate a class to be a fundamental and critical responsibility of a teacher. When asked "What would you look for in a high school teacher to determine if they were a good teacher?" he responded with a list of criteria heavily skewed toward organizational and operational concerns. His list included: (a) the kids are paying attention; (b) gives directions clearly and the kids respond to directions showing that they heard; (c) what he said made good sense; (d) organized drills, organized calisthenics, lesson didn't get bogged down; (e) didn't let a few kids take over the lesson; and (f) didn't get distracted from where he wanted to go.

Bob relied upon few resources in deciding the organizational and operational patterns of his classes. It was, perhaps, the improvisational character of a classroom that forced Bob to look primarily to his experience and beliefs in crafting his operational procedures and organizational patterns (Doyle, 1986; Kelsay, 1991; Leinhart & Greeno, 1986). He explained that

> There have been so many times I have had a structured program and then something comes along and changes it at the last second. . . . So you just, I guess it is out of necessity or survival, you just make do. Some things work and some don't and you just throw out the things that don't and you go to something else.

The fundamental criterion for evaluating his class organization and operation knowledge was Bob's satisfaction with the results of the policy, rule, or procedure. If it worked all was well, for the problem had been solved. The level of evaluation did not go any further.

Outside influence over his operation and organization came on two fronts. The first influence was over his teaching stations. Other members of the school had a greater influence over Bob's teaching station than he. In my time with Bob, I observed the nurse usurp the gymnasium to conduct health screening exams, the custodians claim the football field so that they could mow it for that evening's contest, and the building principal threaten to reallocate the all-purpose room Bob and Kathy used as a teaching station for a student lounge.

The second area of influence that held consequence for Bob's organization and class operation dealt with the consequences for student misconduct. He could set all of the rules he cared to set. There were no formal guidelines or recommendations. How he enforced those rules was another matter. Parents and administrators took a strong interest in the consequences Bob dealt students for misbehavior. Bob explained it this way:

> You've gotta have the right administration, the administrator that is willing to go along with what you see as important, what your values are, a disciplined structured program, and back you up on that. Because if you don't . . . the kids are going to start complaining, which in turn, the parents start complaining. Parents are going to the administration. If the administrator will support you and back you up, then you can.

Bob seemed unaware of an existence of a "shared technical culture" (Lortie, 1975) for matters of classroom operation and organization. The approval of others usually seemed unnecessary. For example, Bob's policy of required student showers was disliked by the students and Kathy alike. He believed that Kathy was entitled to her opinion but his students conformed to his opinion. Bob accommodated opinions from parents and administrators when he had no choice, but he did not see their views as more important than his own. As he was fond of telling his students "In this class, it's my way or the highway."

Teaching Behavior

A significant portion of Bob's everyday actions and activities were devoted to the task of instructing students. Knowledge for meeting these demands was classified by Schulman (1987) as general pedagogical knowledge, for this knowledge transcended a particular subject content. Much of Bob's teaching behavior was characterized by well rehearsed, time-worn rituals. Every class began with student-led exercises while Bob took attendance. Then Bob informed the students of the day's activities. A brief skill demonstration or explanation was followed by a drill. Most classes closed with a game or culminating activity. Sometimes, a game was played for the entire class period. The practices that defined Bob's teaching behavior were largely composed of comfortable habits and familiar routines. In crafting a teaching style, comfort does not appear to be an uncommon criterion among teachers (Lange & Burroughs-Lange, 1994; Russell & Johnston, 1988).

Bob did not actively pursue knowledge that directly affected his instructional practices. The roots of this perspective can be traced to his undergraduate days. "When I was going through college," he said, "they didn't have any methods classes. None. Zero." The fundamental criteria [sic] used to determine the success of a lesson was, therefore, not so much what students learned, but rather their level of enjoyment. During one interview Bob told me that "they really seem to enjoy it (the activity). They develop certain skills. The more skill they develop, the more they seem to enjoy it."

While he did not actively seek effective teaching strategies, Bob recognized its lacking in his repertoire of skills. He told me, "I hear in some cases, teachers drop the ball and let them play. You know, I'm guilty of a little bit of that too, at times, you know." He went on to say "That's one thing I could upgrade my program with, some more creative drill work that would teach the skills I want them to learn and at the same time give them some fun and enjoyment."

Bob's teaching behavior was a nonissue with almost everybody in the school. The structure of the school provided him with no feedback on his teaching behavior, nor was there visible encouragement for him to stimulate greater student achieve-

ment. Students, for example, appeared to have little regard for their learning in physical education. Upon seeing Bob before class, students would invariably ask "What are we gonna play?" "Do we have to dress down?" or "Are we gonna do anything today?" No student ever thanked Bob for something they learned or requested to learn a particular skill or concept.

Although student learning was a concern in Bob's occupational activity, it was not the driving force behind his pedagogical practices. He harbored a stronger concern for maintaining control over the collective social behavior of the students. He showed far greater frustration when there was a breach of order than when students failed to make significant learning gains. The concern for classroom control over educational substance has been a consistent finding in research on physical education teachers' conceptions of their occupational duties and responsibilities (Placek, 1983; Schempp, 1985, 1986).

The immediate and multiple demands placed on Bob's time in school often relegated the learning of his approximately 130 students to the back burner of his priorities. During one observation, Bob and I were in his office between classes and I remarked, "I can't believe all the things you have to attend to." His comment was

> Yeah, there's a lot going on. Right now I'm trying to get a test set up, get the equipment I need for that, worry about the two kids who are on their way to the counselor's office to drop the class, answer kids questions about what we're doing today, think about that indoor soccer ball for next period, I have two home counseling visits coming up, remember to read the announcements this period, and I have an executive school meeting.

He rose out of his chair, picked up his roster book, glanced over a tardy note pushed into his hand by a late student and was on his way to take roll and begin another class.

Time that could be used to evaluate and improve his instructional practices is consumed by the competing requirements of his coaching responsibilities and the many mundane activities he continually has to attend to (e.g., lost locks, attendance records, clean towel supply, field preparation, equipment maintenance). One morning every free moment before and between classes was used to locate a popcorn machine for the concessions that evening at the boys basketball game. His work environment conspired to inform Bob that the operation of the school as a system took precedent [sic] over student learning in a physical education class.

Additionally, there was little incentive for Bob to improve his teaching behavior to stimulate increases in student learning. Administrators held a greater concern for the operation of the school than they did for achievement of students in physical education. Parents were more concerned with how their children were treated than what they learned. Students wanted to play; not learn. Whether students learned in his class or not was a concern that was, from my observations, held only by Bob. And because of the lack of concern from others, it was often not even at the forefront of Bob's concerns. He received no rewards if learning was increased and there were no consequences for a lack of student achievement.

Subject Matter

The content of Bob's classes was described and detailed in a curriculum guide he had compiled. Objectives for each program were identified and the policies used to conduct the program were also described. The largest portion of the guide was composed of the specific subject-matter units. When asked about the resources used to complete the guide, Bob told me that most of the units came from an undergraduate curriculum course assignment. He has added to the guide materials and resources gathered at in-service programs.

Although the guide was a 148-page document and included an outline of each subject taught, it was used sparingly. Over the course of my time with Bob, I observed him using the guide perhaps a half dozen times, mostly to review teaching points for an upcoming lesson or remind himself of game rules. The guide did not hold the majority of subject matter Bob taught, for experience has taught him that he must "keep most of the (subject matter) knowledge organized in my head and I can't write it down because everything is situation specific."

Bob acquired new subject-matter knowledge based upon these criteria: (a) perceptions of his own competence in teaching the subject, (b) personal interest in the subject matter, (c) perceptions of student interests, (d) actual student demand as demonstrated by elective class enrollments, (e) time investment necessary to teach or prepare to teach the subject, (f) the novelty of the subject, and (g) facility and equipment constraints.

Bob reported that gymnastics and outdoor education were two content areas recently dropped. Gymnastics was no longer offered because Bob did not like teaching it and had a concern for liability. Outdoor education was no longer part of the curriculum because the individual who taught the course had left the school and Bob did not want to give up his weekends for the activities. Weight training was a new subject added to the course offerings because of student demand, Bob's personal interest in teaching the subject, and the availability of an adequate facility. Personal understanding and meaning of subject matter plays an important role in Bob's acquisition and use of content knowledge. Teachers in other subject areas also appear to rely on personal understanding in selecting content (Wilson & Wineburg, 1988).

By his own admission Bob is not an expert in many of the areas he teaches. Rather, he knows enough to teach a 10-day unit in the selected subject. He would draw from the subject areas in which he had expertise to bolster areas that were unfamiliar. For example, soccer drills were structured very much like basketball drills. Bob was required to teach over 93 different units in any given year. It would be difficult for any teacher to be knowledgeable in so many different subjects.

Bob gave this example of how and why new subject knowledge was selected:

I had never heard of pickleball until last year. I happened to be looking through a magazine and it looked like a neat game. So I wrote to them and I cheated a bit. It said, "We'll give you some free materials if you order a program." And I wrote to them and said we didn't receive our teaching sheets and they sent me one. Once I saw what it was all about, I wanted to implement it in our program. I wrote back and got the equipment.

The company supplied both the equipment necessary for instruction as well as the content to be taught. Bob was able to incorporate the content immediately into his program with no prior knowledge of the subject. Because the game strongly resembled tennis, a subject he had taught for many years, Bob used the same drills and skill demonstrations he used in his tennis unit. Thus, the combination of his previous experience and information from an equipment manufacturer supplied all the content knowledge necessary for a new instructional unit.

Perhaps it was the lack of expertise in subject matter that provided the flexibility that allowed Bob to change content so readily and amenably. It is also the lack of expert knowledge in these areas that forces Bob to use noneducational rational [sic] in selecting subject matter for his classes. "They got some enjoyment out of it. . . . They wanted to keep playing it (pickleball) forever, but I said 'Hey, we gotta stop and go on to something else . . . but that was a success."

Pedagogical-Content Knowledge

Shulman (1986) defines pedagogical-content knowledge as content knowledge "which goes beyond knowledge of subject matter per se to the dimension of subject matter for teaching" (p. 9). Years of experience have forged a mode of operation, a routine, which frames the knowledge Bob imparts to his students. Bob seeks curricular content that fits his teaching style. In pedagogical practice, he teaches an activity in terms of its essential skills by giving

brief explanations and sometimes demonstrations, then has students practice these skills through drills, and after varying amounts of practice the students are then given the rules and play the game. These procedures have been used for years by Bob with all varieties of subject matter. He is, therefore, more inclined to select new activities that fit his mode of operation than he is to look for new ways to teach old subject matter. Further, Bob was less likely to teach subject matter in depth and more likely to teach many activities at the introductory level. The more new information conveniently fit into familiar routines, the more likely it would be incorporated.

Bob's content knowledge appeared to not only influence what he teaches, but how he teaches. Activities, particularly skill drills, were borrowed from better-known subject lessons and adapted and applied in lesser-known subject areas. In concept explanations, metaphors and images were drawn from parallel concepts in better-known subjects and used to help explain subject concepts that he did not know well. Bob does not appear unique in this regard. Teachers of mathematics (Leinhart & Smith, 1985; Marks, 1990), social studies (Gudmundsdottir & Shulman, 1987), and English (Grossman, 1989, 1990; Gudmundsdottir, 1991) all seem to follow this process in acquiring and developing pedagogical-content knowledge.

As Bob screened new content knowledge for his pedagogical practice, he used the term *practical* to identify acceptable pedagogical-content knowledge. For example, in explaining why he takes few university courses, he stated he had "a great deal of difficulty finding coursework of relevance for a teacher in my situation. A lot of philosophy, theory, etc., but not many practical, time-proven methods which I can use in my class." Another time, he identified coaching clinics as more worthwhile than teaching workshops because the clinics "offer practical information that can be directly implemented into our program." Content that could be incorporated into the existing classroom routines and rituals was highly valued. Previous research reveals that Bob is not alone in his regard for knowledge that is easily imported into existing classroom practices (Alexander, Muir, & Chant, 1992; Elbaz, 1983).

External Conditions

Conditions originating outside the classroom, and removed from Bob's immediate control, came to bear on several pedagogical decisions. These conditions include local regulations and requirements that were imposed by the administration and school board as well as regulations and laws handed down from state and federal agencies. Therefore, the wishes and demands of administrators, students, parents, and state agencies factored into Bob's procurement of knowledge. The influence of administrators, parents, and students on Bob's knowledge was discussed above. School and state regulations also influenced him, but to a far lesser degree.

Bob passively resisted school and state imperatives that ran counter to his personal beliefs and his interpretation of the community moral standards. For example, in discussing coed classes, he reported that:

> We used to (have coed classes) but it was a hassle. . . . We had a lot of nondressers and got a lot of complaints from parents. It just wasn't worth it. So we have boys and girls separate the first year and together after that. We got a little pressure from the state about Title IX, but I think we're in compliance.

When he and I discussed the new state curricular guidelines, Bob expressed frustration that change seems to negate previous work. To him, it was not so much that the new ideas were better or worse than old ones, but that all his previous work on curriculum development was for naught. He felt frustrated that the amount of work that had gone into developing his curriculum was ignored by those in state agencies. "Hillcrest has always prided themselves on being a leader. Now we'll have to throw them (present guidelines) out for no apparent reason or justification." As he had in the past, he would continue as before making only token modifications to existing practice. External conditions were only a minor consideration in Bob's acquisition of knowledge.

CONCLUSION

After years of service, Bob had a well developed set of criteria to guide his acquisition of occupational knowledge. These criteria allowed Bob to identify gaps in his knowledge and to assess new knowledge in light of its potential contribution to his teaching. Contrary to the belief of many students, administrators, and colleagues, Bob continually reviewed and screened new information and then made attempts to integrate this knowledge into his professional practice. Because the criteria used in acquiring new knowledge were primarily comprised of experiences, interests, values, beliefs, and orientations, Bob's professional knowledge appeared personal and idiosyncratic (Carter, 1990; Zeichner, Tabachnick, & Densmore, 1987). Bob was, by his own admission, set in his ways. Therefore, the changes and alterations he did make were neither dramatic nor overtly visible. In short, little changed in the observable practices of Bob's day-to-day activities as a teacher and he became fairly predictable in his course of action.

Classroom order and operation held the highest priority in Bob's pedagogical knowledge. Subject matter that fit his personal interests, workplace conditions, and would result in student enjoyment had the greatest chance of penetrating the curriculum. New knowledge that conformed to his well-worn classroom practices passed Bob's test of valued professional knowledge. He acknowledged a lack of information regarding effective teaching behavior, and given his workplace conditions, this situation appears to have little chance to change. Will Bob ever change? He is, in fact, always changing as new information comes to him and is incorporated into his professional knowledge base. In the final analysis, however, Bob's time in service has made him well aware of who he is, what he does, why it does it, and what knowledge is required for him to meet the demands of teaching in a public school.

References

Alexander, D., Muir, D., Chant, D. (1992). Interrogating stories: How teachers think they learn to teach. *Teaching and Teacher Education, 8,* 59–68.

Carter, K. (1990). Teachers' knowledge and learning to teach. In W. R. Houston (Ed.) *Handbook of Research on Teacher Education* (pp. 291–310). New York: Macmillan.

Clandinin, D. J. (1985). Personal practical knowledge: A study of teachers' classroom images. *Curriculum Inquiry, 15,* 361–385.

Clandinin, D. J. & Connelly, F. M. (1986). Rhythms in teaching: The narrative study of teachers' personal practical knowledge of classrooms. *Teaching and Teacher Education, 2,* 377–387.

Doyle, W. (1986). Classroom organization and management (pp. 392–431). In M. Wittrock (Ed.) *Handbook of Research on Teaching* (3rd ed.). New York: Macmillian.

Elbaz, F. (1983). *Teacher thinking: A study of practical knowledge.* London: Croom Helm.

Glaser, B., & Strauss, A. (1967). *The discovery of grounded theory: Strategies for qualitative research.* Chicago: Aldine.

Goetz, J. P., & LeCompte, M. D. (1984). *Ethnography and qualitative design in educational research.* Orlando: Academic Press.

Grossman, P. (1989). A study of contrast: Sources of pedagogical content knowledge for secondary English. *Journal of Teacher Education, 40,* 24–32.

Grossman, P. (1990). *The making of a teacher: Teacher knowledge and teacher education.* New York: Teachers College Press.

Gudmundsdottir, S. (1991). Ways of seeing are ways of knowing: The pedagogical content of an expert English teacher. *Journal of Curriculum Studies, 23,* 207–218.

Gudmundsdottir, S., & Kristjansdottir, E. (1989, March). *The content of pedagogical content knowledge: Case studies of learning to teach.* Paper presented at the American Educational Research Association Annual Meeting, San Francisco, CA.

Gudmundsdottir, S., & Shulman, L. (1987). Pedagogical content knowledge in social studies. *Scandinavian Journal of Educational Research, 31,* 59–70.

Kelsay, K. L. (1991). When experience is the best teacher: The teacher as researcher. *Action in Teacher Education, 13,* 14–21.

Lange, J. D., & Burroughs-Lange, S. G. (1994). Professional uncertainty and professional growth: A case study of experienced teachers. *Teaching and Teacher Education, 10,* 617–631.

Lather, P. (1986). Issues of validity in openly ideological research: Between a rock and a soft place. *Interchange, 17,* 63–84.

Leinhart, G., & Greeno, J. (1986). The cognitive skill of teaching. *Journal of Educational Psychology, 78,* 75–95.

Leinhardt, G., & Smith, D. A. (1985). Expertise in mathematics instruction: Subject matter knowledge. *Journal of Educational Psychology, 77,* 247–271.

Lortie, D. C. (1975). *Schoolteacher: A sociological study.* Chicago: University of Chicago Press.

Marks, R. (1990). Pedagogical content knowledge: From a mathematical case to a modified conception. *Journal of Teacher Education, 41,* 3–11.

Miles, M. B., & Huberman, A. M. (1984). *Qualitative data analysis: A sourcebook of new methods.* Beverly Hills: Sage Publications.

Patton, M. (1980). *Qualitative evaluation methods.* Beverly Hills: Sage Publications.

Placek, J. (1983). Conceptions of success in teaching: Happy, busy and good? In T. Templin & J. Olson (Eds.) *Teaching in Physical Education* (pp. 46–56). Champaign, IL: Human Kinetics.

Russell, T., & Johnston, P. (1988, April). *Teachers' learning from experiences of teaching: Analysis based on metaphor and reflection.* Paper presented at the annual meeting of the American Education Research Association, New Orleans, LA.

Schempp, P. G. (1985). Becoming a better teacher: An analysis of the student teaching experience. *Journal of Teaching in Physical Education, 4,* 158–166.

Schempp, P. G. (1986). Physical education student teachers' beliefs in their control over student learning. *Journal of Teaching in Physical Education, 5,* 198–203.

Schon, D. A. (1983). *The reflective practitioner.* New York: Basic Books.

Shulman, L. S. (1986). Those who understand: Knowledge growth in teaching. *Educational Researcher, 15,* 4–14.

Shulman, L. S. (1987). Knowledge and teaching: Foundations of the new reform. *Harvard Educational Review, 57,* 1–22.

West, W. G. (1975). Participant observation research on the social construction of everyday classroom order. *Interchange, 6*(4), 35–43.

Wilson, S., & Wineburg, S. (1988). Peering at history through different lenses: The role of disciplinary perspectives in teaching history. *Teachers' College Record, 89,* 525–539.

Yinger, R. J. (1980). A study of teacher planning. *Elementary School Journal, 80,* 107–127.

Zeichner, K., Tabachnick, R., & Densmore, K. (1987). Individual, institutional and cultural influences on the development of teachers' craft knowledge. In J. Calderhead (Ed.) *Exploring teachers' thinking* (pp. 21–59). London: Cassell.

CHAPTER 11

ETHNOGRAPHIC RESEARCH

Arvella Johnson just completed the requirements for an elementary teaching certificate. Although she grew up in a relatively homogeneous culture in the United States, she is applying for several jobs in a nearby state with a high proportion of immigrant families from Central and South America. To prepare for her job interviews, she decided to do some reading about the cultures of ethnic-minority youngsters.

By doing a literature review, Arvella located ethnographic research studies that related to her problem. Some are about the cultures of Central and South American countries, while others describe the culture shock and adjustment that students from these countries face as they enter U.S. society and schools. After reading this research, she felt almost as if she had seen and talked with students like those she expects to encounter in her first teaching assignment. Also, the research stimulated Arvella's reflections on what she might do as a teacher if she learned that some of her students faced the issues that were described.

In this chapter you will see how the findings of ethnographic research can help educators understand and respond more effectively to the cultural characteristics of the varied groups they encounter in their work.

OBJECTIVES

After studying this chapter, you will be able to

1. describe the major characteristics of ethnographic research.
2. explain what ethnographers mean by culture and why they view it as worthy of systematic study.
3. explain how ethnographers collect and analyze data about the phenomena they study.
4. describe the issues that ethnographic researchers face in their efforts to understand and improve educational practice.

KEY TERMS

agency
critical ethnography
cultural acquisition
cultural transmission
culture

emic perspective
enculturation
ethnography
ethnology
ethnoscience

etic perspective
holistic ethnography
microethnography
participant observation
thick description

THE CHARACTERISTICS OF ETHNOGRAPHIC RESEARCH

Ethnography can be defined as the attempt to describe culture or aspects of culture. Readers of ethnographic research reports can expand their awareness of cultures much different from their own, and also develop more understanding of their own culture.

Ethnography was developed by anthropologists, but researchers in other disciplines, including sociology and psychology, have also contributed to this research tradition. Since the 1960s, some educational researchers who became disenchanted with positivism and the methods of quantitative research have turned to ethnography as an alternative approach. The main features of ethnographic research are described below.

1. *Focus on culture or aspects of culture.* Early ethnographies focused on providing a comprehensive description and analysis of the entire culture of a group of people. This research tradition sometimes is called *holistic ethnography*. Most current ethnographies are more modest in scope; they focus on particular aspects of culture. These studies sometimes are called *microethnography* to reflect their narrowed focus.

Some ethnographic studies bear labels that characterize the phenomena that were studied or the research methods that were used. For example, critical ethnography involves the use of ethnography to study oppressive power relations in a specific culture, while ethnoscience involves cataloging the semantic systems used by a culture or subculture (e.g., elementary school children) to describe important social phenomena, such as work and play.

2. *Naturalistic study of individuals in the field.* Many early ethnographers lived in another culture for a period of years in order to investigate the origins of such cultural phenomena as religious beliefs, sexual practices, and the learning of work skills and social roles. They typically sought to provide a holistic description of non-Western cultures, whose presumably more "primitive" cultural practices were expected to reveal universal patterns in the development of such phenomena. Today, ethnographers often study subcultures in their own vicinity, but they still carry out data collection in the natural setting of the members of the culture. They rely on unobtrusive data collection methods, such as informal observations and conversations, with which field participants will be comfortable. They also seek to immerse themselves in the setting, both to increase participants' trust of them and to deepen their own understanding of cultural phenomena.

3. *Making the familiar strange.* One part of ethnographers' mission is to reflect light on phenomena that members of a culture overlook because they are taken for granted. This research helps us understand the hidden meanings in patterns of language, behavior, and arrangement of physical space that are characteristic

of different groups or types of people. For example, an ethnographer studying the culture of college sports teams might notice varied patterns of acceptable and unacceptable behavior beyond those contained in the game rules, such as differences in the way that starters and bench players cluster around the coach during time-outs.

Ethnographers can make the familiar strange either by immersing themselves in a culture far different from their own, by studying a subculture in their own community with which they are unfamiliar, or by investigating a subculture with which they are familiar but looking at it from the perspective of the subculture's members rather than from their own perspective.

4. *Thick description.* In writing their research report, ethnographers typically describe the field setting in great detail and use extensive quotations from field participants. This "thick" description is intended to bring the culture alive for the reader. Also, ethnographers often write their descriptions in the present tense, which creates the impression of permanence or even universality—that is, the sense that the description applies not just to the specific cases that were studied, but to any and all similar cases.

Some of the characteristics of ethnography match those of a qualitative case study, as described in Chapter 10. As in a case study, the ethnographer focuses on a case or cases, which can range from a single individual to an entire community, society, or institution. Likewise, in ethnographic research the researcher makes an in-depth study of the phenomenon of interest (a culture or some aspect of culture); studies the phenomenon in its natural context; and represents both the field participants' (emic) and researchers' (etic) perspectives. For this reason, David Lancy (1993) claimed that ethnography is "the prototype for the qualitative method" (p. 66).

Because qualitative case studies draw so extensively from ethnography, the entire body of qualitative research sometimes is referred to as *ethnographic research*. It was in this sense that Paul Schempp, the author of the article reprinted in Chapter 10 on case study research, described his research as using "ethnographic techniques."

While educational ethnographies are similar to other case studies, they differ in several ways. First, ethnographies focus specifically on aspects of culture, whereas case studies may focus on a wide range of phenomena, such as the life history of a teacher or the effectiveness of an instructional program. Second, ethnographies usually involve a longer, more in-depth period of data collection than a typical educational case study. Third, ethnographers often make cross-cultural comparisons to further explore and explain the phenomena with which they are concerned. The comparative study of cultures (i.e., *ethnology*) is the primary focus of some ethnographers. In contrast, case study researchers usually limit themselves to a single cultural context.

ETHNOGRAPHIC CONCEPTIONS OF CULTURE

Culture is the central concept in ethnographic research. The term originated with the development of efforts to assist the growth of specific organisms, as in agriculture. Early ethnographers viewed "native" cultures as representing earlier stages of cultural evolution than those of supposedly more "civilized" Western cultures. Researchers today view the peoples of the world as being grouped into many cultures, each with positive qualities and unique characteristics.

Culture can be defined as the pattern of traditions, symbols, rituals, and artifacts that characterize a particular group of individuals. Different cultural features are viewed as being systematically related to each other, forming an integrated whole. On close examination, however, the culture of a given group of people might appear more like what Murray Wax (1993) called "a thing of shreds and patches" (p. 101) than a consistent whole. Also, Lancy notes that today's world is becoming increasingly homogeneous with respect to culture. Wealth, rather than influences unique to their culture, is now the principal force that differentiates individuals' lifestyles.

Ethnographers believe that the influence of culture in human beings' lives is what makes us unique as a species. Culture allows a particular group of people to live together and thrive through a system of shared meanings and values, but that same system also may lead them to oppose or oppress groups with different shared meanings and values. Ethnographers also believe that certain aspects of human culture have a particularly strong influence on individual and group life. These aspects include patterns of social organization, socialization, learning, family structure, religious practices, and ceremonial behavior. For example, ethnographers might focus on the celebratory rituals marking transitional events in the lives of members of the culture, including school graduations, weddings, and baby showers. Because such aspects of culture are interrelated, ethnographers must study not only one aspect of a culture, but also attend to other aspects to which it is closely related.

The study of culture might be compared to creating a mosaic. Each ethnographic study contributes fragments of information to a broad description of the culture. However, certain parts of the mosaic are likely to be more differentiated and complete than others. For example, with respect to American school culture, more research exists about the culture of teachers than about the culture of school boards and administrators, in part because groups in power often are less inclined to communicate openly to researchers about their cultural life.

Lancy identified three major cultural themes on which educational ethnography has focused: (1) enculturation, which is the process by which cultural practices and beliefs are transferred to the youth or other new members of a culture; (2) how communities adapt to or resist the efforts of formal educational institutions to shape and control the learning processes of their youth; and (3) the culture and subculture of individuals in various social roles (e.g., teacher, student, principal) in educational institutions. We give examples of research reflecting each of these themes in the sections that follow.

THE METHODS OF ETHNOGRAPHIC RESEARCH

The following discussion of ethnographic procedures corresponds closely to the steps in doing a case study, which we described in Chapter 10. These procedures involve formulating a research problem and selecting a case, collecting field data, analyzing and interpreting the data, and reporting study findings.

Formulating a Research Problem

To formulate a research problem for ethnographic research, the researcher must first define the aspect of culture to be explored. Sometimes this step occurs after the culture to be studied has been selected. This selection process sometimes capitalizes on accidental or forced circumstances. For example, a study of the Trobriand Islanders in New Guinea by Bronislaw Malinowski (1922) was occasioned, or at least lengthened, by the advent of World War I and his detention on the islands in the status of an enemy alien. Similarly, a trilogy of studies about the high school dropout "Brad" by Harry Wolcott (1994) began when the researcher discovered the youth living on a corner of his property in the forest outside a small city.

Ethnographers often first formulate their problem and then select a setting that fits it. For example, Margaret Mead (1930) wanted to study the relationship between children's thinking processes and spontaneous animism (i.e., beliefs in the existence of spirits that were thought to develop independently of any external influence). Mead selected Melanesia because it contained many "primitive" groups and had been characterized by previous researchers as a region filled with the phenomena usually associated with spontaneous animism. She then narrowed her focus to the relatively unknown Manus tribe for practical reasons, including the availability of some texts in the native language and of a school boy willing to act as an interpreter.

The research study by Kenneth Anderson and AnnE McClard (1993) that is reprinted in this chapter involved a team of ethnographic researchers who explored two aspects of university student culture: the meanings that students attributed to the construct of *study*, and the students' perceived and actual use of time. The researchers also explored the effects of computers on these aspects of student culture.

Collecting Field Data

Ethnographers use the full range of qualitative data-collection methods, and also quantitative methods when appropriate. For example, Mead observed the Manus children at play, in their homes, and with their parents. She collected

spontaneous drawings from the children, who had never before held a pencil in their hands, and asked them to interpret ink blots. Because the entire Manus tribe included only 210 people, Mead was able to follow all current events in the village "with careful attention to their cultural significance and the role which they played in the lives of the children" (p. 291). Records of conversations and interpretations were all taken down in the native language. Mead avoided technical terms, couching her descriptions "in the field of the novelist" (p. 292). She also used detailed record sheets to organize her notes. For example, the household record sheet included headings for the house owner's children by each marriage, who financed his marriages, and what marriages he was financing. Mead made a detailed analysis of the composition of a subculture of the Manus tribe (the Peri population), recording the number of married couples, widows, and widowers and the average number of children per married couple.

In his ethnography of a school principal, Wolcott (1973) shadowed the principal for a period of time while making continuous entries in a notebook. He then collected "time and motion" data, recording what the principal was doing, where, and with whom, at 60-second intervals over a carefully sampled two-week period at school. The researcher also carried out analyses of official school notices, quantitative records, and census data for the community in which the school was located.

Wolcott engaged in almost constant note taking so that participants in the setting that he studied would become comfortable with it. His longhand notes were typed onto 5" × 8" cards, each describing a single event. The researcher did not return to the school until he had completed his notes from the last visit. To avoid becoming overidentified with the principal, he visited often with teachers and staff members. Wolcott also carried out visits with the principal's family at home and observed the principal's errands and community activities around town and at special social events.

Only after he had spent over half a year at the school did Wolcott add interviewing as a data-collection method. He conducted and taped several one-hour interviews with the principal (e.g., about the principal's forecast of the coming school year, his family life, and what had occurred at the school since Wolcott's last visit). The ethnographic research also included individual interviews with 13 faculty and two staff members about their perceptions of the principal as a school administrator. All fifth- and sixth-grade students were asked to write brief, anonymous comments about the principal.

Wolcott concluded his fieldwork by distributing a 10-page questionnaire to all faculty and staff: "The questionnaire was particularly valuable in enabling me to obtain systematic data about the staff, as I could see no point in holding a long taped interview with each of the twenty-nine members of the regular and part-time staff" (p. 123).

In the ethnographic study that is reprinted in this chapter, the research team spent an entire academic year investigating the college students living in a freshman residence hall at their university that had just been outfitted with

computers. The researchers describe participant observation as their chief method of data collection. One of the researchers actually lived in the residence hall for the entire study year, thus serving as an almost constant participant observer. Other information was obtained from formal and informal interviews and from written questionnaires (referred to in the article as *surveys*). The questionnaire data included quantitative measures of students' self-reported use of computers and their time allocations to study and other activities. Another quantitative measure was the amount of each student's computer and network use. These data were collected directly by a computer program that tracked the use of computers in the residence hall network.

Thus, although ethnography generally is a qualitative method of inquiry, there can be exceptions. In qualitative research, as in quantitative research, researchers are free to use any methods that help them understand the phenomena they are studying.

Analyzing and Interpreting Ethnographic Data

As we explained in Chapter 10, data analysis in qualitative research usually begins while the data are being collected, and affects subsequent data-collection efforts. For example, Mead's research led her to an emerging sense that the hypothesis guiding her study (i.e., that the concept of animism arises spontaneously in children's thinking) was not going to be supported by the data. Nonetheless, she continued collecting data in order to discover and support an alternate interpretation of what she was observing:

> The results of this research were negative, that is, evidence was found to support the view that animism is not a spontaneous aspect of child thinking nor does it spring from any type of thought characteristic of immature mental development; its presence or absence in the thought of children is dependent upon cultural factors, language, folk lore, adult attitudes, etc., and these cultural factors have their origin in the thought of individual adults, not in the misconceptions of children. (p. 289)

Mead's admission of her failure to support her original hypothesis reflects the requirement that ethnographers look for disconfirming evidence and then modify their hypotheses, theories, and interpretations to reflect whatever they discover in the field.

The use of theory to interpret ethnographic data is illustrated by a study of Christian schooling in a U.S. community that was conducted by Alan Peshkin (1986). Using data obtained by interviews, questionnaires, and observations, Peshkin examined many aspects of the culture that a fundamentalist Christian high school sought to establish, including how it originated from, and in turn influenced development of, the beliefs of teachers, students, and students' parents. Peshkin applied a particular sociological theory to describe the culture of Bethany Baptist Academy as that of a "total institution." By this he meant that the school had pervasive effects on its members, effects that were "unrestricted

in time and space, neither limited to a term or a sentence nor confined to a building or a particular setting" (p. 274).

Reporting Ethnographic Research

Marion Dobbert (1982) described an ethnographic report as having five parts: (1) a statement of the research questions and the situations and problems that led to them, (2) a description of the background research and theory used to refine the study's questions and design, (3) a detailed review of the research design, (4) a presentation of the data, and (5) an explanation of the findings. Dobbert described the presentation of data as the "heart and soul" of the report. To her, this presentation should be a detailed description of the cultural scene under investigation, presented in organized fashion and based on a low-level (i.e., descriptive or low-inference) categorical analysis of data.

In reporting about the student culture involving the constructs of study and time described in this chapter, Anderson and McClard use several long quotes from individual students. Their narrative also explains the meaning of these constructs from the students' emic perspective:

> Study breaks were an integral part of study time. Indeed, students often spent more time on study breaks than they spent studying. Because study breaks were a social activity, it appeared to the outsiders that students goofed off a lot. Clearly, the study break, as defined by the student, was actually study time. The academic problems that the students worked out during a break could not be worked out in more formal settings or on their own. The study break was a secure environment for testing ideas. (pp. 165–166 in the original article)

The authors thus paint a sympathetic, but revealing, picture of how typical college students define and use their time, likening it to the time orientation of farmers rather than to that of "9-to-5 workers."

Ethnographic reports often have a story-like flavor, because of ethnographers' concern for thick description and conveying the emic perspective. This story-like quality is illustrated by Mead's description of an interaction between a six-year-old child, Popoli, and his father:

> [H]e whines out in the tone which all Manus natives use when begging betel nut: "A little betel?" The father throws him a nut. He tears the skin off with his teeth and bites it greedily. "Another," the child's voice rises to a higher pitch. The father throws him a second nut, which the child grasps firmly in his wet little fist, without acknowledgment. "Some pepper leaf?" The father frowns. "I have very little, Popoli." "Some pepper leaf." The father tears off a piece of a leaf and throws it to him. The child scowls at the small piece. "This is too little. More! More! More!" His voice rises to a howl of rage. (pp. 20–21)

The story concludes with the father rationally explaining why he cannot give his son more pepper leaf, accidentally dropping his knife into the water and requesting that his son get it, and the son refusing: "No. I won't, thou, thou stingy one, thou hidest thy pepper leaf from me." The child swims away, leaving his father to climb down and rescue the knife himself. And Mead leaves it to the reader to infer the quality of parent-child relationships in the Manus culture.

To do a holistic ethnography of a culture, or even a complete study of one aspect of a culture, is a major undertaking, as our examples illustrate. Some ethnographers devote their entire career to the continuing study of one culture. Often a single report represents only one aspect of the total culture. The culture might be revisited repeatedly in order to study different aspects and changes over time. For example, George Spindler and Louise Spindler (1982) have carried out a comparative ethnography of two schools and their communities in Germany and the United States for a period of several decades.

APPLYING ETHNOGRAPHIC RESEARCH FINDINGS TO EDUCATIONAL PRACTICE

Ethnography has provided educational researchers a means to explore in depth the various ways in which cultural factors affect teaching and learning. Studies that reveal the cultural milieu in which students find themselves when outside of school, for example, obviously can help teachers better understand the students and hopefully foster their learning. However, you should take care to read ethnographic research reports critically, just as you would any other type of research report, rather than accept their findings at face value.

As we explained in Chapter 10, qualitative researchers use different criteria than quantitative researchers to judge the credibility, trustworthiness, and applicability of their findings. Some of these criteria involve reader judgment, whereas others involve principles of sound research design and thoroughness of data-collection and analysis procedures. These same criteria apply to ethnographic research, which relies primarily on qualitative methodology.

In addition to applying these general criteria, you should know about issues of credibility, trustworthiness, and applicability that are specific to ethnographic research and the ethnography of education. Sensitivity to these issues will help you read ethnographic research reports with greater understanding and a more critical eye. We discuss seven of these issues below.

1. *Equating schooling and education.* One danger that ethnographers of education face is that of equating schooling and education. In many cultures, formal educational institutions control the provision and validation of learning among the members of the culture. However, many individuals have important learning experiences in other contexts, including family units, peer groups, or the workplace. A holistic ethnography of education would need to include explorations of the teaching-learning process as it occurs in varied contexts.

2. *Learning as a cultural process.* Ethnographers of education face the issue of whether it is better to view learning primarily as a process of cultural transmission or of cultural acquisition. Research on cultural acquisition puts the focus on how individuals seek to acquire, or to avoid acquiring, the concepts, values, skills, and behaviors that are reflected in the common culture. In contrast, research on cultural transmission puts the focus on how the larger social structure intentionally intervenes in individuals' lives in order to promote or, in some cases, to discourage, learning of particular concepts, values, skills, or behaviors.

This issue plays a central role in efforts to understand differences in educational success among the members of various cultural groups. Lancy cites a number of research studies that explored the adaptation to public schooling of young people whose cultures were in transition:

> All document persistent "failure" in the sense that one sees little pleasure in either the teaching staff or the children. There is no evidence that students are making satisfactory academic progress, enabling them to "climb out of the ghetto," "leave the reservation," or "become self-sufficient." Increasingly, anthropologists who study minority education now take student failure as their point of departure. . . . (p. 41)

In seeking the cause of many minority students' lower level of academic success compared to that of students in the mainstream culture, John Ogbu (1978) carried out research based upon a theoretical model of education and caste. The model focuses on learning as cultural acquisition, and the claim that native-born members of minority groups who have suffered a long history of economic discrimination in the United States tend to withhold their investment in education, because they do not perceive it as having any economic payoff. Other qualitative researchers interested in cultural acquisition have studied individuals' sense of agency, which refers to the assumed ability to shape the conditions of one's life, whatever one's cultural situation.

Spindler and Spindler (1992) observed that the focus on cultural acquisition makes it easy to slip into a "blame-the-victim" interpretation of individuals' learning problems. They argued that ethnography can best contribute to the understanding of learning by showing how societies use their cultural resources to organize the conditions and purposes of learning. Their research focuses on how schools and other agents of cultural transmission (e.g., families) facilitate or hinder specific types of learning by individuals from various cultures.

Still another position is that both cultural acquisition and cultural transmission can figure in a given individual's or group's learning. In this view, the task of educational ethnography is to determine how cultural factors and human agency interact to codetermine what individuals and groups learn.

3. *Conveying culture accurately.* Some educators question the ability of ethnographic research to convey the richness and complexity of cultural phenomena. Clifford Geertz (1973) claimed that ethnographies are "fiction," in that they are not an accurate description of the culture but rather a story told by the

researchers using various literary conventions and devices. Critics argue that the genre of writing used in typical ethnographic reports imposes an order on cultural phenomena that might not accurately reflect the variety and ongoing changes occurring in the culture being described. As a result, different role groups (e.g., teachers or administrators) might accept ethnographic findings as applying to the individuals or groups with whom they have contact (e.g., students or parents) without checking their actual applicability to those individuals or groups. As Lancy notes, "one must be extremely skeptical of the cherished assumption [in ethnography] of cultural homogeneity" (p. 63).

4. *Reflecting privileged male discourse.* Some feminist theorists argue that traditional ethnographies reflect a privileged male discourse that maintains unequal relationships between researchers and the members of the culture who are studied. Such criticisms have prompted some ethnographers to adopt a "dialogic" stance in which they conduct their research as a collaboration between the researcher and the members of the culture being studied. In fact, some educational ethnographers have sought not just to describe, but also to change, a particular culture to promote student learning and empowerment. For example, some ethnographic researchers have actively sought to change the school curriculum in order to match the unique cultural characteristics of students from minority ethnic backgrounds (Weisner, Gallimore, & Jordan, 1988; Collier, 1988). In addition, the specialization of critical ethnography enables ethnographers to engage in critical inquiry about cultural phenomena (see Chapter 12).

5. *Difficulty in making the familiar strange.* Because educators who become researchers typically valued and did well in school themselves, they may have difficulty in discovering the hidden meanings of school culture as it is experienced by individuals with different values about, and experiences with, education. As Wolcott (1987) puts it:

> Being so totally immersed in and committed to formal education, they are as likely to "discover" school culture as fish are likely to discover water. The cross-cultural and comparative basis that helps ethnographers identify something they are tentatively willing to describe as culture in someone else's behavior—because it is readily distinguishable from their own—is lacking. (p. 50)

Wolcott recommends that students learning ethnographic research methods do their first major fieldwork in a distant society or with a dramatically different microculture before attempting to study the all-too-familiar culture of the school or classroom.

6. *Overidentification with informants.* In their attempt to reflect the emic perspective, ethnographers sometimes overidentify with one or more of the cultural groups from whom they seek their informants. In studying school culture, for

example, they might give the impression that the students' perspective is more truthful or ethical than that of the teachers with whom they have contact.

7. *Balancing the emic and etic perspectives.* It is not easy for ethnographers to balance the emic and etic perspectives obtained about a group's culture. The emic perspective involves the perceptions and language categories used by members of the culture to describe and explain the culture. That perspective helps readers understand a culture as a unique social reality, but does not always provide a sound basis for discovering regularities of social life that can be used to describe and explain other cultures. Some critics argue that the ethnographers' etic perspective, which is oriented to standard categories for describing a culture, might provide a better basis for the discovery of cross-cultural regularities.

Lancy recommends that ethnographers attempt to reconcile the etic and emic perspectives by checking the correspondence between field participants' thoughts about their setting and their actual behavior in that setting. For example, Lancy (1976) conducted an ethnographic study using research methods based on ethnoscience to explore the activities in which students engage while at school, from the perspective of the students themselves. He developed a taxonomy of activities from information obtained in student interviews. The taxonomy included main categories of student activities (working, helping, making, playing, and fooling/messing around), and subcategories for each. He then used the categories derived from the student interview data to develop a behavior observation checklist of students' in-school activities. In subsequent observations of the students in six different school settings, he found a good match between the taxonomy categories and students' actual behavior.

CONCLUDING THOUGHT

Imagine that you have landed on a desert island and found it occupied by a tribe of human beings unlike any that you have met before. Out of curiosity and a desire for connection, you decide to mingle with these people and learn about their way of life. Gradually you learn to communicate with them. As an educator, you take special interest in what the tribe does to teach its youngest members basic living skills, acceptable ways to express their boundless energy, and how to relate to others in the tribe and contribute to its welfare through their labor. You also try to understand how the tribe makes sense of and justifies these activities, some of which appear to take the form of ritual behavior. At the same time, you find yourself constantly reflecting on the ways in which such learning typically occurs in your own culture.

This imaginary situation corresponds to how ethnographers approach the study of specific cultural phenomena involving education. The findings of ethnographic research provide a rich picture of a cultural phenomenon, one that ideally is based on a balance between the etic perspective of researchers and the emic perspective of the members of the culture whom they study. Reading reports of ethnographic research involving aspects of culture that relate to your work should give you a richer understanding of the teaching-learning process and a better basis for improving your professional practices.

SELF-CHECK TEST

1. When researchers study a subculture in their own vicinity with which they are unfamiliar, they are fulfilling the intent of ethnographic research to
   a. carry out naturalistic observations of participants in the field.
   b. make the familiar strange.
   c. provide a thick description of a cultural phenomenon.
   d. do a cross-cultural comparison.

2. Ethnographers focus on the study of culture because they believe that
   a. the influence of culture in human beings' lives is what makes them unique as a species.
   b. the study of primitive cultures can show how Western cultures evolved.
   c. an increasing number of distinct cultures are emerging in the world.
   d. the similarities observed between people from different parts of the world are best explained in terms of enculturation.

3. Ethnographers
   a. rely exclusively on qualitative methods of data collection.
   b. begin analyzing their data only after concluding their fieldwork.
   c. sometimes present their findings in a story-like format.
   d. continue collecting data until they have confirmed their hypotheses.

4. In providing a holistic description of a culture, ethnographers generally seek to
   a. compare the culture to other cultures.
   b. give primacy to the views of high-status members of the culture.
   c. use their own perspective to reconcile conflicting views of the culture.
   d. balance the emic and etic perspectives.

5. Some educational ethnographers consider the main reason for minority students' lower academic performance than mainstream students to be their tendency to withhold their investment in education because they do not perceive it as having any economic payoff. This viewpoint focuses on the effects of _____ on students' performance.
   a. cultural acquisition
   b. cultural assimilation
   c. school organization
   d. teacher bias

6. Referring to ethnographies as "fictions" reflects primarily the view of some scholars that
   a. ethnographers can never reflect the emic perspective; they can only reflect the etic perspective.
   b. ethnographers are biased toward conveying cultural aspects in the most negative terms.
   c. ethnographies are stories told by researchers using various literary conventions and devices.
   d. only holistic ethnography can truly represent the characteristics of a culture.

CHAPTER REFERENCES

Anderson, K. T., & McClard, A. P. (1993). Study time: Temporal orientations of freshmen students and computing. *Anthropology and Education Quarterly, 24,* 159–177.

Collier, J. (1988). Survival at Rough Rock: An historical overview of Rough Rock Demonstration School. *Anthropology and Education Quarterly, 19,* 253–269.

Dobbert, M. (1982). *Ethnographic research: Theory and application for modern schools and societies.* New York: Praeger.

Geertz, C. (1973). *The interpretation of cultures: Selected essays.* New York: Basic Books.

Lancy, D. F. (1976). The beliefs and behaviors of pupils in an experimental school: Introduction and overview. *Learning Research and Development Center Publication Series 3.* ERIC Document Reference No. ED 127 301.

Lancy, D. F. (1993). *Qualitative research in education: An introduction to the major traditions.* White Plains, NY: Longman.

Malinowski, B. (1922). *Argonauts of the Western Pacific.* New York: Dutton.

Mead, M. (1930). *Growing up in New Guinea: A comparative study of primitive education.* New York: William Morrow.

Ogbu, J. U. (1978). *Minority education and caste: The American system in cross-cultural perspective.* New York: Academic Press.

Peshkin, A. (1986). *God's choice: The total world of a fundamentalist Christian school.* Chicago: University of Chicago Press.

Spindler, G., & Spindler, L. (1982). Roger Harker and Schoenhausen: From the familiar to the strange and back again. In G. Spindler (Ed.), *Doing the ethnography of schooling* (pp. 21–43). New York: Holt, Rinehart, & Winston.

Spindler, G., & Spindler, L. (1992). Cultural process and ethnography: An anthropological perspective. In M. D. LeCompte, W. L. Millroy, & J. Preissle (Eds.), *Handbook of qualitative research in education* (pp. 53–92). San Diego: Academic.

Wax, M. (1993). How culture misdirects multiculturalism. *Anthropology and Educational Quarterly, 24,* 99–115.

Weisner, T. S., Gallimore, R., & Jordan, C. (1988). Unpackaging cultural effects on classroom learning: Native Hawaiian peer assistance and child-generated activity. *Anthropology and Education Quarterly, 19,* 327–353.

Wolcott, H. F. (1973). *The man in the principal's office: An ethnography.* New York: Holt, Rinehart, & Winston.

Wolcott, H. F. (1987). On ethnographic intent. In G. D. Spindler & L. Spindler (Eds.), *Interpretive ethnography of education* (pp. 37–57). Hillsdale, NJ: Erlbaum.

Wolcott, H. F. (1994). *Transforming qualitative data: Description, analysis, and interpretation.* Thousand Oaks, CA: Sage.

RECOMMENDED READING

Atkinson, P., & Hammersley, M. (1994). Ethnography and participant observation. In N. K. Denzin & Y. S. Lincoln (Eds.), *Handbook of qualitative research* (pp. 248–261). Thousand Oaks, CA: Sage.

Describes key issues that have developed within the ethnographic research tradition, and summarizes contemporary perspectives on those issues.

LeCompte, M. D., & Preissle, J. (1993). *Ethnography and qualitative design in educational research* (2nd ed.). San Diego: Academic Press.

Describes how to design and carry out ethnographic research in education. Traces the origins of ethnography from anthropology as well as more recent influences on educational ethnography from sociology, psychology, and other fields.

Spindler, G., & Spindler, L. (1992). Cultural process and ethnography: An anthropological perspective. In M. D. LeCompte, W. L. Millroy, & J. Preissle (Eds.), *Handbook of qualitative research in education* (pp. 53–92). San Diego: Academic Press.

Explains the nature of cultural phenomena and the strategies used by ethnographers to study enculturation in and across cultures.

SAMPLE ETHNOGRAPHIC RESEARCH STUDY:
STUDY TIME: TEMPORAL ORIENTATIONS OF
FRESHMEN STUDENTS AND COMPUTING

Anderson, K. T., & McClard, A. P. (1993). Study time: Temporal orientations of freshmen students and computing. *Anthropology and Education Quarterly*, 24, 159–177.

In the rest of this chapter you will read a research article that illustrates an ethnographic research study. It is preceded by comments written especially for this book by the authors of the article. Then the article itself is reprinted in full, just as it appeared when originally published. Where appropriate, we have added footnotes to help you understand the information contained in the article.

Researchers' Comments, Prepared by Kenneth Anderson and Ann McClard

Background

We wrote the article that is reprinted here when we were both predoctoral graduate students in anthropology at Brown University, employed by the Institute for Research in Information and Scholarship (IRIS). Before this study we were involved in IRIS's three-year research project on the effectiveness of using an early network-based, hypermedia educational software product (Intermedia) in the classroom. (The World Wide Web is an example of this technology as it has evolved.)

On the IRIS project we had done extensive ethnographic work in school classrooms and computer laboratories, under the direction of William Beeman. We focused on the question of whether and how the Intermedia technology was changing the way students learned. Although we found this work interesting, we also felt that we were missing "the big picture" concerning the nature of students' knowledge acquisition. It seemed to us that much of what the students were learning came through informal means, and was more related to social networks than to computer networks. As a consequence, we and two colleagues who had also worked on the Intermedia project decided to redirect our research on technology.

Some of the questions that compelled us to undertake this research were: (1) How do students go about learning on a day-to-day basis? (2) What practices do students employ to mediate their college experience? (3) What "interpretive lenses" do students use to navigate through college, both socially and academically? We wanted to explore through ethnography the less formal learning environment of the university, where students live, work, and spend the majority of their time. The college dormitory provided us with a naturally occurring social unit to study. Although residential life studies were numerous at the time of our research, we knew of none that focused on the social aspects of learning.

We were also interested in the effects of technology on learning, but not in a conventional sense. Instead, we sought to look at technology from the perspective of a cultural anthropologist. With a few notable exceptions (Blomberg, 1987; Orr, 1987a, 1987b; Suchman, 1983a, 1983b, 1986; Suchman & Trigg, 1986), cultural anthropologists had not done much research on technology in the United States. Most technology studies in the 1980s focused on evaluation: Researchers sought to test the hypothesis that technology has an impact on human behavior. By contrast, our focus was on the *human process of making sense* of something—in this case, network-connected computers as part of the university living experience.

We were interested in how students construct meaning—how their experience of technology is shaped through their mediated understanding of what it is and how they can use it. To put it another way, people's use of technology relies upon their understanding, which is culturally constructed and contextually situated. Technologies do not have meaning apart from the ways that they are used and experienced in a particular context.

This said, the end product of such cultural inquiry is not meant to be a dictionary-like treatment that implies it conveys the "true" meaning of things. Rather, the result of an ethnographic analysis should serve as an arbiter of what meaning the members of a particular culture are likely to construe. We feel that our article failed in this regard. People often read it and conclude that *study time* is X, Y, or Z. Instead we viewed study time as a "native category," that is, a conceptual framework that had many different hooks on it. We wanted to convey the point that students understood, interpreted, and enacted study time in many different ways. Study time is an acknowledged and even institutionalized part of the student experience, but it is not an instance of "shared meaning."

Perhaps our extensive use of the present tense and various authoritative and declarative statements in the article gave readers the impression that we were making statements of fact, but that was not our intention. Were we to write the article today, the tone would be considerably different. Rather than conforming to the positivistic style of scientific writing, we would make more extensive use of stories in order to reflect the diversity of perspectives that were represented among the students living in Ford Hall.

Our Research Experiences

The Dorm Project field study, as we called it, lasted for one year. Each of the four team members had differing experiences and roles. There were three ethnographers: the two of us, and Gail Bader. Anderson lived in the dormitory for the entire academic year. Bader and McClard were itinerant participant observers, and they each played a key role in interviewing and in the ethnographic data analysis. The fourth member of the team, Jim Larkin, was responsible for quantitative data collection (electronic tracking and scoring of questionnaires), data management, and computer-based data analysis. He spent very little time in the dorm or talking with its residents.

People often refer erroneously to "the ethnographic method," as if it were a single research approach. In fact ethnographers typically use a variety of approaches to conduct a research study. The key tools of ethnographic research are participant observation and interviewing, but ethnographers use whatever data-collection tools are the most appropriate to answer the questions at hand. In the case of the Dorm Project, we used both qualitative and quantitative approaches, but it was participant observation that served as the "glue" that helped us piece together the sometimes incomprehensible results churned out by our structured interviews, questionnaires, and electronically collected data.

"Doing ethnography," which in the 1990s has come into vogue in many disciplines beyond anthropology, is often equated with participant observation. To many, participant observation appears to be little more than "hanging out," watching what people are doing, and taking a few notes. We believe strongly that good participant observation is never just "hanging out." Participant observation requires the active, systematic collection of information. The participant observer must constantly reflect on the data that have been collected to develop new directions of inquiry. Additionally, because it is a reflexive process, seemingly irrelevant information that is noted at one time often turns out to be critical at a later time. Ethnographic inquiry is not an unmediated process; one cannot simply take notes, type them up, stick some pseudonyms in, and summarize events in an impressionistic way. Ethnographic research requires complex social, practical, and personal skills to sustain a role in the field.

We approached the dorm just as we would have approached a village in a foreign country. After all, the youngest of us was ten years older than the oldest freshman in Ford Hall. At the outset we felt culturally quite distant from the students and their everyday experiences. For the most part we did not share common cultural references with them. As a result, we needed to find our way into their "village," to learn how to be accepted and gain their confidence so that we could understand the village from *their* perspective. Participant observation was the approach to data collection that allowed this to happen.

As the name implies, the participant observer must find a means to participate in a meaningful way. He or she cannot simply stand by passively as a witness to things that are happening, but must become a part of the social context. Anderson's role as an older dorm resident was critical to gaining a depth of understanding of the students' experiences. Having multiple ethnographers of different genders and ages was also important, because ethnography is "perspective based." We felt that it was important to capture a wide range of perspectives among the freshmen.

Each ethnographer on the project interacted with the dorm residents in a unique way. Where one ethnographer had difficulty developing rapport with a particular resident or group of residents, another did not. The students in the dorm became a significant and integrated part of our lives, and we became a part of theirs. In this way we were able to gain a breadth of understanding that would not have been possible had only one participant observer been on the job. On the other hand, we soon learned that participant observation, done right, is neither easy nor quick.

In retrospect, we wish we had focused less on some of our other data-collection activities and more on the qualitative side of the work. The structured interviews and questionnaire instruments provided the least interesting information, simply documenting what people said they believed or said they did. We gained a much better understanding of the unspoken, inchoate, and taken-for-granted aspects of peoples' lives that underlie their beliefs and behaviors from computer-generated behavioral data (collected electronically), daily informal conversations, observations, and contextually elaborated interviews.

Aftermath

After the Dorm Project was completed, the computers were distributed to various campus locations, and the freshmen moved on to other places. The project had been funded because it was a technology initiative—a hot topic—not because of its focus on the nature of social learning. One of the things we had hoped was that the university would see the educational value of network computing, and that this would lead to all the residential halls on campus getting "wired." While this did not happen immediately, Brown was on the forefront in providing computer networks in residential halls. We do not know if the Dorm Project informed these decisions or not.

Soon after we completed our study, IRIS folded and the team disbanded. Bader, who was then a postdoc, now holds a faculty position in educational anthropology at Ball State University. Larkin started a consulting company that specializes in technical writing and Web publishing.

We (Anderson and McClard) got married and embarked on our dissertation research. While we could have used the data from our previous two studies for our dissertations, we wanted to have the "traditional" anthropological experience of doing research in a foreign country. We therefore went to the Azore Islands, an autonomous region of Portugal. Anderson's work focused on another aspect of technology—television and its meaning in that culture. McClard studied the annual cycle of festivals in the region. We are currently employed in a research division of a Regional Bell Operating Company, where we are involved with ethnographic studies of technology and education.

Implications

A decade has passed since we carried out the Dorm Project research described in this article. Since then we have been involved with numerous studies of innovation in society. Themes and issues raised in our analyses from the Dorm Project continue to be relevant. The tentative conclusions we drew have been validated in multiple contexts.

While we can't say with any degree of certainty that this work has been enormously influential for educators or technologists, we do know that it was tremendously important for our own development as professional anthropologists.

References

Blomberg, J. (1987). Social interaction and office communication: Effects on users' evaluation of new technologies. In R. Kraut (Ed.), *Technology and the transformation of white collar work* (pp. 195–210). Hillsdale, NJ: Lawrence Erlbaum Associates.

Orr, J. E. (1987a). Narratives at work: Story telling as cooperative diagnostic activity. *Field Service Manager: The Journal of the Association of Field Service Managers International, 11*(6), 47–60.

Orr, J. E. (1987b). Talking about machines: Social aspects of expertise. Contract Report No. MDA903-83-C-0189. Alexandria, VA: Army Research Institute.

Suchman, L. (1983a). Office procedures as practical action: Models of work and system design. *ACM Transactions on Information Systems, 1*(4), 320–328.

Suchman, L. (1983b). The role of common sense in interface design. In D. Marschall & J. Gregory (Eds.), *Office automation: Jekyll or Hyde? Highlights of the International Conference on Office Work and New Technology.* Cleveland, OH: Working Women Education Fund.

Suchman, L. A. (1987). *Plans and situated actions.* Cambridge: Cambridge University Press.

Suchman, L., & Trigg, R. (1986, December). A framework for studying research collaboration. In the *Proceedings of Conference on Computer Supported Cooperative Work,* Austin, TX.

STUDY TIME: TEMPORAL ORIENTATIONS OF FRESHMEN STUDENTS AND COMPUTING

Kenneth T. Anderson
Brown University

Anne Page McClard
Brown University

This article presents an ethnographic examination of the student domains of "study" and "time," and how these domains relate to a technological innovation in a freshman residence hall. We argue that technological innovations in education warrant attention as part of the more general movement toward reform in higher education. We believe that a closer examination of student life is necessary before discussing effects of educational reform. In this article we point out some of the ways in which students' conceptions and configurations of time differ from those of others, including university administrators and professors, and the implication of their differing perspectives on the way they use personal computing facilities in a residence hall. COMPUTER USE, EDUCATIONAL REFORM, UNIVERSITY STUDENT CULTURE

Anderson, K.T., & McClard, A. P. (1993). Study time: Temporal orientations of freshmen students and computing. *Anthropology and Education Quarterly, 24,* 159–177. Reprinted with permission of the American Anthropological Association. Copyright © 1993 by AAA.

Americans are once again clashing over the goals and methods of higher education. At the time we were doing the research for this article there was a proliferation of exchanges on the topic of educational reform. During the intervening five years, interest has continued to grow. Two critiques of higher education, Allan Bloom's *Closing of the*

American Mind (1987) and E. D. Hirsch, Jr.'s *Cultural Literacy* (1987), became best-sellers. Beyond the popular press, many people in the field published critiques of education, such as Ernest Boyer's *College* (1987) and reports by former Secretary of Education William Bennett. Furthermore, a survey conducted by the American Council on Education (ACE) in 1987 indicated that 95 percent of all two- and four-year higher education institutions in the United States either had overhauled their curricula in the last few years or intended to do so in the near future (Ottinger 1987).

Across the country, universities and colleges have been scrambling to computerize their campuses. Increasingly, courses are being taught with the computer as an integral component. Technical innovations, however, have not drawn the amount of attention that ideological innovations have. Although technical innovation is perceived as revolutionizing education and educational possibilities, it has not been seen or studied as part of the general movement toward reform.

Although this article is neither a call for educational reform nor an essay refuting the need for it, it is a call for a close examination of the population that will be most affected by both technological and ideological reforms: students. We are asking, in short, for more ethnographic research in educational situations in which the student is viewed as a vital element who actively shapes the educational community and institution.

This article contains an analysis of our research at Brown University as it relates to the addition of technical innovations. Specifically, we will deal with the domains of "studying" and "time"—the way that students categorize their time (study and non-study)—and discuss some of the ways in which the computer has fit into their lives as students.[a]

METHODS

The analysis presented here is based on data collected over the course of the 1987–88 academic year. For this project we placed IBM Model 30 computers in 33 of the 34 rooms at Ford Hall, a freshman residence hall at Brown University. During the project, Ford was home to 63 students. Of these, 61 agreed to participate in the project. The rooms were fairly spacious by Brown standards, and most rooms had two windows. The halls were dark and narrow, perhaps because the residence hall was built in 1925. The dorm was coed by room; that is, each room was occupied by same-sex roommates, but both males and females lived on the same floor. Only the more senior class counselors were allowed to have individual rooms. In Table 1 we compare the Ford Hall population with the 1987 freshman class as a whole with respect to sex and race.[b]

TABLE 1   Sex and Race of Ford Hall Residents Compared to All Freshmen

Ford Hall Residents	47	53	73	10	6	10
All Freshmen	53	47	81	7	3	9

Each computer came with a word processing package, a presentation manager, a relational database, and a number of games. In addition, each computer was linked to an IBM PC AT—the server for a laser printer (IBM 3813) that was placed in a common area. Along with the server, an IBM Model 30 and a PC AT were available as "public machines." The local area network (Novell Netware 2.0) allowed the students to send and receive electronic mail (e-mail), exchange files, and play the network

---

a. The authors' reference to the domains of "studying" and "time" means that studying and time both are constructs about which a good deal of research and theoretical work has carried out.

b. Table 1 does not include the information about gender and race to which the authors refer in the article. At our request, the authors provided the following interpretation: The numbers in each data column of the table are percentages, with those in data columns 1–2 representing students' gender and those in data columns 3–6 representing the main racial groupings of Brown students. The similarity between the two numbers in each data column indicate that Ford Hall residents (row 1) are fairly representative of all freshmen at Brown University (row 2) with respect to their gender and race.

game "Snipes." Finally, a terminal emulation package (N3270) was available that allowed the students to reach the campus mainframe via BRUNET using mainframe facilities. The equipment and software were set up for the students before they arrived, and support was provided by two members of the residence hall who were hired by the project as consultants.

We used a variety of ethnographic methods to collect data for this project: surveys, computer and network use data, time and task diaries, informal and formal interviews, and participant observation.

We conducted three surveys during the academic year to gain a broad perspective on the project. The questions we asked in the surveys emerged from our interviews, participant observation, and the other mentioned sources of data, allowing us to draw on a large number of the residents of Ford Hall to substantiate ideas that may have originated with just one student. Response rates were 85 percent, 62 percent, and 62 percent for the first, second, and third surveys respectively. In addition to the project-specific surveys, all incoming freshmen were asked to complete a brief computing questionnaire the summer before they arrived at Brown. The response rate for this survey was 85 percent. Furthermore, a shorter version of the third Ford questionnaire, which had been administered in the spring, was administered to a sample of all students at Brown. These two non–Ford Hall surveys served as a comparative frame for certain measures. The analysis of these quantitative data also provided us with broad parameters within which our ethnographic endeavors were framed.

We collected computer use data in two ways: (1) from student use logs (self-reported use) and (2) from an automated network use tracking system. These sources had to be interpreted carefully. Self-reported computer use data are not the same as actual use data. Some students discovered ways to defeat the network tracking devices by breaking out of the menu system supplied by the project. Consequently, those users, who naturally were among the heaviest and most sophisticated users, were not fully represented in our tracking data.

Given these limitations, however, the data are still useful if treated not as absolutely descriptive but as relatively descriptive. For example, although we cannot provide an exact figure for the amount of time students spent using their computers on weekday mornings, we can with confidence say that they used them in the mornings substantially less than they did in the afternoons and evenings. Furthermore, we can say they used them more for word processing (as opposed to games or electronic mail) during the mornings than at any other time.

To understand how computers fit into student work and life patterns, we first had to understand those patterns. The time and task sheets were designed to provide an "insider's" perspective. A group of student volunteers recorded their activities for several one-week periods during the academic year. A wide range of students kept the time and task self-reports. Each report was organized into half-hour sections. The students were asked to describe for each time frame what they were doing and where they were doing it. We tried also to monitor different weeks in the semester so that we would not overlook important pattern shifts during the academic year.

The research staff conducted formal and informal interviews. On a regular basis we held formal interviews with standardized questions about computing attitudes, behaviors, educational goals, and work habits. Twenty-three students were interviewed during the first semester of the academic year. Ten of these students were interviewed in the third and fourth weeks of the semester, and 13 others were interviewed just before final exams. During the second semester, we changed our approach to interviewing: we developed a third interview protocol based on discussions and findings from the interviews in the first semester. Instead of interviewing all students at specific points, as we did in the first semester, we interviewed students at different times throughout the final semester. This allowed us to ask a "core" set of questions and to amend the interviews quickly to trace the changes in dorm life as they occurred over time. By the end of the second semester, we had formally interviewed all but four residents of Ford Hall at least once.

In addition to the formal interviews, the staff conducted informal interviews in a variety of contexts. These sometimes took the form of conversation over coffee, a discussion with a student about a recent exam while walking to class, or a few quick questions to students while they were watching television. Although formal interviews provided standardized data from which generalizations could be drawn, informal interviews were a valuable means of gathering complementary information on student life. In other words, scheduled, formal interviews with specific questions may have elicited informant responses that were deliberate and calculated, but less than candid. Informal interviews occurred in a variety of contexts and elicited spontaneous and situationally relevant responses.

Participant observation was the most central research activity of the project. A male participant observer lived in the residence hall throughout the year. Two female observers visited Ford Hall on a regular basis, noting what students were doing, what they said they were doing, and how they talked about what was going on. Participant observation was used to obtain information on the social context of computing in the residence hall. It allowed us to get a firsthand look at how students go about work and play, and enabled us to create a detailed picture of student life in a freshman dormitory. The ethnographer's understanding and experience of the complex web of social life in the dorm was critical to this research and ultimately provided an interpretive framework for all other forms of data.[c] For example, without the ethnographer we could not have seen the subtle way in which residents established rules of appropriate computing. In watching the process by which the rules were developed, we could see how group pressure was exerted to "move" other students to comply.

This article is organized to give the reader an ethnographic perspective on student life at Ford Hall. In the first section, we discuss how student categories of time relate to student patterns of leisure and work. We point out some of the ways in which time was configured differently for students at Ford Hall than it is for the average working American. In the second section, we examine several time events over which the students have little control. These events are tied to institutional time (i.e., the semester and the day). In the third section, we explore student orientation toward time. Here we discuss attitudes toward the present and future, student goal setting, and choices. Finally, we show how the computer, an example of educational innovation, was subsumed under student categories of time, work, and leisure, and how it was integrated into student living patterns.

FRESHMEN CATEGORIES OF TIME

A freshman walks along the green, returning from a double feature at the movie theater, and into her dorm. A few minutes later a friend drops by her room and asks "What have you been up to?"

She answers, "I've been studying all day."

"Well," responds the friend, "let's take a study break then and go get some coffee."

"Sure," she agrees.

Later in the evening a computer consultant helps the same woman print a letter to her mother. She writes to apologize for not writing sooner. She says "she has been busy studying."

The scenario above is fictional, but it is similar to incidents that took place at Ford Hall. The young woman who claimed that she had been studying all day had been at the movies for several hours, had socialized over coffee, and had written a letter to her mother. The observer might be inclined to think that the woman was lying or irrational. To her way of thinking, however, she was studying, as we explain below.

Differing concepts of time across cultures have been of long-term interest to anthropologists from Benjamin Whorf to Edward T. Hall. Cultures, like individuals, are in some sense time bound, and, like individuals, each of them has a slightly different atti-

c. This reference to *the ethnographer* means the male participant observer who was a member of the research team and who lived in the freshman residence hall where the research was carried out.

tude toward, and configuration of, time. In an attempt to understand the students at Brown we began with their notion of time.

Much of daily life in any society consists of necessary habitual activities. For some people, in the United States for instance, this involves planning social and other activities around an eight-hour work day, a five-day work week, and a two-week paid vacation. For others, the structuring of time revolves around cultural interests. For example, Hallowell reported that the Andamanese developed their calendar on the basis of a succession of dominant smells of flowers and trees, and used the plants as reference points for activities (Hallowell 1937). The Ford Hall story is not as exotic as that of the Andamanese. However, the freshman concept of time is quite different from the American 9-to-5 worker's concept of time.

The first-year students we studied at Brown had two general time-planning categories under which all of the others were subsumed: study time and free time (social time). Study time, taken in the most general way, was from Sunday afternoon through Friday morning. Free time was from Friday afternoon through Sunday afternoon. Free time was the primary "social time." We will argue that it was free not in terms of task completion, but by definition.

One might guess, based on the two categories, that the primary activity of these students from Sunday afternoon through Friday morning was studying, and that from Friday afternoon through Sunday afternoon the primary activity was socializing. Surprisingly, the activities that took place Sunday afternoon through Friday morning were not all that different from the activities that took place during the remainder of the week—at least as viewed by an outsider. Brown students, however, perceived and acted on them as being fundamentally different.

The category of "social time" on Friday night and Saturday night included such activities as going to sports events, going to movies, going to parties, "hanging out," going to eat. The category of "study time" during the rest of the week was divided into three segments: "studying," "time spent in class," and "study breaks." "Studying" consisted of such

activities as "reading on my bed," "reading at my desk," "reading in the library," "studying in the library," "doing a problem set," "reviewing for an exam," and "writing a paper." We found that, on the average, students spent about ten hours a week on such "studying" activities. Additionally, students said that they did two kinds of study: "serious" study and "social" study. The distinction drawn here is best exemplified by one student's response when asked how much studying she did.

> How much actual studying, or how much time do I sit at my desk daydreaming and pretending to study? . . . [I study at my desk] maybe like five hours a day, but I don't [really] study that much. I write letters, and I listen to music, and then sometimes I study. . . . When I am in my room studying, like if I study in my room for two hours, I might actually get 45 minutes of studying done, because people come in and talk so you are sitting at your desk pretending to study but you are really socializing.

Oddly, freshmen did not generally see the time that they spent in class as being an integral part of studying, and they frequently skipped classes, especially discussion section.

"Study breaks," which seemed to take up the most time from Sunday night through Friday, included all of the same activities that are included in the category of "social time." Students took study breaks when they were "fed up" with working, had "had it," or were just "tired." Also, a study break was something earned by working hard. Such phrases as "I deserve to take a study break" or "I have gotten to the point where I need to take a study break" were not unusual. On several occasions students were known to have spent the whole night on a study break. The next day, when asked what they did the night before, they answered, of course, "I studied." During "study time" students are supposed to study. To their way of thinking, they do.

On just about any day of the week, students went to parties, to the movies with friends, out to eat, over to friends' rooms to "hang out," but the way they framed these activities on different days varied. For example, going to a movie on a Wednesday evening might have been considered a "study break," whereas going to a movie on a Saturday would not be considered a study break because Saturday was designated for social activities.

Students performed two different acts in "going to the movies" on Wednesday or "going to the movies" on Saturday, although to the outsider it appeared as the same act done on different days. "Study time" had meaning to them in the sense that it directed the action. "Going to the movies" meant different things during "social time" and "study time." If the student went to the movies during study time, then the action of going to the movies was viewed as a short-term respite from the ongoing action of studying. The action of going to the movies was seen as having the function of bringing the student back to a place where it was possible to study. The explicit aim of "free time" was to relax, which in most cases means avoiding study. In this context, movie-going is seen as a part of relaxing, "having fun," "hanging out" with friends.

Study breaks had another important function: they were a frame within which students could discuss academic subjects informally with one another. For example, during a pizza study break students covered a variety of topics related to their current class assignments. One student discussed a political science paper, another tried to figure out how to approach a paper topic in a literature course, and yet another student discussed topics in a geology course. Oddly, students did not view this informal discussion time as studious activity in the way that they did "sitting at their desks."

Students discussed academic problems informally all semester. They seemed continually aware of their assignments, and they used the informal and social nature of the study break to play with ideas and to develop their thoughts for a later time, when they would actually use them in either an examination, a formal discussion, or a paper.

Study breaks were an integral part of study time. Indeed, students often spent more time on study breaks than they spent studying. Because study breaks were a social activity, it appeared to the out-

siders that students goofed off a lot. Clearly, the study break, as defined by the student, was actually study time. The academic problems that the students worked out during a break could not be worked out in more formal settings or on their own. The study break was a secure environment for testing ideas.

During "social time," however, the student avoided studying. Indeed, those who tried to study during this time were pressured by peers not to study—particularly on Friday and Saturday nights. People caught studying at these times were verbally forced into non-study behavior by "dorm mates." This is exemplified by a conversation that was overheard at Ford Hall:

Student A: What are you doing studying on a Friday night. Let's go out and party.

Student B: No I can't. I have this paper due on Monday and I'll never get it done if I go with you over to Ellen's and party.

Student A: Oh come on! You don't really have that much to do. I wrote a five-page paper last Sunday night for Philosophy with no problem so I know that you can do it too. Chip and Fluffy are coming too and they'll be disappointed if you don't come. At least come up and have a quick beer and then you can decide.

In the end, Student B decided to go have a beer, and she never went back to her room to work on the paper. If one person did not succeed at talking the student into partying, reinforcements were sometimes brought in to convince the student to go to the party. In other instances, students even started a party in the violator's room to prevent him or her from studying.

There were several factors operating in these situations. As an example, take the first instance in which the student was coerced into partying. First the student was challenged because she was working on a Friday night—she was violating a time category. Second, we can see by her response that she had calculated her time and felt that she needed the extra time afforded by the weekend—"non-study" time in the student's mind—to complete the task. The response of the other student illustrated that she was wrong in her expectation about the amount of time required to write the paper. He claimed to have written a five-page paper the previous Sunday. Furthermore, he went on to say that it was for his Philosophy class. In their world this translated as an assignment for a "hard" class, not a "B.S." class. He then brought in another dimension—significant others. He told the woman that her friends Chip and Fluffy would be there. Without allowing the woman to say "no," the young man took yet another tack by offering a compromise: he suggested that she take only a short break for a drink. The implication was that she could then just drift back downstairs. Once upstairs with her peers, however, she would not stand much chance of escaping.

Conversely, people who attempted to disrupt the residence hall environment during the week with loud music, games, and partying faced another set of problems. Although it was recognized that most of these activities constituted a "study break" for the student, the atmosphere in which they were done was extremely different. On weekends, such activities were usually open and loud. During the week, however, the tendency was to keep these activities under control. Through the social network, most people knew when and where things were happening (who was going to the movies when, who might have been polishing off a case of beer or smoking marijuana). Study-time parties were not advertised, nor were they usually in violation of another person's rights to study. On the rare occasion when studying rights were violated, a request by the studying student to the violator was usually sufficient. If it wasn't, the resident counselors were called in.

There was another set of activities that crosscut the two major time categories: "extracurricular" activities, which could be both educational and social, but did not necessarily fall neatly into either study or social time. Freshman year at Brown is largely a time for experimentation. Many of the students were involved with a variety of nonacademic and academic clubs, which ran the gamut from the sailing club to the Society for Creative Anachronism to CIAO (keeping the CIA off campus). Some of these activities took up an enormous amount of time.

There are a few possible explanations for why freshmen saw their time divided into study time and social time, even though the activities during the different periods were not inherently different. One obvious explanation derives from the course schedule. There were no classes held on Saturday or Sunday, so there was no pressure on Friday and Saturday nights for the students to get work done.

Another explanation may lie in expectations of what college is supposed to be like. Most come to college thinking that they should study all the time. This view is represented in statements made by students, such as "I'm not exactly sure what I am going to do when I get done with my education at Brown. All I know is for now I have to study and study hard. I mean, that is why I am here." People come to college to get an education for the unknown future. Typically, the way that one achieves this desired goal is to study. Because students think they ought to be studying all the time, they sometimes say they are studying when they aren't.

A third possible explanation may be found in the way the students categorized their time in high school. Most said that there were several things that were different about college life: (1) their mother wasn't there, (2) they weren't in classes all day long, (3) they had classes at all hours of the day, and (4) college work was more difficult and more interesting than the work they did in high school. In short, they had much more freedom in college than they did in high school.

To give us a better idea of what he meant about the differences, one freshman gave us an example of how he spent his time when he was in high school:

> In high school I would be in school from nine in the morning until three. Here, I am in school from nine to twelve. And I would have class everyday, and it was less work every night but

more tedious during the day in class and stuff. Here, the work, if you let yourself get behind in the work, it seems like a lot of quantity, but I guess if you do it when you are supposed to do it, it is not that much. . . . It is a lot different socially. I guess the big difference is that on week nights in high school you are isolated and you did whatever it is that you do after school. I was involved in a couple of things after school in high school, and then you go home. And then from say 6 o'clock until you go to bed you are by yourself. Here you have say 49 people of your own age around and that is the social environment. There is always somebody around if you want to take a break from studying. . . . On the weekends I guess there is not much difference. A lot of people here like to go out and drink on weekends and a lot of people in high school like to go out and drink on weekends.

The striking feature of this passage is that it reveals the same time categories that we have found among the freshmen at Ford Hall—parties on the weekends, studying during the week. What has been introduced since high school is an enhanced social environment that allows "study breaks." Therefore, perhaps freshmen time categories are a carry-over from high school.

OTHER TIME EVENTS

Although "study time" and "social time" are two of the primary structuring time frames within which the students operate, there are others that affect the students' strategies of organization and pacing within these two time units. These are the semester and the day.

The Semester

The semester is the imposed time frame within which the student operates. At Brown, the semester is 16 weeks. The semester has a cycle of its own over which the student has little control. There is a beginning, a middle, and an end. Within this framework students have to choose, plan, and prioritize their activities. Assignment due dates largely regulate the flow of the semester for students and directly affect the "study time" and "study break" process. Many classes require that work be handed in regularly, whereas others require it sporadically. Usually, the most time-consuming assignments are due at the end of the semester.

The events that lie between the beginning and the end of the semester are somewhat random. Aside from classes there are no regularly recurring events. Assignment due dates and exams drive the time frame. This in turn is determined by which courses the students have chosen. Additionally, the students must juggle time and resource demands.

Most freshmen are not semester planners; they plan for the student week. As a consequence, they end up working intensively in spurts around midsemester and at the end of the semester.

The Day

The final unit of time is the day. The structure of the day is highly dependent on how it fits into "study time" and "social time." Each day is then framed by these notions. "Social study" (studying with other people) and "study breaks" are fluid components of "study time" that occur randomly during the course of the day. Freshmen are not very good at estimating how much time any one studying activity will take, so they are not as skilled as they might be at apportioning time.

Within the day there are better times to study than others. Most social study occurs in the evening, whereas individual study occurs in the afternoon and late night. Classes, a daytime activity primarily, are not a primary time frame within which the students operate. Classes can be turned into study break time for any number of reasons, including "I worked hard last night, I don't need to go to class today" or "I don't feel like going—I think I will just read the material instead."

These explanations embody two important concepts that were mentioned earlier. In the first, we can see evidence of the notion of deserving a study break. After a large effort has been put into an assignment, a break is deserved. We saw this on smaller scale when we discussed regular reading assignments. After reading so many pages, the person can justify taking a study break. On larger assignments where a product is due, the reward is greater. We can also see the importance placed on critical due dates as opposed to classes. Classes are not necessarily critical for students to complete their assignments, and as such, they can be missed. Students do only what is necessary; they read only what they have to; they attend class only if it is necessary to. The necessity of an activity is directly related to whether the students will be evaluated on the basis of their performance.

Related to this, we can see in the second explanation that replacement strategies are in operation. If a lecture is the same as a reading, then it is possible, depending on how the person is evaluated in the course, to skip one or the other.

The student day is not one that is governed by a clock; rather, the number and type of activities that a student has to do govern its flow. Certain amounts of text have to be read, papers written, exams reviewed for, and classes attended, but these are not time-bound events—they are activities that shape the day.

Study can occur in the morning, afternoon, evening, or late night; it doesn't matter to the student. Their concept of when a day begins or ends is not dependent on a clock, but on what they have to do. Consequently, when they are studying, they are in many ways unaware of hours of the day or night, but they are aware of tasks that must be accomplished—tasks that are often done at the expense of sleep.

Many students find themselves "cycling" through days. Cycling refers to being completely off a "normal" schedule; that is, their work and sleep patterns do not reflect those of the outside world (i.e., working until 4 a.m., getting up at 8 a.m., sleeping again from 2 to 4 p.m., then working again until 3 or 4 a.m., and repeating the cycle). The pattern most often develops during crisis times, although some students operate on this kind of schedule more or less all the time. By examining the temporal orientation, we can see the effects of living by "study time."

TEMPORAL ORIENTATION

In the previous section we discussed some of the over-arching categories and units of time for the student, but we have neglected to discuss their temporal orientations. Temporal orientations often pique the interest of anthropologists. A classic example of temporal orientation is found among the Iroquois; they see themselves as servants to the past and the future. Any decision made in the tribe requires asking, "How does the decision that we make today conform to the teaching of our ancestors and to the yearnings of our grandchildren?" (Lyons 1980). Thus, temporal orientation refers here to attitudes toward time—the value a people places on events occurring in the present and their relationship to events that took place in the past or that will happen in the future.

The students' temporal orientation differs dramatically from that of the Iroquois, as one might suspect. Students orient their activities to the present, the near future, and the distant future. The past is not very important when they are deciding how to spend their time. Their perspective arises from the time structure of the semester and from their educational goals for the distant future. Student orientation to the future is reflected by goal setting and the means by which goals are achieved—both short-term and long-term—whereas orientation to the present is reflected in what must be done right now to get the grades that will allow long-term goals to be realized.

First, there is the immediate goal of getting a grade. Although Becker et al. (1968) formulated the idea that all student life revolves around the grade, this is not true for the students at Brown, at least not in terms that Becker described. Instead of the grade being the currency of the campus, as Becker suggests, the grade has other meanings. At Brown there is no grade lower than a C. It is impossible to have a failing grade. Yes, a student can "flunk," but then that course is dropped from the record. To get above a C is the driving force. The search for the B shapes the student's attitude toward the present. Students do what has to be done "now" to get the B at the end of the semester, which will in turn give them passage to their professional careers in the distant future.

The quest for the B had ramifications for interaction in the residence hall. Because as we mentioned earlier, the events of the semester are somewhat randomly dispersed, with pockets of crisis, students in the residence hall developed an interactional style that allowed them to ask other residents for help. Crises for students led to the need for help "right now." "Right now" could be at three o'clock in the morning or at one o'clock in the afternoon. A crisis could be needing help retrieving something on the computer, needing to work out an idea for a paper that was due the next day, getting information that could help on an exam, or getting assistance with a problem set. By "knowing" everyone in the residence hall students were able to seek help or just talk to anyone they came into contact with in the building. Other students were important academic resources when it came to periods of or even moments of crisis.

Students at Ford Hall lived in a present-oriented world, like the pioneers of old—facing unknown hardships each day that seemed to emerge from no place. And like pioneers, they did not cross the wilderness (college) alone, but in a "wagon train" (the residence hall) with others who were going through the same experience, who helped when they were able, and who, in return, asked for help when they needed it.

Is every moment a crisis time, a time when students need help? No. Students are, in many ways, much more like farmers in their time orientation than the 9-to-5 workers we mentioned earlier. The farmer, like the student, sometimes has to work

from dawn until dusk, and at other times hardly at all. His clock, like the student's clock, depends on tasks that have to be done. Crises often hit farmers all at once, and so too for students; they are barraged at times with crises—papers, exams, and so forth.

The future is what comes at the end of the semester and lies beyond school. The student's orientation toward the future goes far beyond school, but it relates to the courses chosen in school. In choosing courses, students ask themselves two future-oriented questions: (1) "Does this course make me a more well-rounded person?" and (2) "Will this course assist me in fulfilling my career choices?" The second question is secondary to the first for freshmen. Students use these long-term goals to select courses. Once courses are selected, these goals determine the amount of time students will spend working on course-related activities. The amount of time allotted to a particular course-related activity depends primarily on the course's importance to career goals, and then on the student's personal interest in the course and desire to get a good grade.

INTERVENTION OF THE COMPUTER

Because we did not have a control group residence hall, and because this was not a pre-test/post-test situation, we are unable to make conclusive claims about changes brought about by the computer. The data we present here about possible changes in how students use and view "time" and "studying" are based on what students reported themselves about how the computer changed their work and play patterns. Primarily, the computer, as it was integrated into the residence hall during the course of the year, provides another example of how students understood and manipulated the fundamental categories of time.

The computer is potentially valuable to students, especially because of their particular orientation toward time. The computer can increase the amount of work that students do within bounded periods of time. When students are under a crunch and have to work in crisis mode, they need a tool that allows them to increase the rate at which they work. Just as pioneer farmers needed better plows at planting time, and better equipment at harvest time, when more intensive labor was required, students need tools that allow them to complete their work more efficiently at times of crisis. Unfortunately, at Ford Hall, the computers were not as helpful to students during crisis times as they might have been.

For example, a primary crisis time in the residence hall came during midterms and finals. Students "crammed" the night before an exam so that the information learned would be recalled more easily at the time of the exam. At Ford Hall, the computer did not facilitate studying for exams. Only when computers are an integrated feature of a course are they used as tools for study in this way (Beeman et al. 1988).

The computer was useful for routine writing assignments and major term papers. As described previously, students "talked through" their papers and developed their ideas long before they wrote them. We found out that this informal talking often took place while students were in their rooms studying with friends or during meals. Having the computer immediately available, or available soon after a late night "study break," allowed students to write things down in an unstructured form that could later be included or developed into a larger corpus.

Furthermore, in the actual production, our data show that students usually had papers done further in advance than they did formerly, so they had time to revise. One of the most common claims students made was that it allowed them to redistribute time from one stage of writing to another. The time they used to spend typing the final draft of a paper could now be used for editing and revising:

Let's say that I write my rough draft and it has been five hours recopying that paper. That is absolutely busy work. . . . I can spend those five hours . . . actually going over the paper . . .

rereading it . . . going away from it for a while, coming back and rereading it. I can do that and make minor adjustments.

Students felt that revisions were less laborious when done on the computer. Even students who wrote their first drafts by hand (because they did not feel comfortable composing on the computer) liked rewriting on the computer and felt that it saved an enormous amount of time. A paper was no longer finished once the assigned number of pages had been typed. To further illustrate this point, when students' papers were a page longer than was assigned, with only a couple hours left before it was due, they were able to (1) edit it easily or (2) play with the type style and formatting. Over the year, students became increasingly interested in making their papers good in form as well as in content.

As we have mentioned, student schedules are erratic in many ways. The personal computer is useful for students because it can be used at any time of the day or night. As we have described, students tend to write at night, and often late into the night. Unlike students using the public areas at Brown, the students at Ford Hall were able to use the computer whenever they wished; they were not tied to the institutional restrictions that apply at the clusters. The advantages of this situation were explained by a student from Ford:

Well, for writing papers, having a computer in your room, you can use it at any time, at any time of night and not have to worry about going over and walking some place, worrying about whether or not you are going to get a computer or have to wait for a computer. And with the printer downstairs, you just print out and you can go. A lot of times it is ten minutes before you have to get to class and you finish up the last thing and you print it out and go, which wouldn't be possible otherwise.

Accessibility to computers is important. Crises tend to come up for groups of students at the same time; they are not spread out. Personal computers in individual rooms reduce the competition for resources. Nothing is more detrimental to students than not having access to the materials necessary for writing a paper. Often, there are long waits to use equipment at computer clusters on campus. Even when the student finally gets on the computer, he or she has a limited amount of time. As a consequence, computers are often used only as typewriters at the clusters, rather than as tools for writing.

We have focused on how the computer is useful for the students at the residence hall when they are in "crisis mode," but the computer has served several other important purposes as well. As we pointed out, "study time" includes "serious study," "pretend study," "study breaks," and "classes." The computer has played a role for the students in each of these categories.

In discussing the computer with respect to "crisis times" in the residence hall, we have touched on some of the ways it has entered into serious study time and the ways that it integrated with classes, but there are several other aspects of computer use.

One curious phenomenon that we discovered is that students used the computer as a "warm-up" for doing "serious study." Warming up to study consisted of reading and sending electronic mail or playing a quick computer game. These two activities also fall under the category of "pretend study"—those occasions when students sit at their desks intending to study, but end up daydreaming, writing notes, and so on. Being occupied at the desk gives the activity a feeling of studying. The computer activities also appear under the category of "study break." The student has been studying and takes a break on the computer. One student explained:

> Sometimes when I get tired of studying I just sit and make pictures [on the computer]. I need a break from work. . . . I love being able to sit at my own desk in my own room to create them. It's one of the best things about having the computer here.

Computer games were a primary way to take a "study break" at Ford Hall. They were much less time consuming and expensive than a movie or a pizza. As such, the computer provided the student with a valuable new tool for study breaks. One did not have to spend large amounts of time on it, although some computer games were more involved than others. Regardless of what game the student played, he or she had control over the duration. The types of computer games with which students took breaks generally required little thought, and yet they were engaging enough to constitute actual breaks. These breaks differed considerably from the formally held breaks in which the students worked out their academic problems with others. Playing a computer game is genuinely a break from thinking about academic subjects.

In the previous section we discussed how an ethic of "knowing others" arose at Ford. It was important for students in the residence hall to get to know one another. The computer arrangement at Ford Hall, rather than having an isolating effect, promoted different types of social behavior; it opened a new avenue for meeting, communicating, and playing with other students in the residence hall.

As we mentioned, Snipes was one of the games on the computer network. It is a group game requiring a certain amount of coordination. Six players play at once, all logging on to their computers at the same time. Students at Ford created a communication network in their building that facilitated this process. "Runners" were stationed at the stairwell entries. They would count down so that the individual players could log on to the computer at the same time. One student explained how it worked:

> Snipes was fantastic, I mean, just the idea of six people playing each other, you know, in a hunt-chase, hunt-and-kill game throughout the dorm. It's like, we used to yell down the hall, "Okay, we're starting now! Everybody log on . . . Go!" And it was it was, like, you could hear yells down the hall, and it was a lot of fun.

Students played other games together too— games that were not on the network. Not only did they compete with one another at these games, but they also worked together to develop strategies to win, or they just sat with a person who was playing for the vicarious thrill it provided. The ultimate goal was not to beat your friends, but to beat the machine.

Besides the games, another social component was provided to the student through the new medium of electronic communication. Students used the mail system at Ford Hall in a variety of ways. Some people were "heavy" users, using the system every day for sending and receiving personal messages from friends in the building. Others used computer mail only to check on "happenings" in the residence hall through postings or announcements on the mail system. The kinds of things that could be posted varied from the sale of bicycles (public notices) to people seeking rides (requests for assistance) to debates about political candidates (opinion forums).

Although all the students had access to the campus-wide mainframe computing system that has a mail system of its own, only four freshmen had used it by the end of the first semester. Even then, they were not using it extensively, but on a weekly basis. Here, once again, we feel that the "knowing others" ethic comes into play. Although the campus-wide mailing service offered the student access to every person on campus, and through BITNET and ARPANET access to people around the world, it was not used much.[d] The reason is clear—most of the people to whom they wanted to send e-mail were in their residence hall. These people were the people they needed to "know" to survive.

Aside from communication channels opened by e-mail, other new communication channels were spontaneously opened with the presence of computers in Ford Hall. For example, an unexpected consequence of having a common area for the printers was that students would run into one another when picking up printed material. This time allowed just one more opportunity, which did not exist before, to "get to know" others in the residence hall. The following example illustrates this phenomenon:

> I was working on a paper that was due at 9 a.m. and I didn't want to stay up all night. I just wanted to get the thing done. I shut my door, I worked on the machine as stand alone until I had to print so no one knew I was there. I didn't even turn on my stereo. Then I printed and headed down to pick up my output to see what I had done. I went out the door and made it as far as the printer before I was compelled into conversation. Normally it probably takes about three minutes to make it from my room down to the printer. That night it was like running a gauntlet because I ran into so many people. It ended up taking me an hour. I was waiting for the paper [to come out of the printer]. My paper was behind a couple others. One of them was Robin's. Robin and a couple others convinced me to go credit [go get a snack] and then come back. Since my paper wasn't coming out right away I did. But I have never made it down to the printer and back without seeing someone.

Another spontaneous channel of communication sprang up. The friends of students who did not live in Ford Hall frequently came to use the facilities there.

The examples we have shown here illustrate that the computers in Ford Hall were used by the students in ways that were consistent with their fundamental understandings of "time" and "studying." For the students, having a computer in the room was as

---

d. The acronym *BITNET* stands for the *Because It's Time/Because It's There Network*. This network was created in 1981 to connect IBM computing centers around the world. It is a cooperative network in which members pass traffic to other sites for free, and software developed by one is made available to all. By 1994 BITNET encompassed over 1,400 organizations in 49 countries around the world. The acronym *ARPANET* stands for the *Advanced Research Projects Agency Network*. The precursor to the Internet, this network was developed in the late 1960s and early 1970s by the U.S. Department of Defense as an experiment in wide-area-networking that was intended to survive a nuclear war.

a beneficial tool, allowing them maximum flexibility in their work schedules. The computer has come to be more than a neutral tool that sits on students' desks; it has come to have social meaning as an object that is understood and used in the social context of the residence hall.

CONCLUSIONS

In this article we have drawn some conclusions about the way that students categorize their time and the strategies they use in accomplishing academic goals. We have presented the freshmen as sharing a particular orientation toward time and having specific strategies for dealing with it. Furthermore, we have drawn some conclusions about the ways that the computer fits into these time constructs.

We have argued that technological innovations in education warrant the attention that ideological innovations have received, and that the resulting changes must be considered if we are to understand student life from the student perspective. As we have shown, the student perspective differs markedly from the outsider's perspective. We have discovered that there are problems with implementing technical innovations when it is assumed that students operate on a schedule that is the same as the rest of the world's. People in the world do not necessarily share a concept of "time" or "work"—not even all Americans share such concepts.

The student world is one full of randomly interwoven events over which students have little control. Students must respond and develop specific time strategies that will allow them to accomplish immediate tasks and long-term goals. Personal computers fit well into the student world when implemented appropriately. We have attempted to show that students' concepts of time and studying result in certain types of actions, and that their categories are not merely linguistic. Understanding the meaning of these categories and their resultant actions may

allow us to understand the process of the adaptation of innovations by society.

Kenneth T. Anderson and **Anne Page McClard** are doctoral candidates at Brown University.

Notes

Acknowledgments. The research reported here was supported by a Joint Study Grant from Brown University and IBM. We gratefully acknowledge their support. We also thank the 1987–88 freshmen of Ford Hall who invited us into their lives.

References Cited

Becker, Howard S., Blanche Geer, and Everett C. Hughes. 1968. Making the Grade: The Academic Side of College Life. New York: John Wiley.

Beeman, W. O., K. Anderson, G. Bader, J. Larkin, A. McClard, and P. McQuillan. 1988. Intermedia: A Case Study of Innovation in Higher Education. Final Report to The Annenberg/CPB Project on A Network of Scholars Workstations in a University Environment: A New Medium for Research and Education. Providence, RI: Office of Program Analysis, Institution for Information and Scholarship, Brown University.

Bloom, Allan. 1987. The Closing of the American Mind: How Higher Education Has Failed Democracy and Impoverished the Souls of Today's Students. New York: Simon & Schuster.

Boyer, Ernest L. 1987. College: The Undergraduate Experience in America. New York: Harper & Row.

Hallowell, A. Irving. 1937. "The Temporal Orientation in Western Civilization and in Preliterate Society." American Anthropologist 39(4):647–670.

Hirsch, E. D., Jr. 1987. Cultural Literacy: What Every American Needs to Know. Boston, MA: Houghton Mifflin.

Lyons, Oren. 1980. "An Iroquois Perspective." In American Indian Environments: Ecological Issues in Native American History. Pp.171–174. Christopher Yecsey and Robert Venables, eds. New York: Syracuse University Press.

Ottinger, Cecilia A., Comp. 1987. Fact Book on Higher Education. New York: Macmillan.

CHAPTER 12
CRITICAL-THEORY RESEARCH

Pauline Casey and John Beedle married while both were graduate students, Pauline in business and John in social psychology. They have done training and computer consulting in many business organizations. Now they have been hired as consultants to help a large school district expand and update its computer programs. In preparing for this consultancy, they read about recent work by educators in Brazil and Australia that applies concepts of critical theory to the use of instructional technology. These educators view the computer as a mediator that can help teachers and students interact with each other and discover new ways to meet the students' learning needs.

Pauline and John embrace this critical-theory perspective on computer use. As consultants, they decide to design opportunities for teachers and students in the district to develop greater awareness of each other as people and as learn-

ers. Then the students and teachers can codiscover how computers fit into their learning goals. Their discoveries will be developed into action plans and then implemented. Both teachers and students will keep reflective journals on how well their action plans worked in practice and how they might need to be revised. The process of implementation, reflection, and revision constitutes a kind of research that is controlled by those who are the subjects of the research (i.e., teachers and students) rather than by external investigators.

Educators who learn about critical theory often find that new light has been shone on their professional practice, revealing tensions and possibilities that may have been only dimly felt before. In this chapter you will learn how critical theory can be applied to both educational research and practice, and the benefits of doing so.

OBJECTIVES

After studying this chapter, you will be able to

1. describe the goals and underlying assumptions of critical theory as applied to educational research.

2. explain the meaning of hegemony, voice, and internalized oppression from the critical-theory perspective.

3. describe the methods of inquiry used by researchers who work within the critical-theory framework.

4. explain the unique perspective that critical theory offers to the study of educational phenomena.

5. give possible reasons why critical theory has not had a greater impact on educational research and practice.

KEY TERMS

agency	feminisms	normative-evaluative truth
border pedagogy	Hawthorne effect	claims
critical ethnography	hegemony	norms
criticalist	hidden curriculum	objective truth claims
cultural studies	instrumental rationality	reconstructive analysis
deconstruction	internalized oppression	subjective truth claims
dialogical data generation	monological data generation	voice

THE NATURE OF CRITICAL THEORY

Critical theory represents a broad school of thought that involves uncovering the nature of power relationships in a culture, and that also seeks through its inquiries to help emancipate members of the culture from the many forms of oppression that operate within it. Developed primarily in Europe and Latin America, critical theory is showing increased impact on educational research and practice in the United States.

Basic to work in the critical-theory tradition is cultural critique. The term *critical* is used in critical theory to refer to a systematic process of review and analysis (i.e., critique) of cultural phenomena. In the process, hidden assumptions underlying accepted but problematic cultural practices are exposed, along with their negative aspects.

Joe Kincheloe and Peter McLaren (1994) list seven basic assumptions that are accepted by a *criticalist*, that is, "a researcher or theorist who attempts to use her or his work as a form of social or cultural criticism" (p. 139). We summarize these assumptions below and suggest their implications for education and educational research.

ASSUMPTIONS OF CRITICAL THEORY

1. *Certain groups in any society are privileged over others.* For a cultural group to be privileged means that the members of that group have greater power, resources, and opportunity to express themselves and enjoy life's comforts than the members of other groups. For example, in his critical analysis of life in schools, Peter McLaren (1998) emphasizes the educational inequities experienced by individuals who are not members of the dominant race, gender, or class categories of western societies.

Criticalists believe that the widespread cultural oppression in contemporary societies is most forcefully reproduced when nonprivileged groups accept their lesser social status as natural, necessary, or inevitable. The reproduction of cultural oppression means that accepted patterns of inequity are transmitted to new members who are born to or join the culture. The acceptance of these patterns takes the form of internalized oppression, meaning that individuals help to maintain their oppression through thoughts and actions that are consistent with their disempowered status.

Hegemony refers to the ways in which privileged groups maintain their domination over subordinate groups through various cultural agencies that exert power (e.g., the media, corporations, governmental bodies, and educational systems). The dominant culture exercises hegemony by framing the experiences of individuals through a steady stream of "terms of reference" (e.g., clichés about "the good life," media images, and stories) that individuals use to construct and evaluate their own reality. According to McLaren, hegemony thus involves "a struggle in which the powerful win the consent of those who are oppressed, with the oppressed unknowingly participating in their own oppression" (p. 182).

Critical theory seeks to disclose the true interests (i.e., the needs, concerns, and advantages) of different groups and individuals. Those who are privileged always have an interest in preserving the status quo in order to protect their advantages. Critical theory strives to highlight the sense of frustration and powerlessness that nonprivileged groups feel with respect to their opportunities to realize their potential, and to provide insight to guide them toward greater autonomy and ultimately, emancipation.

2. *Oppression has many faces.* Criticalists claim that focusing on only one form of oppression at the expense of others (e.g., class oppression vs. racism) obscures the interconnections among them. Both to understand and to combat oppression, they consider it necessary to examine all the cultural categories that are used to separate and oppress different groups, and to consider their joint operation and effects. For example, in seeking to understand why a teacher views a particular student as defiant in class, one must consider not only the student's ethnic identity, but also the student's gender and social class background, as well as other cultural characteristics (e.g., being identified as gifted, hyperactive, or learning disabled).

3. *Language is central to the formation of subjectivity (conscious and unconscious awareness).* Individuals' awareness is both expanded and constrained by the language that they have available for encoding their experience. Students whose first language is Spanish, for example, will have a different conscious and unconscious experience of a classroom lesson or a school football game than students whose first language is English. The formal and informal language that occurs in classrooms, as well as instructional programs involving different forms of discourse (e.g., bilingual education or whole language instruction), are examples of how language can be utilized by schools to maintain or contest hegemony.

The concept of voice is used by criticalists to study particular expressions of domination and oppression. Voice refers to the degree to which individuals occupying particular social categories or identities are privileged, silenced, muted, or empowered through the operation of discourses that maintain or contest dominant and subordinate cultures in a society. Henry Giroux (1992), who has played a central role in applying critical theory to education, asserts that voice "provides a critical referent for analyzing how students are made voiceless in particular settings by not being allowed to speak, or how students silence themselves out of either fear or ignorance regarding the strength and possibilities that exist in the multiple languages and experience that connect them to a sense of agency and self-formation" (pp. 205–206).

4. *The relationship between concept and object and between signifier and signified is never stable or fixed and is often mediated by the social relations of capitalist production and consumption.* This assumption implies that every human act of inscribing experience into discourse is fluid, and that most such acts are affected by culturally determined conceptions involving the production and exchange of material wealth. Further, any discourse, object, or event has communicative value and thus can be viewed and analyzed as a "text."

According to criticalists, the form and content of most texts reflect the values of the dominant culture and are consistent with standards derived from a capitalist value framework. For example, how a textbook author (the signifier) writes a textbook (the signified) involves basic political and economic considerations, such as concerns for avoiding controversy or efforts to reach the widest possible market.

Criticalists continually subject to critical analysis both the texts of the hegemony (e.g., law statutes, textbooks, operas) and those that convey popular culture. Texts include everything in the environment, whether permanent or momentary, with communicative content. They include spoken or written language (e.g., comic books, songs on MTV, or product packaging such as a can of cola; signs (e.g., the flagpole outside a school); and events as perceived by others (e.g., a gay rights march or a confrontation between a traffic cop and a motorcycle driver).

The critical analysis of texts, which originated in philosophy and literary criticism, is called *deconstruction*. Deconstructionism asserts that a text has no definite meaning, that words can refer only to other words, and that "playing" with a text can yield multiple, often contradictory interpretations. Criticalists view most of the texts in education and research as problematic (i.e., capable of misrepresenting experience) and therefore deserving deconstruction. In deconstructing a written statement, for example, they examine the connotations of each term, thus opening the text to multiple interpretations, with none privileged over any other. Criticalists even question the authority of their own emancipatory agenda by deconstructing the terms and statements that comprise the text expressing that agenda.

To understand how any cultural object or event can be treated as a text, and thus deconstructed, let us consider the case of professional sports. Many individuals watch football games, golf tournaments, and other sporting events, viewing them as a harmless form of entertainment and diversion from work. However, other interpretations of sporting events are made possible through the process of deconstruction. For example, consider this deconstructive analysis by Pierre Bourdieu (1991):

> More than by the encouragement it gives to chauvinism and sexism, it is undoubtedly through the division it makes between professionals, the virtuosi of an esoteric technique, and laymen, reduced to the role of mere consumers, a division that tends to become a deep structure of the collective consciousness, that sport produces its most decisive political effects. (p. 364)

Its constant probing of the other possible meanings of every cultural expression is what makes deconstructionism refreshing to some and tiresome, or terrifying, to others.

5. *All thought is fundamentally mediated by power relations that are socially and historically constituted.* In the context of education, this assumption implies that the beliefs and activities of students, teachers, and the other groups involved in education are inevitably affected by their experiences with power and dominance, both within and outside the educational system. Thus, the particular beliefs and activities of such groups or individuals can only be understood in reference to the unique context in which they occur. For example, say that a student ignores a teacher's command to stop talking in class. Depending on students' views of the teacher, their history of experience with that particular classmate, and what is occurring in the classroom at the moment the teacher utters his command, some students might regard the student who keeps talking as a trouble maker, while others might see the student as a buddy or a hero.

6. *Facts can never be isolated from the domain of values or removed from some form of ideological inscription.* The first part of this assumption reflects critical theory's rejection of the notion that educational researchers' quest for truth is an objective, value-free process. Indeed, criticalists question the notion of objective reality itself. Like other qualitative researchers, criticalists believe that all so-called facts about human nature and behavior are socially constructed, thus open to many interpretations, and subject to modification through human action.

Some scholars associate critical theory with postmodernism. As we explained in Chapter 1, postmodernism is a philosophy based on the assertion that no one approach to developing knowledge about the human world is privileged over (i.e., preferable to) any other. Criticalists are indeed skeptical of any theory or method that claims to have timeless or universal application to understanding or improving the human condition. Nonetheless, they remain committed to forms of social inquiry and action that promote the emancipation of nonprivileged individuals and groups, thereby affirming what Kincheloe and McLaren call "resistance postmodernism" (p. 144).

The second part of this assumption refers to ideological inscription. As applied to education, ideological inscription means that ideas about how teaching and learning operate always involve preformed systems of values and beliefs, which usually reinforce the power of dominant groups in society. A criticalist would hold that educational concepts like achievement, reform, innovation, and standards are categories constructed by, and serving the interests of, certain privileged groups in the educational hierarchy.

7. *Mainstream research practices are unwittingly implicated in the reproduction of systems of class, race, and gender oppression.* The epistemology of positivism has guided the majority of educational research, which has been carried out primarily by middle- or upper-class Caucasian males. This research rests on assumptions about truth, science, and good that have been accepted as universal, but which, according to criticalists, have served to maintain the oppression of groups who represent other cultural categories. Criticalists particularly oppose educational research that focuses on prediction and control for the purpose of maximizing educational productivity. In their view, such research reflects the operation of instrumental rationality, which involves a preoccupation with means (e.g., computer technology) over ends or purposes (e.g., the development of effective writing or study skills). Rex Gibson (1986) views the IQ testing movement as a key example of the shortcomings and injustices that this preoccupation involves:

> Instrumental rationality is the cast of thought which seeks to dominate others, which assumes its own rightness to do so, and which exercises its power to serve its own interests. Coldly following its narrow principle of efficiency and applying a crude economic yardstick, its results are all too obvious . . . the interests least served are those of comprehensive schools and pupils from working class homes. (pp. 8–9)

Criticalists thus spotlight problems that affect the members of nonprivileged groups at a much more personal and pervasive level than other groups. Yet they also help clarify the ways in which the members of other groups also suffer from the same problems. Education is meant to address the needs of every student. Educators therefore must attend to the increasingly negative consequences experienced by all the members of a culture, even those belonging to privileged groups, from cultural practices that privilege some and oppress others. For example, in his study of suburban youth Ralph Larkin (1979) observed that:

> [Middle-class] students experience a two-fold alienation: from adult society wherein lies the power, and from each other as invidious competition and mobility undercut authenticity and understanding of each other. They are isolated as a class and as monadic individuals. Most lives are characterized by lack of depth. . . . They live at the surface, fearful yet desirous of what might happen should they "bust out" of their not quite Edenic existence . . . [they] are terrorized by their fears. (p. 210)

Despite the widespread effects and taken-for-granted nature of much cultural oppression, criticalists seek to balance their criticism with hope, and a deep belief that the emancipation of nonprivileged groups will improve the life conditions of all groups and individuals.

Some individuals denounce critical theory because of its critical view of capitalism, the worldwide spread of the market culture, and a politics in the United States and other western societies that equates national well-being with domination of the global marketplace. However, critical theory stands "in opposition to crude material or economic determinism" (Seymour-Smith, 1986, p. 59). Thus, while it shares with Marxism a critique of the inequities of the capitalist system, it promotes democratic principles as the best way to discover and correct those inequities. The scholarship based on critical theory can stimulate much critical reflection about dominant forms of educational practice and research.

METHODS OF INQUIRY

Criticalists do not subscribe to a unified, formal methodology. Instead, they draw upon methods from a wide range of research traditions. For example, Cary Nelson, Paul Treichler, and Lawrence Grossberg (1992) describe cultural studies as an interdisciplinary tradition that involves critical investigation of cultural phenomena as expressed in literature, art, history, and other disciplines.

Critical theory is particularly concerned with "economic, ethnic, and gender structures that constrain and exploit humankind" (Guba & Lincoln, 1994, p. 113). Gender and race as cultural categories have each formed the basis for specialized fields of study within critical-theory research.

Feminist research involves such varied foci and methods that scholars such as Virginia Olesen (1994) describe it in the plural, as *feminisms*. According to Olesen, critical work in feminist studies has had two main foci: (1) the study of females' lived cultures and experiences and how they are shaped by the cultural meanings that circulate in everyday life; and (2) the production and meaning of cultural objects as texts. Critical feminists have done much work to identify and deconstruct cultural texts, such as those in film and popular literature, that contain and circulate depictions of women primarily or only as: (1) sexual objects for men; (2) responsible for domesticity, housework, child rearing, and caregiving; (3) the weaker or secondary sex; and (4) normally as well as normatively heterosexual (Agger, 1992). Later in the chapter we discuss an example of critical feminist research concerning the depiction of young women's sexuality in an education context.

With respect to race, critical research on each of the commonly identified racial or ethnic groups is being carried out, some conducted by members of the groups being studied but still a good deal by Caucasian researchers. John Stanfield II (1994) argues that the more empowering and normality-revealing aspects of Afro-American intellectuals "have been ignored, marginalized, or reinterpreted to fit into the more orthodox norms of social scientific communities" (p. 177). Stanfield suggests how indigenous qualitative methods that draw from the cosmos of people of color will diverge from previous mainstream forms of investigation. He recommends "the collection of oral histories that allow the examined people of color to articulate holistic explanations about how they construct their realities" (p. 185), and that American researchers engaged in such research discard their own notions of time, space, and spirituality in order to grasp the meaning of indigenous people's stories.

Perhaps the only method that is common to the research and theory building of criticalists is critique—of the phenomena being studied, of methodology, and of the researchers' own perspective and values. In Phil Carspecken's (1996) words:

> Criticalists find contemporary society to be unfair, unequal, and both subtly and overtly oppressive for many people. We do not like it, and we want to change it. (p. 7)

While criticalists may condemn particular educational structures or actions, because they strive to do work consistent with the theme of empowerment, they rarely practice negative evaluation of individuals, or of cultural groups as a whole.

In his book covering procedures for conducting critical research in education, Carspecken uses the term *critical ethnography* to apply to critical qualitative research in general. Below we summarize Carspecken's model of critical ethnography to illustrate how research based on critical theory uses methods that are consistent with the assumptions described by Kincheloe and McLaren.

Stages of Critical Ethnography

Like other qualitative research, critical ethnography begins with the identification of a phenomenon (e.g., a specific social site, group of people, or social problem) that researchers wish to study. In his book Carspecken illustrates the research model with an example of a phenomenon he investigated, namely, evaluation of a program (Project TRUST) designed to increase the conflict-resolution skills and self-esteem of elementary school students who were perceived as disruptive in their classrooms.

As a preliminary step, Carspecken recommends that researchers create a list of research questions related to the phenomenon, followed by a list of specific items for study. For Project TRUST, the researcher's questions included questions about how students were picked to be part of the program, what was taught in the TRUST classroom both intentionally and unintentionally, and what relationships existed between TRUST and the elementary school in which it was housed, the immediate neighborhood, and the broader social-economic forces of the community. He then defined the items he wished to study, including the social routines of Project TRUST participants and the constraints and resources that affected those social routines.

Carspecken also recommends that researchers explore their value orientations at the very start of the study, preferably with the help of a colleague. This step "helps to raise awareness of your own biases and check for them while compiling your field notes and formulating your research questions" (p. 41).

Once the preliminaries are completed, critical ethnography involves five stages, which are detailed below.

Stage One: Compiling the Primary Record Through the Collection of Monological Data.   The information collected during this stage is called *monological* because only the researchers directly "speak," writing the primary record in the third person from the perspective of an uninvolved observer. The researchers make themselves as unobtrusive as possible to observe interactions within a social site. Passive observation is used to produce a thick record of social routines in a naturalistic form relatively free of the Hawthorne effect, that is, changes in field participants' behavior due to the presence of observers. The later examination of differences between the data collected during this stage and during stage three, when the researchers shift from being passive observers to being facilitators of talk and discussion, are crucial in analyzing the findings.

The researchers build up the primary record, also called a *thick description* of the site, through note taking, audiotaping, and possibly videotaping. This description includes not only verbalizations, but body movements and postures; uses a low-inference vocabulary; and includes frequent time notations, bracketed observer comments, necessary context information, and visual diagrams to describe spatial arrangements and individuals' movements. Besides intensive field notes, the researchers also keep a looser journal detailing observations and conversations in and around the site.

The purpose of monological data collection is to collect as much objective data as possible. Findings that satisfy the validity requirements for being considered objective truth claims are ones to which there is multiple access, meaning that other observers would generally agree with the researchers' truth claims.

Stage Two: Preliminary Reconstructive Analysis.   The researchers begin analyzing the primary record in order to determine interaction patterns and the apparent meaning of those patterns. They reconstruct the information obtained in stage one by putting into words the cultural themes and system factors that underlie the primary record, but which are not directly observable nor usually articulated by the participants themselves.

Much of the researchers' work during reconstructive analysis involves speculating about the subjective and normative-evaluative truth claims that will be tested during stage three, when the researchers engage in direct communication with the field participants.

Subjective truth claims prioritize the first-person perspective, that is, they refer to the presumed state of an individual while she is engaged in an action or interaction. The validity of a subjective truth claim is based on the principle of privileged access, meaning that only the individual herself has access to the experience on which the claim is based. Thus, researchers must test subjective truth claims for validity by engaging individuals in dialogue (during stage three) to facilitate their self-exploration and self-representation.

Normative-evaluative truth claims are intersubjective and are based on sets of norms that operate conjointly in a social setting. Norms are unstated background sets of rules and assumptions that influence social acts. The validity of normative-evaluative truth claims depends on position-taking with others to clarify shared assumptions about the world as it is or should be. During dialogue with the researchers, a new normative context is created for field participants, in which slightly new identities may be claimed and new norms referenced. That is the reason that individuals will often express themselves in new or less common ways in an interview or group discussion than they did during the situations observed by the researchers during monological data collection.

Stage Three: Dialogical Data Generation. At this point in the study, the researchers cease to be the only voices involved in building up the primary record. Through interviews and discussions, the researchers begin conversing intensively with the field participants (that is, engaging in a dialogue, the outcomes of which are data to be analyzed). The new data that are collected often challenge information collected during previous stages. According to Phil Carspecken and Michael Apple (1992), dialogical data generation is essential to critical fieldwork for several reasons:

1. It is necessary in order to complete the normative reconstructions that were begun in stage two.
2. Dialogical techniques yield data that can be contrasted with the data obtained during monological data collection.
3. Dialogical techniques aid in the discovery of normative structure.
4. Dialogical methods are empowering to the groups being studied, helping them to name previously undisclosed or even unknown aspects of their oppression.
5. Dialogical data generation allows the people under study some control over the research process, yielding a more democratic form of knowledge production.

Carspecken recommends semistructured interviews to collect dialogical data. Semistructured interviews provide balance between structure and flexibility in the interview process. In his Project TRUST study the researcher used specific lead-off questions to put the respondent in a concrete mind-set, such as asking the teacher: "Yesterday I saw you and Samuel in dispute over a test. Can you pretend I wasn't even there and just tell me everything that happened?"

Carspecken also lists appropriate follow-up questions and suggests a typology of interviewer responses to help ensure that the interviewer gets the necessary information to grasp the field participant's perspective and to test his understanding. The interviewer's response options, ordered from 1 to 6, range from low to high with respect to the extent to which they direct the interviewee's next response, and from high to low with respect to the frequency with which Carspecken recommends that each response be used. An example of each response is given below.

1. *Bland encouragement*. A one-word utterance or a facial expression to encourage the interviewee to continue: "Right," or nodding and making eye contact.
2. *Low-inference paraphrasing*. Restating what the interviewee just said without adding content: "So you went back to college after your divorce."
3. *Nonleading leads*. Indicating interest to elicit more information: "Tell me more about that."
4. *Active listening*. Putting into words feelings that the interviewee expressed indirectly: "Sounds like you are upset with her."
5. *Medium-inference paraphrasing*. Stating one's speculations about the meaning or implications of the interviewee's statement: "You have no control over the situation."
6. *High-inference paraphrasing*. Stating suspected background beliefs not explicitly stated by the interviewee: "I think you're saying that life is like a ladder, and some people can keep climbing while others get stuck on the lower rungs."

Stage Four: Discovering System Relationships.   In this stage of the study, the researchers compare the findings obtained in the social site being investigated with findings discovered in other social sites having some relation to this site. This process corresponds to cross-case analysis in case study research, but here the cases chosen for comparison are specifically selected to reflect the critical focus of the research.

The type of system relationships that critical ethnography can discover is illustrated by Paul Willis's study (1977) of working-class "lads." Willis discovered correspondences, which he termed a *reproductive loop*, between the lads' behavior in three different social sites—the school, the home, and the job setting. He reported that the lads sought to avoid activities in school (e.g., doing the assigned work) that could conceivably help them to move out of the working class into the middle class, but that they viewed as a rejection of their home-based culture. In the home site, the lads' fathers had stayed within the working class in seeking work. The lads in turn moved into jobs involving physical labor when they left school.

Carspecken describes how individual students in Project TRUST sought to "renegotiate" classroom settings that were stressful. For example, Ricardo, a Latino, defied school culture through confrontations with Alfred, an African-American. When Alfred exerted his dominance, Ricardo often began singing or speaking in Spanish, the language of his home and neighborhood. According to Carspecken, this behavior "referenced an opposition between 'us' and 'them' that was lacking for Samuel," (p. 199), a student of mixed white and African-

American heritage. In this way Ricardo asserted a self-defined superiority over both the school culture and Alfred's culture. The researcher's reconstructive analysis of Ricardo's behavior exemplifies his discovery of system relationships during stage four of critical ethnography.

Stage Five: Seeking Explanations of the Findings Through Social-Theoretical Models. Here the level of inference rises as the researchers seek to explain the findings obtained in earlier stages by reference to existing or emergent system theories. The analysis goes beyond that in stage four, because interests and power relations discovered at the system level now are used as explanatory factors. Carspecken notes that during this stage

> . . . a critical researcher is able to suggest reasons for the experiences and cultural forms she reconstructed having to do with the class, race, gender, and political structures of society. Often, it is this fifth stage that really gives one's study its force and makes it a contribution to real social change. (p. 43)

To identify broad system features, Carspecken suggests noting the cultural products that impact the participants. For example, for elementary-age children, relevant cultural products might include video games, textbooks, comic books, TV shows, popular music, and movies. The researchers should reflect on the possible symbolic and cultural meanings of such products for the field participants, and conduct interviews and group discussions to get their perspective.

Because of time limits and other constraints, Carspecken carried out only a rough analysis of the system relationships that might explain the findings of the Project TRUST study. He described the difficult living conditions of the students and their families: "Children were both used to harsh forms of discipline at home and to seeing their parents actively resist any efforts of others to dominate" (p. 205). At school the children, through their behavior, reproduced these and other conditions of the home environment. Teachers had only limited success in helping these students, in part because they were constrained by state-mandated testing requirements. To understand why communities like the one in which Project TRUST was housed exist, and why standardized tests are imposed on such schools, Carspecken speculates:

> During a period of economic decline, lower-class people lose jobs in large numbers. When the economy picks up, the unemployed are reabsorbed into the most menial of positions. The economic system of the United States creates groups like the [Project TRUST setting] . . . Schools end up keeping children like those in the TRUST study off the streets, but the students ill prepared to do anything but unskilled labor. (p. 206)

Carspecken notes that some critical qualitative research studies are conducted only through stage three, but that the whole picture emerges only when a study is carried through stage five. During this stage the researchers use core concepts from macrolevel social theory to build a systems analysis from the experiences and cultural terms of the research participants, with the following intended result:

> Ideally, use of these concepts in dialogue with your subjects will result in a fusion of horizons; the researcher attaining an insider's view of the cultural group, and group members attaining an insider's view of researcher culture. (pp. 206–297)

By using epistemological models of the social system that are built from a third-person insider perspective and are intelligible and consented to by as broad a cultural audience as possible, the researchers approach the goal of doing fully democratic research. Carspecken concludes: "Making your research project as democratic as possible, from start to finish, is the best way to help rather than harm" (p. 207).

Other Critical Forms of Inquiry

We have described Carspecken's model of critical ethnography in detail because it uses specific procedures to increase the validity of the truth claims made by critical researchers. In searching for literature on critical theory, educators should understand that not all critical research is labeled as *critical ethnography* or *critical qualitative research*, and some of it does not use the methodology described above.

Some critical research is descriptive and highly polemic, journalistic, or even autobiographical. For example, cultural studies is a growing field in higher education, in which criticalists representing various disciplines and academic orientations explore and deconstruct many aspects of capitalist culture that other researchers trivialize or ignore. Many of the writings of cultural studies researchers are quite abstract and do not appear to involve any fieldwork as such.

At the same time, critical theory's descriptive analyses often involve critique of the educational settings in, or genres through which, criticalists carry out their work (e.g., schools, universities, conferences, journals). Thus their descriptions have direct applications to educational practice. For example, in a presentation on the theoretical underpinnings of cultural studies, Stuart Hall (1992) speaks autobiographically, from his own experience as a "critical intellectual" (p. 277).

Criticalists reject some of the canons that guide much educational research. At the same time, they often address the practical applications of their discoveries more directly than many researchers who do quantitative research, or who work in other qualitative traditions. As we noted earlier, their goal is not merely to spotlight inequitable societal conditions, but to change them. As a result, critical theory has great potential to affect both educational research and practice. Below we describe some of the ways that it has already done so.

THE IMPACT OF CRITICAL THEORY ON EDUCATION

One of the main educational problems studied by criticalists is the disproportionate levels of school failure among various cultural groups. As described earlier, Willis explored how lads from working-class backgrounds expressed values consistent with their background and actively resisted school activities that challenged those values. Critical research by Jean Anyon (1980) showed how cultural oppression operates in the other direction, namely, how schools shape nonprivileged and privileged individuals' educational experiences differently in ways that maintain hegemony.

Anyon studied the hidden curriculum in schools, that is, the implicit instruction in attitudes and habits that schools continually transmit by their structure and the way that they organize activities. Anyon found that schools whose students are primarily from working-class families teach them skills and values that prepare them for working-class lives (e.g., mindless obedience, tolerance for repetitive tasks, and respect for authority). In contrast, Anyon found that schools serving mainly students from upper socioeconomic classes teach them skills and values that prepare them for middle- and upper-class lives (e.g., leadership, problem solving, critical thinking, and creativity).

While research like Willis's and Anyon's is enlightening, criticalists like Michael Apple (1997) argue that it is not possible to understand the reasons for educational inequity in U.S. society without consideration of students' race or ethnicity. Many researchers have investigated, or sought to change, the social and cultural conditions of minority students, but criticalists find much of this work questionable, claiming that it is based on middle-class Caucasian values and perspectives. In his discussion of the need for ethnic modeling in qualitative research, Stanfield comments that "only recently have people of color in some disciplines, the humanities in particular, been allowed to speak in different legitimated voices" (p. 180), citing bell hooks as one such scholar. In her writings hooks (1992) refers openly to her personal experience and uses literary discourse, rather than strictly research discourse, to critique educational research and practice.

Criticalists also are interested in the role of schools and other institutions in silencing or muting the voices of nonprivileged groups and perpetuating hegemony. For example, Michelle Fine's (1988) critical ethnography of sex education and school-based health clinics illustrates critical feminists' concern for the ways in which educators' views of gender and class issues jointly conspire to limit how students, especially females, are educated for adulthood. Fine interviewed high school girls, observed sex education programs, and analyzed curriculum materials in U.S. schools in order to explore the desires, fears, and fantasies that shape the silences and voices concerning sex and sex education for female students.

Fine found that female students, particularly those from low-income families, have minimal access to school-based health clinics and courses providing information that is relevant to their developing sexuality. Where such clinics and courses are provided, their prevailing discourse and practice tend to discourage rather than to encourage students to use their services.

Fine defined three discourses of female sexuality that prevail within the public school system: (1) sexuality is described essentially as violent and coercive, (2) sexuality is associated with victimization, because males are cast as potential predators, and (3) interventions designed to influence females' sexual decision making center on the value of premarital abstinence. Fine saw all three of these discourses as designed to discourage adolescent females from sexual activity, even though research findings she reviewed indicate that they generally engage in responsible sex practices (e.g., ensuring the use of contraceptives).

Fine argued for a fourth possibility: the discourse of desire. This discourse would acknowledge the possibility of desire, pleasure, and sexual entitlement among female students. She concluded that this discourse "remains a whisper inside the official work of U.S. public schools" (p. 33). As a result, many of the students whom she studied viewed the efforts of school-based sex education programs and health clinics as largely irrelevant or opposed to their perceived needs. Fine concluded that such educational practices actually hinder females' development of sexual responsibility, thereby contributing to their continued disempowerment: "How can we ethically continue to withhold educational treatments we know to be effective for adolescent women?" (p. 50).

Like Fine, many criticalists have examined whether and how educators confirm the oppression of students who are members of nonprivileged groups. Others have looked at how the voices of teachers are silenced, or at least muted, by the prevailing structure of public and private educational systems. For example, the research article that is reprinted in this chapter describes how Nancy Kraft, a staff development specialist, uses concepts and procedures based on critical theory in an effort to empower the teachers with whom she works. In her workshops, Kraft shares her perceptions of her role as a facilitator of teachers' learning; structures their learning experiences on the principles of adult education theory; assists participants in examination of their own beliefs, values, and assumptions about teaching and learning; and actively fosters teachers' reflection on, and sharing of, their experience and the "rich knowledge of their craft" (p. 34 in the original article). Thus Kraft attempts to help teachers deconstruct traditional models of school change. By first analyzing why their own voices are not part of most debates about school reform, teachers gain more understanding of the sources of student resistance and disempowerment.

Criticalists also are at the forefront of investigations into educational influences beyond those of the schools, particularly the products of popular culture. In a recent book titled *Kinderculture: The Corporate Construction of Childhood*, Shirley Steinberg and Joe Kincheloe (1997) argue that the prevailing economic and technological climate in the United States has created a "crisis of childhood," in which corporations have become the major educators of children through such channels as the entertainment media. *Kinderculture* makes a strong case that the impact of corporate culture on education requires a new response from educators, beyond that based on the traditional forms of cultural transmission involved in curriculum, pedagogy, and schooling.

THEORY BUILDING IN CRITICAL THEORY

Critical theory emphasizes the value of theory in explaining society and in contributing to the emancipation of its participants. Henry Giroux (1988) is among those scholars who have played a major role in developing a body of critical theory that is applicable to American education.

For his development of a theory of critical pedagogy, Giroux takes as his starting point the assumption that U.S. public education is in crisis. He sees this condition reflected most clearly in the contrast between the hegemonic rhetoric that equates U.S. culture with democracy in its ultimate form and numerous indicators of the falsity of this rhetoric, including low voter participation and growing illiteracy rates among the general population, and the increasingly common perception by U.S. citizens that social criticism and social change are irrelevant to the meaning of American democracy.

Giroux proposes a liberatory theory of "border pedagogy" to replace what he describes as the "politics of difference" that characterizes much of the current dialogue about educational problems and solutions. For Giroux, the term *border* reflects the notion of permeable, changing boundaries to describe differences between individuals and groups, as opposed to the rigid, "either-or" nature of conventional social categories.

In Giroux's theory, difference is linked to a broader politics, and schools and pedagogy are organized around a sense of purpose that makes difference central to a critical notion of citizenship and democratic public life. This concept of difference is postmodern in that it recognizes the need to acknowledge the particular, the heterogeneous, and the multiple; and it views the political community as a diverse collection of subcommunities in flux. Giroux asserts that schools must empower students by giving them opportunities to analyze how the dominant culture creates borders "saturated in terror, inequality, and forced exclusions," and to "construct new pedagogical borders where difference becomes the intersection of new forms of culture and identity" (p. 209).

Giroux asserts a pedagogy in which educators at all levels of schooling engage in redefining the nature of intellectual work and inquiry itself. Giroux views the ultimate outcome of this pedagogy as "nothing less than providing the conditions for educators and their students to become knowledgeable and committed actors in the world" (p. 208).

Application of Giroux's theory as a guide for educational practice would require that students no longer study unified subjects, but instead explore the "borderlands" between diverse cultural histories as sites for critical analysis and a potential source of experimentation, creativity, and possibility. Power would be explicitly explored, both to help students understand how forms of domination are historically and socially constructed and to explore how teachers can use their authority to aid students in their emancipation from such domination. Finally, students would be educated to read critically not only how cultural texts are regulated by various discursive codes, but also how such texts express and represent different ideological interests.

STRENGTHS AND WEAKNESSES OF CRITICAL THEORY

The assumptions and methods of critical theory have provoked considerable criticism from educators and researchers representing other traditions. For example, Charlene Spretnak (1991) argues that criticalists' preoccupation with the deconstruction of every possible form of rhetoric or other text leads to groundlessness being "the only constant recognized by this sensibility" (p. 13). In other words, their critics view criticalists as hypercritical. They argue that deconstruction, if taken to an extreme, can lead to a sense of hopelessness rather than to hope for emancipation.

In practice, however, at least some researchers in the critical theory tradition fulfill its emancipatory agenda. The work of such criticalists as Henry Giroux and Michelle Fine suggests fresh directions for educators to explore in order to better meet the needs of traditionally underserved students.

Another limitation of critical theory is the complicated terminology of many researchers who work in this tradition. Rex Gibson (1986) described the problem in these terms:

> The writings of criticalists do not exactly help their cause. Turgidness, unnecessarily complex sentence structures, a preference for their own neologisms (newly-coined words), and an almost wilful refusal to attempt to communicate directly and clearly with the lay reader, characterize many of their books and articles. The impression conveyed is of "cliquishness," or exclusion; of insiders writing only for insiders. (pp. 16–17)

If one assumes that understanding is a part of what emancipation involves, this inaccessibility of the language of many criticalists to ready understanding tends to belie its claim to foster the emancipation of oppressed groups. The solution to this problem is obvious: to employ a writing style that is more accessible to educators who lack expertise in this research tradition. To their credit, some criticalists make considerable effort to translate their ideas into familiar language. For example, Peter McLaren's book *Life in Schools* is designed for use by teachers, and for the most part it minimizes the use of abstractions and complex sentence structure.

CONCLUDING THOUGHT

To be effective, educators must find ways to make sense of the social and economic inequities that they observe in today's world. Those who address such concerns can convey greater hope and guidance to their students. If you have concerns about the directions in which education is moving, or question its capacity to foster the learning of all students, the ideas and findings of critical theory can provide useful insights and guides to action.

SELF-CHECK TEST

1. What most clearly distinguishes critical theory from other research traditions is its
   a. focus on cultural phenomena.
   b. commitment to an emancipatory agenda.
   c. attention to societal problems.
   d. examination of the positive aspects of culture.

2. In the view of critical theory proponents, mainstream research practices have maintained cultural oppression primarily by
   a. neglecting the study of racial and ethnic minorities.
   b. upholding hegemonic assumptions about truth, science, and good.
   c. questioning the meaning of all texts.
   d. not distinguishing between the effects of class, race, and gender on individuals' cultural attainments.

3. Criticalists refer to the tendency of certain researchers to become preoccupied with means over ends or purposes as
   a. instrumental rationality.
   b. voice.
   c. cultural assimilation.
   d. deconstruction.

4. Hegemony refers to
   a. emancipatory methods as conceptualized by criticalists.
   b. a conception of social justice advocated by criticalists.
   c. differences among the emic perspectives of members of a nonprivileged cultural group.
   d. the domination of nonprivileged cultural groups by privileged cultural groups.

5. In a critical ethnography, it is desirable to
   a. involve field participants in all phases of data collection.
   b. demonstrate consistency between the data collected through passive observation and data collected through dialogue with field participants.
   c. collect primarily data that meet objective truth claims.
   d. analyze the findings from the specific research site in terms of existing or emergent theory about system relationships.

6. One reason for the limited impact of critical theory on educational research to date is its relative
   a. neglect of issues of central importance to educational practice.
   b. preference for everyday mundane language over scientific terminology.
   c. emphasis on deconstructing any form of rhetoric or text.
   d. lack of a foundational theory.

CHAPTER REFERENCES

Agger, B. (1992). *Cultural studies as critical theory*. Washington, DC: Falmer.

Anyon, J. (1980). Social class and the hidden curriculum of work. *Journal of Education, 162,* 67–92.

Apple, M. W. (1997). Introduction. In M. W. Apple (Ed.), *Review of Research in Education,* vol. 22 (pp. xi–xxi). Washington, DC: American Educational Research Association.

Bourdieu, P. (1991). Sport and social class. In C. Mukerji & M. Schudson (Eds.), *Rethinking popular culture: Contemporary perspectives in cultural studies* (pp. 357–373). Berkeley: University of California Press.

Carspecken, P. F. (1996). *Critical ethnography in educational research: A theoretical and practical guide*. New York: Routledge.

Carspecken, P. F., & Apple, M. (1992). Critical qualitative research: Theory, methodology, and practice. In M. D. LeCompte, W. L. Millroy, & J. Preissle (Eds.), *The handbook of qualitative research in education* (pp. 507–552). San Diego: Academic.

Fine, M. (1988). Sexuality, schooling, and adolescent females: The missing discourse of desire. *Harvard Educational Review, 58,* 29–53.

Gibson, R. (1986). *Critical theory and education*. London: Hodder & Stoughton.

Giroux, H. A. (1988). Critical theory and the politics of culture and voice: Rethinking the discourse of educational research. In R. R. Sherman & R. B. Webb (Eds.), *Qualitative research in education: Focus and methods* (pp. 190–210). New York: Falmer.

Giroux, H. A. (1992). Resisting difference: Cultural studies and the discourse of critical pedagogy. In L. Grossberg, C. Nelson, & P. A. Treichler (Eds.), *Cultural studies* (pp. 199–212). New York: Routledge.

Guba, E. G., & Lincoln, Y. S. (1994). Competing paradigms in qualitative research. In N. K. Denzin & Y. S. Lincoln (Eds.), *Handbook of qualitative research* (pp. 105–117). Thousand Oaks, CA: Sage.

Hall, S. (1992). Cultural studies and its theoretical legacies. In L. Grossberg, C. Nelson, & P. A. Treichler (Eds.), *Cultural studies* (pp. 277–294). New York: Routledge.

hooks, b. (1992). *Black looks: Race and representation*. Boston: South End.

Kincheloe, J. L., & McLaren, P. L. (1994). Rethinking critical theory and qualitative research. In N. K. Denzin & Y. S. Lincoln (Eds.), *Handbook of qualitative research* (pp. 138–157). Thousand Oaks, CA: Sage.

Larkin, R. W. (1979). *Suburban youth in cultural crisis*. New York: Oxford University Press.

McLaren, P. (1998). *Life in schools: An introduction to critical pedagogy in the foundations of education* (3rd ed.). New York: Longman.

Nelson, C., Treichler, P. A., & Grossberg, L. (1992). Cultural studies: An introduction. In L. Grossberg, C. Nelson, & P. A. Treichler (Eds.), *Cultural studies* (pp. 1–22). New York: Routledge.

Olesen, V. (1994). Feminisms and models of qualitative research. In N. K. Denzin & Y. S. Lincoln (Eds.), *Handbook of qualitative research* (pp. 158–174). Thousand Oaks, CA: Sage.

Seymour, Smith, C. (Ed.) (1986). *Dictionary of anthropology.* Boston: G. K. Hall.

Spretnak, C. (1991). *States of grace: The recovery of meaning in the postmodern age.* New York: HarperCollins.

Stanfield, J. H. II (1994). Ethnic modeling in qualitative research. In N. K. Denzin & Y. S. Lincoln (Eds.), *Handbook of qualitative research* (pp. 175–188). Thousand Oaks, CA: Sage.

Steinburg, S. R., & Kincheloe, J. L. (1997). *Kinderculture: The corporate construction of childhood.* Boulder, CO: Westview.

Willis, P. (1977). *Learning to labour: How working class kids get working class jobs.* London: Gower.

RECOMMENDED READING

Carspecken, P. F. (1996). *Critical ethnography in educational research: A theoretical and practical guide.* New York: Routledge.

Provides a clearly written guide to the conduct of critical qualitative research in education. The theoretical foundations of such research and validity issues are emphasized.

McLaren, P. (1998). *Life in schools: An introduction to critical pedagogy in the foundations of education* (3rd ed.). New York: Longman.

Explains critical pedagogy and the effects of race, class, and gender on student failure. The book includes the author's journal, written while he taught in an inner-city elementary school in Canada, and discussion questions to help teachers consider how they would address the issues described in the journal.

Morrow, R. A., & Brown, D. D. (1994). *Critical theory and methodology.* Thousand Oaks, CA: Sage.

The authors present the history of critical theory and explain its major tenets. Various methods for conducting research in the critical-theory tradition are described.

Wink, J. (1997). *Critical pedagogy: Notes from the real world.* White Plains, NY: Longman.

The author provides a readable explanation of the theory and concepts of critical pedagogy. The many stories and simple models help educators apply critical pedagogy to their professional development and teaching practice.

SAMPLE CRITICAL-THEORY RESEARCH STUDY: THE DILEMMAS OF DESKILLING: REFLECTIONS OF A STAFF DEVELOPER

Kraft, N. P. (1995). The dilemmas of deskilling: Reflections of a staff developer. *Journal of Staff Development, 16,* 31–35.

In the rest of this chapter you will read a research article that illustrates research based on critical theory. It is preceded by comments written especially for this book by the author of the article. Then the article itself is reprinted in full, just as it appeared when originally published. Where appropriate, we have added footnotes to help you understand the information contained in the article.

Researcher's Comments, Prepared by Nancy Kraft

Critical theory has been highly influential in shaping the way I facilitate the professional development of other educators. It has provided a means to critically reflect on my role in educational systems and how I perform it.

Viewing the world critically was always part of my life, having been raised in a household with a grandmother who was a socialist from Finland and with a father who encouraged me to question everything. However, it was not until I began facilitating seminars for agricultural extensionists from developing countries, and working toward a Ph.D. in educational policy studies at the University of Wisconsin–Madison (UW), that I was able to name the philosophical orientation that reflects my way of looking at and participating in the world. These experiences enabled me to view the world from a new perspective, built upon a critical awareness of how government and economic systems perpetuate an inequitable distribution of power and monetary resources. Through my own work and my interactions with peers who had critical perspectives, I came to know and value the work of criticalists, especially Jürgen Habermas's theory of knowledge-constitutive interests (Held, 1980).

Critical theory also influenced my work as an educational consultant for a statewide evaluation consortium that was connected with an outreach department at UW. The culmination of this five-year experience was my dissertation research: a critical analysis of the role of external change agents in facilitating change in schools (Kraft, 1997). This research was grounded in a critical social science paradigm and an action research philosophy and methodology. Briefly, I discovered the difficulties of facilitating change in situations where a propensity exists for maintaining the status quo. My study showed the power of hegemony in hindering school educators from critically reflecting on their own beliefs, values, and assumptions and how this negatively impacts their practice.

Ironically, this critical perspective generally was not valued or welcomed in the work I did at UW. Critical theory, which at its core involves questioning the basis of power relations, was perceived as threatening by some people in positions of power at UW.

It wasn't until I began working for a private educational research firm, where I am now employed, that this perspective and the concomitant passion I had in situating my practice within it was acknowledged, tolerated, and even valued by my colleagues and peers. In my current role, I have been asked to organize and facilitate professional development internally for my colleagues. This has afforded me the opportunity to integrate a critical perspective in selecting readings and structuring dialogue around important educational issues that confront us in schools.

In the present study my goal was to assist a group of Chapter 1 (now Title I) educators to critically question their own beliefs, values, and assumptions about teaching and learning. More specifically, I wanted to help them understand how their perceptions of Title I children and parents influence the ways they interact with and structure learning experiences for these children.

Children who qualify for Title I traditionally come from lower socioeconomic backgrounds and are often children of color. These facts alone often lead teachers to assume that instructional practices for such children should be remedial in nature. The focus is generally on memorization of mathematics facts and vocabulary, not on engaging the children in analytical or critical thinking and giving them a voice in their own learning program. Also, their instruction is rarely grounded in the kinds of accelerated learning practices that are commonly used in instruction for students in talented and gifted programs. Critical theory provides a means to reveal to educators that some of their beliefs and attitudes may be ideological illusions that perpetuate an inequitable status quo.

As in all my work, my intent at the workshop described in the study that is reprinted here was to help teachers understand the negative effects of power relationships within schools, including the relationship between teachers' limited voice in decision-making processes and the lack of students' voice and ownership in instructional decision making. While I rarely name social science theories such as positivism, interpretivism, critical theory, or postmodernism in my workshops, I do describe how these different philosophical orientations influence the ways that we educators look at the world, and our practices in schools. I try to show that a critical world view permits individuals to better understand why the conditions under which they operate are often frustrating, and that it can foster discoveries of the kinds of actions that may be required to eliminate the sources of those frustrations.

I use participatory and structured dialogue to involve educators in the tasks of critical analysis of their own situations, with a view to transform them in ways that will improve educational situations for students, teachers, and society. My goal in these professional development experiences is to help participants come to realize their collective potential as the active agents of history and change. According to Carr and Kemmis (1986):

> . . . critical educational science has a view of educational reform that is participatory and collaborative; it envisages a form of educational research which is conducted by those involved in education themselves. It takes a view of educational research as critical analysis directed at the transformation of educational practices, the educational understandings, and educational values of those involved in the process, and the social and institutional structures which provide frameworks for their action. (p. 156)

Focusing on entitlement programs that serve marginalized and disenfranchised groups in society makes it generally easy to introduce concepts of power relationships in schools and society. If we first address the way that teachers' own voices are silenced, it then becomes easier for them to acknowledge and talk about the silenced voices of students.

Another technique that I utilize to encourage discussion of such issues is to include exercises that challenge participants to identify their own beliefs, values, and assumptions about teaching and learning, knowledge and curriculum, and children's capabilities. I expose participants to critical literature such as *Rethinking Schools*, a journal published by teachers in Milwaukee, Wisconsin, which focuses on issues of social justice and equity.[1] I also cite books on educational issues that present an alternative perspective to the linear, rational models that form the basis of much of the mainstream literature on educational reform and change processes.

Critical educational science requires that teachers become researchers into their own practices, understanding, and situations. Because I consider my role as a staff developer congruent with that of a teacher, I have always researched my own practice as a staff developer. While the participant whom I quote at the beginning of my research report indicated on the reflection sheet that her attendance was required, I didn't want to brush off her comment as merely that of a disgruntled teacher. Instead, her negative comments confirmed to me that I always need to look for meaningful ways to validate participants' knowledge and involve them in their own learning. Therefore I used her comments as an opportunity to critically reflect on the content and process of this three-day workshop and the way that I try to structure learning for adults. I reread several books that had shaped my practice as an educator. I then wrote an extensive reflection paper that was included in my professional portfolio. This paper formed the basis for the present article.

Interestingly, I had an opportunity to present another workshop to the same group of educators one year later. Because I wanted to stress the value of teachers engaging in reflective practice as well as to model what that looked like, I read portions of my article on the dilemmas of deskilling to these teachers. I explained to them how I had used negative participant feedback from the previous year's workshop to critically reflect on my own practice. I indicated how analysis from a broader socioeconomic, political, historical, and cultural perspective helped me examine power relations in schools. I also noted that outside consultants typically are afforded expert status, whereas teachers themselves have expertise but few forums in which to share it. I explained that as a result of this individual's comments, I had incorporated an activity in which the participants would generate strategies for having a greater voice in effecting needed change in the schools.

I continue to find critical theory a useful framework to guide my own understanding of the ways that schools silence both teachers' and students' voices in identifying directions for meaningful educational reform. It is much more than a framework or an analytical tool, however. It has become a way of life and thinking that provides me a lens to look at and deconstruct the world. Using critical theory, I can continually analyze and reflect on how the broader socioeconomic, political, historical, and cultural context impacts my life and the lives of those with whom I interact on a professional and personal basis.

References

Carr, W., & Kemmis, S. (1986). *Becoming critical: Education, knowledge and action research*. London: The Falmer Press.

Held, D. (1980). *Introduction to critical theory: Horkheimer to Habermas*. Berkeley: University of California Press.

Kraft, N. P. (1997). A critical analysis of the role of change agents in facilitating change. *Dissertation Abstracts International, 57*(12), 5018A. (University Microfilms No. AAG97-11786).

Note

1. *Rethinking Schools: An Urban Education Journal* is edited by Robert Lowe, Bob Peterson, and Rita Tenorio and is available from Ed Press in Milwaukee, WI.

THE DILEMMAS OF DESKILLING: REFLECTIONS OF A STAFF DEVELOPER

Effective staff development programs need to minimize teacher deskilling practices and instead engage participants in critical, democratic, and participatory learning experiences.

Nancy P. Kraft

I have been a staff developer for the past 10 years working with teachers and educators to help them learn about their teaching through the processes of self-study, reflective practice, and action research. I believe that staff development should encourage educators to be more critical, self-analytical, and reflective.

Unfortunately, much of today's staff development consists of giving teachers the "nuts and bolts" and the "how-to's" rather than creating learning opportunities for teachers to examine the nature and processes of educational change and reform initiatives. In effect, these practical staff development approaches without self-study and reflection actually cause teachers to be deskilled, to limit their improvement.

The deskilling approaches separate the conception of curriculum from execution of curriculum; these approaches have experts do the "thinking" while teachers are reduced to doing the "implementing." Giroux (1988) concludes that "the effect is not only to deskill teachers, to remove them from the processes of deliberation and reflection, but also to routinize the nature of learning and classroom pedagogy" (p. 124). If one major outcome of education for children is to create individuals who are critical thinkers and problem solvers, how will teachers be successful in doing this if they, themselves,

Nancy P. Kraft is a research associate, RMC Research Corporation, Writer Square, Suite 540, 1512 Larimer St., Denver, Colorado 80202, (303) 825-3636.

Kraft, N. P. (1995). The dilemmas of deskilling: Reflections of a staff developer. *Journal of Staff Development, 16*, 31–35. Reprinted with permission of the National Staff Development Council. Copyright © 1995 by NSDC.

aren't given opportunities to engage in critical discourse about educational issues.

As a professional who has devoted many years to thinking through educational processes through inquiry into my own practice, and as a person who adamantly resists my own deskilling, I refuse to perpetuate a model of staff development for others which ultimately contributes to their deskilling as well. Thus, this article presents a story about a recent dilemma that I confronted regarding deskilling practices. In addition to sharing my journal reflections from this workshop, I describe a set of strategies that I use as a staff developer to encourage teachers to actively participate in their own learning.

THE EMPEROR IS WEARING NO CLOTHES

"*The emperor's new clothes are here. There she is parading before the audience. No one is telling her she got nothing.*" As I read these words written on the reflection sheet I received from one participant during the second day of a three-day workshop, I suddenly felt very dejected and extremely discouraged. I was facilitating learning for 35 Chapter 1 teachers in a workshop which covered a broad array of topics ranging from "getting in touch with your beliefs, values, and assumptions about knowledge and learning" to "how to get meaningful parent involvement in Chapter 1 programs."

In my own journal, I had noted resistance from some of the participants who were expecting the traditional "sit and get" type of workshop, but I thought that by the end of the first day I had been rather successful in presenting a different kind of staff development opportunity—one that required the participants to think and engage in critical discourse. After all, I reflected in my journal, attendees had been actively participating in their own learning, exploring their beliefs about education and assumptions of Chapter 1 students, and willingly sharing their craft knowledge and expertise with each other. Even though I had encouraged critical reflection on the events of the workshops, the criticism by this participant hurt me.

I questioned the source of this participant's criticism: Was it my style or the content of my workshop? Was it because I was requiring her to think and become more analytical about her own teaching situation (something she may not have had to do in a long time)? I wondered how I could find ways to validate her feelings, but at the same time find ways to help her reconceptualize staff development as an opportunity to reflect and engage in critical discourse.

APPROACHES TO STAFF DEVELOPMENT

I see two approaches to staff development—the traditional approach which essentially tells teachers what to do and the critical theory approach which has teachers engage in critically reflective analyses of educational constructs and their beliefs, values, and assumptions.[a]

The Traditional Approach

So much of staff development has traditionally focused very narrowly on effecting change through telling teachers what to do and how to do it. Teachers haven't been involved in either conceptu-

alizing what change should look like or in deciding how best to initiate and implement that change. They are typically relegated to technician status in implementing others' ideas or "recipes" for change. In a critique of the process of educational reform, Giroux (1988) says:

> Many of the recommendations that have emerged in the current debate either ignore the role teachers play in preparing learners to be active and critical citizens or they suggest reforms that ignore the intelligence, judgment, and experience that teachers might offer in such a debate. Where teachers do enter the debate, they are the object of educational reforms that reduce them to the status of high-level technicians carrying out dictates and objectives decided by experts far removed from the everyday realities of classroom life. The message appears to be that teachers do not count when it comes to critically examining the nature and process of educational reform. (p. 121)

The Critical Theory Approach

The critical theory approach allows teachers to examine society from the perspective of power relationships within that society; it allows staff developers to engage participants in questioning power relationships within schools. Thus the critical theory approach allows teachers to deconstruct traditional models for enacting school change (i.e. questioning why their voices aren't part of the school reform debate, engaging in historical analyses of teacher roles in school change, and understanding feelings of teacher resistance and alienation in school change efforts).[b]

---

a. Educational constructs are concepts (e.g., hyperactivity, intelligence) that are inferred from observed phenomena and then are used as explanations of other instances of such phenomena.

b. To deconstruct a concept or model involves analyzing it as though it were a "text." Deconstruction is based on the assumption that no text has a definite meaning, but rather any text can have multiple interpretations, with no single interpretation privileged over any other.

Reaching this understanding helps teachers to collectively generate strategies which might bring about meaningful change. This deconstruction, generally, also provides them with the means to understand sources of student resistance, alienation, and disempowerment, as well.

Carr and Kemmis (1986) and Apple (1983), who ground their work in critical theory, criticize the traditional model of teacher involvement in staff development that views teachers as mere "operatives" in an education factory, carrying out the dictates of others. In the traditional model, the outside expert or consultant is brought in, often as an extension of administrative control, with the charge of "telling" others how to go about effecting change.

While it has become popular in recent years to involve teachers in staff development focused on action research, teacher research, reflective practice, and collaborative inquiry processes, most of these efforts have perpetuated a deficit model of teachers' knowledge in that the emphasis of these efforts is often on the development of teachers' skills as the sole means of school improvement. These collaborative processes, however, are detrimental to teachers' perceptions of their own abilities and possibilities (Miller, 1990).

A common belief is that teachers only need to change their behavior to improve schools. Staff development based on the critical theory paradigm, however, allows teachers to look more critically at their own practices and also to become more analytical and critical about the conditions which shape their lives as professionals and impact student learning.

My Approach With Critical Theory

While I strongly believe that teachers, for too long, have not been treated as intellectuals, I continue to be frustrated by teachers, themselves, who prefer to participate in their own deskilling, who want to go away from an inservice session with a "bag of tricks" or ideas for "what to do on Monday morning" in the classroom.

Myles Horton, an adult educator instrumental in using adult education for social change, maintains that teachers sometimes prefer the traditional approach because they have had limited opportunities to make important decisions in their professional lives and thus come to the workshop expecting to be taught rather than be challenged to create solutions to their own problems (Kohl & Kohl, 1991).

As a staff developer who relies on a critical theory framework to inform and guide my own practice, I have tried to become more cognizant of the broader social, political, economic, historical, and cultural context which shapes teachers' lives and their professional practice. Thus, the staff development that I plan is heavily influenced by constructs of knowledge and power emanating from a critical theory social science paradigm.[c]

Consequently, I take deliberate steps to negate the power afforded me in the privileged role of the external consultant. These steps include: (a) sharing perceptions of my role as a facilitator of learning with the participants; (b) structuring the learning experience to reflect adult education theory; (c) assisting participants in examining their beliefs, values, and assumptions about teaching and learning, knowledge and curriculum, and learners; and (d) providing opportunities for reflection throughout the staff development experience.

Sharing Perceptions of My Role

Regardless of the topic of my workshop, I always begin by sharing with participants my own philosophy of learning which is consistent with constructivism. I explain this concept as involving others in constructing meaning through acknowledging participants' histories and experience and validating them as capable and thinking beings. Thus the program

---

c. A social science paradigm is a particular model of inquiry based on agreed-upon concepts, procedures, and standards of judgment. Chapter 1 described two major paradigms in social science, the positivist and interpretivist paradigms. Some scholars view critical theory as a third paradigm.

will not be a "make it and take it" workshop, but will instead involve them in critical thinking and reflection. I share with participants who I am (my own background as an adult educator with an interest in school change/reform) and how I see my role (as a facilitator of a learning experience for them).

Even though I am designated presenter or speaker, I also share with them that I view myself as a learner and that I will use this opportunity with them to become more reflective, myself, on my role as a staff developer. My own journal keeping is visible throughout the workshop with my recording of incidents as they occur. Killion and Harrison (1991/1992) refer to this as reflection-in-action, or the mental processing of actions as they occur. I believe that the most effective way to present reflective practice is to model, that is to "walk my talk."

I relate the connections I see between theory and practice, sharing with them I believe there is nothing as practical as a good theory—that theory guides everything we do and believe as educators. I tell them that, as part of my role, I will be using theory as the bases for both the process and content of our shared learning experience.

Structuring the Learning Experience

At this point in my workshops, I usually share with participants adult learning theory delineating the following characteristics of adult learning as identified by Smith (1982):

- adults bring a different orientation to education and learning than children (which results from adults having multiple roles, tasks, responsibilities, and opportunities);
- adults have an accumulation of experience (deriving from their vast range of roles and responsibilities) which I make integral to the workshop content;
- adults pass through developmental phases that are different from those experienced by children and youth; and

- adults bring a degree of anxiety and ambivalence to learning (given multiple roles and responsibilities).

I also share with participants the theory (Smith, 1982) regarding conditions for adult learning:

- adults feel the need to learn and have input into what, why, and how they will learn;
- adults' previous experiences are taken into account when designing both the process and content of the new learning experience;
- what is to be learned is related optimally to the individual's developmental change and life tasks;
- the learning experience provides the learners with the necessary training to adequately complete the task (i.e., making learners more independent for self-directed learning and interedependent for collaborative learning);
- adults learn best in a climate that minimizes anxiety and encourages freedom to experiment; and
- adult learning styles are taken into account.

By realizing that adults have an accumulation of experience, I often begin my workshops with an acknowledgement of this experience. During the initial introductions, I generally ask participants to share how many years of experience they have as educators, and then systematically provide opportunities for them to share their experience throughout the workshop. I believe that one of my roles as a staff developer is to create the conditions (e.g., a climate that minimizes anxiety and provides encouragement for experimentation) that will foster their willingness to share their vast array of experience, wisdom, and expertise.

Barth (1990) says that adults who work in schools carry around with them extraordinary insights about curriculum, staff development, community relations, leadership, and other issues; the challenge is to create the conditions under which they will reveal this rich knowledge of their craft so that it may become part of the discussion.

In this particular workshop (where one participant reflected about the "emperor's new clothes), the 35 educators had 611 years of collective experience, wisdom, and knowledge. I made a point at that workshop, as [sic] all others, that their collective experience would be the basis for examining and critiquing the designated content together. Given the vast experience of these particular participants, one of the unplanned activities became a "teacher exchange" where participants had a formal opportunity to share ideas with each other.

Participants appreciated the teacher exchange, as reflected by several who commented, "Thank you for opening up to teacher idea exchanges," and "I was impressed with the presenter and how she took the time to listen to *our* concerns instead of being a presenter and filling us with all kinds of material that you might forget two days after. It was useful because it opened my eyes to new ideas for my classes. Also the ideas from the other teachers were very, very helpful!" and "Allowing lots of interaction between the teachers and sharing of ideas and concerns was very helpful."

As a means to give them input into the what, why, and how they will learn, we generally co-construct a list of ground rules for how the learning will be structured throughout the workshop. As a co-participant, in addition to being the facilitator of their learning, I list my expectations of their participation in the workshop. Ground rules include such things as:

- the experience of all participants is valued and drawn upon;
- people share/debate/discuss what they are learning with others;
- participants feel respected/listened to;
- participants have input into how teaching and learning happens;
- the learning experience models democratic relations between learner and leader;
- the learning experience includes both reflection and action; and

- the learning experience will be an enjoyable one.

While participants are always given the opportunity to co-construct ground rules, I find that generally few take me up on this offer. For the most part, participants are surprised that they can have direct control over their learning, as this has not been the norm of past staff development experiences. Common sense procedures, such as mutually developed ground rules, establishes [sic] a climate that is conducive to learning and supports participants' willingness to share and interact with each other.

Assisting Participants

I always encourage participants to get in touch with their own beliefs, values, and assumptions about teaching and learning and the knowledge and curriculum they hold as educators. This establishes a precedent of critical thought for the entire workshop.

Brookfield (1987) believes that such a process entails much more than the skills of logical analysis and should involve, "calling into question the assumptions underlying our customary, habitual ways of thinking and acting and then being ready to think and act differently on the basis of this critical questioning" (p. 1).

I believe that only through this kind of reflection, we are able to imagine and explore alternatives. But at the same time, it can be threatening to call into question the values and beliefs that shape the ways in which we look at the world. Consequently, we use non-threatening activities, such as personal reflection with small-group sharing or a graffiti exercise wherein participants write down and share their reactions to a series of questions, as a means to explore personal values, beliefs, and assumptions.

Coming to grips with this part of themselves enables participants to better understand their own resistance and frustrations regarding change. These exercises generally provide an excellent means to redirect those negative feelings into positive strategies and action.

Participants willingly engage in these activities and found it to be valuable as reflected by one teacher who said, "This (workshop) was like a retreat in that we took time from the busy work of teaching to reflect on 'why' we do what we do and/or why and what can be improved. It has helped me get in touch with myself as a professional." Or another, who commented, "A belief, value, or view that is presented should be reflected on and experimented with, but not taken as 'etched in stone' simply because someone presents it as such." And a final comment, "Reflection through journaling, discussion with other teachers, reflective thought, etc. can enable me to evaluate my teaching at present as well as new teaching ideas, to see if I am/can be teaching at the standard of my beliefs and ideals."

Providing Opportunities for Reflection

Frequent check-ins and opportunities for feedback from the participants are incorporated throughout the workshop. Participants are encouraged to challenge and question continuously, and are given opportunities to anonymously share their perceptions. One such strategy asks participants to reflect on the positive points, the negative points, and the interesting or intriguing points about the ideas, opinions, or activities discussed and conducted as part of the workshop. Participant feedback at the end of the workshop generally invites participants to reflect critically, practically, and artistically on any of the ideas discussed during the workshop (Gage & Berliner, 1989).

In reflecting critically, participant comments included: "(The workshop) caused me to identify and analyze my beliefs/values/assumptions regarding teaching and learning," "For one thing, it makes sense to say that educational reform begins in the classroom with the teacher rather than with a state or federal mandate most often designed by others who have no real working knowledge of what goes on in classrooms today," and "I need to be more aware of the research, its applicability to our situation or to that of individual children either before

buying into something or as a guide in designing action research for evaluating current practices."

Practical reflections encompassed, "I'm going to start using my computer to document student progress," and "Using journals seems very practical and of great value for sorting thoughts and feelings and planning action." Viewing new learning artistically included comments such as: "I now take notes on each class and student—what we did, special notes I want to remember about a student, things I want to do with them. With a little more time, perhaps I can expand this into a journal with anecdotal records, my response, notes on my reactions, feelings, kids, etc;" "I think journaling has a wide variety of uses. For me personally, it would probably give me a feeling of continuity with my students. My day is spent doing a variety of jobs. I finish the day feeling disconnected sometimes. It would help me take time to reflect;" and "I would set up an educational tracking plan for my students that includes opportunities for his or her discussion and reflection of the worth of what is being learned."

RECOMMENDATIONS FOR STAFF DEVELOPERS

The adage, "The more things change, the more they stay the same," comes to my mind as I reflect on the stories I have heard, witnessed, and recorded about the ways schools operate and use staff development to effect change. If staff developers ever hope to have an impact in facilitating meaningful change, there are several lessons that can be learned from my narrative.

First, we should be aware of our own ideological positioning and theoretical framework which guides and shapes our work as staff developers. This framework will influence the way we view educators and their capacity to change as well as the nature of change itself. Grounding my work in critical theory has assisted my understanding of teacher resistance to change and provided ways that I can counter that resistance to engage teachers in more meaningful processes to facilitate change. Therefore, staff developers need to understand how social science paradigms affect and influence our own practice.

Second, starting points for staff development experiences should take into consideration the four points outlined in this article. I establish a tone for staff development that actively involves participants in engaging in their own learning by assuming a facilitator role versus role of "expert"; structuring workshops on adult education theory; encouraging critical examination of participants' beliefs, values, and assumptions; and providing ample opportunities for participant reflection. This engagement has generally led to participants' willingness to at least consider trying the new ideas which were the basis of the staff development experience in the first place.

Third, personal reflection via journaling has been a powerful tool for me to become more reflective about my own successes and failures in facilitating others' growth and change. My journal entries have been the basis for writing stories which I often share with participants in other workshops. I use these stories as a means to assist participants in analyzing and understanding their own feelings towards change. If we as staff developers aren't ourselves reflective, how can we expect others to become more reflective.

As this narrative has shown, positive teacher comments serve as a validation that what I am doing is on the right track. But negative comments, such as those of the participant alluding to the "emperor's new clothes," have caused me to think and critically reflect on ways that I can involve even the most resistant person in actively participating in his or her own learning.

My reflections about this experience have shown me that I need to look for ways to validate these feelings and discern their sources. Part of my own growth as a staff developer needs to focus on understanding resistance and continuing to look for ways to encourage active participation on the parts of all learners.

References

Apple, M.W. (1983). Curricular form and the logic of technical control. In M.W. Apple & L. Weis (Eds.), *Ideology and practice in schooling* (pp. 143–165). Philadelphia, PA: Temple University Press.

Barth, R. (1990). *Improving schools from within: Teachers, parents, and principals can make the difference.* San Francisco, CA: Jossey-Bass Publishers.

Brookfield, S. (1987). *Developing critical thinkers: Challenging adults to explore alternative ways of thinking and acting.* San Francisco, CA: Jossey-Bass Publishers.

Carr, W., & Kemmis, S. (1986). *Becoming critical: Education, knowledge and action research.* London: The Falmer Press.

Gage, N.L., & Berliner, D.C. (1989). Nurturing the critical, practical and artistic thinking of teachers. *Phi Delta Kapan, 71*(3), 213–214.

Giroux, H.A. (1988). Teachers as transformative intellectuals. In H.A. Giroux, (Ed.), *Teachers as intellectuals: Toward a critical pedagogy of learning* (pp. 121–128). Granby, MA: Bergin & Garvey Publishers, Inc.

Killion, J., & Harrison, C. (1991/1992, December/January). The practice of reflection: An essential learning process. *The Developer.*

Kohl, H., & Kohl, J. (1991). *The long haul: An autobiography of Myles Horton.* New York: Doubleday.

Miller, J. (1990). *Creating spaces and finding voices: Teachers collaborating for empowerment.* Albany, New York: State University of New York Press.

Smith, R. (1982). *Learning how to learn: Applied theory for adults.* New York, NY: Cambridge.

CHAPTER 13

HISTORICAL RESEARCH

Conrad Timms is a curriculum coordinator for a large urban school district. Sandy du Vall, head of the science department at one of the district's high schools, has asked Timms for help in writing a grant proposal to try out a new constructivist-based curriculum for teaching science.

Timms remembers the new science programs that were introduced in the 1960s following Sputnik, and the widespread perceptions back then that students needed better science instruction. He wonders how the assumptions and techniques of the new science program differ from those of the earlier ones, so he tells du Vall: "Fine, but first let's do a literature search on the history of science education." Together they conduct a search of the ERIC database, entering the descriptor *Science Education History* and related terms. They locate several useful journal articles, including a special issue in the *Journal of Research in Science Teaching* on "Science Curriculum Reform." One article gives suggestions for undertaking science reform today in light of some of the errors made during the curriculum reform efforts of the 1960s. After reading this and other articles, Timms and du Vall feel prepared to write a strong grant proposal, in which they will cite several historical studies that support their ideas for implementing the proposed science program.

Historical research helps educators improve education by its insights into the past, present, and future. This chapter explains the methods used by historical researchers so that you can draw on their studies to understand educational phenomena of interest to you from a historical perspective.

OBJECTIVES

After studying this chapter, you will be able to

1. describe several ways in which the study of history figures as a central concern for educators.
2. explain the major steps of a historical research study.
3. explain the role and relative value of primary and secondary sources in historical research.
4. describe the types of primary sources that historical researchers might study.
5. describe the procedures used by historical researchers to determine the authenticity of primary sources.
6. describe the procedures used by historical researchers to determine the accuracy of primary sources.

7. explain the unique contribution that quantitative records make to historical research.

8. explain several key issues that are involved in interpreting and applying historical research findings.

KEY TERMS

archive

concept

document

external criticism

futurology

historiography

internal criticism

oral history

preliminary source

presentism

primary source

quantitative materials

reconstructionist

record

relic

repository

revisionist historian

secondary source

text materials

variant source

THE NATURE OF HISTORICAL RESEARCH

The education literature is rich with historical studies of educational leaders, institutions, policies, and procedures. The range of issues and subjects investigated by historical researchers is suggested by the following list of published studies:

Candoli, C. (1995). The superintendency: Its history and role. *Journal of Personnel Evaluation in Education, 9,* 335–350.

Fultz, M. (1995). African American teachers in the South, 1890–1940: Powerlessness and the ironies of expectations and protest. *History of Education Quarterly, 35,* 401–422.

Hernandez, D. J. (1995). Changing demographics: Past and future demands for early childhood programs. *Future of Children, 5,* 145–160.

Wagner, L. A., Ownby, L., & Gless, J. (1995). The California Mentor Teacher Program in the 1980s and 1990s: A historical perspective. *Education and Urban Society, 28*(1), 20–39.

Historical research is the process of systematically searching for data to answer questions about a past phenomenon, in order to better understand the phenomenon and its likely causes and consequences. Historians have engaged in this process for thousands of years, using methods of inquiry that today we might call *qualitative*. With the rise of positivism in the twentieth century, historical research shifted toward the compilation of historical "facts" and causal interpretations of the relationship between such facts. Today historical research continues to undergo further shifts. For example, some historians now use computer technology to retrieve and analyze data about the past.

Contemporary historians tend to dismiss much of the historical literature of bygone eras as mere chronicles of events and lives. Their own writings generally are shorter, and they subordinate historical facts to an interpretive framework within which those facts are given meaning and significance. In this chapter we treat historical research as a qualitative research tradition because of its reliance on, although not exclusive use of, interpretivist approaches to data collection and analysis.

The types of research that we describe in other chapters of this book involve the creation of data. For example, researchers create data when they make observations or administer tests to determine the effectiveness of an instructional program. In contrast, most historical researchers primarily discover already existing data in such sources as diaries, official documents, and relics. On occasion, though, historical researchers interview individuals to obtain their recollections of past events. This form of historical research, called *oral history*, does involve data creation.

The Role of History in Education

The past is of great interest to both educational researchers and educational practitioners, although not necessarily for the same reasons. In the following sections, we describe various ways in which educators use historical research methods and findings in their work.

A Subject in the Curriculum.   History is a standard component of the social studies curriculum in most schools in the United States and many other countries (Downey & Levstik, 1991). The emphasis on history in the curriculum reflects the belief of policy makers and the general public that students need to learn a great many facts about previous political leaders, wars, economic shifts, and technological advances involving their own and other countries in order to become well-informed, contributing citizens as adults.

Presumably historical knowledge of their country's culture gives students an appreciation of their cultural heritage, and a commitment to fostering and maintaining that heritage. Robert Bellah and his colleagues (1985), for example, argue that the individualism and scientific rationalism that permeate society today provide little guidance to help individuals make sense of life and form moral judgments. In their view, study of the past provides a reminder of traditions that involved a defined moral and social order to which most members of a community subscribed. In fact, many religious and ethnic groups seek to keep their collective past alive through ritual and documentation in an attempt to preserve a sense of moral and social order.

A Foundation for the Theoretical and Knowledge Base of the Education Profession.   Educational researchers must reflect on past findings and methods of investigation (e.g., research designs and data-collection measures) in order to arrive at fruitful ideas about what to study and to decide whether new methods of investigation need to be developed. In fact, almost every research report includes a review of the literature related to the topic that the researchers addressed. If educational researchers did not conduct these reviews of past research, they would be much more likely to test hypotheses that had been shown to be unproductive, to reinvent research methodology, to "discover" what was already known, and to continue making the same methodological errors as their predecessors.

The study of the past also is important for educational practitioners: Most teachers are required to take a course on educational history during their pre-service preparation. The creation of the many educational activities and institutions that exist in society today reflect particular values and views of society that have a long history. Study of that history can inform the way in which teachers and other educational practitioners view present and proposed educational practices. For example, research into the past can shed light on current approaches to science instruction, bilingual education, educational standards, parent involvement, student assessment, and teacher certification.

At the beginning of the chapter we provided examples of the types of historical research studies to be found in the education literature. As we scanned computer printouts from our search for such studies, we were impressed with the wide range of topics that educational researchers have addressed from a historical perspective. When you carry out a literature search you might want to include *History* as a descriptor, connected by *and* with your subject descriptors (see the discussion of computer searching in Chapter 3). In this way, you can locate possible historical studies on the topic that you are investigating. Obtaining a historical perspective on your topic can prove invaluable in understanding and considering possible changes in the strategies you have used thus far to address the topic in your practice.

A Tool in Planning the Future.   Thomas Popkewitz (1997) observed that researchers disagree in their conceptions of such history-related notions as time, development, and progress. Nonetheless, they generally agree that knowledge of the history of educational phenomena can help us predict, and to some extent plan, what the future of those phenomena will be. In fact, a type of research called *futurology* specifically examines what the future is likely to be. Some futurology studies are based on surveys of current trends, while others use simulation and gaming involving various imagined future scenarios. The predictions are based largely on statistical logic or rational reasoning derived from the study of past events.

Another purpose of historical research, then, is to assist educators in defining and evaluating alternative future scenarios involving a particular educational phenomenon. If we know how certain individuals or groups have acted in the past, we can predict with a certain degree of confidence how they will act in the future. For example, we can make a good prediction of how specific legislators will vote on an upcoming education bill by doing research on their past voting records.

As in other types of educational research, however, prediction rarely is perfect. New social, political, or economic conditions continually arise, thus creating discontinuities in educational practices. In Oregon, for example, the passage in 1991 of Measure 5, a voter-approved initiative, fundamentally changed the basis for funding public schools. Thus, pre-1991 practices in Oregon education may no longer serve as a reliable guide for projections concerning schools' budget allocations, organization, or educational programs.

Some historical researchers, generally called *revisionist historians,* carry out historical research to point out aspects of a phenomenon that they believe were missed or distorted in previous historical accounts. Their larger goal is to sensitize educators to past practices that appear to have had unjust aims and effects but that have continued into the present, and thus require reform. For example, Michael Katz (1968) studied educational innovation in mid-nineteenth-century Massachusetts and demonstrated how it functioned to serve dominant economic interests and to thwart democratic aspirations. Katz's study serves to alert educators to the possibility of similar problems with current educational innovations so that they can be avoided or corrected.

Methods of Historical Research

Historiography is the study of the procedures that historians use in their research. In a discussion of historiography, the historian E. H. Carr (1967) described how he carries out research:

> For myself, as soon as I have got going on a few of what I take to be the capital sources, the itch becomes too strong and I begin to write—not necessarily at the beginning, but somewhere, anywhere. Thereafter, reading and writing go on simultaneously. The writing is added to, subtracted from, re-shaped, cancelled, as I go on reading. The reading is guided and directed and made fruitful by the writing: the more I write, the more I know what I am looking for, the better I understand the significance and relevance of what I find. (pp. 32–33)

Educational researchers conducting historical research often use procedures similar to those Carr described. In the next sections of this chapter we describe these procedures as a series of steps. Keep in mind, though, that many researchers skip back and forth between steps, or modify their procedures based on the particular research questions being asked, the circumstances of their search for historical data, and the interpretive framework they use to understand the data.

SELECTING HISTORICAL SOURCES

As we explained previously in the chapter, historical researchers primarily seek to discover, not create, the data that are relevant to their research problem. Those data are available in various existing sources. However, before researchers begin an active search for sources, they first must reflect on the types of sources that are likely to exist. They then can consider what kinds of individuals or institutions are likely to have produced the types of sources they need, whether those sources would have been saved, and if so, where they are most likely to be stored. As their interpretive framework develops, or as sources point them toward still other sources that deserve exploration, researchers can revise their tentative search plan.

In searching for sources, historical researchers use the three basic types of sources that we described in Chapter 3—preliminary, secondary, and primary sources. Below we describe sources of each type that are relevant to historical research.

Preliminary Sources

A literature search for historical research studies usually begins with the use of a preliminary source. You will recall from Chapter 3 that a preliminary source is an electronic or hard-copy index to secondary and primary sources on various topics. Most preliminary sources related to history are indexes of secondary sources, but some list primary sources as well.

Many of the general preliminary sources listed in Appendix 1 are useful for doing a search of historical literature. This appendix also lists some specialized preliminary sources for historical research, such as directories of historical societies and indexes to different types of historical publications.

Secondary Sources

A secondary source in historical research is a document (or other type of recorded information, such as a videotape) in which the author describes an event or situation at which the author was not present. Authors of secondary sources base their accounts on descriptions or records of events generated by other individuals who witnessed or participated in the events. For example, many newspaper articles and TV news broadcasts are secondary sources, because the reporters relied on interviews with eyewitnesses in order to obtain the information. Annual reports of educational programs and school operations also can be considered secondary sources if they are prepared by individuals who relied on data collected from other individuals who were the actual administrators, instructors, and students to whom the data refer.

Most historical researchers read a number of secondary sources early in their research study in order to clarify their research problem and determine the types of primary sources that are relevant to the problem. Sometimes researchers decide to accept the information given in a secondary source about a relevant primary source, rather than tracking down the primary source itself. In other cases, they might decide that they need to examine the primary source directly. In making their decision, they consider the reputation of the author of the secondary source, the degree of compatibility between that author's interpretive framework and their own, and whether it is feasible to gain access to the primary source.

Primary Sources

A primary source in historical research is any source of information (e.g., a diary, a song, a map, a set of test scores) that has been preserved from the past, or that is created to document a past phenomenon by someone who witnessed or participated in it. Virtually any object or verbal account can be a primary source in historical research.

Four main types of primary sources are studied by historical researchers:

1. *Text materials*. Text materials, whether written or printed, are the most common type of primary source for historical research. Yvonna Lincoln and Egon Guba (1985) classify such materials as either documents, which are prepared for personal use only (e.g., a letter to a friend or a private diary), or records, which have an official purpose (e.g., a legal contract, a will, or a newspaper article). Documents and records might contain handwritten, typed, or computer-generated text, be published or unpublished, and use various genres (e.g., newspaper articles, poetry, or novels).

The text materials examined by historical researchers might include both materials that were intentionally written to serve as a record of the past (e.g., a memoir or a school yearbook), and materials that were prepared only to serve an immediate purpose (e.g., school memoranda or a teacher-prepared test), with no expectation that they might be used as a historical source at a later time.

2. *Oral history*. Unlike primary sources that were produced in the past, oral history represents a source that is created in the present, but provides information about the past. Many cultures use ballads, tales, and other forms of spoken language to preserve a record of past events for posterity. Some historical researchers make transcripts of such oral expressions. Others conduct interviews of individuals who witnessed or participated in events of potential historical significance, recording and transcribing the interviews to produce a written record. The tapes and transcripts of research informants' recollections are primary sources, but when historical researchers summarize and comment on the information obtained from informants, the summaries become part of a secondary source (the historical research report).

An example of oral history is *Missing Stories*, a book by Leslie Kelen and Eileen Stone (1996). These researchers studied eight minority communities in the state of Utah. They conducted lengthy interviews with 352 individuals, taped the interviews, and transcribed them. The book presents the stories of 88 of the individuals, who share recollections of their past as it relates to the minority community that each represents. For example, the epilogue to the chapter on the Chicano-Hispano community is the story of a Chicano woman who is an assistant principal of an intermediate school. She describes her father's struggle to obtain an education and become a teacher, and how she as an educator continues his commitment to "reject rejection," despite living in an environment still tempered with racial stereotypes.

3. *Relics*. Relics include any object whose physical or visual properties provide information about the past. School supplies, computers, a blueprint of a

school building, textbooks, worksheets, and instructional games are examples of relics that researchers could examine for information about historical educational practices.

4. *Quantitative materials*. Materials providing quantitative information about educational phenomena are another important primary source. Like documents and records, they are recorded and preserved in some print form or as computer files. Census records, school budgets, school attendance records, teachers' grade sheets, test scores, and other compilations of numerical data can provide useful data for historical researchers. Later in the chapter, we will discuss the unique value of quantitative materials in historical research.

Some primary sources used by historical researchers fit more than one of the four types of sources that we have listed. For example, a school memorandum might include a discussion of plans based on the results of a survey of teachers (documenting the number of teachers for, against, and having no opinion) concerning a proposed change in the intramural sports program. This memorandum is both a written record and a quantitative record, because it includes numerical information as well as text.

Other primary sources might be classified as both text materials and relics, depending on how they are used in a historical study. For example, in a study of the printing methods used in producing textbooks, a specific textbook would be classified as a relic, because one of its physical properties is being examined. The same textbook would be considered a record in a study of how textbooks of different periods explained a particular mathematical operation, because the content of the textbook now is the focus of study.

Written primary sources such as diaries, manuscripts, or school records and relics such as old photographs or classroom paraphernalia might be found in regional museums. Such primary sources sometimes are accumulated for storage in archives (also known as *repositories*). Archives are special locations for storing primary sources in order to preserve them in good condition and control access to them.

The repositories of primary sources related to education include university libraries and the files of public and private organizations. Repositories vary in the ease of access they permit to primary sources. The holdings of official archives usually are well indexed, and an archivist might be available to assist a historical researcher seeking information. In other situations no help is available, so the researchers must learn the institution's filing system or its system for generating and storing quantitative data (e.g., a software program) in order to find the sources they need.

Historical researchers must learn and follow any required procedures for getting access to a primary source, such as making a written request to an archive for permission to study the records, indicating the length of time they will need the records, how they will record information, and perhaps even the use to which they plan to put the information. Some institutions might place restrictions on the use of historical sources—for example, permitting documents only to be examined but not directly quoted, or allowing only certain portions to be copied. Before historical researchers can reproduce documents that might at some time be published for profit, they must follow any legal procedures regarding copyright, such as quoting only short passages of any source, or obtaining publisher permission to reproduce a table or figure from a source.

VALIDATING HISTORICAL EVIDENCE

Educators who wish to apply the findings of historical research need assurance that the historical sources that were used by the researchers as a basis for their interpretations are valid. Historical sources are valid to the extent that they are authentic and contain accurate information. In the following sections we present procedures that are used to validate the authenticity of historical sources and the accuracy of their information.

Procedures for Determining the Authenticity of Historical Sources

Determining the authenticity of the primary sources that are used to describe and interpret past events is an important part of historical research. This process sometimes is called *external criticism*, because it is concerned not with the content of the primary source but rather with the issue of whether the apparent or claimed origin of the source corresponds to its actual origin. The term *origin* refers to such matters as the primary source's author, place, date, and circumstances of publication.

The citation for a primary source should include its author, place of origin, date of publication, and publisher or sponsoring institution. While the author of a primary source usually is listed in the source itself, this indicator may not be reliable. Some primary sources, such as recorded speeches, are ghostwritten by someone other than the individual who is identified as the author. In other cases, authors use pseudonyms to conceal their identity. If a primary source has multiple authors, it might be impossible to determine who wrote the parts of it that are relevant to a historical research problem. Still another issue relating to authorship is the possibility of forgery. A forgery is a fabrication that is claimed to be genuine—for example, a diary written by someone other than the person whose experiences are described.

The place of origin of a primary source often is apparent from where it is stored, or from indications in the source itself. The date of origin might be more difficult to ascertain. If no date is given, it might be possible to infer the date from references in the primary source, or from its sequential location in a file cabinet. Dates on primary sources should be viewed critically, because people often make innocent errors. For example, at the start of a new year it is not uncommon for someone to make the mistake of recording the previous year.

The possible existence of variant sources is another problem in judging the authenticity of a primary source. Variant sources are materials that have been altered in some way from the original version. For example, in going through the files of an educational institution, researchers might discover file copies (i.e., copies stored in the organization's official records) of internal memoranda that relate to their study. However, it is possible that the file copy was not distributed in exactly that form to all its intended receivers. Perhaps the author of a memo added a personal note to one receiver's copy of the memo. In this situation, both versions of the memo could be considered primary sources, each of which reveals different information about a past event.

Typewriters were not available before about 1880. Before then, most documents were written in longhand, and copies were prepared in the same manner. In working with pre-1880 documents, then, researchers need to determine whether more than one copy was made, and if so, compare their content for errors.

To determine the authenticity of a primary source, researchers must generate and test alternative hypotheses about each aspect of its reputed origin. For example, they might hypothesize that a particular primary source was written by a subordinate in the organization rather than the person designated as the author. As they collect information showing that this and other hypotheses are untenable, they increase the probability, though never to the point of absolute certainty, that the source is genuine. Any doubts that a researcher has about the authenticity of a source should be noted in the research report.

Procedures for Determining the Accuracy of Historical Sources

The process of determining the accuracy of a primary historical source is called *internal criticism*. To guide internal criticism, researchers ask such questions as: Is it likely that people would act in the way that the writer described? Is it physically possible for the events described to have occurred this close together in time? Do the budget figures mentioned by the author seem reasonable? However, the researchers' sense that an event or situation described in a historical source seems improbable might not be sufficient basis for discounting the source. Most people can recall highly improbable events that actually occurred in their lifetime.

Internal criticism requires researchers to judge both the reasonableness of the statements in a historical source and the trustworthiness of the person who made the statements. Criteria that are used in judging the trustworthiness of a source's author include: (1) the author's presence or absence during the events being described; (2) whether she was a participant in or an observer of the events; (3) her qualifications to describe such events accurately; (4) her level of emotional involvement in the situation; and (5) whether she might have a vested interest in the outcomes of the event.

Even competent and truthful witnesses often give different versions of events that took place. When researchers discover widely differing accounts of an event, they need not conclude that all are equally true or false. As Carr (1967) notes, "It does not follow that, because a mountain appears to take on different shapes from different angles of vision, it has objectively either no shape at all or an infinity of shapes" (pp. 30–31). Carr argues that the historical researchers' task is to combine one or more witnesses' accounts, admittedly subjective, and to interpret them (also a subjective process) in an attempt to discover what actually happened.

Accounts of historical events need to be checked carefully for bias. A bias is a set to perceive events in such a way that certain types of facts are habitually overlooked, distorted, or falsified. Individuals with strong motives for wanting a particular version of a described event to be regarded as "the truth" are likely to produce biased information. For example, if a school memo describing a dispute between the superintendent and members of the school board was written by the superintendent, researchers might suspect that the superintendent's side of the argument would be presented in the most favorable light.

Many biased reports of events can be traced to people's tendency to make a story more dramatic, or to exaggerate their role in events. Historical researchers examine such factors as the ethnic background, political party, religious affiliation, and social status of those whose views are conveyed in a historical source, in an effort to appraise the likelihood of bias. They also examine use of emotionally charged or intemperate language, which can reflect commitment to a particular position on an issue.

Biased reports are especially likely when the social or political position of individuals requires them to make socially acceptable statements, even if they do not honestly feel that way. For example, a school principal we know was questioned about internal difficulties with particular teachers and classified staff at her school. The principal made claims about high staff morale and cohesiveness at her school. Such claims probably were made to avoid compounding the problem, and to guard against putting the speaker in a negative light. For similar reasons, some people in public life make mild statements about a colleague or rival, even when those statements do not reflect their true feelings. Recently the opposite trend has emerged in political campaigns, that is, a tendency to "blast" one's opponent regardless of the verifiability of one's statements.

If researchers discover a difference between someone's public and private statements, the discrepancy does not necessarily mean that the public statements have no value as historical evidence. Rather, the discrepancy itself is evidence about the person making the statement, and about the social environment in which he functioned.

INTERPRETING THE INFORMATION OBTAINED FROM HISTORICAL SOURCES

In explaining internal criticism, we noted that witnesses to an event report different impressions based on their competence, personal position, and relationship to an event. Historical researchers are in a similar position. Historians will write different histories about the past depending upon the evidence that they have chosen to collect and how they have interpreted it.

Because history inevitably involves interpretation, historical researchers continually reconstruct the past as their interests and knowledge change. The last few decades of historical research in education have seen the emergence of revisionist historians (also known as *reconstructionists*). As we explained earlier in the chapter, such researchers take a different view of educational history than the conventional or popular view. Revisionist historians tend to believe that past educational practices reflect particular political, economic, or other social forces and motivations more than they reflect rationality, good will, or pedagogical considerations. As a result, Sol Cohen (1976) notes that historians of education ". . . are now disclosing phenomena long hidden by official pieties: the maltreatment of immigrants and ethnic groups, the discriminatory treatment of women and minority groups, the connections between schools and politics and between education and social stratification" (p. 329).

In Chapter 12 we discussed critical-theory research, which is similar to revisionist history in that both take a critical stance toward much educational practice, and seek historical explanations for many practices that they view as negative or problematic. Critical theory also is aligned with recent historical research on the importance of investigating nonschool influences that affect the socialization and learning of young people and adults. This research reflects critical theory's resistance to "essentializing" one definition of education over any other.

Historical researchers need to be especially careful to avoid a type of interpretive bias known as *presentism*. Presentism is the interpretation of past events based on concepts and perspectives that originated in more recent times. Historical researchers need to discover how various concepts were used in the time period and setting that they are investigating, rather than attach present meanings to them.

For example, there has been much interest recently in school choice, which refers to such phenomena as allowing parents to send their children to any public school in the district in which they reside, or providing tuition vouchers so that parents can send their children to private schools instead of state-supported public schools. Researchers interested in the history of school choice during the nineteenth century might look for data on the choices then available to parents about their children's education. Educators then might have used a term similar to *school choice*, but it might have meant something quite different—for example, whether children whose parents kept them home to work during harvest season would be considered absent from school and thus responsible for making up missed schoolwork.

The Importance of Concepts to Interpret Historical Information

As in other types of qualitative research, researchers doing historical research develop concepts to organize and interpret the data that they have collected. Concepts are terms that can be used to group individuals, events, or objects sharing a common set of attributes. For example, without a concept such as *progressive education*, a great many past phenomena that share common characteristics might be seen as separate and lacking historical significance.

Concepts, however, also place limits on historical researchers' interpretation of the past. For example, a researcher conducting a historical study of teaching might consider the defining attribute of the concept of *teaching* to be paid work done by someone who holds a state certificate that signifies completion of a college-level teacher education program. This definition of teaching will cause the researcher to study some individuals from a certain historical period but to exclude others (e.g., teacher aides and school volunteers) who would have been considered to be teaching if a different definition of the concept were used.

Historical researchers should determine whether the definition of each concept used in their research applies to the historical phenomena that they wish to study, and if necessary, provide definitions of important concepts in their research report. Many educational terms (e.g., *intelligence, distance learning, multicultural education*) have become part of people's everyday vocabulary, but readers need to understand how such terms are used in the context of a research study.

Historical researchers have made increasing use of concepts from the social sciences and other disciplines. In their investigation of historical studies that had won awards during a certain time period, T. C. R. Horn and Harry Ritter (1986) found that all the studies that were judged to be outstanding had drawn upon conceptual frameworks from other disciplines. Interdisciplinary concepts are useful tools. For example, in applying the concept of *bureaucracy* to the public school system that developed in the United States during the mid-nineteenth century, Michael Katz (1987) defined it with reference to the definition set forth by Carl Friedrich, a sociologist.

Using Quantitative Materials in Historical Research

One reason for the growing use of quantitative materials in historical research is that conclusions based on large amounts of carefully selected quantitative data are considered to be more generalizable than conclusions based on case studies. Another benefit of quantitative materials is that they allow researchers to characterize the historical views and experiences of many people, which sometimes is referred to as the *common-man approach* to historical research. By contrast, older historical studies tend to focus on a few prominent individuals.

H. Warren Button (1979) referred to the common-man approach as "history from the bottom up—grassroots history" (p. 4). Because historical records typically give minimal attention to grassroots perspectives, Button argued that historical researchers must mine every source in order to reflect those perspectives:

> For instance, for a quantitative study of Buxton, a black antebellum haven in Ontario, it is necessary to assemble data from perhaps fifteen thousand entries in the census manuscripts of 1861, 1871, and 1881; from town auditors' accounts, and church records. . . . The research necessity for compila-

tion and statistical treatment, by unfortunate paradox, produces history almost without personalities, even without names. Still, this new history has and will produce new understandings and will counterweight our long-standing concern for "the better sort." (p. 4)

Thus, a historical research study that includes the analysis of quantitative materials (sometimes referred to as *quantitative history*) provides information beyond that available from a purely qualitative historical research study. In turn, it requires the researchers to use sampling techniques, to define and measure variables, and to conduct statistical analyses.

Causal Inference in Historical Research

An essential task of historical research consists of investigating the main causes of past events. Examples of causal questions that could guide historical studies are: What were the forces and events that gave rise to the intelligence-testing movement? Why did U.S. educators adopt so readily the British open-classroom approach several decades ago? How did the role of school principal originate in this country?

Causal inference in historical research is the process of reaching the conclusion that one set of events brought about, directly or indirectly, a subsequent set of events. Historical researchers cannot prove that one past event caused another, but they can make explicit the assumptions that underlie their causal inferences concerning sequences of historical events.

Some historical researchers make the assumption that humans act similarly across cultures and across time. Thus, they might use a currently accepted causal pattern to explain an apparently similar pattern in the past. For example, a researcher might find an instance in nineteenth-century U.S. education when students at a particular college stopped attending classes and began making public protests against some college administrators. Suppose that the researcher also discovered that this event was preceded by administrative rulings at the college that diminished students' rights and privileges. He might infer—perhaps correctly—that these rulings led to the student revolt, his reasoning being that a similar chain of events precipitated student protests in many U.S. colleges during the 1960s.

Historians generally believe, however, that historical events are unique, and therefore that history does not repeat itself. In this view, occurrences at one point in time can illuminate, but do not explain, occurrences at another point in time. Even historians who see past occurrences as a harbinger of later events must be wary of presentism, which we described previously as the use of concepts that now have different meanings to interpret events from an earlier time period.

Historical researchers have emphasized various types of causes in their attempts to explain past events. They might attribute past educational occurrences to the actions of certain key persons, to the operation of powerful ideologies, to advances in science and technology, or to economic, geographical, sociological, or psychological factors. Some historians take an eclectic view and explain past events in terms of a combination of factors. For example, David Tyack (1976) studied the rise of compulsory education in the United States. He concluded that until about 1890, Americans built a broad base of elementary schooling that attracted ever-growing numbers of children. During that period most states passed compulsory attendance legislation, but did little to enforce those laws. Tyack calls this phase the *symbolic* stage of compulsory schooling.

Tyack concluded that a second stage, which he calls the *bureaucratic* stage, began in the United States shortly before the turn of the twentieth century. He notes that during this era

> . . . school systems grew in size and complexity, new techniques of bureaucratic control emerged, ideological conflict over compulsion diminished, strong laws were passed, and school officials developed sophisticated techniques to bring truants into schools. By the 1920s and 1930s increasing numbers of states were requiring youth to attend high school, and by the 1950s secondary school attendance had become so customary that school-leavers were routinely seen as dropouts. (p. 60)

The question arises, Why did schooling in the United States gradually become compulsory under force of law? Tyack examined five causal interpretations to see how well each answered this question. For example, the ethnocultural interpretation argues that compulsory education came about because of the belief that it would inculcate a single "correct" standard of behavior. This interpretation is based in part on a recognition of efforts then being made to address challenges to the U.S. economy and culture resulting from the influx of immigrants from southern and eastern Europe, which provoked considerable concern among some religious and ethnic groups already established in this country. Another interpretation, drawn from the economic theory of human capital, states that compulsory schooling grew out of a belief that education would improve the productivity and predictability of the workforce.

Each of Tyack's interpretations of the main reason for the growing strength of compulsory schooling in the United States explains some historical evidence, leaves other evidence unexplained, and suggests new lines of research. Tyack notes that such alternative interpretations help historians "to gain a more complex and accurate perception of the past and a greater awareness of the ambiguous relationship between outcome and intent—both of the actors in history and of the historians who attempt to recreate their lives" (p. 89).

The more researchers learn about the antecedents of a historical event, the more likely they are to discover possible alternative causes of the event. Therefore, it probably is more defensible to identify an earlier event as *a* cause, rather than *the* cause, of a later event. Moreover, by their choice of language in the research report, researchers can convey their interpretation of the strength of the causal link (e.g., "It was a major influence . . ." or "It was one of many events that influenced . . .") and of its certainty (e.g., "It is highly likely that . . ." or "It is possible that . . .").

Generalizing from Historical Evidence

Like other qualitative researchers, historical researchers do not seek to study all the individuals, settings, events, or objects that interest them. Instead, they usually study only one case or a few instances of the phenomenon of interest. The case that is chosen is determined partly by the availability of sources. For example, suppose that a historical researcher wished to examine the diaries, correspondence, and other written records of elementary school teachers in the 1800s in order to understand teaching conditions during that time. The study necessarily would be limited to teachers whose writings had been preserved, and to which the researcher could gain access. The researcher also would need to consider the possibility that teachers who kept written records of their work might not be typical of teachers in general.

Before generalizing the study's findings to other teachers of the period, the researcher should consider whether other teachers would have provided similar data. One way to determine whether similar results would be found for other types of teachers would be to examine how teachers in different circumstances viewed their teaching experience. For example, the researcher might ask: Did teachers who wrote about their work for publication describe similar conditions as did teachers who wrote about their work in private diaries and correspondence?

Another potential problem in historical interpretation involves the generalizability of historical data related to a single individual. For example, a historical researcher might discover a primary source in which an educator stated an opinion about a particular educational issue. The statement does not prove that this educator held the same opinion at a later or earlier time. The researcher must look for more data that will help her decide whether the expressed opinion was characteristic of this educator.

As in any research project, historical research findings are strengthened by increasing the size of the data set on which they are based. Conducting an extensive search for primary and secondary sources relating to the topic will help historical researchers expand their data set. If the evidence is limited to only a few sources, the researchers should exercise restraint in the generality of their interpretations. For example, they might phrase a generalization about teaching as "Teachers in rural schools of 50 or fewer students during the period 1860 to 1870 . . ." rather than "Teachers during the period 1860 to 1870. . . ." Historical researchers wishing to make the latter generalization could strengthen their case by presenting statistical analyses based on representative quantitative data.

Reporting of Historical Research Findings

The presentation of findings in a historical research report varies. Some historical reports present historical facts in chronological order. Another method of presentation involves organizing historical facts according to topic or theme.

The research article reprinted at the end of this chapter involves a combination of these approaches. The author, Terese Volk, analyzed the development of multicultural music education by doing a chronological analysis of the issues of a major journal for music educators published over a 25-year period. Four "milestone issues" of the journal provided the time frame for her analysis. The author also tracked certain themes in the development of multicultural music education, using the publication of a 1966 speech by a leading music educator as her source in defining those themes. For example, she described a session from a national conference reported in the journal:

> The nearly three hundred music educators who participated in the Symposium sang songs and learned dances for both the Native American and Asian-American segments of the event. They had opportunities to perform in a Chinese percussion ensemble, play Andean raft-pipe instruments, see an excerpt of Chinese opera, and attend a dance party with salsa and other Latino dance music. (p. 146 in the original article)

Through this style of reporting, Volk brings the past alive, showing how earlier events led to the present acceptance of multiculturalism in music education, and how some problems of practice still are in need of solution.

CONCLUDING THOUGHT

Historical researchers provide a unique perspective on the current state of educational beliefs, values, and practices by identifying their roots in the past. Educators who have a historical perspective on an issue that concerns them can think about it in greater depth and select a wiser course of action.

SELF-CHECK TEST

1. All educational researchers can be regarded as historians in the sense that they generally
   a. review past research as a basis for designing their own research studies.
   b. seek causes for present-day phenomena by investigating past phenomena.
   c. interpret the practical significance of their research findings.
   d. suggest desirable directions for future research on the topics they have studied.

2. In historical research, the literature review typically
   a. is a relatively minor part of the research process.
   b. provides the research data.
   c. is conducted after the data have been collected.
   d. focuses on secondary sources.

3. Historical researchers typically read secondary sources relating to their research problem in order to
   a. gain an overview of historical information relevant to their problem.
   b. obtain the most accurate information possible about a past event.
   c. identify relevant preliminary sources.
   d. eliminate the necessity of examining primary sources.

4. In historical research, a private journal written by a nineteenth-century school principal most likely would be considered
   a. oral history.
   b. a relic.
   c. a document.
   d. a secondary source.

5. In historical research, physical objects preserved from the period being studied are called
   a. records.
   b. secondary sources.
   c. repositories.
   d. relics.

6. The procedure for determining whether a source of historical data is authentic sometimes is called
   a. internal criticism.
   b. external criticism.
   c. historiography.
   d. revisionism.

7. Internal criticism of documents is used to
   a. detect forgeries.
   b. determine the accuracy of the information in the document citation.
   c. locate variant sources.
   d. determine the accuracy of the information in the document text.

8. In historical research, presentism refers to the
   a. belief that the present is more important than the historical past.
   b. use of contemporary concepts to interpret past events.
   c. belief that the present cannot be understood by the study of past events.
   d. set of assumptions underlying revisionist history.

9. Historical researchers generally consider quantitative materials superior to other types of primary sources for
   a. exploring the unique aspects of a historical phenomenon.
   b. investigating the history of nonliterate cultures.
   c. writing grassroots historical accounts.
   d. describing prominent individuals of past periods.

10. Causal inference in historical research is a process by which researchers
   a. narrow the cause of a historical phenomenon to one set of factors.
   b. explain past events in terms of contemporary concepts.
   c. take a critical view of past practices that previously were viewed positively.
   d. use interpretation to ascribe causality to a sequence of historical events.

CHAPTER REFERENCES

Bellah, R. et al. (1985). *Habits of the heart: Individualism and commitment in American life.* Berkeley: University of California Press.

Button, H. W. (1979). Creating more usable pasts: History in the study of education. *Educational Researcher, 8*(5), 3–9.

Carr, E. H. (1967). *What is history?* New York: Random.

Cohen, S. (1976). The history of the history of American education, 1900–1976: The uses of the past. *Harvard Educational Review, 46*, 298–330.

Downey, M. T., & Levstik, L. S. (1991). Teaching and learning history. In J. P. Shaver (Ed.), *Handbook of research on social studies teaching and learning* (pp. 400–410). New York: Macmillan.

Horn, T. C. R., & Ritter, H. (1986). Interdisciplinary history: A historiographical review. *The History Teacher, 19*, 427–428.

Katz, M. B. (1968). *The irony of early school reform: Educational innovation in mid-nineteenth century Massachusetts.* Cambridge, MA: Harvard University Press.

Katz, M. B. (1987). *Reconstructing American education.* Cambridge, MA: Harvard University Press.

Kelen, L. G., & Stone, E. H. (1996). *Missing stories.* Salt Lake City, UT: University of Utah Press.

Lincoln, Y. S., & Guba, E. G. (1985). *Naturalistic inquiry.* Beverly Hills, CA: Sage.

Popkewitz, T. S. (1997). A changing terrain of knowledge and power: A social epistemology of educational research. *Educational Researcher, 26*(9), 18–29.

Tyack, D. B. (1976). Ways of seeing: An essay on the history of compulsory schooling. *Harvard Educational Review, 46*, 55–89.

Volk, T. M. (1993). The history and development of multicultural music education as evidenced in the *Music Educators Journal,* 1967–1992. *Journal of Research in Music Education, 41*, 137–155.

RECOMMENDED READING

Barzun, J. (1998). *The modern researcher* (6th ed.). Fort Worth: Harcourt Brace College.
   Provides a comprehensive description of historical researchers' work, including strategies for fact finding, criticism, interpretation, and reporting.

Burton, O. V., & Finnegan, T. (1990). Teaching historians to use technology: Databases and computers. *International Journal of Social Education, 5*, 23–35.
   A brief introduction to the databases, database management programs, and statistical procedures used in quantitative history. The authors highlight the computer skills needed to use these tools effectively.

Tuchman, B. W. (1982). *Practicing history: Selected essays*. New York: Ballantine.

A collection of essays on the uses of history and the craft of doing historical research. Examples of the author's historical studies are included.

Yow, V. R. (1994). *Recording oral history: A practical guide for social scientists*. Thousand Oaks, CA: Sage.

The author explains interviewing strategies and the ethical issues involved in oral history. Includes an in-depth description of three types of oral history projects—community studies, biographies, and family histories.

SAMPLE HISTORICAL RESEARCH STUDY: THE HISTORY AND DEVELOPMENT OF MULTICULTURAL MUSIC EDUCATION AS EVIDENCED IN THE *MUSIC EDUCATORS JOURNAL*, 1967–1992

Volk, T. M. (1993). The history and development of multicultural music education as evidenced in the *Music Educators Journal*, 1967–1992. *Journal of Research in Music Education, 41*, 137–155.

In the rest of this chapter you will read a research article that illustrates a historical research study. It is preceded by comments written especially for this book by the author of the article. Then the article itself is reprinted in full, just as it appeared when originally published. Where appropriate, we have added footnotes to help you understand the information contained in the article.

Researcher's Comments, Prepared by Terese Volk

Historical research to me is not merely a study of the past. The excitement and wonder I feel when I hold a 150-year-old manuscript or songbook in my hand, or when I suddenly discern a definite trend evolving over time, brings history alive for me in a way that reading historical accounts rarely does. My task as a historian is to try to convey that sense of aliveness to my readers through the discipline of historical research. My hope is to present the past in a way that sheds light on the present, and on the future as well.

The Evolution of This Research

I originally wrote the article reprinted here as an assignment for a History of Music Education class during my graduate studies. I selected it because of my long-standing interest in multicultural music education and the many articles I had read on that topic in the *Music Educators Journal* (*MEJ*). I also noticed that the literature contained very little historical review of the development of this "new" component in music education since 1967, despite the many individual articles about it. I sensed a need to collect all this information and make it accessible in one place. At first it was merely a topic for a paper to satisfy a grade requirement. However, as I began work on my paper I found that the task required more than simple chronicling.

I became engrossed with my research, and slowly realized that I had been bitten by the "historical research bug." My investigation of this topic became so intense that I nearly neglected my other courses that semester! I, who previously had trouble finding a question upon which to design experimental research, could not stop the flow of questions this historical paper generated. I knew I had finally found my mode of research, and a focus for my doctoral dissertation.

The present article is the finished paper from my course, further polished with the assistance of a knowledgeable and caring editor on the board of the *Journal of Research in Music Education* (*JRME*). The *JRME*, the research journal for the Music Educators National Conference (MENC), is a refereed journal that accepts only articles with implications for the entire profession. Whereas *JRME* is obtained only by subscription, every dues-paying member of the MENC receives *MEJ*. The *MEJ* is partly an organizational newsletter, partly an advertising medium for both professional activities and school materials, and partly a collection of articles on various topics of interest to music educators. The articles in *MEJ* are more conversational in tone, and offer more immediate practical classroom applications, than the more formal research reports demanded by *JRME*.

Methodology

There are several useful methodologies for doing historical research. Probably the most familiar is the *historical narrative*, that is, simply telling the story using primary source material to document trends or clarify events. This method relies heavily on written documentation, but it may also include *oral history* (interviewing people to obtain new information or to confirm written sources). Other examples of methods to chronicle and draw inferences from historical events include *content analysis* (the literal counting of topics or even words across a selected literature and time span), *collective biography* (comparisons drawn from information about the lives of a large group of individuals), and *statistical analysis* (a quantitative method, frequently used to compile data from such sources as U.S. census reports or immigration files).

For this article, I chose to use primarily the historical narrative approach. I selected a single set of documents (the issues of *MEJ* from 1967 to 1992) and a single topic to examine (the growth of multicultural music education). I then set about obtaining an overall picture of what was happening with regard to this topic by reading through every journal issue in this time period. I also read many earlier articles in *MEJ* and its predecessor, the *Music Supervisors Journal*.

Next I focused on locating specific *MEJ* articles that would help me discern the larger trends that were developing over the 25-year time span I had selected. As part of my research I employed content analysis. While I did not actually do a statistical word count, I tracked trends denoted by specific phrases in the articles, such as *ethnic musics*, *world musics*, and *multicultural music education*, and noted when the usage changed from one term to another.

Because *MEJ* had published four milestone issues with implications for multicultural music education beginning in 1967, the headings for my paper were somewhat predetermined for me. I worked chronologically within the time framework covered in these special issues.

Beyond the simple compilation of events and articles dealing with multicultural music education, a second focus of my paper was to discover how far multicultural music education had progressed over the 25-year time period I examined. The points of reference I chose were the problems Egon Kraus identified in 1966. Kraus's speech touched on eight problems. In the article I quote the first five of them directly (note 1) and paraphrase the other three, which were of a more international nature (note 2). These problems provided me with both the overall trends I sought to track as I read the *MEJ* issues and the reference points for some evaluative conclusions I reached at the end of the narrative. I have found this format (moving from predictions or problems, to historical chronology, to a summary of trends, and finally to evaluation) to be particularly effective for me as a researcher.

Writing the article was not without its difficulties. It went through three reviews by *JRME* before it satisfied the review editor's queries. The most difficult revision for me was defining *culture* and *music* (words that, as a student, I thought were self-explanatory!) in a way that would be acceptable to both the editor and the general reader. I also was asked to clarify the reasons why I chose *MEJ* as my literature base and to explain how I was going to delimit the enormous number of articles contained in it. It was not until I found Kraus's speech that I felt I had found the framework that would give the article its focus and make it compelling reading.

Commentary

Seeking "what happened" is frequently the most enjoyable part of historical research. The sleuthing involved in digging out the documentation of past events often carries a thrill of discovery akin to an archeological find. However, because most documented events have already been identified in some way, just asking "What happened?" is not always sufficient for historical research. Such questions as: "Why and how did it happen?" "Was it part of a trend?" "Does it have repercussions today?" and "Does it have applications for current practice?" provide a greater immediacy and purpose for the research. It is these kinds of questions that are the basis of my article. Perhaps that is one reason why the article has proven useful to many music educators, both in the general classroom and in college classes.

Educators have thanked me on various occasions for writing this article. Teachers have specifically mentioned how much it helped them to access needed information about various music cultures, and to incorporate world musics into their curriculum. College professors have told me that they use the article with their preservice students to help the students find articles directly applicable to their future teaching situations, to give them information about specific musics, and to provide them with an overview of the changes in multicultural music education over the last quarter-century.

The article also prompts questions about the future of multiculturalism and education. Perhaps the most urgent question relates to teacher preparation. Conference sessions and innumerable articles may help to educate in-service teachers, but they are not sufficient to prepare future educators of music or of any other subject. Changes must be made within the teacher education preparation programs at colleges and universities in order to ensure a multicultural perspective for every new teacher, but such changes are never easy to accomplish.

In music education, I see the core music curriculum, teacher education courses, performance, and repertoire all as areas that need to address multiculturalism. A few colleges and universities have begun doing so, and there are more such situations today than there were in 1992, when my historical review concluded. Perhaps, as my research shows, there is a growing awareness among educators that multiculturalism isn't just a fad, but is an important and expanding component of music education. Because music education tends to follow the direction of general education, it probably is safe to say that there also is a greater awareness of multiculturalism in general education today than ever before.

Nonetheless, George Heller's conclusion that multiculturalism in music education is more practiced than it is written about in historical accounts (note 7) remains true today. My desire to tip the scales toward a more balanced representation of the true impact of multiculturalism on music education was another reason for my writing this article, and why I chose to follow it with a more complete history of multicultural music education as my dissertation (Volk, 1993). Today my book, *Music, Education, and Multiculturalism* (Volk, 1997), is one of the few available texts that are devoted entirely to the topic. One never knows where a single research article may lead!

References

Volk, T. M. (1993). A history of multicultural music education in the public schools of the United States, 1900–1990. *Dissertation Abstracts International, 55*(03), 0501A. (University Microfilms No. AAG94-22423.)

Volk, T. M. (1997). *Music, education, and multiculturalism: Foundations & principles.* New York: Oxford University Press.

THE HISTORY AND DEVELOPMENT OF MULTICULTURAL MUSIC EDUCATION AS EVIDENCED IN THE *MUSIC EDUCATORS JOURNAL*, 1967–1992

Terese M. Volk
Kent State University

In 1967, secretary-general of ISME Egon Kraus challenged music educators to become multicultural in their perspective, a challenge spurred on by the Tanglewood Symposium. Music educators in the United States have long been interested in the musics of other cultures. Often they have learned about these musics and how to implement them in the classroom through the pages of the *Music Educators Journal (MEJ)*. The *MEJ* has covered multicultural perspectives in music through its articles, special issues, book reviews, and reports from MENC conferences and symposia. A study of the *MEJ* from 1967 to 1992 revealed the growth of multicultural music education. During the 1970s, a greater depth of interest in, and knowledge about, world musics developed. Throughout the 1980s, this initial interest grew steadily into a need for methods and materials for the implementation of multicultural music studies in the classroom, as did the need for teacher training in these musics. A formal declaration of commitment to multicultural music education was adopted at the MENC Multicultural Symposium in 1990, leading to a broad world perspective for music education. The three *MEJ* special focus issues on multicultural music education epitomized each of these growth areas.

For copies of this article, contact Terese M. Volk, 808 Woodstock Avenue, Tonawanda, NY 14150.

Volk, T. M. (1993). The history and development of multicultural music education as evidenced in the *Music Educators Journal, 1967–1992. Journal of Research in Music Education,* 41, 137–155. From *Journal of Research in Music Education,* Summer 1993. Copyright © 1993 by Music Educators National Conference. Reprinted with permission.

The confrontation of the cultures is the destiny of our times, and the bringing about of this confrontation in a meaningful manner is the great cultural-political task of our century. We, the music educators, can contribute significantly.—*Egon Kraus, secretary-general, ISME, 1966*

In January 1967, the *Music Educators Journal (MEJ)* published a speech given by noted German music educator Egon Kraus at the International Society for Music Education (ISME) conference the preceding summer. In that speech, Kraus argued that a one-sided view of music from either East or West was no longer appropriate, and that an open mind leads to better understanding and knowledge. He outlined eight problems that he challenged ISME and music educators in general to solve in the future. He asked for:

(a) proper regard for foreign musical cultures in music teaching at all educational levels,

(b) methodological realization of the music of foreign cultures, past and present,

(c) renewal of ear training, rhythmic training, and music theory with a view to inclusion of the music of foreign cultures,

(d) reviewing of school music textbooks and study materials (also with regard to prejudice and national and racial resentments),

(e) preparation of pedagogically suitable works on the music of foreign cultures with special attention to authentic sound recordings....[1]

He also sought the establishment of international seminars and some way for all nations to share multicultural music education concerns, as well as continuing cooperation with the United Nations Educational, Scientific, and Cultural Organization (UNESCO).[2] He concluded with the quotation at the beginning of this article. Kraus's speech was a sign of the changes in music education at the end of the 1960s. Music educators had begun to see with a multicultural perspective.

INTRODUCTION

Throughout their existence, the public schools of the United States have presented an essentially white, Eurocentric education. Therefore, it is not surprising that historical accounts of American music education have said little about multicultural perspectives in music in the schools. Edward B. Birge does not include references in his textbook either to African-American music or any musics that immigrant peoples brought to the United States.[3] Theodore A. Tellstrom has two paragraphs in which he tells of the rising interest in world musics and recommends that the well-rounded music program include such study.[4] James A. Keene and, more recently, Michael L. Mark and Charles L. Gary refer briefly to the study of world musics when summarizing the Tanglewood Symposium.[5] In addition, Mark and Gary mention "ethnic [music], rock, pop, and jazz" when discussing the changing music of urban classrooms.[6] This evidence seems to concur with George N. Heller's assessment that multicultural music education has been more practiced than documented in the published histories of music education.[7]

The following three publications deal specifically with the history of multicultural music education. In 1983, Heller wrote a broad retrospective discussing early Music Educators National Conference (MENC) involvement with musics from various cultures through its conference sessions, describing the founding of ISME, and commenting briefly on the increased activity within the profession since the Tanglewood Symposium.[8] William M. Anderson provided a more detailed view of multicultural music education from 1916 through 1970, beginning with the work of Satis Coleman, a music teacher at the Lincoln School of Teachers College, Columbia University in New York and ending with the beginnings of research in multicultural music education following Tanglewood.[9] A recent study by Christine E. Brett focused on trends in multicultural music education from 1960–1989. The main thrust of her work, however, was not historical documentation but rather the philosophical development of the movement and the implementation of this philosophy in the Silver Burdett Music Series.[10]

Since there has been scant historical documentation of the development of multicultural music education during the last twenty-five years, one purpose of this research was to trace its history and development as documented in the *Music Educators Journal (MEJ)* from 1967 to 1992. A second purpose was to see, by studying this history, how well music education has approached solutions for the problems posed by Kraus. I hope that this will give music educators some perspective of how far they have come and of how far they may have yet to go in addressing these problems.

For the purposes of this study, "culture" is defined as learned ways of thinking and behaving that enable an individual to survive in a society.[11] If "music education" is the transmission of that part of culture that is expressed through music,[12] "multicultural music education" enables one to function effectively in multiple music cultures.[13] "Music" is defined as a human expression using patterned behaviors in sound that are agreed upon by the members of the society involved.[14] Therefore, the phrases "musics of many cultures" and "musics from a variety of cultures" will be used to mean the musics from any assortment of cultures, worldwide. Although this definition of music encompasses the art, folk, and popular traditions of any culture, this study will focus primarily on the global perspective in music education that developed through the addition of musics from many cultures to the music curriculum.[15]

The *MEJ* has been selected as the source for information for this study for the following reasons. First, it is the official journal of the MENC, the largest music teacher organization in the United States, and organizational activities can be traced through conference announcements and reports in the pages of the *MEJ*. Second, as Maureen D. Hooper noted, the *MEJ* is a means of communication between the leadership of the organization and its membership.[16] She also noted that

> Authors from outside music education play an important role in the communication of the concerns of society as they relate to the music program. . . . [and] Officials of the Music Educators National Conference carry the major responsibility for the formulation and communication of the organized theoretical foundation for music education.[17]

In voicing both the needs of society and the views of the leadership of the MENC, the *MEJ* takes on the role of "guide" for the profession. Third, as John W. Molnar's study showed, looking at the *MEJ* in retrospect can reveal trends in music education, applicable at least to the membership of the MENC, and, as far as the MENC membership constitutes a representative sample of music educators in the United States, for music educators across the country.[18]

Evidence for this study was taken from articles, MENC conference program listings and follow-up reports, announcements and reports of MENC activities, advertisements, and monthly features such as the "Book Review" and "MENC Adviser" columns. It was beyond the scope of this study to include every article or report on the subject in the *MEJ*. A reasonable attempt has been made to identify those that seemed to point most toward the development of multicultural music education, and in particular those articles that would indicate direction taken in providing solutions for Kraus's problems. It is acknowledged that these are not all-inclusive. Articles that dealt with comparative music education (i.e., how music is taught in the schools of other countries) were omitted from this study, as were biographical and autobiographical articles.

OVERVIEW TO 1967

Music educators have long been interested in musics from around the world, and it has been the *Music Educators Journal* (and its predecessor the *Music Supervisors Journal*) that has documented multicultural music education in the music classrooms of the United States. As early as 1918, the *Music Supervisors Journal (MSJ)* carried the program listing for that year's annual meeting of the Music Supervisors National Conference (MSNC), which included a lecture-recital of folk songs presented by Walter Bentley and an address by Elizabeth Burchenal on "Folk Dancing."[19] In 1919, the *MSJ* published an article by John Wesley Work titled "The Development of the Music of the Negro from the Folk Song to the Art Song and Art Chorus."[20]

There was a stronger emphasis on world musics throughout the 1920s and 1930s. MSNC annual meetings often included folk songs and dances.[21] In 1928, the *MSJ* announced the formation of the MSNC Committee on International Relations,[22] and over the next decade music supervisors from Europe, the United Kingdom and the United States met during the summer to exchange information about music and music education.[23]

Interest in inter-American music education began through the cooperation of the State Department Division of Cultural Relations and the MENC in 1939,[24] and in 1944, the Advisory Council on Music Education in the Latin American Republics was established in cooperation with the Pan American Union.[25] Along with this, MENC developed a program called "American Unity Through Music." Through the *MEJ*, teachers were encouraged to include both American folk musics and Latin American musics in their classes.[26] A gradually widening world view in music education led to the establishment of ISME in 1953.[27] The interest in the musics of other cultures continued throughout the late 1950s and into the 1960s and was given added strength by the civil rights movement.

The impetus to include music from a variety of cultures as part of the curriculum in the music classroom began with the Yale Seminar in June 1963. Its call for a school music repertoire that included non-Western and folk musics[28] was answered by the Juilliard Repertory Project, begun in 1964.[29] The Repertory Project was reported in the pages of the *MEJ* and, although the Yale Symposium was mentioned only briefly, the anthology itself was considered a "welcome addition to our [music educators'] resources."[30]

The International Seminar on Teacher Education in Music took place at Ann Arbor, Michigan in August 1966. Along with issues relating to the education of music teachers, the musical training of general classroom teachers, and technical media for education, "Papers were presented and discussions held relative to the importance of the use in schools of the music of all cultures."[31] Egon Kraus gave his speech the next week at the ISME conference at Interlochen.

1967: THE TANGLEWOOD SYMPOSIUM

Spurred by the Yale Seminar and the Juilliard Repertory Project, MENC undertook a major self-evaluation of the profession and its goals for music in the schools. Meeting at Tanglewood in the summer of 1967, this Symposium was titled "Music in American Society." To stimulate national thinking on the Symposium's topics, a series of questions was developed for each area to be discussed, and these were published in the April 1967 issue of the *MEJ*. Music educators were asked to voice their opinions as input for the discussions at the symposium. Addressing "Music in our Time," some questions dealt specifically with the issue of musics from a variety of cultures in the schools: "Polycultural curriculums are developing rapidly. Should music of other cultures be included? For what purposes? Few centers exist in this country for such studies. What are the implications?"[32]

The Tanglewood Symposium was fully reported in the November 1967 *MEJ*. The final declaration of the Symposium opened the door for all musics to be taught in the public schools with the statement: "Music of all periods, styles, forms, and cultures belong[s] in the curriculum . . . including avant-garde music, American folk music, and the music of other cultures."[33] In the same issue, Charles Fowler's editorial supported the need for studying world musics. He stated, "Music education, by latching on to diversity, by being comprehensive in its coverage of the musics of the world, will insure that the tastes of the public are based on choices made from acquaintance with all that constitutes the art of music."[34]

David McAllester's speech at Tanglewood was printed in its entirety in the *MEJ* in December 1968. In it, he emphasized the fact that a rapidly shrinking world was one of the forces shaping music education. He asked, "How then can we go on thinking of

'music' as Western European music, to the exclusion of the infinitely varied forms of musical expression in other parts of the world?"[35]

During 1967, the *MEJ* carried articles by Zoltán Kodály and Kwabena Nketia both validating and advocating the use of folk song in music education.[36] Lucius Wyatt's article included museum photographs of instruments from around the world.[37] This article is notable because it is the first in the journal to contain pictures of authentic instruments from a variety of cultures in the period under study.

From 1968 to 1972, there was an increase of articles on the musics from a variety of cultures in *MEJ*. The journal acted to encourage music educators to implement the statements of both Yale and Tanglewood. There was a special report on the use of popular music in the classroom, and the foundation of the National Association of Jazz Educators (NAJE), also reported in the *Journal,* gave impetus to jazz education.[38] Articles early in this period mainly gave information about various musical cultures, but gradually more were included on how to use these musics in the classroom. Many of these dealt with African-American music, hardly unusual in the light of the growing awareness of African-American culture in the United States.[39] Informative articles were published on the music of India and Hudson Bay Native Canadians, and another on Native American music in the classroom.[40] In an article based on her research, Elizabeth May reported "An Experiment with Australian Aboriginal Music" in the classrooms of Los Angeles, California.[41] A working collaboration between ethnomusicology and music education was suggested by Donald Berger,[42] and John M. Eddins[43] spoke of both comprehensive and cross-cultural trends in teaching music.[a]

It did not take long for the MENC to include musics from various cultures around the world in its national conferences. At the 1968 conference in Seattle, the University of Hawaii presented a program of songs and dances illustrating the diverse heritage of the Hawaiian islands.[44] At this same conference, jazz concerts were introduced and quickly became a mainstay for all subsequent MENC national conferences. There was a series of sessions at the 1970 Chicago conference called an "Ethnic Musics Institute." These sessions all featured a lecture and demonstration by a specialist in the field and concluded with a special session devoted to teaching resources.[45] The 1972 conference in Atlanta included sessions on ethnic musics,[46] as did the 1974 conference in Annaheim. This conference featured sessions ranging from a demonstration by an African drum ensemble, to choral and instrumental performance practices in various parts of the world, to the implications for music education dealing with the "culturally different student."[47] The 1976 conference in Atlantic City offered ways to incorporate African and Native Alaskan musics in the elementary classroom. Discussions of the problems and perspectives of multicultural music education in grades K–12, as well as the role of multicultural music education in higher education, were also part of the program. Concert music featured a combination steel drum and wind ensemble, and a balalaika orchestra.[48] Members attending the 1978 conference in Chicago could choose from sessions focusing on musical concepts taught through the music of many cultures, or on African and Japanese musics.[49]

The name of the Ethnic Musics Committee of the MENC was changed by the 1978 Chicago meeting to the Ethno and World Musics Committee. The word "Ethnic" apparently was too limiting, as if the committee only represented an interest in various "ethnic" (folk?) musics, hence the addition of "and World," which would include the art and popular traditions of music systems worldwide. In 1974, the Minority Concerns Commission also sponsored sessions at the biennial conferences. Its name changed to the Minority Awareness Commission by the 1978 meeting. It became the Multi-Cultural Awareness Commission in 1979 to better reflect both the many musics found in the United States and around the

---

a. According to Volk, ethnomusicology is the study of music in, and as, culture. Ethnomusicology focuses on the ethnographic study of the people who make the music as well as on the musicological study of the sounds that they produce.

world, and the committee's role in the MENC.[50] Although the commission was restructured in 1982, the name "Multi-Cultural Awareness Commission" remained.

THE FIRST MULTICULTURAL "SPECIAL ISSUE"

The *MEJ* has often devoted sections of individual issues to some specific topic. In November 1971, MENC published a special issue of the *MEJ* devoted entirely to African-American music. This issue covered research, the impact of music and African-American culture, and a program in African music established at Howard University.[51] The issue also included a selected resource list for studies in African-American music.[52] This is the first time such compilation of materials for any culture was made available to the *MEJ* readership.

OCTOBER 1972 SPECIAL FOCUS ISSUE: "MUSIC IN WORLD CULTURES"

Titled "Music in World Cultures," the October 1972 issue of *MEJ* was designed as a resource issue for music educators and was divided into three sections. The first section presented an overview of world musical cultures. Beginning with "Music is a Human Need" by Margaret Mead,[53] the articles proceeded through the musics of Northeast Asia, Southeast Asia, South Asia, West Asia–North Africa, and Africa south of the Sahara, European folk traditions, the Americas, and Oceania.[54] A unique aspect of this issue was the inclusion of two soundsheets with musical examples from cultures representative of each of these world regions. The soundsheets were accompanied by a listening guide that included pertinent information about the source, context, and content of each selection.

While the first section provided basic information about these varied musical cultures, the second section contained articles on the need to use these musics in the schools. Malcom Tait wrote "Increasing Awareness and Sensitivity through World Musics,"[55] Ricardo Trimillos said that musical experiences must be expanded to fit today's world,[56] and Charles Seeger put forth a challenge to American schools to use world musics.[57] Educators were also shown some ways to use musics from a variety of cultures in the classroom. Hawaiian and African-American musics could involve students in other cultures from within the United States. Rhythm concepts could be taught from a multicultural perspective, and a greater understanding of various ethnic musics could be obtained through movement experiences with the music.[58] The authors of the articles in this issue were, and still are, leaders in the field and experts on their particular area of musical culture.

The third section of this issue was a compilation of resources for classroom music teachers. With the exception of the resource list on African-American music compiled in 1971, there had not been another effort made like this one. The issue contained a glossary of terms, a bibliography/discography, and filmography of available materials for many cultures. Also included were nearly ten pages of pictures of musicians and instruments from around the world, as well as a list of the societies and archives for ethnomusicology and the names of colleges and universities offering courses in ethnomusicology.[59]

The "Book Reviews" column of this particular issue is worth noting.[60] Up to this point there were few, if any, books reviewed that had anything to do with multicultural approaches in music. This was due in part to the scarcity of books written, but also to the fact that the *MEJ* published reviews of books that its readership would find useful. Up until 1967, the musics from cultures around the world were simply not very high on the "useful" list for most teachers. All the books reviewed for this issue, however, dealt with some facet of these musics. These reviews became a further resource for the teacher looking for more depth on the subject of various cultures, or ethnomusicology in general. From this issue onward, the *MEJ* either reviewed publications about world musics, or listed them in the "Book

Browsing" or "Study Shelf" columns.[61] In 1989, these columns were supplemented with "Video Views," which often included reviews of video materials on the musics of other cultures.[62]

Over the next ten years, the pages of *MEJ* continued to include articles about musics from many cultures. The topics were eclectic, ranging from "A Practical Introduction to African Music," to Eskimo string-figure games, to American popular and rock music.[63] Readers learned the joys of a Scottish pipe-and-drum band, about the folk music of Jamaica, and how to make a Tsonga xylophone.[64] The musics of Argentina, China, Tibet, and of Native Americans were brought to the attention of music educators,[65] and there were articles on Appalachian traditions, gospel music, and the training of Indian musicians.[66] Along with these more explanatory articles, there were some thought-provoking essays. Among them, Malcom Tait suggested keeping a balance between attitudes and strategies when working with world musics, and Albert McNeil wrote on the social foundations of the music of African-Americans.[67]

During this same period, the advertisements in *MEJ* for college and university summer study began to include notices of courses and workshops in multicultural music education. Although ads containing these notices were more plentiful in the magazine's pages during the 1970s than they are today, summer multicultural music education classes and workshops have continued to be offered at various locations across the country to the present.[68]

Other advertising also began to reflect a more global perspective. Advertisements included bilingual songs among new choral releases, the musical instruments from other cultures, and folk dance albums for educational use, as well as books dealing with the music of other cultures, or classroom applications of these musics.[69] MENC regularly announced its publications and resources for multicultural music education in the pages of the *MEJ*.[70]

By 1980, the study of musics from many cultures in the schools had increased, and educators became aware of the commitment that teaching these musics would require in the curriculum. The September 1980 issue of *MEJ* included a section on multicultural awareness. In his article "Teaching Musics of the World: A Renewed Commitment," William Anderson said, "Because of the ethnic diversity within our country, schools need to ensure that representative examples of a variety of musics are in the curriculum. . . . There are a number of highly sophisticated musics in the world, and Western art music is just one."[71]

If educators were to implement music from a variety of cultures, multicultural training would be necessary, especially in graduate teacher education.[72] In October 1980, the Report of the MENC Commission on Graduate Music Teacher Education was published.[73] The MENC recommendations for minimal requirements for a master's degree now also included "Basic knowledge of music literature, including jazz, popular, ethnic, and non-Western music; An acquaintance with instructional materials for multicultural needs; Techniques for motivating and relating to students of diverse cultures."[74]

Although teacher education remained an issue, some educators were starting to make use of their new knowledge in their classes. Early in the 1970s, Paul Berliner had told of his methods of incorporating a world perspective in his music classes.[75] Now other teachers wrote to give their colleagues ideas about what worked for them.[76]

A multicultural perspective was starting to pervade other areas of music study as well. Along with articles on many forms of improvisation in the classroom and in jazz, the January 1980 special focus issue on improvisation devoted an entire section to world musics. Improvisation was addressed specifically in the musics of Latin America, West Africa, the Near East, and Korea.[77]

"THE MULTICULTURAL IMPERATIVE": SPECIAL ISSUE, MAY 1983

It had been ten years since an entire issue of *MEJ* was devoted to multicultural music education.

While the 1972 special issue had focused on acquainting music educators with musics from around the world, the May 1983 special issue, "The Multicultural Imperative," emphasized the fact that music educators needed to teach music from a multicultural perspective. This issue had four main topic areas: the multicultural imperative, educational tactics, tools for teaching world musics, and selected resources. The articles in the first section all stressed the fact that no educator could ignore the cultural diversity in the classrooms of the United States.[78] The second and third sections of this issue offered assistance with classroom applications.[79] In addition, there were ideas for using the community as a resource,[80] and annotated resources for Hawaiian and Samoan musics.[81] There were especially pertinent reviews in both "Book Browsing" and "Study Shelf" columns.[82] The issue concluded with a selected resource list. This list was not as extensive as the bibliographical list found in the 1972 special issue; however, it also included reports, committee results, and upcoming events such as the ISME conference scheduled for 1984 in Oregon.[83] The MENC national conferences during the 1980s continued to offer sessions to assist music educators with the implementation of musics from various cultures. The 1980 conference in Miami Beach offered several sessions on African-American music as well as reading sessions devoted to the music of African-American composers.[84] String teachers began to focus on multiculturalism at the 1982 conference in San Antonio with an international round table of artists as well as a viola lecture/recital of music by Spanish and Latin American composers. In addition, one elementary session introduced oral tradition as a teaching practice in musics of various cultures, and another featured a student demonstration of folk dances.[85]

Many of the conference sessions at the 1984 conference in Chicago were, like the topics of the 1983 special issue, focused on teacher training, resources, and teaching methods. There were also groups performing Latin American chamber music and East European instrumental music.[86] *MEJ* did not announce the conference programs for the 1986 and 1988 MENC biennial conferences. Instead, this information was carried in the *MENC Soundpost* newsletter.

In addition to the national conference, MENC, Wesleyan University, and the Theodore Presser Foundation jointly sponsored in August 1984 the Wesleyan Symposium on the Application of Social Anthropology to the Teaching and Learning of Music. The emphasis of the symposium was "on exploring practical implications of research findings in other cultures for U.S. music teachers in their daily instruction."[87] Even though this symposium focused "principally on a transcultural approach" and did not deal specifically with curricula for classroom use, it was the first time the MENC sponsored a gathering of anthropologists and ethnomusicologists for the purpose of a face-to-face exchange with the music educators who would use the results of their scholarship.[88]

Although it was not a special issue, the March 1985 issue of *MEJ* had several articles dealing with musics from many cultures. Elsie Buck told of her successful approach to incorporating world musics in her general music class. In addition, Samuel Miller wrote about the blues, and Martha Giles discussed the improvisational techniques of Indian flute music.[89]

TEACHER TRAINING

The need for teacher training courses in multicultural perspectives for music education continued to be emphasized. René Boyer-White issued a call for teacher training in approaches to multicultural music education in colleges because of the growing diversity of students within America's classrooms.[90] Marvin V. Curtis was even stronger in his views on teacher training: "Educators cannot teach what they themselves do not understand. Schools of higher education must make multicultural music education a part of the training of teachers to prepare them to deal with the black aesthetic experience along with other cultural experiences."[91]

David G. Klocko advised not just a single course of study in multicultural perspectives in music, but an integrated approach including music history and literature courses for a better overall understanding. He said, "The Eurocentric world view is outdated; a more global perspective must replace it."[92] He pointed out the multicultural thrust of the newest resources developed by the MENC, and he also mentioned the fact that the MENC's Eastern Division conference to be held in Boston in March of 1989 would have an international theme.[93] (Although musics from many cultures had previously been included in divisional conferences in one form or another, this was the first time that an entire conference carried a multicultural theme.)

The emphasis during the late 1980s tended to be twofold. Multicultural perspectives in musics were studied not only to increase students' knowledge about the musics of other peoples, but to increase understanding about the people who made these musics. In addition to Klocko's and Curtis' articles on teacher training, which stressed a world view and the fact that teachers cannot teach understanding if they themselves do not understand, Patricia Shehan recommended using multicultural musics as "windows" to cross-cultural understanding.[94]

As teachers became more exposed to musics from many cultures through the pages of the *MEJ* and through MENC conference presentations, they became aware of their own shortcomings in this area. A questioner in the "MENC Adviser" column in February 1990 asked, "How can I incorporate world music into my classroom when I have never been exposed to it? I live in a rural district that has just started to emphasize global education."[95] The need for teachers not just to know, but to experience and thereby be able to teach better, was growing.

SYMPOSIUM: MULTICULTURAL APPROACHES TO MUSIC EDUCATION, 1990

The Multicultural Symposium was presented by the MENC in cooperation with the Society for Ethnomusicology, the Smithsonian Institution's Office of Folklife Programs, and MENC's Society for General Music. It preceded the 1990 National Biennial In-Service Conference in Washington, D.C., and targeted the culture and music of four ethnic groups: African-American, Asian-American, Hispanic-American, and Native American. An ethnomusicologist, performers from the culture, and a music educator well versed in that musical tradition presented material from each culture.[96]

The speakers at the Symposium provided much for music educators to reflect on. Bernice Johnson Reagon's keynote address for the Symposium, as reported by Anderson, stressed the need to help students "understand the relationship between people and their music."[97] Along the same lines, David McAllester said, "We need to learn how to live together even though we belong to different cultures."[98] Perhaps even more powerful was the following statement by Edwin Shupman:

> I believe the potential role of a music educator has not yet been realized in terms of broadening the multicultural horizons of their students, of promoting human understanding, and tolerance for racial and cultural differences.[99]

The nearly three hundred music educators who participated in the Symposium sang songs and learned dances for both the Native American and Asian-American segments of the event. They had opportunities to perform in a Chinese percussion ensemble, play Andean raft-pipe instruments, see an excerpt of Chinese opera, and attend a dance party with salsa and other Latino dance music. Special concert performances featured Nguyen Dihn Nghia and his family performing on Vietnamese traditional instruments, and the Kings of Harmony, an African-American brass band.[100]

At the close of the Symposium, a Resolution for Future Directions and Actions was adopted by the participants. This resolution, quoted below, forms a statement of commitment to multicultural musics for not only the MENC as an organization, but for all music educators:

Be it resolved that:

We will seek to ensure that multicultural approaches to teaching music will be incorporated into every elementary and secondary school music curriculum,

Multicultural approaches to teaching music will be incorporated into all phases of teacher education in music,

Music teachers will seek to assist students in understanding that there are many different but equally valid forms of musical expression,

Instruction will included [sic] not only the study of other musics but the relationship of those musics to their respective cultures; further, that meaning of music within each culture be sought for its own value,

MENC will encourage national and regional accrediting groups to *require* broad, multicultural perspectives for all education programs, particularly those in music.[101]

In addition to the Symposium, the MENC 1990 biennial conference featured performing groups from Hungary, Australia, Taiwan, and Canada.[102]

Also in 1990, *MEJ* carried an article by Marsha Edelman that described ways to incorporate Jewish music in the music curriculum.[103] In a special issue on creativity, Patricia Shehan Campbell viewed the topic of musical creativity from a cross-cultural perspective.[104] In addition, Ellen McCullough-Brabson described a successful museum/school project.[105] One of the highlights of this project was allowing the students hands-on exploration with instruments from around the world. Demonstrations at the 1992 biennial conference in New Orleans included a similar hands-on technique with musical instruments, Native American dances for classroom use, and the musics of the various cultures from southern Louisiana. There were discussions on the philosophical implications of music education in a multi-value culture, and on multicultural concerns in music teacher education.[106]

1992 SPECIAL FOCUS ISSUE: "MULTICULTURAL MUSIC EDUCATION"

For the third time in twenty years, *MEJ* offered a special issue on multicultural music education. Teachers had learned about other cultures in 1972, learned of the necessity of classroom applications in 1983, and now were challenged to incorporate the music from many cultures into all their music classes—choral and instrumental as well as general music.

This issue had a slightly different format from the previous multicultural issues in that it was not divided into sections as were the past issues. Each article had an individual focus. Anthony Seeger presented an opening article that was an encouragement for multicultural music education. After commenting that "Music is an effective way to experience at least one aspect of another culture first-hand,"[107] he went on to say that the musical traditions students bring with them into the classroom should be welcome. These traditions can then be supplemented through exposure to others' musical traditions.[108]

Patricia Shehan Campbell offered several pedagogical techniques to foster the infusion of musics from a variety of cultures in the general music curriculum.[109] Practical lesson plans followed her article for Native American, African-American, Filipino, and Latin American musics.[110] Judith Tucker's multicultural resource list included texts, audiotapes and videotapes, and culture-specific books and recordings.[111] The possibilities of incorporating a multicultural perspective in the instrumental and choral programs were examined by Will Schmid and Joan Conlon respectively.[112] Selected lists of repertoire in these areas followed their articles.[113]

Anderson's article presented a view of multicultural music education in teacher training. He argued that if students are to be taught music from a multicultural perspective, then music teacher education also needs this perspective. Anderson suggested broadening the entire music curriculum for future teachers from theory and history classes to methods classes and performance opportunities in such areas as Asian, Latin American, and African-American musics.[114]

CONCLUSION

In 1967, Egon Kraus challenged music education to become multicultural in its perspective. He left music educators with the goals of developing multicultural attitudes and classroom methodologies, integrating multicultural approaches in other music courses, reviewing textbooks and study materials for multicultural perspectives, providing source materials, holding international seminars, cooperating with UNESCO, and sharing multicultural music education concerns with other countries. How far has the music education profession come in meeting these goals?

Over the last twenty-five years, MENC, through the *MEJ*, has guided the profession with many informative articles about the music of other cultures. This is especially evident in the 1972 special focus issue on "Music in World Cultures." The *MEJ* also emphasized the need for a multicultural perspective in the music classroom. It is safe to say that all these articles were aimed at helping educators develop what Kraus called "proper regard for foreign musical cultures." The declaration of the 1990 Multicultural Symposium provides the clearest indication of the positive attitude many music educators now have toward the musics of other cultures.

MENC and the *MEJ* supplied various strategies and resources for applying the musics of many cultures, both through the publication of multicultural music articles throughout the 1970s and 1980s (particularly in the 1983 "Multicultural Imperative" issue) and through the inclusion of sessions on musics from a variety of cultures in national conferences. The most outstanding of these were the sessions provided at the 1990 Multicultural Symposium. In addition, both MENC and the *MEJ* continued to voice the need for teachers trained in multicultural approaches to music, especially in graduate programs. The Multicultural Symposium provided a model for in-service training for music educators. "Methodological realization" has certainly been addressed.

Although there is little evidence in the *MEJ* of educators reviewing school music textbooks with the purpose of making improvements in multicultural perspectives, the *MEJ* has, since 1967, regularly reviewed textbooks and study materials that deal with the musics of other cultures in the "Book Review" and "Video Views" columns. By bringing these resources to the attention of its readership, the *MEJ* kept music educators aware of current scholarship in the field and encouraged further personal investigation. It is music educators who are knowledgeable about multiple music cultures who can demand more authenticity and less prejudice from the school music textbook publishers.

Contributors to the *MEJ* assisted greatly with the preparation of multicultural resource lists for music educators. These included bibliographies, discographies, and lists of audiocassette and video recording. Although these were selected lists, they were also fairly comprehensive in scope. It seems that music education took Kraus's injunction to prepare "pedagogically suitable works" with "authentic sound recordings" to heart. The publications and films that MENC produced from the multicultural symposium are further evidence of this.

Integrating a multicultural perspective into other music areas such as ear training and music theory is beginning to be more commonplace. The solution to the problem posed by this type of integration has not yet been found, although there is some progress to be seen. The 1992 "Multicultural Music Education" special focus section of the *MEJ* emphasized a global perspective in all aspects of music education—choral, general, and instrumental. In other issues, there have been articles about improvisation, and creativity in a variety of cultures. In addition, Klocko and Anderson both recommended that schools of music incorporate multicultural approaches in music history, music theory and teaching methods classes.

Work with UNESCO and "international cooperation and seminars" perhaps appear to be more the role of ISME than MENC; however, MENC did cosponsor the Wesleyan Symposium. International scholars were among the presenters at this Symposium, and music educators were afforded the opportunity to meet them and discuss the educational implications of their research.

The final resolution/declaration drawn up by MENC and ratified by the teachers at the Multicultural Symposium in Washington, D.C., is a culmination of the past twenty-five years' growth of multicultural approaches to music in music education. History will show if this declaration will have the impact on the profession that the Tanglewood declaration had in opening the doors of the classroom to greater implementation of musics from many cultures. The hope, at least as expressed by the educators at this symposium, is that these beginnings in multicultural music education will become the foundation for a global understanding of music.

Music educators today face an even broader diversity of students in their classrooms than they did in either 1967 or 1980. The need is even greater for teachers themselves to understand the musics these children bring with them into the classroom, to understand the various music systems in the world, and, as pointed out in the 1992 special focus on "Multicultural Music Education," to teach music from a global perspective. Only then can they help their students to understand music in its many forms, to see music as a mode of human expression, and perhaps to help them understand the people who make the music. The declaration of the Multicultural Symposium could be considered a report card for how far the profession has come since 1967. Music education has not solved the problems posed by Kraus, but it has come close on some and has begun work on others. The need for teacher training remains essential. If the past twenty-five years are an accurate indication, the *MEJ* will continue to publish articles and MENC will continue to sponsor conference activities that will assist music educators in accomplishing this task.

Notes

1. Egon Kraus, "The Contribution of Music Education to the Understanding of Foreign Cultures, Past and Present," *Music Educators Journal* 53, no. 5 (January 1967): 91.

2. *Ibid.*, 91.

3. Edward B. Birge, *History of Public School Music in the United States* (Boston: Oliver Ditson, Co., 1928).

4. Theodore A. Tellstrom, *Music in American Education: Past and Present* (New York: Holt, Rinehart, and Winston, 1971), 280.

5. James A. Keene, *A History of Music Education in the United States* (Hanover, NH: University Press of New England, 1984), 362–363; Michael L. Mark and Charles L. Gary, *A History of American Music Education* (New York: Schirmer Books, division of Macmillan, Inc., 1992), 311–313.

6. Mark and Gary, *A History of American Music Education*, 366–367.

7. George N. Heller, "Retrospective of Multicultural Music Education in the United States," *Music Educators Journal* 69, no. 9 (May 1983): 35.

8. *Ibid.*, 35–36.

9. William M. Anderson, "World Musics in American Education, 1916–1970," *Contributions to Music Education*, no. 3 (Autumn 1974): 23–42.

10. Christine E. Brett, "A Study of Trends and Developments in Multicultural Music Education (1960–1989) and their Manifestation in Silver Burdett Music Series" (Master's thesis, Florida State University, 1990).

11. Norris B. Johnson, "On the Relationship of Anthropology to Multicultural Teaching and Learning," *Journal of Teacher Education* 28, no. 3 (May/June 1977): 10.

12. Derived from J. H. Kwabena Nketia, "Music Education in Africa and the West," in Lusaka, ed., *Education and Research in African Music, 1975*. Cited in Barbara Lundquist, "Transmission of Music Culture in Formal Educational Institutions," *The World of Music* 29, no. 1 (1987): 67–68; and Kwabena Nketia, "The Place of Authentic Folk Music in Education," *Music Educators Journal* 54, no. 3 (November 1967): 41.

13. This idea is derived from David Elliott, "Music as Culture: Toward a Multicultural Concept of Arts Education," *Journal of Aesthetic Education* 24, no. 1 (Spring 1990): 158; Barbara Lundquist, "Transmission of Music Culture," 75. For examples of different views of the purpose of multicultural music education, see Abraham Schwadron, "World Musics in Education," *ISME Yearbook* 9 (November 1984), 92; Keith Swanwick, *Mind, Music, and Education*. London: Routledge, 1988, 180.

14. Alan Merriam, *The Anthropology of Music* (Evanston, IL: Northwestern University Press, 1964), 27.

15. Though jazz is included in this definition, and does have its place in multicultural music education, this article is not intended to provide a history of jazz education. For a brief overview of the jazz education movement, see Bryce Luty, "Jazz Education's Struggle for Acceptance," *Music Educators Journal* 69, no. 3 (November 1982): 38–39+ and "Jazz Ensembles' Era of Accelerated Growth," *Music Educators Journal* 69, no. 4 (December 1982): 49–50+.

16. Maureen D. Hooper, "Major Concerns of Music Education: Content Analysis of the *Music Educators Journal*, 1957–1967" (Ed D. diss., University of Southern California, 1969) *Dissertation Abstracts International*, 30 10A, 4479–80.

17. Ibid.

18. John W. Molnar, "Changing Aspects of American Culture as Reflected in the MENC," *Journal for Research in Music Education* 7, no. 2 (Fall 1959): 174–184.

19. Music Supervisors National Conference, Program listing for annual conference in Evanston, IL, *Music Supervisors Journal* 4, no. 4 (March 1918): 4–5.

20. John Wesley Work, "The Development of the Music of the Negro from the Folk Song to the Art Song and Art Chorus," *Music Supervisors Journal* 6, no. 1 (September 1919): 12–14.

21. Music Supervisors National Conference, Program listing for annual conferences in Cincinnati, *Music Supervisors Journal* 10, no. 3 (February 1924); in Detroit, *Music Supervisors Journal* 12, no. 3 (February 1925), 48; in Chicago, *Music Supervisors Journal* 16, no. 3 (February 1930): 19+.

22. Paul J. Weaver, "British and American Educators Plan Unique Meeting," *Music Supervisors Journal* 15, no. 1 (October 1928): 7–15.

23. Percy Scholes, "An International Movement in Musical Education—Is It Possible?" *MSNC Journal of Proceedings, 1930):* 96; William M. Anderson, "World Music in American Education, 1916–1970," *Contributions to Music Education,* no. 3 (Autumn 1974): 25.

24. Charles Seeger, "Inter-American Relations in the Field of Music," *Music Educators Journal* 27, no 4 (March–April 1941): 17–18+.

25. Hazel Hohavec Morgan, ed., *Music Education Source Book* (Chicago, Music Educators National Conference, 1947), 208.

26. For examples see: Music Educators National Conference, "Music for Uniting the Americas," *Music Educators Journal* 28, no. 2 (November/December 1941): 13–14; MENC Committee on Folk Music of the United States, "American Songs for American Children," published in each issue beginning with *Music Educators Journal* 30, no. 3 (January 1944) and ending with *Music Educators Journal* 31, no. 4 (February/March 1945); Harry E. Moses, "A Good Neighbor Policy for Appreciation Classes," *Music Educators Journal* 32, no. 1 (September/October 1945): 22–23; Hazel Kinsella, "Folk Music Aids," *Music Educators Journal* 38, no. 4 (February/March 1952): 52.

27. Hazel Hohavec Morgan, ed., *Music in American Education* (Chicago, IL: Music Educators National Conference, 1955).

28. Claude Palisca, *Music in Our Schools: A Search for Improvement* (Washington, D.C.: U.S. Government Printing Office, 1964), 11.

29. *Juilliard Repertory Library,* Reference/Library edition, (Cincinnati, OH: Canyon Press, 1970), 192–232.

30. Wiley Housewright, editorial, *Music Educators Journal* 53, no. 2 (October 1976): 76.

31. Vanette Lawler, "International Seminar on Teacher Education in Music," *Music Educators Journal* 53, no. 3 (November 1966): 55.

32. Robert Choate and Max Kaplan, "Music in American Society—Introduction to Issues," *Music Educators Journal* 62 [sic] no. 8 (April 1967): 77.[b]

33. Robert A. Choate, "The Tanglewood Declaration," *Music Educators Journal* 54, no. 3 (November 1967): 51.

34. Charles Fowler, "Joining the Mainstream," *Music Educators Journal* 54, no. 3 (November 1967): 69.

35. David P. McAllester, "The Substance of Things Hoped For," *Music Educators Journal* 54, no. 6 (February 1968): 50.

36. Zoltán Kodály, "Folksong in Pedagogy," *Music Educators Journal* 53, no. 7 (March 1967): 59–61; Kwabena Nketia, "The Place of Authentic Folk Music," 41–42+.

37. Lucius Wyatt, "The Brussels Museum of Musical Instruments," *Music Educators Journal* 53, no. 6 (February 1967): 48–51.

38. See the several articles under "Youth Music—A Special Report," *Music Educators Journal* 56, no. 3 (November 1969): 43–74; Music Educators National Conference, "National Association of Jazz Educators," *Music Educators Journal* 68 [sic] no. 8 (April 1968): 57.[c]

39. See, for example, Barbara Reeder, "Afro-music—As Tough as a Mozart Quartet." *Music Educators Journal* 56, no. 4 (December 1969): 88–91; and "Getting Involved in Shaping the Sounds of Black Music," *Music Educators Journal* 59, no. 2 (October 1972): 80–84; Dominique de Lerma, "Black Music Now!" *Music Educators Journal* 57, no. 3 (November 1970): 25–29; Kwabena Nketia, "Music Education in Africa and the West: We Can Learn From Each Other," *Music Educators Journal* 57, no. 3 (November 1970): 48–55.

40. Marie Joy Curtiss, "Essays in Retribalization: India," *Music Educators Journal* 56, no. 1 (September 1969): 60–62; Don DeNevi, "Essays in Retribalization: Hudson Bay," *Music Educators Journal* 56, no. 1 (September 1969): 66–68; Louis Ballard, "Put American Indian Music in the Classroom," *Music Educators Journal* 56, no. 7 (March 1969): 38–44.

41. Elizabeth May, "An Experiment with Australian Aboriginal Music," *Music Educators Journal* 54, no. 4 (December 1968): 47–56.

42. Donald Berger, "Ethnomusicology Past and Present," *Music Educators Journal* 54, no. 7 (March 1968): 77–79+.

43. John M. Eddins, "Two Trends in Teaching Music: The Comprehensive and the CrossCultural, *Music Educators Journal* 56, no. 4 (December 1969): 69–71.

44. Music Educators National Conference, "Seattle in Pictures," *Music Educators Journal* 55, no. 1 (September 1968): 46.

45. Music Educators National Conference, Program listing for biennial conference, Chicago, *Music Educators Journal* 56, no. 6 (February 1970): 38–40+

46. Music Educators National Conference, Program listing for biennial conference, Atlanta, *Music Educators Journal* 59, no. 6 (February 1972): 25–33.

47. Music Educators National Conference, Program listing for biennial conference program, Annaheim, *Music Educators Journal* 60, no. 5 (January 1974): 30–39.

48. Music Educators National Conference, Program listing of biennial conference program, Atlantic City, *Music Educators Journal* 62, no. 6 (February 1976): 64–71.

49. Music Educators National Conference, Program listing for biennial conference, Chicago, *Music Educators Journal* 64, no. 6 (February 1978): 74–104.

50. Ella J. Washington, "Multi-Cultural Awareness Committee: New Directions," *Music Educators Journal,* 69, no. 9 (May 1983): 67.

51. Otis D. Simmons, "Research, the Bedrock of Student Interest," *Music Educators Journal* 58, no. 3 (November 1971): 38–41; Harry Morgan, "Music—A Life Force in the Black Community," *Music Educators Journal* 58, no. 3 (November 1971):

b. For note 32 of the article, the correct citation is: *Music Educators Journal, 53*, no. 8 (April 1967): 77.

c. For note 38 of the article, the correct citation for Music Educators National Conference, "National Association of Jazz Educators" is: *Music Educators Journal, 55*, no. 8 (April 1968): 57.

34–47; Beverely Blondell, "Drums Talk at Howard," *Music Educators Journal* 58, no. 3 (November 1971): 45–48.

52. Music Educators National Conference, "Selected Resources in Black Studies in Music," *Music Educators Journal* 58, no. 3 (November 1971): 56+.

53. Margaret Mead, "Music is a Human Need," *Music Educators Journal* 59, no. 2 (October 1972): 24–27.

54. See the *Music Educators Journal* 59, no. 2 (October 1972): 30–64.

55. Malcom Tait, "Increasing Awareness and Sensitivity though World Musics," *Music Educators Journal* 59, no. 2 (October 1972): 85–89.

56. Ricardo Trimillos, "Expanding Music Experience to Fit Today's World," *Music Educators Journal* 59, no. 2 (October 1972): 90–94.

57. Charles Seeger, "World Musics in American Schools: A Challenge to be Met," *Music Educators Journal* 59, no. 2 (October 1972): 107–111.

58. See the *Music Educators Journal* 59, no. 2 (October 1972): 73–84, 95–99, and 100–104.

59. Music Educators National Conference, Bibliographies and photography sections, *Music Educators Journal* 59, no. 2 (October 1972): 65–72 and 112–141.

60. Music Educators National Conference, Book Reviews section, *Music Educators Journal* 59, no. 2 (October 1972): 145–161.

61. Examples include: David Reck, review of *Teaching the Music of Six Different Cultures in the Modern Secondary School,* by Luvenia George, in *Music Educators Journal* 64, no. 9 (May 1977): 15–16; Will Schmid, review of *Lessons From the World: A Cross-Cultural Guide to Music Teaching and Learning,* by Patricia Shehan Campbell, in *Music Educators Journal* 78, no. 6 (February 1992): 64–65. Content descriptions were included in the "Book Browsing" and "Study Shelf" sections. Many were found in the 1983 special issue (see Note 82). Other examples include: Dena Epstein, *Sinful Tunes and Spirituals: Black Folk Music to the Civil War,* in "Book Browsing," *Music Educators Journal* 65, no. 1 (September 1978): 22; Jeff Todd, gen. ed., *Worlds of Music: An Introduction to the Music of the World's Peoples,* in "Book Browsing," *Music Educators Journal* 71, no. 4

(December 1984): 71; William Anderson and Patricia Shehan Campbell, *Multicultural Perspectives in Music Education,* in "Book Browsing," *Music Educators Journal* 16, no. 1 (September 1989): 66; C. W. McRae, *Sing 'Round the World: International Folksongs,* in "Book Browsing," *Music Educators Journal* 77, no. 2 (October 1990): 65.

62. See, for example, Jo Ann Baird, review of *Arabic Musical Instruments* in "Video Views," *Music Educators Journal* 76, no. 3 (November 1989): 11–14; William Anderson, review of *The JVC Video Anthology of World Music and Dance,* in "Video Views," *Music Educators Journal* 77, no. 7 (March 1991): 51–52. Content descriptions were also published. See *The Hawaiian Show,* in "Video Views," *Music Educators Journal* 76, no. 7 (March 1990): 16; *Pan in 'A' Minor: Steel Bands of Trinidad,* in "Video Views," *Music Educators Journal* 78, no. 5 (January 1992): 70.

63. Carleton L. Inniss, "A Practical Introduction to African Music," *Music Educators Journal,* 60, no. 6 (February 1974): 50–53; Thomas F. Johnston, Matthew Nocolai, and Karen Nagozruk, "Illeagosuik! Eskimo String-Figure Games," *Music Educators Journal* 65, no. 7 (March 1978): 54–61; for articles on popular/rock musics, see *Music Educators Journal* 66, no. 4 (December 1979): 26–34 and 54–59.

64. John C. Laughter, "Bagpipes, Bands, and Bearskin Hats," *Music Educators Journal* 63, no. 3 (November 1976): 66–69; Olive Lewin, "Biddy, Biddy, Folk Music of Jamaica," *Music Educators Journal* 63, no. 1 (September 1976): 38–49; Thomas F. Johnston, "How to Make a Tsonga Xylophone," *Music Educators Journal* 63, no. 3 (November 1976): 38–49.

65. Nick Rossi, "The Music of Argentina," *Music Educators Journal* 59, no. 4 (January 1973): 51–53; Fred Fisher, "The Yellow Bell of China and the Endless Search," *Music Educators Journal* 59, no. 8 (April 1973): 30–33+; Ivan Vandor, "Cymbals and Trumpets from the 'Roof of the World,'" *Music Educators Journal* 61, no. 1 (September 1974): 106–109+; Paul Parthun, "Tribal Music in North America," *Music Educators Journal* 6, no. 4 (January 1976): 32–45.

66. Randall Armstrong, "The Adaptable Appalachian Dulcimer," *Music Educators Journal* 66, no. 5 (February 1980): 38–41; Horace Boyer, "Gospel Music," *Music Educators Journal* 64, no. 9 (May 1978): 34–43; Michael Stevens, "The Training of Indian Musicians," *Music Educators Journal* 61, no. 8 (April 1975): 33–39.

67. Malcom Tait, "World Musics: Balancing Our Attitudes and Strategies," *Music Educators Journal* 61, no. 6 (February 1975): 28–32; Albert J. McNeil, "The Social Foundations of the Music of Black America," *Music Educators Journal* 60, no. 6 (February 1974): 47–49.

68. Examples are: New York University, Advertisement, *Music Educators Journal* 55, no. 8 (April 1969): 114; Indiana University and Wesleyan University, Advertisements, *Music Educators Journal* 58, no. 8 (April 1972): 116–118; Northwestern University, Advertisement, *Music Educators Journal* 64, no. 8 (April 1978): 92, and 71, no. 8 (April 1985): 58; Central Connecticut State University, Advertisement, *Music Educators Journal* 74, no. 8 (April 1988): 58; University of Hartford, Advertisement, *Music Educators Journal* 78, no. 7 (March 1992): 77.

69. For examples, see: Associated Music Publishing, Inc., Advertisement, new choral releases, *Music Educators Journal* 54, no. 3 (November 1967): 22; Inter Culture Associates, Advertisement, instruments of India, *Music Educators Journal* 58, no. 8 (April 1972): 17; RCA Records, Advertisement, *Music Educators Journal* 58, no. 8 (April 1972): 8; Kent State University Press, Advertisement, *Music Educators Journal* 69, no. 9 (May 1983): 77; MENC Publications, *Music Educators Journal* 78, no. 4 (December 1991): 68; Silver Burdett and Ginn, Advertisement, school music textbooks, *Music Educators Journal* 75, no. 4 (December 1989): back cover; Macmillan/McGraw-Hill, Advertisement, school music textbooks, *Music Educators Journal* 78, no. 7 (March 1992): inside back cover.

70. Although a particularly extensive listing of professional resources published by MENC is found in *Music Educators Journal* 52, no. 3 (November 1985): 47–54, *MENC Professional Resources* is now a separate catalog, published annually.

71. William M. Anderson, "Teaching Musics of the World: A Renewed Commitment," *Music Educators Journal* 67, no. 1 (September 1980): 40.

72. Bette Yarbrough Cox, "Multicultural Training," *passim.*

73. Chuck Ball et al., "Report of the MENC Commission on Graduate Music Teacher Education," *Music Educators Journal* 67, no. 2 (October 1980): 46–53+.

74. Chuck Ball et al., "Report of the MENC Commission," 48.

75. Paul Berliner, "Soda Bottles, Whale Bones, Sitars, and Shells—A World Music Perspective," *Music Educators Journal* 59, no. 7 (March 1973): 50–52+.

76. Jerry and Bev Praver, "Barb'ra Allen, Tom Dooley, and Sweet Betsy from PS 42," *Music Educators Journal* 70, no. 5 (January 1984): 56–69; Patricia Shehan, "Teaching Music Through Balkan Folk Dance," *Music Educators Journal* 71, no. 3 (November 1984): 47–51; Martha Holmes, "Israeli Folk Dance: A Resource for Music Educators," *Music Educators Journal* 67, no. 2 (October 1980): 36–39.

77. See "Improvisation in World Musics," *Music Educators Journal* 66, no. 5 (January 1980): 118–147; and "Improvisation at the High School and College Levels," *Music Educators Journal* 66, no. 5 (January 1980): 86–104.

78. Anderson, "Teaching Musics of the World," 40–41; Jack P. B. Dodds, "Music as a Multicultural Education," *Music Educators Journal* 69, no. 9 (May 1983): 33–36; Robert Garfias, "Music in the United States: Community of Cultures," *Music Educators Journal* 69, no. 9 (May 1983): 30–31; Bess Lomax Hawes, "Our Cultural Mosaic," *Music Educators Journal* 69, no. 9 (May 1983): 26–27.

79. See "Educational Tactics," *Music Educators Journal* 69, no. 9 (May 1983): 39–51; "Tools for Teaching World Musics," *Music Educators Journal* 69, no. 9 (May 1983): 58–61.

80. Emma S. Brooks-Baham, "Collecting Materials in Your Community," *Music Educators Journal* 69, no. 9 (May 1983): 52–55.

81. Barbara Smith, "Musics of Hawaii and Samoa: Exemplar of Annotated Resources," *Music Educators Journal* 69, no. 9 (May 1983): 62–65.

82. Music Educators National Conference, "Book Browsing" and "Study Shelf," *Music Educators Journal* 69, no. 9 (May 1983): 22–25.

83. Music Educators National Conference, Resource Listing, *Music Educators Journal* 69, no. 9 (May 1983): 66–70.

84. Music Educators National Conference, "Miami Beach Conference Program Preview," *Music Educators Journal* 66, no. 7 (March 1980): 86–88.

85. Music Educators National Conference, Program listing of biennial conference, San Antonio, *Music Educators Journal* 68, no. 4 (December 1981): 58–62.

86. Music Educators National Conference, Program listing for biennial conference, Chicago, *Music Educators Journal* 70, no. 5 January 1984): 62–64.

87. Music Educators National Conference, Advertisement for Wesleyan Symposium, *Music Educators Journal* 70, no. 8 (April 1984): 57–58.

88. David P. McAllester, project director, *Becoming Human through Music* (Reston, VA: Music Educators National Conference, 1985): 2.

89. Elsie Buck, "Mom, Pack My Bags for Music Class," *Music Educators Journal* 70, no. 6 (February 1985): 33–35; Samuel D. Miller, "Lessons in the Blues," *Music Educators Journal* 70, no. 6 (February 1985): 39–40; Martha Giles, "Improvising on an Indian Flute," *Music Educators Journal* 70, no. 6 (February 1985): 61–62.

90. René Boyer-White, "Reflecting Cultural Diversity in the Music Classroom," *Music Educators Journal* 75, no. 4 (December 1988): 50–54.

91. Marvin V. Curtis, "Understanding the Black Aesthetic Experience," *Music Educators Journal* 77, no. 2 (October 1988): 23–26.

92. David G. Klocko, "Multicultural Music in the College Curriculum," *Music Educators Journal* 75, no. 5 (January 1989): 39.

93. Klocko, "Multicultural Music in the College Curriculum," 40.

94. Patricia K. Shehan, "World Musics: Windows to Cross-Cultural Understanding," *Music Educators Journal* 75, no. 3 (November 1988): 22–26.

95. Music Educators National Conference, "MENC Advisor" column, *Music Educators Journal* 76, no. 5 (January 1990): 10.

96. Music Educators National Conference, Advertisement for Multicultural Symposium, *Music Educators Journal* 76, no. 3 (November 1989): 15.

97. William M. Anderson, "Toward a Multicultural Future," *Music Educators Journal* 77, no. 9 (May 1991): 30.

98. *Ibid.,* 31.

99. *Ibid.,* 31.

100. *Ibid.,* 32.

101. *Ibid.,* 33.

102. Music Educators National Conference, "Conference Connection," *Music Educators Journal* 76, no. 7 (March 1990): 9–10.

103. Marsha B. Edelman, "Exploring the Rich Tradition of Jewish Music," *Music Educators Journal* 77, no. 1 (September 1990): 35–39.

104. Patricia S. Campbell, "Cross-Cultural Views of Musical Creativity," *Music Educators Journal* 76, no. 9 (May 1990): 43–46.

105. Ellen McCullough-Brabson, "Instruments from Around the World: Hands-On Experiences," *Music Educators Journal* 77, no. 3 (November 1990): 46–50.

106. Music Educators National Conference, "1992 Conference Performing Groups and Education Sessions," *Music Educators Journal* 78, no. 6 (February 1992): 39–43.

107. Anthony Seegar, "Celebrating the American Music Mosaic," *Music Educators Journal* 78, no. 9 (May 1992): 29.

108. *Ibid.,* 26–29.

109. Patricia Campbell, "Cultural Consciousness in Teaching General Music," *Music Educators Journal* 78, no. 9 (May 1992): 30–33.

110. See *Music Educators Journal* 78, no. 9 (May 1992): 33–36.[d]

112. Will Schmid, "World Music in the Instrumental Music Program," *Music Educators Journal* 78 no. 9 (May 1992): 41–44; Joan C. Conlon, "Explore the World in Song," *Music Educators Journal* 78, no. 9 (May 1992): 46–48.

113. See *Music Educators Journal* 78, no. 9 (May 1992): 44–45 and 49–51.[d]

114. William M. Anderson, "Rethinking Teacher Education: The Multicultural Imperative," *Music Educators Journal* 78, no. 9 (May 1992): 52–55.

d. The correct citation for the missing note 111 of the article is: Judith Cook Tucker, "Circling the Globe: Multicultural Resources," *Music Educators Journal* 78, no. 9 (May 1992): 37–41.

PART V

APPLICATIONS OF RESEARCH METHODOLOGY

The final part of the book examines two major thrusts in educational research that involve the direct application of research methods to practice. These research applications—evaluation research and action research—both have the goal of improving practice, and can involve either, or both, quantitative and qualitative research methods.

Chapter 14 describes the uses of evaluation research in education and the major differences between quantitative and qualitative models of evaluation research.

Chapter 15 explores the unique opportunity that action research provides educational practitioners to conduct research studies in their own setting. We describe how various approaches to action research foster the professional development of educators and help them improve their effectiveness.

CHAPTER 14

EVALUATION RESEARCH

Amy Tanner is the assistant superintendent of instruction for her school district. Her superintendent has asked her to determine whether changes should be made to the science curriculum to help students understand and apply scientific knowledge. He says that some parents in the district have expressed concerns about whether their children are developing the science skills that they will need for life in the twenty-first century.

From a literature search Amy finds an article that reviews new curriculum programs based on recently established national standards for science education. She learns that the programs have been evaluated to varying degrees. One of the programs integrates mathematics and science teaching, which Amy thinks might appeal to many of the school district's stakeholders.

Amy reports to the superintendent that she wants to conduct a needs assessment with various stakeholder groups, including school site councils, to determine which of the new science programs have the features that they value. Then she will review the evaluation data and costs for these programs so that she can do a cost-benefit analysis. Finally, she will submit a report of her findings and recommendations to the stakeholder groups.

The superintendent believes that Amy's approach to evaluating science curriculum programs will result in a sound adoption decision, and so he gives her approval to proceed.

This chapter describes the advantages of using published research findings to evaluate curriculum programs and other aspects of educational practice about which you may need to make judgments and decisions. We explain the aspects of educational practice that evaluators commonly examine, major types of evaluation research, and quantitative and qualitative approaches to evaluation. We also describe criteria for judging an educational evaluation.

OBJECTIVES

After studying this chapter, you will be able to

1. describe the advantages of using published research findings to evaluate educational phenomena about which educators need to make decisions.

2. describe several types of educational phenomena that have been the subject of evaluation research.

3. describe how needs assessment, cost-benefit analysis, and educational research and development can contribute to the evaluation of educational phenomena.

4. describe the difference between formative and summative evaluation and the value of each.

5. describe the typical focus of quantitative approaches to educational evaluation.

6. describe the similarities and differences between responsive evaluation and educational connoisseurship and criticism.

7. describe four criteria that a good evaluation research study should satisfy.

KEY TERMS

cost-benefit analysis
educational connoisseurship
   and criticism
educational research and
   development
efficiency effect
enabling objective

formative evaluation
meta-evaluation
National Assessment of
   Educational Progress
needs assessment
performance objective
program evaluation

R&D product
responsive evaluation
stakeholder
summative evaluation
systems approach

THE VALUE OF USING EVALUATION RESEARCH IN EDUCATIONAL DECISION MAKING

Educational evaluation is the process of making judgments about the merit, value, or worth of any component of education, such as the eight aspects of educational practice described in the next section of the chapter. The conduct of educational evaluations has greatly expanded in the past 40 years, and it continues to grow. The importance of evaluation research is evidenced in various ways, including the fact that all educational programs receiving federal funding must undergo formal evaluation, the presence of evaluation teams on the staff of many school districts and state departments of education, and the employment of institutional researchers to evaluate the operations of most colleges and universities.

Some educators rely primarily on personal experience or expert advice to make such decisions as the determination of educational goals, the selection of textbooks, and the design of needed instructional programs. However, as we explained in Chapter 1, those sources of information may contain bias and error, and in any case, they are incomplete. A well-done evaluation study is a valuable aid because it helps educators and policy makers weigh a wider range of factors that are relevant to a major decision. In addition, a carefully designed evaluation can yield persuasive evidence that makes educators less vulnerable to protests by individuals or groups who might disagree with their decisions, and that helps them justify the costs associated with a decision.

Various individuals and groups have a stake in the decisions that involve schools and students. Therefore, it is important to identify relevant stakeholders at the outset of an evaluation study. Stakeholders are the individuals who are involved in the phenomenon that is being evaluated or who may be affected by or interested in the findings of an evaluation. For example, stakeholders in the evaluation of a school career guidance program might include career education teachers, parents whose students might participate in the program, school counselors, and employees of businesses that are likely to hire graduates of schools where the program is offered.

Some stakeholders want input into the design of an evaluation, the collection and analysis of information, the interpretation of the findings, and the decisions based on the evaluation. However, different types of stakeholders often hold conflicting positions on the value of a given educational phenomenon. Thus evaluators and the educators who plan to make decisions based on evaluation findings face challenges in conducting evaluations ethically, and in reflecting and reconciling the varied views of relevant stakeholders. The reconciliation of stakeholders' views is one of the most helpful aspects of good evaluation research, but it is not easy to perform.

ASPECTS OF EDUCATIONAL PRACTICE INVESTIGATED BY EVALUATORS

Evaluation research is conducted on many different aspects of the educational enterprise. Below we describe eight aspects of educational practice that frequently are the focus of evaluation research.

Instructional Programs

An instructional program can be defined as a sequence of activities that is guided by a plan, is designed to accomplish particular learning outcomes, and provides instruction to new groups of learners on a continuing basis. Head Start, the language arts curriculum in a high school, and the sequence of courses and field experiences that preservice teachers must complete in order to be certified are examples of instructional programs. Programs often are evaluated to determine whether they have been implemented as intended, and to assess their effectiveness in promoting the learning of students.

Richard Dukes, Jodie Ullman, and Judith Stein (1996) carried out an evaluation to determine the long-term effectiveness of the Drug Abuse Resistance Education (D.A.R.E.) program in one district. D.A.R.E. involves a trained police officer delivering a curriculum to fifth or sixth graders once a week for one semester. The curriculum is designed to build students' self-esteem and resistance to peer pressure, increase peer bonding, and delay the onset of experimentation with alcohol, tobacco, and other drugs.

Three years after the D.A.R.E. program was first offered in the school district, a questionnaire survey was administered to a random sample of ninth graders, most of whom would have had the opportunity to take the program, if they chose. Survey responses of the 497 students who reported they had received D.A.R.E. and the 352 students who reported that they had not received the program were compared.

The evaluators carried out statistical analyses to identify target outcomes that were presumed to reflect the long-term effectiveness of D.A.R.E.: (a) age of onset of use of marijuana and current use of drugs; (b) age of onset of drinking and current use of alcohol; and two items from a measure of self-esteem. The presumed predictor variable, participation in D.A.R.E., did not significantly predict any of the D.A.R.E. target outcomes. The evaluators concluded that D.A.R.E., like most drug-use prevention programs, manifests its strongest effects shortly after program implementation, with a decay over time. They suggest approaches that might improve the program's long-term effectiveness.

The D.A.R.E. follow-up study is unusual, because it reports nonsignificant results. Most evaluation studies in which the tests of statistical significance show no support for the study's hypotheses are never published. Over time this publication bias tends to skew the education literature toward an overestimate of the effectiveness of particular programs. D.A.R.E.'s continuing popularity, despite such nonsignificant findings, also illustrates the fact that many educational programs remain in existence for reasons other than their demonstrated effectiveness. For example, some schools might continue an ineffective program because parents or politicians support it.

Instructional Methods

Educators want to know which instructional methods are most effective, for example, the lecture versus the discussion method of teaching, the whole-language approach to reading instruction, or the use of manipulatives in teaching English as a Second Language (ESL). Kevin Miller (1995) evaluated a well-known instructional method, cooperative learning, to determine its value in stimulating conversational interaction between mainstreamed deaf and hard-of-hearing students and their hearing peers and teachers at the middle-school level. Three general-education teachers of social studies with a hard-of-hearing student in their class participated in the research, which involved a single-subject experimental research design using the A-B-A format (see Chapter 9).

During the first A phase (days 1–3), the teachers used a traditional teaching style, in which each teacher lectured to his or her entire class, students functioned independently of one another, and the teacher determined which students spoke at various points in the lesson. During the B phase (days 4–6), each teacher established a cooperative learning group that included the hard-of-hearing student, and used a cooperative learning style (which the teachers had learned during a pre-intervention workshop). During the second A phase (days 7–9), the teachers again used a traditional teaching style.

Each teacher's class was videotaped for about an hour on each of the nine days of the experiment. The dialogue of the teacher and of each student during the first 10 minutes of each videotape was later transcribed and coded. Then the number of conversational turns, conversational initiations, requests for information, and informational comments for each hard-of-hearing student was calculated for each day.

Miller found that both the hard-of-hearing students and other students who had displayed low levels of conversation during the first A (baseline) phase tended to increase their participation during the cooperative-learning (treatment) phase. Having the hard-of-hearing student play the role of recorder was particularly effective in stimulating his or her increased conversation with hearing peers and the teacher. Thus the study gave a positive evaluation to cooperative learning as a method of fostering conversational interaction among hard-of-hearing students and their hearing peers and teacher.

Instructional Materials

Educators and students spend large amounts of money each year on textbooks and other curriculum materials. Educators count on these materials to help students achieve intended learning objectives. However, reviews of the textbook publishing industry indicate that publishers focus far more on market conditions than on evidence of effectiveness to promote their products (Lockwood, 1992; Apple, 1991). Evaluation research can reveal the relative effectiveness of textbooks and other instructional materials.

The research article that is reprinted at the end of this chapter, by Roberta Ogletree, Barbara Rienzo, Judy Drolet, and Joyce Fetro, involves a comparative evaluation of 23 school-based sexuality education curricula. The authors summarize the philosophy, content, skill-building strategies, and teaching strategies of each curriculum, point out general strengths and weaknesses of the curricula, and suggest strategies for overcoming major weaknesses. A similarly designed evaluation of K–8 science curriculum materials by Dana Johnson, Linda Boyce, and Joyce VanTassel-Baska (1995) is described later in the chapter, where we use its design to illustrate a set of professional standards for evaluation research.

Specific Groups or Organizations

Any educational group or organization (e.g., a support group for minority students, or an organization for parents who home-school their children) can be evaluated, and its operations can be compared to its own organizational goals or to the operations of other organizations. For example, David Porretta, Michael Gillespie, and Paul Jansma (1996) conducted an evaluation of the Special Olympics organization that was commissioned by the organization directors. The authors note that, with over one million athletes participating, Special Olympics currently is the largest sports organization in the world for athletes with mental retardation.

The evaluation involved a questionnaire mailed to 232 respondents representing various agencies throughout the United States (e.g., Special Olympics executive directors, parent organizations, state directors of special education, university-affiliated programs) that provide services to individuals with disabilities. The questionnaire addressed four research questions involving: (1) the prevailing philosophy of agencies servicing individuals with mental retardation, (2) the terminology used by agencies to describe mental retardation, (3) strategies employed by leading agencies in the United States to attract people with disabilities to service delivery systems, and (4) agency professionals' prevailing perception of the Special Olympics' mission.

The research report shows the percentage of respondents giving various responses to each question or its component subquestions. For example, in response to the question, "What is your agency/organization's philosophy related to servicing people with disabilities?" 66 percent indicated, "Least Restricted Environment Based," meaning that the majority of agencies/organizations provide their services in an environment characterized as least restrictive. The researchers summarized the responses as showing that

(1) the mission of Special Olympics should be to place more emphasis on inclusion opportunities, (2) there appears to be a trend away from the term "mental retardation" toward other terms, (3) Special Olympics should provide opportunities to a wider variety of individuals with disabilities, and (4) Special Olympics should examine its mission statement in order to stay abreast with current philosophies being espoused by other agencies/organizations that serve individuals with disabilities. (p. 44)

Educators

Teachers and many other types of educators must take tests or demonstrate certain competencies in order to obtain certification or employment. Performance appraisals in relation to salary reviews and promotions also may occur. These forms of evaluation focus on an individual's merits in comparison to other individuals or to some standard. The personnel evaluation standards set by the Joint Committee on Standards for Educational Evaluation (1988) are meant to guide such evaluations.

Educators who must make decisions about educational programs, materials, and methods also need general information about the qualifications of the educators who will administer such programs, materials, and methods. Many evaluation research studies thus evaluate educators not in comparison to each other but more generally, in order to determine the quality of the human resources available to carry out specific educational activities. For example, Kenneth Sirotnik (1983) described an observational study of over 1,000 school teachers that was conducted by John Goodlad and his colleagues. Sirotnik notes that the researchers were startled by the low level of corrective feedback that teachers provided in any of the classrooms observed:

. . . in the elementary classes observed, on the average, just under 3 percent of the instructional time that the teacher spent interacting with students involved corrective feedback (with or without guidance). At the secondary level, this estimate is less than 2 percent. . . . Thus, one of the most touted pedagogical features of classroom instruction—immediate corrective feedback—rarely occurs. (p. 19)

Sirotnik concludes from the evaluation findings that teachers in American school systems need better supervision and staff development in order to provide effective instruction to students.

Students

Students in schools and other educational institutions are assessed regularly to guide decisions about their school grades and awarding of diplomas or degrees. Many students also periodically take various placement and aptitude tests that affect their access to higher education and employment opportunities.

Teachers are given the responsibility for designing, administering, and scoring many of the tests used to assess student performance. National organizations, such as the Educational Testing Service, focus on standardized assessments that allow for comparisons of student performance to national norms. Increasingly, states are administering assessments to determine whether their students are achieving state-level standards of academic performance in different content areas.

Tests and Assessment Procedures

Because so many decisions about students hinge on their test performance, the tests themselves must be evaluated as to their validity, reliability, fairness, and other relevant factors. In Chapter 5 we described the procedures used to assess the validity and reliability of tests and other measures. For example, the research article by Marvin Simner that is reprinted in Chapter 8 involves the validation of a shortened version of a test designed to predict a disposition for later school difficulty in kindergarten students.

In a more broad-scale evaluation of assessment procedures, Fred Newmann (1990) reported test results from 51 classrooms that used a model National Assessment of Educational Progress essay examination to evaluate higher-order thinking among high school social studies students. The report concluded that the test accurately assesses higher-order thinking competencies in all curriculum subjects.

Evaluations

Because of the major impact that evaluation studies have on both individuals and institutions, educators have developed increasing interest in the evaluation of evaluation studies themselves. The process of evaluating an evaluation study (sometimes called *meta-evaluation*) is illustrated later in the chapter, when we describe a set of standards that were developed to assess evaluations of educational programs.

COMMON FORMS OF EVALUATION RESEARCH IN EDUCATION

Three types of evaluation research studies that are common in education are needs assessment, cost-benefit analysis, and educational research and development. Below we describe each of them in order to illustrate the various purposes, stakeholders, and procedures that specific evaluation research studies might involve. While specific studies of each type may involve only quantitative or only qualitative research, in our view both the quantitative and qualitative evaluation approaches described later in the chapter can contribute to each of these types of evaluation research.

Needs Assessment

Needs assessment is a set of procedures for identifying and prioritizing needs related to societal, organizational, and human performance (Kaufman & Thiagarajan, 1987). A *need* usually is defined as a discrepancy between a desired and an existing state or condition. Thus, for example, the evaluator seeks to obtain information concerning the current quality or level of success of an educational program, and to compare the information to what is desired or expected of the program.

Assessment of needs can involve perceptions of needs or observations of actual performance. In a discussion of needs assessments as a basis for a training program, A. Rossett (1987) identified five types of questions that educational evaluators can ask prospective learners in order to determine training needs. Evaluators can ask questions that lead learners to (1) identify problems that they experience in a particular learning domain, (2) express feelings about a particular course or skill, (3) demonstrate particular skills, (4) identify possible (including both instructional and noninstructional) solutions to a problem, and (5) express priorities among possible topics or skills for a training experience.

When needs are carefully analyzed, proposed solutions are more likely to address the real needs of program participants. For example, one of the authors once coordinated an educational program for parents of at-risk middle-school students. The students participated in an intensive personal growth course and then were assigned mentors for a year-long follow-through program. Soon after the intensive course, all the parents received a telephone call asking about their relationship with the student since the course and about the kinds of support that the parent would like as the student made the transition to high school. Parents also were asked to rate their level of interest in several topics that speakers planned to address in subsequent meetings. Based on the results, several aspects of the parent program were redesigned.

Cost-Benefit Analysis

Evaluation research has become an important tool in helping educators determine whether programs or other educational phenomena that are in operation or being considered for adoption produce benefits that justify their costs. According to Robert Brent (1996), cost-benefit analysis involves an attempt to maximize the difference between the benefits (B) and costs (C) of a program (that is, B minus C). Estimation of C is based on what resources consumers are willing to give up for the program, while estimation of B reflects what they are willing to receive as compensation for this relinquishment of resources. The difference between B and C represents the *efficiency effect* of a program, or the additional resources that are made available by its implementation.

If only one program among several alternatives can be implemented, the program with the greatest efficiency effect should be adopted. However, according to Brent, the costs and benefits of funding a public program such as those in the public schools must first be weighted for various other factors before being compared. For example, the annual net benefit in dollars must typically be reduced by a discount rate to reflect the perceived rate of interest, or economic value of the funds that must be given up now in order to receive a future benefit. Another factor is the marginal cost of public funds (MCF), which estimates the excess burden beyond the dollar cost of a program that is involved in funding it. (For example, one aspect of the excess burden relevant to educational programs is the effect of tax evasion on the generation of the public funds needed to support education.)

Brent explains that cost-benefit analyses of educational programs usually are based on the assumption that "education leads to a future income stream that would be higher than if the education had not taken place" (p. 221), while forgone earnings during schooling represent the costs that must be given up now to get the higher future income. Because private expenditures for education usually are supplemented with public expenditures, the total costs of education almost always exceed the private costs to students of tuition, books, forgone earnings, and so forth.

Brent describes a cost-benefit analysis conducted by C. Constantatos and E. G. West (1991). Their study showed that the social returns from Canadian students' education are relatively higher for elementary education than for secondary education, and lowest for higher education. To arrive at their conclusion, the authors estimated the MCF for each school level and the proportion of differential income that is due to students' ability, independent of the effects of the education they receive. According to Brent, the authors of the study concluded that "there may be evidence of overinvestment in higher education in Canada, depending on one's assumptions concerning the cut-off level for the opportunity cost of public funds. . . . Evidence of external benefits for higher education must be strong in order to ensure that public expenditure on higher education is clearly worthwhile" (p. 223).

The evaluators of Canadian education took several factors into account in estimating the efficiency effect of education at the three school levels. However, Brent notes that they also should have weighted in their analysis a portion of the increased income that students receiving higher education will earn. This study thus illustrates the many factors affecting costs and benefits that must be taken into account before a comparison of instructional programs in terms of their overall efficiency effects is made.

A form of governmental financial reporting that also can be used to analyze the costs and benefits of educational programs is called *service efforts and accomplishments* (SEA) reporting. Its use in program evaluation for elementary and secondary education, colleges and universities, and other types of public institutions is described by Harry Hatry and his colleagues (Hatry et al., 1990).

Educational Research and Development

Evaluation is central to the educational research and development (R&D) process, which is a systematic process involving the development and refinement of educational programs and materials (referred to hereafter as R&D *products*).

Walter Dick and Lou Carey (1996) advocate the systems approach model of educational R&D. The 10 steps of this model are shown in Figure 14.1. You will note that step 1 involves needs assessment, which we described earlier in the chapter. In this model, a needs assessment is carried out in order to identify the goals of the product to be developed. Step 2, instructional analysis, involves identification of the specific skills, procedures, and learning tasks that are involved in reaching the instructional goals identified by the needs assessment. Step 3 is designed to identify the level of entry behaviors (sometimes called *enabling objectives*) that learners bring to the learning task, as well as other characteristics of the learners (e.g., specific personality traits such as test anxiety), or of the settings in which instruction will occur and the learned skills will ultimately be used.

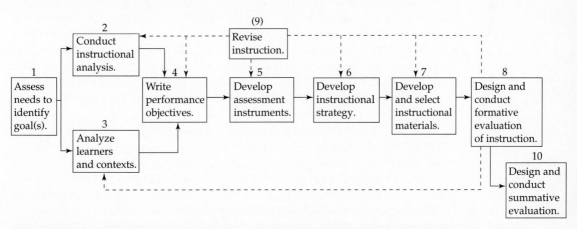

FIGURE 14.1   The steps of the systems approach model of educational research and development (R&D)

Source. Adapted from figure on pp. 2–3 in: Dick, W., & Carey, L. (1996). *The systematic design of instruction* (4th ed.). New York: HarperCollins. Copyright © 1996 by Walter Dick and Lou Carey. Reprinted by permission of HarperCollins Publishers, Inc.

During step 4, the developers write specific statements (called *performance objectives*) of what the learners will be able to do after instruction. Then assessment instruments to test achievement of the objectives are developed (step 5); the appropriate instructional strategy is formulated (step 6); and instructional materials are developed, or possibly selected from available materials (step 7).

Steps 8, 9, and 10 of the systems model involve the distinction between formative and summative evaluation, which was formulated by Michael Scriven (1967). Scriven observed that, in practice, evaluation serves two different functions. Formative evaluation (step 8) involves collecting data about an educational product while it is under development, in order to provide information to guide the developers in revising the product or deciding to discontinue development, if appropriate. By contrast, summative evaluation (described below) is conducted to determine the final product's worth in an operational setting, when compared to other available products.

Formative evaluation occurs throughout the development process. The results of formative evaluation then are used to revise (step 9) any of the work carried out during steps 1 to 7. For example, the developers might carry out a formative evaluation of the product's objectives during step 4, examining such issues as the clarity and comprehensiveness of the objectives. Based on the results, they might eliminate some objectives, rewrite others, and add new objectives. Once they have developed instructional materials (step 7), they might do more formative evaluation and further revise the performance objectives to better match the product content.

Formative evaluation is conducted under field-test conditions. Field tests usually involve a smaller number of research participants, more hands-on involvement of the developers, and a more controlled environment than the normal operating conditions in which the final product is meant to be used.

Once a product completes the development process, it must be evaluated in terms of its effectiveness, and perhaps in relation to its unintended effects as well. Summative evaluation (step 10) is conducted to determine how beneficial the final product is, especially in comparison with competing products. This evaluation usually is carried out by someone other than the developers, but it also can be done by members of the development team if appropriate controls are used to reduce researcher bias.

As an educator examining the evaluation research literature, you probably will be most interested in evaluations of instructional programs, methods, and materials that have been tested under operational conditions. Such summative evaluations will help you determine whether the programs, methods, or materials are effective under conditions similar to your own situation. Sometimes, though, it may be worthwhile to examine studies that involve only formative evaluation. If you must implement a solution to your problem quickly, you might want to know about new products that have not yet been the subject of summative evaluation, but for which formative evaluation results are promising. Learning about a promising product while it still is under development will give you a head start on determining its suitability as a solution to your problem. You might even be able to volunteer your local setting as a field-test site to participate in its evaluation.

QUANTITATIVE AND QUALITATIVE APPROACHES TO EVALUATION RESEARCH

In the following sections, we describe some approaches to evaluation that are based on quantitative research and others that are based on qualitative research. It also is possible for evaluators to combine both quantitative and qualitative approaches in conducting an evaluation research study.

Quantitative Approaches

Objectives-Based Evaluation.   Quantitative approaches to evaluation usually focus on the extent to which an educational program or method helps students achieve the intended learning objectives associated with it. Earlier in the chapter, we referred to an evaluation study involving the National Assessment of Educational Progress (NAEP). The NAEP, a congressionally mandated project of the National Center for Education Statistics of the U.S. Department of Education, is a large-scale, continuing assessment of what a representative sample of students in the United States know and can do in various subject areas (Campbell et al., 1997).

The NAEP is based on Ralph Tyler's model of objectives-based curriculum evaluation. Tyler claimed that school instruction should be organized around specific objectives and that the success of such instruction should be judged on the basis of how well students reach those objectives. The NAEP involves quantitative analysis of the percentage of youth at various age levels who are competent in performing tasks that reflect skills viewed by subject matter experts as necessary for effective functioning in school and society.

Many research studies, particularly those involving experimental designs, involve quantitative evaluation of how well research participants who receive an innovative instructional program perform on a criterion measure compared to participants receiving a traditional program or no program. The quasi-experimental research study by William Lan that is reprinted in Chapter 9 is an example of such a study.

Context-Input-Process-Product (CIPP) Model.   Daniel Stufflebeam and his colleagues (1971) developed the CIPP model to help practicing educators evaluate both instructional and noninstructional programs. During context evaluation, needs and problems are identified, including both those associated with the program and those that the program is intended to alleviate. Input evaluation involves making judgments about the resources and strategies needed to accomplish the intended program goals and objectives. Process evaluation involves the collection of evaluative data concerning the program in operation. Finally, product evaluation involves the assessment of the extent to which program goals have been achieved.

In the CIPP model, evaluators work closely with the client in determining what types of information are needed for each phase of the evaluation, and in synthesizing the information so that it can be used for decision making. Because the collection and analysis of evaluative data are viewed primarily as technical activities, these aspects of the evaluation usually are delegated to the evaluator. While the CIPP approach has been used primarily in quantitative evaluation research, it also appears suitable for evaluation research based on a qualitative orientation.

Qualitative Approaches

Qualitative approaches to evaluation are based on the assumption that judgments of worth depend heavily on the values and perspectives of the individuals doing the judging. Various qualitative approaches have been developed (see Pitman & Maxwell, 1992), including the two that we describe here.

Responsive Evaluation.   Robert Stake (1991) developed one of the first qualitative approaches to evaluation, called *responsive evaluation*. It focuses on being responsive to stakeholders' issues (i.e., points of contention among different stakeholders) and concerns (i.e., matters about which stakeholders feel threatened or that they want to substantiate). Concerns and issues tend to provide a much wider focus for evaluation study than the goals and objectives that are central to quantitative approaches to evaluation.

The four phases of responsive evaluation are (1) initiating and organizing the evaluation, (2) identifying key issues and concerns, (3) gathering useful information, and (4) reporting results and making recommendations (Guba and Lincoln, 1981). During the first phase, stakeholders are identified; also, the evaluator and client negotiate a contract to specify such matters as the phenomena to be evaluated, the purpose of the evaluation, rights of access to records, and guarantees of confidentiality and anonymity.

In the second phase, key issues and concerns are identified through direct involvement with a variety of stakeholders. The evaluators seek to clarify the values of different stakeholders that underlie the issues and concerns expressed. For example, in an evaluation of a particular school system's governance structure, the evaluators might discover that some stakeholders value a high-quality curriculum and accountability, whereas others place greater value on equality of representation in decision making and a rational decision-making process.

In the third phase of the evaluation, the evaluators collect more information about the concerns, issues, and values identified by the stakeholders, descriptive information about the phenomena being evaluated, and standards to be used in making judgments about it.

The final phase of a responsive evaluation involves preparing reports of results and recommendations. Frequently a case study format (see Chapter 10) is used to describe the concerns and issues identified by stakeholders. The evaluators, in negotiation with stakeholders, then make judgments and recommendations based on the information that has been collected.

In doing a responsive evaluation, evaluators do not specify a research design at the outset of their work. Instead, they use an emergent design, meaning that the design of the evaluation changes as evaluators gain insights into stakeholders' primary issues and concerns. Consistent with the purposeful sampling methods described in Chapter 10, responsive evaluators continue obtaining information from stakeholders until the information they are receiving becomes redundant with information already collected.

Advocates of responsive education claim that after sufficient communication, stakeholders can be guided to consensus on the evaluation outcome, despite their differing values and needs. However, Pitman & Maxwell view this claim as unrealistic given "that constructions are *socially situated* and, thus, unlikely to come to be shared by individuals in very different social positions" (p. 742).

Educational Connoisseurship and Criticism.   Elliott Eisner (1979) developed an approach to qualitative evaluation research called *educational connoisseurship and criticism*. This approach depends heavily on the evaluator's professional expertise. The first part of this approach, connoisseurship, involves appreciating (in the sense of becoming aware of) the qualities of an educational program and their meaning. The educational connoisseur is assumed to be aware of more nuances of the program being evaluated than a typical educator or lay person would be. The evaluator thus must have expert knowledge of the program being evaluated, as well as of other comparable or competitive programs. The second part of the approach, criticism, is the process of describing and evaluating what has been appreciated. The evaluator needs to be sensitive to both the strengths and the weaknesses of the program.

While Eisner's approach to evaluation is explicitly artistic in nature, he does not discount the value of scientific and quantitative approaches to evaluation. Instead, he asserts that both artistic and scientific evaluation strategies contribute to the understanding of complex phenomena. Because the evaluation methods used in educational connoisseurship and criticism are defined entirely by the individual evaluator, this approach to evaluation is not easy to validate or disconfirm. However, when this approach is used by a talented and well-trained evaluator, it illuminates the unique nature and value of a program in ways that are less likely to occur with other evaluation approaches.

In seeking to determine the validity of the findings of educational connoisseurship and criticism, we recommend that you look for other studies, ideally carried out by different evaluators, to determine whether they obtained similar findings. You also should determine how similar the evaluator's experience and values are to your own, or to those of the stakeholders whom you must consider in making an educational decision.

CRITERIA FOR JUDGING AN EDUCATIONAL EVALUATION RESEARCH STUDY

In reading evaluation research, educators need guidelines for judging the adequacy of the study. The Joint Committee on Standards for Educational Evaluation (1994) created a set of standards for this purpose. The Joint Committee defined *program evaluation* to include the evaluation of the types of phenomena that we described earlier as the subjects of evaluation research. The Committee excluded the evaluation of educators, which is covered by the Joint Committee's personnel evaluation standards (see Chapter References).

The standards for program evaluation were developed by a committee consisting of representatives from 12 major educational organizations in the United States, including the American Association of School Administrators, the American Federation of Teachers, and the American Educational Research Association. You can use these standards to judge the adequacy of evaluation research studies that you read, or to design your own evaluation research.

The Joint Committee specified 30 standards for program evaluation and grouped them under four criteria that can be used to evaluate an evaluation research study: seven standards for the criterion of utility, three standards for the criterion of feasibility, eight standards for the criterion of propriety, and twelve standards for the criterion of accuracy. Below we explain the four criteria by applying them to an evaluation of K–8 science curriculum materials (Johnson et al., 1995).

Utility

The Joint Committee's utility standards are intended to ensure that an evaluation will serve the information needs of intended users by being designed and carried out so as to be informative, timely, and influential.

Johnson and his colleagues conducted their evaluation of K–8 science curricula for high-ability learners under the auspices of the National Science Curriculum Project for High-Ability Learners. They describe the project's mission as to merge (a) curriculum reform principles advocating high-level standards in all traditional curricular areas, (b) the recommendations of recent national standards projects, and (c) key principles of appropriate curriculum for gifted learners.

To address this mission, the members of the review team (the study authors) needed to bring varied competencies to the evaluation. The report describes one reviewer as a materials specialist with a background in library science and gifted education, the second as a scientist with research experience in university and pharmaceutical laboratories, and the third as an educator with expertise in curriculum and gifted education. In their report, the researchers describe how they located materials for possible review and then narrowed their review to 27 sets of K–8 science curriculum materials "based on breadth of use, likelihood of appropriateness for high-ability students, or reputation as innovative or prototypical materials" (p. 37).

Because the article's citations involve recent work on standards and curriculum for gifted learners, the evaluation appears to be timely. The article's description of reviewers' competencies, clear organization of review procedures and findings, and publication in the *Gifted Child Quarterly* confirm that this study is an informative evaluation that is likely to be influential, particularly among educators in gifted education.

Feasibility

The Joint Committee's feasibility standards are intended to ensure that an evaluation will be realistic, prudent, diplomatic, and economical.

The evaluation process used by Johnson and his colleagues appears realistic in that they first categorized the 27 curricula by what appeared to be their primary function: (a) basal stand-alone texts intended for a particular age or grade level; (b) modular curricula packaged into independent units organized around large concepts; and (c) supplementary materials with a precise focus, and comprised of either loosely connected activities or fully developed units to enrich an existing curriculum.

The reviewers concluded that the sets of materials classified as basal textbooks failed to meet new science curriculum standards for all students, but were especially weak for high-ability learners. The sets of materials that were classified as modular programs or supplementary materials were found to be superior to basal textbooks on most dimensions. For example, with one exception the modular programs tended to be rated the highest in their ability to meet the different needs of high-ability learners, because of their in-depth emphasis on important concepts and their flexibility in use that allowed for faster pacing. The basal stand-alone texts are not identified by name, which reflects a prudent and diplomatic treatment of those curricula rated lowest.

While no mention of the cost of the review is given, it probably was considerable. A note on the first page of the article entitled "Putting Research to Use" indicates that the evaluation process was developed and carried out over an 18-month period. The review procedures described (independent ratings, followed by preparation of a narrative review of each rated curriculum) probably took a great deal of time to complete. However, given the potential benefits of improving science instruction for not only high-ability students but for all students if the reviewers' recommendations are followed, the review appears to be economical (i.e., cost effective).

Propriety

The Joint Committee's propriety standards are intended to ensure that an evaluation will be conducted legally, ethically, and with due regard for the welfare of those involved in the evaluation, as well as those affected by its results. Rather than endorsing one or more specific programs, the authors briefly describe positive features of each of the 21 recommended curricula. They suggest that both pull-out programs and self-contained classes should draw from a number of the available modular and supplementary curricula to meet the needs of gifted students adequately.

In their report, the authors make clear their reasons for advocating the use of these materials over the basal texts. The review thereby gives a sense of having provided legal and ethical treatment of the producers of the curricula that were reviewed, while giving specific recommendations to help stakeholders apply the findings of the evaluation.

Accuracy

The Joint Committee's accuracy standards are intended to ensure that an evaluation will convey technically adequate information about the features that determine worth or merit of the program being evaluated.

Johnson and his colleagues cite two other published reports about the K–8 science curriculum evaluation that describe the evaluation procedures and findings in greater detail. While their report appears to be fairly comprehensive, it is reassuring to know that additional information about the study is readily available.

Johnson and his colleagues independently assessed features of the general curriculum design, classroom design, and technology of each set of K–8 science curriculum materials that were deemed appropriate for review. They also independently rated each curriculum for its treatment of science content and process, and examined its responsiveness to the needs of intellectually gifted learners, science-prone students, girls, minorities, and students with disabilities. The article includes information on the percentage of agreement among the reviewers' ratings during each of three phases of review and for each of five major features on which each curriculum was rated. The review thus appears to be technically adequate and sound in its conclusions. In addition, readers who question the conclusions, or wish further information about specific curricula, have the option of referring to the other reports that are cited.

CONCLUDING THOUGHT

Many educators are involved in selecting instructional programs, methods, and materials and deciding how to allocate limited funds among competing priorities. Having up-to-date evaluation information helps clarify the many factors that bear on such decisions. This chapter has described the kinds of evaluation information that can be found in the education literature to help educators make decisions.

SELF-CHECK TEST

1. Published evaluation research studies generally help education practitioners make better decisions because usually they:
   a. widen the range of factors for educators to consider in making the decision.
   b. include definitive evidence of the effectiveness of instructional programs, methods, and materials.
   c. confirm decision preferences that are based on personal experience.
   d. reduce the costs associated with specific decisions.

2. A research study shows the number of students with interest in pursuing advanced math before and after viewing a series of videotapes about well-paying careers that require advanced math skills. This research study most likely involves the evaluation of
   a. tests and assessment procedures.
   b. educators.
   c. specific groups or organizations.
   d. instructional materials.

3. In evaluation research the term *stakeholder* refers to
   a. the individual who initiates the request for an evaluation.
   b. anyone who will be affected by the evaluation findings.
   c. an evaluator who uses cost-benefit analysis to evaluate a phenomenon.
   d. an evaluator who uses personal interpretation to evaluate a phenomenon.

4. Needs assessment typically involves
   a. interviews of everyone with an opinion about the phenomenon being evaluated.
   b. measurement of the discrepancy between an existing condition and a desired condition.
   c. estimation of the costs and benefits of a proposed intervention.
   d. development and evaluation of a product designed to meet an identified need.

5. The efficiency effect of a program is
   a. an estimate of the difference between the benefits and costs of the program.
   b. the excess burden beyond the dollar cost of the program that is involved in funding it.
   c. a measure of consumers' willingness to pay for the program.
   d. a measure of the benefits to be received from the program.

6. The primary purpose of formative evaluation in educational research and development is to:
   a. demonstrate the effectiveness of the product under operational conditions.
   b. obtain information to guide revision and further development of the product.
   c. evaluate the product once development has been completed.
   d. test the extent to which learners have achieved the product objectives.

7. Unlike formative evaluation, summative evaluation of an educational R&D product generally
   a. occurs throughout the development process.
   b. is conducted to determine whether development of the product should be discontinued.
   c. involves determination of the extent to which learners achieve the product's performance objectives.
   d. does not reveal whether the product is effective under conditions similar to a practitioner's situation.

8. Quantitative approaches to program evaluation in education usually focus on:
   a. comparisons of the costs of different educational programs.
   b. evaluators' interpretations of the inherent value of a program.
   c. the extent of agreement or disagreement among stakeholders about a program's value.
   d. the extent to which a program helps students achieve the intended learning objectives.

9. Context-Input-Process-Product (CIPP) evaluation places emphasis on the
   a. refinement of a product to prepare it for operational use.
   b. evaluation of a product by external evaluators.
   c. evaluators working closely with the client to determine information needs and evaluation results.
   d. clients' involvement in data collection.

10. A central feature of responsive evaluation is its
    a. focus on identifying the issues and concerns of stakeholders.
    b. specification of the evaluation design prior to data collection.
    c. concern with the goals and objectives of the phenomenon being evaluated.
    d. specification of procedures for reconciling the different perspectives of various stakeholders.

11. Educational connoisseurship and criticism differs from other approaches to evaluation research primarily in its
    a. precise specification of the qualifications that evaluators must possess.
    b. efforts to demonstrate the validity of the evaluators' judgments.
    c. use of artistic methods of perceiving and representing the phenomenon that is evaluated.
    d. reliance on humanities scholars to judge the worth of educational programs in literature and the arts.

12. Some of the program evaluation standards of the Joint Committee on Standards for Educational Evaluation are concerned with the technical adequacy of an evaluation. These standards are intended to ensure an evaluation's
    a. utility.
    b. feasibility.
    c. propriety.
    d. accuracy.

CHAPTER REFERENCES

Apple, M. W. (1991). The culture and commerce of the textbook. In M. W. Apple & L. K. Christian-Smith (Eds.), *The politics of the textbook* (pp. 22–40). New York: Routledge.

Brent, R. J. (1996). *Applied cost-benefit analysis*. Brookfield, VT: Edward Elgar.

Campbell, J. R., Voelkl, K. E., & Donahue, P. L. (1997). NAEP 1996 trends in academic progress: Achievement of U.S. students in science, 1969 to 1996; mathematics, 1973 to 1996; reading, 1971 to 1996; writing, 1984 to 1996. Washington, DC: National Center for Education Statistics. (ERIC Document Reference No. ED 409 383)

Constantos, C., & West, E. G. (1991). Measuring returns from education: Some neglected factors. *Canadian Public Policy, 17*, 127–138.

Dick, W., & Carey, L. (1996). *The systematic design of instruction* (4th ed.). New York: HarperCollins.

Dukes, R. L., Ullman, J. B., & Stein, J. A. (1996). Three-year follow-up of Drug Abuse Resistance Education (D.A.R.E.). *Evaluation Review, 20*, 49–66.

Eisner, E. W. (1979). The educational imagination: On the design and evaluation of school programs. New York: Macmillan.

Guba, E. G., & Lincoln, Y. S. (1981). *Effective evaluation*. San Francisco: Jossey-Bass.

Hatry, H. P., Sullivan, J. M., Fountain, J. R., Jr., & Kremer, L. (Eds.). (1990). *Service efforts and accomplishments reporting: Its time has come*. Norwalk, CT: Governmental Accounting Standards Board.

Johnson, D. T., Boyce, L. N., & VanTassel-Baska, J. (1995). Science curriculum review: Evaluating materials for high-ability learners. *Gifted Child Quarterly, 39*, 36–43.

Joint Committee on Standards for Educational Evaluation. (1988). *The personnel evaluation standards*. Newbury Park, CA: Sage.

Joint Committee on Standards for Educational Evaluation. (1994). *The program evaluation standards: How to assess evaluations of educational programs* (2nd ed.). Thousand Oaks, CA: Sage.

Kaufman, R., & Thiagarajan, S. (1987). Identifying and specifying requirements for instruction. In R. M. Gagne (Ed.), *Instructional technology foundations* (pp. 113–140). Hillsdale, NJ: Erlbaum.

Lockwood, A. (1992). Whose knowledge do we teach? *Focus on Change, 6*, 3–7.

Miller, K. J. (1995). Cooperative conversations: The effect of cooperative learning on conversational interaction. *American Annals of the Deaf, 140*, 28–37.

Newmann, F. M. (1990). A test of higher-order thinking in social studies: Persuasive writing on constitutional issues using the NAEP approach. *Social Education, 54*, 369–373.

Pitman, M. A., & Maxwell, J. A. (1992). Qualitative approaches to evaluation: Models and methods. In M. D. LeCompte, W. L. Millroy, & J. Preissle (Eds.), *The handbook of qualitative research in education* (pp. 729–770). San Diego: Academic Press.

Porretta, D. L., Gillespie, M., & Jansma, P. (1996). Perceptions about Special Olympics from service delivery groups in the United States: A preliminary investigation. *Education and Training in Mental Retardation and Developmental Disabilities, 31*, 44–54.

Rossett, A. (1987). *Training needs assessment.* Englewood Cliffs, NJ: Educational Technology Publications.

Scriven, M. (1967). The methodology of evaluation. In R. E. Stake (Ed.), *Curriculum evaluation*, American Educational Research Association Series on Evaluation, No. 1 (pp. 39–83). Chicago: Rand McNally.

Sirotnik, K. A. (1983). What you see is what you get: Consistency, persistency, and mediocrity in classrooms. *Harvard Educational Review, 53*(1), 16–31.

Stake, R. E. (1991). Retrospective on "The countenance of educational evaluation." In M. W. McLaughlin & D. C. Phillips (Eds.), *Evaluation and education: At quarter century* (pp. 67–88). Chicago: University of Chicago Press.

Stufflebeam, D. L., Foley, W. J., Gephart, W. J., Guba, E. G., Hammond, R. L., Merriman, H. O., & Provus, M. M. (1971). *Educational evaluation and decision making.* Itasca, IL: Peacock.

RECOMMENDED READING

The CRESST Line: Newsletter of the National Center for Research on Evaluation, Standards and Student Testing (CRESST). Los Angeles: Center for the Study of Evaluation and Graduate School of Education & Information Studies, University of California at Los Angeles.

Each quarterly issue of *the CRESST Line* contains articles on topics and events relating to evaluation theory, procedures, methodologies, and practice. Available from the UCLA Center for the Study of Evaluation, CSE/CRESST, 301 GSE&IS MAILBOX 951522, Los Angeles, CA 90095-1522; Web address: <www.cse.ucla.edu>.

Newman, D. L., & Brown, R. D. (1996). *Applied ethics for program evaluation.* Thousand Oaks, CA: Sage.

The book provides practitioners of program evaluation a theoretical model and practical guidelines for ethical decision making.

Udinsky, B. F., Osterlind, S. J., & Lynch, S. W. *Evaluation resource handbook: Gathering, analyzing, reporting data.* San Diego, CA: EdITS.

Contains 39 articles, written in outline format, providing tools and information on key issues in evaluation research. Primarily oriented toward quantitative research, the articles include research findings and real-world examples.

Witkin, B. R., & Altschuld, J. W. (1995). *Planning and conducting needs assessments: A practical guide*. Thousand Oaks, CA: Sage.

Based on their work in educational planning and evaluation, the authors provide a framework (primarily qualitative) for systematic needs assessment and application of the findings. Describes the use of such methods as focus groups, strategic planning, and futuring techniques.

Worthen, B. R., Sanders, J. R., & Fitzpatrick, J. L. (1997). *Program evaluation: Alternative approaches and practical guidelines* (2nd ed.). New York: Longman.

The authors discuss the purposes, origins, and likely future of program evaluation and provide detailed treatment of seven different approaches to program evaluation. The book gives practical guidelines for planning, conducting, and using evaluations.

SAMPLE EVALUATION RESEARCH STUDY: AN ASSESSMENT OF 23 SELECTED SCHOOL-BASED SEXUALITY EDUCATION CURRICULA

Ogletree, R. J., Rienzo, B. A., Drolet, J. C., & Fetro, J. V. (1995). An assessment of 23 selected school-based sexuality education curricula. *Journal of School Health, 65*, 186–191.

In the rest of this chapter you will read a research article that illustrates an evaluation research study. It is preceded by comments written especially for this book by the authors of the article. Then the article itself is reprinted in full, just as it appeared when originally published. Where appropriate, we have added footnotes to help you understand the information contained in the article.

Researchers' Comments, Prepared by Roberta Ogletree, Barbara Rienzo, Judy Drolet, and Joyce Fetro

The following research report is the result of a collaborative effort among four Certified Health Education Specialists (CHES)[1] with a long-standing interest in sexuality education. Judy Drolet and Barbara Rienzo have taught the professional preparation courses in human sexuality education at their respective universities for many years. Joyce Fetro, a curriculum specialist for a school district, has participated in several research and evaluation studies examining the effectiveness of sex education programs in preventing pregnancy and the spread of the human immunodeficiency virus (HIV). Roberta Ogletree's primary focus has been the study of sexual coercion. As a result of our shared interest in sexuality education, we have presented numerous papers and coauthored dozens of articles on this topic.

Our decision to undertake an evaluation of published, school-based curricula for sexuality education resulted in the report that follows. We believed that this evaluation would give teachers, curriculum specialists, administrators, parents, and caregivers information that could help them identify published curricula to better meet the needs of children, youth, and families concerning sexuality. All of us became acquainted through our membership in the American School Health Association, and more specifically, on the Council on Sexuality Education. Three of us have been recognized as Fellows of the American School Health Association (FASHA).

Our initial analysis of the curricula described in this assessment resulted in the publication by ETR Associates of *Sexuality Education Curricula: The Consumer's Guide* (Ogletree et al., 1994). The purpose of this publication was to offer, in the chart style of *Consumer Reports*, an evaluation of each individual curriculum, with no analysis or comparison offered. In addition, we included sexuality curricula designed specifically for special education.

ETR Associates provided financial support for two author meetings and clerical support for preparing the *Consumer's Guide*. While working on the *Consumer's Guide*, we also decided to carry out a more detailed and comparative assessment of the most recent and comprehensive school-based sexuality education programs, which resulted in the present article.

While this assessment does not include special education curricula, it extends well beyond the scope of the *Consumer's Guide*. In it we examine the overall results for 23 curricula that met our selection criteria. For each curriculum covered in the assessment, we sought to provide a description of the curriculum focus, the lesson format, and the contents of the curriculum package, along with publisher and cost information. We designed a matrix to show the presence or absence of specific content characteristics that we considered appropriate for the age/grade levels that each curriculum addressed. Finally, we used an evaluation matrix to rate each curriculum on each of the evaluation criteria that we had established.

The major challenge to our collaborative process was the physical distance among the four of us. One author was located on the West Coast and another on the East Coast, while the remaining two were at the same university in the Midwest. We were aware that we could meet in the same location for only two days on two different occasions during the course of the project. Although we knew that two or more of us would be able to meet periodically at professional meetings, we could not count on all four of us being together for more than the two scheduled work sessions. As a result, we had to clearly define each of our roles and ensure tight coordination of our efforts.

Rienzo had the original idea for the evaluation, having heard many requests from school personnel for information about and access to "quality" sexuality education. Teachers often report that they do not have access to suitable materials for this purpose. Because we located numerous materials that appeared questionable in terms of their effectiveness, we felt that an evaluation of existing curricula was critical.

Fetro conceptualized what the final product would look like, and her vision and coordination efforts with ETR Associates guided the project. Fetro and Rienzo took on the task of developing the curriculum attributes and evaluation criteria to be used in the actual evaluation of the curricula. They decided that the key elements necessary for an effective sexuality education program were twofold: prevention (that is, promotion of individuals' delay of the initiation of sexual intercourse), and protection (that is, provision of information to foster individuals' adoption of appropriate practices to protect themselves and others from such effects as unintended pregnancy or sexually transmitted diseases).

Ogletree and Drolet were responsible for the identification, collection, and description of available curricula that met our criteria for inclusion in the assessment.

Responsibilities for all tasks were clearly defined and assigned, which helped promote smooth, timely progress.

By the time of our first authors' meeting, we had determined the curriculum attributes and evaluation criteria and had developed easy-to-use matrices to simplify the evaluation process. The goal of our first meeting was to assess the contents of the curricula. Fetro and Rienzo worked together as a team, as did Ogletree and Drolet. Each pair examined about half the 23 curricula to identify the philosophy and content of each. Next we switched and reviewed the other half, and then we compared the results for a reliability check.

A noteworthy aspect of the project was our solicitation of teacher input as a part of the evaluation. We believed that teachers would be the group most able to offer a pragmatic evaluation of each curriculum based on their experience in actually implementing sexuality education in schools. Therefore, we each identified teachers at the four different curriculum levels (early elementary, upper elementary, middle/junior high school, and high school) who had experience in teaching sexuality education. We recruited eight teachers from Florida, seven from California, and seven from the Midwest. Each teacher reviewed the curricula at his or her teaching level for developmental appropriateness, cultural sensitivity, and ease of implementation.

At our second authors' meeting, we compiled the individual teacher evaluations and rated each curriculum on the evaluation criteria. Again we paired up. Each pair evaluated half the curricula, then the other half, and compared the results for a reliability check.

The advantages of this collaborative effort were many. All of us are members of the same profession (health education), with a similar interest in sexuality education. Our shared interests and experience ensured sufficient professional knowledge and skill to increase the soundness of our effort. Furthermore, because as a group we represent two different educational settings (public school and university), we brought different perspectives to the process, which strengthened the usefulness of the finished product. We all attacked our responsibilities with relish and maintained progress on our tasks and time line. Our ability to collaborate on the project itself also paid off in preparing these comments.

When we created the *Consumer's Guide*, we had voiced to each other several concerns that did not appear in the *Guide* but that we articulated in the "Assessment Implications" section of the report reprinted here. We are well aware of the fact that sexuality education is teeming with controversial issues, yet they are issues that we felt should be addressed explicitly, not kept hidden.

The report expressed our concern with the lack of clear philosophies in most of the curricula that we reviewed. A curriculum's philosophy needs to be responsive to community beliefs and values regarding sexuality. Perhaps most of the authors chose not to clarify the philosophy of their curricula in order to increase the acceptability of the curricula to a broad range of potential users. However, it is important that a sexuality education curriculum reflect local community values.

In study after study, support for sexuality education in the schools is reported to be over 80 percent, and more often about 90 percent. That is overwhelming support. Committees that help make decisions regarding which curriculum is to be used must truly be representative if students are to get the education that parents want them to have, instead of something that is dictated by small numbers of individuals or groups who happen to be vocal but who do not truly represent the overall community.

We also feel that it is desirable for a sexuality education curriculum to promote not only abstinence but also responsibility and protection. Some youth will hear and heed the messages encouraging abstinence. Those who do not heed those messages, however, must hear messages that promote responsible decision making and protection. Exclusive emphasis on abstinence would neglect the need to convey messages regarding safer sex practices, and might fail to portray sexuality in a positive light.

It was clear to us that the curriculum developers gave inadequate attention to evaluation of the curricula. We know that many people are fearful of or uncomfortable with the notion of program evaluation. Even so, evaluation is an essential component of curriculum development, and it should be addressed early in the process rather than as an afterthought (or no thought at all).

Sexuality educators run risks when they address controversial issues in their attempts to help youth sort out the wide range of information about sexuality available in our modern world. But wouldn't they run even graver risks by not addressing these issues? For example, sexual orientation is highly controversial, yet there is a need for all youth, as well as their teachers and counselors, to understand this issue. All the problems caused by myths and misunderstanding (including harassment and violence) make this an issue that needs to be addressed in a sexuality education curriculum.

We also feel strongly that sexuality education should affirm the positivity of sexuality and contribute to helping learners adopt health-enhancing behaviors. The Sex Information and Education Council of the United States published *Guidelines for Comprehensive Sexuality Education* (National Guidelines Task Force, 1991). These guidelines promote six key concepts that sexuality education should address: human development, relationships, personal skills, sexual behavior, sexual health, and society and culture. Under each concept, specific age-appropriate developmental goals are recommended. As we stated in the article, acquiring the necessary knowledge, attitudes, and skills to achieve these goals can best occur within a comprehensive school health program.

Our recommendation would dictate the inclusion of sexuality education in a planned, sequential, developmentally appropriate, and culturally relevant prekindergarten through twelfth-grade curriculum. Such a curriculum needs to integrate the mental, social, emotional, and physical dimensions of health, develop personal and social skills (for example, decision making and communication), and provide opportunities for students to demonstrate appropriate knowledge, attitudes, and behaviors. With this approach, human sexuality would be placed within the context of related events, rather than treated as a separate life entity. It would require programs beyond classroom instruction, including peer education and efforts to educate and involve parents, community organizations, and religious institutions. Through such efforts, the interrelationships among various risk behaviors of youth could be demonstrated, while at the same time reinforcing positive sexuality messages.

Notes

1. The designation of Certified Health Education Specialist (CHES) is a nationally recognized certification in health education offered through the National Commission for Health Education Credentialing, Inc.

References

Ogletree, R. J., Fetro, J. V., Drolet, J. C., & Rienzo, B. A. (1994). *Sexuality education curricula: The consumer's guide.* Santa Cruz, CA: ETR Associates.

National Guidelines Task Force. (1991). *Guidelines for comprehensive sexuality education: Kindergarten–12th grade.* New York: Sex Information and Education Council of the United States.

AN ASSESSMENT OF 23 SELECTED SCHOOL-BASED SEXUALITY EDUCATION CURRICULA

Roberta J. Ogletree, Barbara A. Rienzo, Judy C. Drolet, Joyce V. Fetro

Abstract

While quality sexuality education curricula are available, those responsible for selecting a curriculum may not feel confident to choose one to meet the needs of their students and community. This paper presents a method to guide in selecting sexuality education curricula as well as results from an evaluation of 23 school-based sexuality education curricula. School administrators, curriculum specialists, health educators, school nurses, teachers, and parents involved in curriculum adoption or development can use the process described to select or develop a sexuality education curriculum to meet the needs of their school and community. (J Sch Health. 1995;65(5):186–191)

During the past two decades, increases in sexuality-related behavior among teen-agers and young adults

Roberta J. Ogletree, HSD, CHES, Assistant Professor; and Judy C. Drolet, PhD, FASHA, CHES, Professor, Dept. of Health Education and Recreation, Southern Illinois University, Carbondale, IL 62901; Barbara A. Rienzo, PhD, FASHA, CHES, Professor, Dept. of Health Science Education, University of Florida, FLG-5, Gainesville, FL 32611-2034; and Joyce V. Fetro, PhD, FASHA, CHES, Supervisor, School Health Programs Office, San Francisco Unified School District, 1512 Golden Gate Ave., San Francisco, CA 94115. This article was submitted November 24, 1994, and revised and accepted for publication April 13, 1995.

Ogletree, R. J., Rienzo, B. A., Drolet, J. C., & Fetro, J. V. (1995). An assessment of 23 selected school-based sexuality education curricula. *Journal of School Health, 65,* 186–191. Reprinted with permission of the American School Health Association. Copyright © 1995 by ASHA.

prompted development of numerous sexuality education curricula. As school administrators, curriculum specialists, health educators, school nurses, and classroom teachers make decisions about sexuality education curriculum selection, a number of questions arise. Is the curriculum content developmentally appropriate for students? Does the curriculum include skill-building strategies proven effective? Do the instructional strategies address individual needs and learning styles? Can the curriculum be implemented easily and without additional teacher training?[1]

While teachers seek to assist students in acquiring the information and skills they need to avoid the negative consequences of undesired or unprotected sexual activity, many teachers do not feel adequately prepared to do so. Specifically, teachers claim they need more information on many topics, better instructional materials, and better teaching strategies.[2–4] Although quality sexuality education curricula exist, many teachers and administrators may not feel confident in their ability to select a curriculum to meet the needs of their students and community.

CURRICULUM ASSESSMENT

This project developed a method to guide selection of appropriate sexuality education curricula to meet school and community needs, and evaluated existing published and marketed school-based sexuality education curricula. This information was intended for use by school administrators, curriculum specialists, health educators, school nurses, teachers, and parents involved in curriculum adoption or development.

Curricula Identification

School-based sexuality education curricula were identified through a computerized library search using the Education Resources Information Center and referring to Publisher's Guides. In addition, resource lists were obtained from the Sex Information and Education Council of the United States (SIECUS) and the Comprehensive Health Information Database (CHID).

From the above sources, 68 curricula were identified for possible inclusion in the assessment. Selected curricula were limited to those that met the four following criteria: school-based, published and/or revised since 1985, did not focus on a single sexuality issue such as HIV infection or pregnancy prevention, and available for review by [sic] the publisher.

Twenty-three curricula met the requirements and were reviewed for this assessment. The 23 curricula were classified into age/grade levels, according to SIECUS guidelines.[5] Figure 1 lists the SIECUS levels, number of curricula at each level that were evaluated, grade classification, age range for the level, and developmental stage.

Most of the 23 curricula were designed to stand alone, although some encouraged individual instructors to add or delete material to meet student needs. Variability existed with regard to the amount

of time allotted for the curricula with as few as five lessons to as many as 43, with a mean of 18 lessons.

Assessment Process

The curricula were assessed in two ways: by evaluating the attributes of the curriculum for inclusion of key elements, and by evaluating potential quality of curricula based on how well each met criteria associated with effectiveness. Two matrices were developed to assess these aspects of curricula—the Attributes Matrix and the Evaluation Matrix.

Attributes Matrix. Fetro's[6] analysis of effective prevention programs determined that certain key elements are necessary for sexuality education program success: accurate information about the short-term and long-term physical, psychological, social, and legal consequences or risks of sexually related decisions, internal and external influences on personal health practices and the normative behavior of the peer group, activities to enhance self-esteem, opportunities to build personal and social skills, a peer helper component, and parent/guardian involvement. "Newly developed or adopted curricula should be carefully examined to determine if they include these key elements."[6] Evaluation of published curricula for inclusion of these elements would assist school personnel in identifying those that best meet their needs and thereby provide better educational offerings for students.

To identify components of an individual curriculum, an Attributes Matrix was developed with four

FIGURE 1   Summary Description of Curricula

SIECUS Level	Number of Curricula	Grade	Age Range	Developmental Stage
Level 1	1	Early Elementary	5–8	Middle childhood
Level 2	3	Upper Elementary	9–12	Preadolescents
Level 3	9	Middle/Junior High	12–15	Early adolescents
Level 4	10	High school	15–18	Adolescents

categories: philosophy, content, skill-building strategies, and teaching strategies. The underlying philosophy of each curriculum was identified/extrapolated from the purpose, goal statements, and/or objectives. Developmental messages and student activities included in the curriculum were reviewed for consistency with the philosophy statements.

Age-appropriate content was identified based on the SIECUS *Guidelines for Comprehensive Sexuality Education: Kindergarten-12th Grade*[5] and *Sexuality Education Within Comprehensive School Health Education.*[7] Since all content areas are not appropriate at all age/grade levels, certain content areas were not expected to be addressed at different levels.

Two sources were used to identify key skill-building strategies that should be included. The SIECUS *Guidelines for Comprehensive Sexuality Education*[5] was consulted, and a review was completed of evaluations of prevention programs.[8-14]

A variety of teaching methods were identified for use in both elementary and secondary health education curricula.[15-17] Variety in teaching techniques is important due to the variety in objectives, student needs and interests, and different senses used in learning.[18]

To assure reliability in the assessment of age-appropriate content attributes in each curriculum, the four authors worked in pairs to determine if each attribute was addressed in a specific curriculum. Both sets of assessments were compared. If discrepancies occurred between pairs, the curriculum was reviewed a third time to resolve the discrepancy.

Evaluation Matrix. The Evaluation Matrix consisted of criteria based on related literature describing components of effective sexuality education and health education curricula.[5,7,19-22] These criteria generally are accepted in the profession as the most relevant. Twelve distinct categories were identified for evaluating potential effectiveness of sexuality education curricula. A brief overview of these categories follow.

Comprehensiveness was measured by the *breath* [sic] and *depth* of inclusion of developmentally appropriate concepts and subconcepts as outlined in SIECUS *Guidelines for Comprehensive Sexuality Education.*[5] *Content accuracy/currency* was based on presentation of information from current research. *Skill-building variety* (*breath* [sic] and *depth*) was judged based on variety of personal and social skills included, sequential development of those skills, and opportunities for practice and rehearsal. The curriculum's use of a variety of instructional strategies to meet the diverse needs and learning styles of students was examined to assess *methods variety. Developmental appropriateness* was assessed as to whether material was related to the cognitive, emotional, and social development levels of the targeted groups.

Bias in terms of race or ethnicity, sex or gender roles, family types, sexual orientation, and/or age as well as whether a variety of social groups and lifestyles were depicted in the text and pictures were examined to evaluate *cultural sensitivity. Ease of implementation* determined "user friendliness" based on inclusion of all materials needed to implement the curriculum. The *evaluation* component considered whether the curriculum provided methods and/or instruments for evaluating student knowledge, attitudes, and skills consistent with the goals and objectives of the curriculum. *Appearance/production quality* was judged based on print quality and layout as well as likelihood of stimulating and maintaining student interest. Finally, an *overall quality* rating was given based on the 11 preceding components.

To rate curricula components for the Evaluation Matrix, the authors worked in pairs using a five-point, Likert-type scale.[a] Ratings included unacceptable, inadequate, fair, good, and excellent. In addition to comparing the authors' assessments, classroom teachers and health educators from across the country evaluated each curriculum for developmental appropriateness, cultural sensitivity, and ease of implementation. A minimum of four reviewers with teaching experience at the appropriate grade level

---

a. A Likert-type scale is a measure that asks individuals to check the extent of their agreement or disagreement (often on a five-point scale) with various statements about a topic. Here the authors are using the term simply to signify the use of a five-point rating scale.

examined each curriculum. When discrepancies occurred between the authors' ratings and the curriculum reviewers' ratings, the authors again examined the curriculum in question to resolve differences in ratings.

ASSESSMENT RESULTS

Philosophy

The percentages of curricula at each level and the type of underlying philosophy are listed in Table 1. Of the 23 curricula, 43% had an underlying philosophy of "healthy sexuality." Such a philosophy promotes sexuality as a natural and healthy part of life. Physical, psychological, emotional, social, ethical, and spiritual dimensions of healthy sexuality were addressed.

The Level 1 curriculum was determined to have a "healthy sexuality" philosophy. Of the Level 2 curricula (N = 3), 33% promoted healthy sexuality, 33% promoted abstinence only, and the philosophy of 33% of the curricula could not be determined.

Most (74%) of Level 3 and 4 curricula (N = 19) promoted abstinence as the safest and most effective means of preventing sexually transmitted diseases, HIV infection, and pregnancy. Sixty-eight percent recognized that some adolescents will have sexual intercourse and discussed using protection, if adolescents were sexually active. Sixty-eight percent also supported each individual's right and responsibility to make decisions about their sexuality. Forty-two percent expressed a philosophy of healthy sexuality.

Content

Content attributes of the selected sexuality education curricula and the percentages of curricula that addressed those attributes based on SIECUS levels are listed in Table 2.

The single Level 1 curriculum included in the study contained 75% of the 12 content attributes considered appropriate for the Level 1 age group. However, body image, sexual identity and orientation, and STD transmission issues were not addressed.

Puberty, relationships, and sexual exploitation were covered in all Level 2 curricula (N = 3). Sixty-seven percent included gender roles, reproductive anatomy and physiology, and HIV transmission and prevention. Content areas missing from all three Level 2 curricula included body image, sexual identity and orientation, parenting, STD transmission and prevention, and pregnancy prevention.

As expected, Level 3 and 4 curricula (N = 19) covered the greatest number of content attributes. All but four content attributes were covered by at least half of the Level 3 curricula (N = 9). Forty-

TABLE 1   Percentages of Sexuality Education Curricula with Underlying Philosophy by Level

	Level			
	1	2	3	4
Underlying Philosophy*	(n = 1)	(n = 3)	(n = 9)	(n = 10)
Promotes healthy sexuality	100	33	44	40
Promotes responsibility for decisions	0	0	67	70
Promotes abstinence	0	33	78	70
Promotes using protection, if sexually active	**	0	56	80
Philsophy not clear	0	33	0	0

* A curriculum may have more than one underlying philosophy.

** Not developmentally appropriate for this level.

TABLE 2 **Percentages of Sexuality Education Curricula with Content Attributes by Level**

	Level			
	1	2	3	4
Sexuality-Related Content	(n = 1)	(n = 3)	(n = 9)	(n = 10)
Puberty	*	100	67	*
Body image	0	0	22	10
Gender roles	100	67	78	40
Reproductive anatomy and physiology	100	67	89	70
Conception and birth	100	33	78	60
Sexual identity and orientation	0	0	22	40
Relationships	100	100	78	80
Parenting	100	0	56	40
Sexual expression	100	33	56	50
STD transmission	0	0	89	80
HIV transmission	100	67	89	90
Abstinence	*	33	78	80
Pregnancy prevention	*	0	67	90
STD prevention	*	0	78	70
HIV prevention	*	67	78	80
Sexual exploitation	100	100	44	60
Reproductive health	100	33	33	40

* Not developmentally appropriate for this level.

four percent addressed sexual exploitation and 33% included reproductive health issues. However, only 22% included body image or sexual identity and orientation.

Seventy-five percent of the content areas considered developmentally appropriate for high school students were included in 50% of Level 4 curricula (N = 10). However, only 10% addressed body image. Forty percent discussed gender roles, sexual identity and orientation, parenting, or reproductive health.

Skill-Building Strategies

In the category of skill-building strategies, 78% (18) of all 23 curricula including [sic] decision-making skills and identifying consequences of decisions. Also 17 (74%) addressed accessing community resources

and 16 (70%) included building general communication skills. Ten (44%) included goal-setting skills, but only seven (30%) included activities to examine perceived risk. Four curricula (17%) addressed peer norms or goal-setting skills, while two (9%) included conflict management. The percentages of curricula at each level that included skill-building strategies are identified in Table 3.

Specifically, the Level 1 curriculum did include self-esteem building skills, skills for examining the consequences of decisions, accessing community resources, building assertiveness, conflict management, and decision-making skills. Skill-building strategies omitted included examining personal values, influences on decisions, perceived pregnancy risk, and perceived STD/HIV risk, addressing peer norms, building refusal skills, and planning/goal-setting skills.

TABLE 3 **Percentages of Sexuality Education Curricula with Skills-Building Strategies by Level**

	Level			
	1	2	3	4
Skill-Building Strategy	(n = 1)	(n = 3)	(n = 9)	(n = 10)
Examining personal values	0	0	67	50
Increasing self-awareness/building self-esteem	100	33	67	40
Examining influences on decisions	0	67	89	80
Identifying consequences of decisions	100	67	89	90
Addressing peer norms	0	0	22	30
Examining perceived pregnancy risk	0	0	33	40
Examining perceived STD/HIV risk	0	0	56	50
Accessing community resources	100	67	78	70
Building general communication skills	100	67	78	60
Building assertiveness skills	100	33	100	60
Building refusal skills	0	33	78	20
Building conflict-management skills	100	0	11	0
Building decision-making skills	100	67	78	80
Building planning/goal-setting skills	0	0	44	60

TABLE 4 **Percentages of Sexuality Education Curricula with Teaching Strategies by Level**

	Level			
	1	2	3	4
Teaching Strategy	(n = 1)	(n = 3)	(n = 9)	(n = 10)
Groundrules	0	67	78	80
Anonymous questions box	0	67	67	40
Teacher lecture	100	100	100	100
Large-group discussion	100	100	100	100
Student worksheets	0	67	89	100
Journals/story writing	100	0	56	20
Cooperative learning/small group	100	67	89	100
Case studies/scenarios	100	100	100	100
Skills practice and rehearsal	100	100	100	80
Audiovisual materials	0	100	100	80
Community speakers/involvement	100	0	44	30
Peer helper component	0	0	22	0
Parent guardian involvement	0	67	67	70

None of the Level 2 curricula (N = 3) included all of the skill-building strategies. Sixty-seven percent examined influences on and consequences of decisions, how to access community resources, and building general communication and decision-making skills. Six skill-building strategies were not addressed in any Level 2 curricula: examining personal values, perceived pregnancy risk, perceived STD/HIV risk, addressing peer norms, building conflict management skills, and planning/goal-setting skills.

Most skill-building skills were included in 67% of Level 3 curricula (N = 9). Building assertiveness skills was included in 100% of curricula in this level. Eighty-nine percent included examining influences on decisions and consequences of decisions. Four skill-building strategies were addressed in less than half the curricula: building planning/goal-setting skills (44%), examining perceived pregnancy risk (33%), addressing peer norms (22%), and building conflict-management skills (11%).

Level 4 curricula (N = 10) tended to include fewer skill-building strategies than those in Level 3. Less than half included strategies to build self-esteem (40%), examine perceived pregnancy risk (40%), address peer norms (30%), and build refusal skills (20%). None addressed conflict-management skills.

Teaching Strategies

All 23 curricula include large-group discussion, lecture, and case studies. Ninety-one percent of curricula at all levels include skill practice and rehearsal as well as cooperative learning/small-group activities. Only 9% included a peer helper component. These results are reported in Table 4.

In the Level 1 curriculum, seven of the 13 (54%) teaching strategies were included. In Levels 2 and 3 (N = 12), five strategies were included in all curricula: lecture, large-group discussion, case studies/scenarios, skills practice and rehearsal, and audiovisual materials. In Level 2 (N = 3), three strategies—journals/story writing, community speakers/involvement, and peer helper component—were not used. All Level 4 curricula (N = 10) included lecture, large-group discussion, student worksheets, and case studies/scenarios. The peer helper component was missing from all 10.

Evaluation Attributes

The Level 1 curriculum earned ratings of "good" or "excellent" on all attributes with the exception of evaluation. Those attributes receiving "excellent" ratings were content accuracy/currency, developmental appropriateness, cultural sensitivity, and appearance/production quality.

All Level 2 curricula (N = 3) merited an overall quality rating of "fair." They were strong in content accuracy/currency, developmental appropriateness, ease of implementation, and appearance/production quality. Sixty-seven percent were rated "unacceptable" on evaluation, while 33% rated "inadequate."

Thirty-three percent of Level 3 curricula (N = 9) merited an "excellent" overall quality rating. Four others (44%) were rated "good" while the remaining two (22%) earned "fair" ratings. Fifty-six percent received "excellent" ratings in methods variety, developmental appropriateness, and appearance/production quality. Again, evaluation was weak with only one curriculum assigned an "excellent" rating, while five were rated as "unacceptable."

Of the Level 4 curricula (N = 10), seven (70%) were given an overall quality rating of "good" and three (30%) were "fair." The single attribute for which at least half of the curricula merited an "excellent" rating was appearance/production quality. Other strong areas were content accuracy/currency, methods variety, and ease of implementation. Consistent with other levels, the evaluation component was noticeably weak with 60% of curricula receiving "unacceptable" ratings.

ASSESSMENT IMPLICATIONS

Most authors designed their curricula to stand alone as the sexuality education curriculum for students. However, sexuality education should be a part of a comprehensive school health education program.[7] A resolution adopted by the American School

Health Association recommends that sexuality education occur within a comprehensive school health program so the interrelationship of health behaviors can be examined.[23]

Within the curricula examined in this assessment, variability existed with regard to time allotted for the curriculum lessons. While it was not within the scope of this project to assess length of time for sexuality education units, nor to prioritize content within curricula, the variation found within these curricula confirms a need for research on how these characteristics affect districts' programs. For example, are these components related to districts' ability to implement programs, how programs are incorporated, and to their effectiveness? At this point, school district personnel should strive to provide a program of sufficient length and content to meet identified needs and community standards, ideally within a comprehensive health education program.[7,23]

Few school-based curricula have been developed and published for Level 1 children, although young children at the early elementary level have sexuality education needs.[24] Only one curriculum was identified for this age group. Most curricula were developed for Level 3 and 4 (middle and high school students), perhaps due to a perception that prepubescent children have no need for sexuality education or that sexuality education is more acceptable at higher grade levels.

In most cases, the underlying curriculum philosophy had to be extrapolated from curriculum goals and objectives statements. This omission is disturbing because philosophy provides the blueprint for sexuality education curricula that should "reflect a community's beliefs about sexuality, sexuality education, and how sexuality education should be taught."[25] Philosophy provides the guiding framework, offers a rationale and justification, and can protect a curriculum from attack by opponents.[15]

For a curriculum to be identified as one with a philosophy of healthy sexuality, sexuality had to be presented as a natural and healthy part of everyday living and the curriculum had to address all dimensions of sexuality including physical, emotional, ethi-

cal, and social. Only 53% of curricula were classified in the "healthy sexuality" philosophy category. While this fact raises some concern, it may be due to failure of curriculum authors to see the need for a clearly stated philosophy. When healthy sexuality was missing as an underlying philosophy, the areas of sexual expression and reproductive health usually was missing from curriculum content.

Upon careful examination of the content of the 23 school-based curricula, it was apparent that many curricula do not provide knowledge and skills consistent with their underlying philosophy. Some curricula with philosophy statements purporting to promote responsible decision-making did not offer skills-building activities in decision-making.

The breadth and depth of content areas covered tended to be acceptable. However, body image and sexual identify [sic] and orientation were two areas that seldom were addressed. No attention was given to these topics in any Level 1 and 2 curricula (N = 4) and very little in Level 3 and 4 curricula (N = 19). Body image is one topic area that falls under the SIECUS National Task Force Guidelines' six key concepts (key concept: human development) in a comprehensive sexuality education program. Body image should be addressed at all four levels because "people's image of their bodies affect [sic] feelings and behaviors."[5] "Positive responses lay the foundation for sexual health and self-esteem by helping children feel good about their bodies, good about being male or female . . ."[24]

At the same time, sexual identity and orientation is another content area recommended for inclusion under human development and for which developmental messages are appropriate at all four levels.[5] According to one sexuality education expert, exclusion of sexual orientation from so many of these curricula likely reflects its history of being "considered inappropriate."[26] Research also demonstrates that students and teachers have inadequate knowledge about and high levels of discomfort with the topic of homosexuality.[4] Recent resolutions at the national level by professional organizations, such as the American School Health Association, Association for Supervision and Curriculum Development, and the

National Education Association, along with some educators, assert the need for schools to address the needs of gay, lesbian, bisexual, and questioning youth.[27-30] Curricula that include education about sexual orientation, particularly those with a teacher training component, will help schools meet these identified needs.

More recently published curricula are focusing greater attention on building personal and social skills. General skills for building communication, assertiveness, and decision-making capacity were given ample attention in the selected curricula. Although the depth of skill-building strategies was acceptable, the breadth of skill-building strategies was weak because specific skills, such as refusal skills and conflict-management skills, need greater attention and inclusion.

Although several skill-building strategies are appropriate for Level 1 and 2 students, they were not addressed by those curriculum authors. Given current concern with violence, conflict-management skills were noticeably absent. This absence, particularly violence in relationships, may be a reflection on the curriculum publication date since date rape and domestic violence are relatively recent public concerns.

A variety of teaching strategies should be employed to meet individual needs and learning styles of students. The selected curricula (N = 23) used at least seven different teaching strategies. However, 91% need to be revised/updated to include a peer helper component. It is important for curriculum developers to incorporate skills and teaching strategies that reflect current research findings related to effectiveness.[15,18]

Upon evaluation of the curricula, areas of strength were developmental appropriateness and appearance/production quality. Curriculum authors are writing for their levels and are producing visually appealing curricula. Content accuracy/currency and ease of implementation are additional strengths. It is apparent that evaluation, a critical component of curriculum development, is not being addressed despite its usefulness and value as a tool for measuring the effectiveness of a curriculum.

CONCLUSIONS

Although the curricula assessed in this project were generally rated "good" overall, a need exists for improvement. The upper elementary curricula (Level 2), in particular, need much improvement related to comprehensiveness, skill-building and teaching strategies, cultural sensitivity, and evaluation. Most of the selected curricula should be revised to include current, accurate information and additional skill-building strategies as well as evaluation.

While many schools and districts select prepared sexuality education curricula, many elect to develop their own. The process and instruments developed for this assessment should be helpful with such efforts. Local school districts should incorporate the process and matrices developed to examine their existing curricula [sic] for comprehensiveness and inclusion of key elements related to its potential effectiveness. In addition, school districts planning to develop their own sexuality education curricula should consider using the matrices to guide development. Another potential use of this process is for curriculum adoption, particularly if specific curricular attributes are desired such as an abstinence-based curriculum or a strong skills-building component.

References

1. Ogletree RJ, Fetro JV, Drolet JC, Rienzo BA. *Sexuality Education Curricula: The Consumer's Guide.* Santa Cruz, Calif: ETR Associates; 1994.
2. Allen Guttmacher Institute. *Risk and Responsibility: Teaching Sex Education in America's Schools Today.* New York, NY: Allen Guttmacher Institute; 1989.
3. Forrest JD, Silverman J. What public school teachers teach about preventing pregnancy, AIDS, and sexually transmitted diseases. *Fam Plann Perspect.* 1989; 21(2):65–72.
4. Richards CL, Daley D. Politics and policy: Driving forces behind sex education in the United States. In: Drolet JC, Clark K, eds. *The Sexuality Challenge: Promoting Healthy Sexuality in Young People.* Santa Cruz, Calif: ETR Associates; 1994:47–68.
5. National Guidelines Task Force. *Guidelines for Comprehensive Sexuality Education: Kindergarten-12th*

Grade. New York, NY: Sex Information and Education Council of the United States; 1991.

6. Fetro J. Evaluating sexuality education programs. In: Drolet JC, Clark K, eds. *The Sexuality Challenge: Promoting Healthy Sexuality in Young People*. Santa Cruz, Calif: ETR Associates; 1994:555–581.

7. Neutens JJ, Drolet JC, DuShaw ML, Jubb W, eds. *Sexuality Education Within Comprehensive School Health Education*. Kent, Ohio: American School Health Association; 1991.

8. Bell CS, Battjes RJ, eds. *Prevention Research: Deterring Drug Use Among Children and Adolescents*. Rockville, Md: National Institute on Drug Abuse; 1987. NIDA research monograph 63, US Dept of Health and Human Services publication ADM 87-1334.

9. Botvin GJ, Wills TA. Personal and substance use prevention. In: Bell C, Battjes R, eds. *Prevention Research: Deterring Drug Use Among Children and Adolescents*. Rockville, Md: National Institute on Drug Abuse; 1985:8–49.

10. Eisen M, Zellman GL, McAllister AL. Evaluating the impact of a theory-based sexuality and contraceptive education program. *Fam Plann Perspect*. 1990; 22(6):261–271.

11. Fetro J. *Personal and Social Skills: Understanding and Integrating Competencies Across Health Content*. Santa Cruz, Calif: ETR Associates; 1992.

12. Howard M, McCabe JB. Helping teenagers postpone sexual involvement. *Fam Plann Perspect*. 1991; 22(1):21–26.

13. Kirby D, Barth RP, Leland N, Fetro JV. Reducing the risk: The impact of a new curriculum on sexual risk-taking. *Fam Plann Perspect*. 1991;23(6):253–263.

14. Schaps E, DiBartolo R, Moskowitz J, Palley C, Churgin S. Primary prevention evaluation research: A review of 127 impact studies. *J Drug Issues*. 1981; 11:17–43.

15. Ames EE, Trucano LA, Wan JC, Harris MD. *Designing School Health Curricula*, 2nd ed. Dubuque, Iowa: William C Brown: 1995.

16. Creswell WH, Newman IM. *School Health Practice*. St. Louis, Mo: Times Mirror/Mosby; 1989.

17. Pollock MB, Middleton K. *Elementary School Health Instruction*. St Louis, Mo: Times Mirror/Mosby; 1989.

18. Fodor JT, Dalis GT. *Health Instruction: Theory and Application*. Philadelphia, Pa: Lea and Febringer; 1989.

19. Association for Sexuality Education and Training. *What Criteria can be used to Assess Sexuality (or HIV/AIDS) Curricula*. Oak Harbor, Wash: Association for Sexuality Education and Training.

20. Cassidy DC. *Family Life Education Curriculum Guidelines*. Minneapolis, Minn: National Council on Family Relations; 1990.

21. English J, Sancho A, Lloyd-Kolkin D, Hunter L. *Criteria for Comprehensive Health Curricula*. Los Alamitos, Calif: The Southwest Regional Educational Laboratory; 1990.

22. Rogers T, Howard-Pitney B, Bruce BL. *What Works? A Guide to School-Based Alcohol and Drug Abuse Prevention Curricula*. Palo Alto, Calif: Health Promotion Resource Center, Stanford Center for Research in Disease and Prevention; 1990.

23. ASHA takes a stand. *The PULSE of the American School Health Association*. 1995;16(1):4.

24. Brick P. Sexuality education in the early elementary classroom. In: Drolet JC, Clark K, eds. *The Sexuality Challenge: Promoting Healthy Sexuality in Young People*. Santa Cruz, Calif: ETR Associates; 1994:105–122.

25. LaCursia NL, Beyer CE, Ogletree RJ. What's behind the curriculum? The importance of a philosophy in sexuality education. *Fam Life Educator*. 1994;13(1): 4–9.

26. Yarber WL. Past, present and future perspectives on sexuality education. In: Drolet JC, Clark K, eds. *The Sexuality Challenge: Promoting Healthy Sexuality in Young People*. Santa Cruz, Calif: ETR Associates; 1994:3–28.

27. Blumenfeld WJ. Gay, lesbian, bisexual and questioning youth. In: Drolet JC, Clark K, eds. *The Sexuality Challenge: Promoting Healthy Sexuality in Young People*. Santa Cruz, Calif: ETR Associates; 1994:321–341.

28. Lipkin A. The case for a gay and lesbian curriculum. *The High Sch J*. 1993–1994;77(1–2):95–107.

29. Remafedi G. The impact of training on school professionals' knowledge, beliefs, and behaviors regarding HIV/AIDS and adolescent homosexuality. *J Sch Health*. 1993;63(3):153–157.

30. Sears JT. The impact of culture and ideology on the construction of gender and sexual identities: Developing a critically based sexuality curriculum. In: Sears JT, ed. *Sexuality and the Curriculum: The Politics and Practices of Sexuality Education*. New York, NY: Teachers College Press; 1992:139–156.

CHAPTER 15

ACTION RESEARCH

Tom Eppler teaches in a state that requires all public school teachers to earn continuing professional development (CPD) units in order to retain their teaching credential. He decides to take an in-service course on motivational techniques to earn some of the CPD units that he needs.

The course instructor has asked that each teacher do a project of his or her own design as the major assignment. Some teachers plan to write a paper based on library research; some are developing curriculum units. Still others, like Tom, want to try out some of the motivational techniques that the course covered to determine their effectiveness for their students.

They would like to document their efforts in a way that is useful for them and their colleagues.

Action research is an ideal method of investigation for teachers in Tom's situation. As you will find in this chapter, action research enables teachers, administrators, school counselors, and other education practitioners to investigate and improve their performance in systematic, personally meaningful ways. You will learn that action research draws upon the techniques of investigation that you have studied in other chapters of this book, but for the purpose of improving local practice rather than producing theory or scientific generalizations.

OBJECTIVES

After studying this chapter, you will be able to

1. describe the advantages of conducting action research in order to solve an educational problem.
2. explain several approaches that are commonly used to conduct action research in education.
3. describe the seven steps in the model of action research that is presented in this chapter.
4. describe nine differences between formal research and action research.
5. describe the conditions that facilitate action research projects.
6. state criteria for judging the quality of an action research project.

KEY TERMS

collaborative action research
proactive action research
responsive action research

THE PURPOSE AND ADVANTAGES OF ACTION RESEARCH

Action research is a type of systematic investigation conducted by practitioners involving the use of scientific techniques in order to improve their performance. It would require considerable training to master any of the types of research described in other chapters in this book and then to conduct a research study and report it at a conference or in a research journal. However, action research is well within the reach of education practitioners. This is because the quality of an action research project depends on how well the project serves a practitioner's immediate, local needs rather than on how well the project fulfills the criteria of sound research design and interpretation that preoccupy professional researchers. The steps of an action research project are fairly simple, and they are grounded in the practitioner's interests and workplace.

The term *action research* can be traced back to the social psychologist Kurt Lewin (1946). Lewin was concerned that the methods and findings of academic researchers could result in scholarly publications that had little effect on society or the work of practitioners. Therefore, he developed action research as a type of investigation that could be used by community members and professional practitioners to promote positive social change. For example, in a study conducted during World War II, Lewin brought together groups of housewives to discuss the possible use of organ meats in meal preparation. This was during a time when the U.S. government wanted to promote cheaper cuts of meat because of a shortage in normal meat supplies. The study demonstrated the value of group discussion in changing people's attitudes about, and subsequent actions toward, a significant social issue.

Action research was widely used in the 1940s and 1950s, but its use in the United States declined thereafter as the term *research* came to be equated primarily with laboratory-based experimentation and statistical significance testing. Australian and British educators brought action research back to the fore in the 1960s, and they continue to use this approach extensively. Today action research is becoming increasingly popular in the United States, especially among teacher educators.

Action research has at least five advantages for education professionals. First, it contributes to the theory and knowledge base needed for enhancing practice. When educators carry out their own action research, they learn to reconstruct educational theory and findings in terms that are understandable to them, and to develop more effective practices in their work settings. They then might read formal research reports about similar practices with more comprehension and insight. Furthermore, action research can serve as a wellspring of creativity for new practices. For example, Stephen Jobs and Steve Wozniak were not trained as researchers, but their tinkering in a spare garage—a type of action research—led to the development of the personal computer. Closer to home, Madeline Hunter was the director of the laboratory school at UCLA when she began informally experimenting with ways to improve teachers' classroom instruction. Her individual creativity resulted in the development of a method of instruction called ITIP (Instructional Theory into Practice—Hunter, 1994). This method has had a major impact on contemporary teaching practice, and it has stimulated various formal research studies of its effectiveness (e.g., Pratton & Hales, 1986).

Second, action research supports the professional development of practitioners by helping them become more competent in understanding and applying research findings, and in carrying out research themselves when appropriate. By carrying out action research, practitioners not only develop needed skills in doing research, but also improve their ability to read, interpret, and apply the research of others.

Third, action research can build a collegial networking system. Action research often involves several educators working together; students, parents, and others also may be involved. The communication network that develops during the research project helps reduce the isolation often experienced by the individual teachers, administrators, or specialists working in the education field. The improved communication patterns foster support and sharing of information among practitioners, and thus continue to benefit both staff and students over time.

Fourth, action research helps practitioners identify problems and seek solutions in a systematic fashion. It requires practitioners to define problems clearly, to identify and try out possible solutions systematically, and to reflect on and share the results of their efforts. Thus, action research shows practitioners that it is possible to break out of the rut of institutionalized, taken-for-granted routines and to develop hope that seemingly intractable problems in the workplace can be solved.

Fifth, action research has the advantage that it can be used at all levels and in all areas of education. It can be carried out in specific classrooms or departments, throughout an educational institution, or at the regional or national level.

The benefits of action research have been documented in various projects reported in the literature. For example, Cathy Caro-Bruce and Jennifer McCreadie (1995) described a district-wide initiative in which 40 elementary and middle-school teachers conducted action research projects over the course of a school year. Caro-Bruce and McCreadie reported that the teachers

> . . . have become more reflective in their practice. They have grown professionally, developing a greater sense of efficacy and professionalism. They also have learned that their experience and expertise are valid and valued. . . . Some teachers have found that when they shared their projects with their students, the students became involved and contributed meaningfully to the research. (p. 162)

Elizabeth Soffer (1995), a school principal, described an action research project in which she experimented with ways to reduce some serious discipline problems at her school. She concluded that

. . . my project has benefited both me and the school. Not only did my disciplinary practice improve, but the overall disciplinary climate improved. In their evaluations of my performance, teachers noted improvement but still marked discipline as an area of concern. (p. 124)

Anchalee Chayanuvat and Duangta Lukkunaprasit (1997), two English-language instructors at a university in Thailand, conducted an action research project to determine how best to design a course that would further develop the English-language skills of gifted students entering their university. As a result of their project, they developed recommendations for a special class for these students:

Among other things, we have recommended more emphasis on speaking and writing, inclusion of external reading materials which are more difficult and challenging, and exploitation of students' learning activities outside class in our English program, e.g., an oral discussion following the watching of an assigned film. We also suggested that we should make the students aware of the learning skills that have helped them better their English, and also encourage them to develop other learning skills not many of them think very useful or necessary. (p. 164)

These few examples illustrate the range of action research projects that can be undertaken and the benefits that they can yield. We recommend that you conduct your own review of the literature, using the methods that we described in Chapters 2, 3, and 4, in order to identify successful action research projects in areas of professional practice that are of interest to you.

APPROACHES TO ACTION RESEARCH

Over time, various researchers have developed different approaches to action research, depending upon the goals and values that they seek to emphasize.

Some approaches to action research emphasize the professional development of educators in school settings (Noffke, 1992; Kemmis & McTaggart, 1988) or in higher education (Zuber-Skerritt, 1992). One focus of this type of action research is the enhancement of practitioners' reflection on their teaching so that they can become more sensitive to discrepancies between their intentions and actual practices (e.g., Dadds, 1995; Whitehead, 1993).

Other approaches to action research focus on encouraging practitioners to undertake investigations to help build a knowledge base for their own teaching and for their fellow practitioners (Elliott, 1991), or in the service of school reform (Hollingsworth & Sockett, 1994). Several journals (e.g., *Educational Action Research, Teaching and Change, Teacher Research*) specialize in reporting action research projects that education practitioners have conducted.

Still other approaches emphasize the use of action research to promote democratic forms of education and collaboration among teachers, students, and others in the educational community. Some of these approaches (e.g., Carr &

Kemmis, 1988) look to critical theory as a source of inspiration and concepts for framing action research projects. Among projects of this type are interventions designed to empower aboriginal peoples to assume greater control over their schooling (e.g., Bunbury, Hastings, Henry, & McTaggart, 1991).

The work of Kurt Lewin has inspired other action researchers who desire to promote democratic, collaborative forms of education. Richard Sagor (1992) and Richard Schmuck (1997) are two prominent action researchers in this tradition. Sagor emphasizes collaboration as a feature of action research. His approach to designing and conducting an action research project involves five steps: (1) A group of practitioners define a problem of concern to them; (2) They collect data about the problem; (3) They analyze the data for themes and patterns; (4) They report the results of their data analysis to significant stakeholders; and (5) They prepare and implement a plan for action.

Schmuck's approach to action research is more differentiated than Sagor's, involving a distinction between proactive and responsive action research. In proactive action research, projects are initiated when practitioners try out new practices that interest them. In contrast, a responsive action research project begins with the practitioner carefully diagnosing the situation and collecting data before proposing a new practice for tryout. Schmuck identified six steps in each type of action research, as shown in Table 15.1.

In this chapter we describe an action research model that includes seven steps. The model is inclusive of the various aspects of action research that different proponents of this approach have identified. At the same time, it is more

---

TABLE 15.1 The Steps of Proactive and Responsive Action Research

Proactive Action Research

1. A new practice is tried in order to have a different effect on others, or to bring about better outcomes.
2. Hopes and concerns are incorporated into the new practice.
3. Data are collected regularly to keep track of participants' reactions and behavioral changes.
4. The meaning of the data is checked.
5. Reflection on alternative ways to behave is carried out.
6. Another new practice is tried, and the sequence circles back to step 1, with revisions to the original practices to improve their effectiveness.

Responsive Action Research

1. Data are collected to diagnose the situation.
2. The data are analyzed for themes and ideas for action.
3. The data are distributed to others, and changes to be tried are announced.
4. A new practice is tried, in order to have a different effect on others.
5. The ways in which others are reacting are checked.
6. Data are collected to diagnose the situation. The sequence circles back to step 1, with the general methods now supplemented with specific questions on the particular issues being addressed.

Source. Adapted from Figure 3.3 on pp. 32–33 and Figure 3.4 on pp. 35–36 of: Schmuck, R. A. (1997). *Practical action research for change.* Arlington Heights, IL: IRI/Skylight.

closely linked to the traditions and procedures that formally trained researchers follow in conducting research. (These are the traditions and procedures described in the preceding chapters of the book.) The seven steps of the action research model are: (1) defining the problem, (2) selecting a design, (3) selecting research participants, (4) collecting data, (5) analyzing data, (6) interpreting and applying the findings, and (7) reporting the findings.

We consider the collection and analysis of data (steps 4 and 5) to be the most important aspects of action research. Most practitioners periodically reflect on their work or try new strategies. However, they rarely collect systematic data to determine the problems that their clients are experiencing, what discrepancies might exist between their intentions and their practices, or whether their strategies are working. The defining feature of action research is that it involves the collection and analysis of personally meaningful, local data as a guide to improving practice.

We will now explain the steps of the model by presenting three examples of actual action research projects. The examples illustrate the different contexts in which action research can be used, the various types of educators who do it, and the wide range of problems in professional practice that can be addressed.

EXAMPLES OF ACTION RESEARCH

Example 1. Determining Common Student Concerns in Studying

Summary. Two of the authors of this book (Joyce Gall and M. D. Gall) asked the teachers who participated in our study skills instruction workshops over a one-year period to administer a checklist of student concerns when they returned to their classrooms, and to send us the results. Responses were tallied for each classroom, and the concerns most commonly checked by elementary, middle/junior high, and high school students were identified.

1. *Define the problem.* We have offered teacher workshops on study skills instruction for many years. In our workshops we give teachers a 14-item checklist that they can use to assess their students' most common concerns about study and schoolwork. Some years ago we wished to determine what concerns were most common among elementary, middle, and high school students who responded to the checklist. We thought that it would be useful to include this information when presenting the checklist to teachers in the future, and that it would help us decide which aspects of study skills instruction to emphasize in our workshops.

2. *Select a design.* In every workshop or course that we conduct, we administer the checklist to participants (primarily teachers) and recommend that they in turn administer the checklist to their own students. We decided to conduct a survey by asking the teachers to send us their results. We promised to compile the results for students at each school level—elementary, middle/

junior high, and high school—and to forward them to all teachers who participated in the survey.

3. *Select research participants.* The volunteer sample consisted of all teachers who participated in our courses and workshops over a one-year period and who accepted our invitation to send us the results of their administration of the checklist to their classes. After about eight months we had received usable responses from five classrooms in four elementary schools, nine classrooms in four middle schools, and seven classrooms in three high schools. Most of the schools were in Oregon, where we live, but there were also schools in Canada and Panama.

4. *Collect data.* The primary measuring instrument in this project was the Checklist of Student Concerns from the *Study for Success Teacher's Manual* (Gall & Gall, 1995), which is shown in Figure 15.1. Each student who responds to the checklist is asked to check the five items (out of the 14 that are listed) of greatest personal concern. Each teacher had received a copy of the checklist in our workshop or course and had been encouraged to make copies to administer to students. We gave the teachers self-addressed return envelopes. We asked them to send us their students' responses to the checklist and information about the number of students, their grade level, and the subject of the class in which the checklist was administered.

5. *Analyze the data.* To analyze the data, we calculated the percentage of students in each classroom who checked each of the 14 items by dividing the

Check the FIVE (5) items below that most concern you about schoolwork. (If any of your top concerns aren't listed, write them in the blank spaces below item #14.)

_____   1.   Feeling too tired to study.
_____   2.   Feeling like I'm wasting my time in school.
_____   3.   Procrastinating instead of studying.
_____   4.   Handing in my assignments late.
_____   5.   Misplacing materials I need for doing my schoolwork.
_____   6.   Not understanding what the teacher is talking about.
_____   7.   Not remembering what the teacher talked about in class.
_____   8.   Knowing the answer to the teacher's question but not feeling comfortable to speak up.
_____   9.   Forgetting what I read soon after I read it.
_____   10.   Coming across words in my reading that I don't understand.
_____   11.   Can't seem to get ideas for my writing assignment.
_____   12.   When I write something, feeling it's not as good as it could be but not knowing how to make it better.
_____   13.   Getting nervous about a test coming up.
_____   14.   Running out of time before I finish a test.
_____   15.   _____
_____   16.   _____
_____   17.   _____
_____   18.   _____
_____   19.   _____

FIGURE 15.1   **Checklist of student concerns from the *Study for Success Teacher's Manual***

Source. From Unit 1, Lesson 1, p. 2 of: Gall, M. D., & Gall, J. P. (1995). *Study for success teacher's manual* (5th ed.). Eugene, OR: M. Damien Educational Services.

number of students checking that item by the total number of students who had filled out the checklist. We ranked the items for each classroom, with the item checked most often receiving a rank of 1, the item checked next most often receiving a rank of 2, and so forth. We then made a master ranking of the items checked most often by elementary, middle, and high school students by averaging the rankings across all the classrooms at each level, weighted by the number of students responding in each classroom.

The top three concerns for elementary students were (1) getting nervous about a test coming up, (2) not understanding what the teacher talked about in class, and (3) coming across words in their reading that they don't understand. The top three concerns for middle or junior high school students were (1) feeling too tired to study, (2) getting nervous about a test coming up, and (3) knowing the answer to the teacher's question but not feeling comfortable in speaking up. The top three concerns for high school students were (1) procrastinating instead of studying, (2) feeling too tired to study, and (3) when they write something, feeling it is not as good as it could be but not knowing how to make it better.

6. *Interpret and apply the findings.* Our interpretation was that students at different school levels have somewhat different concerns about study and schoolwork, corresponding to the new challenges that confront them at each level of schooling. We concluded that teachers could help their students deal with these concerns more effectively if they explicitly taught the students study skills that address those concerns.

We now routinely present these results to teachers in our workshops and courses. We point out, however, that each classroom in our sample had somewhat different results. Thus we continue to recommend that teachers carry out their own action research by administering the checklist to their students and collecting data as they try out classroom procedures and instructional activities to help students with various study concerns.

7. *Report the findings.* We prepared tables showing the rankings of the checklist items for each classroom in the sample. We wrote a three-page letter summarizing the study and sent it, along with the tables, to all teachers who had sent us data for our survey. As mentioned above, we also present the findings in each workshop or course we offer.

Example 2. Fostering Cooperative Learning Among Elementary Students

Summary.   In this project, Patricia Wood (1988), an elementary school teacher, arranged cooperative work groups in her classroom. She and several colleagues carried out observations as students worked on a series of classroom activities. Based on her analysis of the data from each classroom activity, she introduced modifications to subsequent activities and to the cooperative learning procedures used to complete them. Wood found that the modifications, along with the students' accumulated practice in working cooperatively, ultimately led to a high degree of success in students' ability to learn cooperatively.

1. *Define the problem*. Wood had supervised a student teacher who conducted an action research project on cooperative learning. She then enrolled in a university course that required her own action research. Wood selected cooperation as her problem to study, for four reasons: (1) She perceived the children in her class to be having a difficult time working and playing together cooperatively; (2) She saw the social groups in the class as strongly defined and closed; (3) She had read articles about cooperative activities but had not found time to organize a sequence of lessons for promoting cooperation; and (4) She wanted to continue the thinking about cooperation that she had engaged in earlier when supervising her student teacher.

2. *Select a design*. Wood's design involved guiding small groups of students in isolated cooperative activities for two weeks. Then a framework emerged for the remainder of her project. It consisted of finding at least one block of time each week to introduce a specific cooperation skill, assigning a small-group activity in which children could apply the skill, and debriefing the activity by conducting a class discussion on how the children had worked together. The cooperative activity was scheduled for a time when three other adults were available to assist in data collection—a student teacher, an assistant teacher, and a parent or other staff person in the school.

Examples of Wood's cooperative small-group activities were: (1) giving a title to a picture showing an Olympic sport; (2) generating ideas about making a group decision and then creating a list of three jobs that all the students' mothers had done; (3) hearing a presentation about the difference between critiquing people's ideas and criticizing the people themselves and about how to include everyone in a group activity, and then designing an imaginary map that included a title, map key, island, and lake; and (4) after a pre-activity of listing cooperative comments in a recording of a previous class discussion, cooperatively building a structure that had to include several features (e.g., a bridge or tunnel) by using a different medium (e.g., Legos, blocks, or sand).

3. *Select research participants*. The research participants were Wood's elementary classroom students, who ranged in age from six to eight and included both boys and girls.

4. *Collect data*. All the adult participants in Wood's action research project had an opportunity to observe the students' cooperative behavior in the small-group activities and then to record the results in ways that would be most helpful in the reflection phase of the research. The data collection consisted of (1) daily recordings noting students' social patterns, (2) anecdotal records of what children did and said during structured group activities, (3) samples of group projects, and (4) tapes of children talking about working together at various times during the semester.

5. *Analyze the data*. After each activity, Wood reflected by looking at the data and trying to understand what happened and why. By examining outcomes that contradicted her beliefs about teaching, she was led to question and then to reaffirm her philosophy of teaching and to become more receptive to suggestions and observations from colleagues.

6. *Interpret and apply the findings.* After reflection on each activity, Wood used her impressions to design a new plan of action for the next cooperative activity. For example, the published report describes her reflections following the first activity:

> The picture-titling activity was a disaster. All of the adults were shocked at how challenging this simple task had been. . . . I was confused about what to do next. I hadn't found a curriculum or teacher's guide to give me specific activities or lessons to try. Are there skills that I should teach about cooperation or should children struggle through and discover the process? (pp. 141–142)

Based on these reflections, Wood had students generate ideas about making a group decision before their next cooperative activity. After this activity, her reflections included these comments:

> I shared my project with another colleague. She helped me realize that I was approaching the problem at a level that was too advanced for this age group (something that I was feeling also). I then read two articles about the impact of children's play on group problem solving. Reencouraged, I decided to continue teaching group skills and roles starting at a more appropriate level. (p. 143)

7. *Report the findings.* Wood's action research project was carried out in part as her project for a university course. She wrote a paper for the course, which along with some later reflections on action research, was subsequently published as an article in the *Journal of Education for Teaching* (Wood, 1988).

Example 3. Identifying the Critical Factors That Superintendents Consider in Administrative Restructuring

Summary.   James Martin and George Wilson (1990) conducted semistructured interviews of superintendents in nearby school districts who had carried out a successful restructuring of the district's administrative staff. Martin is a school district supervisor for secondary education, and Wilson is a professor of educational administration. Using a composite list of organizational and environmental factors derived from a literature review, they identified which of these factors were most critical in the superintendents' restructuring efforts. They also made recommendations for superintendents of other districts who are considering administrative restructuring.

1. *Define the problem.* Current pressures to improve schools and the fact that many school administrators are approaching retirement age have led many school districts to adopt some form of administrative restructuring. Martin and Wilson wished to determine the critical factors considered by school superintendents whose school districts are undergoing this process. They

believed that this information would make other superintendents aware of the most important factors involved in restructuring, and help them reflect on decisions to restructure before actually attempting to reorganize the administrative hierarchy.

2. *Select a design*. Martin and Wilson chose the action research method "because it is the conventional approach for a study which intends to provide information which is practical and directly relevant to an actual situation in the working world" (p. 35). They interviewed superintendents whose districts had undergone administrative restructuring during their tenure.

3. *Select research participants*. Eligible superintendents in western Pennsylvania constituted the sample. Superintendents were considered eligible based on the following factors: (a) The district had completed a successful restructuring of the administrative staff within the tenure of the current superintendent; (b) At least six central office administrators were employed in the district; and (c) The superintendent played a prominent role in the experience.

4. *Collect data*. A semistructured interview was designed. Direct questions and probes were constructed and field tested, and each interview was recorded on audiotape and transcribed.

5. *Analyze the data*. The interview responses were categorized and then compared with a list of factors that had been identified through a review of literature as being critical to administrative restructuring of a school district. The list included both environmental factors (which were not considered to be under the direct control of the superintendent) and organizational factors (which were considered to be under the direct control of the superintendent).

6. *Interpret and apply the findings*. The major environmental factors identified as considerations in administrative reorganization were declining enrollment, local culture, school board influence, and politics. The major organizational factors identified were organizational politics, long-range and strategic planning, and teacher empowerment. Of the 12 reasons that superintendents offered for restructuring, four dominated: (a) declining enrollment, (b) increased attention to curriculum, (c) a need to strengthen a particular area of the organization, and (d) existence of a long-range plan that called for restructuring.

Martin and Wilson reached ten conclusions based on their research, including the following: (1) Few superintendents saw a need to use a consultant for assistance in designing an administrative reorganization plan; (2) Superintendents were aware of the political nature of their positions and of the need to generate a support base for their actions through effective communication with stakeholders; and (3) Superintendents should engage in more long-range planning and become more proactive in planning for change.

7. *Report the findings*. Martin and Wilson wrote an article reporting their study that was published by *Planning and Changing*, a journal that specializes in analyses of current trends in educational administration (Martin & Wilson, 1990). Publication of the study was consistent with their purpose for doing the research, namely, to develop and disseminate guidelines for superintendents considering administrative restructuring within their school districts.

DIFFERENCES BETWEEN FORMAL RESEARCH AND ACTION RESEARCH

Although both formal research and action research aim to increase knowledge and understanding, they differ in important ways, nine of which are described hereafter.

1. *Skills needed by the researchers.* Most researchers need extensive preparation before they are able to use formal research methods skillfully. Individuals who conduct quantitative research studies need to be skilled in using various measurement techniques and inferential statistics. Those who conduct qualitative research studies need specialized skills in collecting and interpreting intensive data on selected cases. By contrast, most education practitioners can carry out action research, whether on their own, in collaboration with colleagues, or with the aid of a research specialist. They do not need advanced skills in research design and interpretation. In the second case example described earlier, an elementary school teacher was the researcher. In the study that is reprinted in this chapter, Beverly Jatko, a teacher of a talented and gifted program in a number of schools in one school district, designed and conducted action research with involvement from three fourth-grade teachers whose students participated in the research.

2. *Goals of the research.* The goals of formal research are to develop and test theories, and to produce knowledge that is generalizable to a broad population of interest. Action research, by contrast, is aimed at obtaining knowledge that can be applied directly to the local situation. It also has the goal of contributing to the preparation, and hence the competence, of education practitioners. In the second case example, Wood's primary goal was to improve her own teaching by fostering cooperation among her students. Her purpose in publishing her study was primarily to encourage other teachers to use action research to improve their own teaching, rather than to present generalizable findings about cooperative learning in elementary school instruction.

3. *Method of identifying the problem to be studied.* In formal research, problems for investigation usually are identified through a review of previous research. Researchers often study problems of personal interest, but they tend to be problems that do not relate directly to the researchers' work responsibilities. In action research, however, educators investigate precisely those problems that they perceive to be interfering with their efficacy, and perhaps that of their colleagues, or that involve important goals they want to achieve in their work. In the third case example, we assume that Martin, as a supervisor for secondary education, had a personal commitment to improving the procedures by which superintendents design administrative restructuring efforts.

4. *Procedure for literature review.* In formal research, an extensive literature review, focusing on primary-source materials, is necessary. The review is needed in order to give the researchers a thorough understanding of the current state of knowledge about the problem being investigated. This knowledge enables them to build on the knowledge accumulated by others in designing

and interpreting their own research. For action research, researchers need only to gain a general understanding of the area being studied. Hence, a more cursory literature review, focusing on secondary sources, usually is adequate. In the second case example, all of Wood's references appear to be books or reports providing guidelines for conducting action research; none are concerned with cooperative learning. If she had intended her study to be a formal study of cooperative learning, she would have needed to do a thorough review of research in this area before conducting her study.

5. *Selection of research participants.* In formal research the researchers aim to investigate a representative sample of the population, so as to increase the generalizability of their findings and to eliminate sampling bias as a factor confounding the meaning of the findings. Action researchers, however, do their research with the students or other individuals with whom they typically work. In the first case example, our research participants were teachers who participated in our workshops and courses and chose to send us the results of their use of the Checklist of Student Concerns.

6. *Research design.* Formal research emphasizes detailed planning to control for extraneous variables that can confuse the interpretation of the results. For example, in quantitative research, major attention is given to maintaining similar conditions in experimental and control groups, except for the variable being compared. Rigorous controls also are used in qualitative research, especially in checking the credibility and trustworthiness of the data that are collected. Thus the time frame for carrying out formal research typically extends over a period of many months. Action researchers, by contrast, plan their procedures less extensively, freely make changes that appear desirable during the action phase of the research, and move quickly between data collection, interpretation, and modification to their practice. Little attention is paid to control of the situation or elimination of sources of error or bias. Because the researchers tend to be personally involved, bias typically is present. However, it is not generally viewed as a problem, because the results are intended for use primarily by those very researchers.

In the second case example, Wood continued to redesign her study as she obtained and reflected on the results from each cooperative learning activity. However, the action research project that is reprinted at the end of the chapter used a more formal research design, involving descriptive statistics. We see, then, that sometimes an action researcher also wants to encourage other practitioners to undertake their own action research on the same problem, so as to foster more general and more rapid improvements to education practice. Such researchers are likely to use a more rigorous research design, and to produce a publishable report of their work.

7. *Data-collection procedures.* Researchers who do formal studies, particularly quantitative researchers, attempt to collect their data using valid and reliable data-collection methods. As a result, they might first evaluate available measures and conduct a pilot study of the measures prior to conducting the main study. Action researchers, instead, often use convenient methods of data collection (e.g., observing or talking with students) and available measures, such

as those routinely administered during classroom instruction (e.g., conventional classroom tests). In the case examples presented above, the only measure utilized was the Checklist of Student Concerns. This measure has not been subjected to extensive testing to determine its reliability or validity.

8. *Data analysis*. Formal research often involves complex analysis of data, but raw data rarely are presented. Tests of statistical significance are usually emphasized. In formal qualitative research, the researcher engages in careful, reasoned analysis of case data to determine their consistency with the theory in which the research is grounded. Most action research, however, involves simpler analysis procedures, with a focus on practical significance rather than statistical significance. Also, the subjective opinion of the researchers often is weighted heavily. All the examples of action research in this chapter involve only descriptive statistics (means and percentages in the first case example, percentages and cumulative problem-solving scores in Jatko's reprinted article) or general observations that are not quantified or grounded in theory (in the second and third case examples).

9. *Application of results*. Researchers who do formal research emphasize the meaning and the theoretical significance of their findings and possible directions for further research. They may discuss the practical implications of their results, but this is not a requirement or a reflection on the study's merit. In action research, however, the practical significance of the results is of foremost importance. Action researchers report their findings mainly in an effort to clarify how the findings might affect their own work and to inform their colleagues about the possible implications for professional practice. Although colleagues might adopt strategies found to be effective in someone else's action research project, they usually do so without concern for careful replication of the original research procedures.

FACILITATING CONDITIONS FOR ACTION RESEARCH

For action research to be successful, practitioners should have sufficient time, the opportunity to collaborate with colleagues, an openness to change, and both the opportunity and commitment to write about the research process and outcome. In addition, they should value data collection and analysis as a guide to improving professional practice.

Educators usually need release time from some of their normal work responsibilities to carry out an action research project. The time is needed for designing the project, doing it, reflecting on and sharing the findings, and modifying one's work practices according to what has been found. Educators who enroll in graduate degree programs often find it desirable or necessary to obtain a leave from their regular positions during their period of study. Thus it is not surprising that much action research by educators occurs as a part of university coursework.

As we explained in the preceding section, some approaches to action research emphasize the desirability of collaboration among education practitioners in conducting an action research project. The collaborative circle can also extend to include the clients for whom the research activities are intended. Schmuck (1997) describes many helpful techniques (e.g., positive social support, critical friendship, probing conversation) to develop the type of collaborative relationships that facilitate this approach to action research.

In their guide for teacher-researchers, Marian Mohr and Marion MacLean (1987) describe their experience in helping teacher-researchers form small groups (four or five teachers) based on common interests. Each group typically included teachers from various grade levels and disciplines. They met regularly; got to know one another and one another's work; and discussed their individual research logs, data, analysis, findings, and drafts of reports. Through this process, both individual and joint action research projects were defined, applied, refined, and reported. Mohr and MacLean documented the positive effects of this process on both teachers' classroom instruction and their planning and research skills.

Another type of support needed by educators is an openness to modifying their daily routines. This means that administrators, school staff, and clients need to feel sufficient trust and freedom to acknowledge and confront workplace practices that need improvement. Once consensus on action has been reached, all stakeholders need to give the teachers or other implementers support for trying it. Verbal support might be sufficient, but depending on the action research project, implementers also might need materials, facilities, assistants, and release time.

Action researchers need to respect data as a guide to action. Practitioners who rely exclusively on their personal belief systems as a guide to their practice are not likely to undertake or support action research projects. Such practitioners will be reluctant to challenge those belief systems by comparing them with diagnostic data at the start of an action research project or with data collected after a new practice has been tried. On the other hand, administrators and staff members who respect data as a guide to practice will encourage each other to engage in ongoing action research projects. When this happens, the organization as a whole improves.

Finally, action researchers should have the opportunity to report about their projects. Stephen Tchudi (1991), describing the teacher-as-researcher model of action research, notes:

> The teacher-as-researcher is, above all, a writer. Such a teacher designs questions about curriculum and teaching, creates trials or experimental lessons and activities, collects a variety of evidence, and writes up the findings. The data collected by this teacher/writer/researcher are wide-ranging. . . . While gathering these data, the teacher keeps a learning log, recording and analyzing in the manner of the ethnographic researcher, as a participant observer. (p. 86)

As we explained in the preceding section, various journals publish action research projects conducted by education practitioners. Also, the findings of such projects increasingly are reported at professional conferences.

JUDGING THE QUALITY OF ACTION RESEARCH

The conditions that facilitate action research, described in the preceding section, suggest five criteria that can be used in judging the quality of an action research project. Each criterion is explained below.

1. *Adequate time commitment.* An essential criterion is that the action researcher is able to devote sufficient time to carry out the project. It takes time to reflect on a problem and a possible solution, to design a suitable data-collection method, and to collect and analyze data. Reporting the findings to one's colleagues requires an additional commitment of time. If an action researcher proceeds hastily because of other work demands, the quality of the project is likely to suffer.

2. *Collaborative effort.* If the action research project involves two or more colleagues, the quality of their collaboration can be examined. Were the most appropriate colleagues and clients involved? Were steps taken to ensure that a sound climate for interpersonal communication and mutual assistance was established? Did colleagues and clients derive a lasting benefit from the project? If questions such as these can be answered affirmatively, the action research project can be considered successful.

3. *Openness to change.* As we indicated earlier, action researchers need to work in an environment that is open to the modification of routines through systematic experimentation. Therefore, we can examine the extent to which the action researcher was free to try out creative solutions, versus being constrained by organizational norms or reluctant colleagues and administrators. While an open environment does not ensure creativity in designing and conducting an action research project, it is more likely than a closed environment to permit possibilities for educators' professional growth and the tryout of innovative solutions.

4. *Quality of data collection and analysis.* Perhaps what most differentiates research, including action research, as a guide to action from more routine or common-sense approaches is the practitioners' systematic collection and analysis of specific information about the problem that they are addressing and their attempts to solve the problem. We can examine the types of information that they obtained, the sources used to obtain the information, and whether it appears to be valid or trustworthy information. The availability of descriptive statistics, such as a table showing the percentages of different types of students who demonstrate a desired behavior before and after the action researcher institutes a new practice, is a persuasive indicator of a sound action research project. We can also ask whether the conclusions that were drawn from such information appear to be reasonable.

5. *Impact on practice.* Effective action research should result in improvement in the researchers' practice. We can examine whether the action researchers were persuaded by their data to change their practices, and whether those changes appear to have had a beneficial effect on the practitioners themselves, their colleagues, or their clients.

To judge the quality of an action research project, you might have little information available to you. Such a project typically is not presented in a complete, formal report. This limitation can be overcome by interviewing the action researcher—and perhaps colleagues and clients, too—in order to learn how the steps of action research that we described earlier in the chapter were carried out. It might also be possible to examine some of the data that the action researcher collected.

CONCLUDING THOUGHT

Now that you have read several examples of action research, we would like you to consider doing your own action research to improve your effectiveness as an educator. One situation in which action research is appropriate occurs when you have read the research literature and have arrived at a tentative solution to a problem that has arisen in your work, and you now wish to put the solution into practice. Using action research will enable you to collect your own evidence of the solution's effectiveness. Or perhaps you have not found a satisfactory solution to your problem in the research literature. In that case, you might develop a tentative solution and test it by conducting an action research project.

SELF-CHECK TEST

1. Action research has all the following purposes except
   a. supporting the professional development of practitioners.
   b. building theory and generalizable knowledge.
   c. building a collegial networking system among educators.
   d. helping practitioners identify problems and seek solutions systematically.

2. The quality of an action research project is *least* dependent on its
   a. use of well-designed methods of data collection and analysis.
   b. promotion of collaboration between the researcher and his or her colleagues.
   c. contribution to the knowledge base for education.
   d. impact on the researcher's practice.

3. Encouraging practitioners to reflect on their teaching most clearly serves the goal of action research involving
   a. the development of a knowledge base to guide education practice.
   b. the creation of collaboration among members of the educational community.
   c. the promotion of practitioners' professional development.
   d. the involvement of research experts in guiding teacher research.

4. The problem to be addressed by an action research project typically is identified by
   a. practitioners' consideration of obstacles that exist to achieving their work goals.
   b. reviews of the education literature.
   c. a systematic needs assessment.
   d. consultation with the researcher's supervisor.

5. When action researchers seek to publish their studies, their primary goal most likely is to
   a. present generalizable findings to the widest possible audience.
   b. encourage other educators to undertake action research projects on the problem that they investigated.
   c. demonstrate the rigor that action research can involve.
   d. publicize the solution to an immediate, local problem.

6. For an action research project to be considered a success, it is important that the researchers
   a. receive extensive preparation to develop their research knowledge and skills.
   b. review the education literature before designing the action to be taken.
   c. discuss the theoretical implications of their results.
   d. apply the findings to their own practice.

CHAPTER REFERENCES

Bunbury, R., Hastings, W., Henry, J., & McTaggart, R. (1991). *Aboriginal pedagogy: Aboriginal teachers speak out*. Geelong, Victoria, Australia: Deakin University Press.

Caro-Bruce, C., & McCreadie, J. (1995). What happens when a school district supports action research? In S. E. Noffke & R. B. Stevenson (Eds.), *Educational action research: Becoming practically critical* (pp. 154–164). New York: Teachers College Press.

Carr, W., & Kemmis, S. (1988). *Becoming critical: Educational, knowledge and action research*. London: Falmer.

Chayanuvat, A., & Lukkunaprasit, D. (1997). Classroom-centered research at Chulalongkorn University Language Institute. In S. Hollingsworth (Ed.), *International action research: A casebook for educational reform* (pp. 157–167). London: Falmer.

Dadds, M. (1995). *Passionate enquiry and school development*. London: Falmer.

Elliott, J. (1991). *Action research for educational change*. Philadelphia: Open University Press.

Gall, M. D., & Gall, J. P. (1995). *Study for success teacher's manual* (5th ed.). Eugene, OR: M. Damien Educational Services.

Hollingsworth, S., & Sockett, H. (1994). *Teacher research and educational reform*, the ninety-third yearbook of the National Society for the Study of Education, Part I. Chicago: NSSE.

Hunter, M. (1994). *Enhancing teaching*. New York: Macmillan.

Kemmis, S., & McTaggart, R. (1988). *The action research planner* (3rd ed.). Geelong, Victoria, Australia: Deakin University Press.

Lewin, K. (1946). Action research and minority problems. *Journal of Social Issues, 2*(4), 34–46.

Martin, J. A., & Wilson, G. (1990). Administrative restructuring: The first step in public school reform. *Planning and Changing, 21*(1), 34–40.

Mohr, M. M., & MacLean, M. S. (1987). *Working together: A guide for teacher-researchers.* Urbana, IL: National Council of Teachers of English.

Noffke, S. E. (1992). The work and workplace of teachers in action research. *Teaching and Teacher Education, 8,* 15–29.

Pratton, J., & Hales, L. W. (1986). The effects of active participation on student learning. *Journal of Educational Research, 79,* 210–215.

Sagor, R. (1992). *How to conduct action research.* Alexandria, VA: Association for Supervision and Curriculum Development.

Schmuck, R. A. (1997). *Practical action research for change.* Arlington Heights, IL: IRI/Skylight.

Soffer, E. (1995). The principal as action researcher: A study of disciplinary practice. In S. E. Noffke & R. B. Stevenson (Eds.), *Educational action research: Becoming practically critical* (pp. 115–126). New York: Teachers College Press.

Tchudi, S. (1991). *Planning and assessing the curriculum in English language arts.* Alexandria, VA: Association for Supervision and Curriculum Development.

Whitehead, J. (1993). *The growth of educational knowledge: Creating your own living theories.* Bournemouth, England: Hyde.

Wood, P. (1988). Action research: A field perspective. *Journal of Education for Teaching, 14,* 135–150.

Zuber-Skerritt, O. (1992). *Action research in higher education: Examples and reflections.* London: Kogan Page.

RECOMMENDED READING

Bernhardt, V. L. (1998). *Data analysis for comprehensive schoolwide improvement.* Larchmont, NY: Eye on Education.

Targeted at non-statisticians, the book shows school personnel how to gather, analyze, and report information about their school and use the information in school improvement efforts.

Hollingsworth, S. (Ed.) (1997). *International action research: A casebook for educational reform.* London: Falmer.

The chapters in this book provide an overview of how action research is being implemented by education practitioners in different countries. Many examples of specific action research projects are described.

Noffke, S. E. (1997). Professional, personal, and political dimensions of action research. In M. W. Apple (Ed.), *Review of research in education* (vol. 22, pp. 305–343). Washington, DC: American Educational Research Association.

The author provides a comprehensive overview of the development of action research in education and other fields, and the various approaches to action research that have developed around the world.

Sagor, R. (1992). *How to conduct collaborative action research.* Alexandria, VA: Association for Supervision and Curriculum Development.

The author describes explicit procedures for conducting action research to improve schools and classrooms. The book is based on the author's experience with a consortium of schools in the northwestern United States involved in collaborative action research.

Schmuck, R. A. (1997). *Practical action research for change.* Arlington Heights, IL: IRI/Skylight.

This book provides many practical procedures for designing and conducting an action research project. The author provides many specific examples of action research projects that practitioners can use as a guide for designing their own studies.

SAMPLE ACTION RESEARCH STUDY: USING A WHOLE CLASS TRYOUT PROCEDURE FOR IDENTIFYING ECONOMICALLY DISADVANTAGED STUDENTS IN THREE SOCIOECONOMICALLY DIVERSE SCHOOLS

Jatko, B. P. (1995). Using a whole class tryout procedure for identifying economically disadvantaged students in three socioeconomically diverse schools. *Journal for the Education of the Gifted, 19,* 83–105.

> In the rest of this chapter you will read a research article that illustrates an action research study. It is preceded by comments written especially for this book by the author of the article. Then the article itself is reprinted in full, just as it appeared when originally published. Where appropriate, we have added footnotes to help you understand the information contained in the article.

Researcher's Comments, Prepared by Beverly Jatko

Background

During my first year as a teacher in an inner-city talented and gifted (TAG) program, I was constantly questioned by the classroom teachers about the curriculum I was using, and about the whys and hows of the selection process for TAG. I felt unable to give the teachers a satisfactory answer, and I myself was not happy with the results.

For the most part, I had depended on my coworkers for advice in designing my TAG curriculum and in selecting the children to participate in the TAG program. Children with proven academic abilities who attended schools in more affluent communities were easily identified by their test scores and thus were selected for participation in TAG. But what could I do when few if any test scores revealed abilities among inner-city students that needed to be addressed by my program? Did this mean a TAG program was not needed by children in inner-city schools, or just that I did not know how to identify the children who needed the program?

The inner-city classroom teachers were willing to share their ideas about how to identify children in their classes who possessed what they saw as the characteristics of deserving (that is, gifted) students, namely, being quiet, cooperative, and obedient. At the same time that I was discussing with the classroom teachers their ideas about giftedness, I was also conducting a review of the research literature on the characteristics of economically disadvantaged students that are indicative of giftedness. During my literature search I discovered the "whole classroom tryout technique." I sensed that it would be an ideal way to view children in a natural setting and give everyone in the classroom an opportunity to display the gifted traits that I hoped to uncover.

I pulled all my ideas together to present to the classroom teachers in the form of a joint research project to be carried out in three elementary schools in my area. The teachers were eager to participate, because in this project all students would be considered deserving (gifted) until they demonstrated otherwise.

One problem remained: What program could I use to give students who were creative in thinking, bubbling with ideas, and curious about life in general an opportunity to shine, in contrast to the teachers' more stereotyped ideas of the "model" (that is, a quiet, cooperative, and obedient) student? I decided that the Future Problem Solving (FPS) program was the answer. The teachers and I worked out a weekly schedule for my "tryouts," and the fun began.

Experiences

Working in each classroom, with the classroom teacher serving as an observer, was an eye-opening experience—for the teacher! Teachers began to see students in a new light due to the different activities and expectations that FPS involves. In a regular classroom setting, teachers usually have a set answer in mind—what they consider to be the "right" answer. By contrast, our activities had no right or wrong answers. The activities that the students engaged in at times depended on individual inspiration and at other times required teamwork. Students whom the teachers had barely noticed before began to emerge. Instead of focusing on the most quiet, cooperative, and obedient students, the teachers began to comment about the students who were the most curious, eager, imaginative, creative, and ingenious during the various FPS activities.

While working individually on activities, one student at Battle Road generated two to three times as many responses as any of the other students from his class. The amazing thing about this child is that he was labeled SED (severely emotionally disturbed), and was not functional in terms of regular classroom expectations. His teacher had never seen this child in a successful school situation prior to my study. Before the year was over, he won the fourth-grade geography bee and was awarded first prize in an art contest sponsored by the Parent Teacher Association of his school. His previous teachers, who had warned his new teacher about the difficulties in store for her, asked what had happened to turn this child around. Teachers began to see other children "turn around," too.

Aftermath

The FPS program publishes a large number of materials designed to stimulate higher-level thinking. The classroom teachers who had participated in the study with me requested copies of all these materials so that they could use similar activities to stimulate thinking with their classes in the future. The students with whom I worked truly enjoyed the format and style of the FPS materials. Teachers also appreciated the fact that these materials can be adapted to the educational level of every student.

Implications and Future Directions

The impact of this study reached beyond the participating classrooms. Many teachers and students from other classrooms heard about what we were doing and how much fun we were having. I was asked to share this experience with the entire school the following year. I shared materials and strategies with everyone who showed an interest. The techniques can be used every day in the regular classroom. Students enjoy the change from being passive learners to being active learners.

In addition to the effect that this study had on the participating schools, I learned valuable information about how to select children from lower socioeconomic areas for a TAG program. In the future, if I try something similar to the "whole classroom tryout," I will not try to form intact teams for a TAG program but instead will use it to select individuals to participate in TAG.

I hope that other researchers will adapt the "whole classroom tryout" technique with classroom teachers in lower socioeconomic areas as a way to stimulate thinking and enthusiasm among their students. The classroom teachers in my study told me that their students looked forward to these activities every week. A teacher in any subject area or grade level would have no difficulty incorporating creative thinking into each class period using these activities.

I once observed a teacher in a lower-level radio/TV class for sixth graders demonstrate how a sponge is like a piece of audio- or videotape, that is, it could hold only so much before it is full. After class, she asked me what I thought about the higher-level thinking that she required of her students. When I told her that I had seen no evidence of higher-level thinking, she reminded me of the sponge demonstration. I explained to her that she could have stimulated the desired thinking from her students if she had asked how *they* think a sponge might be like a piece of audio- or videotape. After listening to their brainstorming session, the teacher probably would have been impressed to hear the *many* ways a sponge can be like a piece of audio- or videotape. After all, learning is more fun, and it takes students to a higher level of thinking, when it involves not just demonstration but participation.

USING A WHOLE CLASS TRYOUT PROCEDURE FOR IDENTIFYING ECONOMICALLY DISADVANTAGED STUDENTS IN THREE SOCIOECONOMICALLY DIVERSE SCHOOLS[a]

Beverly Porter Jatko

The identification of children from low-income populations for participation in talented and gifted programs has been problematic for the field of gifted education. An action research approach was used to evaluate the effectiveness of a nontraditional identification technique for economically disadvantaged students known as the "whole classroom tryout technique." Fourth-grade students from three socioeconomically diverse schools were selected for participation in Future Problem Solving (FPS), one component of this teacher's talented and gifted curriculum. The students selected by the tryout technique competed on Future Problem Solving against students selected by traditional means. Data were collected: (a) to chart the progress of individual teams, (b) to compare the performance of teams within each school based on the mode of selection, and (c) to compare the teams as a competitive sample. The analysis showed that the whole classroom tryout can be an

Beverly Porter Jatko is a teacher in East Tennessee.

Journal for the Education of the Gifted. Vol. 19, No. 1, 1995, pp. 83–105. Copyright © 1995 The Association for the Gifted, Reston, Virginia 22091.

Jatko, B. P. (1995). Using a whole class tryout procedure for identifying economically disadvantaged [gifted] students in three socioeconomically diverse schools. *Journal for the Education of the Gifted, 19,* 83–105. Reprinted with permission of the University of Tennessee. Copyright © by the Association for the Gifted.

a. For clarity, the title of the article would include the word "gifted" before the word "students"; this word was left out through an oversight.

effective means to identify economically disadvantaged students for a talented and gifted program and could be used in combination with traditional techniques.

INTRODUCTION

As an inner-city teacher in a talented and gifted program (TAG), I became concerned that economically disadvantaged children with gifted traits were being overlooked because of established methods of identification. I talked with inner-city classroom teachers (who had the responsibility of nominating children for the TAG program) about the relationship of certain traits to the goals of the program and the Future Problem Solving program, a part of the required curriculum. Anecdotal evidence from those teachers suggested that the children deemed by them to be the most creative and the best problem solvers on day-to-day tasks were not always selected for the talented and gifted program. Even though I encouraged those teachers to make recommendations, I received the name of only one student. Children who were missed by the established methods of identification did not have access to the TAG program, and I did not have an opportunity to observe their gifted traits in another setting. This situation was troublesome and presented an opportunity for me to conduct research aimed at addressing the problem of identification and selection of economically disadvantaged gifted students for participation in my portion of the talented and gifted program.

The Problem

The identification and selection of students from low-income populations has been a persistent problem for the field of gifted education. These populations are consistently underrepresented in talented and gifted programs. While critics of gifted education call the programs elitist and skewed to the wealthy white child (Margolin, in press), proponents argue for more sensitive identification measures to increase the proportion of children from low-income populations in these programs (Borland, 1989; Mitchell, 1988; Richert, 1987). When stan-

dardized tests are the only measure used to identify giftedness, socioeconomic factors can account for large differences in incidence of identification. Because economically disadvantaged students are overlooked by standardized tests that are insensitive to their gifted traits, and established methods used for identification are not as successful in identifying them as we would like (VanTassel-Baska, Patton, & Prillaman, 1989), nontraditional identification techniques have been proposed. Coleman (1985) noted that children get missed for a variety of reasons ranging from instruments that do not appropriately measure their abilities, to misguided teacher judgment, to children whose behavior is not deemed indicative of giftedness. He suggested that a school should construct a sign advertising a gifted program and allowing the children who decided that they were "it" to sign up. VanTassel-Baska et al. (1989) recommended that all children be allowed to tryout on gifted activities in the regular classroom. The "whole classroom tryout" technique gives all children an equal opportunity to participate in "gifted-like" activities and to be judged on their readiness to perform in a specific component of a talented and gifted program's curriculum. I decided to use the tryout technique in addition to the established methods to identify children for the program.

Rationale for the Study

My study examined the utility of a tryout technique for the identification of economically disadvantaged children in my TAG program. Three pieces of information influenced my conception for the study: (a) the Tennessee Comprehensive Achievement Program (TCAP) scores, (b) traits of gifted children, and (c) the Future Problem Solving (FPS) program. The school system in which I teach uses the TCAP, a standardized test, as a primary means to identify students for the TAG program. The TCAP test measures a student's progress (compared with other students on the same grade level) in five subject areas: reading, math, language, science, and social studies. A total battery score is derived from the reading, math, and language scores. The students receive six national percentile scores, one in each subject area plus one in total battery. The percentile scores indicate the percentage of students who performed equal to or below that student's level (Tennessee State Department of Education, 1994). Two scores at or above the 96th percentile automatically qualify a student for TAG. Because the number of students who automatically qualify for this program from inner-city (lower socioeconomic) schools has been significantly smaller than the number who qualify from schools in the more affluent suburbs, teachers adjusted the TCAP criterion for inner-city schools to one score at the 96th percentile. Even with this change, very few economically disadvantaged students were identified, yet classroom teachers reported that they had bright children in their classrooms.

Economically disadvantaged children can exhibit traits associated with being gifted that cannot be identified by standardized test scores. Barbara Clark (1983) listed 21 traits that can be observed but not always verified through testing of economically disadvantaged gifted children. A subset of the 6 traits seemed promising:

1. alertness, curiosity,
2. initiative, eagerness to do new things,
3. imagination in thinking,
4. flexibility in approach to problems,
5. originality and creativity in thinking, and
6. ability to solve problems by ingenious methods.

These traits were relevant to the TAG program because they are necessary for the successful performance of students in FPS. The association between traits and performance is significant because authorities (Coleman, 1985; Feldhusen, Asher, & Hoover, 1984; Gallagher & Gallagher, 1994) in gifted education have argued that selection should be based on a program's objectives.

Future Problem Solving, one component of the TAG program, is a competitive program designed to encourage the development of creative-thinking and problem-solving skills. I wondered how children,

identified by my observation of these untestable gifted traits, would compare on the FPS program to children identified through TCAP scores. If children identified by these traits performed as well on FPS as the children identified by TCAP scores, then I would have a new and useful identification procedure for disadvantaged children. If economically disadvantaged children identified by these traits performed as well on FPS as advantaged children identified by using TCAP scores, then the procedure would have even greater value for the program. The value would lie in dispelling the idea of some teachers that economically disadvantaged children in inner-city schools cannot be competitive against children from the more affluent suburbs. To insure that the technique picked children appropriate for this TAG program, I compared (using performance in the Future Problem Solving program) economically disadvantaged students selected by using the whole classroom tryout technique (a) to students selected in the same school using standardized test scores for identification and also (b) to children from an affluent community who were selected using standardized test scores.

Research Questions

In this study I combined the ideas of identification by gifted traits, the importance of these traits to my curriculum, and the tryout technique. This combination offered all of the students in three classrooms an opportunity to display their untestable gifted traits on problem-solving activities as a tryout for the TAG program by becoming part of FPS.

I had one general and three specific questions for this study. My general question was: Will the whole classroom tryout technique prove to be effective in identifying children for the TAG program? My three specific questions were:

1. Would selection for Future Problem Solving through a tryout or by TCAP scores produce a more effective team?
2. Would socioeconomic factors play a role in the effectiveness of the selection process or in the rate at which problem-solving skills were acquired?

3. Could inner-city teams be competitive with teams from the more affluent suburbs based on equal access to instruction and materials?

Because my interest was to make a practical difference for the children in the schools in which I taught within a larger TAG program and because my teaching situation was not generalizable to those described in the literature, action research was the research methodology that was appropriate for gathering data to answer these questions.

METHODOLOGY

Action research has been called "an emergent and potentially powerful form of research" (Tomlinson, 1995). This type of research, however, is not new. Even though teachers in Great Britain have used this practice for more than 30 years to gather data on aspects of the curriculum that they considered questionable, action research has not been favored in the United States. In recent years, teachers in the United States who believe that traditional research does not address their concerns have begun to use this avenue for gathering practical information.

Comparing Action Research with Traditional Research

Even though action research and more traditional forms of research share some common goals of increasing knowledge and improving understanding, these methods differ in the training of researchers, in the goals of research, in the research process (problem identification, purpose, and application of research), and in the application of the findings (Borg, Gall, & Gall, 1993). Whereas extensive training and experience are necessary for traditional academic research to be conducted properly, most teachers possess the skills necessary to be an effective action researcher. Traditional research strives to produce a generalizable theory; action research seeks to produce knowledge for a specific problem or situation. An investigator in typical academic research tends

to identify a problem through familiarity with the literature; however, an investigator in action research selects problems that interfere directly with her or his work. The selection of a sample is either random or purposeful in traditional research; but in action research, the students with whom the practitioner is already working comprise an appropriate sample to directly answer his or her questions. Empirical research seeks statistical significance while action research focuses on practical significance. Traditional research emphasizes theory plus implications for further research, but action research emphasizes applying the findings immediately to improve one's teaching situation (Borg et al., 1993). This ability to immediately improve a situation was attractive to me because the action research process can be more readily incorporated into one's teaching than is the process of more traditional research.

The Process

Several models for conducting action research that divide the process into steps have been proposed (Borg et al., 1993; Perry-Sheldon & Allain, 1987; Wood, 1988). Tomlinson (1995) has proposed a more user-friendly model. She advocates a "systematic reflection" time period in which the teacher asks a question such as, "How might I modify what I am doing so that it is more effective?" The teacher begins to take notes about questions that arise and then writes observations into a daily journal. Notes and journal entries are reviewed periodically so that patterns become evident. During this time period, Tomlinson suggests that teachers may examine information in publications.

Systematic reflection may last for an extended period of time, even months, before the teacher is ready to pose an initial research question. At this point, the teacher is directed to consult with colleagues or a university professor if possible. The additional contacts may provide suggestions for data collection methods or resources that are likely to make the action research project more workable.

In the data gathering phase, detailed records and information are essential so that the experience can be preserved and verified. Questionnaires, checklists, surveys, interviews, tape recordings, and anecdotes, in addition to a detailed journal, are a few of the suggested means for gathering data. The use of multiple data sources supports the credibility of the research for those with whom the information is shared when the project is complete.

The next phase is data gathering and data analysis, and these occur almost simultaneously in action research. As the teacher observes and notes occurrences, patterns begin to emerge. Tomlinson (1995) suggests that the teacher find a "critical friend" to help guide the analysis and to help expand the teacher-researcher's thinking. At the conclusion of this phase, the teacher implements the changes and may well begin the cycle all over again to judge the effectiveness of the changes. The final phase of action research is a formal sharing of insights. Even though improvement of one's teaching is of primary importance in this type of research, sharing information that is gained from this hands-on approach may "have a ripple effect beyond the individual classroom and practitioner at the core of the research endeavor."

A PLAN OF ACTION

Anecdotal evidence from inner-city teachers concerning their opinion that the most creative and best problem-solving students were often overlooked during the identification and selection process for Future Problem Solving and TAG precipitated a period of systematic reflection. I asked myself, "What can I do to improve my identification and selection process for inner-city children so that a larger percentage of these children with untestable gifted traits will have an opportunity to be included in the talented and gifted program?" Approximately five months were spent researching the literature on disadvantaged gifted populations and identification techniques.

Review of the Literature

Teacher recommendation, parent referral, and peer nomination are commonly used to supplement standardized test scores in the identification process. The most frequently used technique is teacher recommendation (Butler & Borland, 1980; Cox, Daniel, & Boston, 1985; Marland, 1972). For teacher recommendation to be a useful technique in identifying students, the checklist of behaviors that the teachers are asked to complete should directly address the characteristics of the students being sought for the program (Borland, 1989). This checklist reduces the chance that a teacher will use a recommendation just as a reward for appropriate behavior instead of basing the recommendation on a child's gifted behaviors.

In addition to teacher recommendation, parent referral can be a useful tool for including children in a talented and gifted program (Jacobs, 1971; Richert, Alvino, & McDonnel, 1982). Parents, knowing their children better than anyone else, are in a good position to fill in gaps in information concerning developmental history, hobbies, activities, and interests (Borland, 1989; Clark, 1983). A problem occurs with economically disadvantaged populations because most disadvantaged students have already been screened out of the identification process before the parent information can be requested (Richert, 1987).

To take advantage of all forms of information available to assist in the identification process, information gained from peer nominations is especially beneficial in locating children with leadership potential and/or creativity (Richert, 1987). Phillip Powell, an educator who recommends additional identification measures for students outside the mainstream of middle-class culture, uses peer nominations first. He believes that children can identify the smartest student in the classroom, just as the street-smart kid can identify the one most likely to be a problem solver and/or survivor (Cox et al., 1985). Rather than asking direct questions concerning who the child thinks is gifted, one needs to ask who has the best ideas for games on the playground or who would be the most helpful on a science fair project (Borland, 1989). The dissatisfaction with the results from the traditional techniques led me to explore the possibility of using nontraditional means to improve the identification process. I wanted to try a technique that allowed me to take a more active role in the identification process.

The whole classroom tryout technique provided the active role in the identification process that I was seeking. This technique (designed to be used by the classroom teacher) promotes the search for gifted traits in students who are not currently in the talented and gifted program (VanTassel-Baska et al., 1989). All students in a regular classroom setting are given an opportunity to perform on "gifted-like" activities. These activities are selected and designed to show readiness for a specific program that is a part of the talented and gifted curriculum. This approach equalizes opportunity for access to the TAG program based on matching a student's traits with those that are needed for successful performance. Armed with this information and Piirto's (1994) recommendation that all students be given an opportunity to experience creative-thinking activities with the ideas and products from these activities being used in the identification and selection process of students for FPS, I developed my plan of action and formed my research question. The general question was: Will the whole classroom tryout technique prove to be effective in selecting children for the program? After formulating the research question, I selected the schools and the individual classrooms for my study.

Schools

The study was conducted in a TAG program of one school system. Three schools in which I teach (that serve elementary-aged students) participated in this study: Old Bay, Battle Road, and Fiske Hill. These schools were selected because of the divergent socioeconomic backgrounds of the school populations. The socioeconomic status of the school population was determined by the percentage of children eligible for the free or reduced-price lunch program.

Fiske Hill is located in an affluent community. The number of children who qualify for a free or reduced-price lunch is approximately 7% of the school population. Battle Road is located in a lower-middle income community with approximately 54% of the school enrollment qualifying for meal assistance. Old Bay is in an older, less stable community with 75% of the school enrollment currently eligible for the free and reduced-price lunch program.

The standardized test scores fall along predicted lines. Seventeen percent of the students at Fiske Hill score at or above the 95th percentile in total battery on the TCAP test and qualify for the TAG program. The percentage falls below seven at Battle Road and falls below three at Old Bay. The fourth-grade TCAP distribution of stanine scores largely mirrors the free-lunch data. Stanines seven through nine represent above-average performance. The student performance at this level was: Fiske Hill (53%), Battle Road (23%), and Old Bay (21%).

Subjects

The students eligible for this study were in the fourth grade (ages 9–10). I selected this grade because the Future Problem Solving program becomes competitive at the fourth-grade level and because fourth grade is the first opportunity for FPS at these schools. None of the children had prior exposure to the FPS process as confirmed by a student survey.

I requested one fourth-grade classroom of students from each of the three schools for participation in the FPS program. The classroom at Fiske Hill contained 25 students with 9 students qualifying for TAG (based on *two* scores at the 96th percentile). The classroom at Battle Road contained 23 students with 5 qualifying for TAG (based on *one* score at the 96th percentile). The classroom at Old Bay contained 28 students with 5 students qualifying for TAG (based on *one* score at the 96th percentile for 4 students plus 1 student with a teacher recommendation). The classrooms were representative of the school population concerning TCAP scores by the percentage of students who had qualified for TAG.

Overview of Future Problem Solving

Future Problem Solving is an international program begun by E. Paul Torrance in 1974 that is designed to encourage creative thinking. FPS consists of a problem (fuzzy) situation that is set 25 or more years into the future. The students (working in teams of four) research the topic, brainstorm possible problems that could arise from this situation, generate alternative solutions for the most important problem, establish a criteria grid to evaluate solutions, and arrive at a best solution. The program encourages the development of teamwork, communication, and research skills (Crabbe, 1991). During the course of one competitive year, two practice problems and one qualifying problem are posed to all FPS teams. Evaluators from across the state assemble three times each year to score these packets. Feedback from the two practice problems is designed to help the competing teams improve their problem-solving skills for the qualifying problem.

Materials for the Study

The primary source of the skill-building exercises used with whole classroom tryout technique was the 1989 edition of *The Activity Book* by Anne B. Crabbe (1989). Other sources were "Puzzles for Problem Solvers" from *Middle Years* (Leighton, 1993a, 1993b) and "Autumn Brainstorming" from *Challenge* (Fisher, 1994) magazine. The materials used in the study were those published by the international FPS *Readings, Research, and Resources* (Future Problem Solving Program, 1994). The Tennessee FPS (1994a, 1994b) published two booklets for all competitive teams. *Practice Problems for 1994–1995* contains a copy of the first and second practice problems for the 1994–1995 school year.

Gathering Data

The Tryout Phase. After the fourth-grade classrooms were selected, I used a systematic approach to teach every student the initial skills needed for Future Problem Solving. Brainstorming, one of the initial skills in the problem-solving model, is an essential technique to learn (Crabbe, 1989). All of the students (randomly sorted into four or five-member teams) were encouraged to generate and to share ideas (no matter how wild or crazy the idea) with teammates. Activities designed to stimulate brainstorming included: list as many items as possible that are red, list as many things as possible that are associated with summer, and plan a party with a guest list containing

people from history. The activities, while designed to stimulate brainstorming, gave each student in these three classrooms an equal opportunity to display eagerness to do new things, to use imagination in thinking, to try flexibility in their approach to problems, to exhibit originality and creativity in thinking, and to demonstrate an ability to solve problems.

While directing these activities, I kept a journal to record my observations of student behaviors as well as collected raw data that chronicled each student's progress. Students also had an opportunity to exhibit teamwork as well as leadership skills; both are necessary on a problem-solving team.

All of the students in each classroom worked in teams for a 45-minute period each week for four consecutive weeks. At the end of the four-week whole classroom tryout period, I reviewed my daily journal. It proved to be invaluable. Instead of having to rely on mental notes to cover the four-week tryout, the journal (complete with observations, anecdotes, behaviors, and comments from the children) brought the entire process vividly into mind. After combining the data in my journal with the raw scores collected from the students' participation on activities, I made a list of the non-TCAP students who had exhibited the traits (or at least the potential to exhibit these traits) necessary for success in FPS. I needed a minimum of five non-TCAP students to have a four-member (plus one alternate) FPS team. I asked each of the three classroom teachers to also compile a list of non-TCAP students whom they had observed displaying these same traits (the six traits mentioned by Clark) on day-to-day tasks. We compared our lists; and surprisingly, after the teachers became aware of the traits to watch for, our lists of non-TCAP students were almost identical.

There was no doubt about the students in the classroom at Old Bay; the teacher and I listed the same 5 students. These students were obvious to both of us because of their eagerness, imagination, and creativity. The teacher at Battle Road and I listed 5 students each, 4 of whom were common to both lists. This made a 6-student team; however, the 1 student from the classroom teacher's list that was not on my list asked to be excused from the process at the end of the first session as part of the non-TCAP team. The teacher at Fiske Hill and I had a more difficult time compiling a list of non-TCAP students for a team. Due to the large number of TAG students in the classroom at Fiske Hill (9 of her 25 students), the remaining pool of students from which to choose a non-TCAP team was much smaller than at the other schools. Each of us listed the same 3 students. To have a non-TCAP team with 1 alternate, we had to select 2 more students. We discussed the remaining 13 students and reached a consensus on 2 of them. All of the teams were set; I would have seven, 5-member teams (four TCAP and three non-TCAP), to work with for my study (the extra TCAP team is the result of so many students qualifying for TAG from Fiske Hill).

The non-TCAP students (whose names appeared on the combined lists) plus the students who had qualified for TAG (based on TCAP scores) were pulled out of the regular classroom (beginning the fifth week) to form FPS teams and begin preparation for the competition. The TCAP students were placed on one FPS team, and the non-TCAP students (selected due to the display of gifted-like behaviors) were placed on another FPS team. To maintain the anonymity of the team members, each team chose a code name that followed them for the duration of the study. Now the students were ready to learn the problem-solving process.

The FPS Phase. I introduced the topic for the first practice problem: Cities. At each school, we read and discussed the research material as a group so that reading levels would not affect the understanding of the vocabulary or the articles. The first practice problem required completion of only three of the six steps: generate possible problems based on the "fuzzy situation," choose an underlying (most important) problem, and generate possible solutions. Each team spent four class periods preparing problem-solving packets and learning steps one, two, and three of the process.

Upon conclusion of practice problem number one, I typed the seven team packets into the FPS problem-solving format. This prevented the recogni-

tion of handwriting over the course of the study. I gave the FPS packets to the state director of the Tennessee FPS so that they could be evaluated. She scored them individually and evaluated them collectively as a sample. Due to the use of code names for the teams, the state director was not aware of members' names or school affiliation. The results were used to chart the progress of the teams within this study. On the return of the evaluated packets from the state evaluator, I discussed with each team the positives and negatives of the team performance. This process was repeated for the second practice problem, Homelessness, except that the teams spent five class periods and steps four (develop criteria), five (evaluate solutions based on the criteria), and six (write a best solution) of the problem-solving process were also completed.

The third and final practice problem was approached differently because it was used as a qualifying problem for the FPS State Bowl. The students and I researched and discussed the third topic, Kids and Violence, for two class periods. The third class period lasted for two and one half hours. We reviewed the entire FPS process with a question-and-answer session. The student teams were then placed in seclusion for a two-hour block so that they could complete the FPS packet as a team. The teams were in individual rooms that had glass panels on the doors so I could observe their group behavior as well as individual behavior during this process. I offered no help but was available in case problems arose. This last session not only required the knowledge of the process but also the self-discipline of the team members to work together and stay on task.

DATA ANALYSIS AND RESULTS

Throughout this study, the FPS teams were evaluated individually and then ranked as a competitive sample on each practice problem. I used the data that were generated in three distinct ways: (a) to chart the progress of the individual teams, (b) to compare the performance of the TCAP and non-TCAP teams within each school, and (c) to compare all of the teams as a diverse and competitive sample. Because improving the identification and selection process for disadvantaged gifted children was my main goal, the knowledge that I gained from the progress of the individual teams and from the comparison of TCAP and non-TCAP teams within the same inner-city schools was more significant to the program than the competitive rankings among the seven teams representing three schools. In this section I have presented the data analysis and results in this order: (a) team information, (b) individual team scoring on each practice problem (depicted by graphs that also show a comparative rate of progress between the schools as a competitive sample), (c) the difference in performance on each of the three practice problems between TCAP and non-TCAP teams within the individual schools, (d) the point spread among the teams on the three practice problems, and (e) individual team assessment profiles based on FPS data and observations of the strengths and weaknesses of the team members.

Team Information

Table 1 offers an overview of the seven teams that participated in my study. Each team consisted of four competing members plus one alternate (in case of the loss of a competing member) except for the TCAP-2 from Fiske Hill, which did not have an alternate. The vast difference in the team averages for total battery on the TCAP test are [sic] evident. I was

not aware that such a drastic difference existed until the study had been completed. Also, note the strong association between the percent of team members receiving meal assistance (free or reduced-price lunch) and the total battery average for the team.

Future Problem-Solving Evaluation Format

Because the evaluation of each of the six steps in FPS results in a numerical assessment, one can determine the progress of each team on the individual steps by comparing the increase or decrease in points earned from one practice problem (PP) to the next. The students received points (scores) on practice problem number one for (a) generating possible problems, (b) choosing an underlying problem (UP), and (c) generating possible solutions. Practice problems two and three received these three scores plus points for (d) developing criteria and evaluating the solutions and for (e) writing a best solution. In addition, they received points for (f) the overall presentation of the problem/solution packet.

The results from practice problems one, two, and three are displayed in Figure 1. This series of graphs show the composition of the scoring and point total for the individual teams. One can also use the graphs to compare the team scores as a competitive sample. The students were allowed 3 hours to work on problem one and a 3-hour 45 minute time frame

TABLE 1   Information Concerning the Teams in This Study

School Affiliation	Mode of Selection	Percent of Team on Meal Assistance	Total Battery Average
Old Bay	Non-TCAP	80%	53.3%
Old Bay	TCAP	40%	87.4%
Fiske Hill	Non-TCAP	0%	88.6%
Fiske Hill	TCAP-1	0%	98.6%
Fiske Hill	TCAP-2	0%	98.0
Battle Road	Non-TCAP	40%	79.4%
Battle Road	TCAP	20%	96.8%

for problem two. Practice problem three (the only timed problem) had a 2-hour limit. The decrease in the points earned in most areas on this third problem was expected because of the time limit. Only one team improved its score between the second and third problem.

TCAP vs. non-TCAP Teams

After assessing the individual progress of each team, I compared the progress of the TCAP and non-TCAP teams within each school setting to determine whether the whole classroom tryout technique was effective in choosing problem-solving teams on an individual-school basis. The non-TCAP FPS team at Old Bay (see Figure 1) performed slightly better on practice problems one and two than the TCAP team. The non-TCAP team had great difficulty on practice problem three due to an observed lack of self-discipline on the part of two of its members. I realized at that moment that creativity and imagination are not all that is necessary under competitive circumstances.

The two TCAP teams at Fiske Hill alternated ranking on top among the three FPS teams at their school (see Figure 1). The non-TCAP team did not seem to "gel." The results from this tryout technique were not as encouraging in this school where so many students already qualify for the talented and gifted program.

The non-TCAP FPS team at Battle Road (see Figure 1) outscored the TCAP team on each of the three practice problems. The non-TCAP team managed to do this on the third problem without their coleader who was ill on the day of the competition. The alternate member had to compete unexpectedly. Apparently this change caused the non-TCAP team (which had placed first in the competitive sample on the two previous problems) to drop in the overall ranking for practice problem three; nevertheless, this tryout technique was an overwhelming success at Battle Road.

A Competitive Sample

I wanted to have the problem-solving packets evaluated as a competitive sample so that I could determine whether socioeconomic factors or lower TCAP scores would have an effect on the performance of the teams. A few teachers have expressed a concern that teams of inner-city children cannot be competitive with teams of children from affluent suburbs. I wanted an opportunity to put that idea to the test while I was evaluating the tryout technique. Even though my results are not generalizable to other programs, they appear applicable to other children in this same program who are also attending inner-city schools.

My data showed that the inner-city TCAP team from Old Bay developed the problem-solving skills at a much slower rate than the two TCAP teams from Fiske Hill; but by the end of the competitive year, this inner-city team had not only reached but surpassed the skill level of these same two teams from the suburbs. The total battery average of the Old Bay TCAP team (87.4%) was at least 9% lower than all other TCAP teams (98.6%, 98.0%, and 96.8%), and Old Bay feeds 75% of the school population with the free and reduced-price lunch program; neither of these factors negatively influenced the outcome. The classroom teacher at Fiske Hill, commenting on her teams' lower than expected placement, stated that perhaps her students had so many opportunities for competition that no single activity seemed important anymore. Her statement made me reflect on the importance of this competition to the inner-city children because so few of these activities are available. All children, regardless of economic status, need activities that are challenging and exciting.

A final look at results from the competitive sample involving the seven teams revealed a surprise for me. After talking with others who are knowledgeable about the progress of problem-solving teams, I assumed that the largest difference in the spread of points would be initially due to economic differences among the teams (children who are economically disadvantaged do not have access to the experiences of more economically advantaged children and may initially score lower). I was incorrect in that assumption. The difference actually grew larger as the competition progressed, and I am not sure why that happened. The teams completed practice

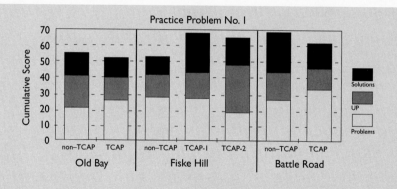

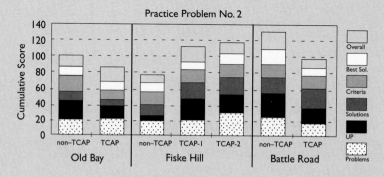

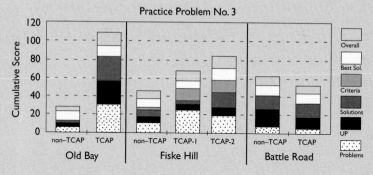

FIGURE 1   **Comparison of school scores[b]**

The figure shows the composition and point total for each individual team score on practice problems one, two, and three. One can also use the figure to compare the team scores as a competitive sample. The categories in which the students could earn points are listed to the right of each graph.

b. The titles of the bars shown to the right of the graphs in Figure 1 have the following meanings:

Overall: Score for the overall presentation of the problem/solution packet
Best Sol: Score for writing a best solution
Criteria: Score for developing criteria and evaluating the solutions
Solutions: Score for generating possible solutions
UP: Score for choosing an underlying problem
Problems: Score for generating possible problems

problem number one with scores that were very similar. After the evaluation for practice problem number two, the difference between the highest and lowest score was fifty-three points. By the end of practice problem three, the difference between the highest and lowest score was seventy-nine points (see Figure 1).

Final Progress Assessments on the Individual Teams

Old Bay. The non-TCAP team from Old Bay (four males and one female) had the lowest TCAP total battery average (53.3%) of any team that competed. Two leaders emerged (one male and one female) who worked hard and carried the team while the three other members added ideas verbally but placed few of them on paper. The leaders, who showed interest and perseverance equivalent to any child I worked with in my program this year, will be placed in TAG program next year with FPS as option if they are interested. The three remaining males will receive periodic enrichment for their creativity but will not be placed in TAG.

The TCAP team from Old Bay was the dark horse team of my study. This team (four females and one male) had the lowest total battery average (87.4%) among all four TCAP teams and second-from-the-lowest average of all teams in the study; however, they made the greatest efforts to improve their team performance each time we had a meeting. The members, collectively, appeared to be the most motivated and self-directed. This was the only team to score higher on practice problem number three (the only timed problem) than it had scored on practice problem number two. They began the study in last place and finished on top. The best part of this study for them was the pride that came when their inner-city team beat three teams from Fiske Hill. I had considered dropping FPS from this school next year, but these students are already talking about the competition when they are in the fifth grade.

Fiske Hill. Even though the non-TCAP team from Fiske Hill had a total battery TCAP average (88.6%) in

the middle of the range for the seven teams, this team remained at or near the bottom of the sample for all three of the FPS problems. The team of four males and one female never learned to work together. They argued more than the other six teams combined.

The TCAP-1 team from Fiske Hill had the highest total battery TCAP average (98.6%) among the seven teams. This team (three males and two females) was a joy to observe because of the self-confidence displayed by the members. Beginning with the first problem, the team members appeared to contribute equally and asked few questions. They worked together well and enjoyed the competitiveness of FPS. This team, however, was never in first place in the competitive sample.

The TCAP-2 team from Fiske Hill, with a total battery TCAP average (98.0%) second only to the TCAP-1 team, were the quietest team in my study. The team of three females and one male worked consistently, the members smiled frequently, but few sounds were made. This team earned the highest cumulative total points scored for the entire study but did not finish any single practice problem in first place.

Battle Road. The non-TCAP team from Battle Road (three females and two males) possessed next-to-the-lowest total battery TCAP average (79.4%); however, one member displayed the most impressive slate of gifted-like traits of anyone (including the TCAP students) in the three classrooms in my study. I am convinced that he is the reason that this team finished in first place in the competitive sample on both the first and second practice problems. This male would not have been in FPS or TAG classes at all without this whole classroom tryout. Finding this child made the entire year-long study worthwhile.

Even though the TCAP team from Battle Road had a seventeen percentage point advantage in total battery average (96.8%) when compared with the non-TCAP team (79.4%) from the same school, they never scored higher than the non-TCAP team on any of the practice problems. The team of four males and one female appeared to work in slow motion and had difficulty completing the problem-solving packets. The difficulty was not due to a lack of understanding but a lack of motivation. I tried several approaches to encourage them, but I did not feel successful. These children will be in TAG next year because of their TCAPS, but I will make FPS optional.

DISCUSSION AND CONCLUSION

My experience with the whole classroom tryout technique has convinced me that this can be an effective tool for increasing the number of economically disadvantaged children in my school system's talented and gifted program. This technique was valuable because it gave me an opportunity to observe the "gifts" of children and to include them into the program when they otherwise would not have access. By the end of the first 45-minute-tryout session, the potential of several of the children in the regular classroom was as obvious to me as if they were waving red flags. I was discouraged to think that some teachers had not recognized their gifts. At the beginning of this study, I had decided that if I found just one student who had been missed by the established identification techniques, I would feel this effort had been successful. Between Old Bay and Battle Road, I identified five economically disadvantaged children who have become a permanent part of the TAG group. Two students from the Fiske Hill team were also permanently added to the TAG program.

The encouraging results did not end with the identification of additional students. The whole classroom tryout technique not only helped to identify disadvantaged children but also promoted goodwill between the classroom teachers and the talented and gifted program. The regular classroom teachers revealed that they considered the tryout an effective procedure for observing all of the children and allowing equal opportunity for access to the program. The teachers told me that they appreciated the extra effort that I was making to include them in the identification process. Several teachers of the other fourth-grade classrooms (that I did not include in my study) came to me and stated that they also had bright children who needed to be included in the program. An additional five students were recommended for my program after the teachers and I

discussed the traits in children who could benefit from the curriculum.

In the end, the students were the major beneficiaries of this technique. Even though the non-TCAP teams (with the exception of the Battle Road non-TCAP team) were not as competitive on the final FPS practice problem as the TCAP teams, these creative children deserve to have access to other facets of my program that can stimulate their interests and enhance their gifts. I will make some adjustments in the use of this technique in the future. The teams, based on my observations, might have been more effective if the TCAP and non-TCAP students had been mixed together on teams instead of separated (this will be my new topic to study next year). I noticed that when teams were heavy with creative minds and lower on TCAP scores, the teams seemed to have a difficult time staying on task. This problem was especially evident with the non-TCAP team at Old Bay. This team functioned well when I monitored the first and second practice problems but fell apart when left to regulate their own behavior on the third problem. Perhaps one's ability to perform well on TCAP tests is also indicative of another characteristic: one's ability to stay on task. I found this characteristic to be evident among the TCAP team members that finished first, second, and third in my study. I would like to help my economically disadvantaged students, who do not possess the important skill of staying on task, to develop that sense of focus.

One conclusion stands out for me. The level of participation in a competitive program by disadvantaged students could not be distinguished from that of the students from the more affluent suburbs. According to the state director of the Tennessee Future Problem Solving, she could not distinguish the FPS packets of the disadvantaged students from the advantaged students based on creativity or quality of ideas. Because a team from one of my inner-city schools finished in first place at the end of the competition, all inner-city TAG teachers should feel encouraged by the prospects of these results.

I am not advocating that this technique replace the identification techniques that are currently in place in the TAG program. I think that we need to access as much information as possible if we are to decrease the chances of missing children who could benefit from our curriculum. This technique along with TCAP scores, teacher recommendation, parent referral, and peer nomination are all needed in our efforts to identify gifted children. My sentiments are well expressed in Richert (1987) concerning the identification of all students with potential:

> It is only when the regular classroom, to which all students have access, becomes a place where gifted potential (i.e. higher level cognitive and affective potential) is evoked that we will be able to identify all students, whatever their configuration of background, characteristics, and exceptional potential. This is a long-range but critical goal for every school that can improve the quality of education for all of America's students. (p. 154)

References

Borg, W. R., Gall, M. D., & Gall, J. P. (1993). Action Research. In W. R. Borg, M. D. Gall, & J. P. Gall (Eds.), *Applying educational research* (pp. 390–410). White Plains, NY: Longman[c]

Borland, J. H. (1989). *Planning and implementing programs for the gifted.* New York: Teachers College Press.

Butler, C., & Borland, J. H. (1980). *Survey of programs for the gifted in New York State.* Unpublished manuscript (from J. H. Borland's, *Planning and implementing programs for the gifted*).

Clark, B. (1983). *Growing up gifted: Developing the potential of children at home and at school* (2nd ed.). Columbus, OH: Charles E. Merrill.

Coleman, L. (1985). *Schooling the gifted.* Menlo Park, CA: Addison-Wesley.

Cox, J., Daniel, N., & Boston, B. O. (1985). *Educating able learners.* Austin: University of Texas Press.

Crabbe, A. (1989). *The activity book* (2nd ed.). Laurinburg, NC: St. Andrews College.

Crabbe, A. (1991). Preparing today's students to solve tomorrow's problems. *Gifted Child Today, 14*(2), 2–5.

Feldhusen, J. F., Asher, J. W., & Hoover, S. M. (1984). Problems in the identification of giftedness, talent, or ability. *Gifted Child Quarterly, 28,* 149–151.

Fisher, A. (1994). Autumn brainstorming. *Challenge, 12*(2), 58.

Future Problem Solving Program. (1994). *Readings, research, & resources.* Ann Arbor, MI: Desktop Services.

Gallagher, J. J., & Gallagher, S. A. (1994). *Teaching the gifted child* (4th ed.). Needham Heights, MA: Allyn & Bacon.

Jacobs, J. C. (1971). Effectiveness of teacher and parent identification of gifted children as a function of school. *Psychology in the Schools, 8,* 140–142.

Leighton, R. (1993a, September/October). Puzzles for problem solvers. *Middle Years.*

Leighton, R. (1993b, November/December). Puzzles for problem solvers. *Middle Years.*

Marland, S. P. (1972). *Education of the gifted and talented: Report to Congress.* Washington, DC.: U.S. Government Printing Office.

Margolin, L. (in press). *Journal for the Education of the Gifted, 19*(2).

Mitchell, B. M. (1988). A strategy for the identification of the culturally different gifted/talented child. *Roeper Review, 14*(3), 163–165.

Perry-Sheldon, B., & Allain, V. A. (1987). *Using educational research in the classroom.* Bloomington, IN: National Council of Teachers of English.

Piirto, J. (1994). *Gifted children and adults: Their development and education.* New York: Macmillan.

Richert, E. S. (1987). Rampant problems and promising practices in the identification of disadvantaged gifted students. *Gifted Child Quarterly, 31*(4), 149–154.

Richert, E. S., Alvino, J. J., & McDonnel, R. C. (1982). *National report on identification.* Sewell, NJ: Educational Improvement Center–South.

Tennessee Future Problem Solving Program. (1994a). *Practice problems for 1994–1995.* Knoxville: TFPSP.

Tennessee Future Problem Solving Program. (1994b). *Tennessee students creating a better tomorrow.* Knoxville: TFPSP.

Tennessee State Department of Education. (1994). *Posttest information—TCAP.* (Pub. Auth. No. 331806). Nashville: State Printing Office.

Tomlinson, C. A. (1995). Action research: An overview and an invitation to teachers of gifted learners. *Journal for Education of the Gifted, 18,* 467–484.

VanTassel-Baska, J., Patton, J., & Prillaman, D. (1989). Disadvantaged gifted learners at-risk for educational attention. *Focus on Exceptional Children, 22*(3), 2–15.

Wood, P. (1988). Action research: A field perspective. *Journal of Education for Teaching, 14*(2), 135–150.

c. The correct citation for the Borg, Gall, & Gall reference is: Borg, W. R., Gall, M. D., & Gall, J. P. (1993). *Applying educational research.* White Plains, NY: Longman.

SELF-CHECK TEST ANSWERS

CHAPTER 1:   Using Research to Improve Educational Practice
1. c   2. b   3. d   4. b   5. d   6. d   7. c   8. c   9. a   10. a

CHAPTER 2:   Conducting a Review of the Research Literature
1. b   2. b   3. d   4. c   5. a   6. c   7. a   8. d

CHAPTER 3:   Using Preliminary Sources to Search the Literature
1. d   2. c   3. d   4. b   5. c   6. a   7. a   8. b   9. b

CHAPTER 4:   Reading Secondary Sources
1. d   2. c   3. a   4. c   5. b   6. a   7. d   8. c   9. d

CHAPTER 5:   Reading Reports of Quantitative Research Studies
1. b   2. c   3. d   4. c   5. a   6. b   7. b   8. d   9. a

CHAPTER 6:   Statistical Analysis of Research Data
1. b   2. a   3. d   4. b   5. d   6. c   7. c   8. a   9. a   10. b   11. d

CHAPTER 7:   Descriptive and Causal-Comparative Research
1. a   2. b   3. c   4. d   5. d   6. a   7. c   8. b   9. c   10. b   11. a   12. d

CHAPTER 8:   Correlational Research
1. b   2. d   3. c   4. d   5. a   6. b   7. a

CHAPTER 9:   Experimental Research
1. c   2. b   3. b   4. d   5. d   6. c   7. b   8. a

CHAPTER 10:   Case Studies in Qualitative Research
1. c   2. b   3. d   4. c   5. b   6. c   7. d   8. a   9. a   10. c   11. b

CHAPTER 11:   Ethnographic Research
1. b   2. a   3. c   4. d   5. a   6. c

CHAPTER 12:   Critical-Theory Research
1. b   2. b   3. a   4. d   5. d   6. c

CHAPTER 13:   Historical Research
1. a   2. b   3. a   4. c   5. d   6. b   7. d   8. b   9. c   10. d

CHAPTER 14:   Evaluation Research
1. a   2. d   3. b   4. b   5. a   6. b   7. c   8. d   9. c   10. a   11. c   12. d

CHAPTER 15:   Action Research
1. b   2. c   3. c   4. a   5. b   6. d

APPENDIX 1
PRELIMINARY SOURCES THAT INDEX THE EDUCATION LITERATURE

Preliminary sources are essential resources for locating educational literature on any topic of interest. They can help you identify books, journal articles, technical reports, or other types of materials.

Many preliminary sources specialize in a particular topic area, such as the *Applied Science & Technology Index* (1958 to date), *Art Index* (1929 to date), and *International African Bibliography* (1971 to date), all published by H. W. Wilson. Too many exist to include them all in the following list, but you can identify them by using your library catalog and the *Bibliographic Index* (see section 1A below).

In Part 1 we list important preliminary sources that educators can use to locate sources covering various topic areas. We provide a brief bibliographic citation for each source, and additional information in some cases. The information provided is current as of the time we prepared this appendix, but keep in mind that indexes may change over time or cease publication. An important recent change is the supplementation of, or substitution for, a hard-copy version of most major preliminary sources with an electronic version (typically, in CD-ROM format). If we were able to determine that an electronic version of a preliminary source is available, it is noted. Otherwise, you can assume that it is published in hard-copy format.

In Part 2 we provide a brief list of preliminary sources that are useful for locating historical research sources.

PART 1. GENERAL PRELIMINARY SOURCES

A. Indexes to Bibliographies

Bibliographic index. (1937 to date). New York: H. W. Wilson.

This preliminary source indexes bibliographies that have been published separately or as parts of books or journals. For example, the 1992 edition of *Bibliographic Index* included bibliographies from an article about distance education, from a book about the history of education, and from an article about bilingual education.

International Bureau of Education, Documentation Centre. (1992). *Current bibliographical sources in education* (4th ed.). Paris: UNESCO.

B. Indexes to Book Reviews

Book review digest. (1905 to date).

Provides citations to and excerpts from reviews of English-language books. Government publications, textbooks, and technical books in the sciences and law are excluded.

Book review index. (1965 to date). Detroit: Gale. Also available in CD-ROM format.
Provides citations to reviews of books, periodicals, and books on tape in a wide range of popular, academic, and professional interest areas. Reviews in more than 600 journals are indexed in this preliminary source.

Contemporary psychology (1956 to date). Washington, DC: American Psychological Association.
This journal specializes in reviews of books (excluding textbooks) and other publications that are relevant to psychology.

Education review: A journal of book reviews. Web address: <http://www.ed.asu.edu/edrev/>
This on-line journal, established in 1997, is designed to publish reviews of important books across the range of current scholarship in the field of education.

C. Indexes to Books

Books in print. (1948 to date). New York: Bowker.

Children's books in print. (1969 to date). New York: Bowker.

El-hi textbooks and serials in print. (1985 to date). New York: Bowker. For earlier editions, see: *El-hi textbooks in print.* (1970–1984). New York: Bowker; *Textbooks in print.* (1956–1968). New York: Bowker.

D. Indexes to Curriculum Materials

ASCD curriculum materials directory. (1992 to date). Alexandria, VA: Association for Supervision and Curriculum Development. Available in hard copy or on MS-DOS diskette.

Film and video locator. (1987 to date). Albuquerque, NM: National Information Center for Educational Media.

Only the best. (1990–1997). Baltimore, MD: Association for Supervision and Curriculum Development. Available in CD-ROM format; 1997/98 edition available in hard-copy format.
This index covers educational software and multimedia programs that received high ratings in various publications that review such software.

E. Indexes to Directories

AERA online registry of educational researchers. Web address: <http://aera.net/resource/>
This registry is designed for educational researchers to enter biographical data about themselves and view entries of other educational researchers; AERA membership is not required.

Biographical membership directory. (1995). Washington, DC: American Educational Research Association.
This directory is updated on a regular basis. If you wish to contact particular educational researchers, it is likely that they will be listed, along with their postal and e-mail addresses.

Directories in print. (1989 to date). Detroit, MI: Gale Research. For earlier editions, see: *Directory of directories* (1st–5th eds.). (1980–1988). Detroit, MI: Gale Research.

Encyclopedia of associations. (1956 to date). Detroit, MI: Gale Research.

Guide to American educational directories (7th ed.). (1994). West Nyack, NY: Todd.

National faculty directory. (1970 to date). Detroit, MI: Gale Research.

F. Indexes to Dissertations and Theses

Dissertation abstracts international. (1969 to date). Ann Arbor, MI: University Microfilms International. It also is available in CD-ROM format.

Dissertation abstracts on disc. Ann Arbor, MI: University Microfilms International. The predecessor of this index was: *Comprehensive dissertation index.* (1861–1972). Ann Arbor, MI: Xerox University Microfilms.

This index provides abstracts for doctoral dissertations submitted by nearly 400 cooperating institutions, mostly in the United States and Canada, but also including a few institutions from other countries.

Master's theses directories. (1993 to date). Cedar Falls, IA: H. M. Smiley. For earlier editions, see: *Master's theses in education* (vols. 1–39). (1951–1990). Cedar Falls, IA: Research Publications.

G. Indexes to Journal Articles, Papers, and Reports

Child development abstracts and bibliography. (1927 to date). Chicago: University of Chicago Press.

An index to articles about child development that appear in over 170 journals in medicine, psychology, biology, sociology, and education. Books related to child development also are reviewed.

Current index to journals in education (CIJE). (1969 to date). Phoenix, AZ: Oryx. Available in hard copy, and in CD-ROM format as part of the ERIC database.

CIJE provides abstracts of articles from almost 800 publications, including many foreign periodicals. Most of the sources covered are educational journals, but when articles relevant to education are published in periodicals such as *Time, Nursing Outlook,* or *Personnel Journal,* these also are abstracted in *CIJE.* Many journals peripheral to education, such as the *Journal of Geography* and the *Journal of Family Issues,* are regularly reviewed for relevant articles.

Education index. (1929 to date). Bronx, NY: H. W. Wilson. Available in hard-copy and CD-ROM formats.

Education Index primarily covers educational periodicals, yearbooks, and monographs from over 400 English-language periodicals related to education. The index includes only bibliographical data. Unlike *CIJE,* no abstract is provided for each citation, but *Education Index* covers journal articles (and books as well) published since 1929.

Educational administration abstracts. (1966 to date). Newbury Park, CA: Sage.

Exceptional child education resources. (1977 to date). Reston, VA: Council for Exceptional Children. For earlier editions, see *Exceptional Child Education Abstracts,* vols. 1–8 (1969–1977).

Published quarterly, this index searches more than 200 journals for articles about exceptional children.

Feather, J., & Sturges, P. (1997). *International encyclopedia of information and library science.* New York: Routledge.

MEDLINE. (1966 to date). Palo Alto, CA: Dialog Information Services. CD-ROM format. This is an index to the biomedical literature.

Monthly catalog of United States government publications. (1951 to date). Washington, DC: U.S. Government Printing Office.

Physical education index. (1978 to date). Cape Girardeau, MO: BenOak.

Psychological abstracts. (1920 to date). Arlington, VA: American Psychological Association. Also available on-line as PsycINFO, and in CD-ROM format as *PsycLIT* (1986 to date). Wellesley Hills, MA: SilverPlatter.

A monthly publication of the American Psychological Association, *Psychological Abstracts* indexes over 1,000 journals, technical reports, monographs, and other scientific reports, including most of the world's literature in psychology and related disciplines. Terms for searching *Psychological Abstracts* are found in the *Thesaurus of Psychological Index Terms* (available in hard-copy format and as part of PsycINFO).

PsychNET. Web address: <PsychNET:www.apa.org>

The American Psychological Association's presence on the Internet, *PsychNET*, provides access to about 370,000 files, including nearly 100 years of abstracts and tables of contents from all APA journals; the *Thesaurus of Psychological Index Terms,* containing all the terms used to index Psychological Abstracts; tables of contents and descriptive information about books published by APA; and information about other APA information sources.

Resources in education. (1966 to date). Washington, DC: U.S. Government Printing Office. Available in hard copy, and in CD-ROM format as part of the ERIC database.

Published monthly by ERIC since 1966, *RIE* reviews "fugitive literature," which consists of educational documents other than journal articles such as transcripts of speeches, final reports of federally funded research projects, state education department documents, and school district reports.

Sage family studies abstracts. (1979 to date). Beverly Hills, CA: Sage.

Science citation index. (1955 to date). Philadelphia, PA: Institute for Scientific Information. Also available in CD-ROM format.

This index covers the literature of medicine, agriculture, technology, and science, including the natural, physical, and biomedical sciences. For an explanation of its purpose and use, see the following entry for *Social Sciences Citation Index.*

Social sciences citation index. (1969 to date). Philadelphia, PA: Institute for Scientific Information. Also available in CD-ROM format.

This index covers the literature of the social and behavioral sciences. Most articles about education are covered in this index, but depending on their topic, articles about psychology may be covered in this index or in *Science Citation Index.*

To understand the purpose of these indexes, suppose that your literature search identifies a key research report that was published some years ago, and you wish to trace its effects on subsequent research. Or, suppose you identify an article that expresses a controversial opinion, and you wish to know what later authors wrote in support of or opposition to it.

By looking up the author of a given reference, you can find where that reference has been cited by later writers. Start your search of *SSCI* with the year that your key reference was published, and check all volumes up to the current one. Under the name of the author of the reference, you will find bibliographical data for all sources that have cited that reference. For example, Arthur Jensen's article in the 1969 *Harvard Educational Review* titled "How Much Can We Boost I.Q. and Scholastic Achievement?" was cited in 20 articles in the 1986 edition of the *SSCI*. A review of these articles would give you a good picture about current thinking in 1986 regarding this controversial topic.

Sociological abstracts. (1953 to date). San Diego, CA: Sociological Abstracts. Also available in CD-ROM format as *Sociofile* (1995). Wellesley Hills, MA: SilverPlatter.

Published five times a year, each issue contains subject, author, and source indexes in addition to abstracts similar to those in *Psychological Abstracts.* The *Thesaurus of Sociological Indexing Terms* should be used to select key words for a search.

Sport discus. (1995). Boston: SilverPlatter. CD-ROM format. Updated regularly.

An index to literature on sport, physical education, physical fitness, and sport medicine.

Women studies abstracts. (1972 to date). Rush, NY: Rush, Inc.

H. Indexes to Magazines and Newspapers

Newspaper abstracts ondisc. (1985 to date). Ann Arbor, MI: University Microfilms International. CD-ROM format.

Readers' guide to periodical literature. (1900 to date). New York: H. W. Wilson.

I. Indexes to Tests and Test Information

ERIC/AE Test Locator Service. Web address: <http://www.aspensys.com/eric>

It is possible to make a comprehensive search for tests on the Internet through the ERIC/AE Test Locator Service, which is provided by the ERIC Clearinghouse on Assessment and Evaluation. You can access such test-related databases as the ETS Test Collection Bibliographies, the Buros Test Review Locator (a database of tests in the *Mental Measurements Yearbook* and *Tests in Print*), and *Test Critiques.*

ETS test collection catalog (2nd ed.). (1993–1995). Phoenix, AZ: Oryx.

The bibliographies of tests prepared by the Educational Testing Service (ETS) cover both published and unpublished tests, thus overcoming a limitation of other preliminary sources. The information for each test is limited to the test name, author, date published, age or grade levels, name and address of publisher, and a brief description of the variables the test is designed to measure. Contact the publisher for information on currently available volumes of the catalog, or Bibliographic Retrieval Services (BRS) for information on the electronic version, the ETS Test Collection Database.

Keyser, D. J., & Sweetland, R. C. (Eds.). (1984–1998). *Test Critiques* (vols. 1–11). Detroit: Gale Research, Inc.

The volumes of this secondary source cover more than 800 widely used measures. Each review includes a detailed description of the test and a summary of its development history; information on administration, scoring, and interpretation of the test; information about the test's reliability and validity; an overall evaluation of the test's merits and weaknesses; and references.

Maddox, T. (1997). *Tests: A comprehensive reference for assessments in psychology, education, and business* (4th ed.) Austin: PRO-ED.

Provides information on more than 3,000 tests, including a statement of the test's purpose, cost, and publisher and a description of the content, administration time, grade range, and scoring information. While helpful in locating tests, this source provides no information on reliability, validity, or norms.

Mental measurements yearbooks. (1938 to date). Lincoln, NE: Buros Institute of Mental Measurements, University of Nebraska.

The *Mental Measurements Yearbooks* are an important source of information on standardized tests. You can use the *MMYB* to obtain specific information about many of the tests that were used in the research projects that you are reviewing. The *MMYB* also can be used to locate and compare available tests on a particular topic to help you select the most appropriate test for your situation. The *Thirteenth Mental Measurements Yearbook*, published in 1998, provides reviews and information on 369 new or revised commercially available tests. Because many educational tests have been in use for 10 years or longer, you also can find useful information in earlier editions.

PART 2. PRELIMINARY SOURCES ON THE HISTORY OF EDUCATION

A. Bibliographies of Bibliographies

Fritze, R. H., Coutts, B. E., & Vyhnanek, L. A. (1990). *Reference sources in history: An introductory guide.* Santa Barbara, CA: ABC-CLIO.

Norton, M. B. (1995). *Guide to historical literature* (3rd ed.). New York: Oxford University Press.

Not only is this preliminary source a bibliography of bibliographies, but it also includes historiographical essays on each section topic. It is designed to provide an overview of outstanding literature in all major areas of history.

The following are examples of bibliographies in the above sources: Beck, F. A. G. (1986). *Bibliography of Greek education and related topics.* Sydney, Australia: F. A. Beck; Cortada, J. W. (1990). *A bibliographic guide to the history of computing, computers, and the information processing industry.* New York: Greenwood; Finley, E. G. (1989). *Education in Canada: A bibliography.* Toronto: Dundurn.

B. Bibliographies of Biographies

Biography and genealogy master index. (1988 to date). Detroit, MI: Gale.

The 1995 edition is an index to more than 455,000 biographical sketches in over 90 current and retrospective biographical dictionaries.

Biography index: A cumulative index to biographical material in books and magazines. (1946 to date). New York: H. W. Wilson. Also available in CD-ROM format.

Slocum, R. B. (Ed.). (1986). *Biographical dictionaries and related works: An international bibliography of collective biographies* (2nd ed.). Detroit: Gale.

C. Directories of Historical Societies

Directory, historical agencies in North America (13th ed.). 1986. Nashville, TN: American Association for State and Local History.

This is an example of a directory to the many historical societies that have been formed in order to advance the historical study of particular regions, time periods, and topics.

D. General Indexes to Historical Publications

America: History and life. (1964 to date). Santa Barbara, CA: ABC-CLIO. Also available in CD-ROM format.

This source indexes articles, dissertations, and reviews of books, films, videos, and documents in microfilm/microfiche format covering the history and culture of the United States and Canada from prehistoric times to the present.

Humanities index. (1974 to date). New York: H. W. Wilson. Its predecessors are: *Social sciences and humanities index.* (1965–1974). New York: H. W. Wilson; *International index.* (1907–1965). New York: H. W. Wilson. Also available in CD-ROM format.

E. Newspaper Reference Sources

United States newspaper program: National union list (4th ed.). (1993). Dublin, OH: Online Computer Library Center. Available in microform and CD-ROM formats.

F. Indexes to Nonpublished Primary Sources

Hitchens, H. B., & Hitchens, V. (Eds.). (1985). *America on film and tape: A topical catalog of audiovisual resources for the study of United States history, society, and culture.* Westport, CT: Greenwood.

National Historical Publications and Records Commission. (1988). *Directory of archives and manuscript repositories in the United States* (2nd ed.). Phoenix, AZ: Oryx.

National union catalog of manuscript collections. (1959 to date). Washington, DC: Library of Congress.

Smith, A. (1988). *Directory of oral history collections.* Phoenix, AZ: Oryx.

APPENDIX 2
ERIC NETWORK COMPONENTS

There are currently sixteen (16) ERIC Clearinghouses, each responsible for a major area of the field of education. Clearinghouses acquire, select, catalog, abstract, and index the documents announced in *Resources in Education (RIE)*. They also prepare interpretive summaries and annotated bibliographies dealing with high-interest topics and based on the documents analyzed for *RIE;* these information analysis products are also announced in *Resources in Education.*

ERIC Clearinghouses:

ADULT, CAREER, AND VOCATIONAL EDUCATION (CE)
Ohio State University
Center on Education and Training for Employment
1900 Kenny Road
Columbus, Ohio 43210-1090
Tel.: 614-292-4353; 800-848-4815; Fax: 614-292-1260

ASSESSMENT AND EVALUATION (TM)
Catholic University of America
210 O'Boyle Hall
Washington, D.C. 20064-4035
Tel.: 202-319-5120; 800-464-3742; Fax: 202-319-6692

COMMUNITY COLLEGES (JC)
University of California at Los Angeles (UCLA)
405 Hilgard Avenue, 3051 Moore Hall
P.O. Box 951521
Los Angeles, California 90024-1521
Tel.: 310-825-3931; 800-832-8256; Fax: 310-206-8095

COUNSELING AND STUDENT SERVICES (CG)
University of North Carolina at Greensboro
School of Education
201 Ferguson
Greensboro, North Carolina 27412
Tel.: 910-334-4114; 800-414-9769; Fax: 910-334-4116

DISABILITIES AND GIFTED EDUCATION (EC)
Council for Exceptional Children (CEC)
1920 Association Drive
Reston, Virginia 20191-1589
Tel.: 703-264-9474; 800-328-0272; Fax: 703-620-2521

EDUCATIONAL MANAGEMENT (EA)
University of Oregon, (Dept. 5207)
1787 Agate Street
Eugene, Oregon 97403-5207
Tel.: 541-346-5043; 800-438-8841; Fax: 541-346-2334

ELEMENTARY AND EARLY CHILDHOOD EDUCATION (PS)
University of Illinois at Urbana-Champaign
Children's Research Center, Room 9
51 Gerty Drive
Champaign, Illinois 61820-7469
Tel.: 217-333-1386; 800-583-4135; Fax: 217-333-3767

HIGHER EDUCATION (HE)
George Washington University
One Dupont Circle, N.W., Suite 630
Washington, D.C. 20036-1183
Tel.: 202-296-2597; 800-773-3742; Fax: 202-452-1844

INFORMATION AND TECHNOLOGY (IR)
Syracuse University
Center for Science and Technology,
4th Floor, Room 194
Syracuse, New York 13244-4100
Tel.: 315-443-3640; 800-464-9107; Fax: 315-443-5448

LANGUAGES AND LINGUISTICS (FL)
Center for Applied Linguistics (CAL)
1118 22nd Street, N.W.
Washington, D.C. 20037-1214
Tel.: 202-429-9292; 800-276-9834; Fax: 202-659-5641

READING, ENGLISH, AND COMMUNICATION (CS)
Indiana University
Smith Research Center, Suite 150
2805 E. 10th Street
Bloomington, Indiana 47408-2698
Tel.: 812-855-5847; 800-759-4723; Fax: 812-855-4220

RURAL EDUCATION AND SMALL SCHOOLS (RC)
Appalachia Educational Laboratory (AEL)
1031 Quarrier Street, Suite 607
P.O. Box 1348
Charleston, West Virginia 25325-1348
Tel.: 304-347-0465; 800-624-9120; Fax: 304-347-0487

SCIENCE, MATHEMATICS, AND ENVIRONMENTAL
  EDUCATION (SE)
Ohio State University
1929 Kenny Road
Columbus, Ohio 43210-1080
Tel.: 614-292-6717; 800-276-0462; Fax: 614-292-0263

SOCIAL STUDIES/SOCIAL SCIENCE EDUCATION (SO)
Indiana University
Social Studies Development Center
2805 East 10th Street, Suite 120
Bloomington, Indiana 47408-2698
Tel.: 812-855-3838; 800-266-3815; Fax: 812-855-0455

TEACHING AND TEACHER EDUCATION (SP)
American Association of Colleges for Teacher Education
  (AACTE)
One Dupont Circle, N W., Suite 610
Washington, D.C. 20036-1186
Tel.: 202-293-2450; 800-822-9229; Fax: 202-457-8095

URBAN EDUCATION (UD)
Teachers College, Columbia University
Institute for Urban and Minority Education
Main Hall, Room 303, Box 40
525 West 120th Street
New York, New York 10027-9998
Tel.: 212-678-3433; 800-601-4868; Fax: 212-678-4048

Sponsor:

EDUCATIONAL RESOURCES INFORMATION CENTER
  (ERIC)
National Library of Education (NLE)
Office of Educational Research and Improvement (OERI)
555 New Jersey Avenue, N.W.
Washington, D.C. 20208-5720
Tel.: 202-219-2289; Fax: 202-219-1817

Centralized Database Management:

ERIC PROCESSING AND REFERENCE FACILITY
Computer Sciences Corporation (CSC)
1100 West Street, 2d Floor
Laurel, Maryland 20707-3598
Tel.: 301-497-4080; 800-799-ERIC (3742); Fax: 301-953-0263

Document Delivery:

ERIC DOCUMENT REPRODUCTION SERVICE (EDRS)
DynEDRS, Inc.
7420 Fullerton Road, Suite 110
Springfield, Virginia 22153-2852
Tel.: 703-440-1400; 800-443-ERIC (3742); Fax: 703-440-1408

Commercial Publishing:

ORYX PRESS
4041 North Central Avenue at Indian School Road, Suite
  700
Phoenix, Arizona 85012-3397
Tel.: 602-265-2651; 800-279-ORYX (6799);
Fax: 800-279-4663; 602-265-6250

Outreach:

ACCESS ERIC
Aspen Systems Corporation
1600 Research Boulevard, 5F
Rockville, Maryland 20850-3172
Tel.: 301-251-5157; 800-LET-ERIC (538-3742);
Fax: 301-309-2084

Source. Inside back cover of: Educational Resources Information Center (ERIC). (December 1997). *Resources in Education,*
32(12). Washington, DC: U. S. Government Printing Office.

APPENDIX 3
PUBLICATIONS CONTAINING SECONDARY SOURCE REVIEWS OF THE EDUCATION LITERATURE

Secondary sources are articles, books, and other publications written by individuals to describe other individuals' research studies, theories, and opinions. Many such secondary sources are reviews of the literature on a particular topic. In Part 1 we list secondary sources covering various topic areas in education. In Part 2 we provide a brief list of secondary sources on the history of education.

The bibliographic information for each source was current at the time we prepared this appendix, but sources are subject to change. Keep in mind, too, that some of the handbooks possibly will appear in a new edition. You can check *Books in Print* for the latest edition.

PART 1. GENERAL SECONDARY SOURCES

A. Annual Reviews

Annual review of psychology. (1950 to date). Stanford, CA: Annual Reviews.

Review of research in education. (1931 to date). Itasca, IL: Peacock.

Yearbook of the National Society for the Study of Education. (1902 to date). Chicago: National Society for the Study of Education.

The two yearly volumes review the literature and provide expert commentary on particular educational topics. Recent topics have included educational reform, bilingual education, gender and education, art education, educational leadership, and Bloom's taxonomy of educational objectives.

B. Encyclopedias

Alkin, M. C. (Ed.). (1992). *Encyclopedia of educational research* (6th ed.). New York: Macmillan.

Husen, T., & Postlethwaite, T. N. (Eds.). (1994). *International encyclopedia of education* (2nd ed.). New York: Pergamon. Also available on CD-ROM.

Williams, L. R., & Fromberg, D. P. (Eds.). (1992). *Encyclopedia of early childhood education.* New York: Garland.

C. Journals Specializing in Literature Reviews

Psychological bulletin. (1904 to date). Washington, DC: American Psychological Association.

Psychological review. (1894 to date). Washington, DC: American Psychological Association.

Review of educational research. (1931 to date). Washington, DC: American Educational Research Association.

D. Handbooks

The following are the topics of 13 recent handbooks of research published by Macmillan Library Reference in New York. Here we list them alphabetically by topic area, followed by the editors and publication date.

Curriculum. Jackson, P. W. (Ed.). 1992.

The education of young children. Spodek, B. (Ed.). 1993.

Educational communications & technology. Jonassen, D. H. (Ed.). 1996.

Educational psychology. Berliner, D. C., & Calfee, R. C. (Eds.). 1996.

Mathematics teaching & learning. Grouws, D. A. (Ed.). 1992.

Multicultural education. Banks, J. A., & Banks, C. A. M. (Eds.). 1995.

School supervision. Firth, G. R., & Pajak, E. F. (Eds.). 1998.

Science teaching and learning. Gabel, D. L. (Ed.). 1994.

Social studies teaching & learning. Shaver, J. P. (Ed.). 1991.

Teacher education (2nd ed.). Sikula, J. (Ed.). 1996.

Teaching (3rd ed.). Wittrock, M. C. (Ed.). 1986.

Teaching the English language arts. Flood, J., Jenson, J. M., Lapp, D., & Squire, J. R. (Eds.). 1991.

Teaching literacy through the communicative & visual arts. Flood, J., Heath, S. B., & Lapp, D. (Eds.). 1997.

Below we list alphabetically by topic area other handbooks of research.

Early childhood education. Spodek, B. (Ed.). (1982). New York: Free Press.

Educational administration. Boyan, N. J. (Ed.). (1988). New York: Longman.

Improving student achievement. Cawelti, G. (Ed.). (1995). Arlington, VA: Educational Research Service.

Music teaching and learning. Colwell, R. (Ed.). (1992). New York: Schirmer.

Reading research. Pearson, P. D. (Ed.). (1991). New York: Longman.

Sport psychology. Singer, R., Murphey, M., & Tennant, L. K. (Eds.). (1992). New York: Macmillan.

E. International Handbooks

The following are the topics of six recent international handbooks published by Kluwer in Hingham, MA. While not specifically on research, they refer to research in the topic areas addressed. Here we list them alphabetically by topic area, followed by the editors and publication date.

Cross national policies on computers in education. Plomp, T., Anderson, R. E., & Kontogiannopoulou-Polydorides, G. (Eds.). (1996).

Educational change. Hargreaves, A., Lieberman, A., Fullan, M., & Hopkins, D. (Eds.). (1997).

Educational leadership and administration. Leithwood, K., Chapman, J., Corson, D., Hallinger, P., & Hart, A. (Eds.). (1996).

Mathematics education. Bishop, A. J., Clements, K., Keitel, C., Kilpatrick, J., & Laborde, C. (Eds.). (1997).

Science education. Fraser, B. J., & Tobin, K. G. (Eds.). (1997).

Teachers and teaching. Biddle, B. J., Good, T. L., & Goodson, I. L. (Eds.). (1997).

Below we list alphabetically by topic area other international handbooks.

Bilingualism and bilingual education. Paulston, C. B. (Ed.). (1988). New York: Greenwood.

Early childhood education. Woodill, G. A., Bernhard, J., & Prochner, L. (Eds.). (1992). New York: Garland.

Educational reform. Cookson, P. W., Jr., Sadovnik, A. R., & Semel, S. F. (Eds.). (1992). New York: Greenwood.

Reading education. Hladczuk, J., & Eller, W. (Eds.). (1992). Westport, CT: Greenwood.

Research and development of giftedness and talent. Heller, K. A., Mönks, F. J., & Passow, A. H. (Eds.). (1993). New York: Pergamon.

Women's education. Kelly, G. P. (Ed.). (1989). New York: Greenwood.

PART 2. SECONDARY SOURCES ON THE HISTORY OF EDUCATION

A. Biographies

Below we list three examples of the many biographical dictionaries that you can use to find information about specific historical figures. To learn what is available, we suggest that you check *Books in Print,* or your university's library catalog, under the subject *Biography.*

Johnpoll, B. K., & Klehr, H. E. (Eds.). (1986). *Biographical dictionary of the American left.* Westport, CT: Greenwood.

Ohles, J. F. (Ed.). (1978). *Biographical dictionary of American educators.* Westport, CT: Greenwood.

Williams, T. I., & Withers, S. (Eds.). (1982). *A biographical dictionary of scientists.* London: A. & C. Black.

B. Histories and History Textbooks

The following are illustrative examples of the many histories and history textbooks that are available.

Button, H. W., & Provenzo, E. E., Jr. (1989). *History of education and culture in America* (2nd ed.). Englewood Cliffs, NJ: Prentice-Hall.

Fee, E., & Acheson, R. M. (Eds.). (1991). *A history of education in public health: Health that mocks the doctors' rules.* New York: Oxford University Press.

Knowles, M. S. (1994). *A history of the adult education movement in the United States* (rev. ed.). Huntington, NY: Krieger.

Osuna, J. J. (1975). *A history of education in Puerto Rico.* New York: Arno.

Litwack, L. F., & Jordan, W. D. (1991). *The United States* (7th ed.). Englewood Cliffs, NJ: Prentice-Hall.

This is an example of a college history textbook that provides information about education in past times. This text contains several index listings for the term *education*, and a bibliography at the end of one chapter lists several relevant references on the history of education. We suggest that you check any data obtained from textbooks against a more scholarly source, because textbooks tend to oversimplify historical events.

C. History Encyclopedias

Bacon, D. C. (1994). *Encyclopedia of the United States Congress.* New York: Simon & Schuster.

Ritter, H. (1986). *Dictionary of concepts in history.* Westport, CT: Greenwood.

Thernstrom, S. A. (Ed.). (1980). *Harvard encyclopedia of American ethnic groups.* Cambridge, MA: Harvard University Press.

D. Geographical Reference Works

Webster's new geographical dictionary. (1988). Springfield, MA: Merriam-Webster.

This is an example of reference works that provide data about the history and characteristics of geographical locations.

E. Statistical Sourcebooks

Statistical sourcebooks contain many tables of numerical data arranged by topic area, as well as introductory essays that provide bibliographic information about other sources on the topic. Below we list two examples of such sourcebooks.

U.S. Bureau of the Census. (1989). *Historical statistics of the United States: Colonial times to 1970.* White Plains, NY: Kraus.

U.S. Bureau of the Census. (1878 to date). *Statistical abstract of the United States.* Washington, DC: U.S. Government Printing Office.

APPENDIX 4

QUESTIONS FOR EVALUATING QUANTITATIVE RESEARCH REPORTS

The following questions can be used to help you evaluate each section of a quantitative research report. For each question we indicate the type of information that you will need to identify in the report to answer the question, and we provide a sample answer. The examples are drawn from our experience in evaluating quantitative research studies.

INTRODUCTORY SECTION

1. Are the research problems, methods, and findings appropriate given the researchers' institutional affiliations, beliefs, values, or theoretical orientation?

   Information needed. The researchers' institutional affiliation often is given beneath the title of a published research report, or it might be at the end of the report or at the end of the journal in which the report appears. Also look for any information in the report that indicates the researchers' beliefs, values, or theoretical orientation with respect to education, and how that affected their research.

   Example. Most of the researchers' prior work has focused on cognitive models of learning. Therefore, they designed their research to show the advantages of cognitively oriented teaching methods compared to behaviorally oriented teaching methods.

2. Do the researchers demonstrate any favorable or unfavorable bias in describing the subject of the study (e.g., the instructional method, program, curriculum, etc., that was investigated)?

   Information needed. Identify any adjectives or other words that describe an instructional method, program, curriculum, and so forth, in clearly positive or negative terms.

   Example. The researchers described the group of students who served as research participants as difficult to handle, unmotivated, and disorganized. No evidence was presented to support this characterization. In the absence of evidence, this description might indicate a negative attitude toward the children who were studied.

3. Is the literature review section of the report sufficiently comprehensive, and does it include studies that you know to be relevant to the problem?

   Information needed. Examine the studies mentioned in the report. Note particularly if a recent review of the literature relevant to the research problem was cited, or if the researchers mentioned an effort to make their own review comprehensive.

   Example. The researchers stated the main conclusions of a previously published comprehensive literature review on the instructional program that they intended to study. They demonstrated clearly how their study built on the findings and recommendations of this review.

4. Is each variable in the study clearly defined?

   Information needed. Identify all the variables (also called *constructs*) that were studied. For each variable, determine if and how it is defined in the report.

   Example. One of the variables studied is intrinsic motivation, which is defined in the report as the desire to learn because of curiosity. This definition is not consistent with other definitions in the research literature, which state that intrinsic motivation is the desire to learn because of the satisfaction that comes from the act of learning and from the content being learned.

5. Is the measure of each variable consistent with how the variable was defined?

   Information needed. Identify how each variable in the study was measured.

   Example. The researchers studied self-esteem but did not define it. Therefore, it was not possible to determine whether their measure of self-esteem was consistent with their definition.

6. Are the research hypotheses, questions, or objectives explicitly stated, and if so, are they clear?

   Information needed. Examine each research hypothesis, question, or objective stated in the report.

   Example. The researcher stated one general objective for the study. It was clearly stated, but it did not provide sufficient information concerning the specific variables that were to be studied.

7. Do the researchers make a convincing case that a research hypothesis, question, or objective was important to study?

   Information needed. Examine the researchers' rationale for each hypothesis, question, or objective.

   Example. The researchers showed how the hypothesis to be tested was derived from a specific theory. They also showed that if the hypothesis was confirmed by the study it would add support to the validity of the theory, which is currently being used in the design of new reading curricula.

METHODS SECTION

8. Did the sampling procedures produce a sample that is representative of an identifiable population, or generalizable to your local population?

   Information needed. Identify the procedures that the researchers used to select their sample.

   Example. The researchers selected several classes (not randomly) from one school. The only information given about the students was their average ability and gender distribution. I cannot tell from this description whether the sample is similar to students in our schools.

9. Did the researchers form subgroups to increase understanding of the phenomena being studied?

   Information needed. Determine whether the sample was divided into subgroups, and if so, why.

   Example. The researchers showed the effects of the instructional program for both boys and girls; this information was helpful. However, they did not show the effects for different ethnic subgroups. This is an oversight, because the program might have a cultural bias that could have an adverse effect on some ethnic subgroups.

10. Is each measure appropriate for the sample?

     Information needed. Determine whether the researchers reported the population for whom the measure was developed.

     Example. The ABC Reading Test was developed 20 years ago for primary grade students. The current study also involves primary grade students, but the test may no longer be valid, because students and the reading curriculum have changed considerably over the past 20 years.

11. Is each measure in the study sufficiently valid for its intended purpose?

     Information needed. Examine any evidence that the researchers presented to demonstrate the validity of each measure in the study.

     Example. The XYZ Test was used because it purportedly predicts success in vocational education programs. However, the researchers presented evidence from only one study to support this claim. That study involved a vocational education program that was quite different from the one they investigated.

12. Is each measure in the study sufficiently reliable for its intended purpose?

     Information needed. Examine any evidence that the researchers presented to demonstrate the reliability of each measure in the study.

     Example. The researchers had observers rate each student's on-task behavior during Spanish instruction in a sample of 30 classrooms. Inter-rater reliability was checked by having pairs of observers use the rating system in the same five classrooms. The pairs typically agreed on 90 percent of their ratings, which indicates good reliability.

13. If any qualitative data were collected, were they analyzed in a manner that contributed to the soundness of the overall research design?

     Information needed. Determine whether the researchers share qualitative information about the research participants, procedures, or findings.

     Example. In seeking to explain the absence of differences between the experimental and control groups' classroom behavior, the researcher mentioned information shared by the students' teacher that students in the control group classroom had reacted positively to the observer's presence.

14. Were the research procedures appropriate and clearly stated so that others could replicate them if they wished?

     Information needed. Identify the various research procedures that were used in the study and the order in which they occurred.

     Example. The researchers administered three types of pretests during one class period the day before the experimental curriculum was introduced. The pretests, though brief, might have overwhelmed the students, so that they could not do their best work. Also, some aspects of the experimental curriculum (e.g., the types of seatwork activities) were not clearly described in the research report, and the researchers did not indicate how soon the posttests were administered after the curriculum was completed.

RESULTS SECTION

15. Were appropriate statistical techniques used, and were they used correctly?

     Information needed. Identify the statistical techniques described in the report.

Example. The researchers calculated the mean score for students' performance on the five tests that were administered. However, they did not give the range of scores (i.e., lowest score and highest score). This would be helpful information, because they studied a highly heterogeneous group of students.

DISCUSSION SECTION

16. Do the results of the data analyses support what the researchers conclude are the findings of the study?

    Information needed. Identify what the researchers considered to be the major findings of the study.

    Example. The researchers concluded that the experimental treatment led to superior learning compared to the control treatment, but this claim was true for only two of the four criterion measures used to measure the effects of the treatments.

17. Did the researchers provide reasonable explanations of the findings?

    Information needed. Identify how the researchers explained the findings of the study and whether alternative explanations were considered.

    Example. The researchers concluded that the narrative version of the textbook was less effective than the traditional expository version. Their explanation was that the story in the narrative version motivated students to keep reading, but that it also distracted them from focusing on the factual information that was included in the test. They presented no evidence to support this explanation, although it seems plausible.

18. Did the researchers relate the findings to a particular theory or body of related research?

    Information needed. Identify any theory or body of related research to which the researchers refer in discussing their findings.

    Example. The researchers discussed the conceptual implications of their findings in relation to theories of reinforcement on learning and task performance.

19. Did the researchers draw sound implications for practice from their findings?

    Information needed. Identify any implications for practice that the researchers drew from their findings.

    Example. The researchers claimed that teachers' morale would be higher if administrators would provide more self-directed staff development. However, this recommendation is based only on their questionnaire finding that teachers expressed a desire for more self-directed staff development. The researchers are not justified in using just this bit of data to claim that teachers' morale will improve if they get the kind of staff development that they prefer.

20. Did the researchers suggest further research to build on their results, or to answer questions that were raised by their findings?

    Information needed. Identify any suggestions that the researchers make for further study of the topic, and the questions that such study might answer.

    Example. The researchers noted that students showed greater levels of problem behavior during the reversal phase of the experiment than during the baseline phase. They recommended further research to explore the conditions under which such "postreversal intensification" tends to occur.

APPENDIX 5

QUESTIONS FOR EVALUATING QUALITATIVE RESEARCH REPORTS

The following questions can be used to help you evaluate each section of a qualitative research report. For each question we indicate the type of information that you will need to identify in the report to answer the question, and we provide a sample answer. The examples are drawn from our experience in evaluating qualitative research studies.

INTRODUCTORY SECTION

1. Are the research problems and methods appropriate given the researchers' institutional affiliations, beliefs, values, or theoretical orientation?

   Information needed. The researchers' institutional affiliation often is given beneath the title of a published research report, or it might be at the end of the report or at the end of the journal in which the report appears. Also look for any information in the report that indicates the researchers' beliefs, values, or theoretical orientation with respect to education, and how that affected their research.

   Example. The researchers taught in inner-city schools for many years before doing this study. This experience would give them knowledge of the issues facing inner-city students and teachers.

2. Do the researchers demonstrate any favorable or unfavorable bias in describing the subject of the study (e.g., the instructional method, program, curriculum, etc., that was investigated)?

   Information needed. Identify any adjectives or other words that describe an instructional method, program, curriculum, and so forth, in clearly positive or negative terms.

   Example. The researchers used a qualitative research method known as *educational connoisseurship and criticism* to study a high school football team. This method is inherently evaluative, so it is no surprise that the researchers made many judgments—both positive and negative—about the impact of the team on individual players.

3. Is the literature review section of the report sufficiently comprehensive? Does it include studies that you know to be relevant to the problem?

   Information needed. Examine the studies mentioned in the report. Note particularly if a recent review of the literature relevant to the research problem was cited, or if the researchers described their efforts to make their own review comprehensive.

   Example. The researchers completed their literature search prior to beginning data collection. This procedure is not desirable in qualitative research, because questions and hypotheses are bound to arise as the data are collected. They should have done an ongoing literature search to discover what other researchers have found concerning the emerging questions and hypotheses.

RESEARCH PROCEDURES

4. Did the sampling procedure result in a case or cases that were particularly interesting and from which much could be learned about the phenomena of interest?

   Information needed. Identify the type of purposeful sampling that the researchers used to select their sample.

   Example. The researchers used intensity sampling to select a high school principal who had received several awards and widespread recognition for "turning her school around." She was a good case to study, given the researchers' interest in administrators' instructional leadership.

5. Were the data-collection methods used in the research appropriate for the phenomena that the researchers wanted to explore?

   Information needed. Examine any evidence that the researchers presented to demonstrate the soundness of their data-collection methods.

   Example. The researchers' primary data-collection method was participant observation. Several quotations suggest that they were accepted as honorary members of the groups they observed. Thus, it appears that they had good access to the kinds of events and behavior about which they wished to collect data.

6. Was there sufficient intensity of data collection?

   Information needed. Identify the time period over which an individual, setting, or event was observed, and whether the observation was continuous or fragmented. If documents were analyzed, identify how extensive the search for documents was and how closely the documents were analyzed. If interviews were conducted, did the researchers build sufficient rapport with field participants before asking in-depth questions, and did they reexplore sensitive topics in subsequent interviews in order to check their data?

   Example. The researchers' goal was to learn how elementary school teachers established classroom routines and discipline procedures at the beginning of the school year. They observed each teacher every day for the first three weeks; this is a good procedure. They assumed, however, that routines and discipline procedures would be explained at the start of the school day, and so they observed only the first hour of class time. The validity of this assumption is questionable.

7. Were the data collected in such a way as to ensure a reflection of the field participants' emic perspective?

   Information needed. Examine any information that the researchers present to demonstrate that they sought to reflect the emic perspective of field participants.

   Example. The researchers wished to learn about children's views of preschool, but noted that children in the culture they studied often become uncomfortable when adults ask them questions in a formal setting. The researchers made the children more comfortable by setting up a playlike environment and asking questions unobtrusively as the interviewer and children played.

8. Did the researchers triangulate their data sources and data-collection methods to test the soundness of the findings?

    Information needed. Examine such information as whether the data obtained from two or more data-collection methods were compared for evidence of confirmation or of meaningful discrepancies.

    Example. The researcher obtained both observational data on students' self-references when with their peers and interview data about students' self-perceptions from one-on-one conversations with the researcher.

9. Were the research procedures appropriate and clearly stated so that others could replicate them if they wished?

    Information needed. Identify the various research procedures that were used in the study and the order in which they occurred.

    Example. The researchers' main data-collection procedure was to ask students questions as they attempted to solve mathematics problems. The problems and questions are available upon request, so it seems that the study could be replicated.

RESEARCH FINDINGS

10. Did the report include a thick description that gives a thorough sense of how various individuals responded to the interview questions and how they behaved?

    Information needed. Identify the amount of vivid detail that is included about what the individuals being studied actually did or said.

    Example. The researchers identified ten issues that mentor teachers faced in working with beginning teachers. Unfortunately the issues were described in rather meager detail, with no examples of what they looked like in practice.

11. Was the research report written in a style that brings to life the phenomenon being studied?

    Information needed. Identify any use of visual or literary structures (e.g., drawings, use of similes or metaphors) or unusual genres (e.g., poetry, songs, story telling) that are meant to convey the unique perspective of individuals in the field.

    Example. The historical research report included photographs to convey what one-room schools and their teacher and students looked like at the turn of the century. A typical school song of the period was included, and a harrowing newspaper account of a boy who became lost in the woods while on his way to school during the winter.

12. In summarizing the findings, did the report present any specific questions or hypotheses that emerged from the data that were collected?

    Information needed. Identify each research hypothesis or question that is stated in the report, and how they are based on the study data.

    Example. The researchers focused almost entirely on writing a narrative account of the events leading up to the teachers' strike. There was no attempt to develop hypotheses about why these events happened, which could be tested in subsequent research.

13. If any quantitative data were collected, were they described and analyzed appropriately?

    Information needed. Identify any quantitative data in the report.

Example. The researchers studied three teachers' aides and made such comments as, "They spent most of their time helping individual children and passing out or collecting papers." Time is easily quantified, so the researchers could have collected some time data and reported means and standard deviations.

14. Did the researchers establish a strong chain of evidence?

Information needed. Identify information in the report that explains the researchers' reasoning with respect to their decisions from the beginning to the end of the study.

Example. The researchers wanted to study how recent immigrants adapted to the manner in which students interact with each other in inner-city high schools. They trained high school students from each immigrant culture to collect observational and interview data. They explained that they chose this method of data collection because they assumed that the students would be able to obtain more valid data than adult researchers could obtain. This explanation appears reasonable, and therefore it contributes to the chain of evidence supporting the soundness of the study's findings.

15. Did the researchers use member checking to ensure that the information they presented about field participants was accurate and reflected field participants' perceptions?

Information needed. Identify information indicating that the researchers asked individuals to review statements in drafts of the researchers' report for accuracy and completeness.

Example. The researchers asked several members of each of the groups they studied—students, teachers, and parents—to review drafts of the report. An individual who spent considerable time on that task and provided helpful feedback was listed as one of the report authors.

DISCUSSION

16. Did the researchers reflect on their own values and perspectives and how these might have influenced the study outcomes, or steps that were taken to minimize their effect?

Information needed. Look for information in which the researchers describe their own thoughts or feelings about the phenomenon being investigated, and how they took their personal reactions into account in collecting and analyzing the data.

Example. The report referred to a discussion among the researchers about their personal disappointment at the ways in which some students treated other students during the research observations. It noted the researchers' agreement to behave in a respectful and friendly manner toward every individual in the field, and then to journal about their personal feelings after each field session.

17. Were multiple sources of evidence used to support the researchers' conclusions?

Information needed. Identify the researchers' conclusions and how each of them was supported by the data analyses.

Example. The researchers concluded that textbook adoption committees were frustrated by the paucity of written information provided by publishers and their inability to question publishers' representatives in person. This frustration was documented by analysis of interviews with selected members of the textbook adoption committees, field notes made by the researchers during committee meetings, and letters written by the chair of the committee to the director of textbook adoption in the state department of education.

18. Did the researchers provide reasonable explanations of the findings?

Information needed. Identify how the researchers explained the findings of the study and whether alternative explanations were considered.

Example. The researchers found that peer coaching did not work at the school they studied, and they attributed its failure to the lack of a supportive context, especially the lack of a history of collegiality among the teaching staff. Another plausible explanation, which they did not consider, is that the teachers received inadequate preparation in peer coaching.

19. Was the generalizability of the findings appropriately qualified?

Information needed. Identify whether the researchers made any statements about the generalizability of their findings. If claims of generalizability were made, were they appropriate?

Example. The researchers made no claims that the results of their case study could be generalized to anyone other than the teacher who was studied. It is unfortunate that they did not discuss generalizability, because the findings have significant implications for practice, if in fact they apply to other teachers. There are not enough data about the teacher's professional education for readers to generalize on their own.

20. Did the researchers draw reasonable implications for practice from their findings?

Information needed. Identify any implications for practice that the researchers drew from their findings.

Example. The researchers found that students who volunteer for community service derive many benefits from the experience. Therefore, they encourage educators to support community service programs for their students. This recommendation seems well grounded in their findings about the benefits of community service that students in their study received.

GLOSSARY

A-B design   A type of single-case experiment in which the researchers institute a baseline condition (A) followed by the treatment (condition B), while measuring the target behavior repeatedly during both conditions.

A-B-A-B design   A type of single-case experiment in which the researchers institute a baseline condition (A), administer the treatment (condition B), institute a second baseline condition (the second A), and readminister the treatment (the second B), while measuring the target behavior repeatedly during all conditions.

Abstract   A brief summary of the information contained in a publication, usually written either by the author or by an indexer who works for the publisher of a preliminary source.

Accessible population   The immediate population from which a sample is drawn for a research study.

Action research   A type of systematic investigation conducted by practitioners that involves the use of scientific techniques in order to improve their own practice.

Age equivalent   A derived score that represents a given raw score on a measure as the average age of the individuals in the norming group who earned that score.

Agency   In qualitative research, individuals' assumed ability to shape the conditions of their lives.

Analysis of covariance   A procedure for determining whether the difference between the mean scores of two or more groups on a posttest is statistically significant, after adjusting for initial differences between the groups on a pretest.

Analysis of variance   A procedure for determining whether the differ-
ence between the mean scores of two or more groups on a dependent variable is statistically significant.

And connector   In an electronic search of a preliminary source, use of the term *and* between two descriptors in order to retrieve only entries that have been coded for both descriptors.

Applied research   Research designed to develop and test predictions and interventions that can be used directly to improve practice.

Archive (also called *repository*)   A facility for storing documents so that they are preserved in good condition and access to them can be controlled.

Artifact   In quantitative research, an atypical variable or condition that affects the outcome of a research study.

Attrition (also called *experimental mortality*)   In experiments, the loss of research participants over the course of the experimental treatment.

Average variation   A measure of the average amount by which the individual scores for a sample deviate from the mean score.

Baseline   In single-case experiments, the A condition or conditions, during which the individual's behavior is observed under natural conditions.

Basic research   Research designed to advance the understanding of the basic processes and structures that underlie observed behavior.

Bibliographic citation   The information needed to describe or locate a publication, typically including the author, title, publisher, publication date, page numbers, and a brief abstract.

Bivariate correlational statistics   A set of statistics that describe the magnitude of the relationship between two variables.

Border pedagogy   A critical theory of education that conceives the differences between individuals and groups as permeable and changing, as opposed to the more rigid, "either-or" nature of conventional social categories.

Canonical correlation   A type of multiple regression analysis that involves the use of two or more measured variables to predict a composite index of several criterion variables.

Case   In qualitative research, a particular instance of a phenomenon that is selected for study.

Case study   A type of qualitative investigation that involves the in-depth study of instances of a phenomenon in its natural context and from the perspective of the participants involved in the phenomenon.

Categories   Variables that yield values that are discrete and nonordered when measured.

Causal-comparative research   A type of quantitative investigation that seeks to discover possible causes and effects of a personal characteristic or behavior pattern by comparing individuals in whom it is present with individuals in whom it is absent or present to a lesser degree.

Causal pattern   In case study research, an inference that particular phenomena within or across cases have a cause-and-effect relationship.

CD-ROM   An acronym for *Compact Disk-Read Only Memory*, meaning a disk from which the user can only obtain data (e.g., information from a preliminary source), not add new data.

Ceiling effect   A situation in which the range of difficulty of a test's items is so restricted that too many research participants earn the maximum score or a score close to it.

Central tendency   The most representative or typical score in a distribution.

Chain of evidence   The presence of clear, meaningful links among a qualitative research study's questions, raw data, data analysis procedures, and findings that attest to the soundness of the study.

Chart essay   A visual presentation that focuses the audience's attention on particular findings from a research study or research review.

Chi-square (χ^2) test   A nonparametric test of statistical significance that is used when the research data are in the form of frequency counts for two or more categories.

Citation   See *bibliographic citation.*

Coding check   In qualitative research, a method for determining the reliability of the process used to develop the categories for coding qualitative data.

Collaborative action research   A type of investigation in which two or more practitioners work together to collect data about a problem, analyze the data, report the results to stakeholders, and prepare and implement a plan of action intended to solve the problem.

Concurrent validity   The extent to which individuals' scores on a new test correspond to their scores on a more established test of the same construct, which is administered shortly before or after the new test.

Connoisseurship and criticism   See *educational connoisseurship and criticism.*

Constant   A construct that is part of the design of a research study but does not vary.

Construct   A concept that is inferred from commonalties among observed phenomena and that can be used to explain those phenomena.

Construct validity   The extent to which a test can be shown to measure a particular psychological characteristic.

Contact summary form   In qualitative research, a form used to summarize the procedures that were employed to collect and analyze data obtained from a field contact in a case study.

Content validity   The extent to which the items in a test represent the domain of content that the test is designed to measure.

Continuous score   A value of a measure that forms an interval or ratio scale with an indefinite number of points along its continuum.

Control group   In an experiment, a group of research participants receiving no treatment or an alternate treatment, to whose performance the experimental group's performance is compared.

Correlation coefficient   A mathematical expression of the direction and degree of the relationship between two measured variables.

Correlational research   A type of quantitative investigation that seeks to discover the direction and degree of the relationship among variables through the use of correlational statistics.

Correlational statistic   A measure of the extent to which the scores on two or more variables covary.

Cost-benefit analysis   In evaluation research, an estimation of the relationship between the costs of a program and its benefits.

Criterion measure   In experimental research, the test or other instrument used to assess the dependent variable that the treatment is intended to affect.

Criterion variable   In correlational research, the variable that researchers seek to predict by the measurement of predictor variables.

Critical ethnography   A qualitative research tradition in which researchers investigate power relationships and forms of oppression in a culture.

Criticalist   A researcher or theorist who attempts to use her or his investigations as a form of social or cultural criticism.

Critical theory   A qualitative research tradition that involves uncovering the nature of power relationships in a culture and seeks through its inquiries to help emancipate members of the culture from the forms of oppression that operate within it.

Cross-sectional research   A type of quantitative investigation in which changes in a population over time are studied by collecting data at one point in time from samples that vary in age or developmental stage.

Cultural acquisition   The process by which individuals seek to acquire, or to avoid acquiring, the concepts, values, skills, and behaviors that are reflected in the common culture.

Cultural studies   An interdisciplinary research tradition that involves critical investigation of cultural phenomena as expressed in literature, art, history, and other disciplines.

Cultural transmission   The process by which the larger social structure intentionally intervenes in individuals' lives in order to promote, or sometimes to discourage, learning of particular concepts, values, skills, or behaviors.

Culture   The pattern of traditions, symbols, rituals, and artifacts that characterize a particular group of individuals and that are transmitted from one generation to the next or from current members to newly admitted members.

Database   In an electronic preliminary source, the citations to all the publications that it indexes.

Deconstruction   The critical analysis of texts, based on the assumptions that a text has no definite meaning, that words can refer only to other words, and that "playing" with a text can yield multiple, often contradictory, interpretations.

Dependent variable   A variable that researchers hypothesize occurred after, and as a result of, another variable (called the *independent variable*).

Derived score   A transformation of a raw score in order to indicate an individual's performance relative to a norming group.

Descriptive research   Research that focuses on making careful, highly detailed observations or measurements of educational phenomena.

Descriptive statistics   Mathematical techniques for organizing, summarizing, and displaying a set of numerical data.

Descriptor   In a literature search, a term that the searcher uses to locate publications that have been classified by that term in a preliminary source.

Dialogical data generation   A stage of a critical ethnography project in which researchers collect data by engaging in dialogue with field participants.

Dichotomy   A categorical variable that has only two values.

Differential analysis   A form of multivariate correlational analysis that involves identifying moderator variables to improve the correlation between a predictor variable and a criterion variable.

Differential selection   In quasi-experiments, the selection of participants for the experimental and control groups by a procedure other than random selection.

Direct observation   The collection of data while the research participants are engaged in some form of behavior or while an event is occurring.

Disconfirming case analysis   The use of purposeful sampling strategies to select extreme cases for study in order to test the basic findings of a case study.

Discriminant analysis   A form of multivariate correlational analysis that involves determining the correlation between two or more predictor variables and a dichotomous criterion variable.

Document   In historical research, a type of text material that is prepared for personal use only, as contrasted with material having an official purpose.

Document analysis   A type of qualitative investigation involving the study of written communications that are found in field settings.

Educational connoisseurship and criticism   A type of expertise-based evaluation involving an appreciation of the phenomenon being evaluated (i.e., connoisseurship) and assessment of the strengths and weaknesses of the phenomenon (i.e., criticism).

Educational research   The systematic collection and analysis of information (sometimes called *data*) in order to develop valid, generalizable descriptions, predictions, interventions, and explanations relating to various aspects of education.

Educational research and development   A systematic process involving the development and refinement of educational programs and materials through formative and summative evaluation.

Educational Resources Information Center (ERIC)   A federally funded agency that maintains the *Current Index to Journals in Education* (*CIJE*), *Resources in Education* (*RIE*), and other information sources for educators.

Effect size   An estimate of the magnitude of a difference or relationship in the population represented by a sample.

Efficiency effect   In cost-benefit analysis, the difference between the estimated costs and benefits of a program; this difference is equivalent to the additional resources that are made available by the implementation of the program.

Electronic preliminary source   A computer-based index to publications of a certain type or on a certain topic; it includes citations for the publications and the software for searching them.

Emic perspective   In qualitative research, the research participants' perceptions and understanding of their social reality.

Enabling objective   An entry behavior that learners are expected to have in order for a program or set of materials to reach its objectives.

Entry   A citation for a publication indexed in the *Current Index to Journals in Education* (*CIJE*).

Epistemology   The branch of philosophy that studies the nature of knowledge and the process by which knowledge is acquired and validated.

ERIC   See *Educational Resources Information Center*.

ERIC clearinghouse   An ERIC-sponsored institution that is responsible for preparing citations related to a particular topic area for use in ERIC preliminary sources; these institutions also produce their own publications.

Ethnography   The study of the features of a culture and the patterns in those features.

Ethnology   The comparative study of different cultures.

Ethnoscience   The study of a culture's semantic systems for the purpose of revealing the cognitive structure of the culture.

Etic perspective   In qualitative research, the researchers' conceptual and theoretical understanding of the research participants' social reality.

Experiment   A type of quantitative investigation that involves the manipulation of a treatment variable to determine the effect on one or more dependent variables.

Experimental group   In an experiment, a group of research participants receiving the treatment that is presumed to affect the dependent variable, to whose performance the control group's performance is compared.

Experimental mortality   See *attrition*.

Experimental research   A type of quantitative investigation in which at least one independent variable is manipulated, other relevant variables are controlled as much as possible, and the effect on one or more dependent variables is measured.

Explained variance (r^2)   In correlational research, a statistic that specifies the percentage of the variance in variable X that can be predicted from the variance in variable Y; it is calculated by squaring the correlation (r) between X and Y.

Exploratory case study method   A method for synthesizing qualitative research studies (as well as quantitative studies and nonresearch accounts of a phenomenon) that acknowledges the unique characteristics of each case, but also identifies concepts and principles that are present across cases.

External criticism   In historical research, the process of determining the authenticity of a historical source, that is, whether the apparent or claimed origin of the source corresponds to its actual origin.

External validity   The extent to which the results of a research study can be generalized to individuals and situations beyond those involved in the study.

Extraneous variable   In experiments, any aspect of the situation that, if not controlled, can make it impossible to determine whether the treatment variable is responsible for any observed effect on the dependent variable.

***F* value**   An inferential statistic that reveals whether the difference between two or more sample means is generalizable to the populations from which the samples were drawn.

Face validity   The extent to which a casual, subjective inspection of a test's items indicates that they cover the content that the test is claimed to measure.

Factor (also called *latent variable*)   A mathematical expression for a feature shared by a particular subset of variables that are found to be correlated with each other.

Factor analysis   A correlational procedure for reducing a set of measured variables to a smaller number of factors (also called *latent variables*) that consist of variables that are moderately or highly correlated with each other.

Feminisms   The study of females' experiences and the manner in which those experiences are shaped by cultural phenomena.

Fieldwork   In qualitative research, the researchers' collection of data while interacting with research participants in their natural settings.

Formative evaluation   A type of evaluation that is carried out while a program or set of materials is under development, in order to improve its

effectiveness or to make a decision to abort further development.

Free-text search   A search of an electronic database that involves requesting every citation in which a particular word or set of words appears anywhere in the citation.

Fugitive literature   Publications that are not easy to obtain (e.g., conference proceedings).

Futurology   A type of research that examines what the future is likely to be.

Gain score   An individual's score on a posttest minus that individual's score on a pretest.

Grade equivalent   A derived score that represents a given raw score on a measure as the average grade level of individuals in a norming group who earned that score.

Hard-copy preliminary source   The paper version of an index to publications of a certain type or on a certain topic.

Hawthorne effect   An observed change in research participants' behavior that is caused by their awareness of participating in a research study, their knowledge of the researchers' hypothesis, or their response to receiving special attention.

Hegemony   The maintenance of privileged groups' dominance over subordinate groups through the cultural agencies that they control.

Hidden curriculum   The knowledge, values, and behaviors that are taught tacitly by schools' typical structure and organization of activities.

High-inference variable   A variable that requires the observer to make a judgment from behavior to a construct that is presumed to underlie the behavior.

Historiography   The study of the procedures that historians use in their research.

History effect   In experiments, the possible effect of events that occur while the treatment is in progress on the dependent variable.

Holistic ethnography   A qualitative research tradition that involves efforts to provide a comprehensive description and analysis of the entire culture of a group of people.

Hypothesis   The researchers' prediction, derived from a theory or from speculation, about how two or more measured variables will be related to each other.

Identifier   Any term (e.g., a proper noun, a test name) used by an ERIC preliminary source to code citations that is not listed as a descriptor in the *Thesaurus of ERIC Descriptors*.

Independent variable   A variable that researchers hypothesize occurred before, and had an effect on, another variable (called the *dependent variable*).

Inferential statistics   A set of mathematical techniques that enables researchers to make inferences about a population based on the scores of a sample that is drawn from the population.

Instrumental rationality   A preoccupation with means over ends; this term is used by criticalists to characterize educational research that focuses on prediction and control and the maximization of educational productivity.

Instrumentation effect   In experiments, a change from the pretest to the posttest that is due to changes in the nature of the measuring instrument rather than to the experimental treatment.

Interaction effect   In experiments, a situation in which the effect of one variable on another variable is influenced by one or more other variables.

Internal criticism   In historical research, the process of determining the accuracy and worth of the information contained in a historical source.

Internal validity   In experiments, the extent to which extraneous variables have been controlled by the researchers such that any observed effects can be attributed solely to the treatment.

Internalized oppression   The process by which individuals help to maintain their disempowered status in society through thoughts and actions that are consistent with that status.

Internet   A worldwide network of computers that enables users to communicate with each other and to access electronic information resources.

Inter-observer agreement   See *inter-rater reliability*.

Interpretational analysis   The process of examining qualitative data to identify constructs, themes, and patterns that can be used to describe and explain the phenomena being studied.

Interpretivism   An epistemological position that regards aspects of the human environment as constructed by the individuals who participate in that environment, and thus asserts that aspects of social reality have no existence apart from the meanings that individuals construct for them.

Interpretivist epistemology   The view that social reality is a set of meanings that are continually constructed by the individuals who participate in that reality.

Inter-rater reliability (also called *inter-observer agreement*)   The extent to which the scores given by one observer or rater on a measured variable correlate with the scores given by another observer or rater.

Interval scale   A measure that lacks a true zero point, and for which the distance between any two adjacent points is the same.

Interview   The collection of data through verbal interaction between the researcher and the individuals being studied.

Item consistency   The extent to which all the items on a test measure the same construct, as determined by one of several correlational methods.

Key informants   In qualitative research, individuals who have special knowledge or status that make them especially important in obtaining an emic perspective of the social reality being studied.

Kruskal-Wallis test   A nonparametric test of statistical significance that is used to determine whether the observed difference between the distribution of scores for more than two groups on a measured variable is statistically significant.

Latent variable   See *factor*.

Latent variable causal modeling   See *structural equation modeling*.

Line of best fit   In correlational research, the line on a scattergram that represents the best prediction of each Y score from the corresponding X score.

Longitudinal research   A type of quantitative investigation that involves describing changes in a sample's characteristics or behavior patterns over a period of time.

Low-inference variable   A variable that requires little judgment on the part of an observer to determine its presence or level.

Mann-Whitney U test   A nonparametric test of statistical significance that is used to determine whether the observed difference between the distribution of scores for each of two groups on a measured variable is statistically significant.

Maturation effect   In experiments, a change from the pretest to the posttest that is due to changes in the research participants during the course of an experiment rather than to the treatment.

Mean   A measure of central tendency corresponding to the average of a set of scores.

Median   A measure of central tendency corresponding to the middle point in a distribution of scores.

Member checking   In qualitative research, a procedure used by researchers to check their reconstruction of the emic perspective by having field participants review statements in the researchers' report for accuracy and completeness.

Meta-analysis   A method for combining the results from different quantitative research studies on the same phenomenon into a single statistic called an *effect size*.

Meta-evaluation   The process of evaluating an evaluation research study in order to assess the soundness of the research findings.

Microethnography   The study of specific aspects of the culture of a group of people.

Mode   A measure of central tendency corresponding to the most frequently occurring score in a distribution of scores.

Moderator variable   In correlational research, a variable, Z, that affects the extent to which variable X predicts variable Y, such that the correlation between X and Y for some values of Z is different from the correlation between X and Y for other values of Z.

Monological data generation   The initial stage of a critical ethnography project, in which only the researchers "speak," compiling a thick description of field participants' activities that is written from the perspective of an uninvolved observer.

Multiple linear regression   A correlational procedure that determines which combination of two or more predictor variables produces the best prediction of a criterion variable.

Multiple-case design   In qualitative research, the study of two or more cases in order to determine the generalizability of findings across cases.

Multiple regression   A statistical procedure for determining the magnitude of the relationship between a criterion variable and a combination of two or more predictor variables.

Multivariate correlational statistics   A set of statistics that describe the magnitude of the relationship between three or more variables.

Narrative summary   A method for synthesizing qualitative research findings that involves using a consistent writing style to create a brief description of each study.

Needs assessment   A set of procedures for identifying and prioritizing discrepancies between desired and existing conditions (i.e., needs).

Negative correlation   A correlation between two measured variables such that the higher the score obtained for variable X, the lower the corresponding score for variable Y.

Nonparametric statistics   Mathematical techniques for analyzing scores that do not involve assumptions about their distribution or form.

Nonparametric test of significance   A type of test of statistical significance that does not depend on assumptions about the distribution or form of scores on the measured variables.

Normal curve   See *normal probability distribution.*

Normal probability distribution (also called *normal curve*)   A distribution of scores that forms a symmetrical, bell-shaped curve when plotted on a graph.

Normative-evaluative truth claims In critical ethnography, assertions by field participants that are intersubjective and based on sets of norms that operate conjointly in the social setting.

Norming sample   A large sample that represents a defined population and whose scores on a test provide a set of standards to which the scores of individuals who subsequently take the test can be referenced.

Norms   In ethnographic research, unstated background sets of rules and assumptions that influence field participants' social acts.

Null hypothesis   The prediction that an observed result for a sample is a chance finding.

Objective truth claims   In critical ethnography, assertions by the researchers about details of the culture to which there is multiple access, meaning that other observers would generally agree with the researchers' assertions.

Observer bias   An observer's mental set to perceive events in such a way that certain events or behaviors are overlooked, distorted, or falsified.

On-line catalog   An electronic version of a library catalog or other database that can be accessed from an off-site computer.

On-line preliminary source   An off-site computer containing an electronic version of a preliminary source that can be accessed directly or by modem from an on-site computer.

Or **connector**   In an electronic search of a preliminary source, use of the term *or* between two descriptors in order to retrieve entries that have been coded for either of the descriptors.

Oral history   A type of historical research in which individuals who witnessed or participated in past events produce recollections of those events.

Outlier   In qualitative research, an individual or situation that differs greatly from other cases that are studied.

Paper-and-pencil test   An instrument that involves measurement of a variable based on individuals' responses to printed text or graphics.

Parameter   A statistic that applies to the entire population rather than just to a sample.

Parametric statistics   Mathematical techniques for analyzing scores that involve particular assumptions about their distribution and form.

Parametric test of significance   A type of test of statistical significance that depends on certain assumptions about the distribution and form of scores on the measured variables.

Participant observation   A qualitative data-collection method in which researchers assume a meaningful place in the culture being studied, but do not engage in activities at the core of the culture's identity.

Path analysis   A statistical method for testing the validity of a theory about causal links between three or more measured variables.

Percentile score   A type of rank score that represents a given raw score on a measure as the percentage of individuals in the sample or

norming group whose score falls at or below that score.

Performance measure   A test that involves evaluating individuals by examining them as they carry out a behavior that involves a complex, real-life task.

Performance objective   A specific statement of what a learner will be able to do after the instruction provided by a program or set of materials.

Population validity   The extent to which the results of a study can be generalized from the sample that participated in it to a particular population.

Positive correlation   A correlation between two measured variables such that the higher the score obtained for variable X, the higher the corresponding score for variable Y.

Positivism   An epistemological position that asserts that there is a social reality "out there" that it is available for study through scientific means similar to those that were developed in the physical sciences.

Postmodernism   A broad social and philosophical movement that questions assumptions about the rationality of human action, the use of positivist epistemology, and any human endeavor (e.g., science) that claims a privileged position with respect to the search for truth.

Posttest   In experiments, a measure that is administered following the treatment in order to determine the effects of the treatment.

Practical significance   The meaning of a research finding in terms of its potential usefulness in professional practice or other real-world settings.

Prediction study   A type of correlational investigation that seeks to predict future behavior or achievement from variables measured at an earlier point in time.

Predictive research   Research that involves the use of data collected at one point in time to predict future behavior or events.

Predictive validity   The extent to which a test is able to predict individuals' subsequent performance on a criterion measure.

Predictor variable   A variable that researchers measure at one point in time and then correlate with a criterion variable that is measured at a later point in time.

Preliminary source   An index or bibliography that cites publications of particular types or on particular topics.

Presentism   A type of bias in historical research that involves interpreting past events with concepts and perspectives that originated in more recent times.

Pretest   In experiments, a measure that is administered prior to a treatment in order to provide a basis for comparison with the posttest.

Primary source   A publication written by the individual or individuals who actually conducted the research or witnessed the events that are presented in the publication.

Primary source analysis   A synthesis of quantitative or qualitative research findings based on the reviewers' reading of reports prepared by the researchers who obtained the findings.

Proactive action research   A cyclical form of action research in which practitioners initiate a new practice based on their interests and needs, collect and analyze data, and then try another new practice based on the results.

Probability value (also called *p value*)   The likelihood that a particular statistical result occurred by chance.

Product-moment correlation coefficient (also called *r value*)   A mathematical expression of the direction and magnitude of the relationship between two measures that yield continuous scores.

Professional review   A synthesis of quantitative or qualitative research findings related to a particular topic that is intended to be read primarily by practitioners.

Progressive discourse   The view that anyone at any time can offer a criticism about a particular research study or research methodology, and if it proves to have merit, it will be listened to and accommodated.

Proportional random sampling   A variation of stratified random sampling that is designed to ensure that the proportion of individuals in each subgroup in the sample is the same as their proportion in the population.

Proximity search   A free-text search of an electronic preliminary source database in which the searcher specifies that the selected words must appear next to, in the same search field as, or within a given distance from each other.

Purposeful sampling   In qualitative research, the process of selecting cases that are likely to be "information-rich" with respect to the purposes of a particular study.

***p* value**   See *probability value.*

Qualitative research   Inquiry that is grounded in the assumption that individuals construct social reality in the form of meanings and interpretations, and that these constructions are transitory and situational; the dominant methodology is to discover these meanings and interpretations by studying cases intensively in natural settings and by reflecting the researchers' own experiences in what they report.

Qualitative research tradition   A group of qualitative researchers and scholars holding a similar view of the nature of the universe and of legitimate questions to ask and techniques to use in its exploration; also, the work of such individuals.

Quantitative research   Inquiry that is grounded in the assumption that features of the social environment constitute an objective reality that is relatively constant across time and settings; the dominant methodology for studying these features is to collect numerical data on the observable behavior of samples and subject them to statistical analysis.

Quasi-experiment   An experimental study in which research participants for the experimental and control groups are selected by a procedure other than random selection.

Questionnaire   A set of written questions that typically measure many variables.

Random assignment   In experiments, the process of assigning individuals or groups to the experimental and control treatments such that each individual or group has an equal chance of being in either treatment condition.

Range   A measure of the amount of dispersion in a score distribution, equal to the difference between the highest and the lowest score plus 1.

Rank score   The position of an individual's score on a measure relative to the positions of other individuals' scores.

Raw score   An individual score on a measure as determined by the scoring key, without any further statistical manipulation.

R&D product   An educational program or set of materials that is developed through the process of educational research and development.

Reconstructionist (also called *revisionist historian*)   A historian who engages in reinterpretation of past events, usually with the intent of demonstrating that past practices reflect particular political, economic, or other social forces and motivations more than they reflect rationality, good will, or professional considerations.

Reconstructive analysis   The process by which critical ethnographers analyze the data collected during monological data generation in order to describe interaction patterns among field participants and the apparent meaning of those patterns.

Record   In historical research, a type of text material that is prepared with an official purpose, as contrasted with material prepared for personal use only.

Reflective analysis   The process by which qualitative researchers rely on their own intuition and personal judgment to analyze the data that have been collected.

Reflexivity   In qualitative research, the researchers' act of focusing on themselves as constructors and interpreters of the social reality that they study.

Refutation   The process of submitting the knowledge claims of science to empirical tests that allow them to be challenged and disproved.

Relational pattern   In case study research, an inference that particular phenomena within or across cases are systematically related to each other, but that the relationship is not necessarily causal.

Relationship research   Any type of quantitative investigation, including causal-comparative and correlational research, that explores observed associations among variables.

Relationship study   A type of correlational investigation that seeks to explore the direction and degree of the relationship between two or more variables that are measured at about the same time.

Reliability   A measure of the extent to which a test or other measure is free of measurement error.

Relic   In historical research, any object whose physical properties provide information about the past.

Replication   The process of repeating a research study with different research participants under similar conditions in order to increase confidence in the original study's findings.

Repository   See *archive*.

Representativeness check   In qualitative research, a procedure used to determine whether a finding is typical of the field site from which it was obtained.

Research and development   See *educational research and development*.

Responsive action research   A cyclical form of action research in which practitioners collect data to diagnose a perceived problem, formulate a new practice and try it out, and collect more data to determine its effects.

Responsive evaluation   A type of evaluation research that focuses on stakeholders' issues and concerns.

Resume   A citation for a publication indexed in *Resources in Education* (*RIE*).

Reversal   In single-case experiments, the process of withdrawing the treatment (condition B) so as to reinstitute the baseline condition (A).

Reviewer bias   With respect to secondary sources, the omission or distortion of research findings that reflects the reviewers' own mental set to perceive events in a certain way.

Revisionist historian   See *reconstructionist*.

r value   See *product-moment correlation coefficient*.

Sampling bias   The use of any procedure to select a research sample that results in a sample that is not representative of the population from which it is drawn.

Sampling error   The difference between a statistic for a sample and the same statistic for the population.

Scale   An instrument that measures personal characteristics by totaling the individual's responses to items having a fixed number of response options.

Scattergram   A graph depicting the correlation between two variables, with the scores on one variable plotted on the x axis and the scores on the other variable plotted on the y axis of the graph.

Scheffé's test   A type of *t* test for multiple comparisons.

Secondary source   A publication in which the author reviews research or other work that was carried out or witnessed by someone else.

Selection-maturation interaction   In experiments, a change from the pretest to the posttest that is due to differential changes in the research participants in the experimental and control groups during the course of the experiment rather than to the experimental treatment.

Simple random sampling   A procedure in which all the individuals in the defined population have an equal and independent chance of being selected as a member of the sample.

Single-case experiment   A type of experiment in which a treatment is administered to a single individual or group in order to determine the effect of the treatment on one or more dependent variables.

Stakeholder   Any individual who is involved in a phenomenon that is being evaluated or who may be affected by or interested in the findings of the evaluation.

Standard deviation   A measure of how much a set of scores deviates from the mean score.

Standard deviation unit   A measure of the position of a score in a score distribution relative to the standard deviation of the score distribution.

Standard score   A derived score that uses standard deviation units to indicate an individual's performance relative to the norming group's performance.

Statistic   Any number that describes a characteristic of a sample's scores on a measure.

Statistical regression   The tendency for research participants who score either very high or very low on a measure to score nearer the mean when the measure is readministered.

Statistical significance   An inference, based on a statistical test, that the results obtained for a research sample can be generalized to the population that the sample represents.

Stratified random sampling   A procedure involving the identification of subgroups (i.e., strata) with certain characteristics in the population and drawing a random sample of individuals from each subgroup.

Structural analysis   The process of examining qualitative data to identify patterns that are inherent features of discourse, events, or other phenomena.

Structural equation modeling (also called *latent variable causal modeling*) A statistical procedure for testing the validity of a theory about the causal relationships among a set of variables, each of which has been measured by one or more different measures.

Subjective truth claims   In critical ethnography, assertions by field participants about their state of being, to which there is privileged access, meaning that only the individual has access to the experience on which the claim is based.

Summative evaluation   A type of evaluation that is conducted to determine the worth of a fully developed program in operation, especially in comparison with competing programs.

Survey research   A form of descriptive investigation that involves collecting information about research participants' beliefs, attitudes, interests, or behavior through questionnaires, interviews, or paper-and-pencil tests.

Systems approach   A model of educational research and development that includes various phases of product development, formative evaluation throughout the development process, and summative evaluation after development is completed.

Target behavior   In experiments, the dependent variable that is measured to determine the effects of the treatment.

Target population   The population to which researchers want to generalize or apply their research findings.

Testing effect   In experiments, the effect of the administration of a pretest, rather than of the treatment, on research participants' posttest performance.

Test-retest reliability (also called *test stability*)   The extent to which individuals' scores on one administration of a test correspond to their

scores on another administration of the test after a delay.

Test stability   See *test-retest reliability.*

Test of statistical significance   A mathematical procedure for determining whether the researchers' null hypothesis can be rejected at a given probability level.

Theme   In qualitative research, a salient, recurrent feature of the case being studied.

Theory   An explanation of particular phenomena in terms of a set of underlying constructs and a set of principles that relates the constructs to each other.

Thick description   In qualitative research, a richly detailed report that re-creates a situation and as much of its context as possible, including the meanings and intentions inherent in the situation.

Treatment   In experiments, the intervention that is administered to the experimental group to observe its effect on the dependent variable.

Triangulation   The use of multiple data-collection methods, data sources, analysts, or theories to increase the soundness of qualitative research findings.

Truncation   A procedure for searching an electronic database for any word that contains a given sequence of letters; for example, a search for the "trunk" *s-i-g-n* will retrieve all instances of such terms as *signify, insignificant,* and *resign.*

***t* test**   A test of statistical significance that is used to determine whether the null hypothesis that two sample means come from identical populations can be rejected.

Tukey's test   A type of *t* test for multiple comparisons.

***t* value**   The computation that results from a *t* test which can be checked in

a table of the *t* distribution to determine the statistical significance of the difference between two sample means.

Unit of analysis   Each instance of a phenomenon that is investigated in a case study.

Validity   The appropriateness, meaningfulness, and usefulness of specific inferences made from test scores; also, the soundness of a research study's findings.

Variability   The amount of dispersion in a set of scores.

Variable   A quantitative expression of a construct.

Variance   A measure of the extent to which the scores in a distribution deviate from the mean score; it is equal to the square of the standard deviation.

Variant source   In historical research, a primary source that has been altered from the original version.

Verisimilitude   In qualitative research, a style of writing that seeks to draw readers emotionally into research participants' world view and leads them to perceive the research report as credible and authentic.

Voice   In critical theory, the extent to which individuals occupying particular social categories or identities are privileged, silenced, muted, or empowered through the operation of cultural forces.

Vote counting   A method of synthesizing the findings of quantitative research studies whereby the studies are classified into four categories based on the direction and statistical significance of the reported results.

Wilcoxon signed-rank test   A nonparametric counterpart of the *t* test of statistical significance.

Name Index

SUBJECT INDEX